Guide to Personal Injury Claims Procedure

Second Edition

Guide to Personal Injury Claims Procedure

Second Edition

John McQuater LLB, LLM

Head of Litigation, Atherton Godfrey Solicitors

Published by
Jordan Publishing Limited
21 St Thomas Street
Bristol BS1 6JS

British Library Cataloguing-in-Publication Data

A catalogue record for this book is available from the British Library.

ISBN 978 1 84661 234 3

Typeset by Letterpart Limited, Caterham on the Hill, Surrey CR3 5XL

Printed in Great Britain by Hobbs the Printers Limited, Totton, Hampshire SO40 3WX

FOREWORD TO THE FIRST EDITION

This really is an excellent book. The guide is very comprehensive and readable, which given the very dry nature of the subject matter is to be welcomed.

It is a book that should be used by all specialist personal injury practitioners.

There is material in this book that would benefit the most experienced practitioner. For example, sections on when to use an expert, when more than one expert of a particular speciality is allowed and indeed the entitlement to facilities to have an expert examine a claimant, are all very comprehensive and thorough. It deals with the relevant authorities, many of which are too easily forgotten.

Practitioners specialising in personal injury, but with limited experience, will also find the guide an excellent resource, as it gives much of the basic information required for conducting a case. For example, the book sets out in some detail the requirements for a witness statement. It explains how to go about making an application to the court. It also gives very useful reminders such as attaching joint statements from experts when sending off the pre-trial checklist.

We should all be grateful to John McQuater for taking the trouble to write such a useful book.

Colin Ettinger
APIL President

PREFACE TO THE SECOND EDITION

In the Preface to the First Edition I wrote that this book attempted to summarise and explain the procedure for dealing with a personal injury claim from receiving initial instructions through to trial or settlement.

Since then much has happened. Indeed, this Second Edition of the book has been a long time in preparation as it has been a real challenge simply to keep pace with all the procedural reforms.

I hope not too many gave up hope of ever seeing the book. I would particularly like to thank all those involved in typing up, proofreading and editing for their help and patience.

Personal injury and clinical negligence cases continue to make significant law on procedure for civil litigation generally, confirming that despite all the changes there have been this remains an important aspect of the legal system for many people.

This edition of the book tries to reflect the law of England and Wales on procedural matters in personal injury claims, as I understand it, as at 17 March 2015.

I do hope this book will continue to assist practitioners dealing with personal injury claims.

John McQuater

Doncaster
March 2015

ASSOCIATION OF PERSONAL INJURY LAWYERS
(APIL)

APIL is the UK's leading association of claimant personal injury lawyers, dedicated to protecting the rights of injured people.

Formed in 1990, APIL now represents in the region of 4,000 solicitors, barristers, academics and students in the UK, Republic of Ireland and overseas.

APIL's objectives are:

- to promote full and just compensation for all types of personal injury;
- to promote and develop expertise in the practice of personal injury law;
- to promote wider redress for personal injury in the legal system;
- to campaign for improvements in personal injury law;
- to promote safety and alert the public to hazards;
- to provide a communication network for members.

APIL is a growing and influential forum pushing for law reform, and improvements, which will benefit injured people.

APIL has been running CPD training events, accredited by the Solicitors Regulation Authority and Bar Standards Board, for nearly 20 years and has a wealth of experience in developing the most practical up-to-date courses, delivered by eminent leading speakers, either publicly or in-house.

APIL training now runs almost 200 personal injury training events nationally each year, plus up to a further 100 meetings of our regional and special interest groups. Topics cover a wide range of subjects and are geared towards giving personal injury lawyers a thorough grounding in the core areas of personal injury law, whilst keeping lawyers thoroughly up to date in all subjects.

APIL is also an authoritative information source for personal injury lawyers, providing up-to-the-minute PI bulletins, regular newsletters and publications, information databases and online services.

For further information contact:

APIL
3 Alder Court

Rennie Hogg Road
Nottingham NG2 1RX
DX 716208 Nottingham 42
Tel 0115 9580585
Email mail@apil.org.uk
Website www.apil.org.uk

CONTENTS

TABLE OF CASES

References are to paragraph numbers.

BCT Software Solutions Ltd v C Brewer & Sons Ltd [2003] EWCA Civ 939, [2004] CP
  Rep 2, [2004] FSR 9, (2003) 26(9) IPD 26057, (2003) 100(35) LSG 35, (2003) 147
  SJLB 874   12.2.2
Beasley v Alexander [2012] EWHC 2715 (QB), [2012] 6 Costs LR 1137, [2013] RTR 7,
  Times, November 2, 2012   11.2.4
Beaumont v Ministry of Defence [2009] EWHC 1258, QB   7.3.2.4.1, 7.9.3
Beck v Ministry of Defence [2003] EWCA Civ 1043, [2003] CP Rep 62, [2004] PIQR 1,
  (2003) 100(31) LSG 31   4.3.1.9.1, 7.8.2, 7.8.2.2
Bell v London Borough of Havering [2010] EWCA Civ 689, [2010] All ER (D) 46
  (Oct)   5.7.3.2
Bellison v McKay unreported, Exeter County Court, 11 March 2008   1.11.4
Belmont Finance Corporation Ltd v Williams Furniture Ltd [1980] 1 All ER 393 3.6.7.5
Belt v Basildon & Thurrock NHS Trust [2004] EWHC 785, QB   1.7.2.2, 11.2.1
Bennett v Compass Group UK and Ireland Ltd & anr [2002] EWCA Civ 642, [2002] ICR
  1177   5.7.2, 5.7.4.5
Berezovsky v Abramovich [2013] EWHC 4348 (Ch)   6.2.3
Bermuda International Securities v KPMG [2001] EWCA Civ 269, [2001] CP Rep 73,
  [2001] CPLR 252, [2001] Lloyd's Rep PN 392, (2001) 98(15) LSG 33, (2001) 145
  SJLB 70, *Times*, March 14, 2001   2.11.2.7
Bethell Construction Ltd v Deloitte and Touche [2011] EWCA Civ 1321   2.10.2.1, 2.10.5.2,
                                                       2.10.8, 11.1.4, 12.2.3.3.1
Bewicke-Copley v Ibeh (Oxford County Court 4 June 2014)   1.12.7, 1.14.4.7.6
Biffa Waste Services Ltd v Maschinenfabrik Ernst Hese GMBH [2008] EWHC 2657
  (TCC)   12.2.4.3.1
Biguzzi v Rank Leisure plc [1999] 1 WLR 1926, [1999] 4 All ER 934, [1999] CPLR 675,
  [2000] 1 Costs LR 67, CA   2.2, 8.2.1.3, 8.2.3, 8.3.2.4
Bim Kemi AB v Blackburn Chemicals Ltd [2003] EWCA Civ 889, [2004] 2 Costs LR
  201   10.9.4
Binks v Securicor Omega Express Ltd [2003] EWCA Civ 993, [2003] 1 WLR 2557,
  [2004] CP Rep 4, [2004] PIQR P13, (2003) 147 SJLB 991, (2003) *Times*, 27
  August   2.2.5, 2.6.6
Birse Developments Ltd v Co-operative Group Ltd [2013] EWCA Civ 474, [2013] BLR
  383, 148 Con LR 264, [2013] 19 EG 96 (CS)   2.12.4
Black v Doncaster & Bassetlaw Hospitals NHS Foundation Trust unreported, Sheffield
  County Court, 20 April 2009   11.4.2.2
Black v Sumitomo Corporation[2001] EWCA Civ 1819, [2002] 1 WLR 1562, [2003] 3
  All ER 643, [2002] 1 Lloyd's Rep 693, [2002] CPLR 148, *Times*, January 25, 2002,
  Independent, December 13, 2001   2.11.2.2, 2.11.2.3
Blackham v Entrepose UK [2004] EWCA Civ 1109, [2004] All ER (D) 478 (Jul), [2004]
  TLR 451, (2004) *The Times*, 28 September, CA   11.5.5.2, 12.2.3.4.7
Blair-Ford v CRS Adventures Ltd [2012] EWHC 1886 (QB)   7.3.1.1, 7.3.2.3
Blake v Sutton [2004] CLY 421   4.2.3.2.1
Blue Sphere Global Ltd v Revenue & Customs Commissioners [2010] EWCA Civ 517,
  [2010] STC 1436, [2010] Lloyd's Rep FC 445, [2010] BVC 638, [2010] STI 1589,
  Times, June 2, 2010   11.5.3.3, 11.5.5.1.3, 12.2.3.1, 12.2.3.4.6, 12.2.3.4.7
Blyth Valley Borough Council v Henderson [1996] PIQR P64   4.3.1.5.3
BMF (Mansfield) Ltd v Galliford Try Constructions Ltd [2013] EWHC 3183 (TCC),
  [2014] CP Rep 3, [2014] CILL 3437   7.9.4.3
Bodycare (Health & Beauty) Ltd, Re [2003] EWHC 1516 (Ch), [2003] All ER (D) 338
  (Jun)   5.3.1, 5.12.3
Bond v Dunster Properties Ltd [2011] EWCA Civ 455, (2011) 108(19) LSG 21, (2011)
  161 NLJ 634   10.12.7.6
Bond v Livingstone & Co [2001] PNLR 30   2.12.1
Boodhoo v A-G of Trinidad and Tobago [2004] UKPC 17, [2004] 1 WLR 1689, 18
  BHRC 429, (2004) 101(15) LSG 28, (2004) *Times*, 9 April   10.12.7.6
Bortniczak v Fresh-Pak Chilled Foods Ltd unreported, Sheffield County Court, 8 July
  2011   7.3.2.3, 7.4.1.2
Bostan v Royal Mail Group plc, unreported, Bradford County Court, 11 June
  2012   1.14.5.2.5, 1.14.5.4.5, 11.5.7.7.7
Botham v Khan [2004] EWHC 2602 (QB)   12.6.5
Bowes v Sedgefield District Council [1981] ICR 234, (1981) 125 SJ 80   3.6.7.3

TABLE OF STATUTES

References are to paragraph numbers.

TABLE OF STATUTORY INSTRUMENTS

References are to paragraph numbers.

TABLE OF PROTOCOLS

References are to paragraph numbers.

CHAPTER 1

PROTOCOLS

1.1 INTRODUCTION

Any legal practitioner instructed by a client seeking damages for personal injuries must be aware of the law relating to liability and quantum. It is also crucial that the lawyer is able to navigate the procedural maze from initial instructions to conclusion of the claim ensuring, throughout, that the claim remains on track to achieve the client's objectives at the earliest opportunity whilst allowing the practitioner to be fairly remunerated for the work done. That is a real challenge.

To successfully meet that challenge the practitioner must be aware of the procedural steps appropriate for the claim and be ready to deal with opponents, whether in the insurance industry or the legal profession, experienced in defending claims.

The starting point, procedurally, for the practitioner will be one of the pre-action protocols, the particular protocol depending upon the nature and potential value of the claim.

1.1.1 The Pre-Action Protocol for Personal Injury Claims

Before 1999 there was no formal procedure for dealing with a personal injury claim until court proceedings had been commenced.

1999 saw the introduction of several pre-action protocols including the Pre-Action Protocol for Personal Injury Claims (the PI Protocol).

These protocols were the advent of major procedural reforms brought fully into effect when the Civil Procedure Rules (the CPR) came into force the same year.

Despite the subsequent introduction of further protocols the PI Protocol remains important as, it is, in many ways, the gateway to the CPR.

The PI Protocol is closely connected with the CPR. The PI Protocol anticipates, and prepares for, the procedural requirements of the rules which will be applicable once court proceedings have been commenced. Equally, the CPR have a bearing on, and shape, certain aspects of the PI Protocol.

The PI Protocol, if followed by the parties, will help guide the claim in a way that should allow it to be resolved, if possible, without the need for court proceedings to be issued.

If the issue of proceedings is necessary, compliance with the Protocol should ensure that the issues have been narrowed and expert evidence controlled which, in turn, should help the proceedings to be dealt with in a proportionate way.

The protocol has been recognised by the courts as reflecting best practice. In *Carlson v Townsend*[1] Brooke LJ observed:

> 'The introduction of pre-action protocols, and of the procedures they suggest for the obtaining of expert evidence, represents a major step forward in the administration of civil justice. Any practitioner or judge with significant experience of personal injuries litigation will have been very familiar with the mischiefs they seek to remedy. Under the former regime, in many disputed cases of any substance nothing very effective seemed to happen until a writ was issued close to the expiry of the primary limitation period. So far as the use of experts were concerned, there were often complaints that they appeared to be playing too antagonistic a role on behalf of the client who was paying for their services, so that it was most unlikely that the other side would accept their report. This led to further delay and expense while the other side instructed their own expert, who might well adopt an equally antagonistic position.'

Brooke LJ went on to say that:

> '(The protocols) are guides to good litigation and pre-litigation practice, drafted and agreed by those who know all about the difference between good and bad practice.'

Whilst the PI Protocol is intended primarily for fast track cases the spirit, if not the letter, is equally appropriate to claims likely to be suitable for the multi-track. Hence in *Carlson* the Court of Appeal observed that the Notes of Guidance to the Protocol state:

> 'the "cards on the table" approach advocated by the Protocol is equally appropriate to some higher value claims. The spirit, if not the letter of the Protocol, should still be followed for multi-track type claims. In accordance with the sense of the civil justice reforms, the Court will expect to see the spirit of reasonable pre-action behaviour applied in all cases, regardless of the existence of a specific protocol.'

1.1.2   Portal protocols

Further protocols, intended to make use of electronic portals and achieve a swift resolution of claims where liability is admitted, for certain types of personal injury claim were first introduced in 2010. The scope of these protocols was expanded in 2013. These comprise:

- the Pre-Action Protocol for Low Value Personal Injury Claims in Road Traffic Accidents (the 2010 RTA Protocol);
- the Pre-Action Protocol for Low Value Personal Injury Claims in Road Traffic Accidents from 31 July 2013 (the (2013) RTA Protocol); and
- the Pre-Action Protocol for Low Value Personal Injury (Employers' Liability and Public Liability) Claims (the EL/PL Protocol).

For claims within scope these protocols will be a preliminary to the claim entering the PI Protocol.

---

[1]   [2001] EWCA Civ 511.

Consequently, claims which exit, or never go into, the RTA Protocol or the EL/PL Protocol will usually enter the PI Protocol and be guided towards the CPR by the terms of that protocol (though the portal protocols identify specific circumstances in which the claimant can move on directly from those protocols to the issue of court proceedings).

1.1.3 Other protocols

There are also other protocols dealing with personal injury claims, in particular clinical negligence and industrial disease claims, which are outside the scope of this book.

1.1.4 Practice Direction – Pre-Action Conduct

Personal injury claims, like any other prospective claim, are also subject to the Practice Direction Pre-Action Conduct which, whilst included in the CPR, deals specifically with behaviour to be expected of the parties as a preliminary to the issue of court proceedings.

Consequently, and with pre-issue behaviour being expected to comply with relevant rules from the outset, it is not surprising that Brooke LJ, in *Crosbie v Munroe*,[2] defined 'proceedings' broadly so as to include:

> '....the dealings between the parties which lead to the disposal of (a claim)...even if the dispute is settled without the need to issue a claim form..'

The editorial introduction in the White Book at C13A.001, notes that the Practice Direction Pre-Action Conduct 'contains provisions describing the conduct the court will normally expect of the prospective parties prior to the start of proceedings' and that 'the court will expect the parties to have complied with that practice direction or any relevant pre-action protocol'.

The protocols and CPR provide a coherent system for dealing with 'proceedings' in most personal injury claims from notification of that claim, through efforts towards early resolution and defining the circumstances in which will be reasonable for the claimant to issue court proceedings.

1.1.5 Professional duties

In addition to the protocols and the CPR all dealings between the claimant's solicitors and the claimant, as well as the defendant, will be governed by the Solicitors' Code of Conduct.

1.2 DEALINGS WITH THE CLIENT

Key aspects of the Solicitors' Code of Conduct, when initially dealing with the client, concern arrangements for funding the claim, reaching agreement on the client's objectives and also the means of achieving those objectives. All of these are important considerations in the era of outcome-focused regulation.

---

2 [2003] EWCA Civ 350.

1.2.1　Funding

Funding arrangements for the claim will need to be discussed, agreed with the client and put in place at the outset. Potential funding options may include any of the following:

- private funding for which the client may have an indemnity under the scope of before-the-event (BTE) insurance cover;
- union funding;
- legal aid (under the Legal Aid, Sentencing and Punishment of Offenders Act 2012 civil legal services are available to an individual if described in Part 1 of Sch 1 though a number of the categories specifically exclude personal injury claims);
- a conditional fee agreement (CFA), which may be accompanied by after-the-event (ATE) insurance cover; or
- a damages based agreement (DBA).

1.2.2　Initial advice

The client should have written confirmation, at the earliest opportunity, of important matters relating to the claim including the following:

- a summary of the action agreed or recommended to achieve the client's objectives (usually that will be the recovery of damages but there may be other considerations with monetary compensation only a subsidiary aim);
- likely timescale;
- confirmation of the name and status of the person dealing with the case;
- information about costs; and
- details of the firm's complaints procedure (and how to follow up a complaint if not resolved by the firm).

1.2.3　Further advice

The client should be kept fully up to date as the matter progresses so that relevant instructions can be taken, appropriate advice given and informed decisions made by the client.

- Care should be taken in obtaining full and accurate instructions on the factual background.
- The client should be advised on the role of experts, the responsibilities of experts and, of course, any reports approved before disclosure (unless prepared on the basis of joint instructions).
- The client should be advised as and when liability is admitted or, if not admitted, the best assessment of the merits that can be made.
- Appropriate information on the value of the claim should be given as the case develops.
- The client should be advised about Alternative Dispute Resolution (ADR), including the availability and potential consequences of Part 36 offers.

1.3 DEALINGS WITH THE DEFENDANT

In *Baron v Lovell*[3] Brooke LJ noted that:

> 'The whole thrust of the CPR regime is to require the parties to behave reasonably towards each other in the conduct of the litigation. The old antagonistic point scoring, which used to drag personal injury cases out and run up costs, should now be at an end.'

It is worth bearing these comments in mind from the first point of contact with the defendant.

1.3.1 Initial contact with the defendant

The defendant, to whom the letter of claim will normally be sent, should be treated courteously. There may often be an ongoing relationship between the parties, for example in an employers' liability case where the claimant remains in the employment of the defendant. There will also be claims in which the incident, that is the subject of the claim, has been distressing for the defendant, as well as for the claimant.

If all relevant protocols are followed that should ensure the defendant is treated considerately. The defendant may be told, and politely reminded if necessary, of the potential consequences which may result from a failure to respond in accordance with the relevant protocol.

1.3.2 Dealings with the defendant's insurers

The relevant protocol will confirm timescales applicable to the defendant and, more generally, what will be appropriate pre-action conduct by the parties.

Consequently, ensuring the terms of the relevant protocol are kept to will ensure the claim is progressed without imposing unreasonable deadlines on the defendant.

The defendant is likely to be regarded as having responsibility for the way insurers deal with the claim. For example, in *Denton Hall Legal Services Ltd v Fifield*[4] Wall LJ observed:

> 'I have to say, however, that I find it distasteful that a large and well known firm of solicitors should not only submit a long–standing and competent employee to a trial at which it called psychiatric evidence in an attempt to show that her symptoms were imaginary, but that even when it rightly abandoned that unattractive argument in this court, it nonetheless sought to escape from its responsibilities to its employee both by attacking clear and compelling findings of fact by the judge relating to its dismissive attitude to its responsibilities under the Regulations, and by persisting in the argument that Mrs Fifield's injuries were not its responsibility. In my judgment, these are not the actions of a responsible employer.'

Having seen the draft judgment written submissions were made on behalf of the defendant, on the basis the appeal had been pursued by their employers' liability insurers. However, Wall LJ continued:

---

3   [2000] PIQR P20.
4   [2006] EWCA Civ 169.

I can, however, only express my surprise in these circumstances that the course favoured by the insurers was not subjected to a more detailed exploration than seems to have occurred in relation to the balance which needed to be struck between the unlikely success of the arguments advanced, its impact on Dentons' standing as employers and the costs involved.

The only concession the court was prepared to make was to substitute the word 'unfortunate' for 'distasteful'.

1.3.3   Dealings with the defendant's legal representatives

While it is important for lawyers to put the interests of their client first, it is generally in the interests of all parties for their legal representatives to maintain a degree of detachment from the conflict that inevitably exists between the parties themselves. Furthermore, the prospects of settlement, which should be the goal throughout the claim, are likely to be enhanced if there is appropriate respect and good faith between the representatives.

Many practitioners now act exclusively for either claimants or defendants. This, coupled with the adversarial nature of the litigation process, can sometimes lead to difficulties in the dealings between the representatives of the parties. Even when it is considered that the representatives of the other party, or that party, are acting in an unreasonable way the correspondence sent should try to focus on the issues and not become personalised. Any action which draws the representatives directly into the conflict between the clients tends to reduce, rather than promote, the prospect of narrowing the issues and achieving outright settlement.

It is possible that, from time to time, intemperate or inappropriate correspondence will be received. Rather than being drawn in to a response in kind, it is better to offer a sensible way forward. However, if that is unavoidable, it may be necessary to make a formal response to the matters raised at that stage or reserve the right to do so at a later stage.

If it really is impossible to get the opponent to deal with the case in a reasonable way it should be remembered that, rather than allowing the correspondence to become antagonistic, conduct is a relevant consideration in relation to costs and that it will be better, when the stage of costs is reached, if the receiving party can refer the court to correspondence which is unreasonable solely on the part of the paying party. Indeed, the court is unlikely to be interested in an exercise of attributing blame where there are intemperate allegations on both sides. It may, perhaps, be better to follow the example of Evelyn Waugh who reportedly, if he received irate correspondence, would reply:

> 'I am sorry to have to tell you that some mad man has got hold of some of your notepaper and is writing preposterous letters and signing them with your name.'

Whilst the representative of a party can be held responsible by the court, personally, for wasted costs, it will not usually be helpful to threaten an application for a wasted costs order whilst the claim is proceeding. Indeed, such a threat may be inappropriate. In *Orchard v South Eastern Electricity Board*[5] Lord Donaldson MR held that:

---

[5]   [1987] 1 All ER 95.

'Whilst there can be no objection to an application (for wasted costs) at the conclusion of a hearing, given appropriate facts, it is quite another matter where such an application is threatened during or prior to the hearing. Objectivity is a vital requirement of professional advisors ... threats to apply on the basis that the proceedings must fail not only make the solicitor something in the nature of a co-defendant, but they may well, and rightly, make him all the more determined not to abandon his client, thereby losing a measure of objectivity.'

The court also has power, in appropriate circumstances, to make a non-party costs order, which potentially could be against the claimant's solicitors. Whilst the prospects of such an application succeeding may be enhanced by warning the non-party of the intention to apply for such an order but when that threat is made to the representatives of a party the observations of Lord Donaldson, on the inappropriateness of such a threat, seem equally applicable.

If inappropriate allegations of impropriety are made against the claimant's representatives the defendant may be visited, to mark the court's disapproval, with indemnity costs as occurred, for example, in *Clarke v Maltby*.[6]

Where the parties are represented by solicitors the conduct of those solicitors towards each other will be regulated, where applicable, by the terms of Solicitors' Code of Conduct.

Furthermore, CPR 1.3 requires the parties to help the Court further the overriding objective which inevitably demands a degree of co-operation.

Case-law has explored what the duty to help further the overriding objective means in what is still an adversarial system.

In *Peacocks Ltd v Chapman Taylor*[7] HHJ Thornton QC recognised that:

'There is an inherent tension between a solicitor's duty to (his) client and to the CPR process. On the one hand, a client's interest is served by not drawing possible procedural failings or procedural errors of the client's opponent's legal team to the attention of that team so as to deprive the client of the advantage which might otherwise accrue to it. On the other hand, the duty of co-operation, and of proportionate procedural conduct imposed on solicitors by the CPR often points to such gratuitous assistance being provided to an opposing legal team.'

Similarly, in *Hertsmere Primary Care Trust v Estate of Balasubramanium Rabindra-Anandh*[8] Lightman J observed:

'CPR 1.3 provides that the parties are required to help the Court to further the overriding objective. In this context that must include assisting the Court to further the objective by co-operating with each other.'

Similar sentiments have since been expressed by the Court of Appeal in *Denton v T H White Ltd*.[9] Although given in the context of applications for relief from sanctions the words of Lord Dyson MR are surely of general application, in relation to dealings between the parties, when he said:

---

6   [2010] EWHC 1856 (QB).
7   [2004] EWHC 2898 (TCC).
8   [2005] EWHC 320 (Ch).
9   [2014] EWCA Civ 906.

'The court will be more ready in the future to penalise opportunism. The duty of care owed by a legal representative to his client takes account of the fact that litigants are required to help the court to further the overriding objective. Representatives should bear this important obligation to the court in mind ....'

1.4 CASE PLANS

Once the client's objectives have been ascertained, the route towards achieving those objectives should be considered and, if appropriate, mapped out by a case plan. Any plan, as well as identifying the objectives and stages to get there, will be shaped by the terms of the relevant protocol and the need for the work done in any particular case to be proportionate.

1.4.1 Format of the case plan

In a straightforward claim, the case plan may be self-evident and not need to be mapped out though practitioners need to be cautious of apparently simple claims which turn out to be more complex than might have been expected. In more complex cases careful thought may be necessary to prepare a case plan which allows for appropriate investigation within a framework that is proportionate to the claim.

1.4.2 Proportionality

A case plan is a good way of focusing on the need for proportionality and, moreover, will demonstrate to the court that account has been taken of this requirement.

In *Jefferson v National Freight Carriers plc*[10] Lord Woolf expressly endorsed the words of HHJ Alton giving judgment in a county court decision when holding that:

'In modern litigation, with the emphasis on proportionality, it is necessary for parties to make an assessment at the outset of the likely value of the claim and its importance and complexity and then to plan in advance the necessary work, the appropriate level of person to carry out the work, the overall time which would be necessary and appropriate to spend on the various stages in bringing the action to trial, and the likely overall costs. While it was not unusual for costs to exceed the amount in issue it was, in the context of modest litigation such as the present case, one reason for seeking to curb the amount of work done, and the cost by reference to the need for proportionality.'

Failing to prepare a case plan may be relevant as and when the court assesses costs. The absence of a case plan, when assessing cots, may be treated as evidence of disproportionality: *O'Leary v Tunnelcraft Ltd*.[11]

1.4.3 Workflow

The RTA Protocol and the EL/PL Protocol each set out a very structured approach for dealing with claims that effectively provides the workflow path and a case plan.

---

[10]   [2001] EWCA Civ 2082.
[11]   SCCO 19 October 2011.

The PI Protocol is less prescriptive but still structured in a way that usefully suggests a pattern for workflow. Any case plan prepared for a claim in the PI Protocol can, as well as identifying the particular steps required to move the case along the workflow path identify which steps can be taken simultaneously and which must be taken sequentially, given the importance of running the case as speedily as possible both for service-delivery reasons and to keep work in progress to a minimum.

1.4.4 Review

The case plan is a working document which will need to be reviewed as the claim proceeds. That is because as von Moltke the Elder observed, though in a different context, 'no plan survives contact with the enemy'.

1.5 LETTER OF CLAIM

If a claim is to proceed in accordance with the PI Protocol, because it is not suitable for a portal protocol or has exited such a protocol, the starting point will be to notify the defendant of the claim by a letter of claim sent in accordance with the terms of the PI Protocol (except where steps already taken in a portal protocol will stand as the letter of claim).

1.5.1 Early notification

The claimant may give the defendant early notification a claim is to be made, before a detailed letter of claim is sent. Early notification may sometimes be appropriate, for example when the claimant is incurring significant expenditure which it is hoped the defendant might pay for or urgent steps are necessary to preserve evidence. Generally, however, such notification will not be required and, if used inappropriately, can lead to unnecessary difficulties, for example by giving the defendant an opportunity to make the first nomination of experts for the purpose of joint selection which, in turn, puts the onus on the claimant to object.

1.5.2 Protocol requirements

Paragraphs 3.1 to 3.5 set out the requirements for a letter of claim to comply with the PI Protocol.

These matters should be dealt with by the letter of claim although, as the Practice Direction – Pre-Action Conduct recognises, compliance is more about substance than form.

Annexe A to the PI Protocol helpfully sets out an example of the format for a letter of claim.

Some specific requirements of the PI Protocol are worth noting.

1.5.2.1   Copies

Two copies of the letter should be sent with a request that one copy be sent on to the relevant insurer and that details of that insurer be given. This is important given that the individual defendant may have no stake in the outcome of the claim. If the insurer is known a copy should be sent direct.

1.5.2.2   Liability

Liability should be dealt with by the letter of claim containing a clear summary of the facts. Additionally, if that is possible, it may be useful to give details of the allegations of negligence or breach of duty based on those facts.

Although the letter will not have the formality of a statement of case, it should set out the claim in appropriate detail. That should allow the insurer to assess risk properly.

To ascertain the facts, and identify appropriate allegations, it will have been necessary to have taken full instructions and then carried out all appropriate investigation on behalf of the claimant. That, in addition to allowing the letter of claim to be properly drafted, will help ensure evidence, particularly evidence that may not otherwise be preserved, is obtained. This also reflects the protocol anticipating no further investigation on liability will be carried out, pending a decision on that issue by the defendant, once the letter of claim has been sent.

It is para 2.10 of the PI Protocol that recommends once the letter of claim has been sent no further investigation on liability should be carried out until a response is receiving indicating whether liability is disputed. This raises some tactical considerations that need to be addressed before the letter of claim is despatched.

- Preliminary investigations, in order to put together the letter of claim in sufficient detail, will, of course, need to be undertaken, for example obtaining the police accident report.
- In many cases once the essential facts have been established it will not be necessary to carry out further investigations on liability, provided these can be followed up, if necessary, should liability be put in issue.
- If it seems likely liability will be an issue and that needs to be investigated before the elapse of further time then those investigations may need to be undertaken before the letter of claim, if they can be pursued without needing facilities from the defendant.
- If investigations may be necessary, but need facilities from the defendant such as permission to inspect premises, the letter of claim will need to be sent and the defendant invited to provide facilities and perhaps even undertake some joint investigations if liability does require those investigations and may be in issue.

1.5.2.3   Quantum

Quantum should be dealt with by an indication of the nature of any injuries suffered and of any financial loss incurred. This should allow the insurer to make a proper reserve on the claim.

It may be useful for the claimant to indicate, in broad terms, whether it is considered the claim, if court proceedings are commenced, is likely to be suitable, in terms of value, for the fast track or the multi-track.

If the claimant indicates at the outset the claim is likely to be suitable for the fast track and investigations, following the letter of claim, suggest the value will exceed £25,000 the defendant should be notified of this development as soon as possible.

If the claim arises out of a road traffic accident the name and address of the hospital providing treatment should be given along with the claimant's hospital reference number.

1.5.2.4 Funding

In certain circumstances the claimant may need to give, in the letter of claim, details of arrangements made for funding the claim.

1.5.2.4.1 Conditional fee agreement with recoverable additional liabilities

If the claimant wishes to recover additional liabilities, under a 'pre-commencement funding arrangement' as now defined by CPR 48.2, it will be necessary to provide information about funding, in the letter of claim, to comply with the Practice Direction – Pre-Action Conduct which, in turn, requires compliance with para 19.4 Costs Practice Direction and CPR 44.3B (as in force prior to April 2013).

- If the funding arrangement is a conditional fee agreement the party must state:
  - the date of the agreement; and
  - the claim or claims to which it relates, including Part 20 claims if any.
  The claimant does not, however, have to provide details of the success fee or the basis on which that success fee has been assessed.

- Where the funding arrangement is an insurance policy the party must:
  - state the name and address of insurer;
  - state the policy number;
  - state the date of the policy;
  - identify the claim or claims to which it relates, including Part 20 claims if any;
  - state the level of cover provided (if the policy was entered into on or after 1 October 2009); and
  - state whether the insurance premiums are staged and, if so, the points at which an increased premium is payable (which reflects the approach to staged premiums adopted in *Rogers v Merthyr Tydfil County Borough Council*[12]).
  The claimant does not, however, have to disclose the amount of the insurance premium.
  Furthermore, although there are some conflicting authorities, most recent case-law suggests the court should not order disclosure of documentation relating to the policy: *Arroyo v BP Exploration Co (Columbia) Ltd*.[13]

- Where the funding arrangement is an arrangement with a relevant body (a collective conditional fee agreement) the party must:
  - state the name of the body;

---

[12] [2006] EWCA Civ 1134.
[13] SCCO 6 May 2010.

- set out the date and terms of the undertaking it has given; and
- identify the claim or claims to which it relates, including Part 20 claims if any.

Paragraph 9.3 of the Practice Direction – Pre-Action Conduct provides that where a party has entered a relevant funding arrangement, that party must inform other parties about such arrangement as soon as possible and in any event either within 7 days of entering into the funding arrangement concerned or, where a claimant enters into a funding arrangement before sending a letter before claim, in the letter before claim.

The sanction, for failing to give such information, is found in CPR 44.3B (as in force prior to April 2013) which states that unless the court orders otherwise a party may not recover:

- Any additional liability for any period during which that party failed to provide information about a funding arrangement as required by any rule, practice direction or court order.
- Any insurance premium where that party has failed to provide information about the insurance policy in question by the time required by any rule, practice direction or court order (and specific reference is then made to para 9.3 of the Practice Direction – Pre-Action Conduct).

Form N251, Notice of Funding, makes provision for all this information to be given in a convenient format and can usefully be completed and enclosed with the letter of claim. Paragraph 19.4(5) Costs Practice Direction (as in force prior to April 2013) makes clear one notice may be used to give information about more than one relevant funding arrangement.

If Notice of Funding has not been properly given appropriate notice should be given at the earliest opportunity, given that the court can grant relief from sanctions (see **2.9.1.5**).

If there is any change to the funding arrangements, once notice has been served, a further Notice of Funding should be served within seven days of that change.

1.5.2.4.2   *Legal aid*

If the claimant is legally aided details of the date of issue of certificate, and certificate reference number, can be usefully be given at this stage to ensure compliance with para 16.3(i) of the LAA Funding Code.

1.5.2.4.3   *Other funding*

There is no requirement to give details of funding, at this or any future stage, unless the claimant wishes to recover additional liabilities or has legal aid (and in either case if there is any change to that funding arrangement).

1.5.3   Further matters

Further matters, which the protocol does not require the claimant to deal with, can usefully be raised with the defendant at the stage of the letter of claim.

- Nomination of experts, usually medical experts but where necessary other experts as well (see **1.8**).
- Proposed use of a medical agency (where the claimant wishes to use such an agency to obtain medical evidence).
- Preservation of documents which might not otherwise be retained, for example:
  - CCTV;
  - Electronic documents.
- Identification of particular categories of documents which seem likely to be relevant (in the event liability is not admitted).
- Preservation, and facilities to inspect, any relevant property or premises.
- The correct identity of the defendant for the purposes of any subsequent litigation.
- Confirmation the insurer will indemnify the defendant in respect of the claim.
- Proposing an appropriate format for ADR, which will usually be negotiation at the outset, and seeking the defendant's commitment to any method of ADR proposed.
- Rehabilitation needs (see **1.10**).
- Earnings details (where the defendant is the claimant's employer).
- Agreement on applicable law (for example in a holiday claim that the standards will be those of the relevant part of the United Kingdom with a view to saving the costs of expert evidence from foreign lawyers about applicable standards where the injuries are suffered outside the United Kingdom).
- Limitation date (to avoid subsequent argument about the expiry of the limitation period).

1.6   ACKNOWLEDGMENT OF THE LETTER OF CLAIM

In accordance with para 3.6 of the PI Protocol the defendant should within 21 days (42 days if the accident occurred outside England and Wales and/or where the defendant is outside the jurisdiction) of the date of posting of the letter of claim have:

- Acknowledged that letter.
- Identified the relevant insurer (if any).
- Identified specifically any omissions.

Accordingly, if the defendant wishes to contend the letter of claim does not comply with the PI Protocol, so that the timetable is not running, it will be necessary to raise this promptly when giving an acknowledgement. Otherwise the time limit, in particular for giving a decision on liability, will run from the date the letter of claim is posted.

1.7   RESPONSE TO THE LETTER OF CLAIM

Rather more significant than the acknowledgment of the letter of claim is the defendant's formal response to the claim.

1.7.1   Timescale

In accordance with para 3.7 of the PI Protocol the defendant must no later than three months (six months if the accident occurred outside England and Wales and/or where the defendant is outside the jurisdiction) from the date of acknowledgement of the letter of claim have completed investigations and:

- replied;
- stated, in the reply, whether liability is denied and if so:
  - given reasons and any alternative version of events relied upon; and
  - enclosed documents in the possession of the defendant material to the issues between the parties.

The obligation to state whether liability is denied implies that, if not, there should, within the same timescale, be an admission.

The requirement for a reply to the letter of claim clearly implies a written response rather than a telephone call, particularly a call of the kind which amounts to a request for further detail of the claim rather than a reply in accordance with the PI Protocol.

1.7.2   Liability admitted

A number of considerations arise if the defendant's response is an admission of liability.

1.7.2.1   Claimant's response

If, but only if, the defendant admits liability a response from the claimant, to afford the defendant the opportunity of settling the claim, is required under the terms of the protocol.

- Any medical reports obtained under the protocol on which a party relies should be disclosed to the other party.
- The claimant should send the defendant a schedule of special damages with supporting documents (strictly this should always be sent as soon as practicable although the protocol adds 'particularly where the defendant has admitted liability').
- The claimant should then delay issuing proceedings for 21 days from disclosure of the medical report and schedule so the parties can consider whether the claim is capable of settlement (which in practical terms should mean the defendant making an offer within that timescale).

If the prognosis is not settled it is appropriate, in the event liability is admitted, to seek an interim payment.

1.7.2.2   What is an 'admission'?

These obligations on the claimant are conditional upon the defendant having made an admission.

Accordingly, there should be a clear and open admission, not made on a 'without prejudice' basis.

Furthermore, an indication of a willingness to enter negotiations, or to try and achieve a settlement of the claim, will not suffice as an admission. Usually, it will be necessary for there to be an admission for words such as 'admit' 'concede' or 'accept' to be used rather than, for example, the word 'offer': *Belt v Basildon & Thurrock NHS Trust*.[14]

Similarly, an offer on liability, or indeed of outright settlement, should be distinguished from an admission under the protocol. An offer cannot amount to a pre-action admission, can be withdrawn if not accepted and, moreover, is likely to be treated as having been made 'without prejudice' even if not expressly stated to be on that basis.

The Compensation Act 2006 provides, by s 2, that an apology, an offer of treatment or other redress shall not of itself amount to an admission of negligence or breach of statutory duty.

1.7.2.3 What is 'liability'?

Liability is not limited to just breach of duty but includes causation, in the sense of the breach having caused some damage. As May LJ observed in *Sam v Atkins*[15] that is because:

> 'Negligence is a composite concept necessarily combining (duty of care, breach of duty, causation and damage).'

Consequently, the term 'liability' will necessarily involve admission of both breach of duty and causation. Strictly, therefore, a purported admission of liability where causation is not admitted, or even denied, is no such thing.

Lord Hoffmann explained why this is so in both *Kuwait Airways Corporation v Iraqi Airways Company*[16] and in *Fairchild v Glenhaven Funeral Services Ltd*[17] when he observed:

> 'One is never simply liable: one is always liable for something ...'

Additionally, if there is an unqualified admission of liability this may well be held sufficient to exclude any argument of contributory negligence. Hence an admission that 'liability will not be raised as an issue' was held sufficient to deprive the defendant of the opportunity to argue contributory negligence in *Roberts v Historic Royal Palaces Enterprises*.[18] Had the phrase 'primary liability' been used the court would surely have allowed contributory negligence to be argued even if not expressly raised at the time.

Whilst the general term 'liability' should encompass both breach of duty and causation a party may, if this is stated clearly, make an admission just on the issue of breach or the issue of causation. This may amount to a pre-action admission of just that issue. For example, an admission of breach of duty was held to be binding, so only causation was left to be tried to determine liability, in *Green v Brunel & Family Housing Association Ltd*.[19]

---

14   [2004] EWHC 785 (QB).
15   [2005] EWCA Civ 1452.
16   [2002] UKHL19.
17   [2002] UKHL 22.
18   (Unreported) Leeds County Court, 19 January 2010.
19   (Unreported) Bradford County Court, January 2008.

1.7.2.4   Can an admission be withdrawn?

This question is likely to depend upon whether the defendant is viewed simply as having made an admission or if the dealings between the parties are such that there is a compromise of the issue of liability, or indeed the claim as a whole.

1.7.2.4.1   Compromise

A compromise will generally involve something more than a mere admission and require: a dispute between the parties; consideration; a complete and unambiguous agreement; an intention to create legal relations.

In *Burden v Harrods Ltd*[20] the court had to consider the relationship between the law of compromise and the provisions of the Protocol and Part 14, as it then read, of the CPR.

The defendant's insurers wrote in terms that they had, 'now completed our preliminary investigations and can confirm we are prepared to concede primary liability…' The letter went on to suggested a 25 per cent deduction for contributory negligence.

The claimant's solicitors replied stating that, 'we confirm that our client is prepared to accept your offer to deal with her claim on a 75 per cent basis in her favour' and argued, when the defendant later sought to resile, this was a binding compromise.

The defendant contended that although binding compromises were still capable of existing they ran counter to the CPR, so the correspondence ought to be looked at in the context of both those rules and the PI Protocol.

The court concluded the defendant's letter could properly be regarded as an offer which was, therefore, capable of acceptance by the claimant to create a binding contract so that even if the defendant sought to resile from its position in good faith, and with an arguable case, the issue of liability could not be reopened.

Where there is a full admission of liability this may constitute a binding compromise if all the elements of a compromise are present: *Telling v OCS Group Ltd*.[21]

If, however, an infant or a protected party is involved any compromise will only become binding when the court has given approval: *Drinkall v Whitwood*.[22]

1.7.2.4.2   Admission

Whilst the protocol no longer contains a presumption the defendant will be bound by an admission CPR 14.1A provides for a 'pre-action admission' where this is made after receipt of a letter of claim sent in accordance with the protocol or where it is stated to be made under Part 14.

---

[20]   [2005] EWHC 410 (QB).
[21]   LTL 02/06/2008.
[22]   [2003] EWCA Civ 1547.

Whilst CPR 14.1A refers to a 'letter before claim' there is a Memorandum of Understanding, agreed by APIL and FOIL amongst others, that this encompasses a letter of claim sent under the Protocol.

A pre-action admission may be withdrawn, by giving notice in writing, before commencement of proceedings, if the person to whom the admission was made agrees, or after commencement of proceedings either with agreement of all concerned or the permission of the court.

Once proceedings have been commenced any party may apply for judgment on the pre-action admission but the party who made it may apply to withdraw it. Paragraph 7 of the Practice Direction to Part 14 sets out specific factors relevant to the exercise of discretion allowing withdrawal of an admission.

- The grounds upon which the applicant seeks to withdraw the admission including whether or not new evidence has come to light which was not available at the time the admission was made.
- The grounds upon which the applicant seeks to withdraw the admission including whether or not new evidence has come to light which was not available at the time the admission was made.
- The conduct of the parties, including any conduct which led the party making the admission to do so.
- The prejudice that may be caused to any person if the admission is withdrawn.
- The prejudice that may be caused to any person if the application is refused.
- The stage in the proceedings at which the application to withdraw is made, in particular in relation to the date or period fixed for trial.
- The prospects of success (if the admission is withdrawn) of the claim or part of the claim in relation to which the offer was made.
- The interest of the administration of justice.

These factors largely reflect the judgment in *Basildon & Thurrock University NHS Trust v Braybrook*[23] which is also an example of circumstances in which the court was not prepared to allow an admission to be withdrawn, that being seen as a largely tactical step on the facts.

Similarly, where a defendant sought to withdraw an admission simply because the claim was worth more than the defendant thought, even though no new information had come to light, withdrawal of the admission, under Part 14, was not allowed: *Roberts v Historic Royal Palaces Enterprises*.[24]

The overriding objective will also be relevant, particularly the need to deal with claims of modest value in a proportionate way which may tell against allowing withdrawal of an admission, as occurred for example in *Green v Brunel & Family Housing Association Ltd*.[25]

---

[23] [2004] EWHC 3352, QB.
[24] (Unreported) Leeds County Court, 19 January 2010.
[25] (Unreported) Bradford County Court, 12 February 2008.

Even without any new evidence, the change in stance simply being dictated by a re-appraisal of the facts, the court may allow withdrawal of an admission as illustrated by the Court of Appeal ruling in *Woodland v Stopford*.[26]

In *Woodland* the letter containing an admission stated: 'we can confirm that liability will be conceded for this claim in full.'

However, subsequently solicitors instructed by the defendant wrote:

> 'The Swimming Teachers Association Ltd hereby now forthwith, and with immediate effect, retracts in full that concession/admission and any other statements or acts that could in any way be construed as any form of admission/concession of liability or responsibility and/or any waiver of rights to alleged contributory negligence and/or to seek a contribution and/or indemnity from any third party.'

In the Court of Appeal Ward LJ noted:

> 'It is quite clear to me that CPR 14.1A(3) confers a wide discretion on the court to allow the withdrawal of a pre-action admission and paragraph 7.2 of Part 14 of the Practice Direction lists the specific factors the court must take into account in addition to the need to have regard to all the circumstances of the case. These factors are not listed in any hierarchical sense nor is it to be implied in the Practice Direction that any one factor has greater weight than another. A judge dealing with a case like this must have regard to each and every one of them, give each and every one of them due weight, take account of all the circumstances of the case and, balancing the weight given to those matters, strike the balance with a view to achieving the overriding objective.'

The potentially precarious position of a claimant who relies on an admission, given the approach taken in *Woodland*, means that, particularly in a case of some potential value where investigations on quantum may take time, it is prudent to consider whether proceedings should be issued and judgment obtained, to put the matter beyond any doubt, at least unless the defendant accepts a binding compromise on the issue of liability has been reached (see **4.3.1.4**).

From April 2013 changes to the overriding objective may result in the court being less ready to allow an admission, which should include a pre-action admission, to be withdrawn: *Henning Berg v Blackburn Rovers Football Club & Athletic plc*.[27]

1.7.2.5   Costs consequences of an admission

The potential costs consequences of an admission mean it is important to discern when there has been an admission and if it is likely to be binding.

In particular, where a conditional fee agreement is entered into after such an admission this is likely to have a bearing on the level of success fee where this is not fixed: *C v W*;[28] *Fortune v Roe*.[29] In *Fortune* the judge concluded liability was only put beyond doubt when judgment on that issue was entered and the possibility, however remote, removed that the defendant might withdraw the admission.

---

[26]   [2011] EWCA Civ 266.
[27]   [2013] EWHC 1070.
[28]   [2008] EWCA Civ 145.
[29]   [2010] EWHC 90180 (Costs).

1.7.3 Liability denied

If liability is denied proper reasons should be given (ideally by reference to the specific allegations made by the claimant) with any alternative version of events relied upon.

Reasons, and any alternative version, should deal with both breach of duty and causation, as appropriate.

If the defendant, in accordance with the guidance given in *Casey v Cartwright*,[30] notifies the claimant within the protocol period the issue of low velocity is to be raised then the claimant, in accordance with further guidance given in *Kearsley v Klarfeld*,[31] should:

- offer the defendant's insurers access to the vehicle involved in the accident for the purpose of early examination if the insurers so wish; and
- give early disclosure, with irrelevant pages redacted if necessary, of any contemporaneous GP or other relevant medical notes.

Documents, material to the issues between the parties, should be disclosed (annex B of the PI Protocol provides specimen, but non-exhaustive, lists of documents likely to be relevant in different types of claim). Paragraph 3.13 of the PI Protocol provides that no charge will be made for providing copies of these documents.

In the absence of an admission by the defendant there is no obligation on the claimant to disclose details on quantum, though the claimant may nevertheless choose to do so and give the defendant a short timescale, certainly not more than 21 days, to make proposals.

If, as well as denying liability, a further party is blamed the claimant may wish, if that has not already been done, to send a letter of claim to that party.

Any such further letter of claim will need to comply, once again, with the requirements of the PI Protocol, including any necessary information on funding. The letter might also outline the steps already taken and response received to the claim from the initial defendant.

The stance taken between defendants under the PI Protocol may be relevant, later, to the incidence of costs: *Maguire v Sefton Metropolitan Borough Council*.[32]

1.7.4 Primary liability admitted (and contributory negligence alleged)

As allegations of contributory negligence are, certainly to an extent, a denial of liability. Accordingly:

- appropriate reasons and any alternative version of events should be given; and
- documents should be disclosed, though these will be confined to those documents relevant to the issues remaining in dispute.

---

[30] [2006] EWCA Civ 1280.
[31] [2005] EWCA Civ 1510.
[32] [2006] EWCA Civ 316.

The claimant should respond to the allegations of contributory negligence before proceedings are issued.

Once again an apology, under the terms of the Compensation Act 2006, will not amount to an admission, in this context on the part of the claimant.

It will be appropriate for the claimant to disclose details on quantum, as to an extent there is an admission of liability, and delay issue of proceedings for 21 days so that the defendant has an opportunity to settle the claim.

1.7.5   Liability not dealt with

Liability may not be dealt with because:

- the defendant fails to provide a reply; or
- there is a reply but this fails to deal with liability because:
    - there is no proper admission; or
    - there is no clear denial.

Once again the absence of an admission will mean there is no obligation on the claimant to disclose details on quantum though the claimant may nevertheless choose to do so.

1.8   EXPERTS

The PI Protocol deals with expert evidence reflecting the general approach, towards expert evidence before court proceedings are commenced, encouraged by the Practice Direction – Pre-Action Conduct.

The Practice Direction contains some provisions very relevant to the terms of the PI Protocol in relation to experts.

- Paragraph 9.4 provides that where the evidence of an expert is necessary the parties should consider how best to minimise expense and refers to the guidance in annex C.
- Paragraph 3 of annex C notes many matters can be resolved without the need for advice or evidence from an expert and provides that if an expert is needed the parties should consider how best to minimise the expense by, for example, agreeing to instruct a single joint expert or an agreed expert.
- Hence para 4 recommends that if the parties do not agree a single joint expert is appropriate the party seeking expert evidence should give the other party a list of experts in the relevant field of expertise. An expert on that list has the potential to be an agreed expert.
- Paragraph 5 of annex C provides for objection to nominated experts. This is by the party receiving the list objecting, within 14 days, to one or more experts and for the party who nominates those experts to instruct an expert who has not been objected to.

This approach is picked up by the terms of the PI Protocol where it deals with the joint selection of experts (as a way of identifying an agreed expert).

1.8.1 Joint selection of experts

The protocol provides for joint selection (as opposed to joint instruction) of experts. The distinction between joint selection and joint instruction is not just a matter of semantics, indeed para 2.14 of the PI Protocol specifically provides the report of a jointly selected expert is not a report for the purposes of Part 35 of the CPR.

The opportunity to jointly select, in accordance with the PI Protocol, is a very effective tool for the claimant which it will often be appropriate to make use of.

The importance of the distinction between joint selection and joint instruction was highlighted in *Carlson v Townsend*[33] where the Court of Appeal reached a number of conclusions.

- The PI Protocol does not provide for joint instruction, but rather joint selection.

- The PI Protocol provides for a practice whereby experts objectionable to one party are eliminated at the outset (which implies that in the absence of an objection a nominated expert may still be jointly selected as this does not necessarily involve agreement of the other party to the instruction of that expert).

- A report obtained from such an expert does not have to be disclosed to the defendant as the PI Protocol does not override the substantive law with regard to privilege (while privilege will not attach to a report prepared on the basis of joint instruction).

- Hence withholding such a report does not amount to non-compliance with the PI Protocol (although one party instructing an expert without giving the other party the opportunity of objecting would amount to non-compliance).

Whilst nothing in the PI Protocol or the CPR can affect privilege which attaches to a report obtained by one party (even if there has been joint selection) that party may yet have to agree to waive privilege as a condition of obtaining court permission to rely on expert evidence: *Edwards-Tubb v JD Wetherspoon plc*[34] (see **1.8.9**).

Consequently, it may sometimes be more appropriate to obtain expert advice, rather than expert opinion following nomination for joint selection, to avoid the risk of having to waive privilege (see **1.8.9** and **1.8.10**).

1.8.2 Range of experts

Whilst recognising the process of joint selection will most frequently apply to medical experts the PI Protocol recognises that, on occasions, this approach may also apply to liability experts. Accordingly, if expert evidence on liability may be necessary, should liability be disputed, it may be sensible to nominate appropriate experts at the outset.

1.8.3 Naming of experts

Selection implies the nomination of more than one expert in any particular field.

---

[33]   [2001] EWCA Civ 511.
[34]   [2011] EWCA Civ 136.

If appropriate experts in a number of specialisms may be nominated, as a range of experts may be necessary either at the outset or as the case develops and it may be useful to establish whether any nominated experts are objected to for the purpose of joint selection (or even joint instruction at a later stage).

However, it is not necessary, until disclosure of the report, to identify the expert who has been instructed nor is it necessary to disclose a copy of the instructions to the defendant as that simply confirms which expert, of those suggested, has been instructed.

1.8.4   Objections to experts

The PI Protocol allows the party receiving the names of experts, with a view to joint selection, to object.

There is a 14 day time limit for giving objections but where experts are nominated in the letter of claim the defendant effectively has 35 days (as in these circumstances the 14 days will not start to run until after the 21 days allowed for acknowledgement of the letter of claim has elapsed).

If there is an objection to an expert, then that expert cannot be jointly selected.

Any objection must be in clear terms, for example if the defendant just expresses preference for one or more expert(s) that is not an objection to the other expert(s) and any of those chosen by the claimant will have been jointly selected.

Where one or more of the experts proposed is objected to it will usually be appropriate to instruct an expert who has not been objected to, so that there is joint selection of a mutually acceptable expert.

The claimant may still instruct an expert who has been objected to but that expert will not have been jointly selected. In such circumstances the defendant may be regarded by the court, at a later stage, as having an attractive argument that permission be given to rely on a corresponding expert selected by the defendant.

If all experts proposed by the claimant are specifically objected to by the defendant the claimant may instruct any of the proposed experts, although the chosen expert will not have been jointly selected. The court will, if necessary, have to decide subsequently whether the defendant acted reasonably and the defendant may face difficulties in justifying objections to all the experts proposed.

Whilst there is no formal requirement, under the PI Protocol, to give reasons for objections it is not unreasonable to seek such reasons as, ultimately, the court may have to decide whether the defendant has acted reasonably if and when permission to obtain/rely upon further evidence from a corresponding expert is sought.

1.8.5   Further experts

When the initial report has been received this may suggest further expert evidence is required.

If so, it may be appropriate to nominate, or re-nominate, experts with a view to further joint selection.

1.8.6 Questions to experts

Either party may send written questions to an agreed expert, in other words putting questions acknowledges the expert has been jointly selected.

The questions must be relevant to the issues and sent via the solicitors who have instructed the expert.

The expert should send answers to the questions separately and directly to each party.

1.8.7 Cost of expert evidence

The cost of an expert's report will usually be paid by the party sending the instructions. Whilst this may involve outlay on behalf of the claimant it is important not to have any invoice sent direct to the defendant, at least pending a decision the evidence of the expert is to be relied upon.

The costs of an expert replying to questions will be met by the party who asks the questions (which is different to the situation prevailing once proceedings have been issued when the party who has instructed the expert will need to meet the costs of dealing with questions, whoever puts those questions).

1.8.8 Defendant's expert evidence

Where there has been joint selection and no suggestion of any range of opinion it will not usually be appropriate for the defendant to obtain medical evidence, at least prior to issue of court proceedings following which the court can consider what expert evidence is reasonably required.

The PI Protocol records that it promotes the practice of the claimant obtaining a medical report which is disclosed to the defendant who then asks questions and/or agrees it without obtaining a corresponding report.

Accordingly, to comply with the PI Protocol, if the defendant does maintain corresponding expert evidence is necessary it would seem appropriate to expect questions and for the defendant either to indicate agreement or any points of disagreement.

If the defendant maintains further expert evidence is required that will often need to be a matter resolved by the court, following the issue of proceedings, at the stage of case management, having regard to the steps taken under the protocol and the terms of Part 35.

1.8.9   Expert advice

The claimant may, rather than obtaining expert evidence whether on the basis of joint selection or joint instruction, prefer to seek, perhaps as a preliminary to an expert's report for potential use as evidence, expert advice.

The distinction between expert advice and expert evidence is recognised by both the Practice Direction – Pre-Action Conduct and Part 35 (see **7.2.3**).

An expert is not precluded from joint selection because advice has already been obtained from that expert.

Expert advice, as opposed to evidence, may be most appropriate where the claimant needs that advice in order to formulate appropriate details for the letter of claim or an advice is required in order to assess whether expert evidence in the relevant field of expertise is likely to be required.

1.8.10   Privilege

Expert evidence obtained by one party, even where there has been joint selection, will be privileged: *Carlson v Townsend.*[35]

Indeed, privilege will still attach to an initial or draft report of an expert who has not been jointly instructed even after a final version of the report is disclosed: *Jackson v Marley Davenport Ltd.*[36]

If, however, court proceedings are commenced any party wishing to rely on expert evidence will need appropriate permission from the court under the terms of Part 35. The claimant, in a personal injury claim will face considerable difficulties establishing much of the claim, at least on quantum, without relevant expert evidence and, accordingly, obtaining permission to rely on such evidence will be essential.

When granting permission to rely on expert evidence the court may impose, under the general case management powers conferred by Part 3, a condition that the claimant disclose to the defendant any report written by a jointly selected expert in the relevant field, even if the claimant does not wish to rely on that evidence: *Edwards-Tubb v JD Wetherspoon plc.*[37]

In *Edwards-Tubb* the claimant's solicitors listed three orthopaedic surgeons, in the letter of claim, and invited objection to any by the defendant. There was no such objection. However, when proceedings were served the Particulars of Claim were supported by a report from an orthopaedic surgeon who had not been nominated in the letter of claim. The Court of Appeal confirmed, in these circumstances, it was proper for the court to give conditional permission to rely on the claimant's chosen expert, the condition being the waiver of privilege, and production to the defendant, of the report prepared by an expert who had been nominated and thus jointly selected.

---

[35]   [2001] EWCA Civ 511.
[36]   [2004] EWCA Civ 1225.
[37]   [2011] EWCA Civ 136.

Expert advice is privileged and, as the Court of Appeal made clear in *Edwards-Tubb*, if there has been no joint selection for the purposes of preparing expert evidence it would not be appropriate to make any conditional order, when giving permission to rely on expert evidence, that privilege attaching to expert advice, or an expert's report where that has been obtained unilaterally without joint selection, be waived.

1.8.11 Consequences of the PI Protocol for future case management under the CPR

The PI Protocol provides that where there has been joint selection of an expert the party who failed to object will be unable to rely on corresponding expert evidence unless the court so directs.

Part 35 of the CPR clarifies the approach the court should take towards experts at the stage of case management and, of course, compliance with the protocol is, in any event, a relevant consideration for the court when deciding what directions to give.

CPR 35.2 confirms the term 'single joint expert' will not encompass an expert who has simply been the subject of joint selection. Rather, to be a single joint expert, it will be necessary for the expert to have been jointly instructed by two or more of the parties, including the claimant.

However, CPR 35.4(3A) provides that where a claim has been allocated to the fast track then if permission is given for expert evidence it will normally be given for evidence from only one expert on a particular issue. That, coupled with the requirement for the court now to consider whether the protocol has been complied with, may mean it is difficult, at least if the case is to remain in the fast track, for a defendant, where there has been joint selection even if that is by default, to gain permission from the court to rely on the evidence of a corresponding expert. It is worth noting this rule uses the phrase 'one expert' rather than the term 'single joint expert', and hence does not necessarily exclude a jointly selected expert.

Consequently, certainly in a case which is likely to be allocated to the fast track, this is a consideration which tells in favour of jointly selecting an expert, despite the risk of having to waive privilege as a condition of getting permission to rely on expert evidence from the court.

1.8.12 Tactics

Care is necessary, before dealing with experts in the letter of claim or other correspondence, about the most appropriate tactics given the opportunity for the claimant to jointly select an expert to give evidence or unilaterally obtain expert advice. There is also the option of inviting the defendant to agree the joint instruction of an expert.

- If the claimant needs the input of an expert to help formulate the letter of claim it may be most appropriate to seek, as a preliminary, expert advice.
- Expert advice, as a preliminary, may be sensible if it is not clear, without that advice, whether expert evidence in the relevant field is likely to be reasonably required.

- Expert advice may also be appropriate if there is a degree of uncertainty about the terms of the evidence the proposed expert may provide. An advice, before joint selection of any such expert, will help guard against the risk of the court later making an order granting conditional permission to rely on expert evidence involving waiver of privilege.

- If the expert evidence is on an issue where both parties are likely to seek an opinion, such as liability, joint selection is a possibility, to avoid the risk of the court later suggesting there should have been a joint expert, but unilateral instruction, for the expert to prepare a report, may nevertheless be appropriate.

- In a case likely to be allocated to the multi-track even evidence that might be suitable for a single expert may, nevertheless, involve unilateral instruction if it is considered likely the court will take the view, at the stage of case management directions, more than one expert in the relevant field will be reasonably required for the purposes of Part 35. The risk, however, is that unilateral instruction will effectively rule out the possibility of a single expert and could, at worst, result in the court directing there be a single joint expert and refusing the claimant permission to rely on the evidence of the expert unilaterally instructed.

- Consequently, in many circumstances it will be appropriate, tactically, to offer experts, in relevant disciplines, for the purposes of joint selection.

- Whilst it will rarely be appropriate to agree to joint instruction of experts prior to the issue of court proceedings from time to time that might be done, for example on an issue where expert input is required but is likely to be relatively non-contentious.

1.9   OBTAINING DOCUMENTS AND GIVING DISCLOSURE

The claimant will be likely, as part of the process of investigating the claim, to obtain relevant documents from the defendant and third parties.

The obligation under the PI Protocol for the claimant to give disclosure is relatively limited, even though the claimant may have documents which are likely to be disclosed under case management directions given following the issue of court proceedings.

1.9.1   Obtaining documents

The PI Protocol provides for the defendant to give disclosure of documents relating to liability, unless an appropriate admission is made.

To obtain relevant documents from the defendant or third parties the claimant can rely on the Data Protection Act 1998 and might also wish to make use of the Freedom of Information Act 2000.

1.9.1.1   *Data Protection Act 1998*

The Data Protection Act 1998 gives individuals, to whom relevant personal data relates, rights of access.

Data means information which:

- is being processed by means of equipment operating automatically in response to instructions given for that purposes;
- is recorded with the intention that it should be processed by means of such equipment;
- is recorded as part of a relevant filing system or with the intention that it should form part of a relevant filing system; or
- does not fall within the above but forms part of an accessible record.

An accessible record is defined by s 68 as including a health record and an educational record.

A Data Controller is a person who determines the purposes for which and the manner in which any personal data is processed.

Personal Data means data relating to a living individual who can be identified:
- from the data; or
- from the data and other information which is in the possession of, or is likely to come into the possession of, the Data Controller.

Processing means obtaining, recording or holding information or data.

An individual is entitled to the right of 'subject access' which means being informed by the Data Controller:
- whether personal data of which that individual is the data subject is being processed by or on behalf of that Data Controller;
- if that is the case a description of the personal data of which that individual is the data subject, the purposes for which that data is processed and the recipients or classes of recipients to whom the data may be disclosed;
- to have communicated in an intelligible form the information constituting any personal data of which that individual is the data subject and any information available to the Data Controller as to the source of the data; and
- be informed by the Data Controller of the logic involved in decision-taking where the processing by automatic means of personal data of which that individual is the data subject is for the purposes of evaluating matters relating to the subject such as work performance, creditworthiness, reliability or conduct and where this is likely to constitute the sole basis for any decision significantly affecting the subject.

The Act applies to all organisations which hold or use personal data. Any such organisations must notify the Information Commissioner about the processing undertaken by that organisation and this information is placed on a public register.

A subject access request can be made by writing to the Data Controller at the organisation holding data.

The organisation may ask for further information to confirm identity and locate the information required. The organisation may also ask for payment of a fee (usually up to £10 but up to £50 for health records which are not held in electronic form).

The Act allows the organisation 40 calendar days to answer the request, starting from the date the request is received.

On application a court can, if satisfied a subject access request has not been complied with, order compliance with that request under the terms of s 7(9) of the Act.

Additionally, the Information Commissioner may serve an enforcement notice so, rather than make application to the court under the Act, a complaint may be made to the Information Commissioner about any failure to properly comply with the subject access request. The Information Commissioner can be contacted at:

The Information Commissioner's Office
Wycliffe House
Water Lane
Wilmslow
Cheshire SK9 5AF

1.9.1.2   Freedom of Information Act 2000

The claimant may wish to rely on the terms of the Freedom of Information Act 2000 to obtain information that, in turn, may help identify whether or not any relevant documents are held by a public authority.

Section 1 of the Act imposes, when a request is made, a duty on a public authority to confirm or deny whether information, of the description specified in the request, is held and, if it is, to have that information communicated.

Section 8 requires a request to:
* be in writing;
* state the name of the applicant and an address for correspondence; and
* describe the information requested.

Schedule 1 to the Act lists public authorities and that list includes:
* any government department;
* the armed forces;
* a local authority;
* a health authority or trust;
* any person providing medical and dental services under the National Health Service Act 1977.

1.9.2   Who should obtain documents?

Care should always be exercised before recommending that the claimant provide authorities for the defendant to obtain documents from third parties. That is because it is the responsibility of the claimant's solicitor, as it is for the representative of any party, to determine, at least in the first instance, which documents properly comprise part of standard disclosure.

This process requires, first, that the issue be defined and, then, that the claimant's lawyer review documents potentially discloseable in the light of those issues. This cannot be done if those documents are obtained by the defendant.

If, however, a decision is made to provide authorities to the defendant that should be on the basis that any documents obtained are forthwith disclosed to the claimant's representatives.

1.9.3 Medical records

The PI Protocol envisages that relevant medical records will be made available to the medical expert by the claimant's solicitor.

There may be, depending on the type of case, records which are obviously not relevant although it may be preferable to obtain all records and ask the medical expert to identify those that are relevant.

Care should be exercised before disclosing any records to the defendant, certainly at this stage. That is because these are confidential documents and it is inappropriate to give what may prove to be unnecessary disclosure at an early stage. Some records may, of course, be identified as relevant by the medical expert, and disclosed with the report, otherwise disclosure may be best dealt with when that stage of any court proceedings is reached.

It is unlikely a defendant would be able to obtain records by an application for pre-action disclosure: *OCS Group Ltd v Wells*.[38] In many cases disclosure of records, or at least all records, will not be appropriate.

If the claim arises out of a low velocity impact, and the defendant indicates it is disputed the claimant suffered any injury, the Court of Appeal indicated in *Kearsley v Klarfeld*[39] that the claimant should give early disclosure, with irrelevant passages redacted if necessary, of any contemporaneous medical notes. This recognition of the need to redact irrelevant material only serves to confirm that disclosure of all records is not the usual or appropriate step, certainly at this stage of the claim.

Different considerations may apply at the stage of disclosure following issue of court proceedings (see 5.7).

A protocol has been agreed between the Law Society and the BMA for obtaining medical records. That involves giving appropriate advice to the claimant concerning the records to be obtained and the extent to which disclosure of those records may take place as well as seeking the records in the agreed format.

1.9.4 Documents supporting the schedule

If liability is admitted by the defendant the claimant should disclose, with the Schedule, supporting documents which may include:

---

[38]   [2008] EWHC 919 (QB).
[39]   [2005] EWCA Civ 1510.

- earnings details;
- receipts for expenditure; and
- documents confirming other losses.

1.9.5   Other documents

Unless liability is admitted any disclosure by the claimant will generally be inappropriate under the PI Protocol.

Even when liability is admitted care should be taken to ensure any disclosure by the claimant is controlled in a way that reflects the need for necessity, relevance and proportionality. Usually it will be more appropriate to give disclosure at the appropriate stage in any proceedings, when the issues will have been defined and the need for disclosure clear.

1.10   REHABILITATION

Part 4 of the PI Protocol deals with rehabilitation.

The parties ought to consider rehabilitation and the opportunity this may offer for improving the immediate difficulties faced by the claimant. The priority for all parties should be the early recovery of the injured claimant, as that will obviously benefit the claimant and may also help to reduce the damages that might ultimately have to be met by the defendant.

The Code of Best Practice on Rehabilitation, Early Intervention and Medical Treatment in Personal Injury Claims sets out a framework for the parties to approach these topics. APIL has also produced the Best Practice Guide on Rehabilitation which provides additional guidance and support in this important area.

Whilst the claimant's representatives should readily embrace effective rehabilitation it may be necessary to exercise caution for a number of reasons.

- The need for any treatment or rehabilitation will normally be identified, in the first instance, by those responsible for treating the claimant.
- Where any treatment or rehabilitation is appropriate the defendant should be asked to fund what is required and the claimant decide by whom that should be provided.
- While the defendant may be able to offer facilities for assessment and/or treatment this should always be undertaken by an agency independent of the relevant insurer and on the basis it will be undertaken completely outside the litigation process. Otherwise, there is a risk of the defendant, in effect, obtaining expert evidence, where that evidence should be limited to jointly selected experts under the protocol. Paragraph 4.4 of the protocol guards against this by providing any report obtained in relation to rehabilitation needs shall not be used in proceedings, the subject of the claim, except by consent.

These difficulties should be avoided if the Code of Best Practice is followed by the parties.

By analogy with the reasoning in *Copley v Lawn*[40] the defendant should not simply be able to stipulate provision of rehabilitation to the claimant. Rather, the defendant should make an interim payment or reimburse the provider of appropriate rehabilitation direct.

1.11 ADR

The PI Protocol and the Practice Direction – Pre-Action Conduct encourage ADR and, if possible, settlement.

1.11.1 Types of ADR

ADR is sometimes thought of in terms just of mediation. However, as para 8.2 of the Practice Direction makes clear, ADR includes any way of resolving the dispute without determination by the court. In personal injury claims, particularly at the pre-action stage, the most appropriate form of ADR is often, therefore, discussion and negotiation.

1.11.2 Advising the claimant of ADR

The claimant should be advised of the options for ADR at an early stage so that any specific wishes can be ascertained and implemented and also because, if and when proceedings are commenced, the court will need to be informed, in the Directions Questionnaire, that such advice has been given to the claimant.

1.11.3 Engaging the defendant with ADR

It may be helpful if the claimant indicates, at the outset, what is considered the appropriate method of ADR, which will usually be discussion and negotiation at that stage. Paragraph 8.1 of the Practice Direction – Pre-Action Conduct acknowledges ADR is not compulsory hence if the defendant does not reciprocate this approach the claimant ought not to be criticised for doing no more at this stage.

1.11.4 When to issue and when to pursue ADR

Paragraph 8 of the Practice Direction – Pre-Action Conduct provides that proceedings should not normally be started when a settlement is still actively being explored. However, if the defendant has not complied with the protocol the parties will not usually be at a stage where settlement is 'actively being explored'.

If the PI Protocol has been complied with, and some negotiations have taken place but the claim not yet been resolved, difficulties can arise in determining whether the terms of the Practice Direction make the issue of proceedings premature. Should the court conclude any proceedings have been issued where settlement is 'actively being explored' that may have a bearing on the costs of those proceedings (given the scope for sanctions identified in para 4.6).

---

40   [2009] EWCA Civ 580, [2010] Bus LR 83.

However, for these purposes case-law indicates the courts should not speculate what would have happened if one or other party had made an offer which, in fact, was not made.

In *Ellison v Fairclough*[41] the court, when considering costs in a case of alleged premature issue, followed the guidance given by the Court of Appeal on this topic in *Straker v Tudor Rose*[42] where Waller LJ held:

> 'If the judge is finding that the case would have settled as opposed to finding that there was a chance it would have settled, that could not have been other than a speculation. In my view it does not come well from a defendant who has paid money into court to argue that if a claimant had been more reasonable he would have offered more. An investigation as to how negotiations would have gone is precisely the form of investigation which should be avoided. In a case about money a defendant has the remedy in his own hands where a claimant is being intransigent. He can pay into court the maximum sum he is prepared to pay.'

The claim in *Ellison* arose out of a road traffic accident in which liability was admitted and the claimant disclosed details on quantum with an invitation proposals for settlement be made within the 21 day period. The defendant made an offer of £1,100. The claimant invited an improved offer and warned proceedings would be issued in default. Following issue the claim settled, within a month, for £1,700. Allowing an appeal from the decision of the District Judge, that only predicable costs be awarded, the Circuit Judge followed *Straker* on the basis the claimant had complied with the protocol and the defendant had made an offer which was outside a reasonable bracket leaving the claimant entitled to issue proceedings. There was no basis for departing from the general rule the claimant was entitled to costs on the standard basis in these circumstances.

In contrast the claimant, though on the basis these would be assessed, recovered only partial costs in *Bellison v McKay*,[43] though in that case there were breaches of the protocol by the claimant and costs of preparing for a full trial were incurrent when, in reality, the only live issue remaining was costs. Similarly, a claimant was restricted to predictable costs in *Turner v Gribbon*.[44] Once again, however, the case had unusual features, not least delay by the claimant which allowed the court to conclude that had appropriate information on the value of the claim been given promptly there would have been no need to issue proceedings at all.

The need to avoid issue of proceedings whilst settlement is still actively being explored must, however, be seen in the context of the overriding objective. The parties have a duty to help further the overriding objective, which includes the need for claims to be dealt with at proportionate cost but also expeditiously. Consequently, even though the sums involved may not be substantial, but the parties are some way apart and negotiations seem likely to be protracted, it may be less costly, and hence more proportionate, simply to get proceedings underway as that may force a resolution of the claim sooner and at less overall cost which is also likely to be most expeditious. It is worth noting that in *Straker* Waller LJ envisaged the defendant offering the maximum he was prepared to pay, surely a warning to defendants against what might be termed 'drip-feed' negotiations.

---

[41] (Unreported) Liverpool County Court, 30 July 2007.
[42] [2007] EWCA Civ 368.
[43] (Unreported) Exeter County Court, 11 March 2008.
[44] (Unreported) Bristol County Court, 27 August 2008.

It is on this basis, perhaps, that an offer, before medical evidence was available, of £500, in a claim which ultimately settled for damages of £1,560, was held to be 'derisory' in *Letts v Royal Sun Alliance plc*.[45] Moreover, although a further offer was made and the proceedings issued on the day the protocol period expired the court held that issue of proceedings was not premature to any material degree and that the amount of costs allowable had the claim settled pre-issue could not simply act as a cap on the costs of assessment (although if proceedings were issued prematurely that would be a relevant factor in assessing the amount of costs).

Whilst the PI Protocol observes both parties should always consider whether to make a Part 36 offer before issuing proceedings it is only necessary to 'consider' rather than to 'make', reflecting the view expressed in *Straker* that the onus is on the defendant to make an appropriate offer if wishing to engage in ADR.

1.11.5 Sanctions for failing to follow ADR

Whilst paragraph 8.1 of the Practice Direction – Pre-Action Conduct recognises ADR is not compulsory it recommends that the parties consider whether some form of ADR might enable them to settle the matter without starting proceedings. This paragraph of the Practice Direction also observes that court proceedings should usually be a step of last resort and not normally started when a settlement is still actively being explored.

Sanctions can be applied, by the court at a later stage, if a party does not engage in ADR. Any such sanction is likely to sound in costs.

In *Halsey v Milton Keynes General NHS Trust*[46] the Court of Appeal held that, if ADR was to have an impact on the application of the general rule that the unsuccessful party should pay the costs of the successful party the onus would be on the party suggesting ADR to show the other party acted unreasonably in refusing it.

However, in *Burchell v Bullard*[47] the Court of Appeal held a building dispute was a case which leant itself to ADR and the only reason a sanction was not imposed on the defendant, for refusing to mediate, was that the claimant's offer to do so was made prior to the decision in *Halsey*. It was observed that:

> '... these defendants have escaped the imposition of a costs sanction in this case but the defendants in a like position in the future can expect little sympathy if they blithely battle on regardless of the alternatives.'

Consequently, in *Rolf v De Guerin*,[48] yet another building dispute, costs sanctions did follow the defendant's refusal to participate in round-table discussions. Rix LJ held:

> '... the facts of the case disclose that negotiation and/or mediation would have had reasonable prospects of success. The spurned offers to enter into settlement negotiations or mediation were unreasonable and ought to bear materially on the outcome of the court's discretion, particularly in this class of case.'

---

[45] [2012] EWHC 875 (QB).
[46] [2004] EWCA Civ 576.
[47] [2005] EWCA Civ 358.
[48] [2011] EWCA Civ 78.

Further impetus towards ADR was given by the Court of Appeal in *PGF II SA v OMFS Company 1 Ltd* (see **12.2.4.1.2**).[49]

1.12   RESOLUTION

If the claim is resolved within the PI Protocol terms of settlement need to be reached for the whole claim and costs dealt with.

1.12.1   Settlement

If settlement is achieved pre-action, it is important that the terms to which both parties agree are clearly set out in correspondence.

A number of matters will need to be covered in most, if not every, case.

*   The sum payable and, as appropriate, how this breaks down between:
    –   any CRU deduction;
    –   any interim payments; and
    –   any balance payable.
*   The timescale for payment.
*   That the defendant is to pay the claimant's costs (as under Part 44, the Part 8 procedure can only be used if the relevant agreement is recorded in writing and includes provision for payment of costs).

1.12.2   2003 Fixed recoverable costs (predictable costs)

Predictable costs will apply to a claim arising out of a road traffic accident which occurred on or after 6 October 2003, where the agreed damages are outside the small claims track limit but do not exceed £10,000.

Predictable costs are not applicable to claims settled within the 2010 RTA Protocol, but do apply to claims which leave that protocol but are settled, for damages not exceeding £10,000, before the issue of court proceedings.

If a claim enters the 2013 RTA Protocol, which will apply to any claim within scope whenever the accident occurred if the CNF was not submitted by 31 July 2013, costs, at whatever stage the claim is settled (subject to certain exceptions), will be in accordance with the tables of fixed costs set out in CPR 45.18 (as the CPR reads from April 2013).

1.12.2.1   Scope

The scope of the scheme, and figures for costs, are set out in S.II Part 45 (as that rule read prior to April 2013).

The Costs Practice Direction (as it read prior to April 2013) gives further detail on the scope of the scheme.

---

[49]   [2013] EWCA Civ 1288.

These rules provide for fixed costs to be recoverable between parties in respect of costs incurred in disputes which are settled prior to proceedings being issued. The section applies to road traffic accident disputes as defined by CPR 45.7(4)(a), where the accident which gave rise to the dispute occurred on or after 6 October 2003.

Injury must be caused by, or arise out of, the 'use' of a motor vehicle on a road (see **1.14.2.2**).

The section does not apply to disputes where the total agreed value of the damages is within the small claims limit or exceeds £10,000.

The section applies to cases which fall within the Uninsured Drivers Agreement but not to cases which fall within the MIB Untraced Drivers Agreement.

Where there is more than one potential claimant in relation to a dispute and two or more claimants instruct the same solicitor or firm of solicitors, the provisions of the section apply in respect of each claimant.

1.12.2.2 Amount

Fixed recoverable costs are calculated by reference to the amount of agreed damages which are payable to the receiving party. In calculating the amount of these damages:

- account must be taken of both general and special damages and interest;
- any interim payments made must be included;
- where the parties have agreed an element of contributory negligence, the amount of damages attributed to that negligence must be deducted;
- any amount required by statute to be paid by the compensating party directly to a third party (such as sums paid by way of compensation recovery payments and National Health Service expenses) must not be included.

The formula for calculating the amount of fixed recoverable costs is to total the following:

- the sum of £800;
- 20 per cent of the agreed damages up to £5,000; and
- 15 per cent of the agreed damages between £5,000 and £10,000.

These figures are exclusive of VAT and any success fee.

Additional costs will be allowed for work in specified areas, namely (within London) the county court districts of Barnet, Bow, Brentford, Central London, Clerkenwell, Edmonton, Ilford, Lambeth, Mayors and City of London, Romford, Shoreditch, Wandsworth, West London, Willesden and Woolwich and (outside London) the county court districts of Bromley, Croydon, Dartford, Gravesend and Uxbridge.

The court can allow, but only in exceptional circumstances, more than predictable costs but if these are assessed at no more than 20 per cent above the predictable figure the claimant will be ordered to pay the costs of both sides for the Part 8 proceedings.

1.12.2.3   Exceptionality

CPR 45.12 allows the court to entertain a claim for an amount greater than fixed recoverable costs, but only if the court considers there are exceptional circumstances making it appropriate to do so.

In *York v Adams*[50] the claimant obtained medical evidence to help assess whether the effect of the trauma resulting from a road traffic accident had accelerated a pre-existing condition, the court accepting further medical evidence was necessary to deal with this and so the case was exceptional.

In *Udogaranya v Nwagw*[51] the court noted the dictionary definition of 'exceptional' is 'unusual or not typical'. Consequently, the predictable costs regime was held to be 'fair enough in the normal run-of-the-mill case'. This, however, was not a 'run-of-the-mill' case given that:

- relevant events took place over two years and eight months;
- the defendant was giving the claimant the 'run-round' which, whilst it may be normal practice in certain cases, is not consistent with the purposes of the fixed costs regime that relevant protocols confirm are intended to bring matters to a conclusion as soon as possible;
- both breach and causation were disputed initially, on the basis that there was either no impact or, if there was, it had been a low velocity impact; and
- extensive requests for further information were made.

Thus, the claimant had to decide whether to accept predictable costs or seek assessment, mindful that under CPR 45.13 the claimant must, at detailed assessment, recover costs of more than 20 per cent above predictable costs or be restricted to predictable costs and also have to meet the costs of the defendant for the detailed assessment.

1.12.2.4   Timescale

In *Scargill v Shah*[52] the claimant, on settlement, asked for predictable costs warning that Part 8 proceedings would be commenced unless payment was made within 14 days. Payment was not made so Part 8 proceedings were commenced and the costs were then paid. The court held, by analogy with CPR 44.8 (which requires payment of costs within 14 days of the date of Judgment or Order providing for those costs), a reasonable timescale for payment of predictable costs was 14 days. Where, as happened in this case, the defendant was silent it was reasonable for the receiving party to treat that silence as an implied dispute and commence Part 8 proceedings. Accordingly, the defendant was ordered to pay the costs of the Part 8 proceedings in addition to the predictable costs.

[50] (Unreported) Sheffield County Court, 27 March 2008.
[51] [2010] EWHC 90186 (Costs).
[52] (Unreported) Chester County Court, 21 December 2004.

1.12.2.5 Indemnity principle?

In *Butt v Nizami*[53] it was held the indemnity principle had no application to predictable costs under Part 45 and hence no need for the paying party to be satisfied any conditional fee agreement was compliant with the regulations. Accordingly:

'In cases falling under CPR 45 S.II the receiving party does not have to demonstrate that there is a valid retainer between the solicitor and client merely that the conditions laid down under the rules have been complied with.'

1.12.2.6 Success fee?

In *Kilby v Gawith*[54] it was held that where the claimant had entered a conditional fee agreement a success fee fixed at 12.5 per cent of the fixed recoverable costs was payable, with no discretion available to reduce or disallow that additional liability.

1.12.2.7 Part 36

If, in a claim to which the terms of s II Part 45 apply, a Part 36 offer is accepted before the issue of court proceedings, the costs payable will be those set out in this section rather than costs assessed on the standard basis: *Solomon v Cromwell*[55] (see **1.12.1.1.1**).

1.12.3 2010 RTA Protocol fixed costs

Claims settled within the 2010 RTA Protocol carry, rather than predictable costs, the costs applicable under CPR 45.29 (as it read until April 2013).

These costs applied, with a variation effective from 30 April 2013, where the CNF was submitted up to 30 July 2013.

1.12.3.1 Profit costs

Profit costs include:

- Stage 1: £200 (£400 where the CNF was submitted by 30 April 2013);
- Stage 2: £300 (£800 where the CNF was submitted by 30 April 2013);
- Stage 3:
  - Type A (the legal representative's costs): £250.
  - Type B (advocate's costs): £250 (the term 'advocate' being defined in CPR 45.37(2) (a) as 'a person exercising a right of audience as a representative of, or on behalf of, a party').
  - Type C (costs for the advice on the amount of damages where the claimant is a child): £150.

These costs do not include:

- London weighting (12.5% on costs of stage 1, stage 2 and type A stage 3 costs);

---

[53]   [2006] EWHC 159 (QB).
[54]   [2008] EWCA Civ 812.
[55]   [2011] EWCA Civ 1584.

- VAT;
- disbursements;
- a success fee.

1.12.3.2   Disbursements

CPR 45.19 deals with disbursements, that can be recovered in addition to profit costs, and which may include the following:

- medical records;
- a medical report or reports or non-medical expert reports as provided for in the relevant protocol;
- an engineer's report;
- DVLA search;
- Motor Insurance Database search;
- court fees (as a result of Part 21 being applicable);
- court fees where proceedings are started as a result of a limitation period that is about to expire;
- court fees for the stage 3 procedure;
- any other disbursement;
- ATE premium (where this is recoverable).

1.12.3.3   Success fees

The former CPR 45.31(3) set the claimant's success fee, if there is a conditional fee agreement which is a 'pre-commencement funding arrangement' as defined by Part 48, at 12.5% for stages 1 and 2 and 100% of relevant stage 3 costs.

The former CPR 45.31(4) provided that where there is a stage 3 hearing and the claimant is to pay the defendant's costs then, if the defendant has entered a conditional fee agreement, the success fee on the defendant's costs is also 100%.

1.12.3.4   Indemnity principle?

As these fixed costs are, like predictable costs, set under Part 45 the indemnity principle should not apply (see **1.12.2.5**).

1.12.4   2013 fixed costs for the protocols

CPR 45.18 contains tables setting out fixed costs applicable to claims which enter either the RTA Protocol or the EL/PL Protocol from 31 July 2013 and which settle within the relevant protocol.

Table 6
Fixed costs in relation to the RTA Protocol

Where the value of the claim for damages is not more than £10,000		Where the value of the claim for damages is more than £10,000 but not more than £25,000	
Stage 1 fixed costs	£200	Stage 1 fixed costs	£200
Stage 2 fixed costs	300	Stage 2 fixed costs	600
Stage 2 Type A fixed costs	250	Stage 3 Type A fixed costs	250
Type B fixed costs	250	Type B fixed costs	250
Type C fixed costs	150	Type C fixed costs	150

Table 6A
Fixed costs in relation to the EL/PL Protocol

Where the value of the claim for damages is not more than £10,000		Where the value of the claim for damages is more than £10,000 but not more than £25,000	
Stage 1 fixed costs	£300	Stage 1 fixed costs	£300
Stage 2 fixed costs	600	Stage 2 fixed costs	1,300
Stage 3 Type A fixed costs	250	Stage 3 Type A fixed costs	250
Type B fixed costs	250	Type B fixed costs	250
Type C fixed costs	150	Type C fixed costs	150

Once again, as these costs are fixed by Part 45, the indemnity principle should not apply (see **1.12.2.5**).

Fixed costs are also provided, by further tables set out in CPR 45.29C, for claims which start, but no longer continue under, the RTA Protocol or the EL/PL Protocol (see **12.2.7.1.3**).

1.12.5   Non-fixed costs

If fixed costs are not applicable on settlement prior to issue of court proceedings the agreement between the parties should provide for the defendant to pay the claimant's reasonable costs, to be the subject of a detailed assessment, if not agreed.

That is because the claimant will, if proceedings were commenced, be entitled to recover costs for pre-action work *In Re Gibson's Settlement Trusts*.[56] Consequently, as the costs incurred could be recovered if proceedings were commenced it is reasonable to expect, in most circumstances, the defendant will agree to meet costs as part of a pre-action settlement.

Conversely, even if proceedings are issued a defendant who successfully persuades a claimant to abandon a claim, pursued under a protocol but not included in the proceedings issued, will be unable to recover costs incurred, in relation to that claim, as incidental to the proceedings subsequently issued: *McGlinn v Walsham Contractors Ltd*.[57]

The claimant will not usually have any liability for costs the defendant may incur unless and until a claim form is issued (see **2.3.10**). Even if a liability for costs arises a defendant who has acted without a solicitor should not be entitled to recover, as a disbursement, fees or expenses paid to a third party for work of a kind which a solicitor could have done: *Agassi v Robinson (Inspector of Taxes) (Costs)*.[58] Hence costs of pre-action work undertaken by loss adjusters was not recoverable, nor even fees paid by the loss adjusters to a solicitor where there was no formal agency agreement, in *Cuthbert v Gair*.[59]

Provided the defendant agrees, in writing, to pay costs then, if those costs cannot be agreed, the claimant can issue a Part 8 claim form in order to have the costs assessed by the court.

Only fixed costs, certainly with an adult claimant, are likely to be recovered if the claim would, on issue of court proceedings, have been allocated to the small claims track. If the claimant is a child, even with a small claim, the position on costs may be different where application is made for approval of a settlement: *Dockerill v Tullett*.[60]

In *Dockerill* the damages, in a claim brought on behalf of a child, had been agreed at £750. The claim was properly issued under Part 8 as CPR 21.10.2(b) provided that this procedure must be followed where the sole purpose was to obtain approval of a settlement or compromise. That being so CPR 8.9(c) provided the claim shall be treated as allocated to the multi-track and in such cases costs were to be the subject of assessment under Part 44. Nevertheless, when assessing costs, the court had to consider whether the costs claimed were proportionate to the issues involved and could, if this were the case, reflect the track to which the claim would have been allocated, if a Part 7 claim form had been issued, when determining what costs were reasonably incurred (applying *O'Beirne v Hudson*[61]).

---

[56]   [1981] 1 All ER 233.
[57]   [2005] EWHC 1419 (TCC).
[58]   [2005] EWCA Civ 1507.
[59]   (2008) 105 (39) LSG 22.
[60]   [2012] EWCA Civ 184.
[61]   [2010] EWCA Civ 52.

1.12.6   Approval

If either party is a child or protected party approval by the court at the settlement should be sought, rather than relying on an agreement in correspondence, perhaps including a parental indemnity, so that the claim is properly finalised.

Approval will require preparation of the appropriate documentation which is likely to include the following:

- Part 8 claim form;
- appointment of litigation friend;
- advice on, or statement about, the settlement giving relevant background and reasons why the settlement is considered appropriate;
- draft order;
- consent of litigation friend;
- Form 320 (for investment purposes);
- notice of funding (if additional liabilities are to be claimed).

1.12.7   Finality

If the parties agree an issue or part of the claim that is likely, as with any agreement, to form a binding compromise even if other issues or parts of the claim remain in dispute: *Bewicke-Copley v Ibeh*[62] (and see **1.7.2.4.1**).

If terms of settlement are reached for the whole claim that will, as with agreement on an issue, generally amount to a binding compromise.

A compromise, like any contract, may be vitiated on grounds such as fraud or mistake, though even with an alleged misrepresentation it may not be possible to re-open the agreement if the issue is one that had emerged and effectively been part of the compromise reached: *Zurich Insurance Co plc v Hayward*.[63]

Should an insurer have dealt directly with the claimant, and not suggested the need for independent legal advice, the court may conclude a breach of fiduciary duty, arising out of undue influence or inequality, allowing any agreement to be set aside if the claimant relied on the insurer: *Horry v Tate & Lyle Refineries*.[64]

1.13   STOCKTAKE

Paragraph 2.17 of the PI Protocol recommends that where the claim is not resolved a stocktake by the parties may be carried out before proceedings are started. The stocktake may be arrived at because the defendant has failed to comply with the terms of the protocol, or because, although the protocol has been complied with, this has not allowed the claim to be resolved.

---

[62]   (Unreported) Oxford County Court, 4 June 2014.
[63]   [2011] EWCA Civ 641
[64]   [1982] 2 Lloyd's Rep 416.

The stocktake may suggest some further negotiations, or other means of resolving the dispute without litigation, will be appropriate, that the case should be discontinued or that proceedings should be issued.

It is important that, if unresolved, the claim does not become stalled and the stocktake is undertaken promptly so that appropriate action can be implemented.

Accordingly, this stocktake should be undertaken unless settlement, under the PI Protocol, is achieved in a timely way.

Any of the following circumstances may prompt at least a consideration of the need to issue court proceedings.

- Failure by the defendant to acknowledge the letter of claim within time.
- Failure by the defendant to give a decision on liability within time.
- Failure by the defendant to give an admission in sufficiently clear terms and/or in a way that is likely to be binding.
- Denial of liability (remembering causation is an aspect of liability).
- A dispute on contributory negligence which prevents agreement on this issue.
- Failure to disclose (all) relevant documents where liability is not fully admitted.
  - Where, despite the absence of disclosure, an assessment of the merits of the case on liability can be made it is likely proceedings will be issued.
  - If disclosure is required in order to assess the merits of the case it may be more appropriate to make application for pre-action disclosure remembering that such disclosure should now have been seen as part of the usual pre-action exchange of information with costs sanctions applying in default.
- Failure to make prompt proposals (21 days in accordance with PI Protocol)for settlement following disclosure of information on quantum.
- Failure to agree quantum despite negotiations bearing in mind the need to balance the avoidance of proceedings at a stage when 'settlement is still being actively explored' (para 8.1 of the Practice Direction) and the need to act proportionately and avoid unnecessary costs (para 6.2).
- Failure by the defendant to make timely proposals for adequate interim payments, in cases where liability has been admitted but there is no firm prognosis or other reasons exist which make final settlement impossible at that stage.
- Where proceedings need to be issued for limitation reasons though, in such circumstances, it may still be appropriate to try and follow the spirit of the protocol:
  - which may be achieved by deferring service (but generally once issued proceedings are best served promptly); or
  - serving proceedings and agreeing, and/or seeking permission from the court, for timescale to be extended whilst steps that would normally have been taken under the protocol are followed.

A review prompted by any of these circumstances should force a decision to issue court proceedings, pursue further negotiations or discontinue the claim. That decision is best made sooner rather than later.

Consequently, following the stocktake, it may be appropriate to engage in further negotiation, seek instructions to discontinue the claim or seek instructions to issue court proceedings.

1.14 THE RTA PROTOCOL

The 2010 RTA Protocol was introduced to deal with personal injury claims arising out of road traffic accidents, occurring after 30 April 2010, so far as such claims were within the scope of, and remained in, that protocol.

The 2010 RTA Protocol has since been largely superseded by the 2013 RTA Protocol.

1.14.1 Overview

Each RTA Protocol comprises stages, with fixed costs for each of those stages.

1.14.1.1 Stages

The process described by each RTA Protocol comprises three stages, namely:

- Stage 1: when the claim is notified to the defendant in accordance with the process and, to keep it within the process, a timely admission made by the defendant.
- Stage 2: when, provided the case remains within the process, details on quantum are disclosed and offers exchanged with a view to reaching settlement.
- Stage 3: for those cases that, whilst remaining in the process, are not resolved in stage 2 and which proceed to a court hearing when quantum can be assessed.

1.14.1.2 Communication

Where each protocol requires information to be sent to a party it must be sent electronically, para 5.1 of the 2013 RTA Protocol confirming this must be sent via www.claimsportal.org.uk (or any other portal address that may be prescribed from time to time). The only exception to this provision is the 'Defendant Only CNF'.

Paragraph 5.1 also requires the claimant to give an email address in the CNF and for all written communications between the parties not required by the terms of the protocol to be sent by email.

1.14.1.3 Costs

Costs in each RTA Protocol are fixed, reflecting the predictable nature, and well-defined parameters, of the process.

1.14.1.4 Preamble

Paragraph 2.1 of each protocol confirms that it describes the behaviour the court expects of parties prior to the start of court proceedings, with a claim that falls within the scope of the protocol, and specifically notes that the CPR enables the court to impose costs sanctions where the protocol is not followed.

1.14.1.5   Aims

Paragraph 3.1 of each protocol sets out the aims which suggest a purposive interpretation should be adopted towards the rules, towards achieving those aims.

1.14.1.5.1   General aims

These are:
- the defendant pays damages and costs using the process set out in the protocol without the need for the claimant to start proceedings;
- damages are paid within a reasonable time; and
- the claimant's legal representative receives fixed costs at each appropriate stage.

1.14.1.5.2   Aims in soft tissue injury claims

Paragraph 3.2 of the 2013 Protocol identifies additional aims in soft tissue injury claims, namely:
- the use and cost of medical reports is controlled;
- in most cases only one medical report is obtained;
- the medical expert is normally independent of any medical treatment; and
- offers are made only after a fixed cost medical report has been obtained and disclosed.

1.14.1.5.3   Significance of aims

These aims, along with the overriding objective, will be significant if the court later has to determine whether parties have behaved reasonably in commencing proceedings. A party is likely to be regarded as having acted unreasonably if that party has sought to 'manipulate' the terms of, and hence defeat the aims of, the protocol, whether this be the claimant (for example *Ilahi v Usman*[65]) or the defendant (for example *Amiri v Haven Insurance*[66]).

Furthermore, by definition, failure to comply with the protocol will amount to unreasonable behaviour (because the party in default will have failed to adopt the behaviour the court expects).

There will also have been a failure to comply with the terms of the Practice Direction Pre-Action Conduct and that will be a relevant consideration, under the terms of CPR 1.1(2)(f), in the event proceedings are issued (so far as further case management and costs are concerned) as well as raising the possibility of a sanction under the terms of the Practice Direction itself (to reflect the breaches that have already occurred).

---

[65]   (Unreported) Manchester County Court, 29 November 2012.
[66]   (Unreported) Birkenhead County Court, 22 January 2014.

In *Patel v Fortis Insurance*[67] Mr Recorder Morgan, recognising these aims, observed, of the RTA Protocol, that:

> 'It is clearly of a different character to other Pre-Action Protocols: it is more prescriptive; it is a largely self-contained scheme; it has a fixed costs regime and it is linked to bespoke court process under CPR Part 8. There are also specific rules as to costs contained in Part V of CPR Part 45 and these link with specific rules as to offers to settle contained in Part II of CPR Part 36.'

Consequently, the behaviour described in the protocol, with a view to achieving the aims of the protocol, should be precisely what the parties are entitled to expect of each other.

1.14.1.6 Rules

The relevant protocol sets out stages 1 and 2.

Stage 3 is dealt with by Practice Direction 8B to the Civil Procedure Rules.

1.14.1.7 Which protocol?

Paragraph 4.2 of the 2013 Protocol confirms that the 2010 Protocol will continue to apply, as it stood immediately before 31 July 2013, to all claims where the CNF was submitted prior to 31 July 2013.

The 2013 Protocol applies to claims, within scope, where the CNF was submitted on or after 31 July 2013 (whenever the accident occurred).

Where, however, the accident occurred on or after 30 April 2010 but before 31 July 2013 the upper limit, even though the claim enters the 2013 Protocol, is £10,000.

The 2013 Protocol has been amended in 2014 so that where the CNF is submitted on or after 1 October 2014 special rules apply to a claim which is a 'soft tissue injury claim'

1.14.2 Scope

Each protocol defines the scope of the process and hence, subject to the specific exceptions, what claims are suitable for, and so will normally be put into, the protocol.

Paragraph 4.1 of each protocol, when dealing with the scope, confirms that it applies to a claim for damages arising out of a road traffic accident occurring on or after 30 April 2010 (the 2010 RTA Protocol) or where the CNF is submitted on or after 31 July 2013 (the 2013 RTA Protocol), where the claim includes damages for personal injury and the claim falls within scope on value.

To determine the precise scope it is necessary to look at definitions given in the protocol as well as rules dealing with the value of claims covered by the protocol.

---

[67] (Unreported) Leicester County Court, 5 December 2011.

1.14.2.1   Road traffic accident

The term 'road traffic accident' means:

- an accident resulting in bodily injury to any person;
- caused by, or arising out of, the use of a motor vehicle on a road or other public place in England and Wales (see **1.13.2.1**);
- unless the injury was caused wholly or in part by a breach by the defendant of one or more of the relevant statutory provisions defined by s 53 Health & Safety at Work etc Act 1974 (which remain in force as part of the criminal law despite the terms of the Enterprise Act 2013), namely:
  - the Control of Substances Hazardous to Health Regulations 2002;
  - the Lifting Operations and Lifting Equipment Regulations 1998;
  - the Management of Health and Safety at Work Regulations 1999;
  - the Manual Handling Operations Regulations 1992;
  - the Personal Protective Equipment at Work Regulations 1992;
  - the Provision and Use of Work Equipment Regulations 1998;
  - the Work at Height Regulations 2005; and
  - the Workplace (Health, Safety and Welfare) Regulations 1992.

1.14.2.2   Use of a motor vehicle

The term 'motor vehicle' means a mechanically propelled vehicle intended for use on roads (see **1.13.2.1**).

'Intended for use' may require the court to identify what use a vehicle might reasonably be intended for, hence a forklift truck without lights, indicators, road tax or MOT certificate was held not to be a 'motor vehicle' in *Conelly v Lancaster*,[68] applying *Burns v Currell*.[69] Where Lord Parker CJ held, when considering the meaning of the word 'intended' that the test was 'whether a reasonable person looking at the vehicle would say that one of its users would be a road user'.

Use of the motor vehicle must be on a road or public place in England and Wales.

A 'road' means any highway and other road to which the public has access and includes bridges over which a road passes.

'Use' requires a sufficiently close causal connection as explained in *Dunthorne v Bentley*.[70] There was no such connection in *Adams v Arla Foods UK*,[71] *Caroe v Stacey*[72] and *O'Brien v Sundown Court Management*.[73] There was, however, a sufficiently close connection in *Schneider v Door2door PTS Ltd*.[74]

---

[68]   (Unreported) Manchester County Court, 4 March 2011.
[69]   [1963] 2 QB 433.
[70]   [1996] RTR 428.
[71]   (Unreported) Altrincham County Court, 12 May 2009.
[72]   SCCO 1 June 2009.
[73]   (Unreported) Liverpool County Court 27 July 2011.
[74]   [2001] EWHC 90210 (Costs).

1.14.2.3 Value

Paragraph 4.1(4) of each protocol confirms that it applies where if proceedings were started the small claims track would not be the normal track for the claim. CPR 26.6 provides the small claims track will not be the normal track in a personal injury claim where damages for pain, suffering and loss of amenity is more than £1,000.

However, perhaps recognising it may be difficult to determine the precise value of a claim at the outset, para 5.9 provides that where the claimant reasonably believes the claim is valued at between £1,000 and £10,000 but it subsequently becomes apparent the true value is less than £1,000 the claimant will be entitled to costs allowed under the process. For example, where damages of £850 were agreed, and that settlement approved by the court, costs under the process were allowed on the basis that it could not be said at the stage when the claim was submitted its value was plainly less than £1,000: *Bromley v Hewson*.[75]

The upper limit is set out in para 1.2(1) of each protocol. The original upper limit, set out in the 2010 RTA Protocol, was £10,000. The 2013 RTA Protocol provides for a revised upper limit of £25,000 where the accident occurred on or after 31 July 2013, but confirms that the upper limit remains £10,000 where the accident occurred on or after 30 April 2010 but before 31 July 2013.

Paragraph 4.1(3) confirms the scope of the protocol is limited by the upper limit, as it only applies where the claimant values the claim at no more than that limit.

The upper limit in each protocol includes pecuniary losses as well as damages for pain, suffering and loss of amenity but, for these purposes, those pecuniary losses exclude, by para 4.3 of the 2010 RTA Protocol and para 4.4 of the 2013 RTA Protocol, vehicle related damages. These, in turn, are defined in para 1.1 as damages for:

- the pre-accident value of the vehicle;
- vehicle repair;
- vehicle insurance excess; and
- vehicle hire.

In assessing the value of the claim any reduction for contributory negligence should be left out of account.

Paragraph 4.2 of the 2010 RTA Protocol and para 4.3 of the 2013 RTA Protocol provide that the protocol will cease to apply if the claimant, at any stage, notifies the defendant the claim has now been revalued at more than the upper limit.

1.14.2.4 Soft tissue injury claim

Some claims arising out of a 'road traffic accident' will be a 'soft tissue injury claim' which is defined as:

---

[75] Medway County Court 6 September 2012.

'"Soft tissue injury claim' means a claim brought by an occupant of a motor vehicle where the significant physical injury caused is a soft tissue injury and includes claims where there is a minor psychological injury secondary in significance to the physical injury.'

Special rules apply, in particular concerning medical evidence and early offers, to a soft tissue injury claim.

1.14.2.4.1   Accredited medical expert

It is proposed that only an 'accredited medical expert' will be able to prepare a report for use in a soft tissue injury claim. This is likely to be an expert:

- registered with MedCo as a provider of reports for soft tissue injury claims; or
- is accredited to provide reports for soft tissue injury claims under the accreditation process approved by MedCo; and
- is in one of the following disciplines:
  - consultant orthopaedic surgeon;
  - consultant in accident and emergency medicine;
  - general practitioner registered with the General Medical Council;
  - physiotherapist registered with the Health and Care Professions Council.

1.14.2.4.2   Fixed cost medical report

A 'fixed cost medical report' means a report in a soft tissue injury claim which is from a medical expert (and it is proposed only an *accredited* medical expert) who, save in exceptional circumstances:

- has not provided treatment to the claimant;
- is not associated with any person who has provided treatment; and
- does not propose or recommend that they or an associate provide treatment.

CPR 45.19(2A) provides for the amount of the fixed cost.

CPR 45.19(2A)(a) provides that the recoverable cost of obtaining the first fixed costs medical report will be £180 (whatever the specialism of the expert).

CPR 45.19(2A)(b) provides that the recoverable cost of a further fixed cost medical report will be:

- £420 for a report from a consultant orthopaedic surgeon (inclusive of a review of medical records where applicable);
- £360 for a report from a consultant in accident and emergency medicine;
- £180 for a report from a general practitioner (registered with the General Medical Council);
- £180 for a report from a physiotherapist (registered with the Health and Care Professions Council).

In these claims the cost of obtaining medical records is limited to no more than £30 together with the direct cost from the holder of the records (and £80 in total) for each set of records required, the cost of an addendum report on medical records (except by consultant orthopaedic surgeons) is fixed at £50 and the fee for answering questions under Part 35 fixed at £80.

Consequently, it is important that experts who are instructed to prepare a fixed cost medical report are aware of the limit on the recoverable cost for writing the report, reviewing records and dealing with questions.

If records are obtained by the lawyers the cost of £30, for each set of records, should be added to the costs (whether or not the claim settles in the protocol).

1.14.2.4.3 Medical expert

The term 'medical expert' (rather than the more specific term 'accredited medical expert') means a person who is:

- registered with the General Medical Council;
- registered with the General Dental Council; or
- a psychologist or physiotherapist registered with the Health and Care Professions Council.

1.14.2.5 Excluded

Some claims which would otherwise fall within each RTA Protocol are, nevertheless, excluded from scope by the terms of para 4.4. This rule specifically excludes claims, otherwise within scope, in any of the following categories:

- a breach of duty owed to a road user by a person who is not a road user (for example the owner of an animal escaping onto the highway or a highway authority);
- a claim made under the Untraced Drivers' Agreement;
- where the claimant or defendant acts as a personal representative of a deceased person;
- where the claimant or defendant is a protected party as defined in r 21.1(2). That definition is:

    'a party, or an intended party, who lacks capacity to conduct the proceedings', with 'lacks capacity' defined in turn as meaning lacks capacity under the terms of the Mental Capacity Act 2005;

- where the claimant is bankrupt;
- where the defendant's vehicle is registered outside the United Kingdom.

Whilst protected parties are excluded, children are included (unless a protected party or otherwise excluded).

1.14.2.6 Importance of scope

The scope of the process is significant both for understanding the extent to which this is available for appropriate claims and also because CPR 45.24 (formerly CPR 45.36) permits the court to limit the claimant to the fixed costs payable under the protocol where, for example, a case within the scope is never put into the process or does enter that process but exits due to the claimant, in the view of the court, unreasonably valuing the claim at more than the upper limit.

It is, similarly, important to identify 'soft tissue injury claims' because of the special rules that apply in relation to medical evidence and sanctions that apply if procedures, particularly concerning medical evidence, for such claims are not followed.

Where a claim is put into the protocol it will usually be subject to fixed costs, even if the claim is resolved outside that protocol, but fixed costs will not apply to a claim that has not entered either the RTA Protocol or EL/PL Protocol (subject to the court applying CPR 45.24).

1.14.3   Stage 1

Paragraph 6 of each protocol deals with stage 1 of the process.

1.14.3.1   Claim notification form

Where the claimant decides a claim is within the scope of the protocol that claim is notified electronically, rather than in a letter of claim, by a claim notification form ('CNF').

1.14.3.1.1   Insurer

Paragraph 6.1 of the protocol confirms the CNF should be sent the defendant's insurer, and as this is required by the protocol must therefore be sent electronically through the portal, whilst a modified version of the form, omitting certain personal details, should be sent direct to the defendant by first class post.

1.14.3.1.2   Defendant

Paragraph 6.2 of the protocol provides the defendant's CNF can be sent, if not at the same time, 'as soon as practicable after the CNF was sent', which may assist in cases where information on the driver is limited.

1.14.3.1.3   Mandatory information

Paragraph 6.3 confirms all boxes in the CNF marked as mandatory must be completed and that the claimant must make a 'reasonable attempt' to complete other boxes.

Paragraph 6.8 indicates that where the defendant considers inadequate mandatory information has been provided in the CNF that shall be a valid reason for the defendant to decide the claim should no longer continue under the protocol. It is implicit that decision will be made within the 15 day period for response as the claim will, otherwise, have already exited the process. The costs implications following such a decision are dealt with by CPR 45.24(2).

1.14.3.1.4   Statement of truth

Paragraph 6.6 deals with signature of the statement of truth in the CNF, which can be by the claimant or the claimant's legal representative (but the latter will need written evidence of authorisation to sign the CNF). Entry of the relevant name in the signature box of the electronic CNF will meet this requirement.

1.14.3.1.5 Funding

The reference to a conditional fee agreement in the CNF relates to a 'pre-commencement funding arrangement', in other words a conditional fee agreement with recoverable additional liabilities. Accordingly, unless the claimant has entered such a funding arrangement the answer to this question will be 'no' (even where the claim is funded by a conditional fee agreement entered from April 2013 onwards).

1.14.3.1.6 Value

The best assessment possible of potential value should be made at the stage the CNF is completed, to confirm whether the value is anticipated as being in excess of £10,000. This may be very relevant to recovery of the cost of an advice from counsel or specialist solicitor.

1.14.3.1.7 Further CNF

Paragraph 5.2 confirms that where the claimant has sent the CNF to the wrong defendant the claimant may, in this circumstance only, send the CNF to the correct defendant.

1.14.3.2 Insurer acknowledgement

Paragraph 6.10 requires the defendant to send to the clamant an electronic acknowledgement the next day after receipt of the CNF.

Despite the requirement for an acknowledgement of the CNF a claim will not leave the protocol if that is not given: *Patel v Fortis Insurance Ltd*.[76]

1.14.3.3 Insurer response

The first substantive step for the defendant, where the protocol sets out consequences for non-compliance, is the insurer response.

1.14.3.3.1 Time limit

Paragraph 6.11 requires the defendant must complete the insurer response form of the CNF and send this to the claimant within 15 days. Once again, as this is a requirement of the protocol, that communication must, in accordance with para 5.1, be through the portal.

If the MIB is dealing with the claim the response must be given, under para 6.13, within 30 days. An insurer may contend, on the basis of Article 75, the right to 30 days for a response. The claimant may wish to challenge this by seeking reasons for any issue on indemnity

---

[76] (Unreported) Leicester County Court, 23 December 2011.

Paragraph 5.3 confirms the reference to 'days' means reference to 'business days', in turn defined by para 1.1(8) as excluding Saturdays, Sundays, Bank Holidays, Good Friday and Christmas Day.

Whilst para 5.5 of the protocol usually allows the parties to vary time periods, this 15-day time limit cannot be varied (see the exceptions to the general rule in para 5.5). Indeed, the portal will police this time limit because it will prevent a purported response outside the relevant timescale.

1.14.3.3.2   Exiting

Paragraph 6.15 confirms that the claim will no longer continue under the protocol where, within the 15 day (or 30 days if the MIB are dealing) period, the defendant:

- makes an admission of liability but alleges contributory negligence (other than in relation to the claimant's admitted failure to wear a seat belt);
- does not complete and send the response;
- does not admit liability;
- notifies the claimant it is considered there is inadequate mandatory information in the CNF; or
- notifies the claimant that if proceedings were issued the small claims track would be the normal track for the claim.

Consequently, any issue about contributory negligence, other than seatbelt issues, will cause the claim to exit the protocol. Even then the case will exit the protocol if there is a factual dispute as to whether or not the claimant was wearing a seatbelt (as this is not an issue the process is capable of resolving).

1.14.3.3.3   Compliance and sanctions

Paragraph 6.16 provides that where the defendant does not admit liability brief reasons must be given in the insurer response.

Whilst para 6.15 does confirm what happens if the insurer response is not given, namely that the claim will exit the protocol, that will still be a failure to comply with the terms of para 6.11, or para 6.13 if the MIB are dealing. This will also amount to a breach of the terms of para 6.16.

Whilst there is no express sanction, within the protocol, for breach if the claim exits the protocol and costs have to be determined under the CPR this may amount to conduct 'out of the norm' sufficient to generate indemnity costs or, even if not, sufficient to apply the 'exceptionality' provisions that will take the case out of fixed costs.

Even if there is a breach of the RTA Protocol it is likely the court will expect the claimant to afford the defendant the time allowed under the PI Protocol, for a decision on liability, where this has not been made in an exiting claim.

In addition to any sanctions imposed by the court, should proceedings be issued, any non-compliance with the spirit, let alone the letter, of the protocol, can be reported to the Behaviour Committee. Whilst any ruling will not impose a sanction, as such, this may be relevant in the event the court has to determine whether any sanction is appropriate, should the default continue and court proceedings subsequently be issued.

1.14.3.4   Admission of liability

To keep the claim within the protocol there must be, within the relevant time limit, an insurer response which admits liability without any allegations of contributory negligence (other than where the claimant has admitted failing to wear a seatbelt).

Paragraph 1.1 of each protocol defines precisely what is meant by the term 'admission of liability' which is that:

- the accident occurred;
- the accident was caused by the defendant's breach of duty;
- the defendant caused some loss to the claimant, but the nature and extent of that is not admitted; and (for claims in the 2013 RTA Protocol)
- the defendant has no accrued defence to the claim under the Limitation Act 1980.

1.14.3.5   Defendant's account

In a soft tissue injury claim para 6.19A provides that on admission of liability (in the limited cases where it is considered appropriate) the defendant's account of the accident may be sent to the claimant at the same time as the CNF response, provided the defendant's insurer has the defendant's written authority to provide that account (and by sending the account the insurer is certifying there is such authority). There is not, however, any requirement for a statement of truth.

If the defendant's account of the accident is provided that will be relevant when medical evidence is obtained.

It is implicit the defendant's account must be consistent with the 'admission of liability'. Consequently, if the account amounts to a denial of causation that should be challenged and consideration given to exiting the protocol if the defendant does not concede some injury as a result of the breach of duty.

1.14.3.6   Destination of claims exiting in Stage 1

Where the claim exits the process at this stage para 6.17 confirms that, generally, it will then proceed under the PI Protocol, entering that protocol at the start of the three-month period given to the defendant to investigate the claim. This means that, in these circumstances, the CNF will stand as the letter of claim and that the 21 days for acknowledgment of that letter will be treated as having elapsed.

The PI Protocol now contains para 2.10A which confirms that, in such circumstances, the CNF can be used as a letter of claim, unless the defendant has notified the claimant there is inadequate information in that form. The claimant may wish to expressly confirm, when a claim exits the protocol at this stage, the CNF is used as the letter of claim for the purposes of the PI Protocol, for the avoidance of any doubt.

1.14.3.7   Costs of Stage 1

Costs of stage 1 are set out in CPR 45.29 (see **1.12.4**).

Paragraph 6.18 provides that stage 1 costs, as provided for in CPR 45.29 are, except where the claimant is a child, payable when liability is admitted within 10 days after the defendant receives the Stage 2 settlement pack.

Where the defendant fails to pay those costs within that timescale para 6.19 allows the claimant to give written notice, within ten days after the last date under which costs are payable in accordance with para 6.18, that the claim will no longer continue under the protocol. Unless such notice is given the claim will, despite non-payment of costs, continue under the protocol.

1.14.4   Stage 2

Paragraph 7 of each protocol deals with stage 2.

1.14.4.1   Evidence

Recognising the need for evidence to deal with quantum, the 2013 RTA Protocol contains provisions dealing with both medical and non-medical expert evidence as well as factual evidence.

1.14.4.2   Medical expert evidence

Medical expert evidence is likely to be required in every case, and in a soft tissue injury claim an aim of the protocol is that offers are made only after a fixed cost medical report has been obtained and disclosed.

1.14.4.2.1   Selection

There is no express provision for the claimant to instruct a jointly selected or agreed expert. The claimant may, accordingly, press ahead and obtain expert evidence without involving the defendant. Whilst, strictly, the terms of the Practice Direction – Pre-Action Conduct still apply these are not likely to be of significance unless the claim subsequently exits the RTA Protocol.

1.14.4.2.2   Content

In claims run under the protocol the medical report is a key document as, in the majority of cases, it will be the only evidence, other than documents supporting expenses and losses, relied on by the parties, or if the matter goes to Stage 3, the court when valuing the claim. Consequently, the report needs to cover all relevant matters, including topics that would be dealt with by factual evidence in claims run outside the protocol.

1.14.4.2.3   Initial report(s)

Paragraph 7.4 of the 2010 Protocol confirms that where it is clear one expert cannot deal with all elements of the injury the claimant may, at the outset, obtain a second report from an expert in a different discipline.

Paragraph 7.5 of the 2010 Protocol confirms any such expert instructed at the outset may separately recommend a further initial report from an expert in a different discipline (hence the claimant may obtain, if so advised, reports from experts in up to four disciplines with the process).

Paragraph 7.2 of the 2013 Protocol notes that it is expected most claims will require a medical report from just one expert, but additional medical reports may be obtained from other experts where the injuries require reports from more than one medical discipline.

If the claim is a soft tissue injury claim para 7.1A requires the initial report to be a fixed cost medical report.

1.14.4.2.4   Subsequent report(s)

Other than a soft tissue injury claim the general provision in para 7.2 will apply, that 'additional medical reports may be obtained from other experts where the injuries require reports from more than one medical discipline'. Furthermore, para 7.8 of the 2013 requires a subsequent medical report from an expert who has already reported to be justified. Examples of a report being justified include where:

- the first medical report recommends that further time is required before a prognosis of the claimant's injuries can be determined; or
- the claimant is receiving continuing treatment; or
- the claimant has not recovered as expect in the original prognosis.

With a soft tissue injury claim para 7.1A(2) provides that any further report must also be a fixed cost medical report.

Furthermore, in a soft tissue injury claim, para 7.8A provides that:

- it is expected that only one medical report will be required; and
- a further medical report, whether from the first expert instructed or from an expert in another discipline, will only be justified where:
  - it is recommended in the first expert's report; and
  - that report has first been disclosed to the defendant.

Accordingly, in a soft tissue injury claim, it may be important to emphasise to the expert instructed at the outset the need for any further report or supplemental report to be identified in that first report. If the need for a further report is not clear from the initial report the expert may need to clarify the report.

Although, in a soft tissue injury claim, any further report must be a fixed cost medical report that just excludes any expert who has provided treatment to the claimant, is associated with any person who has provided treatment and has not proposed or recommended that they or an associate provide treatment. It is proposed, however, a fixed cost medical report can only be provided by an *accredited* medical expert and if that is confined to certain specialisms this could have the effect of restricting the scope of medical evidence in a soft tissue injury claim.

1.14.4.2.5   Medical records

Paragraph 7.4 of the 2013 Protocol provides that the medical expert should identify within the report the medical records that have been reviewed and the medical records considered relevant to the claim.

This rule also stipulates the claimant must disclose with any medical report sent to the defendant the medical records that the expert considers relevant. The rule refers, throughout, to 'medical records'. Whilst it is clearly appropriate for an expert to identify medical records reviewed, for example general practitioner records or hospital records, the documentation to be disclosed must surely be relevant entries within any general category of records as it would seem disproportionate for whole categories of records to be disclosed simply because there are relevant entries within such records.

Indeed, the importance of avoiding disproportionate disclosure is emphasised by the terms of para 7.5 of the 2013 Protocol, which stipulates that in most claims with a value of no more than £10,000 it is expected that the medical expert will not need to see any medical records.

1.14.4.2.6   Photographs

Paragraph 7.6 of the 2013 Protocol also requires any photographs of the injuries on which the claimant intends to rely to be disclosed with the medical report.

1.14.4.2.7   Contributory negligence

Paragraph 7.3 of the 2010 Protocol and para 7.7 of the 2013 Protocol require the medical report, where the claimant was not wearing a seat belt, to contain sufficient information to enable the defendant to calculate the appropriate reduction of damages 'in accordance with principles set out in existing case-law'. This means applying the approach in *Froom v Butcher*[77] (confirmed by the Court of Appeal in *Stanton v Collinson*[78]).

Consequently existing case-law means that there will be:

- no deduction where use of a seat belt would not have made any material difference to the injuries suffered;

- a deduction of 25% where failure to wear a seat belt made all the difference, in other words the claimant would have been uninjured or virtually uninjured; and

- a deduction of 15% in other cases, in other words cases where the claimant would still have suffered an injury but the injury is more severe because of the failure to wear a seat belt.

---

[77]   [1975] 3 All ER 520.
[78]   [2010] EWCA Civ 81.

1.14.4.2.8 Accuracy

Paragraph 7.3 of the 2013 Protocol confirms the claimant must check the factual accuracy of any medical report before it is sent to the defendant as there will be no further opportunity for the claimant to challenge that accuracy thereafter.

1.14.4.2.9 Fixed cost medical report

Paragraph 7.1A requires that, in a soft tissue injury claim, the claimant should obtain a medical report and that any such report must be a fixed cost medical report. Furthermore, if a further report is justified, in accordance with para 7.8A, that must also be a fixed cost medical report.

1.14.4.2.10 Defendant's account

If, in a soft tissue injury claim, the defendant has provided a different account, under para 6.19A, the claimant must provide that as part of the instructions to the medical expert for the sole purpose of asking the expert to comment on the impact, if any, on diagnosis and prognosis if:

- the claimant's account is found to be true; or
- the defendant's account is found to be true.

Despite this reference to what is 'true' there is no requirement the defendant's account contain a statement of truth.

The medical expert should not be asked to express a view on a defendant's account that amounts to a denial of causation, because such a claim ought not to be continuing within the RTA Protocol.

If the medical expert suggests the defendant's account does make a difference to the opinion that may be an issue that cannot then be resolved within the RTA Protocol, given that any stage 3 hearing is concerned only with quantum, not fact finding.

1.14.4.2.11 Cost of further report(s)

Paragraph 7.31 provides that where the claimant obtains more than one expert report the defendant, at the end of stage 2, may refuse to pay or the court, at stage 3, may refuse to allow the cost of any report not reasonably required.

Paragraph 7.31 also provides that where the claimant obtains more than one expert report the reason should be explained in the stage 2 settlement pack (so the defendant can explain why any objection is taken to the cost of such a report).

1.14.4.3 Non-medical expert evidence

Paragraph 7.9 of the 2013 Protocol provides for a report from a non-medical expert where that is reasonably required to value the claim.

The claimant must, as with medical evidence, check the factual accuracy before this is sent to the defendant.

Paragraph 7.31 will, again, apply to the cost of any report not reasonably required.

The claimant, as with a further medical report, should explain, in the settlement pack, why this was obtained and the defendant give any reasons for objecting to the cost.

1.14.4.4 Witness statements

Paragraph 7.11 of the 2013 RTA Protocol notes that in most cases witness statements will not be required, but may be provided where reasonably required to value the claim.

1.14.4.5 Specialist legal advice

Paragraph 7.10 of the 2013 Protocol notes that in most cases the claimant's legal representative will be able to value the claim but recognises that in some cases with a value of more than £10,000 (excluding vehicle related damages) an additional advice from a specialist solicitor or counsel may be justified where reasonably required to value the claim.

The term 'specialist solicitor' is not defined in the protocol but ought to include any solicitor who is a member of the Law Society Personal Injury Panel or an APIL accredited solicitor.

Paragraph 7.31 provides that where the claimant has an advice from a specialist solicitor or counsel the defendant, at the end of stage 2, may refuse to pay or the court, at stage 3, may refuse to allow the cost of any advice not reasonably required.

Consequently, as with supplemental expert evidence, the claimant should explain in the stage 2 settlement pack why such an advice was obtained (and if the cost is disputed the defendant explain why).

1.14.4.6 Interim settlement pack and interim payments

Paragraphs 7.7 to 7.23 of the 2010 RTA Protocol and paragraphs 7.13 to 7.30 of the 2013 RTA Protocol deal with the situation where the prognosis is not settled.

Paragraph 7.12 of the 2013 RTA Protocol provides that where the claimant needs to obtain a subsequent medical report or a non-medical report the parties should agree to stay the process for a suitable period and that the claimant may then request an interim payment.

To request an interim payment para 7.14 of the 2013 RTA Protocol requires the claimant to send the defendant an interim settlement pack with initial medical report(s) and evidence of pecuniary losses and disbursements. If the interim payment requested is £1,000 para 7.18 of the 2013 RTA Protocol requires the defendant to pay that sum within 10 days of receiving the interim settlement pack.

If the defendant fails to make the interim payment of £1,000, where required, by the due date the claimant may start proceedings under Part 7 and apply to the court for an interim payment. However, para 7.30 of the 2013 RTA Protocol requires the claimant, as a preliminary, to give notice to the defendant that the claim will no longer continue under the protocol, and that notice must be sent within 10 days of the deadline for the defendant to make the interim payment.

If the claimant is a child there will be no automatic entitlement to an interim payment, though an interim payment may nevertheless be sought.

The claimant may seek an interim payment in excess of £1,000, which may include sums the claimant has paid for vehicle related damage. If the defendant does make an interim payment of at least £1,000, but less than the sum claimed, the claimant may start proceedings though the court will order the defendant to pay no more than stage 2 fixed costs if, in the event, the interim payment awarded is no more than the amount offered.

Paragraph 7.21 of the 2013 RTA Protocol confirms that where the claim is valued at more than £10,000 the claimant may request more than one interim payment.

Paragraph 7.26 of the 2013 RTA Protocol confirms that the provisions relating to interim payments do not apply where the claimant is a child. Consequently, if an interim payment is reasonably required for a child proceedings must be started under Part 7 and an application for an interim payment made in those proceedings.

Eventually, once the prognosis is settled, the claimant will need to complete a settlement pack. In cases where the initial medical evidence gives sufficient information for the claim to be settled the settlement pack will be completed at that stage.

1.14.4.7   Settlement pack

In cases where the initial medical evidence gives sufficient information for the claim to be settled the settlement pack will be completed at that stage. In other cases, once the prognosis is settled, the claimant will need to follow up the interim settlement pack with the settlement pack.

1.14.4.7.1   Content

Paragraph 7.32 of the 2013 RTA Protocol confirms that the settlement pack must comprise:

- the stage 2 settlement pack form;
- a medical report or reports;
- evidence of pecuniary losses;
- evidence of disbursements;
- any non-medical expert report;
- any medical records/photographs served with medical reports;
- any witness statements.

1.14.4.7.2   Amendment to content

The settlement pack was always intended to be a 'living document'. Consequently, the initial version of the settlement pack may, pending any dispute by the defendant with the figures, only give brief details to explain the sums claimed, on the basis the pack can be amended to explain and justify the claimant's figures if these are not agreed.

1.14.4.7.3   Timescale

Paragraph 7.26 of the 2010 RTA Protocol and para 7.33 of the 2013 RTA Protocol confirm the settlement pack should be sent to the defendant within 15 days of the claimant approving:

• the final medical report and agreeing to rely on the prognosis in that report; or

• any non-medical expert.

This is an important provision as it reflects the privilege inevitably attaching to a report until this is disclosed and the need to follow instructions on whether the opinion is to be relied on.

Approval and agreement may also be relevant to the situation where the prognosis is not stated as settled, but the client believes it is, or vice versa.

If a medical report is not approved by the claimant, and further evidence obtained and relied upon, there may well be an issue about recovering the costs of the first report.

1.14.4.7.4   Soft tissue injury claim

Paragraph 7.32A provides that in a soft tissue injury claim the stage 2 settlement pack is of no effect unless the medical report is a fixed cost medical report. Where the claimant includes more than one medical report, the first report obtained must be a fixed costs medical report and any further report from an expert in any of the following disciplines must also be a fixed cost medical report:

• consultant orthopaedic surgeon;

• consultant in accident & emergency medicine;

• general practitioner;

• physiotherapist.

1.14.4.7.5   Seatbelt contributory negligence

Claims where the defendant alleges contributory negligence on the basis of the claimant's admitted failure to use a seatbelt will remain within the protocol. Although contributory negligence relates, strictly, to liability it is effectively treated as a quantum issue for the purposes of the protocol.

Where the defendant alleges contributory negligence through failure to wear a seatbelt para 7.34 requires the claimant to suggest, in the settlement pack, an appropriate percentage reduction (which the protocols recognise may be 0%) for any seat belt contributory negligence (which for the purposes of para 6.15(1) means the claimant's admitted failure to wear a seatbelt).

1.14.4.7.6   Claimant's offer

The total figure in the settlement pack, net of any seat belt contributory negligence admitted, will be the claimant's offer at this stage.

Moreover, the court is likely to regard each figure for every element of the claim that is set out in the settlement pack as an individual offer, capable of agreement: *Bewicke-Copley v Ibeh*.[79]

Consequently, as well as ensuring the individual figures are approved it will be important to get instructions on the individual figures, as well as the total, as representing sums acceptable to the claimant for the purpose of settlement before these are put to the defendant.

The settlement pack is, in effect, both the claimant's schedule of damages (and like any schedule if the defendant agrees any item that will amount to a compromise on that part of the claimant) as well as an offer to settle the claim as a whole.

1.14.4.7.7   Reasons for report/advice

In accordance with para 7.31 the claimant should explain, in appropriate circumstances, in the settlement pack why more than one expert report or an advice from a specialist solicitor or counsel was obtained. That advice, however, is not for disclosure.

1.14.4.7.8   Communication

As the protocol requires this information to be sent that must, in accordance with para 5.1 be via the portal.

1.14.4.8   The total consideration period

This is the further time allowed in stage 2 for the parties to negotiate.

There is a 35-day period described as 'the total consideration period' comprising:

- up to 15 days for the defendant to complete the stage 2 settlement pack and make an offer: 'the initial consideration period'; and
- the remainder of the total consideration period: 'the negotiation period'.

1.14.4.8.1   The initial consideration period

This timescale can be extended but only by agreement between the parties. Accordingly, unless the claimant agrees to an extension of time, the defendant must provide a response to the settlement pack within 15 business days. Paragraph 7.31 of the 2010 Protocol and para 7.38 of the 2013 Protocol require that response to be an acceptance of the claimant's offer or the making of a counter offer using the settlement pack form. If the defendant fails to take either step the claim will exit the protocol.

---

[79]   (Unreported) Oxford County Court, 4 April 2014.

While the defendant's admission will be binding, unless the parties agree otherwise or proceedings are commenced and the court gives permission to withdraw the admission, the defendant may withdraw the admission in relation to causation at this stage, in accordance with para 7.39 of the 2013 Protocol. The defendant may also contend, at this stage, the small claims track will be the normal track for the claim. That must be done, however, within the 'initial consideration period', namely the period of up to 15 days given to consider the stage 2 settlement pack. If that happens the claim will exit the protocol.

The defendant may accept the claimant's offer, in which case a settlement will have been achieved.

Paragraph 7.34 of the 2010 Protocol and para 7.41 of the 2013 Protocol require a defendant who makes a counter-offer to propose an amount for each head of damage claimed by the claimant. This, in effect, requires the defendant to make an offer which is at least the total for each such item but the rule specifically allows the defendant to make an offer that is higher than the total of the amounts proposed for all heads of damage. This provision specifically recognises that an explanation will assist the claimant when negotiating a settlement and allow both parties to focus on those areas of the claim that remain in dispute. These are those parts of the settlement pack the claimant may wish to expand upon, to justify the claims made, at this stage in the event that the claim proceeds to stage 3. That is because the parties need to be mindful of para 7.66 which provides comments in the pack prepared for stage 3, if that becomes necessary, must not raise anything that has not been raised in the stage 2 settlement pack (though, given this is a living document, that means the final version of the pack).

Paragraph 7.35 of the 2010 Protocol and para 7.42 of the 2013 Protocol require the defendant, where there is a CRU deduction, to state the name and amount of any deductible benefit in the counter offer. It is, of course, important to remember the 'like for like' nature of the scheme for compensation recovery so that deductions of relevant benefits can only be made, and to the extent of, claims for:

- loss of earnings;
- care; and
- transportation.

As the protocol requires this information to be sent, that must, in accordance with para 5.1 be via the portal.

1.14.4.8.2   The negotiation period

If the defendant does not accept the claimant's offer but makes, within the initial consideration period, with any extension of time agreed, a counter-offer, the claimant has, under the terms of para 7.43, until the end of the total consideration period, or further consideration period, to accept or decline the counter-offer.

At this stage there is no requirement for the parties to communicate, hence offers do not have to be made via the portal and can be made in any way the parties choose, whether in writing by email or oral negotiation.

1.14.4.8.3   *The further consideration period*

Paragraph 7.37 provides that where a party makes an offer 5 days or less before the end of the total consideration period, including any extension of time, there will be a further period of 5 days after the end of the total consideration period for the relevant party to consider that offer but during that time no further offers can be made by either party.

1.14.4.8.4   *Compliance and sanctions*

Paragraph 7.38 requires the defendant to respond to the settlement pack within the initial consideration period (as extended if appropriate), hence a failure to do so will be a breach of the protocol and that may be relevant to the approach the court subsequently takes towards case management and/or sanctions.

Non-compliance with the protocol may be regarded as 'out of the norm' or sufficient to trigger the rules on 'exceptionality' in relation to costs.

1.14.4.8.5   *Late settlement*

Where the parties agree a settlement for a greater sum than the defendant had offered during the total consideration period, or further consideration period, and after the court proceedings pack has been sent to the defendant but before proceedings are issued under stage 3, para 7.48 confirms, in addition to the costs otherwise payable, the defendant must pay the fixed late settlement costs provided for in CPR 45.23A, namely stage 3 type A fixed costs of £250.

1.1.4.4.8.6   *Vehicle-related damage*

For those involved with recovery of vehicle related damages paras 7.43–7.53 of the 2010 Protocol and 7.51– 7.62 of the 2013 Protocol deal with the various issues that can arise where additional damages are sought for vehicle-related damage and practitioners involved in such claims need to be aware of these provisions.

1.14.4.9   *Offers and costs*

Paragraph 7.44 confirms that any offer to settle made at any stage by either party will automatically include, and cannot exclude, the fixed costs payable under the protocol.

Paragraph 7.44A confirms that in a soft tissue injury claim an offer to settle made by either party before a fixed costs medical report has been obtained and disclosed will have no adverse costs consequences until after the report has been disclosed (though this provision is only likely to be of significance if the claim exits the protocol).

1.14.4.10   *Withdrawal of admissions*

CPR 14.1A has been in force since 6 April 2007, providing that pre-action admissions will effectively be binding prior to issue of proceedings (unless the parties agree otherwise) but can thereafter be withdrawn if the court gives permission.

The introduction of the 2010 RTA Protocol saw a new CPR 14.1B dealing with the withdrawal of admissions made under that protocol.

- The defendant may withdraw an admission of causation during the 'initial consideration period' (or at any time if the parties agree or following commencement of proceedings if the court gives permission).

- Any other pre-action admission can only be withdrawn following issue of proceedings (unless the parties agree otherwise).

CPR 14.1B reflects the terms of para 7.39, which allows the defendant to withdraw an admission of causation within the initial consideration period (and also to contend that if proceedings were started the small claims track would be the normal track for the claim).

Thus, other than causation (and if this admission is withdrawn the case will exit the process anyway) admissions will effectively be binding for the purposes of the process.

1.14.11   End of Stage 2

Paragraph 7.40 of the 2010 RTA Protocol and para 7.70 of the 2013 Protocol require the defendant, if a settlement is achieved at this stage, to pay the damages, any unpaid stage 1 costs and the stage 2 costs along with disbursements, those costs and disbursements being identified by Part 45 CPR.

Paragraphs 7.55 to 7.66 of the 2010 RTA Protocol and paragraphs 7.64 to 7.69 of the 2013 RTA Protocol deal with the conclusion of stage 2 in the event the parties fail to reach agreement.

- The claimant must send the court proceedings pack to the defendant which must not raise anything not raised in the stage 2 settlement pack (in the version finally exchanged).

- The defendant should check the pack and if it is contended this does include anything not previously raised the claimant should be notified within five days. The defendant should also indicate if a legal representative is to be nominated.

- The defendant, except where the claimant is a child, must pay at this stage the final offer of damages made by the defendant together with any unpaid stage 1 costs, the stage 2 costs and disbursements which have been agreed (and if not agreed such amount as the defendant considers reasonable).

- If these payments are not made within 15 days of receiving the court proceedings pack the claimant may give written notice the claim will no longer continue under the protocol and start proceedings under Part 7 (so a positive election will be necessary by the claimant as to whether it is best to proceed to stage 3 or to issue).

If the claim remains within the protocol, but is not resolved at the end of stage 2, it will proceed to stage 3.

1.14.4.12   Destination of claims exiting in stage 2

The destination will be the PI Protocol at the appropriate point, largely depending on whether liability is admitted.

1.14.4.13   Costs of Stage 2

Costs of stage 2 are those provided for in CPR 45.29 (from April 2013, CPR 45.18) (see 1.12.4).

1.14.4.14   Exits

The protocol specifically provides for the claim to leave the process in certain defined circumstances (both in stage 1 and stage 2).

In other situations, given the general provision found in para 7.76, a claimant may decide the claim is no longer suitable for the protocol. Whether or not that is a reasonable decision is likely to depend upon whether that decision is consistent with the aims of the protocol itself.

Paragraph 5.11 confirms that claims which no longer continue under the protocol cannot subsequently re-enter the process. The only exception to this is that para 5.2 allows for a further CNF 'in this circumstance only' where the claimant has sent the CNF to the wrong defendant when the claimant may send the CNF to the correct defendant. Whether or not a further CNF may be sent will depend on whether the original recipient of the CFA can be regarded as the 'wrong defendant'.

1.14.5   Stage 3

Stage 3 is for those cases which, while remaining within the relevant protocol, have not been resolved in stage 2.

Because stage 3 will involve court proceedings the procedure is set out in Practice Direction 8B, supplementing Part 8 of the CPR.

Accordingly, that Practice Direction applies where the parties have followed the protocol but are unable to agree the amount of damages payable by the end of stage 2 or the claimant is a child so, even if damages are agreed, approval of the court is required.

1.14.5.1   Venue

The claim can be started in any county court.

1.14.5.2   Documents

A Part 8 claim form will be required, for stage 3, along with a number of accompanying documents.

1.14.5.2.1   Claim form

The claim form must state:

• the claimant has followed the procedure in the relevant protocol;

- the date the court proceedings pack was sent to the defendant (unless the hearing is for approval only);
- whether the claimant wants the claim determined on the papers (except where the claimant is a child) or at a hearing (in which case dates the claimant requests should be avoided need to be given); and
- the value of the claim.

1.14.5.2.2   Further documents

The claimant must file with the claim form the following further documents:

- the Court Proceedings Pack (Part A).
  - This must contain the final schedule of the claimant's losses and the defendant's responses. In other words this will reflect any open concessions or agreement on particular heads of claim that differ from the original version of the settlement pack but not the final, Part 36, offers made at the end of stage 2 (as these will be given in Part B).
  - There should also be any supporting comments and evidence on the disputed heads of damage. However, nothing that has not already been raised in the stage 2 settlement pack form should be included, emphasising the need for that form to be developed during stage 2 of the process, dealing with issues as they emerge.
- the Court Proceedings Pack (Part B). This contains the final offer and counter offer from the stage 2 settlement pack and is placed in a sealed envelope;
- copies of medical reports;
- evidence of special damages;
- evidence of disbursements;
- any notice of funding (if the claimant has a 'pre-commencement funding arrangement).

1.14.5.2.3   Figures in Part A and Part B

It is self-evident the figures in Part B will usually not be the same as in Part A, or there would be no need for separate parts of the pack and for this to be put in a sealed envelope.

Part A reflects, for the purpose of the stage 3 hearing, the claimant's schedule of damages which, accordingly, should contain the original, best case, offers by the claimant, unless these have been agreed meanwhile in which case the pack should reflect the agreement reached by stating relevant figures.

Part B will, however, contain the final, Part 36, offers made in stage 2, by both claimant and defendant and hence should not be seen by the court until the conclusion of the hearing, which is why this pack is placed in a sealed envelope.

To complete Part A workaround should be used to change the figures so that these show the initial offers of each party whilst the final version of the pack will comprise Part B.

1.14.5.2.4   Soft tissue injury claim

Paragraph 6.1A prevents the claimant, in a soft tissue injury claim, from proceeding to stage 3 unless the medical report filed is a fixed cost medical report. Where the claimant includes more than one medical report the first report must be a fixed costs medical report and any further report from an expert in the following disciplines must also be a fixed cost medical report:

* consultant orthopaedic surgeon;
* consultant in accident & emergency medicine;
* general practitioner;
* physiotherapist.

1.14.5.2.5   Children

Additional documentation is required where the claimant is a child and the hearing is to approve settlement.

* A draft consent order.
* An advice by counsel, solicitor or other legal representative on the amount of damages.
* A statement verified by a statement of truth and signed by the litigation friend confirming the child has recovered in accordance with the prognosis and whether there are any continuing symptoms (as this will enable the court to decide whether the child will need to attend the settlement hearing).

1.14.5.2.6   Motor Insurers' Bureau

The MIB must be joined as second defendant where the defendant is uninsured and the Bureau has agreed to be joined.

1.14.5.3   Hearing

The terms of the protocol effectively prevent any further evidence being relied upon at the hearing so it is essential that the parties ensure all relevant matters are included in the final version of the settlement pack at the end of stage 2.

1.14.5.4   Costs of Stage 3

Costs of stage 3 are fixed (see **1.12.4**) but, unlike the earlier stages, will follow the event, depending upon a comparison between the amount of damages awarded by the court and the amount of the final offer made by each party for the purposes of Section II Part 36 CPR.

Paragraph 6.2 Practice Direction 8B provides that the filing of the claim form, and accompanying documents, represent the start of stage 3 for the purposes of fixed costs.

1.14.5.4.1   Part 36 CPR

Section II Part 36 deals, specifically, with offers to settle for the purposes of, originally, the RTA Protocol and now, also, the EL/PL Protocol. It comprises CPR 36.16 to 36.22.

The two sections of Part 36 are quite distinct. CPR 36.1 confirms Section I does not apply to an offer where Section II applies, whilst CPR 36.16 (1) confirms that where Section II applies then Section I will not apply.

CPR 36.16 (2) confirms Section II applies only where the parties have followed either the RTA Protocol or the EL/PL Protocol and then started the stage 3 procedure. In other words there is no provision for Part 36 offers in either protocol which pre-empt dealing with the case in accordance with stages 1 and 2. Section II offers are, accordingly, only relevant to the incidence of stage 3 costs.

This, of course, is consistent with para 7.37 of the 2010 RTA Protocol and para 7.44 of the 2013 RTA Protocol, which confirm offers made up to and including stage 2 will automatically include, and cannot exclude, costs under the process up to that point.

1.14.5.4.2   Protocol offer

Accordingly, what is defined in CPR 36.17 as a 'protocol offer' has to be set out in Part B of the court proceedings pack, when stage 3 proceedings are commenced, and will be the final offer by each party made in stage 2.

1.14.5.4.3   Costs consequences of protocol offers

CPR 36.20 prohibits communication of the amount of any protocol offer to the court until the claim is determined and prohibits communication to the court at all of any other offer to settle (emphasising that only the protocol offer can carry any costs consequences for a claim which remains within the relevant protocol).

Once the claim is determined CPR 36.20(3) confirms the court will examine the protocol offers to assess the costs consequences of such offers for stage 3.

The costs consequences of protocol offers, made in accordance with Section II of Part 36, are provided for by CPR 36.21. There are three possibilities so far as the costs of stage 3 are concerned given that, in every care proceeding to stage 3, there will have been a protocol offer by each party.

- If the claimant obtains judgment for an amount of damages less than or equal to the defendant's offer; the claimant will pay the defendant's costs of stage 3 and interest on those costs.
- Where the judgment is for an amount of damages more than the defendant's offer but less than the claimant's offer; the defendant will pay the claimant's stage 3 costs.
- Where the judgment is for an amount of damages equal to or more than the claimant's own offer; the defendant must pay the claimant's stage 3 costs and interest on the damages as well as interest on costs, in each case at a rate not exceeding 10per cent above base rate.

It is notable that CPR 36.21 uses the phrases 'less than or equal to' and 'equal to or more than' for the purposes of comparing the offer and judgment. This is in contrast to the term 'more advantageous' in CPR 36.14 and indicates a simple, and absolute, comparison between offer and judgment in purely monetary terms.

CPR 36.22 confirms the amount of the judgment is less than the defendant's offer where the judgment is less than that offer after deductible benefits, identified in the judgment, are deducted. This is why it remains important, and the rules provide accordingly, for protocol offers made by the defendant to give a breakdown of any deductible benefits.

1.14.5.4.4   Costs consequences of other offers

Whilst CPR 36.13(4) confirms an offer to settle can be made in whatever way a party chooses that rule also confirms that if the offer is not made in accordance with S.II, in a case running under the RTA Protocol or the EL/PL Protocol, the offer will not have any costs consequences.

Accordingly, 'Calderbank' offers, which may be relevant to costs under Part 44 CPR outside the RTA Protocol or the EL/PL Protocol, will not be relevant to the costs of a claim which remains within the RTA Protocol or the EL/PL Protocol.

1.14.5.4.5   Acceptance

It may be that an offer made under Section II Part 36 cannot be accepted, even if not changed or withdrawn, should the claim subsequently exit the relevant protocol: *Bostan v Royal Mail Group Ltd.*[80] If, however, the claim remains within the protocol, but proceeds to stage 3, offers, unless withdrawn, are likely to remain open for acceptance: *Purcell v McGarry.*[81]

Case-law has not yet clarified whether an offer made under Section II Part 36 is subject to the general law of contract, so far as offer and acceptance is concerned. It is clear the general law of contract, where this conflicts with the express terms of Part 36, will not apply: *Gibbon v Manchester City Council.*[82] However, *Gibbon* was concerned with what is now Section I Part 36, in particular CPR 36.9(2), which provides a Part 36 offer may be accepted at any time (whether or not the offeree has subsequently made a different offer) unless the offeror serves notice of withdrawal on the offeree. That rule is now found within Section I Part 36.

CPR 36.A1(2) expressly provides that Section I contains rules about offers to settle other than where Section II applies and CPR 36.1(1) expressly provides that Section I does not apply to an offer to settle to which Section II applies. Similarly, CPR 36.16(1) confirms that where Section II applies then Section I does not apply. There is no equivalent provision to CPR 36.9(2) in Section II which may result in the general law of contract preventing an offer which has been rejected, including rejection by counter offer, subsequently being accepted.

---

[80]   (Unreported) Bradford County Court, 9 June 2012.
[81]   (Unreported) Liverpool County Court, 7 December 2012.
[82]   [2010] EWCA Civ 726.

1.15   THE EL/PL PROTOCOL

Many, but not all, non-RTA personal injury claims are now within the scope of the EL/PL Protocol.

1.15.1   Preamble

Paragraph 2.1 confirms that the protocol describes the behaviour the court expects of parties prior to the start of court proceedings, where a claimant claims damages valued at no more than £25,000 in an employers' liability claim or a public liability claim, and specifically notes that the CPR enables the court to impose costs sanctions where the protocol is not followed.

1.15.2   Aims

The aims of the protocol are set out in para 3.1.

> 'The aim of this Protocol is to ensure that–
> (1)   the defendant pays damages and costs using the process set out in the Protocol without the need for the claimant to start proceedings;
> (2)   damages are paid within a reasonable time; and
> (3)   the claimant's legal representative receives the fixed costs at each appropriate stage.'

1.15.3   Parties

Paragraph 1.1(11) defines 'defendant' as including, where the context indicates, the defendant's insurer or legal representative.

1.15.4   Scope

Paragraph 4.1 sets out the scope of the EL/PL Protocol.

> 'This Protocol applies where–
> (1)   either–
>   (a)   the claim arises from an accident occurring on or after 31 July 2013; or
>   (b)   in a disease claim, no letter of claim has been sent to the defendant before 31 July 2013;
> (2)   the claim includes damages in respect of personal injury;
> (3)   the claimant values the claim at not more than £25,000 on a full liability basis including pecuniary losses but excluding interest ('the upper limit'); and
> (4)   if proceedings were started the small claims track would not be the normal track for that claim.'

(Rule 26.6 provides that the small claims track is not the normal track where the value of any claim for damages for personal injuries (defined as compensation for pain, suffering and loss of amenity) is more than £1,000.)

1.15.5   Definitions

The EL/PL Protocol defines the scope of the process and hence, subject to the specific exceptions, what claims are suitable for, and so will normally be put into, that process.

Scope is clarified by some terms defined within the protocol.

1.15.5.1 Employers' liability claim

Paragraph 1.1(14) defines 'employers' liability claim' as a claim by an employee against their employer for damages arising from:

(a) a bodily injury sustained by the employee in the course of employment; or

(b) a disease that the claimant is alleged to have contracted as a consequence of the employer's breach of statutory or common law duties of care in the course of the employee's employment, other than a physical or psychological injury caused by an accident or other single event;

'Employee' has the meaning given to it by s 2(1) of the Employers' Liability (Compulsory Insurance) Act 1969, namely:

> 'For the purposes of this Act the term 'employee' means an individual who has entered into or works under a contract of service or apprenticeship with an employer whether by way of manual labour, clerical work or otherwise, whether such contract is expressed or implied, oral or in writing.'

1.15.5.2 Public liability claim

Paragraph 1.1(18) provides that 'public liability claim':

> '(a) means a claim for damages for personal injuries arising out of a breach of a statutory or common law duty of care made against:
> (i)   a person other than the claimant's employer; or
> (ii) the claimant's employer in respect of matters arising other than in the course the claimant's employment; but
> (b) does not include a claim for damages arising from a disease that the claimant is alleged to have contracted as a consequence of breach of statutory or common law duties of care, other than a physical or psychological injury caused by an accident or other single event.'

1.15.5.3 Excluded

Some claims which would otherwise fall within the EL/PL Protocol are, nevertheless, excluded. That is because para 4.3 expressly excludes a number of claims from the protocol:

- where the claimant or defendant acts as personal representative of a deceased person;

- where the claimant or defendant is a protected party as defined in r 21.1(2). That definition is:

> '"a party, or an intended party, who lacks capacity to conduct the proceedings", with "lacks capacity" defined in turn as meaning lacks capacity under the terms of the Mental Capacity Act 2005';

- where, in the case of a public liability claim, the defendant is an individual ('individual' does not include a defendant who is sued in their business capacity or in their capacity as an office holder);

- where the claimant is bankrupt;
- where the defendant is insolvent and there is no identifiable insurer;
- where, in the case of a disease claim, there is more than one defendant;
- for personal injury arising from an accident or alleged breach of duty occurring outside England and Wales;
- for damages in relation to harm, abuse or neglect of or by children or vulnerable adults. The term 'vulnerable adult' is defined as having the same meaning as in para 3(5) of Sch 1 to the Legal Aid, Sentencing and Punishment of Offenders Act 2012 namely:

  > 'A person aged 18 or over whose ability to protect himself or herself from abuse is significantly impaired through physical or mental disability or illness, through old age or otherwise.'

  That schedule defines, in turn, 'abuse' as 'physical or mental abuse including sexual abuse and abuse in the form of violence, neglect, maltreatment and exploitation';

- a claim which includes a claim for clinical negligence, which is defined as having the same meaning as in section 58C Courts and Legal Services Act 1990, namely:

  > 'Breach of a duty of care or trespass to the person committed in the course of the provision of clinical or medical services (including dental or nursing services)';

- a claim for mesothelioma;
- a claim for damages arising out of a road traffic accident (as defined in para 1.1(16) of the Pre-Action Protocol for Low Value Personal Injury Claims in Road Traffic Accidents).

1.15.6   Communication

Where there is an identified insurer the EL/PL Protocol intends the portal be used in the same way as the RTA Protocol but, recognising the greater difficulties in identifying insurers in EL, and particularly PL, cases it will not always be possible to do that.

The EL/PL Protocol makes appropriate provision for communication.

The way in which the parties must communicate with each other, whilst a claim remains in the protocol, is set out in para 5.1.

> 'Subject to paragraph 6.1(2), where the Protocol requires information to be sent to a party it must be sent via www.claimsportal.org.uk (or any other Portal address that may be prescribed from time to time). The claimant will give an Email address for contact in the Claim Notification Form ('CNF'). All written communications not required by the Protocol must be sent by Email.'

1.15.7 Stage 1

1.15.7.1 Introduction

The EL/PL Protocol follows stage 1 of the RTA Protocol but reflecting the different nature of EL/PL claims and, in particular, the potential difficulties notifying an insurer of the claim at the outset.

1.15.7.2 Notification

Paragraph 6.1 of the protocol provides:

'(1) The claimant must complete and send–
(a)   the CNF to the defendant's insurer, if known; and
(b)   the Defendant Only Claim Notification Form ('Defendant Only CNF') to the defendant,

but the requirement to send the form to the defendant may be ignored in a disease claim where the CNF has been sent to the insurer and the defendant has been dissolved, is insolvent or has ceased to trade.

(2) If–
(a)   the insurer's identity is not known; or
(b)   the defendant is known not to hold insurance cover, the CNF must be sent to the defendant and no Defendant Only CNF is required.

(3) Where the insurer's identity is not known, the claimant must make a reasonable attempt to identify the insurer and, in an employers' liability claim, the claimant must have carried out a database search through the Employers' Liability Tracing Office.

(4) In a disease claim, the CNF should be sent to the insurer identified as the insurer last on risk for the employer for the material period of employment.'

Paragraph 6.2 provides:

'If the CNF or Defendant Only CNF cannot be sent to the defendant via the prescribed Portal address, it must be sent via first class post; and this must be done, in a case where the CNF is sent to the insurer, at the same time or as soon as practicable after the CNF is sent.'

1.15.7.3 Content

Paragraph 6.3 provides:

'All boxes in the CNF that are marked as mandatory must be completed before it is sent. The claimant must make a reasonable attempt to complete those boxes that are not marked as mandatory.'

Paragraph 6.4 provides:

'Where the claimant is a child, this must be noted in the relevant section of the CNF'

Paragraph 6.5 provides:

'The statement of truth in the CNF must be signed either by the claimant or by the claimant's legal representative where the claimant has authorised the legal representative to do so and the legal representative can produce written evidence of that authorisation. Where the claimant is a child the statement of truth may be signed by the parent or guardian. On the electronically completed CNF the person may enter their name in the signature box to satisfy this requirement.'

1.15.7.4   Acknowledgement

Paragraph 6.9 requires the defendant to send the claimant an electronic acknowledgement the next day after receipt of the CNF.

If, however, the CNF is sent only to the defendant (because the insurer's identity is not known or the defendant is known not to hold insurance cover) para 6.10 applies, which provides:

(a)   the defendant must send to the claimant an electronic acknowledgment the next day after receipt of the CNF and send the CNF to the insurer at the same time and advise the claimant that they have done so;

(b)   the insurer must send to the claimant an electronic acknowledgment the next day after its receipt by the insurer; and

(c)   the claimant must then submit the CNF to the insurer via the Portal as soon as possible and, in any event, within 30 days of the day upon which the claimant first sent it to the defendant.

1.15.7.5   Insurer response

To keep a notified claim within the protocol the defendant must provide an appropriate response within the relevant timescale.

Paragraph 6.11 requires the response section of the CNF to be sent to the claimant within 30 days in an employers' liability claim and within 40 days in a public liability claim.

Paragraph 6.13 confirms that the claim will no longer continue under the protocol where the defendant, within the relevant timescale in para 6.11:

(1)   makes an admission of liability but alleges contributory negligence;

(2)   does not complete and send the CNF response;

(3)   does not admit liability; or

(4)   notifies the claimant that the defendant considers that–
      (a)   there is inadequate mandatory information in the CNF; or
      (b)   if proceedings were issued, the small claims track would be the normal track for that claim.

1.15.7.6   Admission of liability

The definition of 'admission of liability' is found in para 1.1(1) which provides:

'"admission of liability" means the defendant admits that–
(a)   the breach of duty occurred;

(b) the defendant thereby caused some loss to the claimant, the nature and extent of which is not admitted; and

(c) the defendant has no accrued defence to the claim under the Limitation Act 1980.'

1.15.8 Stage 2

1.15.8.1 Introduction

If the claim remains within the EL/PL Protocol then, as with the RTA Protocol, it enters stage 2.

Stage 2 of the EL/PL Protocol is largely the same as stage 2 of the 2013 RTA Protocol.

1.15.8.2 Evidence

Paragraph 7.2 provides:

'It is expected that most claimants will obtain a medical report from one expert but additional medical reports may be obtained from other experts where the injuries require reports from more than one medical discipline.'

Paragraph 7.6 provides:

'A subsequent medical report from an expert who has already reported must be justified. A report may be justified where–

(1) the first medical report recommends that further time is required before a prognosis of the claimant's injuries can be determined; or

(2) the claimant is receiving continuing treatment; or

(3) the claimant has not recovered as expected in the original prognosis.'

Paragraph 7.7 provides:

'(1) In most cases, a report from a non-medical expert will not be required, but a report may be obtained where it is reasonably required to value the claim.

(2) Paragraph 7.2 applies to non-medical expert reports as it applies to expert medical reports.'

Paragraph 7.4 provides:

'(1) The medical expert should identify within the report–

(a) the medical records that have been reviewed; and

(b) the medical records considered relevant to the claim.

(2) The claimant must disclose with any medical report sent to the defendant any medical records which the expert considers relevant.'

Paragraph 7.5 provides:

'Any relevant photograph(s) of the claimant's injuries upon which the claimant intends to rely should also be disclosed with the medical report.'

In addition to medical evidence the protocol recognises specialist legal advice may be required. Paragraph 7.8 provides:

> 'In most cases under this Protocol, it is expected that the claimant's legal representative will be able to value the claim. In some cases with a value of more than £10,000, an additional advice from a specialist solicitor or from counsel may be justified where it is reasonably required to value the claim.'

The medical evidence relied on under the EL/PL Protocol is, just as with the RTA Protocol, crucial because it is the principal material on which the claim will be valued and negotiated as well as, if the claim goes to a stage 3 hearing, the key document on which the court will rely to assess not just the nature of the injuries but the implications of those injuries for the claimant.

Paragraph 7.10 provides:

> 'In most cases, witness statements, whether from the claimant or otherwise, will not be required. One or more statements may, however, be provided where reasonably required to value the claim.'

1.15.9   Stage 3

EL/PL Protocol claims which reach stage 3 will be dealt with in exactly the same way as claims entering stage 3 in the RTA Protocol (see **1.14.5**).

1.16   DESTINATION OF EX-PROTOCOL CLAIMS

1.16.1   Introduction

A personal injury claim which enters either the RTA Protocol or the EL/PL Protocol will, unless resolved under the terms of that protocol, usually move into the PI Protocol.

The terms of the RTA Protocol and the EL/PL Protocol are prescriptive. Those terms may stipulate that, in certain circumstances, the claimant can commence court proceedings under Part 7 CPR. In other circumstances the terms of the PI Protocol and the Practice Direction – Pre-Action Conduct will determine whether the issue of court proceedings is then reasonable and appropriate or, if not, what further steps are necessary as a preliminary.

The ultimate destination of a personal injury claim, which is not resolved in accordance of any of the protocols, will be the CPR, once court proceedings have been commenced.

A fixed costs regime makes it essential to progress cases through the protocols and into the CPR unless reasonable terms of settlement are reached precisely in accordance with the terms of the protocols, given that the costs effectively assume that will happen.

Consequently, it is essential to be aware of the defined circumstances in which a claim will move onto the next stage of the applicable protocol and, where this is not expressly stated as being a proper step to take, when the court is likely to be regard the issue of proceedings as reasonable conduct.

1.16.2 Discontinuing under the RTA Protocol and the EL/PL Protocol

Paragraph 5.11, found in both the 2013 RTA Protocol and the EL/PL Protocol, provides that if a claim does not continue under the relevant protocol it cannot subsequently re-enter that process.

Both protocols define a number of situations in which a claim will leave that protocol, though there are also a number of situations in which one party or another may, in any event, cause the claim to leave the protocol.

However, the claimant needs to remember that CPR 45.24 provides for costs sanctions which may apply if the claimant does not comply with the protocol, elects not to continue with that protocol or never enters a potentially suitable claim into the appropriate protocol. If those sanctions apply the claimant may be restricted to costs which would have been allowed had the claim continued under the relevant protocol.

The costs sanction for a defendant, where a claim does not continue under the relevant protocol, is that at the very least, subject to the terms of CPR 45.24 applying, higher costs are likely to be payable. Furthermore, both the RTA Protocol and the EL/PL Protocol expressly provide, in the preamble to each protocol, that the court can impose costs sanctions where the protocol is not followed. The Practice Direction Pre-Action Conduct expressly provides that these sanctions may include assessment of costs on the indemnity basis.

Stages 1 and 2 of both the RTA Protocol and the EL/PL Protocol identify a number of specific circumstances in which a claim will, or may if a party so decides, leave that protocol.

Furthermore, the claimant may, at any stage, give notice to the defendant that the claim is unsuitable for the relevant protocol. Paragraph 7.76 of the 2013 RTA Protocol gives the example of complex issues of fact or law in relation to the vehicle related damages. Paragraph 7.59 of the EL/PL Protocol gives the example of complex issues of fact or law or where claimants contemplate applying for a group litigation order.

If the claimant gives notice the claim is unsuitable for the relevant protocol that claim will no longer continue within the process but where the court considers the claimant acted unreasonably in giving such notice it will award no more than the fixed costs provided for under Part 45. In these circumstances the claimant may wish to refer the court to the preamble to each protocol.

1.16.3 Entry into the PI Protocol

When a claim leaves either the RTA Protocol of the EL/PL Protocol the claimant, as well as considering the point at which that claim enters the PI Protocol, needs to assess what action is appropriate to comply with the terms of the PI Protocol and to take the steps necessary for investigation of issues that may now have arisen, in particular liability, and, if necessary, prepare the case for the issue of court proceedings.

1.16.3.1   *Letter of claim*

Paragraph 2.10A of the PI Protocol provides that where a claim no longer continues under the RTA Protocol or the EL/PL Protocol the CNF completed by the claimant can be used as the letter of claim, unless the defendant has notified the claimant that there is inadequate information in that CNF.

If the defendant has given such notification a letter of claim will need to be sent. Otherwise the claimant may wish to take stock and write confirming the CNF is to be used as the letter of claim, highlighting the stage the claim has reached under the PI Protocoland dealing with any further matters that now arise.

1.16.3.2   *Liability*

Unless liability is admitted it is likely the claimant will now need to undertake investigations on this issue.

Under the PI Protocol the defendant is required to produce relevant documents where liability is not admitted.

The claimant may wish to seek facilities from the defendant to inspect the scene of the accident and/or any relevant property belonging to the defendant.

1.16.3.3   *Quantum*

If, at the time the claim enters the PI Protocol, quantum has not yet been investigated, and it is now appropriate to do so, further steps may be required.

Neither the RTA Protocol nor the EL/PL Protocol have a mechanism for the joint selection of experts. Accordingly, unless expert evidence has already been obtained the claimant may now wish to nominate experts for the purposes of joint selection under the PI Protocol and establishing an agreed expert under the terms of the Practice Direction – Pre-Action Conduct.

1.16.3.4   *ADR*

The terms of the RTA Protocol or the EL/PL Protocol may expressly provide for the issue of court proceedings in the circumstances that the claim has left the relevant protocol. If not, however, the claimant will need to follow the terms of the PI Protocol and the Practice Direction – Pre-Action Conduct, in particular concerning ADR, before commencing proceedings (see **1.11**)

1.16.3.5   *Stocktake*

Subject to raising any necessary matters with the defendant the claimant may wish, if appropriate upon the claim exiting either the RTA Protocol or the EL/PL Protocol, to move straight on to the stocktake recommended by the PI Protocol (see **1.13**).

1.17 SANCTIONS

The protocols do not stipulate any sanctions that will apply immediately in the event of non-compliance. However, non-compliance by a party with any relevant protocol may be an important consideration for the court once proceedings are underway or in the event of an application for pre-action disclosure.

1.17.1 The RTA Protocol and the EL/PL Protocol

The preamble to each protocol, after confirming the protocol describes behaviour the court will expect of parties prior to the start of proceedings, expressly states that costs sanctions may be imposed by the court where the terms of the protocol are not followed.

The CPR, and in particular CPR 45.24, makes express provision for the imposition of costs sanctions on a claimant, in certain circumstances, where the relevant protocol is not followed (see **1.17.4**).

1.17.2 The PI Protocol

This protocol confirms the standards set out are the normal reasonable approach to pre-action conduct but it is for the court to decide, if proceedings are issued, whether non-compliance should merit adverse consequences without identifying what those consequences might be. For these purposes it would seem necessary, therefore, to turn to the Practice Direction – Pre-Action Conduct.

1.17.3 The Practice Direction – Pre-Action Conduct

The Practice Direction – Pre-Action Conduct links compliance with any relevant protocol to sanctions which may be applicable under the CPR, at the appropriate stage, in the event of the parties having failed to adopt reasonable pre-action behaviour.

Paragraph 2.1 confirms the Practice Direction describes the conduct the court will normally expect of prospective parties prior to the start of court proceedings.

Paragraph 4.1 is a reminder that, once proceedings have commenced, the extent of compliance with the protocol will be relevant to case management of claims, in accordance with CPR 3.1, and to costs, under Part 44.

The focus should, however, be upon compliance with the substance of the protocol rather than minor or technical shortcomings. Specific examples of non-compliance, identified in para 4.4 and thus more likely to attract sanctions, include:

- failing to provide sufficient information to enable the other party to understand the issues;
- failing to act within a time limit set out in the protocol;
- unreasonably refusing to consider ADR; and/or
- failing to disclose documents without good reason.

Accordingly, tactical manoeuvring about technical non-compliance, and efforts to try and show a failure to comply when the alleged failing can have had no significant effect, should be avoided.

It remains important, however, to highlight, and deal with in an appropriate way, a material failure which does have consequences. This is also reflected in the general principles, set out in para 6, about the need for proportionality and the avoidance of unnecessary costs in relation to issues about compliance with the Practice Direction.

Paragraph 4.5 of the Practice Direction confirms the court should look at the overall effect of non-compliance when deciding whether to impose sanctions.

The Practice Direction has also important provisions about pre-action arrangements for obtaining expert evidence, which could, potentially, result in the imposition of sanctions at a later stage if not complied with.

The general tenor of the Practice Directions, and relevant protocols suggests non-compliance will usually result in costs, rather than other, sanctions.

1.17.4   Sanctions on the claimant

If the claimant has commenced court proceedings prematurely, given the terms of para 8 of the Practice Direction – Pre-Action Conduct, that may be relevant in determining what costs have reasonably been incurred and hence should be allowed.

If the claimant has failed to comply with, or elects not to continue with, the RTA Protocol or the EL/PL Protocol the court can, if it considers the claimant acted unreasonably, restrict the claimant to the fixed costs and disbursements, as set out in CPR 45.18 and 45.19, in accordance with the terms of CPR 45.24.

There are, additionally, express sanctions in the RTA Protocol which apply to soft tissue injury claims, within the scope of the protocol, in the event the claimant does not rely on fixed cost medical reports where required to do so.

1.17.4.1   CPR 45.24(1) and (2)

CPR 45.24 (until April 2013, CPR 45.36) applies where the claimant does not comply with the process set out in the relevant protocol or elects not to continue with that process and starts proceedings under Part 7.

Where this rule applies and judgment is given in favour of the claimant the court may order the defendant to pay no more than the fixed costs in CPR 45.18 and disbursements allowed in CPR 45.19 if:

- the court determines that the defendant did not proceed with the relevant protocol because the claimant provided insufficient information on the CNF;
- the court considers that the claimant acted unreasonably:
    - by discontinuing the process set out in the relevant protocol and starting proceedings under Part 7;
    - by valuing the claim at more than £25,000, so that the claimant did not need to comply with the relevant protocol;

– in any other way that caused the process in the relevant protocol to be discontinued; or

– the claimant did not comply with the relevant protocol at all, despite the claim falling within the scope of the relevant protocol.

The power conferred by this rule will need to be exercised at the stage when judgment is given in favour of the claimant and, in this context, the word 'may' appears to confer a discretion.

The terms of CPR 45.24 are reflected by para 7.76 of the 2013 RTA Protocol, which confirms that where the claimant gives notice the claim is unsuitable for the protocol then the claim will no longer continue under that protocol but, if the court considers the claimant acted unreasonably in giving such notice, it will award no more than fixed in CPR 45.18.

Furthermore, it is important, for the purpose of this rule, to keep in mind the general terms of the RTA Protocol, and the similar provisions in the EL/PL Protocol, in particular the following terms.

- Paragraph 2.1, which describes behaviour 'the court will normally expect of the parties prior to the start of proceedings'. Hence where there is a fixed timescale, and the protocol contains no discretion to vary this, it ought not to be unreasonable for the claimant to expect strict compliance by the defendant.

- Paragraph 3.1 confirms the aim of the protocol is to ensure damages and costs are paid by the defendant 'using the process set out in the protocol'. Hence any acts or omissions by the defendant which do not help achieve that objective ought not result in subsequent steps by the claimant being characterised as 'unreasonable'.

The proper approach to these costs sanctions was considered in *Patel v Fortis Insurance*[83] and *Greenway v Davies*.[84]

For these purposes the court may need to decide who has caused the claim not to proceed under the relevant protocol.

In *Boyd v Clark*,[85] the CNF was sent by fax to the defendant's insurers, rather than through the portal, at a time when the terms of the protocol required electronic communication but not necessarily through the portal. The defendant's insurers objected to communication outside the portal and stated they were, accordingly, 'unable to give consideration to the claim'. The proceedings concluded at a hearing where the judge assessed damages in excess of the offer eventually made by the defendant. The defendant argued the claimant should be restricted to fixed costs payable under the RTA Protocol, as the CNF had not been submitted through the portal. The judge rejecting that argument in the court held that the defendant was at fault, having been 'quite excessively and inappropriately pedantic'.

This approach follows the guidance given by the Court of Appeal, against speculation, in *Straker v Tudor Rose*[86] (see **1.11.4**).

---

[83] (Unreported) Leicester County Court, 23 December 2011.
[84] SCCO (Master Simons) 30 October 2013.
[85] APIL PI Focus, Vol 21, Issue 5.
[86] [2007] EWCA Civ 368.

For these purposes both the preamble to and aims of each protocol may be highly relevant.

1.17.4.2   CPR 45.24(3)

CPR 45.24(3) provides that where the claimant starts proceedings to obtain an interim payment and the court orders the defendant to make an interim payment of no more than the amount payable under the relevant protocol the court will, on the final determination of the proceedings, order the defendant to pay no more than relevant stage 1 and 2 fixed costs and disbursements allowed in accordance with CPR 45.19.

Unlike the discretionary terms of CPR 45.24(1) and (2) this provision is expressed in mandatory terms and is likely to make a claimant wary of issuing proceedings to secure a more substantial interim payment unless confident of succeeding in that application.

For these purposes both the preamble to and aims of each protocol may be highly relevant.

1.17.5   Sanctions on the defendant

If there has been material non-compliance with the Practice Direction- Pre-Action Conduct by the defendant, para 4.6 provides that the court may, in accordance with Part 44 CPR, order costs to be assessed on an indemnity basis and that interest on any damages be paid at a rate not exceeding 10% above base rate.

The importance of parties complying with the Practice Direction – Pre-Action Conduct was emphasised in *Thornhill v Nationwide Metal Recycling Ltd*[87] where Sir Henry Brooke observed that:

> '... it is essential that all parties to any prospective litigation and their solicitors should take this Practice Direction seriously ...'

From April 2013, with greater emphasis on compliance with rules, practice direction and orders, the terms of the Practice Direction – Pre-Action Conduct may assume even greater importance.

The issue of court proceedings by the claimant, as a result of non-compliance by the defendant, should not, of itself, be regarded as a sanction on the defendant. That is because the claimant is, in any event, entitled to take such a step and, indeed, issue of court proceedings may be appropriate even if the defendant has fully complied with any relevant protocol. Additional costs inevitably follow the issue of court proceedings so simply to allow those costs is hardly consistent with the imposition, as envisaged by the preamble to each protocol, of 'costs sanctions'. Furthermore, non-compliance with protocols inevitably generates additional costs, hence the linkage between proportionality and the need for compliance expressly stated within Part 1 of the CPR from April 2013

Accordingly, the terms of the Practice Direction – Pre-Action Conduct, regarding indemnity costs, simply endorse the approach that may, in any event, be applicable

---

[87]   [2011] EWCA Civ 919.

under Part 44. So far as compliance with protocol reflects 'normal' pre-action behaviour the failure to comply must be conduct which is 'out of the norm', the touchstone for the award of indemnity costs (see **12.2.6**).

In a case subject to fixed costs, non-compliance by the defendant might, even if indemnity costs are not awarded, result in the court concluding this amounted to 'exceptional circumstances' under CPR 45.29J so that costs should be assessed even if that be on the standard basis.

All of this, whilst considered in the particular context of relief from sanctions, was recognised by the Court of Appeal in *Denton v TH White Ltd*,[88] where Lord Dyson MR held:

> 'Heavy costs sanctions should, therefore, be imposed on parties who behave unreasonably in refusing to agree extensions of time or unreasonably oppose applications for relief from sanctions. An order to pay the costs of the application under rule 3.9 may not always be sufficient. The court can, in an appropriate case, also record in its order that the opposition to the relief application was unreasonable conduct to be taken into account under CPR rule 44.11 when costs are dealt with at the end of the case. If the offending party ultimately wins, the court may make a substantial reduction in its costs recovery on grounds of conduct under rule 44.11. If the offending party ultimately loses, then its conduct may be a good reason to order it to pay indemnity costs. Such an order would free the winning party from the operation of CPR rule 3.18 in relation to its costs budget.'

1.17.6   ADR

Sanctions may be imposed for a failure to engage with or explore ADR (see **1.11.5**).

The terms of any relevant protocol may also inform the courts approach if having to decide whether it would be unjust for the normal costs consequences to follow where a party has made an early Part 36 offer but failed to provide information required under the relevant protocol, particularly if that offer is accepted, though outside the relevant period, once the information does become available: *Webb Resolutions Ltd v Waller Needham & Green*.[89]

1.17.7   Pleading compliance

If court proceedings are started the claimant, to comply with para 9.7, should state in the claim form or particulars of claim whether the Practice Direction, and the protocol, have been complied with.

If the claimant pleads non-compliance by the defendant that becomes a matter the defendant will then need to deal with in the defence, in order to comply with the terms of the CPR.

---

[88]   [2014] EWCA Civ 506.
[89]   [2012] EWHC 3529 (Ch).

CHAPTER 2

ISSUE AND SERVICE

2.1   INTRODUCTION

The protocols, in particular the PI Protocol, and the Civil Procedure Rules (the CPR) are, for reasons set out in chapter 1, closely connected. Consequently, it is appropriate to be mindful, from the outset, about the terms of the CPR as these may have implications on how a claim is run prior to issue of court proceedings. Once a claim form has been issued the case will, in any event, be subject to the CPR.

Furthermore, a number of cases have explained that the term 'proceedings' when used in the CPR can, in context, apply to steps taken under a pre-action protocol before court proceedings have been commenced: *Crosbie v Munroe*;[1] *Solomon v Cromwell*.[2]

Accordingly, before dealing with the procedural aspects of issuing and serving court proceedings some of the pervasive aspects of the CPR, of general application to all 'proceedings', will be considered.

2.2   THE CPR

CPR 1.1(1) provides that the rules are a new procedural code.

These rules must be given a purposive construction as Lord Woolf made clear in the Final Report when, at paragraphs 10 to 11 of chapter 20, he said:

> 'Every word in the rules should have a purpose, but every word cannot sensibly be given a minutely exact meaning. Civil procedure involves more judgment and knowledge than the rules can directly express. In this respect, rules of court are not like an instruction manual for operating a piece of machinery. Ultimately their purpose is to guide the court and the litigants towards a just resolution of the case. Although the rules can offer detailed directions for the technical steps to be taken, the effectiveness of those steps depends upon the spirit in which they are carried out. That in turn depends on an understanding of the fundamental purpose of the rules and of the underlying system of procedure.'

When giving judgment in *Biguzzi v Rank Leisure plc*[3] Lord Woolf MR observed:

---

[1]   [2003] EWCA Civ 350.
[2]   [2011] EWCA Civ 1584.
[3]   [1999] 1 WLR 1926.

'The whole purpose of making the CPR a self-contained code was to send the message which now generally applies. Earlier authorities are no longer generally of any relevance once the CPR applies.'

Accordingly, when interpreting the rules it will usually be appropriate to refer only to cases decided under those rules. However, it has been observed that earlier authorities, whilst not binding, may be of considerable persuasive force and help contribute to a just result: *Garratt v Saxby (Practice Note)*.[4] To this extent cases decided up to 1999 may remain relevant, especially if approved in or consistent with cases decided under the CPR.

2.2.1   The overriding objective

CPR 1.1(1) confirms the CPR is a code with the overriding objective of enabling the court to deal with cases justly and, from April 2013, at proportionate cost.

CPR 1.1(2) explains that dealing with cases justly and at proportionate cost means:

- ensuring that the parties are on an equal footing;
- saving expense;
- dealing with the case in ways which are proportionate;
  - to the amount of money involved
  - the importance of the case
  - the complexity of the issues
  - the financial position of each party
- ensuring the case is dealt with expeditiously and fairly;
- allotting an appropriate share of the court's resources; and (from April 2013);
- enforcing compliance with rules, Practice Directions and orders.

CPR 1.2 requires the court to give effect to the overriding objective whenever it exercises any power or interprets any rule.

CPR 1.3 requires the parties to help the court further the overriding objective.

Accordingly, the overriding objective influences the way the court will deal with every stage of the proceedings. Indeed, as the protocols prepare for, and lead into the CPR all steps taken, from the very outset, should be viewed in the context of the overriding objective.

There is undoubtedly a tension between the different objectives, intended to help the court deal with the case justly, identified in CPR 1.1(2). Some of those objectives might be regarded as deontological in nature whilst others are consequentialist, almost utilitarian. It is for the court to reconcile these potentially conflicting considerations when assessing, overall, what will be just in any given situation.

Expressly reflecting on the factors identified in CPR 1.1(2) is often a useful exercise not just for the court but also practitioners whenever considering how the court may be invited to exercise case management powers.

---

4   [2004] EWCA Civ 341.

The general approach the court should take to the overriding objective was considered in *Holmes v SGB Services Ltd.*[5]

Arden LJ held that:

'... The rules are a new procedural code which has to be construed in its own right, without reference back to prior practice, unless there is some compelling reason for looking at prior practice. So the function of a judge in this situation is to look at the overriding objective and to consider how the case can be dealt with justly in the light of the circumstances placed before the court.'

Buxton LJ, in the same case, observed:

'In looking at CPR Part 1, paragraph 1.1, it is perhaps important to note that 1.1(1) says that the overriding objective is to enable the court to deal with cases justly; but then in 1.1(2) it explains that just dealing with a case includes not only matters such as the parties being on an equal footing but also, much more directly, management questions such as saving expense, dealing with the case in a proportionate way and ensuring that it is dealt with expeditiously. In making a decision under the overriding objective the court has to balance all those considerations that are set out under that heading without giving one of them undue weight. It is essentially, as I have said, a matter for the judge's management, and it would be wrong for this court to give, or judges to seek, any direction suggesting that one or other of those criteria was more or less important.'

In any individual case, of course, a particular facet of the overriding objective may assume particular importance in enabling the court to deal with that case justly.

Hence when considering the need for additional expert evidence, in a clinical negligence claim of potentially very substantial value, the court attached most significance, in the context of that case, to the objective of ensuring the parties were on an equal footing: *ES v Chesterfield and North Derbyshire Royal Hospital NHS Trust.*[6]

Similarly in *Henry v News Group Newspapers Ltd*[7] the court attached particular importance to the need for the parties to be on an equal footing, in the context of costs. Moore-Bick LJ observed that the purpose of costs budgets was:

'... to ensure that one party is unable to exploit superior financial resources by conducting the litigation in a way that puts the other at a significant disadvantage.'

Putting the parties on an equal footing, whilst not a factor that automatically prevails over the other factors identified in CPR 1.1(2), is clearly a consideration of real significance not least in litigation where the parties are, patently, not on an equal footing in terms of the resources that can be devoted to the claim. That was so in the context of a libel claim in *Henry* and will be the case in most personal injury claims where an individual litigant faces a large commercial organisation.

Even under the revised terms of the overriding objective, applicable from April 2013, the value of the claim does not detract from the need to deal with that claim justly. In

---

5   [2001] EWCA Civ 354.
6   [2003] EWCA Civ 128.
7   [2013] EWCA Civ 19.

Layland v Fairview New Homes PLC[8] Neuberger J (as he then was) noted that a claimant with a small claim was entitled to the same treatment, in terms of substantive and procedural justice, as a claimant with a more substantial claim, proportionality being subject to the fundamental and overriding requirement that every case is disposed of justly.

Whilst the change to CPR 1.1(2) made in April 2013 added to, rather than subtracted from, the specific factors found in the rule since 1999 the additional requirement to enforce compliance with rules, Practice Directions and orders may have a significant effect on how the courts approach the meaning of 'dealing with cases justly'. On 22 March 2013, giving the 18th Lecture in the Implementation Programme (for the forthcoming changes to the CPR in April 2013), Lord Dyson MR observed:

> 'Dealing with a case justly does not simply mean ensuring that a decision is reached on the merits. It is a mistake to assume that it does. Equally, it is a mistaken assumption, which some have made, that the overriding objective of dealing with cases justly does not require the court to manage cases so that no more than proportionate costs are expended. It requires the court to do precisely that; and so far as practicable to achieve the effective and consistent enforcement of compliance with rules, PDs and court orders.'

Since April 2013 the courts have put particular emphasis on this new factor as well as attaching greater weight to the existing consequentialist factors, in particular allotting an appropriate share of the court's resources. For example, in *Fons HF v Corporal Ltd*[9] HHJ Pelling QC described court sitting days as 'a valuable national resource'.

The parties should keep the need to deal with the case justly, and at proportionate cost, in mind throughout, given that CPR 1.3 requires those parties to help the court further the overriding objective (see **1.3.3**).

2.2.2   The case management powers of the court

These are extensive, reflecting the case (and from April 2013 costs) management role of the court under the CPR, and comprise:

- the court's duty to manage cases found in CPR 1.4; and
- general case (and from April 2013 costs) management powers found in Part 3.

2.2.3   Time

CPR 2.8 explains how to calculate any period of time for doing any act specified by the rules, a Practice Direction or judgment or order of the court. In particular:

- any period of time expressed as a number of days shall be computed as clear days (which excludes the day on which the period begins and if the end of the period is defined by reference to an event also excludes the day on which that event occurs);
- where the specified period is five days or less then a Saturday, a Sunday, a Bank Holiday, Christmas Day and Good Friday will not count;
- court orders should, wherever practicable, contain calendar dates and the time of day by which any act, subject to a time limit, must be done; and

---

[8]   [2002] EWHC 1350 (Ch).
[9]   [2013] EWHC 1278 (Ch).

- save for certain specific exceptions time limits may be varied by the written agreement of the parties themselves.

With greater emphasis on the need for compliance with court orders, and the terms of the CPR, this rule has become even more important.

When a period of time is specified by the CPR of the terms of a court order there are circumstances in which the parties can agree to vary the relevant time limit and circumstances when they cannot.

2.2.3.1 *When the parties may vary time limits*

CPR 2.11 allows, unless the rules or practice directions otherwise provide, for 'the time specified by a rule or by the court for a person to do any act may be varied by the written agreement of the parties'.

The importance of the word 'written' in CPR 2.11 was considered in *Thomas v Home Office*.[10] The Court of Appeal held that the phrase 'written agreement of the parties' was confined to:

- a single document signed by all parties; or
- an exchange of letters; or
- an oral agreement subsequently confirmed in writing by all parties.

Consequently, an oral agreement recorded in a letter sent by one party to the other, which was not replied to, or an oral agreement only evidenced by internal file notes, even if made by each party, would not constitute a 'written agreement' for the purposes of CPR 2.11.

2.2.3.2 *When the parties may not vary time limits*

Under CPR 28.4 (fast track) and CPR 29.5 (multi-track) an application to the court will be required if a party, even with agreement, wishes to vary the date the court has fixed for:

- a case management conference;
- a pre-trial review;
- the return of the pre-trial checklist;
- the trial; or
- the trial period.

Moreover, CPR 3.8(3) provides that where a rule, Practice Direction or court order requires a party to do something within a specified time and specifies the consequence of failure to comply, the time for doing the act in question may not be extended by agreement between the parties. In these circumstances the parties will need an order varying the timetable even where there is written agreement. There are some important provisions in the CPR which do specify the consequence of failing to comply with a time limit including:

---

[10]   [2006] EWCA Civ 1355.

- CPR 31.21 (disclosure and inspection);
- CPR 32.10 (witness statements); and
- CPR 35.13 (expert evidence).

2.2.4   Sanctions and relief from sanctions

The policy of the CPR is that court orders, and the rules themselves, are to be complied with. Accordingly:

- sanctions will automatically apply (CPR 3.8); but
- relief from sanctions can be given (CPR 3.9).

An application will be necessary, by the party in default, to seek relief from sanctions which the court will consider having regard, as ever, to the overriding objective and to the terms of CPR 3.9 (see **8.10.2**).

CPR 3.9 was amended in April 2013 and, along with the corresponding amendments to the overriding objective, this seems likely to herald a tougher regime towards the enforcement of sanctions by the courts. Lord Dyson MR had this to say about the future approach to sanctions when he gave the 18th Lecture in the Implementation Programme:

> 'The tougher, more robust approach to rule-compliance and relief from sanctions is intended to ensure that justice can be done in the majority of cases. This requires an acknowledgement that the achievement of justice means something different now. Parties can no longer expect indulgence if they fail to comply with their procedural obligations. Those obligations not only serve the purpose of ensuring that they conduct the litigation proportionately in order to ensure their own costs are kept within proportionate bounds. But more importantly they serve the wider public interest of ensuring that other litigants can obtain justice efficiently and proportionately, and that the court enables them to do so.'

Seeking relief from a sanction which already applies should be distinguished from seeking an extension of time before the relevant deadline, imposing the sanction, has been reached. In that situation the court will not be applying the terms of CPR 3.9 but just the overriding objective (though, of course, this also now emphasises the need for the rules, Practice Directions and orders to be complied with).

A number of decisions considering the April 2013 version of CPR 3.9 have confirmed the court will adopt the approach towards relief from sanctions indicated in the Implementation Lectures, in particular the Court of Appeal judgments in *Mitchell v News Group Newspapers Ltd*[11] and *Durrant v Chief Constable of Avon & Somerset Constabulary*[12] and *Denton v TH White Ltd*[13] (see **8.10.2**).

The imposition of a sanction, for non-compliance with the rules, should also be distinguished from a procedural error made by a party, even though this error may result in non-compliance with a rule and so, indirectly, a sanction.

---

[11]   [2013] EWCA Civ 1537.
[12]   [2013] EWCA Civ 1624.
[13]   [2014] EWCA Civ 906.

If there has been an error of procedure, such as a failure to comply with a Rule or Practice Direction, CPR 3.10 provides that the error does not invalidate any step taken in the proceedings unless the Court so orders and, furthermore, the court may make an order to remedy the error.

In *Cala Homes (South) Ltd v Chichester District Council*[14] the applicant issued a claim form, which fully set out the basis and grounds of the proceedings, in the wrong court. After the relevant time limit had expired the respondent contended the proceedings were defective and could not proceed. However, with a view to achieving the overriding objective, the court applied CPR 3.10 to correct the error on the basis that issuing in the wrong court, and therefore using the wrong claim form, did not make the proceedings a nullity.

The scope of CPR 3.10 was considered again in *Steele v Mooney*.[15] The Court of Appeal held the phrase 'error of procedure' should not be given an artificially restrictive meaning, and could include a drafting error, when considering an application by the claimant seeking an extension of time for service of the particulars of claim and supporting documentation. That application omitted express reference to the claim form as a result of an error when the application was prepared. In these circumstances the subsequent application was to correct that error, under CPR 3.10, rather than an application, now out of time, seeking an extension of time for service of the claim form (which would have brought the terms of CPR 7.6(3) into play). Accordingly, the application was allowed.

In *Phillips v Symes (No 3)*[16] Lord Brown put CPR 3.10 into the context of the earlier rules replaced by the CPR, and how those rules were applied when dealing with errors of procedure, when he said:

> 'The court's procedure at that time was governed by the Rules of the Supreme Court and the rule in point was RSC Ord 2, r 1. For present purposes I can see no material differences between that rule and CPR r 3.10. All three members of the court accepted that RSC Ord 2, r 1 was a most beneficial provision, to be given wide effect.'

The views of Lord Brown, with whom all members of the Judicial Committee agreed, were described as 'authoritative guidance on the scope of this provision' by Popplewell J in *Integral Petroleum SA v SCU-Finanz AG*.[17]

2.2.5 Statements of truth

Part 22 and the accompanying Practice Direction require certain documents to be verified by a statement of truth.

The documents to be verified by a statement of truth include:

- a statement of case (and any amended statement of case);
- a response complying with an order under CPR 18.1 to provide further information;

---

[14] [2000] CP Rep 28.
[15] [2005] EWCA Civ 96.
[16] [2008] 1 WLR 180.
[17] [2014] EWHC 702 (Comm).

- a witness statement;
- a schedule or counter schedule of expenses and losses (and any amendment to such a schedule or counter schedule);
- an expert's report; and
- a certificate of service.

If the statement of case does not have a statement of truth it will remain effective, given the terms of CPR 22.2(1)(a), but the statement of case may not be relied on as evidence of the matters set out in it and that statement of case is at risk of being struck out by the court.

The requirement for a statement of truth is an important aspect of the CPR, intended to ensure cases are only pursued and defended on what are likely to be the real issues.

Further, a statement of truth is an important safeguard when, under the CPR, evidence which would previously have been given orally, under oath, is now often admitted in written form. Hence, in *Zurich Insurance Co plc v Hayward*[18] Smith LJ observed:

> 'In the post CPR world, one aim of the rules is to encourage the parties to reach settlement of their disputes. This means that the statements or representations made at the pre-trial stage have taken on an even greater importance than they had under the old rules, where it was expected that their truthfulness and accuracy would probably be tested at trial. The importance of the truthfulness of pretrial statements is evidenced by the new requirement that a statement of case must be accompanied by a declaration of truth. The intention is that a party should be able to rely on a pre-trial statements in reaching settlement. Thus pre-trial statements play a vital role in the administration of civil justice.'

Consequently, care is necessary to ensure facts given in a document supported by a statement of truth are not only accurate but do not give any impression that might be potentially misleading: *Motor Insurers' Bureau v Shikell*.[19]

There can be serious consequences for anyone who signs a document containing a statement of truth where the information is inaccurate and those potential consequences should, therefore, always be made clear to the claimant, witnesses and any others who may, in the course of the claim, need to sign documents which have a statement of truth. CPR 32.14 expressly provides that proceedings for contempt of court may be brought against a person if he makes, or causes to be made, a false statement in a document verified by a statement of truth without an honest belief in its truth.

Signing a statement of truth does not prevent a claimant asserting, in the alternative, that if the defendant's factual case, even if denied by the claimant, is made out the defendant may be liable on those facts if, of course, such facts establish a cause of action: *Binks v Securicor Omega Express Ltd*.[20]

---

[18]   [2011] EWCA Civ 641.
[19]   [2011] EWHC 527 (QB).
[20]   [2003] EWCA Civ 993, [2003] 1 WLR 2557.

2.2.6　Part 36

Part 36 provides a formal, and self-contained, system for the parties to make offers which carry the potential for costs consequences set out in that rule.

CPR 36.3(2)(a) confirms that Part 36 offers can be made, and be effective for cost purposes, before court proceedings are commenced. Indeed, section II of Part 36 deals specifically with making offers relevant to costs within the RTA Protocol and the EL/PL Protocol.

Part 36 is a key aspect of the CPR when considering negotiations and settlement of the claims (see **11.5**).

2.2.7　Workflow

The CPR create, for claims not resolved pre-issue, a workflow path through the court process. The key stages of that path are:

- issue;
- service;
- defence;
- allocation and case management;
- disclosure;
- exchange of factual evidence;
- exchange of expert evidence;
- pre-trial checklists and listing;
- trial;
- costs.

Although it is important to keep the case moving along the workflow path this should always be on the basis that, at all stages, risk is reviewed and reassessed as appropriate with the prospect of settlement being kept in mind throughout.

A challenge for the practitioner is, whilst keeping to the general workflow path, identifying, in any particular case, which steps need, or need not, be taken and the extent to which action can be taken simultaneously or sequentially. That is critical to running the case efficiently, and at proportionate cost, while helping to ensure the claim is concluded sooner rather than later.

2.3　REVIEW BEFORE ISSUING

The stocktake recommended by the PI Protocol, if that does not result in the claim being promptly resolved or discontinued, is likely to suggest the issue of court proceedings. If court proceedings are appropriate that stocktake should prompt a review of all necessary matters prior to issue.

A review, at this stage, should ensure all practical, procedural and tactical considerations are taken into account. That will involve a number of considerations.

2.3.1 Compliance with the Protocol

Each protocol reflects reasonable pre-action standards for the parties to deal with each other. Accordingly, it is sensible, before court proceedings are issued, to check the terms of any relevant protocol have been complied with.

2.3.1.1 *Compliance by the claimant*

If there are any aspects of a relevant protocol the claimant has not complied with, which can be rectified, appropriate action should be taken before issue of proceedings. That will allow confirmation to be given, at the stage of allocation, the claimant has complied with the relevant protocol.

2.3.1.2 *Compliance by the defendant*

If the defendant has not complied with a relevant protocol consideration should be given as to the implications of this and any steps that should be taken as a result.

If there are breaches of the protocol by the defendant, but these do not have a material effect on the decision as to whether or not the main action should be commenced, it may suffice simply to give the defendant the opportunity of rectifying matters and, if this is not done, draw the matter to the attention of the court at the stage of initial case management.

If the claimant is prejudiced by the defendant's conduct that may suggest it is more appropriate for the claimant to make a pre-action application, for an order enforcing the terms of the protocol rather than issue the main action. Any such application is likely to seek an order for disclosure of documents. Additionally, the claimant may seek, under the general case management powers of the court, an order requiring a decision on liability, failing which the defendant will be debarred from contesting liability in any main action, though the court may be reluctant to invoke case management powers of this kind at the pre-action stage.

If compliance with the protocol is required as a preliminary to assessing the strength of the case it will usually be necessary to make a pre-action application, rather than issue the main action and seeking early orders, for example in relation to disclosure, in that action.

If, however, the claimant needs something not provided for by the protocol, perhaps facilities for an inspection of property, issue of the main action, with early application for an appropriate order in that action, may be regarded by the court as justified even though a pre-action application might have been made. That is because such an order will help ensure, at the subsequent stage of initial case management, the claimant will then be ready to deal with likely directions, for example the exchange of expert evidence when getting that evidence will depend upon having appropriate inspection facilities meanwhile.

Pre-action applications are dealt with later in this chapter (see **2.11**).

2.3.2 Issues

One purpose of the Protocol is to focus on the issues between the parties so that those issues, and those only, are addressed with consequent costs savings. Ideally, exchange of information under the Protocol will have identified the issues that remain between the parties so the particulars of claim can, as well as identifying points of agreement, focus on the matters still in issue and the claimant's case on those matters.

The causes of action identified in the case plan should be reviewed, to check whether all of these remain appropriate and/or whether any further causes of action arise.

Additionally, the evidence, which the court is likely to need to determine whether those causes of action can be made out given the matters that remain in issue, will need to be reviewed and any further necessary evidence identified so that steps can be taken to obtain this.

2.3.3 Claimant's identity and status

The claimant will need to be correctly described in the proceedings. Whilst relevant details will have been obtained at the outset it may be necessary to check there has been no change of title or name, by marriage or otherwise.

The claimant must have the legal standing to commence court proceedings relating to the claim and, if not, necessary steps must be taken as a preliminary to those proceedings.

2.3.3.1 *Children and protected parties as claimant*

A litigation friend will be required if the claimant is:
- a child; or
- a protected party.

Capacity, and hence whether a person is a protected party, will be determined in accordance with the Mental Capacity Act 2005. The courts have given guidance about the appropriate test for capacity in civil proceedings in case-law including *Masterman-Lister v Jewel*[21] and *Dunhill v Burgin*.[22]

A certificate, in form N235, will need to be completed and signed by the litigation friend ready for filing at court on the issue of proceedings and those proceedings will need to confirm the claimant proceeds by a litigation friend.

If proceedings are commenced without a litigation friend, when one is required, CPR 21.3(4) allows the court to order that any step in the proceedings, before a litigation friend has been appointed, can take effect.

---

[21]   [2002] EWCA Civ 1889.
[22]   [2012] EWCA Civ 39.

2.3.3.2   *Deceased claimant*

If the injured person has died a Grant of Representation should be taken out.

If the deceased did not leave a will a Grant of Letters of Administration is an essential preliminary to the issue of court proceedings, the absence of which will render any proceedings that are commenced a nullity: *Millburn-Snell v Evans*.[23]

If, however, the deceased left a will that gives the executor authority to commence court proceedings, even without a grant of probate.

Proceedings, on behalf of a deceased claimant, will usually be taken by the executor or administrator of the estate, claims of the estate surviving for such purposes under the terms of the Law Reform (Miscellaneous Provisions) Act 1934.

Section 2(2) Fatal Accidents Act 1976 provides, however, that if there is no executor or administrator of the estate, or if no action is brought within six months after the death by and in the name of an executor or administrator of the deceased, then the action may be brought by and in the name of all or any of the persons for whose benefit an executor or administrator could have brought it. This provision allows dependants, as defined by the Act, to commence proceedings in such circumstances.

2.3.3.3   *Bankrupt claimant*

Section 306 Insolvency Act 1986 vests the bankrupt's estate in his trustee. Even if the bankrupt is subsequently discharged title to any property that has vested in the trustee will remain with that trustee unless and until there is an assignment back to the bankrupt.

For these purposes 'property' is defined by s 436 of the 1986 Act. The definition is broad enough to catch any cause of action, which therefore vests in the trustee (unless the cause of action consists solely of a personal claim, namely pain and suffering).

Consequently, where the cause of action comprises claims for both pain and suffering and for other heads of damage, sometimes termed a hybrid claim, the whole cause of action will vest in the trustee even though damages for pain and suffering, which are personal in nature, will be held on a constructive trust for the bankrupt by the trustee as and when any such damages are recovered: *Ord v Upton*.[24]

Where a claimant has been made bankrupt before proceedings have been commenced, even if subsequently discharged from the bankruptcy but there has been no assignment of property from the trustee, the bankrupt has no title and any proceedings, unless limited to damages for pain and suffering, will be an abuse of process if the claimant commences proceedings at a time when it is known there is no cause of action because that is vested in the trustee. That abuse could not be cured by the bankrupt later acquiring the cause of action by assignment: *Pickthall v Hill Dickinson LLP*.[25]

---

[23]   [2011] EWCA Civ 577.
[24]   [2000] 1 All ER 193.
[25]   [2009] EWCA Civ 543.

Whilst it is an abuse of process to issue proceedings knowing there is no relevantly vested cause of action it does not follow it will be an abuse of process to issue proceedings where a claimant does not know, or is uncertain, whether that claimant has a vested cause of action, because the abuse is the actual knowledge of a lack of title: *Munday v Hilburn*.[26] If the claimant has been bankrupt, subsequently discharged from that bankruptcy and the cause of action arises after the discharge that cause of action will not vest in the trustee and the claimant is entitled to proceed: *Grant v Hayes*.[27]

Consequently, before commencing court proceedings, a bankruptcy search should be made against the proposed claimant. If the proposed claimant is an undischarged bankrupt, or even a discharged bankrupt where the cause of action accrued prior to discharge and there has been no assignment of property as yet from the trustee, the trustee should be approached with a view to selling or assigning the cause of action back to the bankrupt.

2.3.3.4 Anonymity

CPR 39.2(1) confirms the general rule is that any court hearing is to be in public. CPR 39.2(3) allows the court to hold, in appropriate circumstances, a hearing in private. Of more significance, at the stage of commencing proceedings, CPR 39.2(4) allows the court to order that the identity of any party must not be disclosed if the court considers non-disclosure necessary in order to protect the interests of that party.

Consequently, before court proceedings are commenced it is appropriate to consider whether there is any reason to seek an order giving the claimant anonymity under CPR 39.2(4).

If invited to make such an order that is likely to involve the court balancing conflicting rights, under Article 8 and Article 10, in the European Convention on Human Rights 1950: *JXF v York Hospitals NHS Foundation Trust*;[28] *MXB v East Sussex Hospitals NHS Trust*.[29]

Because CPR 5.4 requires the court to keep a publically accessible register of claims which have been issued it will also be necessary for any order, dealing with anonymity, to restrict access, perhaps by requiring there to be an application for leave, on notice to all parties, if any person not a party to the proceedings wishes to have access to court documents under CPR 5.4.

Given the publically accessible register of claims a party may, alternatively, seek permission to start legal proceedings without providing the identify details required by Part 16. Guidance on the correct approach to such an application was given in *CVB v MGN Ltd*.[30]

Further guidance on the issue of anonymity, specifically in claims for personal injuries suffered by a child or a protected party brought before the court for approval, was given

---

[26]   [2014] EWHC 4496 (Ch).
[27]   [2014] EWHC 2646 (Ch).
[28]   [2010] EWHC 2800 (QB).
[29]   [2012] EWHC 3279 (QB).
[30]   [2012] EWHC 1148 (QB).

by the Court of Appeal Tugendhat J in *JX MX v Dartford & Gravesham NHS Trust*[31] where Moore-Bick LJ, giving the judgment of the court, held he stressed:

> 'In our view the court should recognise that when dealing with an approval application of the kind now under consideration it is dealing with what is essentially private business, albeit in open court, and should normally make an anonymity order in favour of the claimant without the need for any formal application, unless for some reason it is satisfied that it is unnecessary or inappropriate to do so. Such an order should be drawn in terms that prohibit publication of the name and address of the claimant and his or her immediate family and also (if not already covered) the name of his or her litigation friend. The court must also recognise, however, that the public and the Press have a legitimate interest both in observing the proceedings and making and receiving a report of them. Accordingly, the Press should be given an opportunity to make submissions before any order is made restricting publication of a report of the proceedings, but for obvious reasons it will be unnecessary to notify the Press formally that an application for an anonymity order will be made. If the Press or any other party wishes to contend that an anonymity order should not be made, it will normally be necessary for it to file and serve on the claimant a statement setting out the nature of its case.'

With that in mind we suggest that the following principles should apply:

(1)   the hearing should be listed for hearing in public under the name in which the proceedings were issued, unless by the time of the hearing an anonymity order has already been made;

(ii)   because the hearing will be held in open court the Press and members of the public will have a right to be present and to observe the proceedings;

(iii)   the Press will be free to report the proceedings, subject only to any order made by the judge restricting publication of the name and address of the claimant, his or her litigation friend (and, if different, the names and addresses of his or her parents) and restricting access by non-parties to documents in the court record other than those which have been anonymised (an 'anonymity order');

(iv)   the judge should invite submissions from the parties and the Press before making an anonymity order;

(v)   unless satisfied after hearing argument that it is not necessary to do so, the judge should make an anonymity order for the protection of the claimant and his or her family;

(vi)   if the judge concludes that it is unnecessary to make an anonymity order, he should give a short judgment setting out his reasons for coming to that conclusion;

(vii)   the judge should normally give a brief judgment on the application (taking into account any anonymity order) explaining the circumstances giving rise to the claim and the reasons for his decision to grant or withhold approval and should make a copy available to the Press on request as soon as possible after the hearing.

The judge did not dissent from the application of a Practice Direction in the Family Division that where the claimant intended to apply for an anonymity order notice should be given to the Press Association.

---

[31]   [2015] EWCA Civ 96.

2.3.4   Defendant's identity and status

Accurate information on the name and status of the defendant is important both to ensure that the claim form can be correctly completed and so that any preliminary steps which may be necessary prior to the issue of proceedings can be taken.

The defendant's insurers will, ideally, have confirmed necessary details of the defendant's identity. If not it may be necessary to undertake further enquiries whilst confirming in writing to the insurers the claimant's understanding of the defendant's identity and reserving the claimant's position should proceedings be commenced accordingly and amendment then prove to be necessary.

Additionally, consideration needs to be given to the defendant's status, including steps necessary to ascertain that status, and any further steps which may then be necessary prior to issuing proceedings.

2.3.4.1   *Children or protected parties as defendant*

If the defendant is a child or protected party a litigation friend will need to be appointed on behalf of the defendant.

If no such person is nominated it may be necessary to approach the Official Solicitor to ask that he act in that capacity for the defendant.

In a case involving the Motor Insurers' Bureau, the Bureau should be invited to be nominate itself.

If no litigation friend is appointed the terms of CPR 21.3(2) permit the claimant to issue and serve a claim form and then apply for the appointment of a litigation friend, but prohibits any other step in the proceedings until a litigation friend has been appointed unless the court gives permission. However, CPR 21.3(4) permits the court to order a step taken before a child or protected party has a litigation friend shall take effect.

2.3.4.2   *Deceased defendant*

If the tortfeasor against whom the claim would have been brought has died the appropriate defendant, and description for the purposes of the claim form, will depend upon whether a Grant of Representation has been issued.

- If a Grant of Representation has been issued, the claim must be brought against the personal representatives of the deceased (CPR 19.8(2)(a)).
- If no Grant of Representation has been issued, the claim must be brought against 'the estate of' the deceased and the claimant must apply to the court for an Order appointing a person to represent the estate (CPR 19.8(2)(b)).
- If it is not known whether a Grant of Representation has been taken out, the claim should be brought against the personal representatives of the deceased, as it will then be treated as having been brought against the estate of the deceased if there is no grant (CPR 19.8(3) and paragraph 5.5 of Practice Direction 7A).

2.3.4.3   *Bankrupt defendant*

If the defendant is an individual, a bankruptcy search should be made to establish whether that defendant is a bankrupt.

If the defendant is bankrupt the trustee may be made a defendant.

Should the defendant be made bankrupt after court proceedings have been issued the court should have a discretion to allow those proceedings to continue under s 285(3) Insolvency Act 1986 *Re Saunders (a bankrupt).*[32]

If the defendant is subject to an individual voluntary arrangement or debt relief order that will not affect the right to bring a claim against the defendant.

If the defendant was bankrupt, but has since been discharged, s 281(5) Insolvency Act 1986 does not release the bankrupt from liability to pay damages for personal injury.

2.3.4.4   *Limited company as defendant*

If the defendant is, or thought to be, a limited company, a company search should be undertaken to confirm the correct name of the company, the current registered office and status of the company.

Usually, a search at the Companies House website will, usually, provide the necessary information about the company.

Further action may be necessary if the company has a receiver, is in administration, a winding-up order has been made, the company is in liquidation or that company has been dissolved.

2.3.4.4.1   *Receivership*

A receiver will usually be appointed by administration order of the court, by the holder of a floating charge over the company's assets or by the company itself or its directors. Most administrations are dealt with under Schedule B1 of the Insolvency Act 1986. Paragraph 43(6) of Schedule B1 provides for a moratorium on legal process against a company in administration, so no claim may be instituted or continued against that company without either the consent of the administrator or permission from the court.

Accordingly, if the company is in administration the consent of the administrator should be sought and, in default, court permission applied for in accordance with paragraph 47(7) of Sch B1 of the 1986 Act.

2.3.4.4.2   *Administration*

Administration is an insolvency procedure giving the company protection from creditors for a period of time.

---

[32]   [1997] 3 All ER 992.

Schedule B1 para 43(6) of the Insolvency Act 1986 prevents legal proceedings being instituted or continued against a company in administration, except with consent of the administrator or with the permission of the court.

Accordingly, the administrator should be requested to give written consent to the claim proceeding. If that is not given permission should be sought from the court in accordance with Sch B1 para 43(7) of the Insolvency Act 1986.

2.3.4.4.3 Company voluntary arrangement

The directors may apply to the court, with the assistance of an authorised insolvency practitioner, for a voluntary arrangement.

The insolvency practitioner will then realise assets and pay creditors, usually a proportion of the sum due.

Such an arrangement may restrict the right to bring legal proceedings, including a personal injury claim. Accordingly, the claimant may wish either to get agreement that the claim is not subject to the voluntary arrangement or, if necessary, apply to the court under s 6 Insolvency Act 1986 on the grounds the arrangement unfairly prejudices the interest of the prospective claimant on the basis that claimant should be able to recover sums due in full from the company's relevant liability insurer.

There is, however, a 28-day time limit running from the date the result of the creditors' meeting is reported to the court or, if no such notice is given, 28 days after the person concerned becomes aware the meeting has taken place.

2.3.4.4.4 Winding-up order

When a winding-up order has been made, or a provisional liquidator appointed, proceedings cannot be commenced, or proceeded with, without leave of the court under the terms of s 130 of the Insolvency Act 1986.

If proceedings have been commenced without such leave these will not be a nullity as the court has power to grant leave retrospectively: *Re Linkrealm Ltd*.[33]

2.3.4.4.5 Voluntary liquidation

Liquidation involves the company being wound up by a liquidator who collects assets and distributes these to creditors.

If the liquidation is voluntary that will not prevent proceedings being commenced or pursued, although s 112 of the Insolvency Act 1986 does allow the liquidator to apply for any such proceedings to be stayed.

---

[33] [1998] BCC 478.

2.3.4.4.6   Compulsory liquidation

Compulsory liquidation will usually follow a winding-up petition presented to the court by a creditor of the company.

Prior to a winding-up order the court may stay proceedings but otherwise no permission of the court is required to continue or commence proceedings. The court may stay proceedings but that will require an application: s 126(1) of the Insolvency Act 1986.

Once a winding-up order has been made or a provisional liquidator appointed any proceedings are automatically stayed and permission of the court is required to continue those proceedings or start new proceedings; s 130(2) of the Insolvency Act 1986.

Once a company has been wound up the name will be struck off the register of companies and when notice to this effect is published in the London Gazette the company will be dissolved.

2.3.4.4.7   Dissolved company

If a company has been dissolved it no longer exists and must be restored in order for legal proceedings to be brought against it.

A claimant proposing a personal injury claim against a dissolved company is likely to apply to the court to restore the company to the register under s 1029(1) of the Companies Act 2006.

Those entitled to make an application include any person with a potential legal claim against the company under s 1030(6) of the Companies Act 2006.

The terms of relevant provisions in the Companies Act 2006 were reviewed by the Court of Appeal in *Peaktone Ltd v Joddrell*[34] where Mumby LJ summed up the issue for determination in the following terms:

> 'This appeal raises as the central issue a short point on the meaning and effect of section 1032(1) of the Companies Act 2006. Specifically, it raises the question whether an order made pursuant to section 1029 of the 2006 Act has the effect of retrospectively validating an action purportedly commenced against a company during the period of its dissolution.'

In *Peaktone Ltd* the defendant company had been struck off the Register of Companies and dissolved under s 652 of the Companies Act 1985 on 31 March 2009.

On 24 August 2009 the claimant issued proceedings against the defendant claiming damages for personal injuries which it was alleged the claimant had suffered during his employment with the defendant.

The claim form and particulars of claim were served by a letter dated 23 December 2009 at what had been the defendant's registered office immediately prior to its dissolution.

---

[34]   [2012] EWCA Civ 1035.

On 10 June 2010 an order was made in the Companies Court under s 1029 of the Companies Act 2006 that the defendant be restored to the Register of Companies.

On 18 June 2010 the defendant issued an application in the personal injury proceedings issued by the claimant for an order striking the claim out. The claim was struck out at first instance and an appeal against that order dismissed.

The Court of Appeal, however, noted the different procedures formerly provided for by s 651 and s 653, respectively, the Companies Act 1985 had been replaced by a new single procedure under the terms of the Companies Act 2006. This new procedure adopted the language of the former s 653 of the Companies Act 1985 meaning that an order restoring the company had the effect of deeming that the company had continued in existence as if it had not been dissolved and hence retrospectively validated the issue of the claimant's claim.

Consequently, under the 2006 Act, proceedings issued against a company which has been dissolved can be validated by subsequent order restoring that company. If expiry of the limitation date is approaching it is, therefore, preferable to issue proceedings, even though the company has been dissolved, and then apply to restore.

If the limitation period has already expired when the court proceedings are to be commenced the claimant, adopting the procedure recommended with applications made under the former s 653, should normally involve the defendant, or on a more practical level the defendant's insurers, in the application to the Companies Court as that will be the substantive way of dealing with the limitation point: *Smith v White Knight Laundry Ltd.*[35]

2.3.4.5 *Partnership as defendant*

Where a claim is brought against two or more persons who were partners, and carried on that partnership business within the jurisdiction at the time the cause of action arose, para5A.3 of Practice Direction 7A provides that, unless inappropriate to do so, the claim must brought against the name under which that partnership carried on business at the time the cause of action accrued.

If proceedings are brought against partners in the name of the partnership para 2.6 of the Practice Direction to Part 16 requires the full name of the partnership to be given in the title to the proceedings followed by the words '(A Firm)'.

Where, however, partners are sued as individuals para 2.6 of the Practice Direction to Part 16 requires the full and abbreviated name of each partner and the title by which that person is known.

To clarify matters, where a partnership name is used, the claimant may wish to request a partnership membership statement, as provided for by paragraph 5B.1 of Practice Direction 7A. Paragraph 5B.3 requires the request to specify the date when the relevant cause of action accrued. Paragraph 5B.2 stipulates the request must be responded to within 14 days and paragraph 5B.1 provides that the response must include a written

---

[35]   [2001] EWCA Civ 660.

statement of the names and last known places of residence of all the persons who were partners in the partnership at the time when the cause of action accrued.

The advantage of using the partnership name of a firm, and obtaining details of all partners at the relevant time, is that use of the firm name ensures proceedings are instituted against all those who were partners at the relevant time as the claim, in substance, is an action against individual partners.

Use of a partnership name may also have advantages when it comes to service of the claim form as the table in CPR 6.9(2), where this is applicable for service, allows an individual being sued in a business name, which is different to that individual's name, of a partnership to be served at the usual or last known residence of that individual or the principal or last known place of business of that partnership (see **2.3.4.6**). Whilst individual partners, where the defendant is a partnership, will still need to be served it may suffice to send the claim form to the business address of the firm, if no other address for service has been given, of the firm: *Brooks v AH Brooks & Co (a firm)*.[36]

2.3.4.6   Business name of individual as defendant

Where the defendant is an individual but carrying on business within the jurisdiction, even if not personally within the jurisdiction, and that business is carried on in a name other than the individual's own name, para 5C of Practice Direction 7A provides the claim may be brought against the business name as if it were the name of a partnership.

Suing in an individual's business name, just like the use of a partnership name, may be helpful when serving the claim form as the table in CPR 6.9(2) confirms that, where that table can be utilised, an individual being sued in the name of a business may be served at the usual or last-known residence of the individual or the principal or last known place of business. This rule will not, however, apply to an individual who happens to be carrying on a business if that is in his own name: *Murrills v Berlanda*.[37]

Where proceedings are taken against an individual carrying on a business in a name other than his own para 2.6 of the Practice Direction to Part 16 requires the title of the proceedings to give the full and abbreviated name of the individual, together with the title by which he is known and the full trading name. The example given in the CPR is 'John Smith trading as "JS Autos"'.

2.3.4.7   Unincorporated association as defendant

If the defendant appears to be an unincorporated association further enquiries or action are likely to be required before proceedings are issued.

Generally, an association may be sued in its own name only if incorporated, for example under the Industrial and Provident Societies Act 1965 or the Friendly Societies Act 1974.

In other circumstances it will be necessary to take representative proceedings in accordance with CPR 19.6. For these purposes a member of an unincorporated

---

[36]   (Unreported), 4 November 2010 Birmingham District Registry.
[37]   [2014] EWCA Civ 6.

association may act as a representative of all the members (expressly excluding the claimant if also a member): *Artistic Upholstery Ltd v Art Forma (Furniture) Ltd.*[38]

The reason for expressly excluding the claimant, where the claimant is a member of the association, in any representative proceedings is that otherwise the claimant would be bringing proceedings against himself or herself.

The claimant is not prevented from bringing a personal injury claim simply because that claimant is a member of the unincorporated association being sued. In *Vowles v Evans*[39] Morland J reviewed and summarised the legal principles when he said, in paragraph 86 of the judgment, that:

> '(i) At common law an unincorporated members club or its officers or committee members owe no duty to individual members except as provided by the Rules of the organisation;
>
> (ii) An individual member of a members club may assume a duty of care to another or be found to owe such a duty according to ordinary principles of law and in those circumstances the fact of common membership of the association will not confer immunity from liability upon the member sued;
>
> (iii) Whether or not such a duty is held to exist would depend upon all the circumstances of the case ...'.'

A duty of care, owed by an individual member of an unincorporated association, may arise from a voluntary assumption of responsibility within that association: *Prole v Allen;*[40] *Owen v Northampton Borough Council.*[41] It is also arguable, though the law on this point is not clear, that the membership of an unincorporated association can be vicariously liable for the acts of individual members: *Melhuish v Clifford.*[42]

The claimant may, in these circumstances, wish to join individual members of the unincorporated association as defendants in addition to suing those members in their capacity as representatives of all members of the association.

2.3.4.8 Transferee of undertaking as defendant

If there has been a transfer under the Transfer of Undertakings (Protection of Employment) Regulations 1981 the tortious liabilities of the transferor are transferred to the transferee, who will therefore need to be the defendant: *Martin v Lancashire County Council.*[43]

2.3.4.9 Insurer as defendant

Whilst, in reality, the claim is likely to be dealt with by an insurer, this will generally not affect the identity of the defendant for the purposes of proceedings except in some specific circumstances.

---

[38] [1999] 4 All ER 277.
[39] [2002] EWHC 2612 (QB).
[40] [1950] 1All ER 476.
[41] [1992] 156 LGR23.
[42] (Unreported) 18 August 1998.
[43] [2000] 3 All ER 544.

- If the claim arises out of a road traffic accident and the defendant is insured, proceedings may be issued against the insurer under the terms of the European Communities (Rights Against Insurers) Regulations 2002. Under those Regulations the proceedings may be commenced against just the relevant insurer, which is particularly useful if the insured is out of the jurisdiction as that will allow the claim to be issued in the courts of England and Wales: *FBTO Schadeverzekeringen NV v Odenbreit*.[44] These Regulations are also useful, for joining the insurers into the proceedings from the outset, if there is uncertainty about the identity of the driver of any vehicle involved in the accident, which is insured by the insurer, or if an issue as to indemnity arises (see **2.3.5.1**).

- If the claim arises out of a road traffic accident and the defendant is an uninsured motorist, for the purposes of the Uninsured Drivers Agreement, the Motor Insurers' Bureau will usually be joined to the proceedings, in addition to the motorist, as a defendant (see **2.3.5.2**).

2.3.4.10   Costs of preliminary applications

If an application, preliminary to the issue of court proceedings, is required, for example to restore a dissolved company or in the Companies Court, that will not be part of the proceedings seeking damages for the claimant's personal injury.

Consequently, the claimant will want, as part of that application, to seek an order that the costs be costs in the proposed personal injury claim so that, ultimately, those costs can be recovered if that claim succeeds.

2.3.5   Indemnity

Unless the defendant is likely to be able to satisfy any judgment debt, it will be important to check that there is an insurer who will indemnify. If there is an insurer but an issue, or potential issues, about the provision of an indemnity the claimant will need to consider taking appropriate steps to enforce any indemnity to which the defendant might be entitled from the insurer.

A check of the claimant's own insurance cover may also be worthwhile, as the claimant may have insurance against an unsatisfied judgment (see **2.3.5.5.3**).

2.3.5.1   Road Traffic Act 1988

If the claim arises out of a road traffic accident the insurers should be given notice of proceedings in accordance with section 152 Road Traffic Act 1988.

If the claimant fails to give notice the insurer may not have to indemnify under s 151 of the Act (which otherwise may require the insurer to meet a judgment in respect of any liability that would have been covered had the vehicle been properly insured as required by law).

In *Wylie v* Wake[45] it was held that:

---

[44]   (C-463/06) [2008] 2 All ER (Comm) 733.
[45]   [2001] RTR 20.

- a letter of claim did not suffice as notice for the purposes of s 152, the court taking the view a prudent solicitor would be well advised to ensure that the Insurer received written notice within seven days after the commencement of proceedings so as to avoid any room for argument; and

- even if the insurer defended the claim, only raising the failure to give notice after judgment, there would be no estoppel that prevented reliance on the absence of notice under s 152 at any stage.

2.3.5.2   Motor Insurers' Bureau

If the claim arises out of a road traffic accident and it appears the defendant was an uninsured motorist it will be necessary to comply fully with the terms of the Uninsured Drivers Agreement to ensure any judgment will be met by the Motor Insurers Bureau.

That agreement requires the claimant to give notice to the Bureau at various stages, making it essential for the claimant to refer to that agreement.

Some of the requirements to give notice will, however, be obviated if the claimant joins the Bureau as a defendant in the proceedings. That will, accordingly, usually be the best course to take and is preferred by the Bureau. The remedy to be sought by the claimant against the Bureau, in these circumstances, is a declaration of the Bureau's contingent liability.

2.3.5.3   *Identifying insurers*

The claimant is entitled to request that the defendant provide details of motor insurers following a road traffic accident, under the terms of s 154 of the Road Traffic Act 1988. In any event a search can be made of the Motor Insurers' Database.

The Employers' Liability (Compulsory Insurance) (Amendment) Regulations 2008 require an employer to display at each place of business the certificate of Employers' Liability Insurance or give reasonable access to this information in electronic form to any relevant employee. Accordingly, these provisions can be relied upon to help identify an insurer in an employers' liability claim.

If the claimant needs to establish details of an employer's liability policy held by the defendant a search can be made of the Employers Liability Tracing Office (ELTO).

Helpful guidance on tracing employer's liability insurers is given in an APIL Briefing Note on Searching for EL Insurers which is available on the APIL website and gives links to past ABI search results and information supplied by APIL members.

With other claims, including public liability, it may be more difficult for the claimant to establish the availability, and scope, of any insurance cover. The defendant, or directors of a defendant company, can be requested to voluntarily disclose details of relevant insurance cover.

If those details are not given voluntarily there is conflicting case-law as to whether information about insurance policies can be requested, during the court proceedings, under Part 18 of the CPR. A request was allowed in *Harcourt v FEF Griffin*[46] but refused in *West London Pipeline & Storage Ltd v Total UK Ltd*.[47]

An alternative approach, relying on the general case management powers of the court conferred by CPR 3.1(2)(m) was accepted in *XYZ v Various*[48] on the basis that knowledge of the insurance position would permit the court to properly case manage the litigation which was in accordance with the overriding objective.

If, however, the insurers are jointed into the proceedings, for a declaration concerning the obligation to indemnify, the terms of the policy are potentially an issue in the claim which may support such a request.

2.3.5.4   Resolving indemnity issues

The provision of an indemnity under the terms of an insurance policy is, strictly, a contractual matter between the defendant and the defendant's insurers and quite distinct from the issue of the liability of the defendant to the claimant.

However, the existence of an indemnity by insurers is often a very material consideration as to whether the claimant presses ahead with proceedings.

Accordingly, it is usually appropriate to seek confirmation that an indemnity will be given by the insurers. If the insurers indicate an indemnity is not to be given, it will be necessary to:

- assess the means of the defendant, and whether the defendant is likely to be able to satisfy any likely judgment and award of costs; and

- seek information as to the reasons for the refusal, in order to assess whether or not the insurer can justify a refusal to indemnify.

Ultimately, the claimant can test the ability of the insurer to refuse an indemnity, if and when judgment is obtained against the defendant, by proceedings under the Third Parties (Rights Against Insurers) Act 1930. The disadvantage of this, however, is that the claimant, meanwhile, has to litigate without knowing whether the judgment will be satisfied and then, if it is not, having to take further proceedings with the risk that the insurer may then be able to show good reason for not indemnifying.

Alternatively, the claimant might consider, at the outset, bringing the insurer into the proceedings, as a further defendant, and to seek a declaration as to whether the insurers are required to indemnify the defendant. Given that, in such circumstances, insurers have successfully applied to be joined as second defendant, it would seem appropriate for a claimant to be able to apply for joinder so that this issue might be determined: *Churchill Insurance v Charlton*.[49]

---

46   [2007] EWHC 1500 (QB).
47   [2008] EWHC 1296 (Comm).
48   [2013] EWHC 3643 (QB).
49   [2001] EWCA Civ 112.

Similarly, joinder of the insurer for the purposes of a declaration was held to be an appropriate means of determining the contingent liability of that insurer to indemnify where there was an issue about the adequacy of notice under s 152 of the Road Traffic Act 1988: *Wake v Wylie*.[50]

2.3.5.5 Alternatives to indemnity

If there is no indemnity by insurers, at least of the party who would be the most obvious defendant in any proceedings, an important consideration, before commencing any proceedings, will be the ability of the proposed opponent to meet a judgment, the viability of pursuing a claim against another party who would be able to meet a judgment or even relying on any insurance cover the claimant may have.

2.3.5.5.1 Defendant's resources

If the proposed defendant is uninsured but has resources likely to satisfy a judgment it may be appropriate to proceed against that party.

With a limited company a company search may reveal relevant financial information. With other prospective defendants it may be necessary for an enquiry agent to be instructed.

If the party to be sued does have insurance cover but the extent of that cover is not known, and it seems unlikely from enquiries made the defendant would be able to satisfy a judgment, the court may be prepared to direct that details of available indemnity be provided: *XYZ v Various*.[51]

2.3.5.5.2 Proceeding against other parties

If the proposed defendant is uninsured and/or not able to satisfy a judgment the claimant will need to consider whether a claim is likely to succeed against a party who is insured or has the resources necessary to meet any judgment.

A particular problem, in practice, can be a limited company that is both uninsured and without any adequate resources, yet behind that company is an individual who would be able to meet the judgment. This problem has been approached in various different ways.

- Where the claimant has been injured at work there may be an individual with sufficient 'control' for there to have been liability under Workplace Health and Safety Regulations, for example *Tafa v Matsin Properties Ltd*.[52] Whilst those regulations no longer give a civil cause of action they remain part of the criminal law and that may be sufficient to generate a duty of care applying general principles (see *Caparo v Dickman*[53]).

- With an occupiers' liability claim such an individual may have sufficient control to be an 'occupier' of the premises where the accident occurred and hence owe a direct duty of care which can be actioned.

---

50 [2001] RTR 20.
51 [2013] EWHC 3643 (QB).
52 [2011] EWHC 1302 (QB).
53 [1990] 2 AC 605.

- If there is a single person in effective control of a company that person may owe personal duties as a director under company law, for example *Brumder v Motornet Service & Repairs Ltd.*[54]

- In appropriate circumstances a parent company may owe a duty of care to the employees of a subsidiary company, such duties being established in *Chandler v Cape Plc*[55] but not in *Thompson v Renwick Group Plc.*[56]

2.3.5.5.3   Claimant's own insurance cover

A number of insurers provide cover, often under household/public liability policies, in the event the insured obtains a judgment which is not satisfied within a given timescale. This cover may extend to any judgment or just to judgments for liabilities covered by the policy (what is termed a 'reverse indemnities' policy).

If the claimant has such cover that may reduce the risk, if the insurance position of the defendant is not known, of being left with an unsatisfied judgment.

Accordingly, especially if issues about recovery of damages seem likely, the claimant's policy should be checked to establish whether these insurers need to be given any advance notice or if there are other terms of the policy to be complied with as a preliminary to recovering an unpaid judgment by this route.

2.3.6   Arrangements for service

Consideration should be given, at the stage of issuing, about the arrangements to be made for service of proceedings. That is both to help ensure the claim form is correctly completed with the appropriate address for the defendant and to plan ahead by facilitating the practical step of serving the claim form.

Paragraph 2.14 of the PI Protocol recommends the defendant's insurer be invited to authorise solicitors to accept service of the claim form. Accordingly, the insurers may be asked for confirmation whether solicitors are to be given as the address for service. The claimant may wish to indicate, if not, the address at which it is proposed to effect service on the defendant, with a request that if this has changed the claimant be notified meanwhile.

2.3.7   ADR

ADR is defined as a 'collective description of methods of resolving disputes otherwise than through the normal trial process' in the glossary to the CPR.

Accordingly, ADR is not synonymous with mediation and a willingness to negotiate is likely to meet any obligation to engage in ADR: *Corenso (UK) Ltd v D Burden Group plc.*[57]

---

[54]   [2013] EWCA Civ 195.
[55]   [2012] EWCA Civ 525.
[56]   [2014] EWCA Civ 635.
[57]   [2003] EWHC 1805 (QB).

The particular form of ADR that is appropriate will depend upon the nature of the claim and the stance adopted by the defendant (see **11.4.9**). It is sensible to review the options for ADR before court proceedings are commenced given the potential costs consequences for a party failing to engage in ADR, as explained in *Halsey v Milton Keynes General NHS Trust*,[58] *Reed Executive plc v Reed Business Information Ltd*,[59] *Burchell v Bullard*;[60] *Rolf v De Guerin*;[61] and *PGF II SA v OMFS CO 1 Ltd*.[62]

2.3.8   Part 36

In addition to a general assessment of ADR any Part 36 offers made or received need to be reviewed at this stage.

2.3.8.1   Offer to settle liability

If liability has been admitted without allegations of contributory negligence then obviously no offer on liability is required or appropriate.

If liability has not yet been admitted, but realistically would not seem to be in issue, it may be preferable, rather than making a Part 36 offer on liability, to indicate that leaving liability in issue is considered unreasonable and that indemnity costs may be sought under Part 44. In other circumstances, an offer on liability may well be appropriate (see **11.4.2.2**).

2.3.8.2   Offer to settle the whole claim

Such an offer will usually be appropriate only when the overall value of the claim can be assessed. Even then, it may be more desirable to seek an opening offer from the defendant (see **11.4.2.1**).

2.3.8.3   Withdrawal or change of claimant's offer

If any extant Part 36 offer by the claimant no longer represents a reasonable settlement of the claim, changing or withdrawing that offer should be considered.

2.3.8.4   Acceptance of defendant's offer

If any extant offer by the defendant now seems an appropriate settlement of the claim, consideration should be given to acceptance either by negotiating terms as to costs or, if this might be too risky, simply giving notice of acceptance.

2.3.9   Risk assessment

A risk assessment should be undertaken as part of the review prior to issue of court proceedings. That is because once proceedings are underway significant further costs are

---

[58]   [2004] EWCA Civ 576.
[59]   [2004] EWCA Civ 159.
[60]   [2005] EWCA Civ 358.
[61]   [2011] EWCA Civ 78.
[62]   [2013] EWCA Civ 1288.

likely to be incurred and, furthermore, the claimant, or any insurer providing appropriate cover, will be exposed to the risk of meeting the defendant's costs should the claim be unsuccessful or have to be discontinued.

The assessment will inevitably involve a review of the merits on liability in the context of likely quantum allowing an overall cost/benefit analysis to be made.

2.3.10   Costs and proportionality

The risk assessment leads into a review of the costs position of the claimant. Depending on the method for funding the claim that will involve questions about the likely costs of both claimant and defendant.

- Is it appropriate to incur further costs on a conditional fee basis?
- Does any costs condition on a legal aid certificate need extending?
- Is there any limit on authority or indemnity, whether on a private basis with BTE cover or ATE cover, which needs to be increased having regard to the likely costs of the defendant in the proposed proceedings?

Issue of proceedings is a significant stage, so far as costs are concerned, because any costs incurred by the defendant, which are unlikely to be recoverable up to this point, are now subject to the discretion of the court and hence, at least potentially, payable by the claimant.

Hence in *Bethell Construction Ltd v Deloitte and Touche*,[63] for example, the claimant was ordered to pay the defendant's costs where service was held to be ineffective, proceedings having been issued which gave the court jurisdiction to make an order as to costs between the parties.

In *Citation plc v Ellis Whittam Ltd*[64] Tugendhat J held, after reviewing relevant authorities, that:

> 'In summary I take the law to be: (1) if no claim form is issued, then there is no litigation and so there are no costs of litigation, whatever costs may have been incurred in complying with a Pre-Action Protocol; but (2) if a claim form is issued, the costs incurred in complying with a Pre-Action Protocol may be recoverable as costs 'incidental to' any subsequent proceedings.'

In *Clydesdale Bank plc v Kinleigh Folkard & Hayward Ltd*[65] Master Bragge held that the power conferred by section 51 Senior Courts Act 1981, under which the court may order a party to pay another party's costs of and incidental to proceedings, is triggered by the issue, rather than service, of a claim form.

Without the issue of proceedings a defendant would have difficulty recovering costs incurred even if these related to dealing with a potential claim in accordance with any relevant protocol. Indeed, even if a claim form is issued the defendant may not be able to recover costs in relation to matters investigated under a relevant protocol but not pursued in the proceedings (see **1.12.5**).

---

[63]   [2011] EWCA Civ 1321.
[64]   [2012] EWHC 764 (QB).
[65]   Unreported, 5 February 2014, Ch D.

The original case plan may need to be reviewed and, as appropriate, amended given developments in the case and the need to keep proportionality very much in mind.

2.4   HOW AND WHERE TO ISSUE

Issuing proceedings seeking damages for personal injuries suffered, along with expenses and losses incurred as a result of those injuries, will require the preparation of some key documents.

Those proceedings will need to be commenced in the correct venue and it will, of course, be necessary for the courts of England and Wales to have jurisdiction.

2.4.1   The key documents

The key documents necessary to commence a Part 7 claim will be:

- claim form;
- notice of funding (if applicable); and
- cheque.

Particulars of claim, a medical report supporting the particulars and a schedule of expenses and losses will, ideally, be filed at court with the claim form but it is not essential to do so in order to commence proceedings.

2.4.2   Where to issue

Most personal injury claims will be commenced in the county court given the terms of paragraph 2.2 of the Practice Direction to Part 7. This provides that, in accordance with the High Court and County Courts' Jurisdiction Order 1991, a personal injury claim must not be started in the High Court unless the value of the claim is at least £50,000.

In the High Court a claim may be issued out of any District Registry or the Royal Courts of Justice, where there are designated Masters for dealing with particular types of claim including mesothelioma and clinical negligence. Paragraph 2.6 of the Practice Direction to Part 29 indicates claims with a personal injury element suitable for trial in the Royal Courts of Justice include:

- professional negligence claims;
- Fatal Accidents Act claims;
- fraud or undue influence claims;
- claims for malicious prosecution or false imprisonment; and
- claims against the police.

Issue of proceedings in the county court does not impose a limit on the sum which may be claimed and, in any event, the case may always be transferred to the High Court, under Part 30 of the CPR, if appropriate at a later stage.

A personal injury claim issued in the county court will be a 'designated money claim' for the purposes of CPR 2.3(1), namely 'a claim for either or both a specified amount of money or an unspecified amount of money'. A claim for damages, even with an upper limit, will be for an unspecified amount of money.

Paragraph 4A.1 Practice Direction 7A requires any designated money claim to be issued in the County Court Money Claims Centre ('CCMCC'). The claim will be issued in the name of the Northampton County Court, though the CCMCC is quite distinct from Northampton County Court itself, being based in Salford. To denote proceedings in the CCMCC, as opposed to Northampton County Court, the proceedings will be headed 'IN THE NORTHAMPTON (CCMCC) COUNTY COURT'.

The postal address for the CCMCC is:

CCMCC Salford Business Centre
PO Box 527
Salford
M5 0BY

The DX address for the CCMCC is:

DX 702634 SALFORD 5

If the limitation period is about to expire court papers may be delivered to any county court who will then forward those papers to the CCMCC (so the court papers should still be in the name of the CCMCC). In accordance with paragraph 5.1 Practice Direction 7A proceedings are 'brought' for the purposes of the Limitation Act 1980, and any other relevant statute, on the date the claim form is received in the Court office (even if issued on a later date).

The claimant's solicitors may request that the court papers, once issued by the CCMCC, be returned for service, though if that is requested the claim form should be marked 'SOLICITOR SERVICE' in bold.

The defendant will need to send the acknowledgement of service and defence to the CCMCC.

Similarly, the claimant will need to make any request for judgment to the CCMCC.

Both parties will need to file directions questionnaires at the CCMCC. However, once any claim for an unspecified amount of money is defended, and ready to be allocated, it will be transferred to the most appropriate court.

Paragraph 4A.2 of Practice Direction 7A requires the claimant to indicate, in the claim form where a claim is issued in the CCMCC, the 'preferred court'. The 'preferred court' is defined by CPR 2.3(1) as the county court the claimant has specified, in the claim form, as the court to which proceedings should be transferred if necessary.

Part 8 claims are not 'designated money claims' and, accordingly, the claimant can select the county court in which to issue any such claim.

Pre-action applications are not 'designated money claims' and, again, the claimant can select the county court in which to make any such application.

2.4.3 Jurisdiction

A claim form may only be issued in the courts of England and Wales if those courts have jurisdiction. If so then service of proceedings may be effected on a defendant outside that jurisdiction provided the rules set out in CPR 6.19 to 6.30 are, where appropriate, followed.

Where the cause of action occurred in England and Wales, the claimant sustained damage within England and Wales (even if also sustained elsewhere) or the defendant is domiciled or resident in England and Wales the proceedings can be commenced within the jurisdiction.

The courts of England and Wales will, additionally, assume jurisdiction if the defendant may be served in accordance with the rules contained in the Brussels Convention or the Lugano Convention and CPR 6.19 (or where these rules do not apply by serving the defendant within the jurisdiction or in accordance with CPR 6.20).

Furthermore, if the claim arises out of a road traffic accident occurring on or after 19 January 2003 it may be possible to rely on the European Communities (Rights Against Insurers) Regulations 2002 if the defendant lives in a country of the European Union: *FBTO Schadeverzekeringen NV v Odenbreit*.[66]

The defendant may apply to stay proceedings on the grounds that England and Wales is not the most appropriate forum (forum non conveniens). In *Spiliada Maritime Court v Cansulex Ltd*[67] Lord Goff explained:

> 'The basic principle is that a stay will only be granted on the ground of forum non conveniens where the court is satisfied that there is some other available forum having competent jurisdiction which is the appropriate forum for the trial of the action, i.e. in which the case may be tried more suitably for the interest of all the parties and the ends of justice.'

The courts of England and Wales may be the most appropriate forum if, for example, the claimant has suffered injury abroad but continues to suffer damage, for example treatment or care, after returning home: *Cooley v Ramsey*;[68] *Stylianou v Toyoshima*.[69]

The defendant may apply to stay proceedings on the grounds that England and Wales is not the most appropriate forum. In *Harty v Sabre International Security Ltd*[70] it was noted that there are three stages to be considered when approaching applications for permission to serve out of the jurisdiction, namely:

- the claimant sustained damage within England and Wales;
- the claim has a reasonable prospect of success;

---

[66]   (C-463/06) [2008] 2 All E.R. (Comm) 73.
[67]   [1987] AC 460.
[68]   [2008] EWHC 129 (QB).
[69]   [2013] EWHC 2188 (QB).
[70]   [2011] EWHC 852 (QB).

- the court is satisfied that England and Wales is the proper place in which to bring a claim (with the burden of proof being on the defendant to demonstrate England and Wales is not the appropriate or convenient forum and that another jurisdiction is more appropriate: *Spiliada Maritime Corp v Cansulex Ltd (The Spiliada)*[71]).

However, even if jurisdiction is assumed by the courts of England and Wales the applicable law may be that of a relevant foreign jurisdiction, for example under the terms of s 11 of the Private International Law (Miscellaneous Provisions) Act 1995 (which will also import the foreign limitation period by s 1 of the Foreign Limitation Periods Act 1984). Liability is traditionally dealt with by applying the law of the locus whilst procedural issues are governed by the law of the forum. Assessment of damages has been held to be a question of procedure (*Harding v Wealands*[72]) but where 'Rome II' applies this approach will be displaced and, in any event, some issue relating to damages will be regarded as matters of substantive law (as explained in *Wall v Mutuelle De Poitiers Assurances.*[73]

The parties may, of course, agree, with a view to saving costs such as expert evidence on foreign law, that the relevant law to be applied on liability will be the same as that applicable in England and Wales to the relevant issue.

2.5   THE CLAIM FORM

Court proceedings seeking damages for injuries suffered will generally be issued under Part 7 by form N1.

In certain circumstances, however, court proceedings should be commenced under Part 8 using form N208, for example where court approval of a settlement is necessary or in costs only proceedings.

To comply with relevant aspects of the CPR, and the Practice Direction to Part 7, particular attention should be paid to a number of points when completing the claim form.

2.5.1   Claimant's details

Accurate details, reflected in the title of the proceedings, must be given, to comply with para 2.6 of the Practice Direction to Part 16, including the full name of each party.

In a personal injury claim the claimant will usually be an individual which will mean giving the full unabbreviated name and title by which the claimant is known.

Details of any litigation friend or representative capacity in which the claim is being pursued should be given.

---

[71]   [1987] AC 460.
[72]   [2006] UKHL 32.
[73]   [2014] EWCA Civ 138.

The claim form must include an address at which the claimant resides or carries on business, to comply with para 2.2 of the Practice Direction to Part 16, even though the claimant's address for service is the business address of the claimant's solicitor.

If there is more than one claimant the title of the proceedings should be set out in accordance with paragraph 4.2 of the Practice Direction to Part 7.

2.5.2 Defendant's details

Accurate details of the defendant must be given, including the defendant's full name, to comply with para 2.6 of the Practice Direction to Part 16.

For these purposes the 'full name' means, where it is known, the following:

- in the case of an individual, his full unabbreviated name and title by which he is known;
- in the case of an individual carrying on business in a name other than his own name, the full unabbreviated name of the individual, together with the title by which he is known, and the full trading name (for example, John Smith 'trading as' or 'T/as' 'JS Autos');
- in the case of a partnership (other than a limited liability partnership (LLP)) –
  - where partners are being sued in the name of the partnership, the full name by which the partnership is known, together with the words '(A Firm)'; or
  - where partners are being sued as individuals, the full unabbreviated name of each partner and the title by which he is known;
- in the case of a company or limited liability partnership registered in England and Wales, the full registered name, including suffix (plc, limited, LLP, etc), if any;
- in the case of any other company or corporation, the full name by which it is known, including suffix where appropriate.

CPR 6.6(2) provides that the claimant must include in the claim form an address at which the defendant may be served, and that address must include a full postcode unless the court orders otherwise.

Additionally, to comply with the terms of para 2.3 of the Practice Direction to Part 16 the claimant should, if able to do so, include in the claim form an address at which the defendant resides or carries on business (even though the defendant's solicitors have agreed to accept service on the defendant's behalf).

Under the terms of para 2.5 of the Practice Direction to Part 16 if a claim form does not show a full address, including postcode, for the claimant and defendant, the claim form will be issued but then retained by the court and not served until the claimant has supplied any full address required, including postcode, or the court has dispensed with the requirement to do so. The court is required to notify the claimant in these circumstances.

Under the CPR what really matters, so far as identification of the defendant is concerned, is that the description of the defendant is sufficiently precise to identify those who are included in the proceedings and those who are not: *Owners of the Sardinia Sulcis v Owners of the Al Tawwab*;[74] *Insight Group Ltd v Kingston Smith*.[75]

2.5.3 Details of the claim

The general nature of the claim should be set out by brief synopsis, for example in a road traffic accident, that the claimant seeks:

> 'Damages for injury and loss caused to the claimant by the negligence of the defendant in the driving, managing and control of a motor vehicle on *1 January 2015* at *Hall Gate, Doncaster*.'

A claim for interest on damages can be confirmed by indicating on the claim form that the claimant seeks:

> 'Interest pursuant to s 69 of the County Courts Act 1984 on the amount found to be due to the claimant at such rate and for such period as the court shall consider just.'

If proceedings are commenced in the High Court interest will be claimed under s 35A of the Senior Courts Act 1981.

2.5.4 Valuation

It is necessary to make at least a broad valuation of the claim by the time that court proceedings are issued for two different purposes.

- First, for the purpose of calculating the court fee (but because these do not necessarily correspond to the statement of value required for CPR 16.3 it may be helpful to state the figure at the upper end of the band to which the court fee relates is the maximum, provisional, value of the claim).
- Secondly, to comply with the requirements of CPR 16.3, which may help facilitate allocation of the claim in due course, by indicating whether the value:
  - is less than £10,000;
  - exceeds £10,000 but is less than £25,000; or
  - exceeds £25,000.

For these purposes there should be disregarded:
- interest and costs;
- any deduction for contributory negligence;
- any counterclaim or set-off; and
- any Compensation Recovery Unit (CRU) deduction.

Additionally, CPR 16.3 requires, in a personal injury claim, the claimant to indicate whether the damages to be recovered for pain, suffering and loss of amenity will be more than £1,000.

---

[74] [1991] 1 Lloyd's Rep 201.
[75] [2012] EWHC 3644 (QB).

Para 2.2 of Practice Direction 7A confirms that in accordance with the High Court and County Courts Jurisdiction Order 1991 a claim for damages in respect of personal injuries must not be started in the High Court unless the value of the claim is £50,000 or more.

The valuation of the claim in the claim form will not restrict the damages which may be awarded, as CPR 16.3(7) confirms the statement of value in the claim form does not limit the power of the court to give judgment for the amount which it finds the claimant is entitled to.

2.5.5 Human rights

No specific human rights point will generally arise in a personal injury claim, so it will be appropriate to complete the 'no' box accordingly.

If, however, there is a specific human rights aspect to the case the claim form should be completed accordingly and appropriate details set out in the particulars of claim.

2.5.6 Particulars of claim

The claim form should confirm whether the particulars of claim are attached or will follow.

If possible the particulars of claim should accompany the claim form. However, particulars are not essential to get court proceedings issued and if necessary, for example for limitation reasons, those proceedings can be commenced on the basis the particulars of claim will follow.

2.5.7 Statement of truth

Ideally, as with all statements of truth, this should be signed by the claimant.

If necessary, for example when proceedings need to be issued urgently for limitation reasons and/or there is delay or difficulty in getting the form signed by the claimant, the legal representative may sign on behalf of the claimant as, generally, that representative will be in a position to confirm the accuracy of the basic information set out in the claim form.

2.5.8 Address for service

The claim form should contain the claimant's address for service of documents relating to the proceedings, to comply with CPR 6.23(1).

That address must be within the United Kingdom and, unless the court otherwise orders, include a full postcode.

Where solicitors are acting for the claimant this address will, therefore, invariably be the business address of the solicitors.

If content to be served by document exchange, fax, email or other means of electronic communication details should be given as part of the address for service.

If it is not proposed to accept service by document exchange, fax, email or other electronic means such information should be omitted from the claim form but care will be necessary when serving the proceedings, as inclusion of relevant details on writing paper used for any covering letter may amount to deemed agreement for service by such means under Practice Direction 6A (see **2.10.2.3**).

It is, of course, also helpful to give details of the file reference given to the matter by the claimant's solicitors and a contact telephone number, for use by the court and the defendant.

2.5.9   Sealing

CPR 2.6 requires the court to seal the claim form on issue.

The court will, ideally, provide the claimant with a sealed copy claim form for the claimant's file together with a sealed copy claim form for service on each defendant. That is because the claimant will usually, but not always, need to serve a sealed copy of the claim form to effect valid service (see **2.10.2.4**).

2.5.10   Date of issue

CPR 7.2 provides that proceedings are started when the court issues the claim form, which in turn is confirmed by the date entered on the form itself by the court.

However, paragraph 5 of the Practice Direction to Part 7 confirms that where a claim form was received by the court on a date earlier than the date it was issued the claim has been 'brought' for the purposes of the Limitation Act 1980, and any other relevant statute, on that earlier date. That date will generally be confirmed by the date stamp on the claim form or the letter that accompanied it. However, particularly where the limitation period is about to expire, it may be safest to deliver the papers by hand, if practicable, and record on the file exactly when the claim form was 'received' by the court in this way. Where the claim should be issued in the CCMCC some courts will forward the papers whilst others will then return those papers for onward transmission to the CCMCC.

It is important, particularly if the limitation period is about to expire, to check the court does return the papers following issue though even if duplicates have to be sent, and the original claim form is never returned by the court, the claim will have been 'brought' if the claimant can establish the original claim form did arrive at the court office within time: *Page v Hewetts Solicitors*.[76]

2.6   PARTICULARS OF CLAIM

The claimant's statement of case will be the particulars of claim.

---

[76]   [2012] EWCA Civ 879.

Whilst particulars of claim do not have to accompany the claim form when proceedings are issued or served these must, in accordance with CPR 7.4(1)(b) be served on the defendant within 14 days after service of the claim form and, given the terms of CPR 7.4(2) in any event by the latest date on which the claim form may be served (that is the calendar day four months after the date of issue).

It is, accordingly, preferable to prepare the particulars of claim, along with the claim form and other documentation, ready for the issue of proceedings whenever that can be done.

2.6.1 Procedural requirements

Part 16 and the accompanying Practice Direction deal with the requirements of statements of case. In particular, paragraph 4 of the Practice Direction to Part 16 deals with any particulars of claim which include a claim for personal injury.

There are also more general requirements found in the Practice Direction – Pre-action Conduct.

All of these procedural requirements need to be considered when preparing the particulars of claim.

2.6.1.1 Part 16

Part 16 sets out some requirements of general application to particulars of claim which:

- must give a concise statement of the nature of the claim, sufficient to establish a cause of action; and
- must also give confirmation of, and the basis for, any claim for interest.

2.6.1.2 Practice Direction to Part 16

There are additional requirements, where a claim for personal injuries is made, which are set out in the Practice Direction to Part 16.

- In all such claims the particulars of claim must:
  - give the claimant's date of birth;
  - give brief details of the claimant's personal injuries;
  - have attached or be served with a report from a medical practitioner about the personal injuries alleged;
  - have attached a schedule of past and future expenses and losses claimed; and
  - set out details of any claim for provisional damages.
- In a fatal claim the particulars of claim must also state:
  - that it is brought under the Fatal Accidents Act 1976;
  - the dependants on whose behalf the claim is made, with the date of birth of each dependant and details of the nature of the dependency;
  - any Law Reform (Miscellaneous Provisions) Act 1934 claim; and
  - any claim for damages for bereavement.
- The particulars of claim must give details of any conviction that the claimant intends to rely upon as evidence.

2.6.1.3   Practice Direction – Pre-action Conduct

Paragraph 9.7 of this Practice Direction provides that the claim form or the particulars of claim should state whether the claimant has complied with the terms of the Practice Direction or any relevant protocol.

Given the Practice Direction puts obligations on all parties the claimant may also wish to state whether or not the defendant has complied with its terms. If not this will, as paragraph 4 of the Practice Direction makes clear, be relevant to case management as well as the incidence of costs as specific sanctions are provided for under paragraph 4.6 of the Practice Direction, which include provision for the claimant's costs to be assessed on the indemnity basis and for enhanced interest. The defendant will need to deal in the defence with any issues raised by the particulars of claim.

The defence will need to deal with each and every matter pleaded in the particulars of claim which should clarify whether or not there is any issue about compliance with the Practice Direction and hence relevant protocols.

2.6.2   Factual background

Concise details of the facts will, in accordance with the requirements of Part 16, suffice.

There are, however, advantages in setting out some detail of the factual background. That will confirm, even if this has not been done already under the relevant protocol, the nature of the case that the defendant has to meet. Additionally, under the terms of the CPR, the defendant will be required to deal specifically in the defence with each and every matter raised in the particulars of claim.

All factual matters necessary to establish the cause of action must be set out. However, there may be further facts, not an essential part of the cause of action, which, if admitted in the defence, will mean that the issues are narrowed and may avoid the need for obtaining and/or calling evidence, resulting in a saving of costs and helping to keep costs, overall, proportionate.

2.6.3   Negligence/breach of duty

Allegations of negligence and breach of duty are at the heart of the particulars of claim as, if these matters are not made out, the claim will fail.

Ideally, allegations set out in the letter of claim (or CNF standing as the letter of claim), allowing for any refinement of the case in the light of information exchanged under the PI Protocol, will remain the basis of the claimant's case on negligence and/or breach of duty.

The allegations of negligence and/or breach of duty set out in the particulars of claim need to be comprehensive, for example in a claim involving injuries suffered at work all relevant breaches of the regulations concerning health and safety in the workplace (even in a purely common law claim).

In appropriate cases it may be possible to place an evidential burden of proof on the defendant; either by reliance on relevant statutory duties or, in any event, by asserting that the fact of the claimant's injuries is, of itself, evidence of the defendant's negligence (*res ipsa loquitur* if Latin terminology now discouraged by the courts is used).

2.6.4   Evidence

Whilst all material facts should be set out in the particulars of claim, matters of evidence should not generally be pleaded.

The distinction between facts and evidence is sometimes difficult to discern. Essentially, facts are matters which need to be proved in order to establish the claimant's claim, whilst evidence is the means of proving those facts. Of course, if relevant facts are admitted, there will be no need for these to be proved and the objective, both under the Protocol and on exchange of Statements of Case, should be to identify and narrow the factual dispute so that the costs of obtaining and adducing evidence can be kept under control.

A conviction recorded against the defendant is, strictly, a matter of evidence rather than fact but is specifically required by the Practice Direction to be included in the particulars of claim if relied on as evidence by the claimant.

2.6.5   Quantum

The particulars of claim will need to set out the nature of the claimant's case on quantum. Most personal injury claims seek an award of damages for pain, suffering and loss of amenity as well as for expenses and losses. Some cases will seek additional heads of claim.

2.6.5.1   Pain, suffering and loss of amenity

A claim for pain, suffering and loss of amenity will usually be made by giving particulars of the injuries alleged.

These are likely to be brief details made by reference to any medical report accompanying the particulars of claim or to be served at a later stage.

2.6.5.2   Aggravated and/or exemplary damages

Given the terms of Part 16, if such damages are sought, the particulars of claim must contain a statement to that effect and grounds. These must include, if there is a claim for aggravated and/or exemplary damages a statement to that effect and the grounds for such a claim.

Aggravated and/or exemplary damages can, in appropriate circumstances, be sought in a personal injury claim, for example *AT v Dulghieru*.[77]

---

77   [2009] EWHC 225 (QB).

2.6.5.3   *Other non-pecuniary claims*

If the claimant seeks other heads of non-pecuniary loss, given the general requirements of Part 16, these should be indicated in the particulars of claim. Such claims may include heads such as:

* disadvantage on the labour market;
* loss of congenial employment;
* loss of marriage prospects;
* loss of expectation of life;
* wrongful birth.

2.6.5.4   *Provisional damages*

If the claimant seeks provisional damages paragraph 4.4 of the Practice Direction to Part 16 requires the particulars of claim to give details, namely:

* that an award of provisional damages is sought under s 32A of the Supreme Court Act 1981 or s 51 of the County Courts Act 1984, as appropriate;
* that there is a chance that at some future time the claimant will develop some serious disease or suffer some serious deterioration in his physical or mental condition; and
* the disease or type of deterioration in respect of which an application may be made at a future date.

2.6.5.5   *Expenses and losses*

Expenses and losses, both past and future, can be set out in the particulars of claim and, if these are modest, it may be appropriate to do so.

Usually, however, the particulars are likely to refer to an accompanying schedule of expenses and losses setting out, provisionally or more substantively, further details of such claims.

2.6.5.6   *Periodical payments*

If a periodical payments order for future pecuniary loss is sought the claimant should confirm as much in the particulars of claim.

Where a periodical payments order is sought the particulars of claim should also indicate the basis on which it is contended future indexation should take place, if that is not to be RPI. A number of decisions have confirmed that indices such as ASHE, rather than RPI, will be appropriate for, for example, future care: *Thompstone v Tameside & Glossop Acute Services NHS Trust*;[78] *Corbett v South Yorkshire Strategic Health Authority*;[79] *Sarwar v Ali*;[80] *RH v United Bristol Healthcare NHS Trust*.[81]

---

[78]   [2006] EWHC 2904 (QB).
[79]   [2006] EWCA Civ 1797, (2007) 151 SJLB 27.
[80]   [2007] EWHC 1255 (QB).
[81]   [2007] EWHC 1441 (QB).

2.6.6   Statement of truth

Part 22 requires any statement of case, such as the particulars of claim, to contain an appropriate statement of truth.

The particulars of claim, unlike the brief details set out in the claim form, will contain details central to the dispute between the parties. These are matters of which only those parties, rather than their representatives, are likely to have first hand knowledge.

Accordingly, the particulars of claim will usually contain a statement of truth signed by the claimant. The claimant should be advised, or reminded, of the importance and consequences of a statement of truth when asked to approve the particulars of claim.

A statement of truth, on the basis of a particular factual scenario, does not prevent the claimant from asserting that liability attaches on the basis of a different factual scenario advanced by the defendant if, in the event, that is accepted by the court: *Binks v Securicor Omega Express Ltd.*[82]

If the statement of truth is not signed the particulars of claim will be effective, but not as evidence of the matters stated and will remain susceptible to a striking out order (para 4 of the Practice Direction to Part 22).

2.6.7   Format

All statements of case, including the particulars of claim, must be headed with the title of the proceedings in accordance with para 4.1 of the Practice Direction to Part 7.

Additionally, para 2.2 of the Practice Direction to Part 5 confirms that every court document, including statements of case, should be:
- on A4 paper of durable quality;
- fully legible and normally typed;
- bound securely;
- have pages numbered consecutively;
- be divided into numbered paragraphs; and
- have all numbers, including dates, expressed as figures (for example £1,000 and 1 January 2015).

2.7   MEDICAL REPORT

Some, but not necessarily all, of the medical evidence upon which the claimant relies will be likely to accompany the particulars of claim.

It is, however, important to note that the CPR does not require the claimant to disclose all medical evidence, let alone all expert evidence, at this stage.

---

[82]   [2003] EWCA Civ 993.

Consequently, the claimant needs to determine the extent to which medical evidence is disclosed with the particulars of claim at the outset or only at a later stage in accordance with case management directions for exchange.

2.7.1   Report disclosed with the particulars of claim

The reason why at least some medical evidence should be provided with the particulars of claim is paragraph 4.3 of the Practice Direction to Part 16. This requires, in a personal injury claim, the particulars of claim to be accompanied by a report from a medical practitioner about the personal injuries alleged in the claim.

This requirement is an exception to the general approach towards expert evidence, that it be exchanged at a later stage, often simultaneously, in accordance with case management directions.

This requirement reflects the policy, underlying the CPR, that statements of case should set out what the claim is really about.

2.7.1.1   Format of report

The medical report accompanying the particulars of claim will often be a report prepared for, and complying with, Part 35. However, all para 4.3 of the Practice Direction to Part 16 requires at this stage is a report 'about the personal injuries which (the claimant) alleges in his claim'. Such information may be contained, for example, in a letter of discharge, following hospital treatment, to the claimant's general practitoner.

In the broadly corresponding provision under the former County Court Rules a letter from a registered medical practitioner, not in the format of a formal report, was held to suffice for the purposes of the rule requiring a report with the particulars of claim: *Edwards v Peter Black Healthcare (Southern) Ltd.*[83]

In a 'soft tissue injury claim' para 4.3A of the Practice Direction to Part 16 requires the report to be a 'fixed cost medical report' including any additional report from an expert in the following disciplines:

- Consultant Orthopaedic Surgeon;
- Consultant in Accident and Emergency Medicine;
- General Practitioner;
- Physiotherapist.

2.7.1.2   Extent of disclsoure

Where the claimant, at this stage, discloses a report from any particular expert, that report must still fairly reflect the complete and current view of the expert (given the terms of para 2.5 of the Practice Direction to Part 35 of the CPR) which will mean disclosing any supplemental report reflecting a change of view from an earlier report.

---

[83]   [2000] ICR 120.

This obligation does not mean that draft reports of the expert have to be disclosed: *Jackson v Marley Davenport Ltd.*[84]

An expert whose report is disclosed at this stage may have already prepared, or be due to prepare, a supplemental report. In the former case, unless the supplemental report reflects a change of view, there is no obligation, at this stage, to go beyond the need to provide 'a report' with the particulars of claim. Any supplemental reports not disclosed at this stage will be the subject of exchange in accordance with case management directions later given by the court.

The obligation, at this stage, on the claimant is only to provide a report 'about the injuries' which, in practical terms, means condition and prognosis. Where the medical evidence, including the evidence of an expert whose report about the injuries is disclosed at this stage, also deals, probably in separate reports, with other issues, such as breach of duty and/or causation, that evidence does not have to be disclosed at this stage. Rather, any such reports will usually be exchanged simultaneously with corresponding evidence relied upon by the defendant, in accordance with the timetable set out under case management directions for such exchange. In *Duce v Worcestershire Acute Hospitals NHS Trust*[85] the Court of Appeal confirmed the report required for the purposes of the Practice Direction relates only to condition and prognosis, hence in a clinical negligence claim (or other claim where medical evidence might deal with liability as well as quantum), only evidence on quantum should be disclosed at this stage.

Furthermore, nothing in the CPR detracts from the law of privilege which allows a party, where an expert has produced a report reflecting a change of view, to withhold material which remains subject to legal professional privilege. However, any party exercising that right must forego reliance altogether on the evidence of the expert concerned, as the court should be made aware of the totality of the expert's opinion. This is quite different to withholding earlier draft reports as these, inevitably, will not reflect the totality of the expert's views by the time reports are finalised ready for disclosure.

2.7.1.3 Accuracy and amendment

Medical evidence disclosed to the defendant, whether under the Protocol or with the particulars of claim, effectively becomes part of the claimant's case and it is, therefore, essential that the reports disclosed are factually accurate and approved by the claimant.

This does not mean that 'expert shopping' should be adopted. However, reports can sometimes contain factual or typographical errors and such matters should always be verified with the expert.

If the claimant does not agree with the expert opinion there may be circumstances in which a further opinion, from an expert in the same field, will be justified and, of course, any report other than one obtained on the basis of joint instructions will be privileged unless and until it is disclosed.

---

[84] [2004] EWCA Civ 1225, [2004] TLR 457.
[85] [2014] EWCA Civ 249.

2.7.2   Subsequent exchange of expert evidence

In a straightforward personal injury claim the expert evidence may be limited to just one report from a single medical expert. In such cases, where the evidence may have already been disclosed in accordance with the appropriate protocol, it is likely that exchange of expert evidence will effectively be completed at the stage of serving the particulars of claim.

In other cases, however, the evidence disclosed with the particulars of claim will only be the first stage of exchanging expert evidence.

2.7.2.1   Further medical evidence

The claimant may not be able to disclose all medical evidence, upon which it will be intended to rely, at the stage of issuing proceedings. That may be because evidence from further medical experts is required, because experts whose reports are being disclosed at this stage will need to prepare supplemental reports at a later stage or because the claimant concludes, tactically but mindful of the obligation where an expert's view on any material matter has changed, not all medical evidence should be disclosed at this stage.

In these circumstances the claimant will need to ensure, at the stage of case management directions, that provision is made in the court timetable for exchange of further medical evidence.

2.7.2.2   Other expert evidence

There is no requirement to disclose non-medical expert evidence, or medical evidence which is not directly 'about the injuries', with the particulars of claim, though the claimant may elect to do so.

Once again, if there is such evidence, the claimant will need to ensure provision in the timetable, at the stage of case management directions, for exchange.

2.7.3   Permission

CPR 35.4(1) provides that a party may not call an expert, or put in evidence an expert's report, without the court's permission.

Consequently, even if expert evidence is disclosed at the early stage of the particulars of claim that does not abrogate the need, at the stage of case management directions, for the claimant to seek permission from the court to rely on such evidence, in addition to seeking, where necessary, directions giving a timetable for exchange and then exchanging by the due date.

2.7.4   Tactics

There are some tactical considerations which arise in relation to expert evidence, given the terms of the CPR about provision of a medical report with the particulars of claim.

- If the claimant does not yet have medical evidence, complying with Part 35, available or a decision has not yet been made as to whether Part 35-compliant reports should be relied upon, the claimant may elect to serve with the particulars just a report complying with the basic requirements of para 4.3 of the Practice Direction to Part 16, such as a discharge letter.

- If the claimant has disclosed medical evidence in accordance with the PI Protocol it is likely all such reports, with any further reports from the experts concerned if these reveal a change of view on any material matter, will accompany the particulars of claim.

- If the claimant has not been obliged, under the terms of the PI Protocol, to yet disclose any medical evidence and/or now has available further medical evidence which it is clear the claimant will seek permission to rely upon, it may be helpful for that to be disclosed with the particulars of claim. That is because those reports will then be filed at court and be available to the judge which may assist the claimant in seeking permission to rely upon the evidence at the stage of case management.

- Whether or not any medical evidence has been disclosed under the PI Protocol, the claimant may wish to retain, for simultaneous exchange, reports not yet disclosed including, unless these indicate a change of view, supplemental reports. That would be appropriate where the defendant may seek to rely on evidence from corresponding experts and the nature of the evidence is such that sequential exchange would put the claimant at a potential disadvantage (which will usually be so if the evidence deals with issues on liability or issues on quantum which are likely to be contentious such as care).

- Where, however, it seems unlikely the defendant will wish to rely on evidence from corresponding experts, or there is a prospect the claimant's expert evidence will be agreed, the claimant may decide to disclose reports from experts, even though not previously disclosed, with the particulars of claim (particularly reports on less contentious quantum issues). Whilst this does run the risk of there being sequential exchange of such evidence, that risk may be outweighed by the prospect of the evidence being agreed, if necessary after questions, and the advantage given at the stage of case management when seeking permission to rely on expert evidence if that has been filed and is available for the court to consider whether it is indeed 'reasonably required' for the purposes of Part 35.

2.8 SCHEDULE OF EXPENSES AND LOSSES

Paragraph 4.2 of the Practice Direction to Part 16 requires the claimant, in a personal injury claim, to attach a schedule to the particulars of claim, giving details of any past and future expenses and losses claimed.

2.8.1 Format

Despite the terms of para 4.2 there are many circumstances in which it will be difficult or impossible, and potentially misleading, to attempt a definitive schedule at the time Particulars of claimare drafted so the claimant will need to serve a provisional schedule.

A provisional schedule may be appropriate because the claimant's condition has not settled, so a firm prognosis cannot be given, or that further expert evidence, necessary to accurately value certain heads of claim, is awaited.

In such circumstances it would be wrong for the claimant to be prevented from issuing proceedings because a detailed, let alone final, schedule cannot yet be prepared particularly when the issue of liability needs resolving.

In any even when liability is an issue that needs to be determined it will be disproportionate to incur significant costs investigating quantum in detail when the case may never get that far, should liability not be established.

Liability may have been admitted but, before all the evidence necessary to calculate expenses and losses accurately has been obtained, the claimant needs to issue proceedings in order to secure an adequate interim payment.

When court proceedings are commenced in any of these circumstances it is unlikely the claimant can do more than serve with the particulars of claim a provisional schedule which may, if all necessary evidence is available, have a calculation of past losses but do no more than indicate likely heads of claim for future loss. If past loss requires evidence that is not yet available, for figures to be calculated accurately, the provisional schedule may have to do no more than outline heads of claim for both past and future losses. Where, however, it is possible to calculate the expenses and losses to be claimed this should be done, whether that be past losses or both past and future losses.

Whilst the defendant, in the event of a provisional schedule, may seek to rely on the terms of paragraph 4.2 of the Practice Direction it is important to note the obligations imposed on the defendant by paragraph 12.1 of the same Practice Direction; that the defence include, or be accompanied by, a counter schedule. It may be necessary to remind the defendant of that obligation and seek confirmation that if there is to be a detailed schedule with the particulars of claim an equally detailed counter schedule will be included in, or accompany, the defence (see **3.6.5.2**).

2.8.2   Content

The content, or at least format, of the schedule is likely to be broadly similar, whether provisional or not. A provisional schedule will however not include all or any of the calculations which will be found in the final version of the schedule.

2.8.2.1   *Preliminaries*

It is helpful for the schedule to set out some preliminaries such as the claimant's date of birth, age and injuries suffered as well as other key information which underpins calculations made in the schedule.

2.8.2.2   *Past expenses and losses*

These will include items such as:
- loss of earnings;
- value of care and attendance received;
- cost of DIY, decorating, gardening;
- purchases;
- travel expenses;

- prescription charges;
- damage to property;
- medical expenses; and
- sundry expenses.

2.8.2.3 Future expenses and losses

If expenses and losses are continuing, or expenses and losses not yet incurred are likely to arise in the future, the schedule should include an estimate of these.

Expenses and losses which accrue will normally be dealt with on a multiplier/ multiplicand basis. Multipliers can be calculated by using the Ogden Tables.

Other future expenses and losses will be claimed on a lump sum basis. These may include:

- loss of earning capacity (if appropriate using the methodology in the 6th Edition of the Ogden Tables);
- loss of pension;
- accommodation.

2.8.2.4 Interest

The schedule is an opportunity to quantify the claim for interest made in the claim form.

Accordingly, interest at appropriate rates, should be claimed on the items of past loss and included in the schedule, if these can be calculated at this stage.

2.8.2.5 Damages for pain, suffering and loss of amenity

The schedule, rather than just dealing with expenses and losses, may be a schedule of damages which also includes a suggested figure, or bracket, for pain, suffering and loss of amenity along with any other non-pecuniary heads of claim which are pursued.

If any figures are given for general damages an additional uplift of 10% should be added, or the right to do so reserved, in applicable cases applying the guidance given in *Simmons v Castle*[86] as clarified in *Simmons v Castle*.[87]

Including a figure to reflect damages for pain, suffering and loss of amenity, at least at the outset, will usually be appropriate only when there is an axiomatic conventional award, which can be stated with some certainty. Otherwise, certainly for the schedule prepared at the outset of court proceedings, it may be preferable to omit claims other than expenses and losses, not least because of the need for the schedule to contain a statement of truth when this part of the claim, save where there is a conventional award, is a matter of legal argument rather than fact.

---

[86] [2012] EWCA Civ 1039.
[87] [2012] EWCA Civ 1288.

2.8.2.6 Summary

Where the schedule contains calculations it may be useful to have a summary, showing the grand total, of the individual heads of claim.

2.8.2.7 Statement of Truth

The schedule must contain a statement of truth. It is, as with the particulars of claim, usually appropriate to have the statement of truth on the schedule signed by the claimant who, once again, should be reminded of the importance, and consequences, of such a statement.

Narrative in the schedule may, however, need to explain the basis upon which the statement of truth is signed and expressly include the right to make appropriate amendments in the light of further evidence or developments.

The schedule, if it does not have a signed statement of truth, will, once again, be effective but cannot be used as evidence of the matters referred to and is susceptible to strike out.

2.8.3 Tactics

It is important, unless this can properly be done, not to attempt a definitive schedule when proceedings are commenced.

That is because preparation of a full schedule without all the necessary evidence, which may not be available when court proceedings are commenced, carries risks for the claimant.

If the evidence later fails to justify all heads of claim, or the extent of the sums claimed under heads which are established, it is likely the defendant will allege the original schedule was exaggerated.

Conversely, if the claimant omits a head of claim, or uses a figure which later proves to be conservative under a head which is included, the defendant is likely to contend it is the original schedule, rather than the later version, which is the more accurate.

If the claimant does not amend the original schedule, even if the evidence which becomes available would support a finding that a particular head of damages should be greater than the sum claimed, the court is likely to restrict the claimant to the figure claimed in the schedule.

- In *Ilkiw v Samuels*[88] Diplock LJ held:

> 'As regards the question of damages, I would put it in this way. Special damage, in the sense of a monetary loss which the plaintiff has sustained up to the date of trial, must be pleaded and particularised. In this case it was so pleaded and particularised in the sum of £77 odd. Shortly before the trial, the special damage (as so particularised) was agreed at £77 by letter. In my view, it is plain law – so plain that there appears to be no

---

[88]   [1963] 1 WLR 991.

direct authority because everyone has accepted it as being the law for the last hundred years – that you can recover in an action only special damage which has been pleaded, and, of course, proved. In the present case, evidence was called at the trial the effect of which was that the plaintiff had sustained special damage of a very much larger sum, amounting, I think it would work out at, to something like £2,000 – at any rate, a very much larger sum than £77. This was not pleaded, and no application to amend the statement of claim to plead it could be made because of the agreement already arrived at, at the sum of £77 for special damage. The evidence about the loss of earnings *1007 in excess of £77 was admissible, not as proof of special damage (which had not been pleaded) but as a guide to what the future loss of earnings of the plaintiff might be.'

- The same approach was taken, more recently, in *Davison v Leitch*.[89]

Similarly, there is a risk that if a figure is given for pain, suffering and loss of amenity at the outset this will be taken as a starting point for negotiation, rather than a realistic valuation. Even if the claimant suggests a range of figures the defendant will invariably seize upon the lower figure in that range as the most that should be agreed for this head of claim.

Whilst it may be more difficult for the defendant to make a well-pitched Part 36 offer in the absence of a full schedule that, of itself, should not result in the claimant having to serve what is intended to be a definitive schedule, with a statement of truth, when that cannot be done with any accuracy at the stage of issuing court proceedings.

2.9 FUNDING

At the stage of issuing a claim form the claimant may need to give information to the court and to other parties about arrangements made for funding the claim.

2.9.1 Additional liabilities

CPR 48.1 (from April 2013) provides that the former provisions of Parts 43 to 48 relating to funding arrangements, and the attendant provisions of the Costs Practice Direction, will apply in relation to pre-commencement funding arrangements as they were in force immediately before 1 April 2013 (subject to any modifications made by Practice Direction).

A pre-commencement funding arrangement is defined in CPR 48.2 (from April 2013) as including, in practice, all pre-1 April 2013 CFAs.

The terms of para 19.2(2) of the Costs Practice Direction (as it was prior to 1 April 2013) mean that where the claimant wishes to recover additional liabilities relevant details must be given to the court, when the claim form is issued, and to other parties, when the claim form is served, even if those details were given when the letter of claim was sent or subsequently whilst dealing with the claim under the Protocol.

---

[89] [2013] EWHC 3092 (QB).

2.9.1.1   Notice

The information to be provided on issue of court proceedings, where there are recoverable additional liabilities, is, as in the letter of claim, that identified in the former paragraph 19.4 of the Costs Practice Direction (see **1.5.2.4.1**).

That information should be given by notice of funding in form N251.

It is essential to give, at this stage, notice of any funding arrangement under which the claimant will ultimately seek additional liabilities, even if that arrangement is no longer extant at the date court proceedings are issued. For example, notice should be given, on issue, of additional liabilities sought by solicitors who have formerly acted for the claimant or where an earlier CFA or ATE insurance policy has been superseded by a later agreement or policy.

A single notice of funding may, in accordance with paragraph 19.4(5), give notice about more than one funding arrangement.

2.9.1.2   Change

If, having given notice, the information on funding is no longer accurate, paragraph 19.3 of the Costs Practice Direction requires filing and service of a further notice of funding in form N251. That may be because a CFA, or ATE insurance policy, has been terminated or because a new CFA is entered into or a new policy issued or the indemnity level on an existing policy varied.

Where such notice is given it may need to be accompanied, in accordance with CPR 44.15(3), with a new estimate of costs.

Where a party has already given notice that a CFA has been entered into with a legal representative and, during its currency, another CFA is made with an additional legal representative, such as counsel, further notification, by service of notice of funding, need not be given.

If, having given notice on those who were then parties, a party is added to the proceedings then notice of funding must be served on any such party, if the claimant intends to seek recovery of any additional liability from that party.

2.9.1.3   Recoverable clinical negligence ATE premium

Part of the premium for an ATE policy, if that relates to clinical negligence proceedings, taken out from 1 April 2013 remains recoverable by the claimant. Consequently, it would still seem necessary for the claimant to give appropriate notice, at all relevant stages, of that funding arrangement.

2.9.1.4   Other claims

For the time being there remain recoverable additional liabilities for certain types of proceedings, including mesothelioma claims, even where the conditional fee agreement is made on or after 1 April 2013. Notice of funding, as required by the rules pre-1 April 2013, should still be served, at all appropriate stages, for such claims.

2.9.1.5 Sanctions

Failure to provide appropriate notice will prevent recovery of additional liabilities, at least until such time as notice has been served, unless relief from this sanction can be obtained.

If relief from sanctions is necessary the claimant should rely on CPR 3.8 and make application, accordingly, at the earliest opportunity.

If appropriate notice has been given at an early stage the court may be prepared to give relief from sanctions in the event of default in giving notice when proceedings are issued: *Montlake v Lambert Smith Hampton Group Ltd;*[90] *Supperstone v Hurst;*[91] *Haydon v Strudwick;*[92] *Scott v Duncan.*[93]

In *Haydon,* whilst allowing a percentage increase on base costs, the court did not allow recovery of an insurance premium when the notice given to the defendants had only referred to 'additional liabilities'.

In *Robinson-Tait v Cataldo*[94] the claimant's notice of funding failed to disclose full details of the ATE policy and the existence of earlier CFAs. Relief from sanctions was given as the mistake concerning the earlier CFAs was held to be small and of little significance. Whilst the mistake regarding the ATE policy was much greater it had not caused the defendant any prejudice and was, to a large extent, remedied within a few months of proceedings being commenced.

With the tougher approach under the revised CPR 3.9, applicable from April 2013, it may be harder, though not impossible, to secure relief from the sanction applicable for failure to serve notice of funding when required: *Forstater v Python (Monty) Pictures Ltd;*[95] *Harrison v Black Horse Ltd,*[96] *Long v Value Properties Ltd.*[97]

2.9.2 Legal aid

A copy of the up to date legal aid certificate should be filed at court along with a notice of issue giving details of the date of the certificate, reference number and scope.

Other details, including any limitation or costs condition, should not be given in the notice of issue.

A copy of the notice of issue, though not a copy of the certificate itself, should be served on all other parties.

---

[90] [2004] EWHC 1503 (Comm), [2004] 20 EG 167.
[91] [2008] EWHC 735 (Ch).
[92] [2010] EWHC 90164 (Costs).
[93] [2012] EWCA 1792 (QB).
[94] [2010] EWHC 9066 (Costs).
[95] [2013] EWHC 3759 (Ch).
[96] [2013] EWHC B28 (Costs).
[97] [2014] EWHC 2981 (Ch).

If a party is subsequently joined into the proceedings notice of issue should be served along with other court papers.

If the legal aid certificate is amended in the course of the proceedings a copy of the up to date certificate can usefully be filed at court. If the amendment concerns the parties or the description of the proceedings a notice of amendment should be filed at court and served on all other parties. It is not appropriate to give notice to other parties of amendment to a limitation or costs condition.

All other parties should be served with notice of amendment if and when the legal aid certificate is revoked or discharged.

The date of revocation or discharge may be significant if the claimant subsequently pursues the claim under a conditional fee agreement. That is because an extant legal aid certificate prevents, under the Civil Legal Aid Regulations, any other method of funding running in tandem, leaving a premature CFA, unless that is expressly stated to be a prospective agreement, invalid: *Allen v East Midlands Strategic Health Authority*.[98] Furthermore, once court proceedings have been issued the Civil Legal Aid Regulations effectively treat the certificate as being effective unless and until notice or discharge or revocation is both filed and served.

2.9.3   Other funding

If the case is privately funded, whether or not there is likely to be an indemnity from BTE insurers, there is no requirement to give details of the funding arrangements or insurance cover.

Where the claim is funded by a CFA, but there are no recoverable additional liabilities the claimant will seek as part of the costs, there is no requirement to give details of that funding arrangement.

If, however, the claimant intends to recover part of the premium, in a clinical negligence claim, under the terms of the Recovery of Costs Insurance Premiums in Clinical Negligence (No 2) Regulations 2013 it may still be prudent to give notice of funding.

2.10   SERVICE

Once issued the claim form should be served on the defendant, ideally with particulars of claim and supporting documentation, as soon as possible.

2.10.1   Warning!

Expedition and care are essential at this stage. In *Anderton v Clwyd County Council*,[99] Mummery LJ warned that:

> 'The consequences of failure to comply with the rules governing service of a claim form are extremely serious for a claimant and his legal advisors. The situation becomes fraught with

---

[98]   (SCCO 18 September 2008).
[99]   [2002] EWCA Civ 933, [2002] 1 WLR 3174.

procedural perils when a claimant or his solicitor leaves the service of a claim form, which has been issued just before the end of the relevant statutory limitation period, until the last day or two of the period of 4 months allowed for service ...'

In *Hashtroodi v Hancock*[100] Dyson LJ added that:

'It has often been said that a solicitor who leaves the issue of a claim form until almost the expiry of the limitation period, and then leaves service of the claim form until the expiry of the period for service is imminent, courts disaster'.

More recently in *Lincolnshire County Council v Mouchell Business Services Ltd*[101] Stuart-Smith J observed:

'Where a party issues protective proceedings hard up against the expiry of the limitation period, it is expected to pursue those proceedings promptly and effectively; and if it subsequently seeks and obtains orders extending time for the service of the claim form or particulars of claim without notice to the other party, it dices with procedural death.'

2.10.2 How to serve the claim form

The available methods for service of the claim form are set out fully in CPR 6.3. Practice Direction 6A imposes some further requirements, in relation to service generally, which may have a bearing on service of the claim form.

2.10.2.1 *What is service*

The CPR do not define exactly what is meant by 'service' other than by prescribing the methods by which this can be achieved and indicating in the glossary service means the 'step required to bring documents used in court proceedings to a person's attention ...'.

In *Olafsson v Gissurarson (No 2)*[102] Sir Anthony Clarke MR observed:

'... the whole purpose of service is to inform the defendant of the contents of the claim form and the nature of the claimant's case ....'

In *Asia Pacific (HK) Ltd v Hanjin Shipping Co Ltd*[103] the court held that what amounted, in any particular case, to service had to be judged objectively by looking at what was done and said between the parties.

- The claimant had sent the claim form to the defendant without stating, expressly, this was sent by way of service and without an accompanying response pack.
- Viewed objectively the claimant had served the claim form, given that this was sent to the defendant at the address for service, by a permitted method of service without any indication the claim form was provided for information only or that it was not to be regarded as having been served.

---

[100] [2004] EWCA Civ 652.
[101] [2014] EWHC 352 (TCC).
[102] [2008] EWCA Civ 152.
[103] [2005] EWHC 2443 (Comm).

- The court distinguished *Cranfield v Bridgegrove Ltd (Claussen v Yeates)*[104] where a claim form was sent specifically only 'in confirmation of the commencement of the proceedings' which, objectively, was not therefore viewed as being sent by way of service

The same approach was taken by the Court of Appeal in *Bethell Construction Ltd v Deloitte and Touche.*[105]

For the avoidance of doubt it is better to confirm, in the covering letter, the claim form is being sent by way of service where that is intended.

2.10.2.2   Methods of service

Under CPR 6.3 methods of service include:

- personal service (in accordance with CPR 6.5);
- first class post;
- document exchange;
- other service which provides for delivery on the next business day (in accordance with Practice Direction 6A);
- leaving the claim form at a place specified in CPR 6.7, 6.8, 6.9 or 6.10;
- fax or other electronic communication (Practice Direction 6A); and
- any method authorised by the court under CPR 6.15 (which will require an application and supporting evidence.

Additionally, the claim form may be served on a limited company by any of the methods of service permitted under the Companies Act 2006 and on a limited liability partnership by any of the methods of service permitted by that Act (as applied with modification by regulations under the Limited Liability Partnerships Act 2004).

2.10.2.3   Further requirements

Practice Direction 6A imposes some further requirements in relation to the service of documents, including service of the claim form.

- Paragraph 2.1 provides that service by document exchange (DX) may only take place where:
  - the address at which the party to be served includes a numbered box at a DX; or
  - the writing paper of the party to be served (or of the solicitor acting for that party) sets out a DX box number; and
  - the party or the solicitor acting for that party has not indicated in writing that they are unwilling to accept service by DX.
- Paragraph 4.1 deals with service by fax or other electronic means and provides:
  - the party to be served, or solicitor acting for that party, must have previously indicated willingness to accept service by fax or other electronic means and given the fax number, Email address or other electronic identification to which the document to be served must be sent; and

---

[104] [2003] EWCA Civ 656.
[105] [2011] EWCA Civ 1321.

– sufficient indication of willingness, for these purposes, will be a fax number on the writing paper of the solicitor acting for the party to be served, or an Email address on the writing paper of the solicitor acting for that party (but only where it is stated that the Email address may be used for service).

However, paragraph 4.2 requires the party intending to serve by these means to first ask the party who is to be served whether there are any limitations on the agreement to accept service by electronic means, for example the format in which documents are to be sent and the maximum size of attachments.

• Paragraph 5 deals with service on members of the regular forces and also the United States airforce.

• Paragraph 6 deals with personal service on a company or other corporation.

2.10.2.4 What needs to be served?

The claimant will need, certainly when serving personally or by post/DX/delivery within the jurisdiction, to serve an original sealed copy of the claim form on each defendant served: *Hills Contractors and Construction Ltd v Struth*;[106] *Davidson v Ageis Defence Services (BBI) Ltd.*[107]

When serving out of the jurisdiction a copy claim form may suffice: *Weston v Bates.*[108]

If a defendant can be, and is, served by fax or other electronic method then, clearly, an original sealed copy of the claim form cannot be served by those means and paragraph 4.3 of Practice Direction 6A expressly provides that, in these circumstances, the party serving the document need not in addition send or deliver a hard copy.

This requirement, as Longmore LJ noted in *Davidson*, is very technical and, accordingly, non-compliance might be remedied by an application under CPR 6.15(2) (see **2.10.5.2**).

Where the claim form is to be served within the jurisdiction CPR 7.5(1) provides that the claimant must complete the 'step required' for the particular method of service chosen before 12.00 midnight on the calendar date four months after the date of issue of the claim form.

Where the claim form is to be served out of the jurisdiction CPR 7.5(2) requires that claim form to be served in accordance with section iv of Part 6 within six months of the date of issue.

2.10.3.1 The 'appropriate step' to serve

The appropriate step, for service within the jurisdiction, will depend upon the method chosen for service. The following table, found in CPR 7.5, identifies the step relevant to each method.

---

[106] [2013] EWHC 1693 (TCC).
[107] [2013] EWCA Civ 1586.
[108] [2012] EWHC 590 (QB).

Method of service	Step required
• First class post, document exchange or other service which provides for delivery on the next business day	Posting, leaving with, delivering to or collection by the relevant service provider
• Delivery of the document to or leaving it at the relevant place	Delivering to or leaving the document at the relevant place
• Personal service under rule 6.5	Completing the relevant step required by rule 6.5(3)
• Fax	Completing the transmission of the fax
• Other electronic method	Sending the Email or other electronic transmission

2.10.3.2 *Extending time for service*

CPR 7.6 gives the power for the court to extend time in which to take the step required for the purposes of CPR 7.5.

2.10.3.2.1   *Within four months*

The general rule, found in CPR 7.6(2), is that an application to extend time must be made within the four month period specified by CPR 7.5.

When considering the earlier version of this rule the courts consistently held that the claimant had to show a good reason for there to be an extension of time, even when the application was made within the 4 month period allowed for service: *Hashtroodi v Hancock*;[109] *Collier v Williams (Leeson v Marsden & United Bristol Health NHS Trust, Glass v Surrendran)*.[110]

The current version of the rule was considered, and the earlier cases followed, in *Imperial Cancer Research Fund v Ove Arup*.[111] After reviewing the earlier cases the court set out the general principles that emerge from these.

- The rule does not impose any threshold condition on the right to apply for an extension of time but the discretion should be exercised in accordance with the overriding objective.
- That will mean it is always relevant to determine and evaluate the reason why the claimant did not serve the claim form within the specified period.
- The pre-conditions in CPR 7.6(3) do not apply but they are relevant to an application under CPR 7.6(2), although the fact the pre-conditions are unsatisfied will not necessarily be determinative of the outcome.
- Matters the court may take into account include:
  - whether the claim has become statute barred since the claim form was issued and, if so, that will be a matter of considerable importance in deciding whether to grant an extension of time;

---

[109]   [2004] EWCA Civ 652.
[110]   [2006] EWCA Civ 20.
[111]   [2009] EWHC 1453 (TCC).

–   whether before the expiry of the four-month period the nature of the claim has been brought to the attention of the defendant; and

–   whether the claimant could not determine if the claim had real prospects of success and not responsibly proceed against the defendant without an expert report which was delayed awaiting a response to proper requests for information from the defendant.

On the facts of the case the claimant was held to have behaved sensibly and reasonably in not wishing to serve the claim form until it was known whether there was a viable claim against the party to be served. Knowing whether there was a viable claim depended upon expert opinion which, in turn, depended upon completion of investigations and reviewing of documentation.

Where, however, enquiries were left until 21 days before the period of service expired an extension of time was not allowed: *F G Hawkes (Western) Ltd v Beli Shipping Co Ltd*.[112]

Similarly, on the basis that having issued a claim form the claimant should have proceeded without undue delay to ascertain the whereabouts of all defendants and then serve them with the claim form, where the limitation period expired a few days after issue of the claim form, an extension of time was not allowed: *Duckworth v Coates*.[113]

No extension of time was allowed even when a member of the case administration unit of the court informed the claimant the judge would grant a short extension: *City & General (Holborn) Ltd v Structure Tone Ltd*.[114]

Lack of funding to pursue the claim is unlikely to be a good reason for there to be an extension of time and, indeed, where an extension of time would deprive the defendant of a limitation defence exceptional circumstances would normally be required for an order to be appropriate: *Cecil v Bayat*.[115]

More recently the case-law dealing with the approach the court should take to an application under CPR 7.6(2) was considered by Tugendhat J in *Hallam Estates Ltd v Baker*[116] in the following terms.

- The power under CPR 7.6(2) must be exercised in accordance with the overriding objective: *Hashtroodi*.

- As the overriding objective is to enable the court to deal with cases 'justly' it is necessary to know the reason why the claimant cannot serve the claim form within the specified period. A claimant who experiences difficulty should normally be entitled to the court's help but a claimant who merely leaves service until too late is not entitled to as much consideration.

- If there is very good reason for failure to serve the claim form an extension of time will usually be granted but the weaker the reason the more likely the court will be to refuse an extension: *Hashtroodi*.

- A defendant's solicitor is under no obligation to reveal the defendant's address for service: Collier.

---

[112]   [2009] EWHC 1740 (Comm).
[113]   [2009] EWHC 1936 (Ch).
[114]   [2009] EWHC 2139 (TCC).
[115]   [2010] EWCA Civ 135.
[116]   [2012] EWHC 1046 (QB).

- Whether the limitation period has expired is of considerable importance, because if an extension is sought beyond the expiry of the limitation period the claimant is effectively asking the court to disturb the defendant who is by that time entitled to assume the defendant's rights can no longer be disputed: *Hashtroodi.*

- The stronger the claim the more important it is the defendant's limitation defence should not be circumvented by an extension of time for serving the claim form save in exceptional circumstances: *Cecil.*

- It is for the claimant to show the 'good reason' directly impacts on the limitation aspect of the problem, for instance the claimant can show delay in service by reasons for which the claimant does not bear responsibility or that the claimant could not have known about the claim until close to the end of the limitation period. Without that the claimant is unlikely to show good, or sufficiently good, reason on the limitation aspect: *Cecil.*

The need for a good reason for there to be an extension of time, particularly following amendments to the CPR in April 2013 and where parties were expected to comply with a pre-action protocol, was emphasised in *Lincolnshire County Council v Mouchell Business Services Ltd.*[117]

2.10.3.2.2   After four months

CPR 7.6(3) deals with the situation where the claimant applies for an order extending time after the end of the four month period specified by CPR 7.5.

This rule stipulates the court may only make an order if:

- the court has failed to serve the claim form; or
- the claimant has taken all reasonable steps to comply with CPR 7.5 but has been unable to do so; and
- in either case, the claimant has acted promptly in making the application.

It seems likely the court will continue to regard this as a self-contained code, so that the claimant will have to show the precise circumstances envisaged by the rule apply: *Vinos v Marks & Spencer plc.*[118]

Furthermore, it is likely the court will continue to prevent other rules, save perhaps for CPR 3.10, to be used as a way of allowing what is forbidden by CPR 7.6: *Godwin v Swindon Borough Council*[119] and *Anderton v Clwyd County Council.*[120]

In *Hakim v Gloucester NHS Trust*[121] Master Cook held that CPR 7.6(3) required, within the four-month period, an attempt to serve the claim form.

---

[117] [2014] EWHC 352 (TCC).
[118] [2001] All ER 784.
[119] [2001] EWCA Civ 1478.
[120] [2002] EWCA Civ 933.
[121] (Unreported) 2 May 2014 (QB).

2.10.3.3   Agreeing an extension of time

The parties may agree an extension of time for service of the claim form, in accordance with CPR 2.11, but for this to be effective there must be a 'written agreement of the parties' as required by the rule: *Thomas v Home Office*[122] (see **2.2.3**).

2.10.3.4   Setting aside an extension of time

Where the court makes an order extending time for service of the claim form without a hearing involving the defendant that order is, under CPR 3.3(5), susceptible to an application by the defendant for an order that it be set aside.

This is not a review but a re-hearing and, consequently, the issue is not whether the judge granting the extension made an order which could not be regarded as plainly wrong but whether, having regard to all the circumstances, the order should have been made.

The risk, therefore, is that the claimant obtains, and relies upon, an order extending time only to find that this is subsequently set aside, leaving the claimant with a claim form that cannot validly be served and, perhaps, a claim where the limitation period has now elapsed.

2.10.3.5   Deemed service of claim form

By CPR 6.14 a claim form will be deemed served on the second business day after completion of the relevant step under CPR 7.5(1).

Whilst it is no longer necessary to ensure the claim form is deemed served within four months of issue, the date of deemed service remains of relevance for calculating when the acknowledgement of service and/or defence will be due.

CPR 6.2 defines 'business day'. It means any day except Saturday, Sunday, a Bank Holiday, Good Friday or Christmas Day. For these purposes 'Bank Holiday' means a Bank Holiday, under the Banking and Financial Dealings Act 1971, in the part of the United Kingdom where service is to take place.

The relationship between CPR 6.14 and CPR 7.5(1) was explored in *T&L Sugars Ltd v Tate & Lyle Industries Ltd*.[123] Flaux J held:

> 'In my judgment these two rules, CPR 7.5 and 6.14, taken together draw a clear distinction between the date when service is actually effected, which is when the relevant step under 7.5 has been completed and the date two business days later when service is deemed to take place under CPR 6.14. If one asks oneself why that distinction is there, it is not ... because service does not actually occur until the deemed day, but because, whereas CPR 7.5 is looking at when actual service takes place, so that a claimant who takes the requisite step, depending upon which method of service he employs, can be sure that he has served within the four months of validity of the claim form (thereby avoiding, if relevant, any limitation issues),

---

122   [2006] EWCA Civ 1355.
123   [2014] EWHC 1066 (Comm).

CPR 6.14 is looking at when service will be deemed to have taken place for the purpose of other steps in the proceedings thereafter, beginning with the filing of an acknowledgment of service.'

2.10.4   Where to serve the claim form

The address at which the claim forms should be served will become a critical issue if the time limit for serving that claim form is about to expire so avoiding this problem a good reason, of itself, for serving the claim form promptly.

CPR 6.6(1) provides that the claim form must be served within the jurisdiction except where a solicitor is instructed to accept service at a business address in Scotland, Northern Ireland or in any EEA state, there is a contractually agreed method for service (so CPR 6.11 applies) or the claim form may be served out of the jurisdiction in accordance with section IV of Part 6.

CPR 6.6(2) requires the claimant to include in the claim form an address at which the defendant may be served and, unless the court otherwise orders, that address must include a full post code.

In some circumstances there will be more than one address at which the defendant may be served but in other circumstances only one such address (which will, therefore, be the address that must be given in the claim form to comply with CPR 6.6(2)).

2.10.4.1   *Address for service given by the defendant*

CPR 6.7 provides the claim form must be served at the business address of that solicitor where either:

- the defendant has given in writing the business address within the jurisdiction of a solicitor as an address at which the defendant may be served with the claim form; or

- a solicitor acting for the defendant has notified the claimant in writing that the solicitor is instructed by the defendant to accept service of the claim form on behalf of the defendant at a business address within the jurisdiction.

The business address of a solicitor does not, however, become the address for service of the claim form simply because a solicitor is acting for the defendant. There must be written confirmation, either by the defendant or the solicitor, the address of that solicitor is the address for service of the claim form: *Brown v Innovatorone plc.*[124]

Under the earlier version of Part 6 the court held an indication by a defendant's solicitor of authorisation to accept service of proceedings by a particular claimant could not ordinarily indicate authority to accept service of a claim, even though arising from the same dispute, by a different claimant: *Firstdale Ltd v Quinton.*[125]

Consequently, even if a solicitor has been acting for the defendant it will be necessary to serve the claim form direct on the defendant unless the solicitor's address is specifically given as the address for service of the claim form. Service direct on the defendant in such

---

[124]   [2009] EWHC 1376 (Comm).
[125]   [2004] EWHC 1926 (Comm).

circumstances was held to be appropriate, even though service for other reasons was ineffective, in *Collier v Williams (Marshall & Rankin v Maggs)*.[126]

The defendant may give an address for service within the jurisdiction, other than the business address of a solicitor. If so CPR 6.8 confirms the defendant may be served at such an address. This implies the claimant may have a choice of addresses at which the defendant may be served. However, caution is necessary where the rules use the word 'may' as, depending on the context, this may confer a choice or indicate a conditional requirement which is, nevertheless, mandatory if the condition is fulfilled (for example the interpretation of the former CPR 45.11(1) in *Kilby v Gawith*[127]).

Even if an address for service is given in accordance with CPR 6.7 a limited company may be served at its registered office as CPR 6.3(2) allows service by any method permitted under the rule or any of the methods permitted under the Companies Act 2006 (and s 1139 confirms a document may be served on a company registered under the Act by leaving it at, or sending it by post to, the company's registered office whilst an overseas company whose particulars are registered under the Act may be served by leaving it at, or sending it by post to, the registered address of any person resident in the United Kingdom who is authorised to accept service of documents on the company's behalf but if there is no such person or any such person refuses service or service cannot for any other reason be effected by leaving it at or sending it by post to any place of business of that company in the United Kingdom). This exception to the general scope of Part 6 was recognised by the Court of Appeal in *Cranfield v Bridgegrove Ltd*.[128]

2.10.4.2 Address for service not given by the defendant

Where neither CPR 6.7 nor CPR 6.8 apply, and personal service is not required or chosen, the starting point is that the claim form must be served on the defendant at the place indicated in the following table which is set out in CPR 6.9(2).

Nature of defendant to be served	Place of service
Individual	Usual or last known residence
Individual being sued in the name of a business	Usual or last known residence of the individual; or principal or last known place of business.
Individual being sued in the business name of a partnership	Usual or last known residence of the individual; or principal or last known place of business of the partnership.
Limited liability partnership	Principal office of the partnership; or any place of business of the partnership within the jurisdiction which has a real connection with the claim.

---

126 [2006] EWCA Civ 20.
127 [2008] EWCA Civ 812.
128 [2003] EWCA Civ 656.

Corporation (other than a company) incorporated in England and Wales	Principal office of the corporation; or any place within the jurisdiction where the corporation carries on its activities and which has a real connection with the claim.
Company registered in England and Wales	Principal office of the company; or any place of business of the company within the jurisdiction which has a real connection with the claim.
Any other company or corporation	Any place within the jurisdiction where the corporation carries on its activities; or any place of business of the company within the jurisdiction.

This provision means that what will amount to the 'usual last known residence' may be significant. That issue was considered in *Varsani v Relfo Ltd (in liquidation)*[129] where the court held it will suffice for an address to be the 'usual or last known residence' if there is a good arguable case the address is such, which is a less onerous test than proof on a balance of probabilities.

Moreover, there may be more than one 'usual' residence given the distinction in CPR 6.9 between 'usual residence' and 'principal' place of business or office. The court recognised, however, the rule contains a number of uncertainties and recommended the CPR Committee re-visit its terms.

Where the defendant occupied only a room at the address to which the claim form was sent it was held, in the absence of evidence the claim form had been suppressed when it arrived at that address or returned undelivered, that service was validly effected: *Akram v Adam*.[130]

If the defendant has never actually resided at the address to which the claim form is sent service is not likely to be effected: *Marshall v Maggs*.[131] In such circumstances the claimant may then need to rely on CPR 6.15(2) (see **2.10.4.3.2**) as if the claimant had no reasons to think the defendant did not genuinely reside at the address where service is attempted that would not appear to prevent an order being made under the rule: *Abela v Baadarani*.[132]

The table in CPR 6.9(2) is only a starting point as CPR 6.9(3) provides that where a claimant has 'reason to believe' the address of the defendant referred to at paragraphs 1, 2 or 3 in the table is an address at which the defendant no longer resides or carries on business reasonable steps must be taken to ascertain the defendant's current residence or place of business, 'the current address'.

In *Murrills v Berlanda*[133] Sir Stanley Burnton dealt with what would, on the facts of the case, have been reasonable steps to ascertain the defendant's address when he observed:

---

[129] [2010] EWCA Civ 560.
[130] [2004] EWCA Civ 601.
[131] [2006] EWCA Civ 20.
[132] [2013] UKSC 44.
[133] [2014] EWCA Civ 6.

'It would not have been difficult to ascertain his residential address, either by enquiry at the professional address or, presumably, in the telephone directory, but in fact no attempt was made to discover it.'

CPR 6.9(4) requires the claimant to serve the claim form at the defendant's current address, if that address is ascertained. If that address cannot be ascertained this rule requires the claimant to consider whether there is an alternative place where, or an alternative method of service by which, service may be effected and, if so, to make an application to the court for an order under CPR 6.15.

If, however, the claimant cannot ascertain an alternative place or an alternative method by which service may be effected, CPR 6.9(6) does permit the claimant to serve the defendant at the address in the table set out in CPR 6.9(2). Where the claimant can rely on that table service will be effective even if the defendant does not receive the papers being served. In *Cranfield v Bridgegrove Ltd (Smith v Hughes)*[134] Dyson LJ held:

'The rule does not say that it is not good service if the defendant does not in fact receive the document.'

Subject to having reason to believe some of the partners may not receive a claim form served at the principal or last known place of business, the table giving place of service found in CPR 6.9 (2) is useful when suing either an individual in a business name or in a partnership name as it allows service at the business, as well as residential, address of that individual.

However, in *Murrills v Berlanda*[135] is also a reminder that where an individual is sued in his or her personal name the address for service in CPR 6.9(2) will be the usual or last known residence, Sir Stanley Burnton explaining:

'An individual is sued in the name of a business when he is sued in the name of a business which is not his personal name. This is the natural reading of CPR 6.9. If the second paragraph of the table under that rule had been intended to apply a person carrying on business in his own name, as well as a person carrying on business in another name, it would have so stated.'

Accordingly, whilst an individual being sued in the name of a business can usually be served at the principal or last known place of business that is not so where the business name and personal name of the defendant coincide. Care is also necessary when serving a defendant sued as a firm, should there be reason to believe some of the partners may not receive the claim form if served at the principal or last known place of business: *Brooks v AH Brooks & Co (a firm)*.[136]

If there is an address within the jurisdiction at which the defendant may be served there will be valid service at that address even if, at the date of such service, the defendant is out of the jurisdiction: *Kamali v City & Country Properties Ltd*.[137]

---

[134] [2003] EWCA Civ 656.
[135] [2014] EWCA Civ 6.
[136] (Unreported) 4 November 2010 Birmingham District Registry.
[137] [2006] EWCA Civ 1879.

2.10.5   Service at an alternative place or by an alternative method

CPR 6.15 allows the court to make an order, prior to the claimant attempting service, under CPR 6.15(1) or, after attempting service, under CPR 6.15(2) for service of the claim form at an alternative place, or by an alternative method, not otherwise permitted under Part 6.

However, before making such an order there must be 'good reason to do so': *Brown v Innovatorone plc*.[138]

2.10.5.1   Prior to attempting service

An application may be made prior to attempting service under CPR 6.15(1).

That application, which will need to be supported by evidence, must specify the method or place of service, the date on which the claim form is to be deemed served and time limits for filing an acknowledgement of service, admission or defence. The application may, however, be made without notice.

Paragraph 9.1 of Practice Direction 6A sets out the evidence required which will include:

- the reason why an order is sought;
- what alternative method or place is proposed; and
- why the applicant believes the document is likely to reach the person to be served by the method or at the place proposed.

2.10.5.2   After attempting service

An application may be made, after attempts to serve, under CPR 6.15(2). The court may order, on such an application, that steps already taken to bring the claim form to the attention of the defendant by an alternative method or at an alternative place is good service.

Paragraph 9.2 of Practice Direction 6A details the evidence that will be required, in support of such an application, which includes:

- the reason why the order is sought;
- what alternative method or alternative place was used;
- when the alternative method or place was used; and
- why the applicant believes that the documents is likely to have reached the person to be served by the alternative method or at the alternative place.

In *Bethell Construction Ltd v Deloitte and Touche*[139] the Court of Appeal, when refusing to make an order under CPR 6.15, adopted the approach in *Kuenyehia v International Hospitals Group Ltd*[140] that this was not a case of 'a minor departure from a permitted method of service or an ineffective attempt to serve by a permitted

---

[138]   [2009] EWHC 1376 (Comm).
[139]   [2011] EWCA Civ 1321.
[140]   [2006] EWCA Civ 21.

method within the time limit'. Consequently, it was not a case of mis-service but a case of non-service. Reliance on CPR 6.15 was not permitted.

In *Abela v Baadarani*[141] the Supreme Court observed that orders under CPR 6.15(1), and hence by implication under CPR 6.15(2), can only be made if there is 'good reason to do so'. Lord Clarke observed:

> 'The question, therefore, is whether there was a good reason to order that the steps taken on 22 October 2009 in Beirut to bring the claim form to the attention of the respondent constituted good service.'

Lord Clarke went on to hold that:

> 'Service has a number of purposes but the most important is to my mind to ensure that the contents of the document served, here the claim form, is communicated to the defendant.'

Overturning the decision of the Court of Appeal the Supreme Court disagreed with the approach that, for there to be an order under CPR 6.15(2) there had to be a 'very good reason' and the circumstances be 'exceptional'.

2.10.6 Special rules

Special rules apply to service of a claim form in the following circumstances:
- in proceedings against the Crown (found in CPR 6.10);
- to service of the claim form by a contractually agreed method (found in CPR 6.11);
- to service of the claim form relating to a contract on an agent of a principal out of the jurisdiction (found in CPR 6.12); and
- to service of a claim form on a child or a protected party (found in CPR 6.13).

2.10.7 Error of procedure: CPR 3.10

CPR 3.10 provides a general power for the court to rectify matters where there has been an error of procedure. This rule may, in some circumstances, assist a claimant with difficulties concerning service of the claim form.

An application under CPR 3.10, relating to service, was allowed in *Steele v Mooney*.[142]
- The claimant had applied for an extension of time for service of the particulars of claim and supporting documentation.
- That application omitted express reference to the claim form as a result of an error when the application was prepared.
- In these circumstances the subsequent application was to correct that error, under CPR 3.10, rather than an application, now out of time, extending time for service of the claim form (which would have brought the terms of CPR 7.6 (3) into play).

---

[141] [2013] UKSC 44.
[142] [2005] EWCA Civ 96.

- The application was allowed. The court accepted, however, CPR 3.10 could not generally be used to achieve something prohibited under another rule (following *Vinos v Marks & Spencer plc*[143]).

The same approach was taken in *Phillips v Symes*.[144]

- Documents had been served on the defendant in Switzerland, except for the English version of the claim form which was removed from the package by a Swiss official because it was erroneously marked 'not for service out of the jurisdiction'.

- Whilst the claim form should have been included in the documents served it was clear that it would have been if not for the error by the Swiss court and as the documents served included a German translation of the claim form the defendant had suffered no prejudice.

- Accordingly, the court was willing to exercise the power under CPR 3.10 to rectify what was regarded as an error of procedure.

CPR 3.10 was, again, held to be appropriately applied in order to deal with a problem concerning service of the claim form in *Stoute v LTA Operations Ltd*[145] where Underhill LJ held:

> '... the principal question is whether the service of the claim form by the Court, in disregard of the Claimant's notification that he wished to effect service himself, constituted "an error of procedure" within the meaning of rule 3.10. In my view it did. What happened in this case seems to me to fall comfortably within the natural meaning of that phrase; but if necessary I would refer to the guidance given by this Court in *Steele v Mooney* [2005] 1 WLR 2819, where it was said that "a broad common sense approach" should be taken to the scope of rule 3.10 (see *per* Dyson LJ, at para. 22 (p. 2824H)). That is in accordance with the case-law about the predecessor provision, RSC O. 2 r. l, which was described as "a most beneficial provision, to be given wide effect": see *Phillips v Symes (no. 3)* [2008] UKHL 1, [2008] 1 WLR 180, *per* Lord Brown at para. 32 (p. 188 A-B), citing *Golden Ocean Assurance Ltd v Martin* [1990] 2 Ll Rep 215.'

2.10.8   Dispensing with service

CPR 6.16 allows the court to dispense with service, thereby overcoming difficulties of place and time, but only in 'exceptional circumstances'.

The current wording of the rule reflects the approach taken by the courts to the earlier version of that rule: *Godwin v Swindon Borough Council*[146] and *Anderton v Clwyd County Council*.[147]

However, in *Asia Pacific (HK) Ltd v Hanjin Shipping Co Ltd*,[148] although not essential to the decision as the claim form was held to have been served, the Court would have dispensed with service under CPR 6.9 had it been necessary to do so. The claimant had sent the claim form, to the right person by a permitted method of service, some 2½ months prior to the expiry of the time limit, and no useful purpose would have been served by requiring the claimant to send the claim form again.

---

[143] [2001] 3 All ER 784.
[144] [2008] UKHL 1.
[145] [2014] EWCA Civ 657.
[146] [2001] EWCA Civ 1478.
[147] [2002] EWCA Civ 933.
[148] [2005] EWHC 2443 (Comm).

In *Phillips v Symes*,[149] in addition to exercising the power under CPR 3.10 to rectify what was regarded as an error of procedure, the court upheld an order made dispensing with service, even if that were to retrospectively validate what would otherwise have been an invalid form of service, as the circumstances were regarded as exceptional.

Similarly, in *Peacocks Ltd v Chapman Taylor*[150] the court held that service would have been dispensed with under CPR 6.9 had it been necessary to do so. The defendant's solicitors had written to the claimant's solicitors stating 'please ensure all subsequent correspondence is sent to ourselves'. The claimant's solicitors subsequently served the claim form on the defendant's solicitors who then contended that reference was only to some arbitration proceedings and that what they said was insufficient to amount to authority to accept service of the claim form. The court held that when determining what was 'an exceptional case' the overriding objective must be applied requiring the court to balance, in a proportionate manner, the needs of efficiency, economy, speed and use in the most effective manner of judicial resources together with the conduct of the parties. Had the defendant's solicitors promptly taken the service point on receipt of the claim form, the claimant could then have served within time direct on the defendant.

The court may now, however, always be satisfied there are exceptional circumstances which justify an order dispensing with service. In *Kuenyehia v International Hospitals Group Ltd*[151] Neuberger LJ held that the power to dispense with service was 'unlikely to be exercised save where the claimant has either made an ineffective attempt in time to serve by one of the methods permitted or has served in time in a manner which involved a minor departure from one of those permitted methods of service'.

Where, however, a firm of solicitors was the defendant and the claim form sent, by fax on the final date available to the claimant to take the 'appropriate step' to serve, service was invalid because the defendant could not be regarded as acting as its own legal representative at the time of purported service, and the fact the defendant was a firm of solicitors did not make it an exceptional case where service could be dispensed with: *Thorne v Lass Salt Garvin*.[152]

Where there is no 'good reason' to make an order under CPR 6.15 it is unlikely there will be 'exceptional circumstances' which would justify an order under CPR 6.16: *Bethell Construction Ltd v Deloitte and Touche*.[153]

2.10.9 Service of the claim form out of the jurisdiction

The rules relating to service of the claim form, and other documents, out of the jurisdiction are found in CPR 6.30 to 6.47 and Practice Direction 6B.

Perhaps the most important aspect of the rules relating to service out of the jurisdiction is that CPR 6.32 allows the claimant to serve a claim form on a defendant in Scotland or Northern Ireland provided the claim is one the court has power to determine under the Civil Jurisdiction and Judgments Act 1982 and the defendant is domiciled in the United

---

[149] [2008] UKHL 1.
[150] [2004] EWHC 2898 (TCC).
[151] [2006] EWCA Civ 21.
[152] [2009] EWHC 100 (QB).
[153] [2011] EWCA Civ 1321.

Kingdom. Furthermore, the claimant can adopt any of the methods permitted in relation to service of the claim form in England and Wales when serving on a defendant in Scotland or Northern Ireland.

Because service out of the jurisdiction amounts to an interference with the sovereignty of the state concerned, an order for service by an alternative method under CPR 6.15 should be regarded as exceptional: *Cecil v Bayat*.[154]

2.10.10   Who should serve the claim form?

CPR 6.4(1) confirms that the court will generally serve the claim form.

However, this rule also allows the claimant to notify the court of the wish to take responsibility for service of the claim form.

The claimant's solicitors may prefer to retain control of service, given the difficulties that can arise if service is not properly effected.

If the court fails to attempt service at all that will be classed as the court having been 'unable' to serve so that the claimant may be able to rely on CPR 7.6(3) for an extension of time: *Cranfield v Bridgegrove Ltd (Claussen v Yeates)*[155].

However, the risk remains that unless wholly the fault of the Court time will not be extended: *Cranfield v Bridgegrove Ltd (Claussen v Yeates)*[156].

Before default judgment can be entered, following service by the claimant's solicitors, form N215 will need to be completed and filed. Where the court has not served the claimant must, under CPR 6.17(2) file a certificate of service, though that is a freestanding requirement independent of CPR 12.3 which does not require a certificate of service as a pre-condition for a default judgment: *Henriksen v Pires*.[157]

2.10.11   Notification on service of the claim form

If arrangements for service of the claim form have not been agreed it is usually appropriate to notify any insurers of the defendant that the claim form has been served. The benefits of giving such notification are that it ensures there is no breach of the defendant's policy of insurance in the event that this requires the insurer to be notified on service of proceedings.

Additionally, giving this information will put the insurer on notice of intention to seek default judgment as well as confirming when it is calculated the claimant will be entitled to request judgment in default from the court.

If the defendant is an uninsured motorist notice the claim form has been served on the defendant must be given, within 14 days after the date when service is deemed to have occurred, in accordance with clause 10 of the Uninsured Drivers Agreement.

---

154   [2010] EWCA Civ135.
155   [2003] EWCA Civ 656.
156   [2003] EWCA Civ 656.
157   [2011] EWCA Civ 1720.

Where the defendant is a NHS Trust the NHSLA should be advised the claim form has been served (certainly if the claim involves allegations of clinical negligence).

2.10.12 Documents requiring service

In a personal injury claim the claimant will be required to serve a number of documents on the defendant.

2.10.12.1 Claim form

The most crucial document, because this confirms the claim has been brought, is a copy claim form which, as a very minimum, must be sent to the defendant by taking the appropriate step required, under CPR 7.5, within the relevant time limit.

Where the claim form is served within the jurisdiction personally or by post/DX/delivery that should be an original sealed copy of the claim form (see **2.10.2.4**).

2.10.12.2 Particulars of claim (and accompanying documentation)

CPR 7.4 requires particulars of claim, if not contained in or served with the claim form, to be served within 14 days after service of the claim form, subject to an overall time limit that these be served no later than the latest time for serving a claim form. This rule, however, is not subject to the self-contained code applicable to an extension of time for service of the claim form found in CPR 7.6 and, accordingly, failure to serve will not, of itself, invalidate service of the claim form. The court can extend time for service of particulars of claim, with accompanying medical report and/or schedule, in accordance with the general case management powers found in Part 3 of the CPR: *Totty v Snowden*.[158] If, however, application is not made before the time limit expires the court may treat the application as needing to meet the criteria for securing relief from sanctions, in accordance with CPR 3.9. In those circumstances that may result in an application, made after the time limit has elapsed, being refused whilst an application made within time would have been granted: *Venulum Property Investments Ltd v Space Architecture Ltd*.[159]

2.10.12.3 Notice of funding

If the claimant wishes to recover additional liabilities from the defendant, under a 'pre-commencement funding arrangement' it is essential to serve notice of funding, giving relevant details of additional liabilities in accordance with section 19 of the Costs Practice Direction (as in force prior to 1 April 2013), when serving the claim form.

2.10.12.4 Response pack

CPR 7.8 requires the claimant, when serving particulars of claim, to accompany these by what is termed the 'response pack', namely a form for defending the claim, a form for admitting the claim and a form for acknowledging service. If, however, the claimant fails to do so service will not be rendered invalid and, whilst a relevant factor when

---

[158] [2001] EWCA Civ 1415.
[159] [2013] EWHC 1242 (TCC).

considering such an application, will not automatically entitle the defendant to get any default judgment set aside: *Rajval Construction Ltd v Bestville Properties Ltd.*[160]

2.10.13   Tactics for service of the claim form

Because service of the claim form is such an unforgiving stage of the proceedings it is worth keeping in mind tactics to avoid, or deal with, problems that may arise.

- Heed the warnings given by the judiciary and serve the claim form promptly following issue (which should also avoid pitfalls about where to serve as there should then be time to put matters right if problems arise).

- Check the address at which the defendant may, or must, be served and seek confirmation of that address whilst stating the address that, in the absence of confirmation, it is understood is the appropriate address and which will be used for the purpose of service.

- Serve a sealed copy of the claim form at the correct address for service and be clear it is being sent to effect service.

- If in doubt consider serving a sealed copy claim form on the defendant at more than one address.

- If necessary apply to the court, prior to attempting service, for an order under CPR 6.15(1) allowing service by an alternative method or at an alternative place.

- If necessary apply to the court, after attempting service, for an order under CPR 6.15(2) that service at an alternative method or at an alternative place be effective.

- Avoid, unless there are insurmountable difficulties in serving the defendant, seeking or agreeing an extension of time for service of the claim form. If that really is necessary:
    – make sure any agreement complies with the requirements of CPR 2.11 (see **2.9.3.3**);
    – if application to the court is necessary ensure this is made under CPR 7.6(2), within the four-month period from issue, and that adequate reasons for seeking an order can be given.
    – if application has to be made under CPR 7.6(3), after four months from issue of the claim form, ensure that the claimant is able to show the specific factors identified in that sub-rule apply.

- If there is an error of procedure consider seeking an order under CPR 3.10.

- Apply to the court for an order under CPR 6.16 dispensing with service, but only if the claimant can show there are 'exceptional circumstances'.

- Serve particulars of claim, and accompanying documentation, no later than the latest date for service of the claim form. If, however, that cannot be done serve just the claim form and apply for an extension of time for service of other documents. That is because whilst completing enquiries to assess the viability of a claim might, in appropriate circumstances, justify an extension of time for service of the claim form a safer course is to serve the claim form and then apply for an extension of time to serve particulars of claim. The disadvantage of this, for the claimant, is that once the claim form has been served the defendant is more likely to incur costs that will be recoverable in the event of discontinuance as service will put the defendant on notice of proceedings in which costs can be assessed although it is the issue of

---

[160]   [2010] EWCA Civ 1621, [2011] CILL 2994.

those proceedings which generates the entitlement to seek costs: *Clydesdale Bank plc v Kinleigh Folkard & Hayward Ltd.*[161]

- Serve the claim form with particulars of claim and/or a schedule that do not have a signed statement of truth where signed versions are not yet available, given that under Part 22 those documents will be effective unless or until the court orders otherwise.

- Following service, even if that service may be defective, wait to see whether jurisdiction is contested by the defendant, filing and acknowledgement of service which does have the appropriate box ticked and, if so, whether the defendant then makes a timely application under Part 11 (see **3.5.1**).

- Issue a further claim form and serve promptly, at the correct address (or apply for an order under CPR 6.15), relying, if limitation is then raised as a defence, on section 33 Limitation Act 1980: *Horton v Sadler;*[162] *Aktas v Adepta;*[163] *Hall v The Ministry of Defence,*[164] *Dowdall v William Kenyon & Sons Ltd.*[165]

- If none of these steps allow the claim to proceed then notify professional indemnity insurers promptly!

2.10.14   Service of other documents

Part 6 also deals with service of documents, within the jurisdiction, other than the claim form.

The special rules, required to ensure the claim form is brought to the attention of the defendant in time, are not necessary for the purpose of serving documents subsequently in the proceedings. Hence the rules for service of documents other than the claim form are grouped in section III of Part 6, from CPR 6.20 to 6.29.

These rules, accordingly, apply to statements of case, application notices, Part 36 offers and all other documents served in the proceedings save for the claim form.

Much of the difficulty associated with service of the claim form is avoided, once that document has been served, because of the requirement, in CPR 6.23, a party to the proceedings must give an address at which that party may be served and the further requirement, in CPR 6.24, to give notice in writing of any change in the address for service, to the court and every other party, as soon as it has taken place.

CPR 6.23(2) provides that, unless the rules allow otherwise, a party's address for service must be:

- the business address either within the United Kingdom or any other EEA state of a solicitor acting for the party to be served; or

- the business address in any EEA state of a European Lawyer nominated to accept service of documents; or

- where there is no solicitor acting for the party or no European Lawyer nominated to accept service of documents:

---

[161]   (Unreported) Master Bragge Ch D 5 February 2014.
[162]   [2006] UKHL 27.
[163]   [2010] EWCA Civ 1170.
[164]   [2013] EWHC 4092 (QB).
[165]   [2014] EWHC 2822 (QB).

- an address within the United Kingdom of which the party resides or carries on business; or
- an address within any other EEA state of which the party resides or carries on business.

The terms of Practice Direction 6A apply, to such address, so far as service by fax and electronic means are concerned.

Whilst CPR 6.22 allows personal service of a document, that is not permitted where the party to be served has given an address for service in accordance with CPR 6.23.

CPR 6.26 identifies in the table that follows, by reference to the method of service, the deemed date of service which may, of course, subsequently be significant for the purposes of complying with the court timetable and also in the making, changing, withdrawing and accepting of Part 36 offers: *Sutton Jigsaw Transport Ltd v Croydon London Borough Council*.[166]

Method of service	Deemed date of service
First class post (or other service which provides for delivery on the next business day)	The second day after it was posted, left with, delivered to or collected by the relevant service provider provided that day is a business day; or If not, the next business day after that day.
Document exchange	The second day after it was left with, delivered to or collected by the relevant service provider provided that day is a business day; or if not, the next business day after that day.
Delivering the document to or leaving it at a permitted address	If it is delivered to or left at the permitted address on a business day before 4.30pm, on that day; or in any other case, on the next business day after that day.
Fax	If the transmission of the fax is completed on a business day before 4.30pm, on that day; or in any other case, on the next business day after the day on which it was transmitted.
Other electronic method	If the Email or other electronic transmission is sent on a business day before 4.30pm, on that day; or in any other case, on the next business day after the day on which it was sent.

---

[166] (Unreported) 27 February 2013, QBD.

| Personal service | If the document is served personally before 4.30pm on a business day, on that day; or |
| | in any other case, on the next business day after that day. |

Whether, in any particular case, service by all of these means will be available depends upon the terms of Practice Direction 6A (see **2.9.2.3**).

The stricter approach to compliance with time limits under the CPR, from April 2013, makes it essential for practitioners to be aware of the method of service available in any particular case and when documents, according to the method of service adopted, will be deemed served as if the deadline is not complied with even a short delay may result in the imposition of a sanction from which relief cannot be obtained.

2.10.15 Claimant's address for service

The claim form will have details of the claimant's address for service and relevant details where service by document exchange, fax, email or other electronic means will be accepted.

However, when serving the claim form it is important to remember that information on the writing paper used may, even if not stated in the claim form, amount to willingness to accept service for the purposes of Practice Direction 6A (see **2.10.2.3**).

2.10.16 Advising the client

Service of proceedings is an important stage at which to report to the client and advise how the matter is likely to proceed.

The client ought to be informed that court papers are about to be received by the defendant, particularly where there is a connection between the parties (for example in employers' liability cases) and the court papers have to be served direct on the defendant.

In any event, this is a timely opportunity to outline the stages in the court process and, so far as possible, give a general indication of likely timescale.

Most clients, if advised of what will happen and when, are happy to let the lawyers get on with the case. If clients are not given that information, this can result, at the very least, in numerous telephone calls, seeking updates and, at worst, a failure to manage expectations. A client who has unrealistic expectations, which have not been adequately managed, will frequently complain about lack of information and delay. Such complaints may not be well founded but are to be expected unless adequate advice and information are given about a process that the client is likely to be unfamiliar with.

2.10.17   Advising experts

The Protocol for the Instruction of Experts to give Evidence in Civil Claims (which can be found as an annex to the Practice Direction to Part 35) provides, in paragraphs 14, for experts to be told of the date reports are disclosed and kept informed of progress with the case.

Consequently, if any experts, whose reports are served with the particulars of claim, have not already been informed about disclosure, or those reports have not previously been disclosed, confirmation of that disclosure should be given at the time of service.

2.11   PRE-ACTION APPLICATIONS

The stocktake, at the end of the Protocol, may result in the decision that further information is required before a decision can be reached whether to issue a claim form or to not proceed with the claim.

Further information, to help reach a final decision, may be obtained by making a pre-action application for disclosure or inspection of property.

2.11.1   Types of pre-action application

There are three main types of pre-action application:

- an application against a proposed defendant for an order relating to, including inspection of, property (CPR 25.5(1)(a));
- an application against a non-party for an order relating to, including inspection of, property that can affect a party who is not a proposed defendant (CPR 25.5(1)(b)), which provision can also be used against a non-party at any stage during the proceedings; and
- an application against a proposed defendant for disclosure (CPR 31.16).

These rules reflect the terms of ss 33 and 34 Senior Courts Act 1981 and ss 52 and 53 County Courts Act 1984.

2.11.2   Pre-action disclosure

CPR 31.16 allows an application to be made to the court for disclosure before proceedings have started.

This provision is particularly useful if there has been a failure to give disclosure of documents in accordance with the protocol.

2.11.2.1   Criteria

CPR 31.16(3) confirms the court may make an order only where:

(a)   the respondent is likely to be a party to subsequent proceedings;

(b)   the applicant is also likely to be a party to those proceedings;

(c)   if proceedings had started, the respondent's duty by way of standard disclosure, set out in r 31.6 would extend to the documents or classes of documents of which the applicant seeks disclosure; and

(d)   disclosure before proceedings have started is desirable in order to:
    –   dispose fairly of the anticipated proceedings;
    –   assist the dispute to be resolved without proceedings; or
    –   save costs.

These sub-paragraphs are jurisdictional in nature, and the first aspect of a two stage test.

2.11.2.2 *Jurisdiction*

The first stage for the court is jurisdictional, namely that the conditions identified in the sub-paragraphs found in CPR 31.16(3) are satisfied.

Sub-paragraphs (a) and (b) do not require proceedings to be likely, only that if subsequent proceedings are issued the applicant and respondent will be parties in those proceedings: *Black v Sumitomo Corporation*.[167]

Moreover, there is no requirement to establish an 'arguable' or 'prima facie' case to establish jurisdiction (although the strength of the case may be a very relevant consideration to the exercise of discretion). In *Smith v Secretary of State for Energy & Climate Change*[168] Underhill LJ held there was no jurisdictional 'arguability threshold' observing:

> 'If there were a jurisdictional requirement of a minimum level of arguability the question would necessarily arise of how the height of the threshold is to be described. But abstract arguments of that kind tend to be arid and unhelpful. It is inherently better that questions about the likelihood of the applicant being able in due course to establish a viable claim are considered as part of a flexible exercise of the court's discretion in the context of the particular case.'

The requirements of sub-paragraph (c) were considered by Rix LJ in *Black* when he observed:

> 'In general, however, it should in my judgment be remembered that the extent of standard disclosure can not easily be discerned without clarity as to the issues which would arise once pleadings in the prospective litigation had been formulated.'

Because sub-paragraph (d) uses the phrase 'anticipated proceedings', this element of the jurisdictional test does require proceedings to be 'anticipated', rather than simply contemplated or a possibility. That requires a real prospect, though there does not have to be a certainty or likelihood, of proceedings between the parties: *PHD Modular Access Services Ltd v Seele GmbH*.[169]

---

[167] [2001] EWCA Civ 1819.
[168] [2013] EWCA Civ 1585.
[169] [2011] EWHC 2210 (TCC).

In *Pineway Ltd v London Mining Co Ltd*[170] it was held that although CPR 31.16 extends to both documents and classes of documents it is inappropriate to obtain pre-action disclosure of documents which would not be subject to standard disclosure by simply calling for classes or categories of documents in which some would be disclosable or to require the respondent to identify which documents are within standard disclosure. In other words, all documents within a class or category must be subject to standard disclosure. This is likely to require highly focussed application.

Longmore LJ gave some general guidance about the proper approach to jurisdiction in *Smith* when he held:

> 'Applications for pre-action disclosure are not meant to be a mini-trial of the action and should be disposed of swiftly and economically. Elaborate arguments are to be discouraged ...'

2.11.2.3   Discretion

In *Smith v Secretary of State for Energy & Climate Change*[171] Longmore LJ went on to explain:

> '... the structure of CPR 31.16 formally requires a two-stage approach. The first stage is to establish whether the jurisdictional thresholds prescribed by heads (a)-(d) are satisfied. If they are, the Court proceeds as a second stage to consider whether, as a matter of discretion, an order for disclosure should be made.'

At this stage the merits of the proposed claim may be relevant to the exercise of discretion. In *Black v Sumitomo Corporation*[172] Rix LJ held:

> 'In general, however, it should in my judgment be remembered that the extent of standard disclosure can not easily be discerned without clarity as to the issues which would arise once pleadings in the prospective litigation had been formulated.'

Even if the jurisdictional tests are met the court needs to consider whether to exercise the discretion, in accordance with CPR 31.16(3)(d), to make an order for pre-action disclosure.

The merits of the proposed claim may be relevant to the exercise of discretion. In *Black* Rix LJ held:

> 'In my judgment, the more focused the complaint and the more limited the disclosure sought in that connection, the easier it is for the court to exercise its discretion in favour of pre-action disclosure, even where the complaint might seem somewhat speculative or the request might be argued to constitute a mere fishing exercise. In appropriate circumstances, where the jurisdictional thresholds have been crossed, the court might be entitled to take the view that transparency was what the interests of justice and proportionality most required. The more diffuse the allegations, however, and the wider the disclosure sought, the more sceptical the court is entitled to be about the merit of the exercise.'

---

[170]   [2010] EWHC 1143.
[171]   [2013] EWCA Civ 1585.
[172]   [2001] EWCA Civ 1819.

For these purposes the court may have regard to whether the claimant can investigate the case and assess liability without the documents sought. If so the overriding objective might mean refusal of an application otherwise meeting the jurisdictional criteria in CPR 31.16 given the discretion available to the court. To an extent this may involve re-assessing some of the matters relevant to the jurisdictional tests.

2.11.2.4 Procedure

An application for pre-action disclosure should be made by application notice in accordance with CPR 23.

CPR 31.16(2) requires the application to be supported by evidence which may usefully set out why it is contended the application meets the requirements of CPR 31.16(3).

CPR 31.16(4) requires any order made to:

- specify the documents or classes of documents which the respondent must disclose; and

- require the respondent, when making disclosure, to specify any of those documents:
    - which are no longer in his control; or
    - in respect of which he claims a right or duty to withhold inspection.

CPR 31.16(5) provides that an order for pre-action disclosure may require the respondent to indicate what has happened to any documents no longer in his control and to specify the time and place for disclosure and inspection.

To help comply with sub paras (4) and (5) of CPR 31.16 it may be helpful if the application is supported by a draft order identifying the documents, or classes of documents, sought, as well as suggesting time limit for disclosure and the means by which inspection is to take place (usually provision of copy documents).

If the scope of disclosure is too wide, or unspecific, it may be more difficult to persuade the court to exercise discretion and order disclosure at this stage.

If the claimant wishes to recover additional liabilities notice of funding should be filed at court, when the application is issued, and served, along with the application notice and accompanying documents, on the defendant. That is because paragraph 19.2(1) of the Costs Practice Direction requires relevant information to be given to the court when issuing the 'claim form', defined for these purposes as including application notice. Accordingly, this will be required even if details of the funding have already been given in the letter of claim.

If, subsequently, the funding arrangement changes the claimant will need to give notice, within seven days, of that change to comply with para 19.2 and CPR 45.15.

2.11.2.5 Other remedies

If an application for disclosure is made the claimant may wish to include in the application any other issues which arise in relation to non-compliance with the protocol by the defendant.

The claimant might, for example, seek orders:

- requiring a decision on liability (with reasons and any alternative version of events should liability be denied); and/or

- debarring the defendant from defending any subsequent proceedings if no decision on liability (or inadequate information given to support any denial) within the timescale stipulated.

The court might just be willing, under general case management powers and with a view to furthering the overriding objective, to make such a provision. If not the claimant will need, in the event of default, to consider other methods of enforcement, which may ultimately require proceedings for contempt.

2.11.2.6   The RTA Protocol and the EL/PL Protocol

Even if a claim is likely to enter the RTA Protocol there may be circumstances in which a pre-action application is, nevertheless, required.

If, for example, the defendant has information which is likely to be contained in documentation, necessary for completion of the claim notification form it may be preferable, rather than waiting for this to be disclosed at the time of the defendant's choosing, to warn that unless the information is disclosed promptly an application for disclosure of relevant documentation will be made.

For these purposes, at least in a claim destined for the RTA Protocol, an application can be made direct against the defendant's insurer given that any such insurer is a potential defendant under the European Communities (Rights Against Insurers) Regulations 2002.

2.11.2.7   Costs

The starting point, so far as costs are concerned, is CPR 48.1(2), which provides that the applicant should meet the costs. However, CPR 48.1(3) allows the court to make a different order as to costs having regard to all the circumstances which expressly include 'whether the parties to the application have complied with any relevant pre-action protocols'.

This starting point explains decisions such as *SES Contracting Ltd v UK Coal plc*,[173] where the claimant did not recover costs but, crucially, in proceedings that were not covered by a specific protocol. Where, however, there is a protocol, providing for early disclosure, the effect of that, coupled with the Practice Direction – Pre-action Conduct, should put the claimant in a strong position to seek costs. That is because paragraphs 4.4(4) and 4.5(2) and (3) of the Practice Direction specifically provide for compliance with a relevant protocol.

Hence, in *Bermuda International Securities v KPMG*[174] the court concluded the failure to comply with a protocol was very relevant to the incidence of costs. In *Sherred v*

---

[173]   [2007] EWCA Civ 791.
[174]   [2001] EWCA Civ 269.

Weston Challenge Housing Association[175] the court declined to follow *SES Contracting Ltd* and ordered the defendant to pay the costs of a pre-action application for disclosure.

Where the defendant has failed to comply with the protocol, making the application necessary, the claimant may seek, in accordance with paragraph 4.6(3) of the Practice Direction Pre-action Conduct, that costs be assessed on the indemnity basis, under Part 44.

If the claimant wishes to recover a success fee that should either be assessed at this stage or adjourned for assessment once the claim is concluded (with most interim hearings in the proceedings the assessment of the success fee would be adjourned but, of course, with a pre-action application there is no guarantee there will be any subsequent proceedings to deal with such assessment).

Where the claimant's solicitors are acting under a conditional fee agreement if that is in the form of the Law Society Model CFA costs of a successful pre-action application are recoverable: *Connaught v Imperial College Healthcare NHS Trust.*[176]

It is important to note that QOCS, which applies generally to personal injury claims from 1 April 2013 except where funded by a 'pre-commencement funding arrangement', will not provide protection from the costs of a pre-action application.

2.11.3 Pre-action inspection of property

A pre-action application may be made, in appropriate circumstances, for inspection of property and, if necessary, other steps such as taking samples of property.

This provision is useful if, for example, the claimant wishes to obtain expert evidence which, in turn, will require an expert to inspect the scene of an accident or, perhaps, relevant machinery or other property.

2.11.3.1 *Criteria*

CPR 25.5(1) applies to applications under s 33(1) Senior Courts Act 1981 and se 52(1) County Courts Act 1984 against a person likely to be a party to subsequent proceedings where an order is sought for:

• the inspection, photographing, preservation, custody and detention of property which appears to the court to be property which may become the subject matter of subsequent proceedings in the High Court, or as to which any question may arise in any such proceedings; or

• the taking of samples to any such property, and the carrying out of any experiment on or with any such property.

---

[175] (Unreported) Manchester County Court, 13 October 2009.
[176] [2010] EWHC 90173 (Costs).

2.11.3.2   Procedure

CPR 25.5(2) requires the evidence in support of an application, if practicable by reference to any statement of case prepared, that the property:

- is or may become the subject matter of such proceedings; or
- is relevant to the issues that will arise in relation to such proceedings.

2.11.3.3   Costs

The applicant for such an order may be at greater risk on costs, than if applying for pre-action disclosure, given the defendant will not be in breach of any specific protocol provision. If, however, the claimant has reasonably requested facilities, which have not been given, that might be seen by the court as a failure to comply with the overriding objective and the Practice Direction – Pre-action Conduct as these require a degree of co-operation between the parties.

2.12   SANCTIONS

The sanction for a claimant who fails to issue or serve a claim form promptly is that the claim, unless the defendant wishes to settle it, cannot proceed. Ultimately, if these steps are not taken and it cannot be settled, the claim will be defeated on the grounds of limitation.

Limitation should not, at least in most cases, be the factor that prompts the issue of court proceedings. Rather, the claimant should follow any applicable protocols, and the terms of the Practice Direction – Pre-Action Conduct, so that proceedings are commenced promptly with claims that cannot be settled in accordance with the relevant protocol.

Nevertheless, given the potential effect of limitation, it is important to be aware of when the limitation period, in any particular claim, will expire so that, if necessary protective, court proceedings can be commenced in time and then duly served.

2.12.1   Primary limitation period

Section 2 of the Limitation Act 1980 provides a general rule that an action founded on tort shall not be brought after the expiry of 6 years from the date on which the cause of action accrued.

A special rule, however, applies, under s 11, in respect of claims seeking damages for personal injury where the time limit is three years. Under s 11 that three-year period starts from the date the cause of action accrued or the date of knowledge, for the purposes of s 14, of the person injured if later.

If the claimant seeks damages for personal injuries the three-year time limit imposed by s 11 applies even if the cause of action is in a tort such as assault rather than negligence: *A v Hoare*.[177]

---

[177]   [2008] UKHL 6.

Similarly, the 3 year time limit applies to personal injury claims based in contract, for example *Bond v Livingstone & Co.*[178]

There are a number of exceptions to the three-year time limit for personal injury claims.

2.12.1.1 Children and protected parties

Section 28 Limitation Act 1980 provides that if on the date when any right of action accrued the person to whom it accrued was under a disability, the action may be brought at any time before the expiration of, in a personal injury claim, three years from the date when that person ceases to be under a disability or dies, whichever occurs first.

Where the claimant is a protected party if capacity is regained the limitation period will start to run and not then cease: *Prideaux v Webber.*[179]

2.12.1.2 Death

If the potential claimant dies within the primary limitation period then the limitation period, for the estate, will be three years from the date of death or date of knowledge of the dependent for whose benefit the action is brought, whichever is the later, in accordance with s 11(5) of the Limitation Act 1980.

2.12.1.3 Fatal accidents

Section 12 of the Limitation Act 1980 imposes a special time limit for actions under the Fatal Accidents Act 1976.

Section 12(1) provides an action under the 1976 Act shall not be brought if the death occurred when the person injured could no longer maintain an action and recover damages in respect of the injury whether because of a time limit under the 1980 Act, in any other Act or for any other reason. For these purposes no account should be taken of the possibility of the time limit being overridden under s 33 of the 1980 Act.

Section 12(2) provides that, rather than other time limits set out in the 1980 Act, the time limit applicable to an action under the 1976 Act will be three years from the date of death or the date of knowledge of the person for whose benefit the action is brought.

2.12.1.4 Defective products

The Consumer Protection Act 1987 inserts s 11A into the Limitation Act 1980 which imposes a general time limit of 10 years on any action for damages under the 1980 Act (usually running from the time of supply) after which any right of action shall be extinguished.

---

[178] [2001] PNLR 30.
[179] (1661) 1 Lev. 31. 263.

2.12.1.5   Injuries on water

There is a two-year limitation period, prescribed by the Athens Convention, where a person travelling on a ship used in navigation suffers personal injury as a result of the fault of another ship.

'Ship' is defined as a sea going vessel, excluding an air cushion vehicle. Small boats are covered by this definition but not jet skis.

A 'passenger' is defined as any person carried on a ship, including being in the course of embarkation or disembarkation.

Navigation means proceeding from an originating place to a terminus, so injuries on boats being used for pleasure purposes rather than navigation are not subject to the two-year time limit.

The Athens Convention is incorporated into the law of England and Wales by the Merchant Shipping Act 1995 and extends to domestic, as well as international, carriage (subject to the requirement of a 'ship' being used in 'navigation').

The limitation period runs from the date of disembarkation or, in the case of death occurring during carriage, from the date on which the passenger should have disembarked.

If the Athens Convention is applicable the two-year limitation period affects claims brought under the Package Travel, Package Holidays and Package Tours Regulations 1992.

It is safest to assume time is not extended for children and protected parties. Furthermore, s 33 Limitation Act 1980 is not available.

2.12.1.6   Injuries in the air

There is a two-year limitation period applicable to injuries sustained when travelling by air.

The Carriage by Air Act 1961 incorporates into English law the provisions of the Warsaw Convention (which was subsequently replaced by the Montreal Convention).

The Carriage by Air Acts (Application of Provisions) Order 1967 applies the two-year time limit to carriage by air not being carriage to which the Convention applies (it other words it applies to domestic as well as international flight).

The two-year period runs from the date at which the aircraft arrived, or should have arrived, at its destination.

After two years the right to damages is extinguished, and that rule is applicable to children and protected parties. No extension of time under the Limitation Act 1980 is available.

Travel by 'aircraft' is covered by the Convention, the term aircraft including, for example, hot air balloons: *Laroche v Spirit of Adventure (UK) Ltd.*[180]

The claimant must be a 'passenger' on the aircraft. Accordingly, a member of the crew will not be a 'passenger' and hence not subject to the Convention: *Fellowes v Clyde Helicopters Ltd.*[181]

Accidents involved in embarking and disembarking the aircraft are included.

A doctor responding to the captain's call when going to the assistance of an ill passenger will be treated as the airline's temporary agent (and hence covered by the airline's insurance).

Bringing an action requires the claimant to bring a claim under the Convention so this must be mentioned in the claim form.

2.12.1.7 Human rights

Section 7(5)(a) of the Human Rights 1998 imposes a time limit of one year, beginning with the date on which the Act complained of took place, for any claim brought under Arts 2 to 12 and 14 of the European Convention on Human Rights.

However, s 7(5)(b) allows proceedings to be brought before the end of such longer period as the court considers equitable having regard to all the circumstances. Time was extended accordingly in *Rabone v Pennine Care NHS Foundation,*[182] but not in *XYZ v Chief Constable of Gwent*[183] as no reason has been given for the delay.

2.12.1.8 Protection from Harassment Act 1997

Section 11(1A) of the Limitation Act 1980 confirms s 11 does not apply to any action brought for damages under s 3 of the Protection from Harassment Act 1997.

2.12.1.9 Fraud, concealment or mistake

Section 32 of the Limitation Act 1980 provides that the limitation period will not begin to run until the claimant has discovered the fraud, concealment or mistake, or could with reasonable diligence have discovered it, if that involves:

* an action based on the fraud of the defendant; or

* any fact relevant to the claimant's right of action has been deliberately concealed by the defendant; or

* the action is for relief from the consequences of a mistake.

---

[180] [2009] EWCA Civ 12.
[181] [1997] AC 534.
[182] [2012] UKSC 2.
[183] [2014] EWHC 1448 (QB).

2.12.1.10   Foreign limitation law

Section 1(1) of the Foreign Limitation Periods Act 1984 provides, subject to other provisions in the Act, that where the law of any other country, in the courts of England and Wales, falls, in accordance with rules of private international law, to be taken into account the law of that other country relating to limitation shall apply.

Issues of private international law are likely to be governed by the terms of the Private International Law (Miscellaneous Provisions) Act 1995.

If, however, both the law of England and Wales and the law of some other country are to be taken into account then the law of England and Wales relating to limitation will apply.

Section 2(1) does provide an exception where the application of the foreign limitation period would conflict with public policy to the extent that its application would cause undue hardship to a person who is, or might be made, a party to the proceedings.

A restrictive approach to public policy causing undue hardship was taken in both *Hardy v Smith*[184] and *Naraji v Shellbourne.*[185]

Foreign limitation periods will, of course, vary from jurisdiction to jurisdiction.

A foreign limitation period may well apply to a claim brought under the Package Travel, Package Holidays and Package Tours Regulations 1992.

2.12.2   Date of knowledge

Section 14 of the Limitation Act 1980 provides that references to a person's date of knowledge are references to the date on which he first had knowledge of the following facts:

- that the injury in question was significant; and
- that the injury was attributable in whole or in part to the act or omission which is alleged to constitute negligence, nuisance or breach of duty; and
- the identify of the defendant; and
- if it is alleged that the act or omission was that of a person other than the defendant, the identity of that person and the additional facts supporting the bringing of an action against the defendant.

Knowledge that any acts or omissions did or did not, as a matter of law, involve negligence, nuisance or breach of duty is irrelevant.

In *Young v Catholic Care (Diocese of Leeds)*[186] the House of Lords confirmed an impersonal standard should be applied under s 14.

---

[184]   [2010] EWCA Civ 78.
[185]   [2011] EWHC 3298 (QB).
[186]   [2008] UKHL 6.

It should not be assumed that a person who had suffered a serious injury would be sufficiently curious to ask questions about it and hence fixed with constructive knowledge of facts he would have learnt if those questions had been asked: *Adams v Bracknell Forest Borough Council*;[187] *Whiston v London Strategic Health Authority*;[188] *Johnson v Ministry of Defence.*[189]

2.12.3 Extension of the limitation period

Section 33(1) of the Limitation Act 1980 allows the court to extend the three-year limitation period under s 11 if it is equitable to do so having regard to the degree to which the provisions of s 11 prejudice the claimant and any decision of the court excepting its operation would prejudice the defendant.

Section 33(3) requires the court, when deciding whether to disapply the primary limitation period, to have regard to all the circumstances of the case some of which are specifically identified, namely:

- the length of and reasons for the delay on the part of the claimant;
- the extent to which having regard to the delay the evidence in the case is likely to be less cogent than if the claim had been brought within time;
- the conduct of the defendant after the cause of action arose including the extent to which the defendant responded to requests reasonably made by the claimant for information relevant to the case;
- the duration of the claimant's disability;
- the extent to which the claimant acted promptly and reasonably once he knew whether or not the act or omission of the defendant might be capable at that time of giving rise to a claim; and
- the steps taken by the claimant to obtain medical, legal or other expert advice.

Drawing these factors together much will depend upon the extent of the delay and how, given the merits of the claim, this is likely to affect a fair trial of the issues.

In *Young* and associated cases the House of Lords confirmed that whilst the individual circumstances of the claimant were not relevant under s 14 they were relevant to the exercise of discretion under s 33.

In *Cain v Francis*[190] the Court of Appeal ruled that, at least where a defendant had early notice of the claim, accrual of a limitation defence should be regarded as a windfall not amounting to prejudice or only a slight degree of prejudice. The disapplication of the limitation period would only be prejudicial to the defendant if the right to a fair opportunity of defending the claim had been compromised by the delay.

That decision, however, does not mean there can never be forensic prejudice if liability has been admitted. In *McDonnell v Walker*[191] liability had been admitted at an early stage but that was on the basis of a substantially different case on quantum to the case

---

[187] [2004] UKHL 29.
[188] [2010] EWCA Civ 195.
[189] [2012] EWCA Civ 1505.
[190] [2008] EWCA Civ 1451.
[191] [2009] EWCA Civ 1257.

which emerged only after the claimant had failed to serve the proceedings initially commenced and, sometime later, sought to serve further proceedings and rely on section 33.

In *Davidson v Aegis Defence Services (BBI) Ltd*[192] the Court of Appeal confirmed there was no conflict between *Cain* and *McDonnell* but emphasised it was the guidance given by Smith LJ in *Cain* which would almost always be of most use to first instance judges asked to disapply the 3 year time limit. That guidance was:

> 'It seems to me that in the exercise of the discretion the basic question to be asked is whether it is fair and just in all the circumstances to expect the defendant to meet this claim on the merits, notwithstanding the delay in commencement. The length of the delay will be important not so much for itself as to the effect it has had. To what extent has the defendant been disadvantaged in his investigation of the claim and/or the assembly of evidence in respect of the issues of both liability and quantum? But it will also be important to consider the reasons for the delay. Thus there may be some unfairness to the defendant due to the delay in issue, but the delay may have arisen for so excusable a reason that, looking at the matter in the round, on balance it is fair and just that the action should proceed. On the other hand, the balance may go in the opposite direction, partly because the delay has caused procedural disadvantage and unfairness to the defendant and partly because of the reasons for the delay or its length are not good ones.'

Since *Horton v Sadler*[193] a claimant has been able to issue a second action, and place reliance on s 33, even though earlier proceedings were commenced within the limitation period (overturning the earlier decision in *Walkley v Precision Forgings Ltd*[194]).

Furthermore, issue of a second action, in these circumstances, will not usually be an abuse of process, unless there are other factors such as intentional and contumelious conduct, want of prosecution or wholesale disregard of the rules: *Aktas v Adepta*;[195] *Hall v The Ministry of Defence*,[196] *Dowdall v William Kenyon & Sons Ltd*.[197]

Under the unified procedure in the Companies Act 2006 for restoring a limited company that has been dissolved time will be deemed to have been running, for limitation purposes during the period the company was dissolved once restoration has taken place. Given that restoration will also validate any proceedings commenced whilst the company was dissolved it is important, if limitation is about to expire, to commence proceedings and then apply to restore, rather than vice versa. If the limitation period has already expired by the time proceedings are commenced against a dissolved company the application to restore may need to deal with any substantive limitation point (see 2.3.4.4.7).

2.12.4   New claims in pending actions

Section 35 of the Limitation Act 1980 deals with new claims in pending actions.

---

[192]   [2013] EWCA Civ 1586.
[193]   [2006] UKHL 27.
[194]   [1979] 1 WLR 606.
[195]   [2010] EWCA Civ 1170.
[196]   [2013] EWHC 4092 (QB).
[197]   [2014] EWHC 2822 (QB).

The scope of this provision was considered by the Court of Appeal in *Birse Developments Ltd v Co-operative Group Ltd*,[198] *Nemeti v Sabre Insurance Co Ltd*[199] and *Bala Peramplam Chandra v Brooke North*.[200]

2.12.5   When is the action 'brought'?

Para 5.1 of Practice Direction 7A provides that:

> 'Proceedings are started when the court issues a claim form at the request of the claimant (see rule 7.2) but where the claim form as issued was received in the court office on a date earlier than the date on which it was issued by the court, the claim is 'brought' for the purposes of the Limitation Act 1980 and any other relevant statute on that earlier date.'

The practical application of this rule was confirmed by the Court of Appeal in *Stoute v LTA Operations Ltd*.[201]

In *Kaur v S Russell & Sons Ltd*[202]the Court of Appeal held that if the court office was not open on the last day within the limitation period the necessary step would be treated as being done in time if done on the next day when the court office was open. Hence when the cause of action accrued on 5 September 1967 and 5 September 1970 fell on a Saturday the proceedings had been 'brought' when issued on 7 September 1970. On this basis it may suffice if, on the last day within the limitation period, the court office is closed and the claim form is received in the court office, even if not issued, on the next day the office is open.

The claimant will, additionally, need to pay the appropriate court fee: *Page v Hewetts Solicitors*.[203]

The claimant will also need to prove, if necessary, the date the claim form was received in the court office: *Page v Hewetts Solicitors*.[204] Consequently, if the claim form is filed close to the expiration of the limitation period it will be important to have some evidence confirming receipt by the court office.

---

[198] [2013] EWCA Civ 474.
[199] [2013] EWCA Civ 1555.
[200] [2013] EWCA Civ 1559.
[201] [2014] EWCA Civ 657.
[202] [1973] QB 336.
[203] [2013] EWHC 2845 (Ch).
[204] [2013] EWHC 2845 (Ch).

CHAPTER 3

DEFENCE

3.1 INTRODUCTION

The defendant, to comply with CPR 15.2 in proceedings commenced under Part 7, must file a defence and, in accordance with CPR 15.6, serve a copy on every other party if all or any part of the claim is to be defended.

If the defendant files an acknowledgement of service that will give some additional time for the filing and serving of a defence.

If the defendant fails, within the appropriate timescale, to file an acknowledgment to service and/or defence the claimant will be entitled to apply to the court for default judgment.

It may be tempting to regard the stage of the proceedings at which the defence is filed as an opportunity for the claimant to adopt a passive role. It is, however, important to take active steps to ensure the defendant does comply with the obligations imposed by the CPR when serving a defence and that, accordingly, the real issues in the case are identified which, in turn, will assist with the next stage in the proceedings, that of case management.

Accordingly, any defence should be carefully checked to ensure compliance with the CPR. The case, as a whole, should be carefully reviewed, on the basis of the issues identified by the defence, to assess what case management should be sought from the court as that will, to a large extent, be shaped by the matters put in issue.

If no defence is filed in time the claimant should promptly seek default judgment and, if appropriate, case management on the basis of such a judgment.

3.2 TIME LIMITS

There are time limits for dealing with any acknowledgement of service and the defence, though these may be varied by agreement between the parties.

3.2.1   Acknowledgement of service

The relevant time limits for filing the acknowledgement of service are given in CPR 10.3. Where the claim form is served within the jurisdiction the time limits on the defendant are:

14 days after service of the particulars of claim, if the claim form states particulars of claim are to follow (CPR 10.3(1)(a)); or

14 days after service of the claim form otherwise (CPR 10.3(1)(b)).

3.2.2   Defence

Where the claim form is served within the jurisdiction the time limits for filing the defence, under CPR 15.4, and for service on the defendant, as required by CPR 15.6, are:

- 14 days after service of the particulars of claim (CPR 15.4(1)(a)); or
- 28 days after service of the particulars of claim if the defendant files an acknowledgment of service under Part 10 (CPR 15.4(1)(b)).

CPR 15.5 expressly provides that the defendant and the claimant may agree the period of time for filing a defence shall be extended by up to 28 days.

3.2.3   Extension of time

An extension of time will often be sought by the defendant for the filing of a defence, occasionally the defendant may seek an extension of time for the acknowledgement of service.

3.2.3.1   *Extending time for the acknowledgement of service*

It will not be usual or necessary to grant an extension of time for the filing of an acknowledgement of service, as that is a straightforward matter which should not require additional time.

Moreover, because the acknowledgement of service should deal with any jurisdictional issues it is important to keep the defendant to relevant timescales imposed by the CPR for raising such issues (see **3.5**).

This approach is reflected by the absence, in Part 10, of any provision which provides expressly for an extension of time to acknowledge service (corresponding to the terms of CPR 15.5 where an extension of time for the defence is envisaged). However, as with any extension of time under CPR 2.11, it will be necessary for that agreement to be recorded in writing by the parties in one of the ways stipulated by the Court of Appeal in *Thomas v Home Office*[1] (see **2.2.3.1**).

---

[1]   [2006] EWCA Civ 1355.

3.2.3.2 *Extending time for the defence*

If requested it is usual to give a reasonable extension of time for the filing and service of the defence.

Indeed, CPR 15.5 anticipates that an extension of time for filing the defence may be appropriate and provides that the deadline may be extended by up to 28 days without the need for a court order. If a longer extension of time is required a court order, which may of course be made by consent, will be necessary.

It is usually courteous and constructive to give up to a 28 day extension of time for the defence readily, if requested to do so, as that will have little overall impact on the timescale of the claim. The defendant's solicitors may have to assimilate a large amount of information, in a relatively short timescale, if only instructed following service of proceedings. Consequently, it is better for the solicitors to have the opportunity of putting together a proper defence, in order to narrow the issues, and also desirable for the representatives to start their dealings with each other in an atmosphere of co-operation and mutual consideration.

An extension of time for the defence beyond 28 days will be less usual, though particular circumstances may make this appropriate.

It may be appropriate, occasionally, for the claimant to agree only an extension of time shorter than 28 days or even for a request extending time for filing the defence to be refused altogether. For example, it might be appropriate not to accede to a request for an extension of time, or at least anything more than a short extension, if the defendant's solicitors have been involved from an early stage and there has been non-compliance with any protocol or other unreasonable delay.

It may be reasonable, if agreeing the defendant's request, for the clamant to impose appropriate terms on an extension of time granted for the filing of a defence.

The claimant may, for example, wish to stipulate that if time is extended the defendant will not make a Part 36 offer within the extension of time, or that, if such an offer is made, the relevant period will not expire until 21 days from the expiry of the extension of time or the filing of the defence if sooner. That will guard against the claimant having to evaluate an offer without knowing the matters in issue.

If the claimant relies on a pre-action admission it would not be unreasonable to grant any extension of time on the basis the defendant, in the defence, abides by the admission.

Unlike the terms of CPR 2.11, which require an agreement in writing by the parties, an extension of time for the defence under the terms of CPR 15.5 only requires the claimant and defendant to 'agree', without this necessarily having to be in writing, although the defendant must notify the court in writing of the agreement to extend time for filing a defence.

3.3   DEFENDANT'S ADDRESS FOR SERVICE

CPR 10.5 requires the acknowledgement of service to be signed and to include an address for service. That address, in accordance with CPR 6.23, must be within the United Kingdom and must, unless the court orders otherwise, include a full postcode.

CPR 16.5(8) requires a defendant who has not filed an acknowledgement of service to give an address for service in the defence.

If the defendant's address for service subsequently changes notice must be given in writing to the court and every other party as soon as that change takes place, as required by CPR 6.24.

The address for service given by the defendant must be used for service of all further documents in the proceedings.

The defendant may confirm, in the acknowledgement of service or defence, willingness to accept service by document exchange, fax, email or other electronic method. Additionally, the defendant may be deemed willing to accept service by such means if the writing paper of the solicitor acting gives relevant details. For example service by:

- a document exchange box number (unless not willing to accept service by this means and this is indicated in writing);
- a fax number; or
- an email address (provided it is stated such address may be used for service).

In each case Practice Direction 6A allows for service of documents, which will be treated as having been sent to the address for service, by those means (see **2.10.2.3**).

Accordingly, as well as noting the defendant's address for service, it is important to be aware of the available methods of service. Those methods which allow for quick communication may be particularly useful when complying with the court timetable, particularly with the added emphasis on meeting time limits from April 2013, as well as when making, changing, withdrawing or accepting Part 36 offers.

3.4   DEFENDANT'S FUNDING

If the defendant wishes to claim an additional liability from the claimant, on the basis of a 'pre-commencement funding arrangement' (as defined by Part 48 from April 2013), the terms of paragraph 19 Costs Practice Direction and CPR 44.15 (as these read prior to April 2013) will need to be complied with.

A defendant, under the terms of paragraph 19.2(3), who has entered a funding arrangement before filing any documents must provide:

- information to the court, by filing notice of funding with the defendant's first document whether this be an acknowledgement of service, defence or any other document (such as an application to set aside default judgment); and
- information to every other party:

- if serving the first document direct by serving a notice of funding with that document; or

- if the court is to serve the first document by providing a copy notice of funding for service with that document.

Subsequently, in the event of any change in funding arrangement, paragraph 19.3 Costs Practice Direction and CPR 44.15 require further notice of funding to be served within seven days. Additionally, that notice may need to be accompanied by a new costs estimate for the purposes of CPR 44.15(3).

The information on funding to be provided is that identified in paragraph 19.4 Costs Practice Direction, corresponding with the information the claimant is required to give on any relevant funding arrangement (see **1.5.2.4.1**).

Whilst this provision may not require details to be given of an enhanced hourly rate payable in certain circumstances (a no 'win – reduced fee' agreement), it does require notice of any intention to seek from the claimant a success fee on base costs or any other additional liabilities, on the basis of such an agreement or otherwise.

If the defendant does not comply with terms of the Costs Practice Direction and CPR 44.15 an application for relief from sanctions will need to be made or the defendant will not be able to recover additional liabilities.

The defendant must, in accordance with the Civil Legal Aid Regulations, serve notice of issue if granted legal aid.

Otherwise, as for the claimant, there is no obligation on the defendant to give details of arrangements made for funding.

3.5 JURISDICTION

The defendant must act swiftly in dealing with the acknowledgement of service if default judgment is to be avoided.

3.5.1 Action required

The defendant must, however, to take care when completing the acknowledgement of service if there may be issues about the jurisdiction of the court. That is because Part 11 provides that if the defendant wishes to dispute the court's jurisdiction:

- the defendant must first file an acknowledgement of service, in accordance with Part 10 (which will not, under CPR 11(4), result in the defendant thereby losing any right there may be to dispute jurisdiction); and

- the defendant must, within 14 days after filing the acknowledgement of service, make an application, make an application, in accordance with Part 23 under CPR 11(4), which is supported by evidence.

If these steps are not taken the defendant will be treated as having accepted the court has jurisdiction to try the claim.

3.5.2   Meaning of 'jurisdiction'

In *Hoddinott v Persimmon Homes (Wessex) Ltd*[2] the Court of Appeal confirmed the term 'jurisdiction' in Part 11 meant not just territorial jurisdiction but also jurisdiction in the sense of the court's power or authority to try a claim.

Accordingly, the reference to 'jurisdiction' in Part 11 was shorthand for both types of jurisdiction.

Service of a claim form out of time did not, of itself, deprive the court of jurisdiction, being no more than a breach of a rule. However, that breach provided the basis for the defendant to argue the court should not exercise jurisdiction to try the claim.

3.5.3   Default

In *Uphill v BRB (Residuary) Ltd*[3] the claimant obtained an extension of time for service of the claim form under CPR 7.5(2). Within the extended time the claim form was sent to the defendant's loss adjustors, which was not the defendant's address for service.

Nevertheless, the defendant's solicitors returned the acknowledgement of service but, while indicating the defendant intended to contest the whole of the claim, did not tick the box indicating the defendant intended to contest jurisdiction.

No application was made by the defendant under CPR 11(4) although there were grounds for challenging the orders, made at first instance, extending time for service and dispensing with service.

The Court of Appeal held that the defendant had waived the right to challenge the validity of service of the claim form by failing to take the steps required under Part 11 and therefore could no longer contend service was invalid.

In *Hoddinott v Persimmon Homes (Wessex) Ltd*[4] the claimant, within the four months allowed for service, made an application under CPR 7.6(2) to extend time. An order, without notice to the defendant, was made extending time. A copy of the claim form was then sent to the defendant 'for information purposes only', following which the defendant issued an application to set aside the order extending time. Subsequently, the claim form was served on the defendant after which the defendant filed an acknowledgement of service indicating an intention to defend all of the claim, but without ticking the box 'I intend to contest jurisdiction'.

At first instance the order extending time for service was set aside but the Court of Appeal allowed the claimant's appeal.

The court confirmed that where the defendant wished to argue the court should not exercise jurisdiction the wording of Part 11 was clear, requiring:

* the defendant to file an acknowledgement of service; and

---

2   [2007] EWCA Civ 1203.
3   [2005] EWCA Civ 60.
4   [2007] EWCA Civ 1203.

- within 14 days after filing the acknowledgement of service to make an application disputing jurisdiction.

Without having taken those steps the Court of Appeal held that the defendant would be treated as accepting the court should exercise jurisdiction to try the claim, notwithstanding late service of the claim form.

These decisions did not determine, as the issue did not arise, whether an extension of time might have been sought to challenge jurisdiction under the general case management powers of the court. Consequently, it might be argued Part 11, like for example CPR 7.5(3), is a self-contained code that excludes the general power to extend time. In any event, because the failure to comply with terms of CPR 11(4) effectively carries a sanction it seems likely the court would need to apply the terms of CPR 3.9 to any such request (and would only give relief if one of the factors identified in *Denton v T H White Ltd*[5] applied).

3.6 CONTENT OF THE DEFENCE

CPR 16.5 and paragraph 12 of the Practice Direction to Part 16 set out the requirements of a defence to a personal injury claim. The content of the defence should, therefore, deal with those requirements if it is to comply with the rules.

If these rules are complied with the defence should help to narrow the issues which, in turn, will ensure the evidence is limited to the real issues and that costs are saved.

With the greater emphasis, from April 2013, on compliance with the rules, and indeed the need to focus on the real issues so that costs are proportionate, the courts might be expected to take a tougher approach to defences that do not contain all relevant information or otherwise fail to comply with the requirements of Part 16 and the accompanying Practice Direction.

3.6.1 General requirements

CPR 16.5 sets out the general requirements of a defence when dealing with allegations made in the particulars of claim.

- The defendant must state which of the allegations in the particulars of claim are denied and where the defendant denies an allegation:
  - the reasons must be stated; and
  - any different version of events from that given by the claimant must be stated.
- The defendant must state which allegations he is unable to admit or deny but which the claimant is required to prove.
- The defendant must state which allegations are admitted.

CPR 16.5(5) expressly provides that a defendant who fails to deal with an allegation, except where the defence sets out the nature of the defendant's case in relation to the issue to which the allegation is relevant, shall be taken to admit that allegation.

---

5   [2014] EWCA Civ 906.

It is important to note that the ability of the defendant to require the claimant to prove an allegation is qualified by the requirement that this is an allegation which the defendant is unable to admit or deny. Whilst there may be matters which are within the knowledge of the claimant, but not the defendant, there will also be many matters about which the defendant does have sufficient knowledge either to deny (with appropriate reasons) or to admit. Accordingly, the defendant should be pressed either to deny allegations, and give reasons, or, whenever that is possible, give an admission.

It might be argued that failing to deal with an allegation means a failure to deal with that allegation in accordance with the requirements of the rules, including the requirement to give reasons for a denial and any different version of events. Failure to deal with an allegation will, of course, mean that the defendant is deemed to admit that allegation under the terms of CPR 16.5(5).

The general requirements set out in CPR 16.5 mean that a defence in a personal injury claim will need to deal specifically with any elements of that claim which are in issue whether that be breach of duty, causation, contributory negligence or quantum. There are also specific rules, applicable to personal injury claims, setting out how the defence must deal with the medical report accompany the particulars of claim and schedule of expenses and losses incorporated in, or sent with, the particulars of claim.

In addition to the requirements of the CPR the general law may require the defendant to positively plead matters where, without that, the claimant's assertions, if proved, will be enough to establish liability.

3.6.2   Dealing with breach of duty

Those general requirements of CPR 16.5 mean that if the defence denies breach of duty the defendant must give reasons for that denial as well as any different version of events relied on.

If the defendant admits breach of duty it will not, usually, be essential to know which particular allegations are admitted. If, however, contributory negligence is alleged it may be important to establish which of the allegations are admitted as the nature of the breach of duty may have a bearing on factors relevant to assessing whether there is any contributory negligence and, if so, the appropriate apportionment. Those factors are causative potency and blameworthiness.

On the question of causative potency there may be breaches of duty which do not exclude a causative contribution to the injuries from the claimant's own conduct. Other breaches of duty relied on by the claimant, but not expressly admitted, may have resulted in the injuries being suffered irrespective of any conduct on the part of the claimant. If so, it is important to clarify which breaches of duty are admitted as that will be very relevant to the causative potency of any conduct on the part of the claimant and without such causation there can be no contributory negligence.

So far as blameworthiness is concerned the courts, particularly when dealing with employers' liability, may be more ready to apportion blame to the claimant when dealing with breach of a common law duty than a statutory duty, the very purpose of which is to guard against the events which occurred: *Mullard v Ben Line Ltd.*[6] Accordingly, knowing which allegations are admitted may be relevant to the question of blameworthiness.

The terms of CPR 16.5 are also significant if the defendant denies liability because another party, whether already joined in the proceedings as a defendant or not, is blamed. That will be a reason for the denial, hence if this underpins the terms of the defence the defendant should state as much. Ultimately, this may be important so far as costs are concerned should the claimant succeed against one, but not all, defendants (whether joined in the proceedings at the outset or brought in as a result of the defence).

3.6.3   Dealing with causation

Causation, of at least some damage resulting from breach of duty, is an integral part of liability for claims based in negligence and related breaches of statutory duty.

Accordingly, care should be taken to ensure that where the defendant purports to admit liability the defence does not only admit breach of duty but also that this has caused at least some damage (see **1.7.2.3**).

The obligation under the CPR to give reasons for any denial is important when causation is denied to establish whether the defendant asserts any positive case, other than the alleged or admitted breach of duty, for the injuries complained of.

There are some circumstances in which the defendant may, in reality, have reasons for denying causation that should, therefore, be given in the defence.

Particular issues can arise in 'low velocity impact' claims and sometimes because the defence, deliberately or otherwise, is somewhat opaque on the issue of causation.

3.6.3.1   *Low velocity impact claims*

The issue in so-called low velocity impact cases is whether, when the breach of duty has resulted in a low velocity impact, the claimant can establish that this breach of duty caused injury.

Reflecting the terms of CPR 16.5 the content required of the defence is likely to depend upon whether the defendant's case is limited to putting the claimant to proof or, in reality, goes beyond that with the defendant seeking to advance, in the evidence subsequently exchanged or arguments made at trial, some positive reason in support of the denial.

In *Lawrenson v Lawrenson*[7] the defence, to a personal injury claim arising out of a road traffic accident, neither admitted nor denied the claim. The claim was dismissed by the district judge but allowed on appeal. Although the appeal was not determined on this point the judge held that a defendant could not seek to defeat a claim on the basis it was

---

[6]   [1971] 1 WLR 1414.
[7]   27 July 2005 Liverpool County Court.

fraudulent without pleading that allegation, and that a defence which merely required the case to be proved was not a plea of fraud or dishonesty. More generally the judge observed:

> 'To the extent that it is the usual practice to plead a non-admission fully intending to deny key allegations in the particulars of claim based on a weaponry of questions arising from documents, that practice should cease. Not to comply with 16.5(1)(a) and 16.5(2) may well lead to "common justice" being disregarded. It is inappropriate for a Defendant to say that, based on a non-admission defence, the Claimant must be prepared for any eventuality including cross examination based on what are in fact un-pleaded and un-particularised denials.'

However, in *Kearsley v Klarfeld*[8] the Court of Appeal, again in a case arising out of a low velocity road traffic accident, observed that the decision in *Cooper v P&O Stena Line Ltd*[9] did not mean it had to be an essential part of the defence in such a case, which therefore had to be dealt with by a substantive allegation that there was fraud or fabrication on the part of the claimant.

The court noted that in *Cooper* the defendant's expert alleged the claimant was fabricating his symptoms, so this had been part of the defendant's case.

In *Kearsley*, by contrast, the defendant's expert asserted only that the claimant could not have suffered the injuries described if the accident occurred, as other evidence suggested it did, at such a low speed. It was the amended defence, following this expert evidence, which went further and alleged fraud.

The Court of Appeal held that where the defendant simply denied causation and invited the judge to draw the inference the claimant had not suffered the injuries alleged there was no burden to plead and prove fraud. If, however, the denial was based on a positive assertion, for example as a result of expert evidence obtained, that the claimant was malingering then the defendant needed to deal with this in the defence so as to comply with the requirements of Part 16. This is because that reflects the need to give reasons for any denial and because, in any event, that would be a positive case that the defendant wished to assert (exactly in the way the defence in *Lawrenson* was developed at trial).

Consequently, if the defendant has raised issues pre-action to suggest the claim arises from a 'low velocity impact' that will need to be made clear in the defence, but it is not necessarily part of the defence in such a case the claimant is acting fraudulently. If, however, fraud is not pleaded the defendant should be prevented from adducing evidence, cross-examining the claimant or otherwise developing an argument that, in the broad sense of alleging dishonesty, inevitably involves allegations of fraud by the claimant.

Where fraud is an integral part of the defence, whether or not issues of low velocity impact arise, then that is a matter the defendant will need to assert (see **3.6.7.5**).

---

8   [2005] Civ 1510.
9   [1999] 1 Lloyd's Rep 734.

The requirement in the PI Protocol for the defendant to give reasons for any denial of liability means that, as the Court of Appeal made clear in *Casey v Cartwright*,[10] if the claim is to raise an issue relating to low velocity impact then this issue on causation should be raised during the protocol period (see **1.7.3**).

If the defendant does not follow this guidance that may be regarded as non-compliance with the PI Protocol and, particularly given the importance of compliance with the protocol from April 2013, might not be allowed by the court to develop any such argument at the stage of the defence.

3.6.3.2 *Other claims*

It may be that defendants fail to appreciate how causation, of at least some injury, is part of the issue of liability in a claim based on negligence or related breach of statutory duty. Perhaps the defendant may appreciate that only too well and try to craft a defence that appears to make an admission but without actually conceding causation.

Consequently, the claimant should be wary of a defence that is sufficiently opaque to potentially leave open the opportunity for the defendant to later assert causation, of at least some injury, and hence that liability has never been admitted. For example, it is not unknown to see a defence that admits liability only in respect of such injury, loss or damage the claimant may prove was sustained as a result of the breach.

The distinction between admission of causation, and hence liability, and denial of this issue may be crucial. With an admission of liability, including causation of at least some injury, the claimant may seek judgment for damages to be assessed and, moreover, will then have won the case, which will allow recovery of costs subject, of course, to the defendant having not made any adequate formal offer to settle.

3.6.4 Dealing with law

The particulars of claim may need to deal with matters of law. If so the defence should, to comply with Part 16, identify what is admitted and what is denied, giving reasons and any alternative case that will mean setting out the defendant's case on the law.

Whilst, in many cases, legal argument will be a matter that is dealt with at trial there are cases where the law will determine what evidence will be required, for example if there are any issues of foreign law.

The court may take the view that the default position is that a pleading assumes the law of England and Wales is to apply. Hence in *Naraji v Shelbourne*[11] Popplewell J held:

> 'It is also contended on behalf of Dr Shelbourne that there is no pleading of a relevant contractual obligation under Indiana law. This is a false point. What is pleaded is a contractual claim, and if a defendant does not assert that it is governed by a foreign system of law which is in a material respect different from English law, the Court assumes that the foreign law is the same as English law.'

---

10 [2006] EWCA Civ 1280.
11 [2011] EWHC 3298 (QB).

3.6.5　Dealing with quantum

The general requirements of CPR 16.5 apply as much to the claimant's pleaded case on quantum as they do to the case on liability.

The defence should, accordingly, give reasons for any denial of matters set out in the particulars of claim relating to quantum as well as, where appropriate, any different version of events asserted by the defendant.

Furthermore, there are important provisions in the Practice Direction to Part 16, which the defence should comply with, that deal with quantum, specifically how the defence should deal with both the medical report that ought to accompany the particulars of claim and the schedule of expenses and losses contained in, or accompanying, the particulars of claim.

3.6.5.1　Medical report

Paragraph 12.1 of the Practice Direction to Part 16 deals specifically with the defence to a claim for personal injuries where the claimant has attached a medical report to the particulars of claim.

In such circumstances, the defendant should state in the defence whether matters contained in the medical evidence are:

- agreed;
- disputed; or
- neither agreed nor disputed but the defendant has no knowledge of such matters.

Reasons for any disputed matters in the medical evidence must be given and the defendant must attach to the defence any medical evidence to be relied on.

Consequently, if the defendant has obtained medical evidence, for example if the claimant has given facilities pre-issue following an admission of liability, available reports should be disclosed with the defence. However, given the terms of the overriding objective, it would seem reasonable to expect that the defendant only disclose evidence corresponding to the evidence disclosed by the claimant accompanying the particulars of claim.

The opportunity for the defendant to state that matters in the medical evidence are neither agreed nor disputed is, as under CPR 16.5, limited to matters of which the defendant has no knowledge. There may be factual matters in the medical evidence of which the defendant does not have knowledge but, so far as matters of opinion are concerned, the defendant ought to indicate whether that opinion is agreed or disputed and, if disputed, give reasons. In more complex cases the defendant may need to rely on medical evidence before indicating whether the claimant's evidence is agreed, but in other cases should be able to identify any matters of dispute in the defence.

Indeed, whether there are any matters of dispute may be a relevant consideration for the court in assessing whether further expert evidence is reasonably required from another expert in the same field at the stage of case management.

3.6.5.2 Schedules

Paragraph 12.2 of the Practice Direction to Part 16 deals specifically with the defence to a claim for personal injuries where the claimant has provided a schedule of expenses and losses.

The defendant should include in the defence, or attach to it a counter schedule, stating:

- items that are agreed;
- items that are disputed;
- items that are neither agreed nor disputed, but the defendant has no knowledge of such matters.

Where any items in the claimant's schedule are disputed the defendant should supply alternative figures, where appropriate.

Only where the defendant has no knowledge of matters should items in the claimant's schedule be neither agreed nor disputed. The defendant will, very often, have sufficient knowledge to either agree or dispute items. For example, where the defendant is the claimant's employer appropriate information should be available to either agree or dispute the calculation of wage loss.

If the claimant is able to do no more than indicate the general nature of the claim for expenses and losses a counter schedule may not be viable at this stage or only be in very general terms.

Where, however, the claimant provides a detailed schedule, even if only for past expenses and losses, the CPR requires the defendant to provide a proper and detailed response at the time of the defence. That requirement is often overlooked but compliance may be important for assessing any Part 36 offer made by the defendant, in helping to identify the scope of the evidence required to deal with individual items of expense and loss and hence, where costs budgeting applies, the costs which will need to be incurred dealing with the issues.

A proper counter schedule, served at the appropriate stage, can help narrow the issues and hence limit the evidence necessary, which in turn will save costs. This is key area where, from April 2013, the courts should be ensuring compliance with rules by the defendant. The problems that can occur, including costs that could otherwise have been avoided, where this does not happen are illustrated, for example, in *Tutas v East London Bus & Coach Company*[12] where service of a counter schedule on the eve of trial raised an issue which ultimately had to be resolved by the Court of Appeal.

3.6.6 Dealing with the statement of value

CPR 16.5 also requires any defendant who disputes the claimant's statement of value to state why it is disputed and, if able to do so, give the defendant's statement of the value of the claim.

---

[12]   [2013] EWCA Civ 1380.

This is likely to be relevant if there is going to be an issue as to the appropriate track for allocation of the claim.

3.6.7 Pleading a positive case

The CPR, and the general law, require the defendant to plead, in appropriate circumstances, a positive case in the defence. This requirement reflects the general obligation, found in the CPR, for the defence to give any version of events asserted by the defendant which are different from those detailed in the particulars of claim by the claimant.

3.6.7.1 Bare denials

The particulars of claim may allege a failure by the defendant to take a positive step. If the defence does no more than make a bare denial of such an allegation that implies, but without giving necessary detail, an appropriate step was taken by the defendant. In these circumstances the defence ought to make positive allegations and a request for further information may be appropriate if no adequate detail is given of what must amount to an assertion that the defendant relies on a different version of events from that given by the claimant.

3.6.7.2 Res ipsa loquitur

If the claimant can properly rely on *res ipsa loquitur* the evidential burden of proof shifts to the defendant and, accordingly, the defence ought to give appropriate positive information to show the basis on which the defendant contends that burden can be discharged.

3.6.7.3 Statutory defences

Where the claimant relies on an alleged breach of statutory duty and that duty contains a statutory defence the defendant must assert that defence if it is to be relied upon. Examples of statutory defences that must be pleaded are:

- a defence of reasonable practicability; *Nimmo v Alexander Cowan & Sons Ltd*;[13] *Baker v Quantum Clothing Group*;[14]
- the defence provided by s 58 of the Highways Act 1980.

The correct forensic approach to defences of this kind has been considered, at the highest level, in a number of cases including *Griffiths v Liverpool Corporation*,[15] *Nimmo v Alexander Cowan & Sons Ltd*[16] and *Baker v Quantum Clothing Group*.[17]

After reviewing relevant case-law the Court of Appeal considered what that meant for the defence served in *Bowes v Sedgefield District Council*[18] where Sir John Arnold P held:

---

[13]   [1967] 3 WLR 1169.
[14]   [2009] EWCA Civ 566.
[15]   [1967] 1 QB 374.
[16]   [1967] 3 WLR 1169.
[17]   [2009] EWCA Civ 566.
[18]   [1981] ICR 234.

'In my judgment the upshot of those authorities is that it is for defendants who wish to confess and avoid, by saying that, in relation to such a provision as is exemplified by section 29 of the Act of 1961 or regulation 6 of the Regulations of 1966, they have failed to provide a safe access or place but it was not reasonably practicable to do so, to aver as a matter of pleading that lack of reasonable practicability. The defendants in this case failed to do so and that was not a mere pleading defect. It was a matter of pleading which had a practical result at the trial in that no evidence was specifically or intentionally called to deal with the question of whether that pleadable point had or had not been made good.'

3.6.7.4   Convictions

If the defendant wishes to deny a conviction, or the relevance of that conviction, relied on in the particulars of claim it will be necessary for that to be asserted, with appropriate reasons, in the defence, given the terms of s 11 of the Civil Evidence Act 1968.

3.6.7.5   Fraud

Fraud has always been regarded as a serious allegation by the courts. That is because, even in civil claims, a finding of fraud is likely to have consequences above and beyond the proceedings in which that finding is made.

Fraud is not, for these purposes, confined to alleging the tort of deceit but includes any allegation which involves an assertion of dishonesty. Accordingly, allegations of malingering, and other forms of deliberate exaggeration, are allegations of fraud which should be properly pleaded. In *Belmont Finance Corporation Ltd v Williams Furniture Ltd*[19] Buckley LJ held:

'An allegation of dishonesty must be pleaded clearly and with particularity. That is laid down by the rules and it is a well-recognised rule of practice. This does not import that the word 'fraud' or the word 'dishonesty' must be necessarily used. The facts alleged may sufficiently demonstrate that dishonesty is allegedly involved, but where the facts are complicated this may not be so clear, and in such a case it is incumbent upon the pleader to make it clear when dishonesty is alleged. If he uses language which is equivocal, rendering it doubtful whether he is in fact relying on the alleged dishonesty of the transaction, this will be fatal; the allegation of its dishonest nature will not have been pleaded with sufficient clarity.'

In *Cooper v P&O Stena Line Ltd*[20] it was held to be unsatisfactory that an allegation as serious as fraud should not be specifically pleaded.

This approach was also adopted in *Haringey London Borough Council v Hines*[21] where the Court of Appeal confirmed that:

'It is a basic principle of fairness that if a party is being accused of fraud, and is then called as a witness, the particular fraud alleged should be put specifically to that party so that he/she may answer it.'

Consequently, it was held that before a finding of dishonesty can be made such allegation must be pleaded and put in cross-examination.

---

[19]   [1980] 1 All ER 393.
[20]   [1999] 1 Lloyd's Rep 734.
[21]   [2010] EWCA Civ 1111.

However, great care must be exercised before pleading an allegation which amounts to fraud. A pleading containing an allegation of fraud should not be drafted unless clear instructions are given to make such an allegation and there is reasonably credible material which, as it stands, establishes the prima facie case of fraud: *Medcalf v Weatherill*.[22]

This approach is reflected in the Conduct Rules in the Bar Standard Board's handbook which provides a barrister must not:

> '... draft any statement of case, witness statement, affidavits or other document containing ... any allegation of fraud, unless (the barrister has) clear instructions to allege fraud and ... reasonably credible material which establishes an arguable case of fraud.'

This may explain why defences sometimes contain what might be regarded as insinuations about the integrity or honesty of the claimant, which the defendant may hope will allow a case based on fraud to be developed at trial. This tactic ought not to be entertained by the courts for the reasons given by Davis LJ in *Hussain v Amin*[23] where he observed:

> 'I would, however, particularly wish to add my own comments about the pleaded defence of the second defendant. It was perfectly proper to join issue on the primary facts alleged in the particulars of claim and as to whether there had indeed been negligence and whether the claimed losses had been caused thereby. But the pleaded defence went much further in paragraphs 7 and 9, setting out a number of matters which, it was alleged, raised "significant concerns" as to whether or not this had been a staged accident requiring further investigation. Possibly, although I have my reservations, such a pleading could be justified as an initial holding defence. But it is a case pleaded on insinuation, not allegation. If the second defendant considered that it had sufficient material to justify a plea that the claim was based on a collision which was a sham or a fraud, it behoved it properly and in ample time before trial so to plead in clear and unequivocal terms and with proper particulars. Thereafter the burden of proof would of course have been on the second defendant to establish such a defence.'

If fraud is not alleged in the defence but the allegation inferred in other ways, for example by factual or expert evidence, the defendant will need to decide whether to amend the defence. Unless an allegation of fraud is clearly made in the defence it may be argued that evidence inferring fraud does not relate to the issues between the parties, as defined by the statements of case, and that such evidence should not be admitted. While the court cannot require a party to amend a statement of case, the court does have the power to restrict evidence outside the scope of the pleadings: *Upton McGougan Ltd v Bellway Homes Ltd*.[24]

Furthermore, without a clear allegation of fraud, the defendant should not be allowed, unless given permission to amend the defence, to develop an argument based on fraud at trial: *Hussain v Sarkar*.[25] Consequently, if the defendant wishes to allege 'fundamental dishonesty' on the part of the claimant it would seem that this should be pleaded, relevant evidence disclosed and that case put to the claimant in cross-examination.

---

[22]   [2002] UKHL 27.
[23]   [2012] EWCA Civ 1456.
[24]   [2009] EWHC 1449 (TCC).
[25]   [2010] EWCA Civ 301.

Although, in civil proceedings, the standard of proof required to establish fraud, like any other issue, is a balance of probabilities the court will generally regard fraud as improbable for the reasons given by Lord Nicholls explained in *Re H (minors)*[26] when he said:

'The balance of probability standard means that a court is satisfied an event occurred if the court considers that, on the evidence, the occurrence of the event was more likely than not. When assessing the probabilities the court will have in mind as a factor, to whatever extent is appropriate in the particular case, that the more serious the allegation the less likely it is that the event occurred and, hence, the stronger should be the evidence before the court concludes that the allegation is established on the balance of probability. Fraud is usually less likely than negligence.'

Lord Nicholls continued:

'Although the result is much the same, this does not mean that where a serious allegation is in issue the standard of proof required is higher. It means only that the inherent probability or improbability of an event is itself a matter to be taken into account when weighing the probabilities and deciding whether, on balance, the event occurred. The more improbable the event, the stronger must be the evidence that it did occur before, on the balance of probability, its occurrence will be established. Ungoed-Thomas J expressed this neatly in *In re Dellow's Will Trusts* [1964] 1 WLR 451, 455: "The more serious the allegation the more cogent is the evidence required to overcome the unlikelihood of what is alleged and thus to prove it."

This substantially accords with the approach adopted in authorities such as the well known judgment of Morris LJ in *Hornal v Neuberger Products Ltd* [1957] 1 Q.B. 247, 266. This approach also provides a means by which the balance of probability standard can accommodate one's instinctive feeling that even in civil proceedings a court should be more sure before finding serious allegations proved than when deciding less serious or trivial matters.'

The need for cogent evidence, to conclude that fraud is established, was emphasised in *Hussain v Hussain*,[27] when the Court of Appeal allowed an appeal against a finding of fraud despite recognising the advantages a trial judge has over an appellate court in making factual findings and drawing conclusions from those facts.

If an allegation of fraud is made but not substantiated the court may be willing to order the defendant to pay the claimant's costs on the indemnity basis, under Part 44, given the nature of such allegations, the need for these to be properly contested and to ensure the claimant is reimbursed for the inevitable additional costs incurred: *National Westminster Bank plc v Kotonou*;[28] *Liptrot v Charte*;[29] *Clarke v Malby*;[30] *Zurich Insurance Company plc v Hayward*.[31]

---

[26] [1996] AC 563.
[27] [2012] EWCA Civ 1367.
[28] [2006] EWHC 1785 (Ch).
[29] (Unreported) Manchester County Court.
[30] [2010] EWHC 1856 (QB).
[31] [2011] EWCA Civ 641.

3.6.7.6   Contributory negligence

It is for the defendant to establish contributory negligence on the part of the claimant. Accordingly, if the defendant wishes to make such allegations these must be set out in the defence: *Fookes v Slaytor*.[32]

3.6.7.7   Limitation

Paragraph 13 of the Practice Direction to Part 16 requires the defendant to give details of the expiry of any relevant limitation period relied on.

3.6.7.8   Mitigation

The defendant may wish to argue the claimant has failed to mitigate loss.

In *Geest plc v Lansiquot*[33] the need for the defendant to give adequate notice of a case based on the claimant's failure to mitigate was stressed. Lord Bingham held that:

> '... it would have been the clear duty of the (Defendant) to plead in its defence that the Plaintiff had failed to mitigate her damage and to give appropriate particulars sufficient to alert the Plaintiff to the nature of the (Defendant's) case, enable the Plantiff to direct her evidence to the real areas of dispute and avoid surprise.'

Accordingly, the defence should deal properly with any allegation of failure to mitigate loss.

3.6.8   Statement of truth

The defence, being a statement of case, must, in accordance with CPR 22.1(1), be verified by a statement of truth.

Paragraph 2.1 of the practice direction to Part 22 sets out the form of the statement of truth, verifying a statement of case:

> '[I believe] [the (*claimant or as may be*) believes] that the facts stated in the [name documents being verified] are true.'

Paragraph 3 of the Practice Direction to Part 22 confirms who may sign that statement of truth.

Paragraph 4 of the Practice Direction to Part 22 confirms a statement of case not verified by a statement of truth will remain effective, but a party may not rely on the contents as evidence and application to the court may be made for an order that unless within such period as a court may specify the statement of case is verified by the service of a statement of truth then that statement of case will be struck out.

---

[32]   [1978] 1 WLR 1293.
[33]   [2002] UKPC 48, [2002] 1 WLR 3111.

3.6.9   Protocols

Any personal injury claim reaching the stage of the defence being filed will have been through at least one, and possibly more than one, of the protocols.

Each of the protocols requires the defendant to give a decision on liability and, where this is not admitted, reasons.

To comply with the Practice Direction – Pre-Action Conduct the particulars of claim may have dealt with compliance, or otherwise, with the terms of that Practice Directions, and the defence should deal with this in any event.

Non-compliance with the Practice Direction – Pre-Action Conduct is, from April 2013, a potentially significant matter for the court. That is because CPR 1.1(2) now explains that dealing with a case justly, and at proportionate cost, includes enforcing compliance with rules, Practice Directions and orders. Where, in accordance with the Practice Direction – Pre-Action Conduct, the issue of compliance is raised in the pleadings the defence may admit non-compliance, or fail to deal with any relevant contention in the particulars of claim so that this amounts to an admission of non-compliance.

As well as the need to comply with Practice Directions each of the protocols describes what ought to be regarded as reasonable pre-action conduct.

Paragraph 1.5 of the PI Protocol expressly recognises the court may consider compliance after court proceedings have begun and the need for the effect of non-compliance to be considered when deciding whether to impose sanctions. This provision is expressly endorsed by the terms of a Practice Direction, namely paragraph 5 of the Practice Direction – Pre-Action Conduct.

Following the Court of Appeal judgments in *Mitchell v News Group Newspapers Ltd*[34] and *Denton v TH White*[35] the courts may more readily impose sanctions for non-compliance with protocols, which ought to include defences raising new matters that go beyond, or seek to resile from, the stance taken by the defendant under the relevant protocol.

3.6.9.1   New matters

A defendant may never have dealt with liability prior to issue of court proceedings. That, in itself, will usually be a breach of the relevant protocol, and sometimes more than one protocol.

The defendant may have denied liability but failed to give any, or any adequate, reasons, which only become clearer when the defence is available. For example, there may be no admission of liability, or even a denial, but only in the defence is an issue of 'low velocity impact' raised.

The court will need to decide whether, having regard to the terms of the relevant protocol, the Practice Direction – Pre-Action Conduct and the CPR this warrants a

---

[34]   [2013] EWCA Civ 1537.
[35]   [2014] EWCA Civ 906.

sanction. If so an appropriate sanction might be to order that matters not previously raised cannot be advanced by striking out the whole or part of the defence.

3.6.9.2   *Resiling from admissions*

The defence may even seek to resile from admissions made under a protocol.

Specific provision is made in the CPR for withdrawal of admissions, and where that is a 'pre-action admission' the terms of CPR 14.1A will apply. Following amendment to the overriding objective in April 2013 the courts may be more reluctant to allow admissions, and that should include pre-action admission, to be withdrawn (see **1.7.2.4**).

3.7   FURTHER INFORMATION

Part 18 of the CPR deals with the provision of further information relating to a party's case.

3.7.1   Pre-CPR

Part 18 replaced rules, under the previous system, which provided for further and better particulars and for interrogatories.

Before the introduction of the CPR an extensive request for further and better particulars frequently accompanied the defence. Tactically, such a request was often concerned more with putting pressure on the claimant than establishing the nature of the claim.

3.7.2   CPR

Further information, under the CPR, is not intended to correlate with the former rules relating to further and better particulars, which would usually be dealt with at the stage the parties exchanged statements of case.

It may now be more appropriate for any further information to be requested at a later stage, following exchange of documents and factual evidence. In this sense a request under Part 18 has more in common with the former practice of interrogatories than further and better particulars.

It is, however, still not uncommon, even though this may be unnecessary, to find the defence is accompanied by a request for further information. There may sometimes be a vestige of the old tactical considerations when a request is made at this stage.

A request might be regarded as tactical, rather than necessary, when it is not required for the party making that request to prepare the case, or understand the case that has to be met, for the purposes of disclosure, factual evidence and expert evidence.

Part 18, and the accompanying Practice Direction, deals with further information under the CPR.

- The court may, at any time, order a party to:
  - – clarify any matter which is in dispute in the proceedings; or
  - – give additional information in relation to any such matter.

- However, by paragraph 1.1 of the Practice Direction to Part 18, a party seeking clarification or information should, before making application to the court for an order, first serve on the party from whom that is sought a written request stating a date by which the response should be served and allow a reasonable time for a response.

- Paragraph 1.2 of the Practice Direction requires the request to be concise and strictly confined to matters which are reasonably necessary and proportionate to enable the party making the request to prepare that party's case and understand the case that has to be met.

- Paragraph 4 of the Practice Direction provides that the party receiving the request is required to inform the party making the request promptly, and in any event within the time stated for a response to be given, if he objects to the request or cannot respond to it within the time stated.

- Where the court makes an order that a party clarify any matter or give additional information, that party must file the response and serve it on other parties.

In accordance with CPR 22.1(1)(b) a response, providing further information, must be verified by a statement of truth.

3.7.3 The court's approach to further information under the CPR

In *McPhilemy v Times Newspapers Ltd*[36] Lord Woolf MR took the opportunity to make general observations about statements of case under the CPR stating:

> 'The need for extensive pleadings including Particulars should be reduced by the requirement that witness statements are now exchanged. In the majority of proceedings identification of the documents upon which a party relies, together with copies of that party's witness statements, will make the detail of the nature of the case the other side has to meet obvious. This reduces the need for Particulars in order to avoid being taken by surprise.'

> 'This does not mean that pleadings are now superfluous. Pleadings are still required to mark out the parameters of the case that is being advanced by each party. In particular they are still critical to identify the issues and the extent of the dispute between the parties.'

> '... excessive particulars can achieve directly the opposite result from that which is intended. They can obscure the issues rather than providing clarification. In addition, after disclosure and the exchange of witness statements pleadings frequently become of only historic interest.'

In *Loveridge v Healey*[37] Lord Phillips MR endorsed the observation of Lord Woolf in *McPhilemy* but added:

> 'It is on the basis of the pleadings that the parties decide what evidence they will need to place before the Court and what preparations are necessary before the trial.'

---

[36] [1999] 3 All ER 775, CA.
[37] [2004] EWCA Civ 173, [2004] All ER (D) 359 (Feb), CA.

Similarly, in *King v Telegraph Group Ltd*[38] Brooke LJ observed that the emphasis, under Part 18, is on what is necessary and proportionate and the avoidance of disproportionate expense. The focus on proportionality is, perhaps, all the more significant from April 2013 following the amendment to Part 1.

Some of the problems caused by extensive requests for further information, and the need to keep in mind the overriding objective, were considered in *Lexi Holdings (In Administration) v Pannone & Partners*.[39] The defendant served a request for further information running to 31 questions. The defendant contended this information was required to complete work on witness statements and fully understand certain aspects of the case which had to be met. The defendant did not, however, suggest the information was needed to plead a full defence or understand the ambit of obligations on disclosure.

The claimant contended the request was not reasonable, necessary or proportionate, objecting to the provision of any of the information requested, even though the costs of dealing with the consequent hearing well exceeded the costs that would have been incurred providing the information. No attempt was made by the parties to compromise or significantly narrow the procedural dispute that arose from the request.

The judge reflected first on the significance of the overriding objective:

> 'It ought not to be necessary, more than ten years after the introduction of the overriding objective and the CPR, to have to say that such an approach to the resolution of interim procedural disputes is wholly unacceptable. The litigation of issues of bad faith and dishonesty may of course generate intense feelings of bitterness on both sides, and a determination to leave no stone unturned, regardless of cost, and all the more so in high value cases such as this one. Nonetheless the parties and their legal teams are obliged by CPR 1.3 to help the court to further the overriding objective. While a case is being prepared for trial this requires the parties and in particular their legal teams to put on one side their understandable feelings of mutual outrage and hostility, and to cooperate with each other in a process of preparation for trial which incurs only proportionate costs and uses no more than an appropriate share of the court's resources.'

With that in mind, and following the guidance in *McPhilemy*, the judge went on to observe:

> 'As will appear from the remainder of this judgment, neither party is solely to blame for the disproportionate expense and court time taken up by this application. In many respects the RFI went well beyond what is contemplated by the CPR, (in contrast with the regime for further and better particulars under the RSC), and was pursued in full in the face of correspondence from the claimant which should have led to a substantial reduction in the information sought. Nonetheless some of the requests were properly made and the claimant's decision to oppose the provision of any of the information requested out of a desire to administer a procedural rap on the knuckles to its opponent was in my judgment equally inappropriate, at least without a serious attempt to identify what might sensibly be provided, at modest cost, by way of response, or some real prior attempt to explore a procedural compromise.'

Mindful of the terms of paragraph 1.2 of the Practice Direction to Part 18, concerning the need for the request to be concise and strictly confined to matters reasonably

---

[38] [2004] EWCA Civ 613.
[39] [2010] EWHC 1416 (Ch).

necessary and proportionate to prepare the requesting party's case or to understand the case to be met, some, but not all, of the requests were allowed.

3.7.4 Scope

Part 18 makes clear the scope of a request for further information should be confined to 'any matter which is in dispute in the proceedings' or 'additional information in relation to any such matter'.

This provision ought not to be construed too narrowly as it may be necessary for the information to be given before it is clear whether there is a disagreement: *Harcourt v Griffin*.[40]

However, reflecting the approach taken pre-CPR, requests for further information should not be allowed if these go solely to cross-examination as to credit because that would have the effect of circumventing the limits on disclosure in such circumstances: *Thorpe v Chief Constable of Greater Manchester*[41] (see **5.1.1.3**).

Similarly, the traditional approach of the courts was to not require further and better particulars that amounted to a 'fishing expedition', in other words requests made to try and find a case about which the party making the request knew nothing and had not yet pleaded: *Hennessy v Wright (No 2)*.[42]

The proper scope of a request for further information ought to be kept in mind, particularly when requests plainly relate to matters of credit, such as allegedly previous inconsistent statements. For example, where it is alleged entries in medical records are inconsistent with a claim subsequently advanced by the claimant those entries are not, themselves, evidence of what did, or did not, happen but, at most, evidence of inconsistency and hence credit: *Denton Hall Legal Services v Fifield*[43] (see **5.7.3**).

Different views have been expressed by the courts, about the proper scope of Part 18, where the claimant seeks information about the existence or extent of insurance cover the defendant has for the claim. A request for information was allowed in *Harcourt v Griffin*[44] but refused in *West London Pipeline & Storage Ltd v Total UK Ltd*.[45] A different approach, of requiring the information about insurance to be given under the general case management powers conferred on the court by CPR 3.1(2)(m) was adopted in *XYZ v Various*.[46]

Whilst a request for further information ought not, at least usually, be used for the purpose of interrogatories, under the former procedure rules, because that will often involve matters beyond the immediate dispute, it does seem appropriate for a request to be made where this is doing no more than requiring the defendant to provide the information that should have been given in the defence if the terms of Part 16 had been complied with.

---

[40] [2007] EWHC 1500 (QB).
[41] [1989] 1 WLR 665.
[42] (1890) 24 QBD 445.
[43] [2006] EWCA Civ 169.
[44] [2007] EWHC 1500 (QB).
[45] [2008] EWHC 1296 (Comm).
[46] [2013] EWHC 3643 (QB).

3.7.5   Compliance

Underpinning the tactics of, in former days, requests for further and better particulars and, nowadays, requests for further information is the prospect of issues arising about compliance with the request, particularly when the court has made an order that further information be provided. Non-compliance may, of course, generate an application to strike out the relevant statement of case.

When the issue of compliance arises it is one the court may need to approach by determining whether the party concerned has made a genuine attempt to provide the information (see **8.3.2.1**). In a sense it might always be said the information given was insufficient so a proportionate approach will be required.

With the added emphasis on compliance with court orders, from April 2013, this may, as it was prior to the introduction of the CPR, become a fruitful area for satellite litigation, despite the potential disproportionality of arguments on the extent of compliance. It is this that, perhaps, still makes the tactical considerations of pre-CPR days of relevance today.

3.7.6   Failure to file a defence

A defendant who fails to file a defence, but never intended to dispute liability, may gain the, unintended by the rule, advantage of avoiding the requirements imposed by the Practice Direction to Part 16 of having to deal with any medical evidence disclosed by the claimant, disclosing any medical evidence the defendant may have obtained and providing a counter schedule.

Consequently, in such circumstances, the claimant may wish to serve a request for further information, under Part 18, requiring the defendant to give the information on quantum which the rules envisage will be provided as a preliminary to initial case management, so as to help define the issues and hence the evidence required to deal with those issues.

Worse still a defendant may not file a defence when causation, at least in relation to some divisible heads of damage, is in issue. That may cause uncertainty, even if there is a judgment, about the range of issues, and hence the evidence necessary to deal with those issues, as occurred, for example, in *Symes v St George's Healthcare NHS Trust*.[47] Consequently, unless the extent to which causation is admitted has already been made clear by the scope of any judgment it would not usually be appropriate to dispense with the need for a defence and, as well as making application for judgment in appropriate terms, the claimant may need to consider use of a request for further information to clarify the position, perhaps as a preliminary.

3.7.7   Tactics

Traditional tactics employed with requests for further and better particulars should not be allowed to prevail with requests for further information under the CPR.

---

[47]   [2014] EWHC 2505 (QB).

It should not, generally, be necessary to seek further information at the stage of exchanging statements of case, except where the relevant statement of case does not give the information that it is required to provide under the CPR or where service of a request would be a proper way of enforcing the rules relating to the format and content of statements of case.

It should not, specifically, be appropriate to seek advance disclosure of the factual evidence of a party by service of an extensive request, as:

- it will be disproportionate, as such information will be provided at the stage of exchanging witness statements, and giving that meanwhile by response to a request for further information will only add unnecessarily to the costs; and

- it will not be consistent with the overriding objective for there to be, in effect, unilateral exchange of factual evidence, as that would not keep the parties on an equal footing.

A request of this kind from the defendant can properly be resisted, though objection to the defendant's request must be made within the time limit for giving the response in order to comply with the Practice Direction to Part 18.

If, however, the request seeks information that ought to have been included within the particulars of claim, or is of a nature that the defendant really needs in order to understand the parameters of the case it may be appropriate to respond to that request.

If the defendant is able to prepare a defence this, of itself, may suggest further information is not reasonably required, certainly at that stage. A more appropriate time for a request might well be after exchange of evidence, in order to clarify any matters still outstanding.

The same considerations apply to any request that the claimant may make.

When faced with what appears to be a tactical request for further information on behalf of the defendant the claimant may wish to object, particularly when the information requested will be provided at a subsequent stage in the proceedings or the request relates to issues of credit, on the basis of the overriding objective.

If, however, the defendant is implacable in seeking the information requested the claimant may need to think carefully about whether any request for information is necessary from the defendant. That would be on the basis both parties then either exchange information at the stage of the proceedings that has then been reached or defer those requests until later, on the basis the information requested will probably have, by then, emerged in any event.

3.8 REVIEW OF THE DEFENCE

The review of the defence is likely to include consideration of various matters which may, depending on the particular case, include some or all of the following.

- Does the defence comply with CPR 16.5 and paragraph 12 of the practice direction to Part 16?

- Are any aspects of the defence inconsistent with admissions made, or information given, under any relevant protocol?
- Are any aspects of the defence inconsistent with any binding compromise the claimant contends has been reached?
- Are the statements of case in order or:
  - is any further information necessary?
  - are any amendments required?
  - is a reply required, perhaps to deal with new issues such as limitation or to put any matters raised by the defence in proper, sometimes legal, context?
- What issues are defined by the statements of case and to what extent, given the need for the parties to narrow the issues and adopt a proportionate approach, are these properly defined?
- Can the key issues, that the case is really about, be ascertained from the statements of case and, if not, can these be identified and agreed between the parties so that further stages in the case can be properly focussed on those issues?
- What evidence will be necessary to deal with the issues?
- What evidence is already available?
- What evidence, on the basis of the issues, may still need to be obtained?
- Can the issues be narrowed or disposed of and in particular:
  - is an application for summary judgment on any issue, particularly liability, appropriate?
  - is a preliminary trial of any issue, particularly liability, appropriate?
- Are the parties correctly identified?
- Does the description of the defendant need amending?
- Do any further parties need to be involved in the proceedings?
- Is specific application to the court required to deal with any matters arising or are all such matters part of routine case management?
- Is any interim remedy appropriate?
- Is there a (sufficient) statement of truth in the defence?
- Should any Part 36 offer be made, changed, withdrawn or accepted?
- In terms of the cost/benefit analysis:
  - is any report to the ATE/BTE insurer, or Legal Aid Agency, required?
  - what further costs will need to be incurred to deal with matters on the basis of the defence?
  - are those costs likely to be proportionate, given the value of the claim and issues arising, and if not does the case plan need to be reviewed and/or efforts made to narrow the issues by agreement between the parties or appropriate case management from the court, particularly if costs are fixed or likely to be restricted by the terms of any costs management order?

Following review of the defence the client should be kept up to date with advice on the matters that remain in issue, any further advice on how best to deal with those issues and information about the next steps in the court process. If any new matters have been raised in the defence instruction will, of course, need to be taken from the claimant.

3.9 ACTION FOLLOWING REVIEW OF THE DEFENCE

There are a number of steps the claimant should take if, following review, it is decided the defence does not deal with the case in a way which is consistent with the requirements of the CPR, there are steps which need to be taken to narrow the issues and, in any event, to prepare the case for the next stage of case management.

3.9.1 Ensuring compliance with CPR 16.5 and the Practice Direction

If the defence does not comply with the requirements of CPR 16.5, and/or paragraph 12 of the Practice Direction to Part 16 the claimant may take a number of steps to deal with this.

- An order might be sought requiring an amended defence complying with CPR 16.5 and/or paragraph 12 which may, perhaps, impose a sanction in default.

- The defendant might be reminded of the requirements of the rules and informed that, unless amended, the claimant will assume that the defendant intends only to rely upon any positive allegations set out in the defence and reserves the right to object to any further matters that may be raised by way of disclosure, evidence or submission at trial.

- A request for further information, which includes requests that will effectively require the defendant to comply with the rules relating to the content of the defence, may be served.

It is important the parameters of the case are defined so that disclosure and evidence, from the point of view of proportionality, is kept to the matters in issue, rather than having to anticipate what may, or may not, need to be dealt with.

3.9.2 The real issues

Even if the defence does properly identify the issues it may still be worth the parties, with a view to cooperating in furthering the overriding objective, trying to identify the real, key, issues.

While the parties should, of course, try to reach agreement on any matters in issue, where that is not possible it may be useful to agree what are the remaining issues which, if agreement is not subsequently reached, the court will need to determine.

As well as helping to further the overriding objective, such an approach will give a template, for the parties to keep in mind, when dealing with the further stages of the case, up to and including the preparation of any case summaries or skeleton arguments for trial.

The key issues in the case may be ascertained from the defence, where liability is in issue, from the defence and/or the medical evidence disclosed with the defence where there are issues about the nature and extent of the injuries and from the counter schedule, assuming the claimant has been able to serve a sufficiently detailed schedule with the particulars of claim, all of which endorses the need for the defendant to comply properly with the terms of the CPR relating to the format and content of defences.

The need for an approach of this kind was emphasised by the Court of Appeal in *PGF II SA v OMFS Company 1 Ltd*.[48]

3.9.3   Request for further information under Part 18

The circumstances under which a request for further information from the defendant will be appropriate, given the role of statements of case under the CPR, are relatively limited. However, such a request may be necessary if, for example, the defence does not comply with Part 16 or the accompanying Practice Direction, especially paragraph 12. By seeking relevant information the claimant may be able to ensure that the defendant complies with the requirements of the rules.

Otherwise, to justify a request, it will probably be necessary to show that, unless the clarification or information is given, the claimant lacks sufficient information about the real issues in order to ensure disclosure is properly dealt with and/or know what evidence should be called to deal, in a proportionate way, with the issues. Defining the issues, to control the extent of disclosure and the evidence in a proportionate way, does seem an appropriate use of a request. Conversely, seeking to obtain unilateral disclosure of the other party's evidence should not be regarded as a proper use of Part 18 as that, in itself, is likely to be disproportionate by causing duplication of work.

3.9.4   Admission of facts

If the defence fails to properly narrow the issues, by not making admissions of fact which ought reasonably to be made, then it may be appropriate to seek the formal admission of facts.

CPR 32.18 provides a notice may be served requiring the admission of facts, and form N266 may be used for this purpose.

Under Part 44 the court may take account of an unreasonable failure to admit facts when considering costs. Whilst, strictly, it would not be necessary to serve formal notice for these purposes it may be helpful if it is clear to the court, at that later stage, the defendant had ample opportunity to narrow the issues and save costs.

3.9.5   Applying for judgment or strike out

Part 24 allows a party to seek summary judgment on the entire claim or on a particular issue. The claimant may, accordingly, make an application for summary judgment on the claim, where the defendant has no real prospect of successfully defending the claim as a whole, or on an issue, where the defendant has no real prospect of successfully defending that issue.

Whether there is a 'real prospect' means there being a realistic, as opposed to fanciful, prospect of success: *Sutradhar v National Environment Research Council*[49] (see **4.3.2.2**).

---

[48]   [2013] EWCA Civ 1288.
[49]   [2004] EWCA Civ 175, [2004] All ER (D) 357 (Feb).

In a personal injury claim any application for summary judgment by the claimant is likely to concern the issue of liability. The requirement in the CPR for a detailed defence supported by a statement of truth, along with the concept of pre-action admissions, has made such applications rarer than they were at one time.

Additionally, CPR 3.4 gives the court specific power to strike out a statement of case which may be another way for the claimant to obtain judgment, at least on the issue of liability, at the stage of the defence being filed.

Under CPR 3.4 the defence may be struck out if it discloses no reasonable grounds for defending the claim. This, essentially, is another way of seeking summary judgment and so the same test, namely whether there is a realistic prospect of the defence succeeding, should be applied under CPR 3.4 as it is under Part 24.

Under CPR 3.4 the defence may also be struck out if it constitutes an abuse of the court process. That might be so if, for example, it is contended the defence seeks to defend matters which are the subject of a binding compromise reached on an issue or on the whole claim.

The court may also strike out the defence under CPR 3.4 where there has been failure to comply with a rule, practice direction or court order. If the defendant has filed what might be termed a holding defence, which fails to comply with the requirements of Part 16, the court might exercise this power to strike that defence out. Following amendment to Part 1 in April 2013 a defendant who has conspicuously failed to comply with any relevant protocol might be at risk of the court exercising this power particularly where the defence raises matters that could, and should, have been dealt with at an earlier stage in accordance with any applicable protocol.

If the defence is struck out the claimant can, in the absence of a defence, seek judgment as appropriate.

CPR 14.1A(4) allows the claimant, following commencement of proceedings, to apply for judgment on the basis of a pre-action admission , though any such application may be met with a cross-application by the defendant for permission to withdraw the admission (see **1.7.2.4.2**).

The claimant should always try to secure judgment, to put matters beyond doubt, whether this be on the basis of an admission or in circumstances where it is considered judgment would be appropriate under Part 3 or Part 24 (see **4.3.1.4**).

3.9.6 Part 36

On the basis that Part 36 offers must be kept under review throughout the case, and particularly at key stages, the status of negotiations is an important consideration when reviewing matters in the light of the defence.

On the basis of the defence it may be appropriate to:
- make an offer on liability or any other issue;
- make an offer to settle the whole claim;
- change or withdraw any earlier offer made by the claimant; and/or

- accept any extant offer made by the defendant.

3.9.7   Statement of truth

The defence, if it has no statement of truth, will, in accordance with paragraph 4 of the Practice Direction to Part 22, remain effective unless and until it is struck out. The claimant is, however, quite entitled to insist that the defendant complies with the requirement the defence have a statement of truth, especially where the defence alleges a factual background different to that given in the particulars of claim.

That is because statements of truth are an integral part of the CPR, there to help confine the statements of case to the real issues (see **2.5.7**).

3.9.8   Further evidence

The issues, set out in the statements of case, may require further evidence.

In any event, the available evidence needs to be reviewed, in the context of the statements of case, in readiness for exchange and may need to be expanded or updated to deal with the issues as now defined.

3.9.9   Interim remedies

Part 25 deals with interim remedies. Review of the defence may prompt an application under this rule.

3.9.9.1   *Interim payments*

CPR 25.6 and 25.7 are concerned specifically with applications for interim payments.

Because CPR 25.6(1) provides that the claimant may not apply for an order that there be an interim payment before the end of the period for an acknowledgement of service, applicable to the defendant against whom the application is made, it is often at, or about, the time of the defence that an interim payment application will be made.

Furthermore, the terms of the defence may have a bearing on whether the claimant is likely to make out the conditions set out in CPR 25.7.

Any application for an interim payment will need to be made in accordance with Part 23 and establish, by reference to CPR 25.7, the basis on which an interim payment may be made (see **4.3.2.3**).

3.9.9.2   *Other interim remedies*

CPR 25 allows the court to give other interim remedies, including the inspection of, as well as experiments on or with, relevant property.

If, on reviewing the defence, any such order seems appropriate application might need to be made following review of the defence.

The general provisions relating to applications for interim remedies are dealt with by CPR 25.2 and 25.3. Any application will need to be made in accordance with Part 23 and reflect the terms of Part 25 (see **4.3.2.4**).

3.9.10   Joinder of parties

The terms of the defence may require the claimant to consider adding or substituting parties.

If there has been an error in the description of the defendant, which might properly be regarded as mis-joinder rather than non-joinder, substitution should be a straightforward matter, perhaps by order at the time of initial case management.

The distinction between mis-joinder and non-joinder may be significant if the limitation period has expired (see **2.12.4**).

If the defendant blames a party not directly involved in the claim (including a party against whom a Part 20 claim is brought), the claimant must decide whether to add that party as a further defendant. That decision is likely to turn upon whether, if the defence is established, the claimant would only have a remedy against that further party.

3.9.11   Notice to produce

If the defence refers to any document which has not yet been produced, the claimant is entitled to seek a copy straight away and should do so by service of a notice to produce in accordance with CPR 31.14 (see **5.2.4**).

3.9.12   Case management directions

It is sensible for the claimant, when reviewing the defence and considering action required, to identify case management directions that seem appropriate to deal with the issues.

The parties should try to agree case management directions so the sooner the draft order can be sent to the defendant, following receipt of the defence, the better as that will give the parties an opportunity to try and agree directions which, in turn, may inform, in multi-track cases, the costs budgets and increase the prospect of these, too, being agreed.

3.10   SANCTIONS

If the defendant fails to comply with the appropriate time limit for filing a defence the sanction will be a default judgment in response to a request by the claimant to the court that judgment be entered.

If a defence is filed but does not comply with the rules, it is likely that the claimant will have to take one of the steps already considered rather than seeking default judgment (though this may be appropriate following any successful application to strike a defence out).

3.10.1   When to apply for default judgment

Default judgment may be applied for, under CPR 12.3, either:

- under CPR 10.3 where the defendant has not filed an acknowledgement of service or a defence within 14 days of service of the claim form (or 14 days of service of the particulars of claim if these follow the claim form); or

- under CPR 15.4 where an acknowledgement of service has been filed but no defence is then filed within 28 days of service of the particulars of claim.

An acknowledgement of service or defence may arrive with the court after the claimant's request for default judgment has been received but before judgment has been entered. Strictly, if the defendant has not filed the acknowledgement of service or defence within the applicable time limit provided by the CPR permission from the court, for late filing, will be required and until that is granted the claimant should be entitled to judgment. In *Coll v Tattum*[50] Neuberger J (as he then was) held:

> 'The Rules are there to be observed, and it seems to me that the general thrust of the Rules is such that where there is no defence or acknowledgement of service or where it is served late, the claimant should have the right to apply for judgment in default, without the defendant automatically "trumping" such an application by the service of a late defence.'

Whilst this approach has not always been followed by the courts the greater focus on compliance with the rules, from April 2013, ought to result in this approach being adhered to.

3.10.2   Procedure for obtaining default judgment

CPR 12.4 confirms that default judgment may be obtained by filing the appropriate request in form N227.

As a preliminary to seeking default judgment, if the claimant has served the claim form, a certificate of service will need to be filed at court in accordance with CPR 6.17(2).

Many default judgments are, of course, relatively straightforward money claims. A personal injury claim is inevitably more complex and, as an unliquidated claim, judgment will only be entered on the issue of liability, for damages and interest to be assessed.

Accordingly, it would not be appropriate, following default judgment in a personal injury claim, for there to be a straightforward disposal hearing. Rather, after entry of judgment, allocation questionnaires will be issued and following return of these in the usual way the court will need to case manage the claim by giving appropriate directions.

---

[50]   (2001) *The Times*, 3 December, ChD.

3.10.3   Setting default judgment aside

Setting aside judgment is dealt with in Part 13, which provides that:

- if judgment was wrongly entered, for example because the relevant time limit had not expired, the court must set the judgment aside; and

- in other circumstances the court may set judgment aside if the defendant shows a real prospect of successfully defending the claim or it appears to the court there is some other good reason for the judgment to be set aside or the defendant be allowed to defend the action, provided the application is made promptly.

It is essential the defendant makes any application to set judgment aside promptly. The meaning of 'promptly' was considered in *Mullock v Price*[51] where the Court of Appeal held that the defendant must act with alacrity or celerity. Even though the delay occurred entirely as a result of the defendant's insurer, the defendant was not permitted to defend the claim after a delay of two years. A delay of less, perhaps considerably less, than two years may still amount to a failure to act with alacrity or celerity.

A strict approach to the need for a prompt application is likely with the greater focus on compliance with the rules from April 2013.

Moreover, the court may approach an application to set aside default judgment, even though made under Part 13, by applying the approach required under CPR 3.9 as set out in *Denton v TH White Ltd*.[52]

Even prior to 2013 the Court of Appeal appeared to recognise that CPR 3.9 was relevant to the court's consideration of an application to set judgment aside under Part 13 in *Hussain v Birmingham City Council*.[53] Subsequently in *Standard Bank Plc v Agrinvest International Inc*[54] Moore-Bick LJ said:

> 'The Civil Procedure Rules were intended to introduce a new era in civil litigation, in which both the parties and the courts were expected to pay more attention to promoting efficiency and avoiding delay. The overriding objective expressly recognised for the first time the importance of ensuring that cases are dealt with expeditiously and fairly and it is in that context that one finds for the first time in rule 13.3(2) an explicit requirement for the court to have regard on an application of this kind to whether the application was made promptly. No other factor is specifically identified for consideration, which suggests that promptness now carries much greater weight than before. It is not a condition that must be satisfied before the court can grant relief, because other factors may carry sufficient weight to persuade the court that relief should be granted, even though the application was not made promptly. The strength of the defence may well be one. However, promptness will always be a factor of considerable significance ... if there has been a marked failure to make the application promptly, the court may well be justified in refusing relief, notwithstanding the possibility that the defendant might succeed at trial.'

In *Samara v MBI Partners UK Ltd*[55] Silber J held that the rationale behind amendments to the CPR in April 2013 changed the approach that should be taken towards failures to comply with all rules and orders, including Part 13. The judge observed:

---

[51]   [2009] EWCA Civ 1222.
[52]   [2014] EWCA Civ 906.
[53]   [2005] EWCA Civ 1570.
[54]   [2010] EWCA Civ 1400.
[55]   [2014] EWHC 563 (QB).

'There is no express statement that CPR Part 13 or that any part of it is excluded from these provisions and I have found nothing in the rules or in the decided cases to show expressly or impliedly that this is so. Further, there is no theoretical justification from excluding this rule from the new regime and the new underlying objectives. Indeed, most importantly, the Master of the Rolls, Lord Dyson, described the effect of the new regime in very general terms and as being of universal application when giving the judgment of the Court of Appeal in *Mitchell v News Group* [2013] EWCA Civ 1537 when he explained that:-

(a)   "[T]he new more robust approach [which] will mean that from now on relief from sanctions should be granted more sparingly than previously" ([46]);

(b)   This approach, which meant an end to the belief that the "culture of delay and non-compliance "would continue (ibid);

(c)   "[T]he starting point should be that the sanction has been properly imposed and complies with the overriding objective" [45];

(d)   Relief would be granted if the default is trivial "provided that an application is made promptly" (ibid [40]) or if there is a good reason for failure to comply (ibid [41]). Good reasons are likely to arise from; circumstances outside the control of the party in default (ibid [43]) and by contrast inefficiency or incompetence of a party's solicitors –for example, the fact that a deadlines is simply overlooked- is unlikely to prove a good reason (ibid [41]) (see Leggatt J in *Summit Navigation Ltd and another v Generale Romania Asigurare Reasigurare SA and another* [2014 EWHC 398 (Comm)[39]); and (e) Applications for relief must be made promptly (ibid [40] and [46]).'

This approach was adopted in *Mid-East Sales Ltd v United Engineering & Trading Co (PVT) Ltd*[56] where Burton J held:

'I am accordingly considering CPR Rule 3.9 but (again pace Lord Dyson in **Matthews**) also Rule 13.3 as in **Hussain**. I am satisfied, as was Silber J in **Samara**, that the new approach described by Lord Dyson's Implementation Lecture and exemplified in **Mitchell** is intended to be of *universal effect*, i.e. across the board in relation to the CPR, by reference at least to the amended Overriding Objective, just as in **Agrinvest** (as set out in paragraph 45(viii) above) it was considered that the introduction of the CPR itself would and should have an accelerating effect.'

This line of authority was again applied by HHJ Richardson QC in *Hockley v North Lincolnshire and Goole NHS Foundation Trust.*[57] Here the parties had agreed, following service of the claim form, to an extension of time, of several months, for service of particulars of claim. After timely service, in accordance with that agreement, of the particulars of claim the defendant filed the acknowledgement of service 13 days late and, meanwhile, the claimant obtained default judgment. That judgment was not set aside, the judge applying the tests set out in *Denton v TH White Ltd*[58] and observing:

'Deadlines set by the rules of the court are there for a purpose and may not be cast aside unless there is agreement by the parties and (where necessary) the approval of the court is sought. It is now to be understood that compliance is not a slide rule to be easily adjusted. The court expects compliance and will take steps which will not be lightly set aside when there is default. Incompetence of a party or its representatives is highly likely to be regarded as a good reason for the removal of a sanction or setting aside an order or judgment. It is, of course, necessary to look at all the circumstances and for the court to avoid trivialities of no reason consequence.'

The judge also observed that:

---

56   [2014] EWHC 1457 (Comm).
57   (Unreported) Kingston upon Hull County Court, 19 September 2014.
58   [2014] EWCA Civ 906.

'The claimant was entitled to invoke the default judgment procedure and take advantage of it by saving much money by not having to prove her case.'

This approach has also been adopted by the Court of Appeal when dismissing an application for permission to appeal the refusal to set aside a default judgment in *Regione Piemonte v Dexia Credop*.[59] The judgment of the court was that:

'CPR 13 makes clear (i) that the power to set aside is discretionary; (ii) that the conditions specified in CPR 13 (1) (a) or (b) are necessary, but not necessarily sufficient, conditions for the exercise of the discretion; and (iii) that the question as to whether the application has been made promptly is a mandatory and obviously, therefore, important consideration. It follows that a court may be entitled to refuse to set a judgment aside even if the defendant shows a real prospect that he may or might succeed in his defence at trial.'

The judgment also explored the relationship between merits and delay when it was observed:

'... it does not seem to me that the merits of any defence are ever irrelevant if by that the judge meant that the court will not even consider them. When it does consider them, it may conclude that they are of little or no weight. The court is engaged in an exercise of weighing delay against merits, which will include considering the nature and extent of the delay, the reason and any justification for it, the strength of the supposed defence and the justice of the case. The stronger the merits (and any justification for the delay) the more likely it is that the Court may be prepared to exercise its discretion to set aside a judgment regularly obtained despite the delay and vice versa. That is not to say that a real or even a good case on the merits will usually lead to the judgment being set aside despite significant delay since delay is now a much more potent factor than heretofore. If there is a marked and unjustified lack of promptness, that, itself, may now justify a refusal of relief because the delay is a factor that outweighs the defendants' prospect of success. As Moore Bick LJ recognised in Agrinvest the climate has changed with the introduction of the CPR from that which applied when this court in JH Rayner (Mincing Lane) Ltd v Cafenorte S.A. Importadora e Exportadora S.A. [1999] 2 Lloyds Rep 750 upheld a decision of his own setting aside a judgment after a delay of 7½ years.'

The Court of Appeal also confirmed that:

'CPR 13.3 requires an applicant to show that he has real prospects of a successful defence or some other good reason to set the judgement aside. If he does, the court's discretion is to be exercised in the light of all the circumstances and the overriding objective. The Court must have regard to all the factors it considers relevant of which promptness is both a mandatory and an important consideration. Since the overriding objective of the Rules is to enable the court to deal with cases justly and at proportionate cost, and since under the new CPR 1.1 (2) (f) the latter includes enforcing compliance with rules, practice directions and orders, the considerations set out in CPR 3.9 are to be taken into account: see Hussein v Birmingham City Council [2005] EWCA Civ 1570 per Chadwick LJ at [30]; Mid-East Sales v United Engineering and Trading Co (PVT) Ltd [2014] EWHC 1457 at [85]. So also is the approach to CPR 3.9 in Mitchell/Denton. The fact that the Court's judgment in Denton was reinforced by the fact that CPR 3.9 was not reworded in the manner proposed by Jackson LJ does not detract from the relevance of CPR 3.9, and what was said about it in Denton, to applications under CPR 13.'

Even where the claimant makes a procedural error when serving the proceedings there may still be a regular judgment which the court will not set aside. For example, where

---

59 [2014] EWCA Civ 1298.

the claimant failed to serve a response pack with the claim form, as required by CPR 7.8(1), that did not prevent a default judgment being entered but was a relevant factor when considering whether any default judgment should be set aside under Part 13: *Rajval Construction Ltd v Bestville Properties Ltd.*[60]

Similarly, where the claimant failed to file a certificate of service before requesting default judgment, but the defendant has suffered no meaningful, prejudice, that judgment was not set aside: *Henriksen v Pires.*[61]

Consequently, a claimant may be able to retain a default judgment even where there appears to be an arguable defence, so care is necessary before agreeing to judgment being set aside.

If, however, it seems very likely the court will set a judgment aside the most constructive approach may be to try and reach agreement on suitable terms. It might, for example, be useful if the defendant will agree that any outstanding matters under the protocol be dealt with and to see if, in principle, a framework can be agreed for case management. Indeed, it may sometimes be possible to agree an apportionment on liability and that default judgment be set aside but there be a judgment reflecting the terms agreed on this issue.

---

60   [2010] EWCA Civ 1621.
61   [2011] EWCA Civ 1720.

CHAPTER 4

ALLOCATION AND CASE MANAGEMENT

4.1 INTRODUCTION

The Civil Procedure Rules (the CPR) introduced active case management by the courts, replacing the previous system of largely automatic directions.

The wide-ranging powers of the court are found in CPR 3.1. Whilst these powers may be exercised at any stage, it is likely that in most claims the key, and sometimes only, stage at which these will be used by the court is at allocation and initial case management.

To assist the court in dealing with allocation and case management each party must complete a Directions Questionnaire (which from April 2013 replaced the former Directions Questionnaire).

Following amendments to the CPR in April 2013 the court, once a defence has been filed, provisionally allocates the claim and informs the parties of that by notice. The notice also requires completion of directions questionnaires which are to be returned by a specified date along with draft directions and, in multi-track cases, a costs budget.

The parties are required, prior to filing directions questionnaires, to cooperate in efforts towards agreeing directions.

Once directions questionnaires have been filed the court may give case management directions without a hearing. If necessary, however, the court will arrange a hearing to decide appropriate directions. Whether or not given at a hearing the case management directions will set out a timetable which the parties must keep to unless these are subsequently varied by the court or, in limited circumstances, by agreement between the parties.

Initial case management is a vital stage of the case which should be approached with care, as the directions given are likely to play a significant part in the way the case proceeds towards trial.

This stage of the case will, ideally, be part of a logical process, following on from the issues being defined under the relevant protocol and/or statements of case, when the parties agree, or the court directs, how those issues should best be dealt with having regard to the overriding objective.

4.2   ALLOCATION (AND TRANSFER)

Once the defence has been filed a court officer will provisionally allocate the claim and notice of that will be issued to the parties also requiring directions questionnaires to be filed, any other steps identified in the notice to be taken and for the claimant to pay the appropriate fee, all by the date given in the notice.

If the claim has been issued in the CCMCC, once all parties have filed directions questionnaires or the time for doing so has expired, that claim will be transferred, to an appropriate county court, at the stage of provisional allocation.

4.2.1   The tracks

The CPR provides for three tracks, namely:

• the small claims track;

• the fast track; and

• the multi-track.

4.2.2   Scope of the tracks

The small claims track and the fast track each have a specific scope whilst the multi-track is, in effect, a residual category.

The scope of the tracks is defined by CPR 26.6.

4.2.2.1   *Scope of the small claims track*

Paragraph 8.1 of the Practice Direction to Part 26 describes the general type of claim suitable for the small claims track as including, along with consumer and certain landlord and tenant claims, 'accident claims'.

However, where the claim is for 'personal injuries' (defined in CPR 2.3 as a claim for damages for personal injury or death) then the small claims track is only the normal track where:

• the value of the claim is not more than £10,000; and

• the value of any claim for 'damages for personal injuries' (defined for this purpose by CPR 26.6(2) as damages for pain, suffering and loss of amenity and does not include any other damages which are claimed) is not more than £1,000.

Accordingly, accident claims, though potentially suitable for the small claims track, will not be allocated to that track if there is an element of personal injury and there is a reasonable expectation that damages for pain, suffering and loss of amenity will exceed £1,000.

Damages for pain, suffering and loss of amenity are likely to exceed £1,000 in most personal injury claims. For example, in *Wilson v Pilley*[1] the Court of Appeal held that

---

[1]   [1957] 3 All ER 525, CA.

general damages for as low a figure of £75, in the money of the day, would only be to compensate pain and suffering in cases which, if not trifling, could properly be classified as slight. The 2015 equivalent of £75 in 1957 is over £1,600.

It is notable paragraph 8.1 of the Practice Direction to Part 26 uses the term 'accident claims'. That would appear to exclude claims for industrial disease and, it might be said, clinical negligence claims. If it were otherwise, the term 'personal injury' might have been expected.

All of these provisions reflect the potential difficulties for a litigant in person dealing with a claim which has a personal injury element, particularly if that does not arise out of an accident.

4.2.2.2   Scope of the fast track

The fast track is the normal track for any claim:

- where the small claims track is not the normal track;
- the claim has a financial value of not more than £25,000;
- provided the trial is likely to last for no longer than one day (for these purposes one day is defined by paragraph 9.1 of the Practice Direction to Part 26 as 5 hours); and
- oral expert evidence at trial will be limited to not more than:
  - one expert per party in relation to any expert field; and
  - expert evidence in two expert fields.

Accordingly, a key feature of the fast track is not just value but a trial which will not exceed a single day in court.

4.2.2.3   Scope of the multi-track

The multi-track is the normal track for any claim for which the small claims track or the fast track is not the normal track.

Allocation to the multi-track will, primarily, be dictated by value. However, it is important to note allocation to the multi-track may be appropriate because of the expert evidence which is to be relied on or other factors which will mean the trial is likely to last for more than a day. The length of trial is highly relevant to allocation given the fast track has fixed costs for the hearing, based on figures which assume a hearing of not more than a day.

Even where a case is within the financial limits of the fast track and the trial is not expected to last more than one day the court may still, having regard to the factors set out in CPR 26.8(1), allocate the case to the multi-track.

Additionally, if the claim issued under Part 8 of the CPR, for example seeking court approval of a settlement, CPR 8.9(c) confirms the claim shall be treated as allocated to the multi-track and therefore Part 26 does not apply to such a claim.

The hallmarks of the multi-track, in relation to case management, are identified in paragraph 3.2 of the Practice Direction to Part 29, namely the ability of the court to deal with cases of widely differing values and complexity and the flexibility given to the court in managing a case appropriate to its particular needs. Thus, the features of any particular case may demand the case management typically found in the multi-track.

4.2.3 Differences between the tracks

The CPR provides for some differences between the tracks both in relation to typical case management and also on costs.

4.2.3.1 Case management

In many respects, the directions given in a personal injury claim may not differ, whichever track the case has been allocated to.

Paragraph 2.1 of the Practice Direction to Part 28 confirms the intention in the fast track is that there will be case management only at the stages of allocation and listing. Consequently, CPR 28.2 stipulates that the court will fix a trial window or trial date and that the standard period of time to trial should be not more than 30 weeks. That is confirmed by para 3.6 of the Practice Direction to Part 28 which also provides that the trial window must not be longer than 3 weeks. The general approach to directions is set out in para 3.9 of the Practice Direction to Part 28.

In the multi-track, however, CPR 29.2 confirms the court, when giving initial case management directions, will not necessarily fix a trial window and, rather, may arrange a further case management conference or pre-trial review.

The multi-track does include cases of significant value and complexity where it may be necessary to give directions which might be regarded as 'tailor-made'.

The hallmarks of the multi-track, in relation to case management, are identified in paragraph 3.2 of the Practice Direction to Part 29, namely the ability of the court to deal with cases of widely differing values and complexity and the flexibility given to the court in managing a case appropriate to its particular needs. Thus, the features of any particular case may demand the case management typically found in the multi-track.

4.2.3.2 Costs

There are significant differences between the various tracks so far as costs are concerned. This distinction may make the issue of allocation important.

4.2.3.2.1 Small claims track costs

If the case is allocated to the small claims track the court is restricted, by CPR 27.14, from making orders for costs between the parties, except for fixed costs and some other expenses associated with bringing the claim such as court fees and experts' fees.

However, CPR 27.14(2)(d) allows the court to make an order for costs between the parties where a party has behaved unreasonably. Examples of unreasonable behaviour are:

- a defendant leaving it very late before settling: *Lincoln v R D Williams Haulage Ltd*;[2]

- the defendant 'drip-feeding' the claim by making a series of offers on liability before ultimately agreeing to settle in full in proceedings that should not have been defended: *Blake v Sutton*;[3] and

- the defendant failing to comply with the Protocol, putting liability in issue and subsequently admitting liability: *Harker v Sheard*.[4]

Additionally, a litigant in person is entitled to seek the cost of legal services reasonably incurred for the conduct of the proceedings under CPR 48.6(3)(b). This rule is unlikely to allow recovery of costs for full representation but might entitle a party to the cost of obtaining specific pieces of advice.

The terms of CPR 27.14 are only applicable once a case has been allocated to the small claims track. If the case settles meanwhile, on the basis costs are to be assessed rather than expressly agreeing that fixed costs will apply in any event, the costs will have to be assessed (although when doing so the court may take account of the value of the claim in deciding what costs were reasonable: *O'Beirne v Hudson*[5]).

4.2.3.2.2 Fast track costs

If the case is allocated to the fast-track, CPR 46.2 provides that the costs of trial will be limited to:

- £485 if the value of the claim is up to £3,000;
- £690 if the value exceeds £3,000 but not £10,000;
- £1,035 if the value exceeds £10,000 (but does not exceed £15,000 and the claim form was issued from 6 April 2009);
- £1,650 if the value exceeds £15,000 (and the claim form was issued from 6 April 2009).

Additionally, CPR 46.3 provides the court may allow £345 for attendance by the legal representative. Because this is discretionary it will usually be necessary to justify such attendance at a fast track trial (see **10.5.3**).

The limit on costs of advocacy at trial reflects the need to ensure allocation to the multi-track if the hearing is likely to last longer than 1 day.

Many personal injury fast track claims will have started in either the RTA Protocol or the EL/PL Protocol. CPR 45.29A provides that section IIIA of Part 45 will apply to such cases which will, therefore, be subject to the fixed costs set out in the relevant table, to be found in CPR 45.29C and CPR 45.29E. In such cases the costs of the defendant,

---

[2]   [2001] CLY 516.
[3]   [2004] CLY 421.
[4]   (Unreported) Doncaster County Court, 22 September 2005.
[5]   [2010] EWCA Civ 52.

though not fixed, will be effectively capped by the terms of CPR 45.29F. Consequently, such fixed costs apply due to the origin, rather than allocation, of the claim.

In other respects costs in a fast track will be dealt with in the same way as a claim allocated to the multi-track (which could include costs budgeting if the court so directs).

4.2.3.2.3   Multi-track costs

There are no fixed costs in cases allocated to the multi-track. If, however, the court, when assessing costs, determines that a case should be allocated to the fast track, perhaps because the party receiving costs has exaggerated either the value or likely length of trial, this may be a relevant factor in assessing those costs.

In *Drew v Whitbread*[6] the Court of Appeal confirmed that, when assessing costs, it was not appropriate simply to treat the case as if it had been allocated to the fast track, and impose trial costs allowed with cases so allocated, but to reflect what costs would have been allowed when determining the costs to be regarded as reasonable and proportionate.

4.2.4   Matters relevant to allocation

CPR 26.8(1) sets out some specific matters to which the court shall have regard when deciding to which track a claim should be allocated. These are:

- the financial value;
- the nature of the remedy sought;
- the likely complexity of the facts, law or evidence;
- the number of parties or likely parties;
- the value and complexity of any counterclaim or other Part 20 claim;
- the amount of oral evidence which may be required;
- the importance of the claim to persons not parties to the proceedings;
- the views expressed by the parties; and
- the circumstances of the parties.

In practice some of these factors are likely to be of particular relevance to allocation.

4.2.4.1   Value

Because value may be the principal basis on which a case is allocated it is important, if the defence disputes the claimant's statement of value in accordance with CPR 16.5(6), that this is a matter the claimant deals with ahead of allocation.

When considering financial value CPR 26.8(2) provides that the court should disregard any amount not in dispute, any claim for interest, costs and any contributory negligence.

The question of value may be most significant in a claim involving minor injuries for which, the defendant may argue, the court might award less than £1,000.

---

6   [2010] EWCA Civ 53.

The claimant, however, is likely to argue that the injuries should not be characterised as 'slight' or 'really trivial'. In any event, as the court is not in a position to make a definitive assessment of quantum at this stage, if there is a reasonable prospect that damages for pain, suffering and loss of amenity will exceed £1,000, the case should be allocated to the fast track.

This approach reflects that taken by the courts prior to the introduction of the CPR when deciding if a case was suitable, on value, for referral to arbitration. The Court of Appeal in *Afzal v Ford Motor Co Ltd*[7] adopted, as the most satisfactory formula in assessing the value for the purposes of reference to arbitration, the question, 'could the plaintiff reasonably expect to be awarded more than £1,000?'.

Similarly, when determining if a case is suitable, on value alone, for allocation to the multi-track the appropriate question for the court should be whether there is a reasonable expectation of the claimant being awarded more than £25,000 (which for these purposes includes both general and special damages).

4.2.4.2 Complexity

Complexity may arise out of the factual background, the legal issues, the number of parties or the nature and extent of the evidence, for example if there are likely to be numerous witnesses of fact.

These factors, whilst relevant in their own terms, may also be of significance when considering whether any trial is likely to last for more than a day and hence be suitable for allocation to the multi-track.

This factor may also be relevant in determining whether, even though personal injury claims are potentially suitable for allocation to the small claims track, it would be appropriate to so allocate such a claim involving an element of personal injury.

In *Diga v Waite*[8] the court noted that where a child's claim settled for £300 and court approval was sought under Part 8 the claim would nominally, if not actually, be allocated to the multi-track. In any event, where the court required expert evidence for the purposes of approval, the claim was held not to be one of the specific types of small dispute for which the small claims route was designed.

4.2.4.3 Views of the parties

Where the parties agree, in their respective directions questionnaires, on the track to which the case should be allocated this will certainly be an important factor for the court. However, and as paragraph 7.5 of the Practice Direction to 25 makes clear, the court will not be bound by any agreement or common view of the parties.

---

7   [1994] 4 All ER 720.
8   (Unreported) Oxford County Court, 21 October 2009.

4.2.4.4   Circumstances of the parties

In a personal injury claim the circumstances of the parties are likely to differ considerably, typically an individual claimant against, in effect, an insurer with considerable resources and plenty of experience in dealing with such claims.

The requirement to consider the circumstances of the parties does, perhaps, also reflect the overriding objective which includes the need to keep the parties on an equal footing.

This factor may be of most significance if the court is considering allocation to the small claims track as the practical effect may be to leave the claimant unrepresented whilst the defendant will remain legally represented (not something that would normally occur with the type of case paragraph 8.1 of the Practice Direction to Part 26 envisages as suitable to the small claims track).

In *Afzal* the Court of Appeal gave general guidance on the referral of personal injury claims to arbitration (the equivalent of allocation to the small claims track under the CPR). Whilst accepting such claims could be referred to arbitration the court went on to observe that:

> 'We have no doubt that the judge was wrong to approach small employers' liability claims as a class of case which it was unreasonable to allow to proceed to arbitration.'

However, after noting trade unions might not be able to fully support small claims of this kind if costs could not be recovered, the court observed:

> 'On the other side, it seems equally questionable whether employers liability insurers' will regard it as commercially justifiable to incur the considerable expense of legal representation at the hearing of such claims which will be irrecoverable.'

This suggests the court anticipated that either all the parties or none of the parties would be represented following referral to arbitration. These remarks have greater resonance following the introduction of the Civil Procedure Rules, and the need to ensure the parties are on an equal footing, as it would seem unfortunate to refer to the small claims track if the nature of the claimant's funding would mean the claimant then becomes unrepresented whilst the defendant continues to have legal support. It would seem particularly unfair if the claimant is a child or a patient when representation, to ensure equality between the parties, is particularly important.

4.2.4.5   Other matters

Whilst the court must have regard to the matters identified in CPR 26.8(1) it is clear, from the rule itself, any other relevant matters may be taken into account.

Conduct may be a relevant matter, hence if the defendant has acted unreasonably this may be an issue relevant to allocation.

In *Duffell v Davies*[9] the claimant obtained default judgment and then had damages assessed at a disposal hearing at under £400 and the case allocated, at that time, to the

---

9   (Unreported) Liverpool County Court, 18 February 2000.

small claims track. On appeal the conduct of the defendant, viewed objectively, was held to be unreasonable as the CPR requires positive investigation and response at an early stage with a view to early settlement of valid claims. Accordingly, it was inappropriate to allocate in a way that would limit the claimant's costs.

4.2.5 TRANSFER

If a claim has been issued in the CCMCC the court will, at the stage of provisional allocation, transfer that claim.

Where the defendant is an individual and the claim is for a specified sum of money that transfer, by CPR 26.2A(3) will be to the defendant's home court. If, however, the defendant in such a claim identifies a preferred court in the directions questionnaire the claim will, in accordance with CPR 26.2A(5), be transferred to that court.

All other claims will, in accordance with CPR 26.2A(4), be transferred to the preferred court. If the claim seeks damages to be assessed that will be a claim for an unspecified sum of money so the preferred court will be the court named by the claimant in the claim form or, if different, the preferred court identified in the claimant's directions questionnaire in accordance with CPR 26.2A(5).

It is possible that the court to which the claim is transferred from the CCMCC will consider further transfer at the stage of case management (see **4.3.1.2**).

4.3   CASE AND COSTS MANAGEMENT

Initial case management, at the stage of allocation, is likely to involve the court giving directions dealing with those matters identified in para 3.9 of the Practice Direction to Part 28, in fast track claims, and para 5.3 of the Practice Direction to Part 29, in multi-track claims.

The court, when giving directions, is able to make use of the wide general powers of case management set out in CPR 3.1.

In multi-track claims the court will also need to deal with costs management in accordance with section II, Part 3.

These matters may, therefore, be regarded as routine case management and will not, therefore, require a specific application, although it may be helpful if the parties identify in draft orders the directions proposed at this stage.

If, however, a party seeks an order which would not be regarded as a matter of routine case management then, as paragraph 5.8 of the Practice Direction to Part 29 makes clear, an application notice, seeking the appropriate order, will be required (unless the parties agree to dispense with that formality).

Accordingly, as well as each party considering what directions are likely to be required, it is necessary to assess whether such directions are simply part of routine case management, so no specific application is required, or not, so that the directions questionnaire can be accompanied by an appropriate application notice.

Whether or not the directions are matters of routine case management these will, once given by the court, set out a timetable taking the case up to the stage of listing or further case management.

4.3.1   Routine case management

The court is likely to consider, in most cases and whether or not specifically raised by the parties, the core topics identified as routine case management in Parts 28 and 29 of the CPR.

There are some other issues the court may, as appropriate, be likely to consider, if the need arises, without specific application.

Accordingly, these core topics, along with similar issues relevant to the particular case, should always be considered when the directions questionnaire, and accompanying documentation is completed.

4.3.1.1   Stay

One or more of the parties may seek a stay in the directions questionnaire. No application should be necessary given that paragraph 3.1 of the Practice Direction to Part 26 confirms that a stay may be sought just by letter.

4.3.1.2   Venue

The court may, of its own initiative or at the request of a party, consider venue at the stage of initial case management and is unlikely to require a formal application before making any appropriate order for transfer.

The question of transfer may arise, at the stage of initial case management, even if the claim has already been transferred from the CCMCC to the court now dealing with case management.

There is no automatic transfer to the defendant's local court under CPR 26.2 unless the claim seeks a specified amount of money. Accordingly, any transfer between courts will be in accordance with CPR 30.2, having regard to the matters set out in CPR 30.3(2) namely:

(a)   the financial value of the claim and the amount in dispute, if different;

(b)   whether it would be more convenient or fair for hearings (including the trial) to be held in some other court;

(c)   the availability of a judge specialising in the type of claim in question;

(d)   whether the facts, legal issues, remedies or procedures involved are simple or complex;

(e)   the importance of the outcome of the claim to the public in general;

(f)   the facilities available to the court at which the claim is being dealt with, particularly in relation to –
    (i)   any disabilities of a party or potential witness;
    (ii)   any special measures needed for potential witnesses; or
    (iii)   security;

(g)   whether the making of a declaration of incompatibility under section 4 of the Human Rights Act 1998 has arisen or may arise;

(h)   in the case of civil proceedings by or against the Crown, as defined in rule 66.1(2), the location of the relevant government department or officers of the Crown and, where appropriate, any relevant public interest that the matter should be tried in London.

In *Tai Ping Carpets UK Ltd v Arora Heathrow T5 Ltd*[10] the defendant failed in an application to transfer an action from the Birmingham District Registry to the Technology and Construction Court in London. That was because many factors relied on by each party cancelled each other out. Even though the defendant was based just outside London, with many witnesses as well as the defendant's lawyers being based in London, the claimant, who had gone to the trouble and expense of starting the proceedings, had requested the claim be run in Birmingham. Additionally, if transferred to London the case would have been more expensive to run.

Value, taking account of the High Court and County Courts' Jurisdiction Order 1991, may prompt transfer from the High Court to a county court, or vice versa. Otherwise, unless there are particular facilities at a court required because of any disabilities of a party or potential witness or security measures demanded by the case, transfer should turn upon whether it would be more convenient or fair for hearings, including the trial, to be held in a particular court.

Accordingly, there should be no automatic transfer to the defendant's local court, as might be expected with a debt claim for example. Prior to the introduction of the CPR it was generally accepted the appropriate venue was the court chosen by the claimant's solicitors who had the 'carriage of the action'. With case management, and the availability of telephone hearings, that may be less of a consideration but, even so, the court should have regard to this factor, along with other relevant matters, when deciding what is most convenient and fair for hearings.

It may be difficult to assess, at an early stage, where it will be most convenient or fair for hearings, including the trial, to take place unless, perhaps, it is apparent all parties have a geographical link with a particular court and that court would be a suitable venue for the trial.

If a case which is to be allocated to the multi-track has been started away from a Civil Trial Centre the court may decide to transfer to that centre before allocation, or to allocate and give case management directions with a view to the trial taking place at that centre in due course.

---

[10]   [2009] EWHC 2305 (TCC).

4.3.1.3 Parties

Whilst addition or substitution of parties may require application, the court will probably be willing to deal with the correction of a party's name, where this is really a question of mis-joinder rather than non-joinder, as part of routine case management.

4.3.1.4 Judgment

If the defence admits liability the court is likely to regard a request for judgment as part of routine case management, not least because with such an admission the entry of an appropriate judgment is unlikely to be contentious.

CPR 14.6 provides, where the claimant seeks an unspecified amount of money and the defendant admits liability, the claimant may request judgment which, if entered, will be for an amount to be decided by the court and costs.

If agreement has been reached providing for an apportionment on liability any judgment should provide that the claimant will recover the appropriate percentage of damages and interest once assessed, rather than a formal apportionment unless that is what the parties specifically intend, to guard against the risk of the claimant conceding any liability for a claim by the defendant (even if there is no formal counterclaim).

In a personal injury claim once judgment has been entered for an amount of damages and interest is to be decided by the court this effectively determines that there has been a breach of duty causative of at least some damage. Depending on the admission made it may be possible for the judgment to confirm the extent of an admission on causation, for example that a particular injury or consequence resulted from the breach of duty. Beyond that the scope of the issues which remain open for determination by the court following judgment will depend on the scope of the issues as defined by the statements of case (which in turn will depend upon whether or not a defence has been filed): *New Century Media Ltd v Makhlay*[11]; *Symes v St George's Healthcare NHS Trust*.[12]

In *Lunnun v Singh*[13] Jonathan Parker J held:

> 'In my judgment, the underlying principle is that on an assessment of damages all issues are open to a defendant save to the extent that they are inconsistent with the earlier determination of the issue of liability, whether such determination takes the form of a judgment following a full hearing on the facts or a default judgment. In this case the judgment was a default judgment.'

In *Lunnun* Clarke LJ agreed with Jonathan Parker J explaining that on the assessment of damages the defendant may not take any point inconsistent with the liability alleged in the statement of claim, such points including contributory negligence, failure to mitigate, causation and quantum. On causation, however, drawing on the judgment of Sir Richard Scott in *Maes Finance Ltd and another v A Phillips & Co*[14] Clarke LJ held that whilst the defendant cannot contend breach of duty was not causative of any loss it might still be argued that such breaches were not causative of any particular items of

---

11   [2013] EWHC 3556 (QB).
12   [2014] EWHC 2505 (QB).
13   [1999] CPLR 587.
14   (1997) *The Times*, 25 March.

alleged loss. Consequently, a judgment should rule out any argument alleging contributory negligence, given that this is an issue on liability rather than purely assessment of quantum (unless there is a defence alleging contributory negligence and the court either declines to enter judgment or provides that judgment be on the issue of primary liability only).

To avoid issues particularly on liability, arising at a later stage a claimant with the benefit of an admission from the defendant would be wise to put matters beyond doubt by inviting the court to enter judgment, for an amount of damages and interest to be assessed, at the stage of initial case management. To rule out any subsequent arguments about causation that judgment will need to identify specific damage caused by the breach of duty, though not necessarily quantification of the damages.

Furthermore, once judgment has been entered any admission, on which such a judgment is based, will no longer be subject only to CPR 14.1A, if a pre-action admission, or CPR 14.1, if the admission is made after commencement of court proceedings, either of which still allows the defendant to make subsequent application for permission to withdraw that admission. Following judgment the defendant has a much more onerous burden, if seeking to resile from the admission, as the defendant will need to show good grounds for the judgment to be set aside. Furthermore, whilst the court may, in accordance with CPR 3.1(7) vary or revoke a case management order, a judgment, even if only for an amount of damages and interest to be decided, is likely to be regarded as a final order to which CPR 3.1(7) does not apply, for example *Roult v North West Strategic Health Authority*.[15]

If judgment is entered in a consent order, that agreement may evidence a binding compromise excluding any general power of the court to vary the order (see **8.2.4.2**).

For these reasons a claimant may wish, even without an admission, to try and secure any judgment which can be obtained at this stage, if necessary by an application under Part 24 (see **4.3.2.2**).

If the claimant seeks judgment under CPR 3.4, by striking out a Statement of Case, under CPR 14.1A, on the basis of a pre-action admission, or under Part 24, on the basis there is no real prospect of succeeding on the claim or an issue, it is likely the court will require an application to be made, given the terms of those rules.

4.3.1.5 Split trial

If any issues can or should be disposed of at any early stage an appropriate order should be sought, in accordance with the case management powers of the court found in CPR 3.1(2)(i) and (j).

If there is to be trial of a preliminary issue that will frequently be liability though limitation may also be dealt with on this basis, either as an issue or in its own right or along with liability.

---

[15]   [2009] EWCA Civ 444.

- a real issue on liability, even if that is only on the extent of any contributory negligence, which needs determining to remove an obstacle to settlement;
- issues on quantum that mean the issue cannot conveniently be dealt with along with liability such as:
    - an unsettled prognosis;
    - the need for further expert evidence on quantum;
    - the defendant wishes to obtain expert evidence on quantum;
    - quantum is otherwise difficult or complex.

The key factor that may identify an issue suitable for a preliminary trial was identified by Lord Hope in *SCA Packaging Ltd v Boyle*[17] when he said:

> 'The essential criterion for deciding whether or not to hold a pre-hearing is whether ... there is a succinct knock out point which is capable of being decided after only a relatively short hearing.'

A more analytical approach was set out by Neuberger J (as he then was) in *Steele v Steele*[18] where a checklist of 10 factors was identified.

> 'The first question the court should ask itself is whether the determination of the preliminary issue would dispose of the case or at least one aspect of the case ... The second question that I think the court should ask itself is whether the determination of the preliminary issue could significantly cut down the cost and time involved in pre-trial preparation or in connection with the trial itself ...Thirdly, if, as here, the preliminary issue is a question of law, the court should ask itself how much effort, if any, will be involved in identifying the relevant facts for the purpose of the preliminary issue ... Fourthly if the preliminary issue is an issue of law, to what extent is it to be determined on agreed facts ... Fifthly, where the facts are not agreed, the court should ask itself to what extent that impinges on the value of a preliminary issue ... That indeed is effectively a sixth factor which the court should at least take into account ... namely whether the determination of a preliminary issue may unreasonably fetter either or both parties or, indeed, the court, in achieving a just result which is, of course, at the end of the day what is required of the court at the trial ... Seventhly, the court should ask itself to what extent there is a risk of the determination of the preliminary issue increasing costs and/or delaying the trial. Plainly the greater the delay caused by the preliminary issue and the greater any possibility of increase in cost as a result of the preliminary issue. The less desirable it is to order a preliminary issue. However, in this connection I consider that the court can take into account the possibility that the determination of the preliminary issue may result in a settlement of some sort. In other cases the court may well decide that, although the determination of the preliminary issue would not result in a settlement, it will result in a substantial cutting down of costs and time ... Eighthly, the court should ask itself to what extent the determination of the preliminary issue may be irrelevant. Clearly the more likely it is that the issue will have to be determined by the court the more appropriate it can be said to be to have it as a preliminary issue ... Ninthly, the court should ask itself to what extent is there a risk that the determination of a preliminary issue could lead to an application for the pleadings being amended so as to avoid the consequences of the determination ... Tenthly, the court should ask itself whether, taking into account all the previous points, it is just to order a preliminary issue. In this connection, it should be mentioned that the nine specific tests overlap to some extent ....'

---

17   [2009] UKHL 37.
18   [2001] CP Rep 106.

4.3.1.5.3   Unsuitable cases?

Even if factors that would normally suggest a split trial are present it may still be appropriate for both liability and quantum to be tried together.

For example, in *Blyth Valley Borough Council v Henderson*[19] it was held that if the defendant alleges malingering, or otherwise attacks the credibility of the claimant on quantum aspects of the case, it may be harder to obtain an order for a split trial as the overall interests of justice may require all issues, in those circumstances, to be determined at the same time. However, that was a case in which there had been significant delay in progressing the claim and it was that delay, together with the allegations of malingering, that led the court to hold it was desirable that both liability and quantum be tried together to avoid the delay and any further prejudice.

In *Hornsby-Clifton v Ministry of Defence*[20] HHJ Reddihough held:

> 'It seems to me that in the circumstances of this case potentially there is going to be a considerable overlap between issues as to causation in particular and as to the quantum of the claim. Thus, in my judgment the same trial judge would be in a very much better position having heard all of the expert and lay witness evidence to determine, if the claimant is successful in establishing negligence, exactly what has resulted from that negligence not only in terms of the claimant's condition and prognosis but also, in relation to the quantum of her claim, what would have befallen her in any event had there not been the negligence in question.'

Consequently, whilst appreciating that if successful in a split trial on liability quantum might then be capable of agreement the judge went on to hold:

> '... it seems to me that all of the issues are so overlapping and intermingled that it is very obvious indeed that all of the issues should be dealt with at one and the same time by the same trial judge. That judge will have a very good impression of the claimant in relation to all of the issues and there would be the risk that if there were to be a split trial on quantum it would be before a different judge who would not have had the advantage of seeing all the various experts and the claimant and other witnesses in relation to the causation and negligence issues. So for all of those reasons I am firmly of the view that it is not appropriate for there to be a split trial on the particular facts and issues of this case and that all issues should be dealt with at one and the same time.'

4.3.1.5.4   Tactics

For the claimant there are a number of advantages in having liability dealt with as a preliminary issue.

Potential costs exposure will be limited, particularly where investigation of quantum may be extensive and expensive if the claimant is unsuccessful. This is important whatever method of funding is adopted by the claimant:

- on a private basis where there is a BTE policy then, as well as protecting the insurers it is essential to keep the indemnity limit, which might cover trial of liability but not the additional costs of investing and trying quantum, in mind;

---

19   [1996] PIQR P64.
20   [2014] EWHC 4412 (QB).

- in a claim funded by a conditional fee agreement it is, again, important to protect the exposure of any ATE insurers and keep within any indemnity limit;
- in legal aid cases the strict cost/benefit ratio may prevent even a case of some potential value being pursued unless the cost of doing so can be controlled but if the claimant succeeds on liability the prospects of success will increase which in turn will justify further work on the quantum aspects.

Furthermore, if liability can be established an appropriate interim payment may then be obtained. In cases of serious injury that may help to put in place, sooner rather than later, suitable accommodation arrangements and an appropriate care regime. Once these are in place it may be more difficult for the defendant to challenge those at any quantum trial (but would find it much easier to raise a challenge if no interim payment has been made, no such measures have been implemented and the claimant is trying to argue, in the abstract, about what reasonable requirements for care and accommodation are).

For these reasons, often under the misguided guise of saving costs, the defendant will object to a split trial. Indeed, the defendant has sound reasons for so doing, though these may not be voiced, including the potential difficulty of making effective offers to settle the whole claim in the absence of detailed evidence on quantum, the effectiveness of Part 36 offers made by the claimant on the issue of liability and, regrettably, the wish to deploy greater resources in out-spending the claimant especially when considerable costs will be required to fully assess quantum in a case which may be difficult on liability.

4.3.1.6 *Further Statements of Case and further information*

Case management directions may be required to deal with outstanding matters concerning Statements of Case.

If the claimant wishes to file amended Particulars of Claim, or the defendant an amended defence, it may be appropriate to seek a direction giving permission, if such amendments have not already been made by the stage of case management.

Amendments will often be allowed, subject to terms on costs, even at a late stage. That approach has been shaped by the observations of Peter Gibson LJ in *Cobbold v Greenwich London Borough Council*[21] where he said:

'The overriding objective (of the CPR) is that the court should deal with cases justly. That includes, so far as is practicable, ensuring that each case is dealt with not only expeditiously but also fairly. Amendments in general ought to be allowed so that the real dispute between the parties can be adjudicated upon provided that any prejudice to the other party caused by the amendment can be compensated for in costs, and the public interest in the administration of justice is not significantly harmed. I cannot agree with the judge when he said that there would be no prejudice to [the defendants] in not being allowed to make the amendments which they are seeking. There is always prejudice when a party is not allowed to put forward his real case.'

However, the new line of defence had been known to the claimant for several months before the application for amendment was made and, accordingly, came as no surprise. Additionally, the amendment concerned just a point of law on facts which were not in dispute.

---

[21] (Unreported) 9 August 1999, CA.

Whilst a party not allowed to make an amendment will always be prejudiced this should be a factor, not the deciding factor, when determining whether to allow the amendment. Consequently, where late amendment would be likely to require an adjournment of the trial the court may rule against allowing an amendment.

In *Swain-Mason v Mills & Reeve (A Firm)*[22] an application to amend a defence made at trial was, on appeal, refused, placing reliance on the observations of Waller LJ in *Worldwide Corporation Ltd v GPT Ltd*[23] that:

> 'Where a party has had many months to consider how he wants to put his case and where it is not by virtue of some new factor appearing from some disclosure only recently made, why, one asks rhetorically, should he be entitled to cause the trial to be delayed so far as his opponent is concerned and why should he be entitled to cause inconvenience to other litigants? The only answer which can be given and which, [counsel for the applicant] has suggested, applies in the instant case is that without the amendment a serious injustice may be done because the new case is the only way the case can be argued, and it raises the true issues between the parties which justice requires should be decided. We accept that at the end of the day a balance has to be struck. The court is concerned with doing justice, but justice to all litigants, and thus where a last minute amendment is sought with the consequences indicated, the onus will be a heavy one on the amending party to show the strength of the new case and why justice both to him, his opponent and other litigants requires him to be able to pursue it.'

In *Cutting v Islam*,[24] however, a late amendment to the particulars of claim was allowed on the basis that prejudice to the claimant, if the amendment was not permitted, outweighed any prejudice to the defendant caused by the grant of permission to amend.

Although costs are likely to be ordered against the party making an amendment it may be difficult to quantify, and summarily assess, those costs pending the trial: *Chadwick v Hollingsworth (No 2)*.[25]

If there is an outstanding request for further information, which it is considered needs a response prior to further stages of the case, an order for a response may need to be sought.

Where there is a Part 20 claim directions will be required relating to Statements of Case and for management of the Part 20 claim, with or separate from the main claim. The court will, generally, wish to manage the main claim and the Part 20 claim together. However, in appropriate circumstances, the claims might be managed separately; for example if liability is not an issue in the main claim, which can therefore be disposed of quickly, whilst there are significant issues in the Part 20 claim, which may therefore require a longer timescale.

4.3.1.7   *Disclosure and inspection*

It will usually be appropriate for each party to give disclosure, by list using form N265, with provision for inspection, on request, of documents disclosed, though the parties can agree to limit disclosure.

---

22   [2011] EWCA Civ 14.
23   (Unreported) 2 December 1998, CA.
24   [2014] EWHC 720 (QB).
25   [2010] EWHC 2718 (QB).

The defendant may suggest that, particularly if liability is not in issue, it is not necessary for the defendant to give disclosure. However, as surveillance evidence is likely to be in a form of a document subject to disclosure (see **5.6**) it would not normally be appropriate to dispense with formal disclosure by the defendant, unless the defendant is able to confirm that there are no documents which would be subject to disclosure (not already disclosed) and that there is no intention to rely on any documents not already disclosed. Even then it may be preferable to generally extend time for service of a list rather than simply dispensing with the need for a list altogether.

In personal injury claims the parties are exempt from the requirement, otherwise applicable in multi-track claims, to prepare a report identifying relevant documents, where and with whom those documents are located, in the case of electronic documents how those documents are stored and the costs of giving standard disclosure. However, and particularly in multi-track cases, the claimant in a personal injury claim should consider carefully the need for electronic disclosure by the defendant and, as appropriate, service of a questionnaire in accordance with Practice Direction 31B of the CPR as a preliminary to disclosure.

4.3.1.8 Exchange of witness statements

A direction for the exchange of witness statements will be necessary, assuming that there is evidence to be given by witnesses of fact.

The requirements of the overriding objective, that the parties are on an equal footing, will normally mean exchange should take place simultaneously. That is reflected by the terms of para 3.9 of the Practice Direction to Part 28, dealing with fast track claims, and para 4.10 of the Practice Direction to Part 29, indicating the general approach to directions in multi-track claims.

The parties may be ready to exchange statements promptly but it will usually be appropriate for exchange to take place after disclosure, so that the statements can deal, as far as necessary, with the documents disclosed or matters arising out of those documents.

If liability is to be dealt with as a preliminary issue exchange, at this stage, will usually be confined to statements on that issue.

4.3.1.9 Permission to use and exchange expert evidence

It is important to secure permission to rely upon expert evidence at the stage of case management directions, whether expert evidence has already been disclosed or is yet to be disclosed, given the terms of CPR 35.4(1), which provides that no party may call an expert or put in evidence an expert's report without the court's permission.

In the most straightforward personal injury claim it will be necessary to seek at least a direction giving permission to rely on the written expert evidence the claimant has already served with the Particulars of Claim.

If the claimant is yet to obtain, or disclose, further expert evidence it will be necessary to seek from the court a direction providing both for permission to rely on such evidence and giving a timetable for exchange, whether simultaneously or sequentially.

In every case the need for expert evidence, and hence permission to rely on such evidence, will need to be carefully considered by reference to the issues defined in the statements of case (see **7.1.4**).

4.3.1.9.1   *Permission*

CPR 35.4(2) deals with the information a party must give the court when applying for the permission, required by CPR 35.4(1), to rely on expert evidence.

This rule requires the party seeking permission to:

* provide an estimate of the costs of the proposed expert evidence;
* identify the field in which expert evidence is required;
* identify the issues which the expert evidence will address; and
* identify, where practicable, the name of the proposed expert.

The cost of the expert evidence will depend upon whether it is proposed the evidence be limited to a written report or if questions and/or joint statements, as well as perhaps oral evidence, may be required.

It may suffice to identify, in broad terms, the issues which the expert evidence will address, for example condition and prognosis, or it may be appropriate to identify those issues by reference to the statements of case.

It will always be necessary to identify the field, or discipline, in which expert evidence is required. Where practicable the name of the proposed expert should be given.

The distinction between an order giving permission to rely on a named expert and an order giving permission by reference to a field of expertise may be important if a party wishes to substitute an expert.

In *Beck v Ministry of Defence*[26] the court gave the defendant permission to rely on the evidence of a named expert. When the defendant wished to instruct a substitute expert the court ordered that, as a condition of being granted permission, privilege would have to be waived and the report of the expert originally named disclosed to the claimant, with a view to preventing 'expert shopping'.

CPR 35.4(3) confirms that if the court gives permission to rely on expert evidence that will be in relation only to the expert names or the field identified and that the order may also specify the issues which the expert evidence should address.

CPR 35.1 requires the court to restrict expert evidence to that which is reasonably required to resolve the proceedings, which is likely to be determined by the admissibility of the proposed evidence and the overriding objective (see **7.3.2**).

---

[26]   [2003] EWCA Civ 1043.

In *Hajigeorgiou v Vasiliou*,[27] however, the order only identified a field of expertise. Accordingly, although upholding the principle in *Beck*, the court concluded that no permission was required when the defendant sought to rely on a substitute expert (which the claimant was aware involved a change of identity because this was not the expert who had carried out an earlier inspection of the claimant's premises). The court reached that conclusion on the basis that the expert was within the same field of expertise as the expert who carried out the inspection, both of whom were experts in the field of expertise identified in the order, and thus further permission from the court was not required. The court took the opportunity of affirming the approach in *Beck*, where the expert is named, rejecting an argument that the decision ignored the law of privilege, on the basis the decision to waive privilege would be made in return for the grant of permission to rely on a substitute expert.

Hence, where expert evidence is available, and the experts upon whom the party is going to rely can be identified, it may well be appropriate to seek an order giving permission in relation to those named experts. In other circumstances it may be wise, if possible, to get permission by reference to a field of expertise. Conversely, if a defendant is seeking facilities to obtain a medical report it would be preferable to ensure any permission is in relation to that named expert so as to ensure that, should the defendant seek facilities to obtain further evidence from an expert in the same field, disclosure of the first report is likely to be required as a preliminary to any permission being granted in accordance with *Beck*.

4.3.1.9.2 *Exchange*

Directions for exchange will be necessary when:

- the claimant wishes to disclose further expert evidence; and/or
- the defendant wishes to disclose further expert evidence; and/or
- the parties have obtained, but not yet disclosed, evidence which ought to be exchanged simultaneously from experts in the same field, for example on liability.

Exchange of reports, at least reports of experts in the same discipline, will normally be simultaneous. However, sequential exchange may be appropriate if the further evidence is from experts in different fields, the evidence is to be from experts in the same fields as those whose evidence has already been disclosed or if there is a likelihood that following disclosure of expert evidence by the claimant the defendant will not seek to rely on corresponding evidence.

Pre-CPR in *Kirkup v British Rail Engineering Ltd*[28] the Court of Appeal endorsed the approach that, generally, exchange of reports should take place simultaneously, although occasionally sequential exchange would be appropriate. The same approach was taken in *Naylor v Preston Area Health Authority*[29] (see **7.10.2**).

Simultaneous exchange will generally remain appropriate under the CPR, reflected by the terms of para 3.9 of the Practice Direction to Part 28, in fast track claims, and the general approach to directions in multi-track claims set out in para 4.10 of the Practice Direction to Part 29.

---

27 [2005] EWCA Civ 236.
28 [1983] 1 WLR 1165.
29 [1987] 1 WLR 958.

4.3.1.9.3   Questions

The directions may provide a timescale for questions, or further questions, to experts and for replies to those questions.

4.3.1.9.4   Joint statements

If the directions contain a provision for exchange of reports between experts in the same field those directions are likely to provide that these experts confer and prepare a joint statement.

4.3.1.9.5   Supporting literature

In certain types of claim the directions should require the expert to identify learned articles, textbook entries and research studies. Standard directions in clinical negligence claims usually make appropriate provision and the same should apply in educational negligence claims: *DN v Greenwich London Borough*.[30]

4.3.1.9.6   Renewing application for permission

Obtaining permission to rely on expert evidence which the claimant will need, to prove those parts of the claim which are in issue, is a key objective at the stage of case management.

There is a risk that should the court refuse permission the trial judge may subsequently find the claimant has, in the absence of appropriate expert evidence, failed to prove relevant parts of the case. At that stage any appeal, on the basis that the trial judge should have allowed an opportunity to call appropriate expert evidence, is unlikely to succeed as it is the case management decision, refusing permission, that has to be appealed or renewed: *Cassie v Ministry of Defence*.[31]

Rather than an appeal the disappointed party may prefer to renew an application for permission to rely on expert evidence, perhaps when further information such as a draft report from the expert, is available. Renewing an application where there has been a material change of circumstance, which might include the availability of a report, may justify a variation of case management directions in accordance with CPR 3.1(7) (see **8.3.3**).

4.3.1.9.7   Written or oral evidence?

If there is only one expert in any particular field oral expert evidence should not be necessary, so any permission can be limited to reliance on the written evidence of such an expert.

If the court gives permission to rely on more than one expert in any field of expertise permission might be given, at the stage of initial case management, to rely on oral expert evidence. Alternatively, the need for oral evidence may be deferred until the stage of

---

30   [2004] EWCA Civ 1659.
31   [2002] EWCA Civ 838.

listing, by which time joint statements should have clarified whether the issues between the experts are such that the trial judge will need to hear those experts give evidence.

4.3.1.10 Schedules and counter schedules

The directions appropriate for schedules will depend upon the stage at which it is likely the claim can be properly quantified and also whether liability is to be dealt with as a preliminary issue.

If the claimant has served a detailed schedule with the Particulars of Claim the defendant should have provided a detailed counter schedule in, or accompanying, the defence. If the defendant has not done so the court should be invited to direct prompt service of a counter schedule so that the issues on quantum, and the evidence to deal with these, can be identified as that, in turn, will help control disclosure, factual evidence and hence costs.

Orders providing for service of schedules, assuming the court is giving directions which include determination of the issue of quantum, will be necessary in other circumstances, including the following circumstances:

- The claimant may not yet have been able to provide a detailed schedule, perhaps because the prognosis is not settled or further expert evidence is awaited.
- The defendant, if given permission to rely on such evidence, may be awaiting expert evidence before being in a position to provide a counter schedule.
- If the claimant is able to do no more than provide a provisional schedule, outlining the broad heads of claim, the defendant is unlikely to be in a position to provide a meaningful counter schedule until a more definitive, even if still provisional, schedule has been served.
- Where the schedules which have been exchanged are complex or substantial these may need to be amended so that interest calculations and multipliers can be brought up to date nearer to trial.

There should generally, either be an exchange of detailed Schedules with the Statements of Case or provision for detailed Schedules after exchange of evidence. It is not appropriate that the claimant, in every case, is obliged to serve a definitive Schedule with the Statement of Case and the defendant only required to respond by detailed Schedule prior to listing, as that ignores the requirement for a counter schedule imposed on the defendant by paragraph 12.1 of the Practice Direction to Part 16.

Schedules provided for under case management directions should generally be in relation to expenses and losses, though these might be schedules of damages setting out figures proposed for pain, suffering and loss of amenity along with other non-pecuniary heads of claim as well.

4.3.1.11 Periodical payments

Paragraph 3A of the Practice Direction to Part 29 and CPR 41.6 require the court to consider whether periodical payments or a lump sum will be the more appropriate form for all or part of an award of damages.

Accordingly, the issue of periodical payments may arise as part of routine case management, even if damages in that form are not sought by the claimant.

At the stage of case management the court may direct the parties to set out details of any claim for, and response to, a periodical payment in the schedules to be exchanged.

4.3.1.12   Listing/further case management

The case management directions will usually stipulate a date by which pre-trial checklists needs to be filed or fix a date for further case management by the court.

Any date given for the filing of pre-trial checklists is important as that cannot be varied just by the agreement of the parties and, moreover, is a deadline the court will expect the parties to work to and comply with.

Accordingly, the timetable for filing the checklist needs to be realistic but, equally, the court will expect the overall timetable to be as expeditious as is reasonably possible.

If this is likely to assist the court, it may be appropriate to provide that, at the stage of pre-trial checklists, copies of Responses to Requests for Further Information, witness statements and/or experts reports be filed. If, for example, it is proposed there be an exchange of reports from experts in the same discipline, with a joint statement from such experts, it is likely these documents will need to be filed so that the court can form a view whether oral expert evidence is required or if written reports with the joint statement will suffice.

4.3.1.13   Trial window

At the stage of initial case management the court may, and in a fast track claim should, go as far as identifying a trial window.

As with the pre-trial checklist, care is required to properly assess the appropriate timetable, as the court will be reluctant, once a trial window has been fixed, to depart from this.

Depending on the arrangements of the particular court, there will, again, need to be a reasonable interval between the date for filing the checklist and the trial window, given that the court will need to review the checklist and give the parties reasonable notice of the trial date.

4.3.1.14   ADR

Paragraph 4.10 of the Practice Direction to Part 29 specifically provides that a direction for ADR will, in the absence of other suggested directions, be considered by the court. That reflects encouragement from the Court of Appeal to use, more widely, the provision for ADR already found in model directions for clinical negligence cases used in the Royal Courts of Justice, see *Halsey v Milton Keynes General NHS Trust*.[32]

---

[32]   [2004] EWCA Civ 576.

The need to properly engage in ADR has been given added impetus by the Court of Appeal judgment in *PGF II SA v OMFS Company 1 Ltd*.[33] Additionally, the 2013 model directions, use of which is encouraged by the CPR, include a direction specifically dealing with ADR.

If a defendant, despite a direction of this kind, still refuses to engage in ADR this may be relevant to costs even if the defendant is ultimately successful in defending the claim (see **12.2.4.1.2**).

If directions include the model order for ADR a party who is not willing to adopt a method proposed by another party will need to comply with the terms of the order in explaining why that is so, and the failure to do so would be a non-compliance with that order which may, of itself, attract a sanction.

Whilst in *Halsey* the Court of Appeal concluded insistence that parties mediate 'would be to impose an unacceptable obstruction on their right of access to the court', in *Wright v Michael Wright (Supplies) Ltd*[34] Sir Alan Ward observed:

> 'Does CPR 26.4(2)(b) allow the court of its own initiative at any time, not just at the time of allocation, to direct a stay for mediation to be attempted, with the warning of the costs consequences, which *Halsey* did spell out and which should be rigorously applied, for unreasonably refusing to agree to ADR? Is a stay really "an unacceptable obstruction" to the parties right of access to the court if they have to wait a while before being allowed across the court's threshold? Perhaps some bold judge will accede to an invitation to rule on these questions so that the court can have another look at *Halsey* in the light of the past 10 years of developments in this field.'

Even if it would not be appropriate for the court to make such an order should the defendant, despite a direction of this kind, still refuse to engage in ADR that may be relevant to costs even if the defendant is ultimately successful in defending the claim (see **12.2.4.1.2**).

4.3.1.15 Costs of routine case management

It will usually be appropriate for costs, in relation to case management, to be costs in the case.

That should be so even if the parties have degrees of success in the extent to which any particular directions are obtained or resisted as some directions will invariably be given, making any hearing at which disputed issues are dealt with an inevitable part of the conduct of the case. Consequently, the costs of any such hearing ought to be costs which reflect the eventual outcome.

It is usually necessary to obtain an order for costs of any court order, even if these are costs in the case, as otherwise, in accordance with CPR 44.13(1) (since April 2013, CPR 44.10(1)), costs will not be recoverable in relation to that order.

---

[33] [2013] EWCA Civ 1288.
[34] [2013] EWCA Civ 234.

If, however, an order is made following an application without notice that, in accordance with CPR 44.13(1A), (since April 2013, CPR 44.10(2)), will be deemed to include an order for the applicant's costs in the case.

4.3.2   Non-routine case management

Further matters, which are not part of routine case management, might conveniently be dealt with at this stage by the court but will normally require specific application.

If any such matters arise it will be usually be appropriate to make application by the time of the directions questionnaire is filed, and indeed the questionnaire asks if any application is to be made. That is because the overriding objective will normally make it appropriate for all case management to be dealt with on one occasion, an approach reflected, for example, by paragraph 2.5 of the Practice Direction to Part 28.

Any such application will need to be made in accordance with Part 23 of the CPR (see 8.4).

A number of issues, even though these are not part of routine case management, may well arise at the stage of allocation.

4.3.2.1   *Parties*

If it is necessary to add, remove or substitute a party this is likely to require an application.

The claimant may, of course, wish to consider joining any Part 20 defendant brought into the proceedings as a defendant to the main claim if that party may be liable in the alternative, rather than in addition to, the original defendant.

4.3.2.2   *Summary judgment*

Under Part 24 of the CPR the court can give summary judgment on the claim or any particular issue, on the basis the defendant has no real prospect of successfully defending the whole of the claim or an issue in it.

The Protocol, and the requirement that defences contain a Statement of Truth, has meant such applications in personal injury claims are less usual than they once were.

Whilst judgment on the basis of an admission in the defence will usually be part of routine case management, judgment under Part 24 will usually require an application, with supporting evidence, complying with the provisions of that rule. It is important to note that:

- the application notice must, in accordance with paragraph 2(2) of the Practice Direction to Part 24 contain a statement that it is an application for summary judgment made under Part 24; and
- under paragraph 2(3) there must be a statement the claimant believes on the evidence that there is no real prospect of successfully defending the claim or issue to which the application relates.

An application for judgment under Part 24, which unless permission of the court is given can only be made once the defendant has filed an acknowledgement of service or defence, may be appropriate in a variety of circumstances:

- Where the claimant relies on a pre-action admission, which the defendant has not obtained permission to withdraw, and the terms of the defence are inconsistent with that admission. That is because CPR 14.1A (4) specifically allows such an admission to form the basis of an application for judgment.

- Where the claimant contends any admission or agreement amounts to a binding compromise of the claim as a whole or any issue in the claim and this is not conceded by the defence. In such circumstances an application for judgment at this stage may be important to avoid an argument by the defendant that the claimant has waived the right to judgment (for example on the basis of the equitable doctrine of approbation and reprobation as occurred in *Ashraf v Devon County Council*).[35]

- If the defendant contests an issue, such as liability, in circumstances such that the claimant can maintain there is no real prospect of successfully defending that issue.

The general advantages of obtaining a judgment, where this is possible, have already been considered (see **4.3.1.4**).

The claimant may, of course, face an application by the defendant for summary judgment. A number of decisions confirm that the court should not too readily deprive the claimant of the opportunity to take a case, even if it may not be the most promising of cases, to trial: *Petrou v Bertoncello*;[36] *Selwood v Durham County Council*;[37] *Smith v Ministry of Defence*;[38] *Duce v Worcestershire Acute Hospitals NHS Trust*.[39]

It is important to keep distinct the ability of the court to enter judgment under Part 3 and under Part 24; *Duce v Worcestershire Acute Hospitals NHS Trust*.

4.3.2.3   Interim payment

CPR 25.6 sets out the general requirements for an interim payment application. Accordingly, if a claimant seeks an interim payment at the stage of initial case management that will generally require an application notice in accordance with Part 23 of the CPR, complying with the formalities of Part 25.

An application for an interim payment cannot be made, under the terms of CPR 25.6(1), prior to the end of the period available to the relevant defendant for filing an acknowledgement of service.

The conditions to be satisfied before the court can order an interim payment, are set out in CPR 25.7(1), hence any application needs to deal with those criteria. This rule provides that the court may only make an order for an interim payment where any of the following conditions are satisfied:

---

[35]   (Unreported) Plymouth County Court, 30 August 2007.
[36]   [2012] EWHC 2286 (QB).
[37]   [2012] EWCA Civ 979.
[38]   [2013] UKSC 41.
[39]   [2014] EWCA Civ 249.

- the defendant against whom the order is sought has admitted liability to pay damages or some other sum of money to the claimant;
- the claimant has obtained judgment against that defendant for damages to be assessed or for a sum of money (other than costs) to be assessed;
- it is satisfied that, if the claim went to trial, the claimant would obtain judgment for a substantial amount of money (other than costs) against the defendant from whom he is seeking an order for an interim payment whether or not that defendant is the only defendant or one of a number of defendants to the claim;
- in a claim in which there are two or more defendants and the order is sought against any one or more of those defendants, the following conditions are satisfied:
  - the court is satisfied that, if the claim went to trial, the claimant would obtain judgment for a substantial amount of money (other than costs) against at least one of the defendants (but the court cannot determine which); and
  - all the defendants are either:
    - a defendant that is insured in respect of the claim;
    - a defendant whose liability will be met by an insurer under section 151 of the Road Traffic Act 1988 or an insurer acting under the Motor Insurers Bureau Agreement, or the Motor Insurers Bureau where it is acting itself; or
    - a defendant that is a public body.

For these purposes a pre-action admission ought to suffice to meet the condition the defendant has 'admitted liability', particularly if the claimant wishes to make application following filing of the acknowledgement of service but before the defence.

CPR 25.7(4) provides the court must not order an interim payment of not more than a reasonable proportion of the likely amount of the final judgment, with CPR 25.7(5) confirming the court must take into account contributory negligence and any counter claim.

An example of the court's approach to assessing a 'reasonable proportion' of damages is *Spillman v Bradfield Riding Centre*.[40]. For these purposes the court took the defendant's valuation of the claim, effectively set out in the counter schedule, discounted that figure by the percentage the parties had agreed to apportion liability and took 75 per cent of the resulting figure as a 'reasonable proportion' of likely damages. From that figure interim payments already made were deducted with the claimant being awarded the balance by way of further interim payment.

However, the court must be cautious if a periodical payments order might be made as it would not be appropriate to award an interim payment at a level which would restrict the options open to the trial judge.

In *Cobham Hire Services Ltd v Eeles*[41] the Court of Appeal indicated, when deciding on a reasonable proportion of the overall damages, the court should usually only take into account damages for pain, suffering and loss of amenity together with past losses and accommodation costs in a case where a periodical payments order might be made at trial.

---

[40]   [2007] EWHC 89 (QB).
[41]   [2009] EWCA Civ 204.

That approach will not be applicable if the trial judge is not likely to make a periodical payments order: *Preston v City Electrical Factors Ltd.*[42]

Even if a periodical payments order may be made at trial the court must still take account of the circumstances of the individual case. Hence in *FP v Taunton & Somerset NHS Trust*,[43] in order to provide suitable accommodation, the judge only excluded future care from the calculation of overall damages for the purpose of assessing an interim payment.

An interim payment will nearly always be appropriate if liability is admitted and can usefully be utilised to fund immediate needs for the claimant, see for example *Daly v General Steam Navigation Co Ltd.*[44] Whilst it might be suggested this can create an 'unlevel playing field', so far as the future assessment of damages is concerned, that is only a factor and not a bar to the making of a substantial interim payment: *Smith* v *Bailey.*[45]

If the defendant contends that contributory negligence is a relevant factor in determining the likely amount of the final judgment the burden of proof is, as at trial, on the defendant to establish an arguable case for contributory negligence at the hearing of an application for an interim payment: *Smith v Bailey.*

In *Smith* Popplewell J also summarised the law guiding the proper approach to interim payment applications following *Eeles* as follows:

'(1)   CPR r. 25.7(4) places a cap on the maximum amount which it is open to the Court to order by way of interim payment, being no more than a reasonable proportion of the likely amount of the final judgment (para 30).

(2)   In determining the likely amount of the final judgment, the Court should make its assessment on a conservative basis; having done so, the reasonable proportion awarded may be a high proportion of that figure (paras 37, 43).

(3)   This reflects the objective of an award of an interim payment, which is to ensure that the claimant is not kept out of money to which he is entitled, whilst avoiding any risk of an overpayment (para 43).

(4)   The likely amount of a final judgment is that which will be awarded as a capital sum, not the capitalised value of a periodical payment order ("PPO") (para 31).

(5)   The Court must be careful not to fetter the discretion of the trial judge to deal with future losses by way of periodical payments rather than a capital award (para 32).

(6)   The Court must also be careful not to establish a status quo in the claimant's way of life which might have the effect of inhibiting the trial judge's freedom of decision, a danger described in *Campbell* v *Mylchreest* as creating "an unlevel playing field" (paras 4, 39).

(7)   Accordingly the first stage is to make the assessment in relation to heads of loss which the trial judge is bound to award as a capital sum (para 36, 43), leaving out of account heads of future loss which the trial judge might wish to deal with by a PPO. These are, strictly speaking (para 43):
    (a)   general damages for pain, suffering and loss of amenity;
    (b)   past losses (taken at the predicted date of the trial rather than the interim payment hearing);
    (c)   interest on these sums.

(8)   For this part of the process the Court need not normally have regard to what the claimant intends to do with the money. If he is of full age and capacity, he may spend

---

42   [2009] EWHC 2907 (QB).
43   [2009] EWCA 1965 (QB).
44   [1980] 3 All ER 696.
45   [2014] EWHC 2569 (QB).

it as he will; if not, expenditure will be controlled by the Court of Protection (para 44). Nevertheless if the use to which the interim payment is to be put would or might have the effect of inhibiting the trial judge's freedom of decision by creating an unlevel playing field, that remains a relevant consideration (para 4). It is not, however, a conclusive consideration: it is a factor in the discretion, and may be outweighed by the consideration that the Claimant is free to spend his damages awarded at trial as he wishes, and the amount here being considered is simply payment at the earliest reasonable opportunity of damages to which the Claimant is entitled: *Campbell* v *Mylchreest* [1999] PIQR Q17.

(9)   The Court may in addition include elements of future loss in its assessment of the likely amount of the final judgment if but only if
        (a)   it has a high degree of confidence that the trial judge will award them by way of a capital sum, and
        (b)   there is a real need for the interim payment requested in advance of trial (para 38, 45).

(10)   Accommodation costs are "usually" to be included within the assessment at stage one because it is "very common indeed" for accommodation costs to be awarded as a lump sum, even including those elements which relate to future running costs (paras 36, 43).'

Popplewell J, giving judgment in *Smith*, also reiterated the point that an interim payment is likely to represent the minimum sum the claimant will be entitled to and judge like any damages awarded at trial an interim payment can be spent as the claimant wishes.

A copy of the application notice, seeking an interim payment, must be served at least 14 days before the hearing of the application and be supported by evidence (which in accordance with CPR 32.6 will be a witness statement setting out relevant matters) in order to comply with the terms of CPR 25.6 (3).

Any respondent to the application must, under the terms of CPR 25.6(4), who wishes to rely on written evidence at the hearing, must file the written evidence and serve copies on every other party to the application at least seven days before the hearing.

4.3.2.4   Preservation and inspection of property

Occasionally, it may be necessary to seek, under the general power given by CPR 3.1(2)(m) or the more specific power in relation to interim remedies in CPR 25.1, an order for preservation or facilities to inspect property.

If, for example, expert evidence on liability is required, which requires inspection of premises or other property, the court may be invited to make an appropriate order at the stage of case management.

In some cases, however, inspection will have taken place at an earlier stage if necessary as a result of a pre-action application (see **2.11.3**).

The approach to such applications was considered in *M3 Property Ltd* v *Zedhomes Ltd*[46] where Akenhead J held:

'So far as the law is concerned, CPR Part 25.1 enables the Court to grant injunctions or orders 'for the inspection of relevant property' or for the 'preservation of relevant property'. It is common ground that that the Court has the power to make the order sought but the

---

[46]   [2012] EWHC 780 (TCC).

order must be both necessary and proportionate. This was confirmed in the case of *Patel v Unite* [2012] EWHC 92 QB. This approach is consistent with the overriding objective.'

The importance of the overriding objective in this context was emphasised by Akenhead J in *McLennan Architects Ltd v Jones*[47] when he held:

'It is primarily to the overriding objective to which one must look as to the basis on which to exercise the discretion to make this type of order. It may be helpful if I list (non-exhaustively) the factors which might properly legitimately be taken into account:

(a) The scope of the investigation must be proportionate.

(b) The scope of the investigation must be limited to what is reasonably necessary in the context of the case.

(c) Regard should be had to the likely contents (in general) of the device to be sought so that any search authorised should exclude any possible disclosure of privileged documents and also of confidential documents which have nothing to do with a case in question.

(d) Regard should also be had to the human rights of people whose information is on the device and, in particular, where such information has nothing or little to do with the case in question.

(e) It would be a rare case in which it would be appropriate for there to be access allowed by way of taking a complete copy of the hard drive of a computer which is not dedicated to the contract or project to which the particular case relates.

(f) Usually, if an application such as this is allowed, it will be desirable for the Court to require confidentiality undertakings from any expert or other person who is given access.'

4.3.2.5 Specific disclosure

CPR 31.12 envisages an application, supported by evidence, where a party seeks an order for specific disclosure or inspection.

An application notice will clearly be required if issues arise out of standard disclosure under the terms of initial case management directions. If, however, there is clearly an issue between the parties at the stage of initial case management on the nature or extent of disclosure the court may treat this as an issue of routine case management not requiring a specific application.

4.3.2.6 Clarification of Part 36 Offers

A party may seek clarification of a Part 36 Offer, under CPR 36.9(1).

If clarification is not given, an application may be made for an Order that it be given, under CPR 36.9(2).

If clarification is sought, but not given, the claimant may rely on the absence of clarification to argue the costs implications of this at a later stage, an approach accepted in *Colour Quest Ltd v Total Downstream UK plc*.[48] Alternatively, the claimant may apply to the court for an order that clarification be given, which can conveniently be done at the stage of allocation and initial case management.

---

[47] [2014] EWHC 2604 (TCC).
[48] [2009] EWHC 823 (Comm).

4.3.2.7   *Costs of non-routine case management*

Where application is made for a specific order costs are likely to follow the event in that application.

Consequently, a claimant who expects to succeed overall will generally prefer to deal with any matters that arise as part of routine case management because, even if the claimant does not succeed in obtaining all the directions sought or is unsuccessful in resisting certain case management directions sought by the defendant, costs will be in the case as such matters are inevitably part of routine case management.

Where, however, an application is made it is much easier for the court to regard the issues as discrete and make provision for costs accordingly.

There are a range of costs orders available to the court when dealing with an interim application, any of which may be applicable to an application dealing with non-routine case management (see **8.9.2**).

4.3.3   COSTS MANAGEMENT

Amendments to the CPR in 2013 introduced costs management for most multi-track claims, following earlier pilot schemes. This followed a recommendation in the Jackson Report, which had described the essence of costs budgeting as being:

> '... that the costs of litigation are planned in advance; the litigation is then managed and conducted in such a way as to keep the costs within the budget.'

The rules relating to costs management are set out in section II of Part 3.

Where these provisions are applicable parties must file and exchange costs budgets, usually with directions questionnaires, so the court can consider whether to make a costs management order.

CPR 3.12(2) confirms the purpose of costs management is that the court should manage both the steps to be taken and the costs to be incurred by the parties to any proceedings so as to further the overriding objective.

This indicates a direct linkage between case management and costs management, the court managing the case in a way that allows matters to be dealt with justly but at proportionate cost. This was recognised by Moore-Bick LJ, dealing specifically with one of the pilot schemes but in words applicable to section II, Part 3, in *Henry v News Group Newpapers Ltd*[49], held:

> '... just as the court has responsibility for managing the proceedings, so also it has a responsibility for managing the costs and that it is expected to manage the costs by managing the proceedings in a way that will keep them within the bounds of what is proportionate.'

---

[49]   [2013] EWCA Civ 19.

Moore-Bick LJ went on to emphasise the importance of the overriding objective in this exercise when he said:

> 'The object of the practice direction, as described in paragraph 1.3, is twofold: (i) to ensure that the costs incurred in connection with the proceedings are proportionate to what is at stake and (ii) to ensure that one party is unable to exploit superior financial resources by conducting the litigation in a way that puts the other at a significant disadvantage. The intention is that both these (objectives) are to be achieved by management of the proceedings in a way that controls the costs being incurred. When paragraph 1.3 speaks of the parties' being on an equal footing it is concerned with the unfair exploitation of superior resources rather than with the provision of information about how expenditure is progressing.'

The approach to costs management varies between courts, as does the linkage between costs and case management. In some courts case and costs management are dealt with together whilst in others the court will give case management directions and subsequently review budgets to deal with costs management.

If a costs management order is made that may well have a bearing on costs eventually recovered by the successful party as CPR 3.18 provides that when assessing costs on the standard basis the court will have regard to the receiving party's last approved or agreed budget for each phase of the proceedings and not depart from that budget unless satisfied there is good reason to do so.

In *Yeo v Times Newspapers Ltd*[50] Warby J gave, in a reserved judgment, some general guidance about costs budgeting topics including:

- whether or not an oral hearing would be required;
- the proper approach to incurred costs;
- the correct approach to approval of figures by the court (and how this differs from conducting a detailed assessment);
- the topics of contingencies and revisions; and
- timing of budgets.

4.3.4   Timetable

The timetable for implementation of case management directions, particularly in a higher value multi-track case, will depend upon the prevailing circumstances, which may include the stage at which medical evidence, giving a definitive prognosis, is likely to be available.

However, paragraph 3.12 of the Practice Direction to Part 28 sets out a typical timetable for a fast-track case which may, as appropriate, apply to cases allocated to the multi-track. That timetable envisages working to the following schedule:

- disclosure within four weeks;
- exchange of witness statements within ten weeks;
- exchange of experts' reports within 14 weeks;
- filing of completed pre-trial checklists within 22 weeks; and
- hearing within 30 weeks.

---

[50]   [2015] EWHC 209 (QB).

This typical timetable gives a useful yardstick of what, for the purposes of preparing a draft order seeking directions, the court may consider an appropriate timescale. In a significant multi-track case, particularly if the prognosis is not settled, the timetable will look very different and is likely to involve a further case management conference rather than a date for listing.

4.4   OBTAINING APPROPRIATE CASE MANAGEMENT DIRECTIONS

Initial case management may be the only stage at which the court gives any significant directions and yet these can have a significant bearing on how the case progresses towards trial.

Accordingly, it is important when preparing the documentation to be filed at court, ahead of allocation, to consider best to persuade the court that the directions sought by the claimant should be ordered and how to resist direction sought on behalf of the defendant which are not considered appropriate.

Consequently, preparation of the necessary documentation, and if necessary negotiations with the defendant's representative, are essential steps at this stage of the claim.

Paragraph 2.3 of the Practice Direction to Part 26 confirms the parties should consult and cooperate in completing questionnaires and in trying to agreed case management directions. That will only be possible if the parties exchange copies of the questionnaires, and accompanying documentation, filed at court.

4.4.1   Claimant's directions questionnaire

The claimant will have to complete the questionnaire in any event, so best use should be made of the form itself to explain, so far as possible, why the allocation and case management directions sought by the claimant are appropriate for the case.

That will require each section in the questionnaire to be considered and completed as required.

4.4.1.1   Stay

The questionnaire invites the parties to indicate whether a stay may be useful.

The court may, in accordance with CPR 26.4, stay the claim, usually for up to one month at a time. Whist the parties might, meanwhile, have requested a stay by letter the directions questionnaire specifically enquires whether a stay is sought.

Generally, even if the case may settle, a stay may not be in the interests of the claimant as it is better for the case to progress forward.

Occasionally, however, it may be appropriate to suggest a stay on behalf of the claimant. For example:

- if some information is awaited that will, once available, allow a settlement to be achieved or perhaps the parties are very close to settlement and need a little additional time; or
- if the claimant has suggested a form of ADR which the defendant has declined, it may be more difficult for the claimant, if necessary at a later stage, to resist an application for the costs of the action by the defendant unless a stay was sought in the directions questionnaire: *Reed Executive plc v Reed Business Information Ltd.*[51]

In these, fairly limited circumstances, a stay might be requested in the claimant's questionnaire.

4.4.1.2 Settlement

Unless not viable, because relevant information necessary to assess proper terms is not available, the claimant will usually want to indicate settlement will be considered at this stage.

That does not, however, mean that it will necessarily be appropriate to suggest mediation, unless perhaps the defendant takes an opposing view to the question of settlement in which case a direction dealing specifically with ADR might need to be sought.

The questionnaire specifically asks for confirmation that the party, on whose behalf the questionnaire is being filed, has been made aware of ADR, hence the need to ensure the claimant is fully appraised of all options available at the earliest opportunity.

4.4.1.3 Compliance with the Protocol

The questionnaire asks the party completing it whether the Protocol has been complied with by that party.

Ideally, as a result of dealing pre-action stages of the case properly, it will be possible to answer this question affirmatively on behalf of the claimant.

Often it might be thought the more relevant question is whether the defendant has complied with the Protocol. As there is no provision in the questionnaire to comment on this aspect of the matter it will be necessary, if there has been non-compliance which is relevant for the purposes of case management, to deal with this by separate case summary.

Compliance with the Protocol is a very relevant issue for the court when managing the case given the terms of paragraph 3.2 of the Practice Direction to Part 28 and paragraph 4.2 if the Practice Direction to Part 29 as well as a mandatory consideration under CPR 3.1(4).

---

[51] [2004] EWCA Civ 159.

4.4.1.4   Experts

The questionnaire should be completed with relevant details of experts on whose evidence the claimant wishes to rely, given that the permission of the court will be required to call such evidence.

CPR 35.4(2) requires a party applying for permission to rely on expert evidence to identify the relevant field of expertise and, where practicable, the name of the expert in that field whose evidence it is proposed to rely upon. Consequently, expert should be named where possible. However, this is not always practicable or prudent, for example if a report is not yet available it is unwise to commit to a particular named expert and better to identify the field of expertise as once an expert is named permission from the court will be necessary to rely on a different expert even in the same expert field (see **4.3.1.9.1**).

In a straightforward case the questionnaire itself will suffice on the topic of experts. If, however, the claimant seeks permission to rely on a number of experts, or conversely argues the defendant does not need to duplicate expert evidence already obtained and disclosed by the claimant, it may be necessary to supplement the questionnaire with further information in a case summary.

4.4.1.5   Proposed directions

The questionnaire asks whether directions are proposed. Wherever possible, draft directions should be set out, as these make clear to the court what directions are proposed and, at the very least, will set the agenda of any case management conference which may be held to determine appropriate directions (see **4.4.2**).

4.4.1.6   Applications

The question about applications is a reminder that if the claimant seeks an order which would not generally be regarded as part of routine case management, an application notice is likely to be required and should be made at the time the questionnaire is filed, so the court can deal with all necessary case management on one occasion.

Routine case management, which will not usually require a specific application, will be the type of matter identified in CPR 28.3 and paragraph 5.3 of the Practice Direction to Part 29 (see **4.3.1**).

It is a question of degree whether formal application is required if a party seeks specific case management not regarded as routine. The court may be willing to take a broad view of case management powers and hence deal with any such matters arising at the case management conference. However, it is prudent for a party seeking non-routine directions to indicate, in the questionnaire or an accompanying draft order, what is to be sought. If that is not done a party faced with such an application, even if made under the guise of a request the court exercise general case management powers, will be able to argue that, in the absence of any prior notification, it was expected only routine matters would arise. In such circumstances it might be contended that it would be wrong for the court to allow a party to be taken by surprise on a contentious point, without a proper chance to prepare for and deal with the issues raised.

4.4.1.7 Other information

The questionnaire invites the party completing it to provide any other information which may assist the court in dealing with allocation and case management.

If largely standard directions are sought no further information is likely to be required.

If, however, it is necessary to go into some detail on the background to the claim and/or why particular directions are required and/or why any directions sought by the defendant are not considered appropriate it is most likely a case summary will be necessary, rather than a very brief summary which is all the box on the questionnaire will allow.

In other circumstances, perhaps one or two brief points on why a particular direction is required, it may be most convenient to complete the questionnaire with information in the relevant box.

4.4.2 Draft order

The directions questionnaire should be accompanied by a draft order setting out the case management directions considered appropriate.

The Appendix to the Practice Direction to Part 28 sets out typical directions that may be appropriate which, coupled with the timetable also found in the Practice Direction to 28, gives a useful template, to which any modifications to suit the particular case can be made.

For multi-track cases there are model directions which can be found on the Ministry of Justice website.

There are more specific types of model directions for particular types of claim which should be used in appropriate cases.

When filing a draft order with the directions questionnaire it may be preferable, as at that stage the date of the order will not be known, to insert into the order the number of weeks after the actual date the order is made each provision is intended to take effect (leaving the court to insert a calendar date as and when the order is made).

If the draft order is prepared for a hearing, or revised prior to a hearing, calendar dates can usefully be inserted, reflecting the timescale proposed by the claimant.

The draft order may also be revised, and amended where appropriate, once the defendant's directions questionnaire, and any accompanying draft order, has been considered.

4.4.3 Costs estimate

Costs estimates have largely been superseded in multi-track claims by costs budgets and costs management orders.

Where, however, no costs management order is made the budget will effectively stand as a costs estimate.

In a fast track cases not subject to fixed costs a costs estimate might still usefully be provided and, as defendant's costs are not fixed, the claimant may wish to obtain an estimate from the defendant.

For cases pre-dating April 2013, where there has been no costs management order, the former section 6 of the Costs Practice Direction, dealing with costs estimates, remains important.

The estimate needs to be realistic, both for costs already incurred and for overall costs. For these purposes that estimate should assume the claim will go to trial rather than settle meanwhile: *Leigh v Michelin Tyre plc*.[52]

Paragraph 6.5A of the Costs Practice Direction provided that if there is a difference of 20 per cent or more between the base costs claimed by a receiving party on detailed assessment and the costs shown in an estimate of costs filed by that party:

- the receiving party must provide a statement of the reasons for the difference with the bill of costs; and
- if a paying party claims to have relied on an estimate of costs or wishes to rely on the costs shown in the estimate to dispute the reasonableness or proportionality of the costs claimed a statement setting out the case on this issue must be included in the points of dispute.

If, following the provision of a costs estimate, developments in the case mean that the estimate is no longer accurate it is important to update the estimate and to do so at the earliest opportunity.

When costs are determined by the court the Costs Practice Direction provides account can be taken, when assessing the costs of the receiving party, of the estimate given by the paying party.

4.4.4 Case summary

In many cases the questionnaire, accompanied by a draft of the directions sought, will suffice but there are circumstances in which, to explain fully why certain directions are sought or resisted, a case summary, dealing with relevant topics, is likely to assist the court.

Guidance on the format of the case summary is given by paragraph 5.7 of the Practice Direction to Part 29.

A case summary, if necessary, can usefully deal with a number of matters.

- The defendant's failure to comply with the terms of any applicable protocol, if that is relevant for the purposes of case management, because otherwise that failure will not necessarily be apparent from answers given in the questionnaires. Particular matters which might be drawn to the attention of the court include:

---

[52] [2003] EWCA Civ 1766.

- explaining steps taken to try to obtain expert evidence in accordance with any relevant protocol;
- where a refusal to co-operate by the defendant means that additional time is required to deal with directions; and
- if facilities to investigate the claim are required because these have not been given pre-issue (either in breach of any specific provisions in a protocol or on the basis of a failure to co-operate as required by the overriding objective);

- to explain why the claimant needs permission to rely on expert evidence, for example evidence dealing with liability or non-medical quantum expert evidence;

- to anticipate, or respond to, any request by the defendant for permission to rely on expert evidence which may duplicate that already obtained and disclosed by the claimant, especially where there has been joint selection under the Protocol and/or a failure to indicate why such further evidence is reasonably required;

- to explain why a split trial is considered appropriate;

- to explain why any other particular directions are considered appropriate in the context of the particular case.

4.4.5 The defendant's directions questionnaire

Given the encouragement in the CPR for the parties to cooperate and try to agree case management directions the defendant should be expected to supply the claimant with a copy of the defendant's directions questionnaire and any accompanying documentation.

If the defendant does not provide the claimant with copy documentation the court should be requested to provide copies.

The defendant's questionnaire should be reviewed to see if, and to what extent, there is any dispute over allocation and appropriate case management directions. It may be appropriate to engage in further consultation and negotiation if it seems likely that this would allow the parties to agree on the directions the court can be invited to give.

4.4.5.1 Stay

Even if the claimant does not think a stay appropriate it may be worth reconsidering this if the defendant suggests as much and it may still be appropriate to try and agree a stay, particularly if the defendant gives a clear indication proposals are to be made.

4.4.5.2 Compliance with the Protocol

The answer to this question should be carefully checked if the defendant does not comply with the Protocol to ensure a candid response is given.

If the defendant gives what appears to be an erroneous answer to this question the matter should, at least, be raised in correspondence by inviting an appropriate amendment to the questionnaire. If the absence of compliance with the Protocol is likely to be relevant to case management issues the claimant may well need, if that has not already been done, to file a case summary setting out the chronology with, by reference to that, alleged breaches of the Protocol by the defendant.

4.4.5.3   Experts

The questionnaire should be carefully reviewed to see whether the defendant wishes to rely on any expert evidence, particularly if the defendant has not sought, or been granted, facilities to obtain such evidence.

In such circumstances, unless the matter is dealt with by case summary or correspondence in reply, a false impression may be created that there is already relevant evidence available which the court ought to give the defendant permission to rely upon, which has the effect of pre-judging whether or not it is reasonable for the defendant to have facilities to obtain such evidence.

There is a particular danger where the defendant seeks permission, in general terms, to rely upon an expert in a particular field as that would allow the defendant permission to rely on any expert within that field and, without more, may allow a degree of 'expert shopping' as illustrated in *Hajigeorgiou v Vasiliou* (2005) (see 7.8.5.1).

4.4.5.4   Proposed directions

If the questionnaire refers to proposed directions then a copy should accompany the questionnaire and, if not, be sought.

Any directions should be carefully reviewed:

- It may be that these are capable of agreement, if appropriate with some modification, in which case negotiations and discussions may be useful.
- The directions may be in relation to contentious points which the claimant needs to deal with either by filing an up to date case summary or correspondence, commenting as appropriate, or by indicating to the court that matters are not agreed and a hearing is probably required.
- The directions sought may even be of such a kind that the defendant ought really to be making formal application in accordance with Part 26, and not just seeking to rely on the general case management powers of the court, albeit the court will generally take a broad view as to what forms part and parcel of general case management.

4.4.5.5   Application

If the defendant makes an application at the time of the directions questionnaire a copy of the application notice and any supporting evidence should, of course, be served on the claimant.

Any such application should be dealt with in the same way as an application made on behalf of the claimant at this stage.

4.4.5.6   Other information

If the questionnaire indicates the defendant invites the court to take account of other information, even where that is the covering letter to the court, the claimant is entitled to see that information, if it is to be taken account of by the court, in accordance with paragraph 2.2 of the Practice Direction to Part 26. So, if any further information is referred to but not supplied this should be sought.

4.4.5.7 Costs budget

Where the defendant's directions questionnaire is accompanied by a costs budget that budget should be reviewed to see whether the parties may be able to agree costs, as well as case, management.

If the case is not subject to costs budgeting the claimant may wish to seek a costs estimate from the defendant, particularly in cases where the claimant's costs are fixed but the defendant's costs are not set, given the potential liability of the claimant for costs.

4.4.5.8 Consultation and negotiation

If it is possible to obtain the directions sought, at least substantially, by agreement, ahead of any court hearing, so much the better.

The outcome of a hearing can never be predicted with certainty and so it is always appropriate to try and agree directions, even if this means agreeing to substantially, rather than wholly, what the claimant would, ideally, seek from the court.

Moreover, consultation and negotiation will help achieve the objective, identified in paragraph 2.3 of the Practice Direction to Part 26, of the parties agreeing case management directions the court may be invited to make.

Furthermore, paragraph 2.2 of the Practice Direction to Part 26 provides that extra information, supplementing the directions questionnaire, should only be taken account of by the court if all parties agree or copies have been provided by the party relying on that information to all other parties.

Accordingly, all or any of the following steps may be appropriate once the claimant's directions questionnaire has been completed:

- Send a copy of the claimant's directions questionnaire, with draft directions, to the defendant inviting agreement of the directions or identification of points of disagreement to see how far apart the parties really are.
- Pick up the telephone and discuss the matter, to see if there really is any significant disagreement.
- Be prepared to compromise and reach an agreement, provided key directions sought can be agreed.
- Confirm the terms in a draft order, endorsed with consent by both parties, which can be filed at court:
    - ideally so that an order can be made before the court makes an order itself and/or ahead of any hearing scheduled; and
    - if a hearing scheduled there is an agreed note before the court from the parties which the court can work to.

4.5   THE CASE MANAGEMENT CONFERENCE

Following the filing of directions questionnaires, the court will, in many cases, make an order allocating the case and giving case management directions without a hearing. This accords with CPR 1.4(2)(j), that the need for attendance at court should be avoided where possible, and paragraph 6.1 of the Practice Direction to Part 26, that the court should only hold an allocation hearing if that is considered necessary.

In other cases the court will, following the filing of directions questionnaires, arrange a case management conference. If such a hearing is arranged then this becomes the focus of the opportunity to secure appropriate directions.

4.5.1   Reasons for a case management conference

The court is likely to fix a case management conference, rather than just give directions on the papers, if, for example:

- the questionnaires indicate a clear disagreement between the parties on the directions which are appropriate; or
- there is a significant disagreement as to the track to which the case should be allocated; or
- if the case is otherwise complex and is likely to require a degree of case management that necessitates a hearing at which the parties can make representations and the court consider what is appropriate after hearing these.

4.5.2   Preparation and tactics

If there is to be a case management conference it is important to approach preparation for the hearing carefully. This may involve a number of steps:

- negotiating with the defendant and trying to agree, or at least narrow, the issues for determination by the court;
- reviewing the file in readiness for the hearing so that any matters that may arise, in relation to case management, can be dealt with which may mean:
  - preparing, or updating, ready for filing a case summary dealing with the issues likely to arise so that these are before the court and the judge will have a good idea of the claimant's stance on case management issues;
  - filing an amended draft order, dealing if appropriate with any agreement reached, incorporating calendar dates;
  - filing any other relevant documents, such as correspondence and reports;
  - filing a skeleton argument as an alternative, or in addition, to case summary if, for example, there are legal arguments it might be helpful for the court to have summarised in written form in support of submissions made orally at the hearing.
- Ensuring documentation filed is in a suitable format, often an indexed and paginated bundle, so that the court and all parties can easily refer to relevant documents at the hearing. This is particularly important if the hearing is to be dealt with by telephone (as explained further at 4.5.3).
- Attending the hearing, which will require efficient diary systems.

- Preparing, if the claimant seeks costs in any event, a costs statement for filing and service ahead of the hearing (though generally a costs statement will not be necessary as case management hearings will normally include provision for costs in the case).

- Remembering the availability of telephone hearings, which are often suited to case management conferences, and seeking the defendant's agreement to this where appropriate.

4.5.3 Telephone hearings

Following a pilot scheme Practice Direction 23A deals with the use of telephone hearings.

The general approach of the court to the availability of telephone hearings was set out by Lord Philips in *Heyward v Plymouth Hospital NHS Trust*[53] where he observed that:

> 'I pause to say that I would commend the practice of carrying out case management conferences or other interlocutory matters by telephone where it is appropriate: but where that is done it is important that the judge who is conducting the hearing should have available before him the appropriate documentary material in a form which the parties to the proceedings are able to duplicate so that their submissions are readily intelligible.'

A telephone hearing will not, however, always be appropriate even when the court is dealing with case management issues. In *Hockley v North Lincolnshire NHS Foundation Trust*[54] HHJ Richardson QC observed:

> 'It is my view telephone hearings are very useful. There are, however, limitations to that method of hearing a case. Over use of telephone hearings is not to be encouraged. One such limitation is that the ethos of the telephone hearing is speed and convenience. There are cases that need a time for reflection and the telephone hearing system does not easily lend itself to that. The milieu is of haste and expediency, not an exercise of reflective examination.'

The judge continued:

> 'Such hearings are amenable to short decision making cases and matters which are truly procedural rather than requiring a fully reasoned exercise of a judgment. A party is entitled to a telephone hearing of any application which is under an hour. In assessing that time, allowance must be made for a judgment to be delivered and even some time for reflection. A case of this kind where there is a demand for the exercise of a judgment in a difficult factual matrix where the consequences are likely to be very significant should not be conducted by telephone hearing.'

4.5.3.1 *When to use telephone hearings*

Paragraph 6.2 of the Practice Direction 23A confirms, unless the court otherwise orders, hearings to be conducted by telephone are:

- allocation hearings;
- listing hearings; and

---

[53] [2005] EWCA Crim 939.
[54] (Unreported) Kingston upon Hull County Court 19 September 2014.

- interim applications, case management conferences and pre-trial reviews with a time estimate of not more than one hour.

Telephone hearings are not, however, appropriate where the application is made without notice to the other party, all the parties are unrepresented or more than four parties wish to make representations at the hearing (though for these purposes where two or more parties are represented by the same person they are to be treated as one party).

The court may order that a hearing which would normally be conducted by telephone will not be and, conversely, that an application not normally dealt with by telephone to be dealt with in that way.

Consequently, the court and the parties should be expected to have regard to the terms of Practice Direction 23A when making an application or fixing a hearing. If that does not occur a request for the hearing to be dealt with by telephone can be made under paragraph 6.4 of Practice Direction 23A, which can be made by letter, rather than application notice and shall be dealt with by the court without requiring the attendance of the parties.

4.5.3.2   *Arranging a telephone hearing*

If the court directs a hearing to be dealt with by telephone it will be necessary to make the arrangements for that hearing in accordance with paragraph 6.5 of the Practice Direction to Part 23:

- the appropriate legal representative (strictly the applicant but in practice usually the representative who has suggested the telephone hearing) must arrange, with an appropriate telecommunications provider, for a telephone conference at precisely the time fixed by the court for the hearing;
- the provider must be given the telephone numbers of all concerned and the sequence in which they are to be called, namely the applicant's legal representative, then the legal representatives of all other parties and then the judge;
- the conference must be recorded by the provider who must then send the tape to the court.

Once an appropriate provider has been arranged, and contact details supplied, that provider should make all necessary arrangements to call those involved at the appointed time and deal with the recording.

4.5.3.3   *Preparing for a telephone hearing*

If a hearing is to be dealt with by telephone it is particularly important that all documentation, to be referred to at any hearing, is filed ahead of the hearing so as to be readily available to the judge. Because the parties will be remote from the judge it may also be useful to ensure any bundles are indexed and paginated for ease of reference.

If the parties have prepared separate draft orders, setting out the case management directions proposed, it may assist a judge to have a single document identifying any terms agreed and denoting where the parties seek orders in different terms.

All documents filed will also need to be served.

4.5.4 Format and objectives of a case management conference

The hearing is likely to be rather more open and wide ranging than the hearing of an application notice. The court is, therefore, likely to look at the case as a whole and deal with any issues relating to case management that arise. Of course, the hearing may have been fixed to deal with a specific issue, such as the need for expert evidence, in which case the hearing is likely to focus on that issue. Nevertheless, the person dealing with the hearing should be ready to deal with any matters raised by the court.

Accordingly, it is important that, if possible, the hearing is dealt with by the person who has conduct of the file. If that is not possible the person dealing with the hearing will need to ensure they are fully familiar with the file and able to deal with any matters that may be raised by the court at the hearing (in accordance with paragraph 6.5 of the Practice Direction to Part 26).

If a draft of the directions sought by the claimant has been prepared this should help to provide an agenda and hence the advantage of ensuring the directions questionnaire is accompanied by a suitable draft.

Similarly, if there is a case summary and/or skeleton argument that may assist in providing an agenda for the hearing.

4.5.5 Scope of the hearing

A case management hearing should not be used as a 'Trojan Horse' so that a party is able to bring before the court, without notice, matters which are not properly part of routine case management.

Even if not the subject of formal application any directions not part of ordinary case management ought at least to be dealt with by draft order served well ahead of the hearing or referred to in the directions questionnaire. Moreover, it is essential that adequate time be allowed and this may be a further reason for excluding other than routine matters without proper notice. In *Basildon & Thurrock University NHS Trust v Braybrook*[55] Summary J observed:

> '... I deplore the attempt to shoe-horn a hearing which, with this judgment has lasted some 4 hours into a half hour hearing. A party who does this will face either the prospect of the application being adjourned or dismissed with costs or, if heard, have to pay the costs whether they succeed or not.'

Conversely, if specific application is made for a matter which could be dealt with by routine case management, and a case management hearing has already been listed, such a step would seen unnecessary. Consequently, it might be argued the costs of the application ought not be allowed, even if the party making it succeeds in obtaining an order along the lines ought, as costs of case management will generally be costs in the case.

---

[55]   [2004] EWHC 3352, QB.

4.5.6   Costs of case management hearings

The appropriate order for costs at a case management hearing, as with any case management, would generally be costs in the case. That is so even if one party has unsuccessfully applied for, or sought to resist, certain directions.

The court can make an order for costs in the same way that it may on the hearing of an application (see **8.9.2**) though this would usually be appropriate only when the focus of the hearing, or the need for a hearing at all, has been a particular aspect of case management on which one party has succeeded and, or course, if there is before the court, at the case management hearing, an application for a specific order.

4.6   ACTION ON RECEIPT OF CASE MANAGEMENT DIRECTIONS

On receipt of the order giving case management directions, or following the hearing if there has been a case management conference, it is important to assess the action required to deal with those directions and ensure the case will be ready for listing in accordance with the timetable given by the court.

4.6.1   Review of directions

When directions have been given by the court, these should be carefully reviewed to check that they are adequate for the steps that need to be taken on the claimant's behalf and that there is provision for costs, usually costs in the case.

If the directions are not suitable it may still be possible to resolve the matter:

*   If directions have been given by the court on the papers, without a hearing, either party may apply back to the court for the directions to be reviewed in accordance with paragraph 4 of the Practice Direction to Part 28 or paragraph 6 of the Practice Direction to Part 29.
*   If there has been a hearing, it will be necessary for any party dissatisfied with the case management directions to appeal that decision. However, any appeal will be a review not a re-hearing, making any challenge to the exercise of discretion very difficult. Furthermore, the terms of paragraph 4.5 of the Practice Direction to Part 52 require the appeal court to take into account, when considering an appeal against a case management decision, whether the issue is of sufficient significance to justify the costs of appeal, whether the procedural consequences of an appeal outweigh the significance of the case management decision and whether it would be more convenient to determine the issue at or after trial (see **10.2.7**).

4.6.2   Planning implementation of the timetable

The timetable set out by the court is not a target, that may or may not be achieved, but a series of deadlines that ought to be kept to.

Indeed, the dates set out in the timetable are the latest dates by which action should be taken and if steps can be taken sooner they should be: *RC Residuals Ltd v Linton Fuel Oils Ltd.*[56]

So, at the very least, the deadline set out in the timetable must be complied with and this will require:

- diary entries being made to ensure any work which will need to be done ahead of the deadline is done well ahead of that deadline;
- diary entries to ensure the claimant does comply, at the latest, by the deadline in the Order;
- diary entries to ensure the defendant complies with directions by the due date.

Any steps that can be taken straightaway should be actioned as soon as possible after the timetable has been given, for example preparing for disclosure and the exchange of evidence.

4.6.3 The defendant

Although the defendant should also have received the order giving case management directions, it is still sensible, and constructive, to agree arrangements, so far as possible, with the defendant for implementing the order, especially as the dates given are the latest dates by which action should be taken and if any steps can be taken sooner so much the better. So:

- It may be useful to confirm to the defendant, following the order, how the claimant intends to implement this, especially if any deadlines can be brought forward and this also guards against the risk of the defendant having not received the Order from the court.
- The defendant should subsequently be reminded, at appropriate stages, in the event the defendant fails to comply with the timetable.

4.6.4 Experts

Paragraph 8 of the Practice Direction to Part 35 provides that where a court order requires an act to be done by an expert, or will otherwise affect an expert, the party instructing that expert must serve a copy of the order on the expert (the claimant serve the order if it is a single joint expert).

4.6.5 Keeping to the timetable

Make sure diary entries are actioned and that the case does keep to the timetable.

Sanctions that apply automatically can, where appropriate, be relied on, though it may be necessary to make application to the court if there are no automatic sanctions or these do not adequately protect the claimant.

Although case management directions envisage compliance by both parties it should be the claimant who remains in the driving seat so far as progress of the claim is concerned.

---

[56] [2002] EWCA Civ 911.

4.6.6   Varying the timetable

If the timetable does go astray steps should be taken, at the earliest opportunity, either to get the case back on track or consider whether the timetable needs to be varied:

- It is better to take steps late than not at all.
- Agreement to vary the timetable can be reached on most stages, so negotiation and co-operation with the defendant can be helpful.
- If agreement cannot be reached it may be necessary to apply to the court either to vary the timetable or seek relief from sanctions. Either way the sooner this is done the better.
- The court must, however, approve any variation to the timetable if this concerns the date fixed for return of the pre-trial checklists, the trial date or indeed the trial window.

4.6.7   Variation of or additional directions

The court can always give additional case management directions, at a later stage, as and when required.

Furthermore, CPR 3.7 gives the court power to vary case management directions, though there will usually have to be a change in circumstances which justifies this. This power can, however, be excluded if the parties have reached an agreement which effectively becomes a binding compromise: *Siebe Gorman & Co Ltd v Pneupac Ltd*.[57] Consequently, care should always be exercised before having an order made 'by consent', as that may prevent even an extension of time being given, and it may be preferable simply to agree the order without expressly stating it is made by 'consent'.

If the court has given judgment, for example on liability, that may amount to a binding compromise but if not may nevertheless be regarded as a final order which cannot then be varied under CPR 3.7: *Roult v North West Strategic Health Authority*.[58]

4.6.8   Reviewing costs budgets

If the court has made a costs management order it is essential to keep track of costs incurred as if these are likely to exceed the budget application to the court, for variation of that budget, should be made at the earliest opportunity: *Elvanite Full Circle Ltd v AMEC Earth and Environmental UK Ltd*.[59]

4.7   SANCTIONS

How will the court approach a case when questionnaires have been filed and what sanctions will there be if there is default?

---

57   [1982] 1 All ER 377.
58   [2009] EWCA Civ 444.
59   [2013] EWHC 1643 (TCC).

4.7.1   General approach

The general approach of the court is set out in paragraph 4 of the Practice Direction to Part 26. So, in dealing with allocation and case management the court will take account of:

- the overriding objective of dealing with the case justly, as set out in Part 1; and

- those parts of the Civil Procedure Rules dealing specifically with case management (26 to 28);

- the Human Rights Act 1998 which provides further assistance in helping to produce a just result and avoiding any violation of the right to a fair trial: *Goode v Martin*[60] and *Woodhouse v Consignia plc*.[61]

4.7.2   Default with directions questionnaire

Sanctions which may apply in the event of default in filing questionnaires are:

- Service of notice requiring payment of the appropriate fee, where the questionnaire is filed without payment of fee (CPR 3.7).

- Exercise of general case management powers, including the power to strike out a Statement of Case, where the questionnaire is not filed at all (CPR 3.4).

- Costs sanctions where a hearing takes place because of the failure to file a questionnaire (paragraph 6.6 of the Practice Direction to Part 26).

After the date for filing has elapsed, the court may issue a notice giving a very short timescale in which to file the questionnaire, providing the claim or defence, as appropriate, be struck out in default. Accordingly, it is important to note, and diarise, the last date for filing the directions questionnaire to ensure that it is filed, at the latest, by that date, duly completed and accompanied by the appropriate fee.

4.7.3   Default with costs budgets

An express sanction is provided in CPR 3.14 for the failure to file a costs budget by the due date, namely that the party in default will be treated as having filed a budget comprising only the applicable court fees.

The courts, notably in *Mitchell v News Group Newspapers Ltd*,[62] have taken a tough approach to the imposition of, and grant of relief from, sanctions relating to the timely filing of costs budgets.

---

[60]   [2001] EWCA Civ 1899.
[61]   [2002] EWCA Civ 275.
[62]   [2013] EWCA Civ 1537.

CHAPTER 5

DISCLOSURE

5.1 INTRODUCTION

Case management directions will usually provide for the disclosure and inspection of documents by all parties.

It is important to deal with the stage of disclosure and inspection carefully to help ensure that documents the claimant has disclosed can be relied on at trial and also that, even if largely dealt with pre-action, all documents which may assist the claimant are made available by the defendant.

Furthermore, dealing with disclosure and inspection as a first step in the implementation of case management directions should mean that the factual and expert evidence subsequently exchanged is based on all appropriate documentation which, in turn, will help ensure that such evidence deals fully with the issues.

The scope of disclosure is, ultimately, tested not by relevancy but necessity. The test of necessity means disclosure of particular documents must be necessary to dispose fairly of the proceedings: *Science Research Council v Nasse*.[1] Hence documents must be relevant to be necessary yet it may not be necessary for all relevant documents to be disclosed.

The CPR need to be seen in the context of this well-established test for disclosure.

5.1.1 CPR disclosure

Part 31 CPR deals with disclosure and contains some important definitions and provisions.

5.1.1.1 Disclosure (CPR 31.2)

A party discloses a document by stating that the document exists or has existed.

5.1.1.2 Document (CPR 31.4)

A document is defined as anything in which information of any description is recorded.

---

[1]   [1980] AC 1028.

5.1.1.3   Standard disclosure (CPR 31.6)

Standard disclosure is defined as requiring a party to disclose:

- documents on which that party relies;
- documents which:
    - adversely affect that party's own case; or
    - adversely affect another party's case; or
    - support another party's case; or
    - are required to be disclosed by a relevant practice direction.

The most relevant practice direction for these purposes is the Practice Direction Pre-Action Conduct which, at para 3.1(4) confirms there should be compliance with any relevant pre-action protocol, hence all documents within the categories identified in the PI Protocol should be disclosed, provided such disclosure is necessary.

'Standard disclosure' does not, however, include documents which, though they may be relevant, are either just part of the background or are what may be termed 'train of enquiry' documents: *Scottish & Newcastle plc v Raguz*.[2]

'Standard disclosure' will also not include documents which relate solely to credit. In *Thorpe v Chief Constable of Greater Manchester Police*[3] Dillon LJ said:

> 'It would indeed be an impossible situation in my view if discovery had to be given of every document, not relevant to the actual issues in the action, which might open up a line of inquiry for cross examination of the litigant solely as to credit.'

In the same case Neill LJ said: 'I am satisfied, however, that it has been the long-standing practice not to order discovery which is directed solely to credit.' *Thorpe* was approved, and applied to the CPR, by the Court of Appeal in *Favor Easy Management Ltd v Wu*.[4]

5.1.1.4   Search (CPR 31.7)

When giving standard disclosure a party is required to make a reasonable search for documents. This is qualified by the terms of para 2 of the Practice Direction to Part 31, which requires the parties to bear in mind the overriding principle of proportionality when determining the extent of a reasonable search.

5.1.1.5   Control (CPR 31.8)

The duty to disclose documents is limited to documents in the control of the party meaning:

- the document is or was in the physical possession of that party;
- that party has, or has had, a right to possession of the document; or
- that party has, or has had, a right to inspect or take copies of the document.

---

2   [2004] EWHC 1835 (Ch).
3   [1989] 1 WLR 665.
4   [2010] EWCA Civ 1630.

When determining whether documents in the physical possession of a third party in the litigant's control for the purposes of CPR 31.8 the court must have regard to the true nature of the relationship between the third party and the litigant: *North Shore Ventures Ltd v Anstead Holdings Inc.*[5]

5.1.1.6 Copy documents (CPR 31.9)

Whilst a party need not disclose more than one copy of a document, CPR 31.9 confirms a copy of a document containing a modification, obliteration or other marking or feature shall be treated as a separate document.

5.1.1.7 Continuing duty (CPR 31.11)

The duty of disclosure continues until the proceedings are concluded.

Accordingly, a party must immediately notify every other party if any document to which that duty extends comes into his possession.

Similarly, if further statements of case, or evidence, broaden the scope of the issues documents not previously but now covered by the scope of standard disclosure should be disclosed immediately.

Any further documents should be disclosed by a supplemental list in accordance with para 3.3 of the Practice Direction to Part 31 (though the parties might agree to do this informally by treating the further documents as having been added to the original list).

5.1.1.8 Specific disclosure (CPR 31.12)

The court may make an order for specific disclosure.

This rule may be relied on in a number of circumstances.

* One party may seek from any other party specific disclosure of undisclosed documents which it is contended properly comprise part of standard disclosure.
* An application may be made under this rule for an order directing a party to carry out a search for specific documents.
* Specific disclosure may be sought where it is contended that it is necessary for there to be disclosure of 'train of enquiry' documents or documents which relate solely to credit, as these categories of document are not part of standard disclosure.

The court may order specific disclosure before standard disclosure has taken place but that will not be usual: *Rigg v Associated Newspapers Ltd;*[6] *Dayman v Canyon Holdings Ltd.*[7]

---

[5]   [2012] EWCA Civ 11.
[6]   [2003] EWHC 710 (QB).
[7]   (Ch D 11/1/2006).

5.1.1.9   Reliance (CPR 31.21)

A party may not rely on a document which that party has failed to disclose or which that party fails to permit inspection of, unless the court gives permission.

It is this rule which imposes a sanction on a party who fails to deal with disclosure. Consequently, there are restrictions, under the terms of CPR 3.8, on any agreement between the parties to extend time for dealing with disclosure and so relief, under CPR 3.9, will be required in the event of sanctions applying (see **8.10**).

5.1.1.10   Use (CPR 31.22)

A party to whom a document has been disclosed may use the document only for the purpose of the proceedings in which it is disclosed, except where the document is read out or referred to at a public court hearing, the court gives permission or the party who disclosed the document agrees. Even in these circumstances the court may restrict or prohibit the use of a document.

5.1.2   CPR inspection

CPR 31 also deals with inspection that will generally, but not always, be permitted where a document has been disclosed.

Once again Part 31 contains some important definitions of provisions.

5.1.2.1   Right to inspect documents (CPR 31.3(1) and (2))

A party to whom a document has been disclosed has a right to inspect that document, subject to the document being in the control of the party who disclosed it, the party disclosing the document having a right or duty to withhold inspection or where the party giving disclosure considers it would be disproportionate to the issues in the case for inspection to be permitted.

5.1.2.1.1   Absence of control

CPR 31.8 defines 'control' (see **5.1.1.5**).

Where a party does not have physical possession of the document but has the right to possession or the right to inspect or take copies of the document then that party will need to take appropriate steps so that, if requested to do so, inspection of the document can be given.

Where a party does not have control of a disclosed document it is likely the party seeking inspection will need to request that document from whoever has possession and consider an application for disclosure, under CPR 31.17, if the party with possession of the document is not a party to the proceedings and fails to allow inspection voluntarily (see **5.9**).

5.1.2.1.2 Privilege

A right or duty to withhold inspection will usually arise where the relevant document is privileged.

Legal professional privilege will often be the basis for claiming a right or duty to withhold inspection as that is a cornerstone of the English legal system, which recognises the need for candour in giving instructions to legal advisors.

- Advice privilege covers communications between a lawyer, acting in the capacity of a lawyer, and a client for the purpose of seeking or giving legal advice: *Three Rivers District Council v Governor and Company of the Bank of England*.[8]

- Litigation privilege protects communications made after litigation has started, or is reasonably in prospect, between not just a lawyer and a client but also between a lawyer and an agent: *Seabrook v British Transport Commission*.[9] However, for privilege to attach the dominant purpose of the communication must be the seeking or giving of advice in relation to the litigation or for the purpose of obtaining evidence, or information which will lead to obtaining evidence, for the purpose of the litigation: *Waugh v British Railways Board*.[10] The dominant purpose of a document will be judged at the time that document is brought into being rather than the use to which that document is subsequently put: *Jones v Great Central Railway Co*;[11] *Alfred Crompton Amusement Machines Ltd v Commissioners of Customs and Excise (No 2)*.[12] It can be difficult to determine, on this basis, whether, for example, reports and investigations into accidents or incidents will be privileged.
  - Where the dominant purpose of the document was to resist a claim for damages the document is likely to be privileged: *Seabrook v British Transport Commission*.[13]
  - Where, however, the focus is on, for example, accident prevention then, even if that document may be used by lawyers if litigation should be commenced, it may well not be privileged: *Lask v Gloucester Health Authority*.[14]

Expert advice and evidence obtained for the purposes of litigation will, accordingly, be privileged (see **7.6.9**).

A claim for privilege must be made in accordance with CPR 31.19 (see **5.1.2.5**).

Communications between client and lawyers are likely to remain privileged so that inspection is never permitted. With evidence obtained for the purpose of the proceedings, however, it is likely that, at an appropriate stage privilege will be waived so the evidence can be relied upon. If the documents, for which privilege is claimed at the stage of disclosure, comprise either witness statements or expert evidence it is important to ensure these are exchanged, at which point privilege will be waived, by the due date under case management directions, failing which the terms of CPR 32.10, for factual evidence, and CPR 35.13, for expert evidence, will impose sanctions.

---

[8]   [2004] UKHL 48.
[9]   [1959] 1 WLR 509.
[10] [1980] AC 521.
[11] [1910] AC 4.
[12] [1974] AC 405.
[13] [1959] 1 WLR 509.
[14] [1991] 2 Med L.R. 379.

The issue of liability will include both breach of duty and causation. Consequently, where causation is, itself, a significant issue the court may need to define, expressly, that the preliminary issue includes the extent of the injuries caused by any breach of duty.

A split trial can be an extremely effective way of dealing with a claim, especially if quantum has any complexity, where liability is a significant issue.

Occasionally, it may be possible to agree quantum, subject to trial on liability only. That may be appropriate if the quantum can be readily assessed but, in other circumstances, it may be preferable to seek a split trial and defer quantum altogether pending determination of liability.

4.3.1.5.1   General approach

The court is likely to approach the question as to whether or not there should be a split trial on the basis of what would be most cost effective.

In one sense a split trial could be said to always increase costs, as potentially there may be two trials rather than one.

However, where liability is a real issue costs are likely to be saved if that issue is dealt with as a preliminary because:

*   if the claim fails it is disposed of relatively quickly and cheaply; but
*   if the claimant succeeds on liability a significant obstacle towards settlement will have been removed and the likelihood is that the case will then be settled without the need for a further trial.

In a fast track case, especially where the expert evidence will be limited to written reports, it will be harder to show that, overall, a split trial will result in a saving of costs, as much of the costs associated with quantum may have been incurred already. Hence in *DHL Air Ltd v Wells*[16] the Court of Appeal expressed concern about a case of relatively modest value where a split trial was ordered. Nevertheless, the court should be willing to order a split trial, even in fast track cases, if, on balance, that is likely to save costs.

In higher value cases where quantum is potentially complex and may require a number of experts, with perhaps oral evidence, it will be more readily apparent costs are likely to be saved by dealing with liability as a preliminary issue.

Adopting the most cost effective approach to the order in which the issues in the case are dealt with is a reflection of the general terms of the overriding objective. A split trial, for the same reasons that costs are likely to be saved, may well involve less use of court resources and may also ensure greater parity between parties who do not have the same resources.

4.3.1.5.2   Suitable cases?

Generally, if there is to be a saving in costs, the case will need to have some features suggesting a split trial is appropriate such as:

---

[16]   [2003] EWCA Civ 1743.

On exchange of evidence a party will expressly waive privilege. Privilege may, however, be impliedly waived so that the party loses the right to withhold inspection. Implying waiver of this kind will often occur when a document, for which privilege is claimed, is mentioned in a statement of case, witness statement or expert's report (see **5.2.4**).

Occasionally inspection of a privileged document may be given inadvertently. CPR 31.20 confirms that when this happens, the party who has inspected the document may use it or its contents only with the permission of the court. The approach the court should take, when considering permission, was considered by the House of Lords in *Al Fayed v The Commissioner of Police of the Metropolis*.[15]

In appropriate circumstances an injunction may be granted to prevent misuse of privileged documents: *Kausouros v O'Halloran*.[16]

It is important to note that even though there may be a valid claim for privilege any document falling within the scope of the disclosure order made by the court, whether this be standard or specific disclosure, must be disclosed. It is appropriate, where necessary, for such documents to be given a generic description in the relevant list, certainly where too specific a description of the document would effectively undermine the privilege to which the document is subject.

While legal professional privilege extends to advice given on the criminal law it does not extend to documents that themselves form part of a criminal or fraudulent act.

5.1.2.1.3   Disproportionality

Where a party considers that it would be disproportionate to the issues in the case for inspection of documents disclosed to be permitted that party is not required to allow inspection if it is stated in the disclosure statement that inspection is objected to on this ground.

This provision allows a party to refuse inspection of documents which are subject to disclosure even though not privileged are subject to the test of disproportionality.

Permitting inspection may be disproportionate on the basis of Part 1 (the relevance of proportionality being expressly endorsed by the terms of CPR 31.3(2)): *Webster v Ridgeway Foundation School Governors*;[17] *Favour Easy Management Ltd v Wu*;[18] *Durham County Council v Dunn*;[19] *Wm Morrison Supermarkets plc v Mastercard Inc*.[20]

This provision is also relevant if permitting inspection of documents would be a disproportionate interference with the right to privacy under Art 8 ECHR. Following the issue of proceedings it is the terms of Part 31, in the context of Art 8, that prevail rather than the provisions of the Data Protection Act 1998 for these purposes: *Durham County Council v Dunn*.[21]

---

[15]   [2002] EWCA Civ 780.
[16]   [2014] EWHC 2994 (Ch).
[17]   [2009] EWHC 1140 (QB).
[18]   [2010] EWCA Civ 1630.
[19]   [2012] EWCA Civ 1654.
[20]   [2013] EWHC 2500 (Comm).
[21]   [2012] EWCA Civ 1654.

5.1.2.2 Specific inspection (CPR 31.12(1))

The court may make an order for specific inspection.

5.1.2.3 Inspection of 'mentioned' documents (CPR 31.14(1) and (2))

Documents mentioned in statements of case, witness statements, witness summaries, affidavits or experts' reports may be inspected, though if that mention is in the report of an expert this is subject to the terms of CPR 35.10(4) (see **5.2.4.3**).

5.1.2.4 Copying (CPR 31.15)

A party with a right to inspect a document must give written notice of the wish to inspect it. That party may request a copy of the document which, subject to paying reasonable copying charges, requires the party who disclosed the document to supply such a copy within seven days of the request.

5.1.2.5 Withholding inspection (CPR 31.19)

A person may apply, before the stage of inspection of documents is reached, for an order permitting that person to withhold disclosure of a document on the ground that disclosure would damage the public interest.

Where a document is subject to disclosure a party may still claim a right or duty to withhold inspection, under CPR 31.19(3). However, that person must state either in the list in which the document is disclosed, or if there is no such list then to the person who wishes to inspect the document, there is such a right or duty and the grounds on which that right or duty is claimed.

Consequently, where there is a list, it is important the list of documents indicates those documents to which the right or duty to withhold inspection applies. That will usually be on the basis that either the documents are privileged or that permitting inspection would be disproportionate (see **5.1.2.1**).

If there is a challenge to the claim of privilege, or that inspection would be disproportionate, that is likely to be by way of application for specific inspection under CPR 31.12(1). CPR 31.19(6) confirms that for the purpose of deciding the validity of a claim for privilege the person seeking to withhold disclosure or inspection of a document may be required to produce that document to the court. Any party making an application for specific inspection, to challenge the validity of a claim for privilege, may wish to seek a direction, as a preliminary to the hearing of the application, that relevant documents be produced to the court if this is not agreed.

5.1.2.6 Authenticity (CPR 32.19)

CPR 32.19(1) provides that a party shall be deemed to admit the authenticity of a document disclosed under Part 31 unless notice to prove the document is served.

Any notice to prove a document must, under CPR 32.19(2) be served:

- by the latest date for serving witness statements; or
- within seven days of disclosure of the document, whichever is the later.

Consequently, if the authenticity of a document disclosed is to be challenged it is important to serve a timely notice (see **5.12.6**).

5.1.2.7   Content (para 27.2 Practice Direction to Part 27)

Para 27.2 of the Practice Direction to Part 27 confirms that all documents contained in bundles which have been agreed for use at a hearing shall be admissible at that hearing as evidence of their contents unless the court orders otherwise or a party gives written notice of objection to the admissibility of particular documents.

Whilst a party will need to have disclosed a document to rely on that document at all, certainly for a final hearing, the combined effect of CPR 32.19 and para 27.2 of the Practice Direction to Part 27 is that where the document is in an agreed bundle and no notice has been given either requiring a document to be proved or objecting to admissibility, that document will be treated as authentic and, moreover, the content will be admissible. Care is, accordingly, required both at the stage of disclosure, if authenticity is challenged, and when agreeing bundles, if there is an issue on admissibility (see **10.2.2**).

It is, equally, important that the claimant disclose all documents to be relied on and ensure these are included in any bundle for use at a hearing which is, if possible, agreed.

5.2   EARLY AND LATE DISCLOSURE

Disclosure and inspection may have taken place at an early stage, either before proceedings were issued or prior to lists of documents being served in accordance with case management directions.

Conversely, disclosure and inspection, at least in relation to some issues, may be deferred until a later stage or even dispensed with altogether.

5.2.1   Disclosure under the PI Protocol

Early disclosure may have been given under the terms of the PI Protocol.

Unless liability is admitted, the defendant should, in accordance with the PI Protocol, disclose all relevant documents within the relevant time limit. If the PI Protocol is followed, disclosure in such cases will be completed within three months of the acknowledgement of the letter of claim.

If, where liability is not admitted, the defendant fails to give full disclosure in accordance with the PI Protocol, the claimant will have had to decide whether to apply for an order requiring pre-action disclosure or to issue the main action and deal with disclosure as part of case management directions.

The claimant should, where the defendant has admitted liability under the PI Protocol, have given early disclosure of documents supporting the schedule of expenses and losses.

Prior to issue of proceedings the terms of the Data Protection Act 1998 will be relevant to the scope of disclosure: *Durham County Council v Dunn*.[22]

5.2.2 Pre-action disclosure

Pre-action disclosure is another way of obtaining early disclosure, particularly when the defendant fails to give disclosure required by the terms of the PI Protocol.

If the defendant fails to comply with the PI Protocol the claimant may wish to make an application for pre-action disclosure, especially where there are documents that may be crucial in assessing the merits of the case.

Where a protocol applies, such as the PI Protocol, the court will be more ready to enforce that protocol by a pre-action order for disclosure. However, such an order is discretionary and if the documents sought are not essential in deciding whether or not to proceed with the claim the court might decline to make an order (see **2.11.2.3**).

5.2.3 Statutory rights of disclosure

The claimant may have made use of statutory rights, prior to issuing proceeding, to obtain disclosure of documents from the proposed defendant and/or other parties at an early stage (see **1.9.1**).

5.2.4 Notice to produce documents

Once proceedings have been commenced a party may be able to obtain early inspection of documents in accordance with CPR 31.14, often ahead of exchange of lists.

Under CPR 31.14(1), a party may inspect any document mentioned in:

* a statement of case;
* a witness statement;
* a witness summary; or
* an affidavit.

Under CPR 31.14(2) a party may apply for an order to inspect a document not already disclosed in the proceedings if it is mentioned in an expert's report, subject to r 35.10(4). This rule does not give an automatic right of inspection and so, unless inspection can be agreed between the parties, a court order will be required.

Initially, any such document can be requested by service of a notice to produce. If inspection of the document requested is not given voluntarily then an application for an order can be made under CPR 31.12(1). Whether the court makes an order for inspection will depend upon whether the document has been mentioned, for the

---

[22]   [2012] EWCA Civ 1654.

purposes of CPR 31.14, and, if it has, whether that amounts to waiver of any privilege that would otherwise attach to the document.

5.2.4.1　Is the document 'mentioned'?

The circumstances in which a document will be 'mentioned' for the purposes of CPR 31.14(1), by being referred to in a statement of case or a witness statement/summary or an affidavit, were considered by Popplewell J in *Wm Morrison Supermarkets plc v Mastercard Inc*[23] in the following passage of his judgment:

> '(1) The test is whether there is a "direct allusion" to, or a "specific mention" of a document. That was the test previously applicable under rules of the Supreme Court, according to Slade LJ in *Dubai Bank Ltd v Galadari (No2)*;[24] and that remains the appropriate test under the CPR.
>
> (2) The mention or allusion must be to the document itself, not merely to the effect or contents of a document.
>
> (3) The document only has to be mentioned; it does not have to be relied upon or referred to in any particular way or for any particular purpose in order to qualify as being mentioned.
>
> (4) Mention of a document within the meaning of Rule 31.14 is treated as a form of disclosure, giving rise to the right of inspection which is enshrined in Rule 31.3.'

Popplewell J went on to observe that any such right of inspection was not automatic, his judgment continuing:

> '(5) The right of inspection under Rule 31.14 is therefore subject to the qualification in Rule 31.3(1)(b) and Rule 31.19(3) that the entitlement to inspection does not arise where the disclosing party has a right or duty to withhold inspection, including a right to withhold on grounds of privilege. Rule 31.19 is of general application to the right of inspection triggered by mention of a document within the meaning of Rule 31.14.
>
> (6) There is what might be called a presumption in favour of inspection by virtue of the fact that the party is to be treated as having already made disclosure.'

Consequently, Popplewell J concluded the right of inspection was subject, among other matters, to the overriding objective, including proportionality that was, in any event, specifically referred to in CPR 31.3(2). Hence there is a discretion to refuse an order allowing inspection where it would not be proportionate, or otherwise in accordance with the overriding objective, for inspection to be permitted.

The right of inspection is, in any event, subject to the important qualification of privilege. In this context the issue is likely to be whether, if the document was subject to privilege, privilege has been waived by mentioning the document.

5.2.4.2　Is privilege waived?

Even if a document is 'mentioned' that does not amount to an automatic and absolute waiver of privilege, rather the terms of CPR 31.3 and 31.19 still remain relevant.

23　[2013] EWHC 2500 (Comm).
24　[1990] 1WLR 731.

If privilege has not been waived a party has the right or duty to refuse inspection even if there has been disclosure through the mention of the document.

In *Expandable Ltd v Rubin*[25] Rix LJ observed that the CPR could not mean 'for the first time in the history of English litigation, the fundamental protection of privilege is automatically abandoned by the mere mentioning of documents'.

If, however, a party is regarded as having sufficiently relied on a document by its mention, that may well amount to a waiver of privilege.

In *Dunlop Slazenger International Ltd v Joe Bloggs Sports Ltd*[26] Waller LJ held:

> 'The key word here is 'deploying'. A mere reference to a privileged document in an affidavit does not of itself amount to a waiver of privilege, and this is so even if the document referred to is being relied on for some purpose, for reliance in itself is said not to be the test. Instead, the test is whether the contents of the document are being relied on, rather than its effect.'

The same approach was taken in *Rigg v Associated Newspapers Ltd*[27] and *Expandable Ltd v Rubin*.[28]

In *ACD (Landscape Architects) Ltd v Overall*[29] Akenhead J quoted, with approval, the notes to the CPR which state:

> 'Mere reference to a privileged document in a statement of case may not of itself lead to an implied waiver of the privilege, but reference to the extent of reliance on the privileged document is likely to do so... [31.14.5]

> As with the statements of case, mere reference to a privileged document in a witness statement may not of itself lead to the implied waiver of the privilege, but waiver will occur where a party is "deploying" the material in court. See *Great Atlantic Insurance Co v Home Insurance Co* [1981] 1 WLR 529... [31.14.6]'

Akenhead J went on to draw a number of propositions from the authorities:

> '(a) Unless there is a good reason otherwise, documents referred to in a witness statement submitted to be used in interlocutory or final court hearings must be disclosed by the party submitting the statement.

> (b) One good reason is that the documents are privileged.

> (c) Privilege will be waived where the otherwise privileged document is actually or effectively referred to in a witness statement and or part of its contents are deployed for use actually or potentially in the interlocutory proceedings or in the final trial, as the case may be.

> (d) A party which deploys part of the privileged document in a witness statement will, at least as a matter of general principle, be required to disclose the whole of the document because it is not just to allow a party by way of cherry picking to rely only on that part.

---

25 [2008] EWCA Civ 59.
26 [2003] EWCA Civ 901.
27 [2003] EWHC 710 (QB).
28 [2008] EWCA Civ 59.
29 [2011] EWHC 3362 (TCC).

(e) The test of whether a document or part of it is being deployed is whether the contents of the document are being relied upon rather than the effect or impact of the document.

(f) Once having referred to the document or part of it in a witness statement, generally at least the court will presume that it is relevant, because the very fact that it is referred to in the statement demonstrates its relevance.'

5.2.4.3   Does CPR 35.10(4) apply?

If a document mentioned in an expert's report is part of the instructions to that expert CPR 35.10(4) provides that, although it is not privileged, the court will decline to order disclosure of a document unless satisfied there are reasonable grounds to consider the expert's statement of instructions inaccurate or incomplete. It would be unusual for such grounds to exist.

Furthermore, the term 'instructions' will be defined broadly and be likely to encompass most, if not all, documents provided to the expert. Accordingly, CPR 35.10(4) seems likely to prevent, in most cases, an order under CPR 31.14(2) for production of documents mentioned by an expert in a report: *Lucas v Barking, Havering and Redbridge Hospital NHS Trust*[30] (see 5.5.3).

5.2.5   Disclosure in stages

Disclosure of some documents may be given late because disclosure is dealt with in stages.

CPR 31.13 confirms that the parties may agree in writing, or the court may direct, that disclosure or inspection, or both, shall take place in stages.

It may be appropriate for the parties to agree, or the court order, disclosure and/or inspection in stages where there is a direction for trial of a preliminary issue, so as to save the costs of disclosure and inspection on issues which are not yet to be tried.

5.2.6   Limiting or dispensing with disclosure

Disclosure may also be delayed because it is limited or dispensed with altogether.

CPR 31.5(1)(b) confirms the court may dispense with or limit standard disclosure while CPR 31.5(1)(c) provides that the parties may agree in writing to dispense with or to limit standard disclosure.

These provisions apply to all personal injury claims. There are similar provisions for non-personal injury multi-track claims found in CPR 31.5(3), which also sets out steps, in such cases, the parties are to take concerning disclosure, no less than 14 days before the first case management conference.

While it may sometimes be appropriate to limit or dispense with disclosure the claimant should exercise care before agreeing to take such a step. That is because, when disclosure

---

[30]   [2003] EWCA Civ 1102.

by the defendant is dispensed with, that may allow the defendant to produce documents at a late stage as, in such circumstances, there will have been no requirement to give disclosure by a specified date and hence no sanction for non-compliance which would otherwise apply (see 5.12).

Accordingly, even if the defendant indicates there are no documents to disclose the claimant may still wish for a formal list or an undertaking there are no documents which are, or are expected to be, disclosable.

5.3   DUTIES WITH DISCLOSURE

There is, obviously, a duty to disclose all documents falling within the scope of disclosure as provided for under case management directions. The duty imposed by the CPR extends to the preservation of, and search for, documents which are, or are likely to be, subject to disclosure. Moreover, compliance with these duties needs to be confirmed by a disclosure statement, signed by an appropriate person, containing a statement of truth. Anyone giving that disclosure statement needs to understand the nature and scope of duties on disclosure.

5.3.1   Preservation of documents

Prospective parties to court proceedings should preserve relevant documents and their lawyers also have professional duties to help ensure this happens.

In *Rockwell Machine Tool Co Ltd v Barrus*[31] Sir Robert Megarry VC described the duty on lawyers as being:

> '...to ensure that their clients appreciate at an early stage of the litigation, promptly after the writ is issued, not only the duty of discovery and its width but also the importance of not destroying documents which might by any possibility have to be disclosed. This burden extends, in my judgment, to taking steps to ensure that in any corporate organisation knowledge of this burden is passed on to any who may be affected by it.'

In *Hedrich v Zimmers*[32] the Court of Appeal approved the observations in *Myers v Elman*[33] that a solicitor's duty is to investigate the position on disclosure carefully and ensure so far as is possible the full and proper disclosure of all appropriate documents is made.

Accordingly, the solicitor should explain to the client the existence and precise scope of the disclosure obligation and the need to preserve documents.

Ideally, the solicitor should supervise the disclosure process, preferably by taking possession of all appropriate documents as early as possible.

This obligation also suggests it is more appropriate for the legal representative of each party to obtain documents within the control of that party, so the representative can determine whether such documents fall within the definition of standard disclosure,

---

[31]   [1968] 2 All ER 97.
[32]   [2008] EWCA Civ 985.
[33]   [1940] AC 282.

rather than the provision of authorities by one party to another allowing documents to be obtained direct from third parties, where there will be no such safeguard.

If it is known the party has concealed relevant documents, with a view to these not being disclosed, the solicitor must not act so as to suggest full disclosure has been or will be given, though this responsibility is limited to taking reasonable steps to ascertain the truth.

If it becomes known a list of documents is inadequate or misleading the solicitor must put this right at the earliest opportunity.

If a party does not preserve documents subject to disclosure and, as a result, there is a real risk of injustice because a fair trial will no longer be possible the court may be prepared to strike out that party's statement of case for abuse of process: *Arrow Nominees Inc v Blackledge*.[34]

Strike out on the basis of an abuse of process may also be applicable where evidence other than documents is destroyed, for example when histological samples had been destroyed in both *Weaver v Contract Services Division Ltd*;[35] *Currie v Rio Tinto plc*.[36] However, in *Matthews v Herbert Collins*[37] the claimant's claim was not struck out following destruction of histological samples as a fair trial was still possible and in the absence of culpable behaviour by the claimant, acting deliberately to prevent a fair trial, it was not just, necessary or proportionate to deprive that claimant the opportunity of having the claim heard.

Consequently, where a party fails to preserve relevant documents, or indeed other evidence, there is a risk, for that party, of the court striking out the relevant statement of case for abuse of process if it would be just to do so, having regard to the culpability of the party concerned and the extent to which the absence of the evidence destroyed will prevent a fair trial. Whilst the cases involving histological samples concerned the destruction of evidence by the claimant exactly the same arguments advanced by the defendants in those cases would be applicable if it were the defendant who had destroyed evidence. That is not uncommon, particularly with ephemeral material such as CCTV images and sometimes electronic documentation. The defendant may be all the more culpable if, for example, the claimant has identified relevant documents, or categories of document, along with other potentially relevant evidence in the letter of claim and even, perhaps, requested that this be preserved.

5.3.2   Searching for documents

CPR 31.7(1) requires a party, when giving standard disclosure, to make a reasonable search for documents falling within the scope of that term (see **5.1.1.8**).

CPR 31.7(2) identifies some specific factors relevant in deciding the reasonableness of the search including the following.

*   the number of documents involved;

---

[34]   [2003] EWHC Ch 1516 ChD.
[35]   LTL 18/2/2010 AC0123425.
[36]   LTL 23/3/2011 AC 0127348.
[37]   [2013] EWHC 2952 (QB).

- the nature and complexity of the proceedings;
- the ease and expense of retrieval of any particular document;
- the significance of any document that is likely to be located during the search.

Practice Direction 31A, in para 2, endorses the terms of CPR 31.7(2) and links those with the need for parties to bear in mind the overriding principle of proportionality set out in Part 1.

Consequently, it will often be appropriate for a party giving disclosure to limit the search for documents, whether this be by deciding not to search for documents coming into existence before a particular date, to limit the search to documents located in some particular places or to restrict the search for documents to those falling within particular categories.

CPR 31.7(3) confirms that where the search for documents has been limited this must be stated in the disclosure statement and CPR 31.10(6)(a) confirms that statement must set out the extent of the search made to locate documents that the party is required to disclose. The practice form list of documents, form N265, usefully contains tick boxes confirming the nature and extent of the search for documents. Care is required to ensure the party giving disclosure has, by proper completion of the list, properly confirmed any limits on the search so that, in turn, other parties can assess whether an appropriate search has been made. That is because this may influence the need for specific disclosure to be sought.

CPR 31.12(2)(b) confirms that an order for specific disclosure may include a requirement for a search to be carried out to the extent stated in that order.

5.3.3 Confirming the duties

The procedure for giving standard disclosure, set out in CPR 31.10, includes a requirement, found in CPR 31.10(5) for any list to include a disclosure statement.

The nature of the disclosure statement is explained in CPR 31.10(6) as requiring the following information:

- confirming the extent of the search made to locate documents which that party is required to disclose;
- certifying that the duty to disclose documents is understood;
- certifying that this duty has been carried out.

Where the party making a disclosure statement is a company, firm, association or other organisation CPR 31.10(7) requires the disclosure statement to identify the person making the statement and explain why he is considered an appropriate person to make that statement. In such circumstances para 4.3 of Practice Direction 31A requires the disclosure statement to include the name and address and the office or position that person holds in the disclosing party or the basis upon which he makes the statement on behalf of that party.

Consequently, the disclosure statement should be signed by, or by an appropriate person on behalf of, the party rather than a legal representative.

In *Prince Abdulaziz v Apex Global Management Ltd*[38] Lord Neuberger observed that:

> '...I incline to the view that the standard form of disclosure by a party does require personal signing by the party. CPR 31.10(6) refers to a "disclosure statement" as being "a statement made by the party disclosing the documents", and the notion that it should be the party himself also seems to get support from CPR 31.10(7). Similarly, that conclusion is supported by para 4 of PD31A, especially subparas 4.2, 4.3, 4.4 and 4.7 (and also the annex to PD31A). It also seems clear that, no doubt when good reasons are made out, the court can permit a departure from this – see CPR 31.5(1)(a) and (b). It is true that para 3.7 of PD22 specifically permits a statement of truth to be signed by a party's solicitor and that para 15 of the Order referred to statements of truth not disclosure statements. However, it seems to me that, although it referred to statements of truth, para 15 was actually referring to disclosure statements – a view supported by paras 1.1 and 1.4 of PD22 and CPR 22.1(1).'

CPR 31.23 confirms proceedings for contempt of court may be brought against a person who makes, or causes to be made, a false disclosure statement without an honest belief in its truth.

5.4 SCOPE OF DISCLOSURE IN PERSONAL INJURY CLAIMS

The PI Protocol is a good guide to what, typically, will be the scope of disclosure in personal injury claims which, in turn, informs the duty to preserve, and search for, appropriate documentation so that the disclosure statement in a list of documents can be properly completed.

5.4.1 The claimant

If liability is in issue, and the claimant has control of relevant documents, disclosure should include documents relating to that issue.

The claimant will always need to disclose documents that support any claim for expenses and losses. Depending on the nature of those claims, that may include wage slips, tax documentation, business accounts as well as receipts.

It is notable the PI Protocol does not envisage disclosure of medical records, simply that these be produced by the claimant's solicitor to the medical expert. Both the RTA Protocol and the EL/PL Protocol anticipate the medical expert will identify relevant records, or perhaps more accurately entries in those records which will effectively be disclosed by attaching copies or citing those entries in the report of that expert.

Disclosure will be governed by necessity and proportionality.

5.4.2 The defendant

The PI Protocol usefully identifies documents, depending on the nature of the case, likely to be necessary if liability is in issue and that should, therefore, be disclosed by the defendant.

---

[38] [2014] UKSC 64.

If the defendant is the claimant's employer documents relating to that employment, including details of the claimant's earnings and, if necessary, earnings of comparators, are likely to be necessary and hence part of standard disclosure to be given by the defendant.

The scope of disclosure will, as it is with the claimant, be governed by necessity and proportionality.

5.4.3 Non-parties

Disclosure by non-parties can often be important in personal injury claims, particularly where none of the parties have control of documentation that will be necessary to fairly determine the issues (see 5.9).

5.5 DEALING WITH STANDARD CASE MANAGEMENT DIRECTIONS

Case management directions will usually provide that all parties give disclosure by list.

CPR 31.5(1)(a) provides that, except for non-personal injury claims in the multi-track, an order to give disclosure is an order to give standard disclosure. Practice Direction 31A, in paragraph 1.1, confirms the normal order for disclosure will be an order that the parties give standard disclosure.

The court may, of course, order otherwise and the parties may agree to limit or dispense with disclosure. Additionally, CPR 31.13 provides the court may direct disclosure or inspection take place in stages which may be appropriate when, for example, the court gives directions for the preliminary trial of an issue and disclosure may conveniently be limited, for the time being, to that issue.

The procedure for standard disclosure is set out in CPR 31.10, requiring each party to make and serve a list of documents with a disclosure statement. Practice Direction 31A, at para 3.1, confirms that the list should be in the format of the relevant practice form, namely N265.

It is important the parties comply with any order for disclosure ahead of the deadline imposed by that order and for disclosure to be dealt with in accordance with the requirements of the CPR.

5.5.1 Disclosure by the claimant

All relevant documents, whether or not in the claimant's control and whether or not privileged, should be disclosed, irrespective of whether those documents support or adversely affect any party's case.

Standard disclosure by list should be completed using the practice form, form N265.

Documents should be disclosed:

- in the first part of the list, if within the claimant's control and there is no claim for privilege; or
- in the second part of the list, if it is asserted that the document is privileged; or
- in the final part of the list, if the claimant no longer has control of the document.

CPR 31.10(3) requires the list to identify documents in convenient order and manner and as concisely as possible. Guidance on what this means when drafting the list is given by para 3.2 of Practice Direction 31A which provides:

> 'In order to comply with rule 31.10(3) it will normally be necessary to list the documents in date order, to number them consecutively and to give each a concise description (e.g. letter, claimant to defendant). Where there is a large number of documents all falling into a particular category the disclosing party may list those documents as a category rather than individually e.g. 50 bank statements relating to account number ...or 35 letters passing between ... and ....'

The disclosure statement must be signed by the claimant or an appropriate person on behalf of the claimant where the claimant is a company, firm, association or other organisation. Where a party is represented any legal representative must, as para 4.4 of Practice Direction 31A makes clear, endeavour to ensure that the person making the disclosure statement understands the duty of disclosure under Part 31.

The duty is to make a reasonable search for documents that adversely affect the case of any party or support the opponent's case. If, however, the search is limited, including a limited search for electronic documents, the disclosure statement must confirm as much.

Where inspection of disclosed documents might be disproportionate the disclosure statement should state as much and identify the documentation concerned (for example medical records 5.7.2).

5.5.2   Disclosure by the defendant

The defendant's list of documents should be carefully checked, on receipt, to ensure disclosure has been dealt with properly.

A review of the defendant's list may involve checking a number of points.

- Has the search for documents been limited and, if so, has a reasonable limit been put on that search?
- Has disclosure of all documents identified as relevant by the PI Protocol to the claim, as now defined by the statements of case, been given?
- Are there any additional categories of document, which appear to be relevant to the issues, that have not been disclosed, which should be sought?
- Are there any further specific documents, especially those referred to expressly or impliedly by documents which are disclosed, that may be relevant to the issues and which should be sought?
- Is it accepted that the defendant makes a valid claim for privilege, where applicable, or should that be challenged, if necessary, by an application for inspection of specific documents?

- Has the defendant disclosed all documents no longer in the control of the defendant and are there any documents the defendant did have, but no longer has, which ought to have been retained to help ensure a fair trial?

- Has the disclosure statement been signed by an appropriate person (usually the defendant in person but where the defendant is a company, firm, association or other organisation an appropriate person, who is adequately identified, for the purposes of CPR 36.10(7) and para 4.3 of Practice Direction 31A)?

If necessary an application can be made under CPR 31.12(1) either for specific disclosure, where it is contended that necessary disclosure is not complete, or specific inspection, where the defendant has failed to produce documents or the claimant wishes to challenge a claim for privilege or proportionality.

The general case management powers of the court, which include the ability to strike out a statement of case, may need to be relied upon if the defendant fails to serve a list of documents at all, provides a list without an appropriately completed and signed disclosure statement or has failed to preserve documents in circumstances that may amount to an abuse of process.

5.5.3 Inspection of the claimant's documents by the defendant

Inspection of documents disclosed must be given, if requested, unless:

- the document is no longer in the control of the party giving disclosure;

- the document is privileged;

- to give inspection would be disproportionate and the party giving disclosure has stated as much in the disclosure statement, as provided for by CPR 31.3(2); or

- the document is 'mentioned' in an expert's report, and therefore potentially disclosable under CPR 31.14(2), but properly regarded as part of the 'instructions' to that expert (so that CPR 35.10(4) applies).

When considering what is proportionate for the purposes of CPR 31.3(2) the court should not be concerned just with the cost of providing copies of the documents requested as CPR 1.1(2)(c) makes reference, when considering proportionality generally, not just to value but also the issues. Furthermore, where Art 8 rights may be affected by giving inspection of documents the concept of proportionality will embrace a consideration of whether to require inspection of relevant documents would be a proportionate interference with those rights: *Webster v Ridgeway Foundation School Governors*;[39] *Favour Easy Management Ltd v Wu*;[40] *Durham County Council v Dunn*.[41]

Under CPR 35.10(4) the court should not order disclosure unless there are grounds for believing the statement of instructions in the expert's report to be inaccurate or incomplete: *Lucas v Barking, Havering and Redbridge Hospitals NHS Trust* (see **5.2.4.3**).[42]

---

[39] [2009] EWHC 1140 (QB).
[40] [2010] EWCA Civ 1630.
[41] [2012] EWCA Civ 1654.
[42] [2003] EWCA Civ 1102 (see **5.2.4.3**).

5.5.4   Inspection of the defendant's documents by the claimant

When documents are received from the defendant, by way of inspection, further action will be necessary.

- A check should be made that copies of all documents disclosed by the defendant, which the claimant will need to see, have been produced by way of inspection. If not copies should now be sought.

- The copies of documents must be complete and fully legible. If necessary better quality copies, and sometimes colour copies, should be requested.

- If there have been adaptations or other markings copies, where available, of the document with and without those annotations should be provided, to comply with CPR 31.9.

- Copies of the documents produced should be sent to the client with:
  - appropriate comments on any matters arising;
  - a request for further instructions on any matters where necessary;
  - advice on the need to check whether the authenticity (though not content) of the documents is accepted, because if not a notice refusing to admit should be served within 7 days of the documents being produced, in accordance with CPR 32.19 (see **5.1.2.6** and **5.12.6**).

- The validity of any claim for privilege, or objection to inspection on the grounds of proportionality, should be considered and, if appropriate, challenged and/or an application for inspection under CPR 31.12(1) should be made.

- If necessary, following production of copies, the defendant should be requested to give facilities for inspection of the documents from which those copies have been produced, ideally the original documentation. Occasionally this may be important, particularly if there have been amendments or adaptations that can more readily be identified by viewing original documents.

- The client should be reminded that documents disclosed are confidential, to be used only for the purpose of the proceedings, unless and until the document has been read to or by the court, or referred to at a hearing held in public (chambers appointments are usually public hearings).

5.5.5   Specific disclosure

If either party is not satisfied with the extent of disclosure, a request for specific disclosure may be made. If the party requesting further specific disclosure is not satisfied with the response, or there is no adequate response to the request, an application may be made under CPR 31.12(1), (2) for specific disclosure. Any such application must identify the documents or classes of documents sought.

When considering whether to order specific disclosure the court has a discretion. The exercise of that discretion may require the court to balance the conflicting rights under Arts 6 and 8 of the ECHR, particularly where documents sought are confidential in nature such as those giving financial disclosure in family proceedings (*Nayler v Beard*[43]) or medical records (*Webster v Ridgeway Foundation School Governors*[44]).

---

[43]   [2001] EWCA Civ 1201.
[44]   [2009] EWCA 1140 (QB).

Even where the documents sought are relevant the court may exercise its discretion, applying the overriding objective, not to order specific disclosure: *A v X and B (Non party)*.[45]

When making an order for specific disclosure the court is not restricted to documents that would form part of standard disclosure but, nevertheless, should be guided by the broad tests of necessity and proportionality. For these purposes it is important to remember that, although the court can do so, disclosure of documents concerned solely with credit will not usually be ordered: *Favor Easy Management Ltd v Wu*.[46]

5.5.6 Specific inspection

CPR 31.12 also deals with specific inspection, which allows a party who is not satisfied with the refusal of a request for inspection can challenge that refusal by application to the court.

5.5.7 Organisation

Documents produced, by way of inspection, on disclosure need to be kept organised so that it is clear which documents have been sent to, and received from, the defendant.

It may be helpful to maintain a bundle of documents which can be added to as the matter progresses for ease of reference and to keep track of all relevant documentation (see **5.11**).

5.6 SURVEILLANCE DOCUMENTS

A video or DVD is a document for the purposes of CPR 31.4: *Rall v Hume*.[47]

Accordingly, surveillance evidence, recorded in this way, needs to be considered at the stage of disclosure.

5.6.1 Timing of disclosure

While legal professional privilege may, until that is waived, apply to surveillance evidence in the form of documents a party wishing to rely on such evidence will need to ensure disclosure is given at the appropriate stage , as under CPR 31.21 a party can only rely on documents which have been disclosed.

Accordingly, surveillance videos and DVDs should, ideally, be disclosed in the relevant party's list of documents if, at that stage, such documents exist.

If such documents come into being after service of the list they should be disclosed forthwith, in accordance with CPR 31.11(2) and the continuing obligation on parties in relation to disclosure.

---

[45]   [2004] EWHC 447 (QB).
[46]   [2010] EWCA Civ 1630.
[47]   [2001] EWCA Civ 146.

Because these documents are likely to have been produced for the dominant purpose of litigation it is likely, though not inevitable, privilege will be claimed but where that is so this does not mean inspection, and waiver of privilege, can be delayed indefinitely. Much will depend on the need to comply with other case management directions.

5.6.2 Timing of inspection

Unless there is a specific direction for disclosure of surveillance documents by a given date there will not, as with witness statements and expert evidence, be a specific date by which privilege must be waived and inspection of surveillance documents given. That does not mean, however, the party wishing to rely on such evidence can assume that it will be admissible even when produced at a late stage.

Should documents comprising surveillance evidence not be admitted by the claimant it may be necessary for the defendant to prove the authenticity of those documents by factual evidence, for example witness statements from surveillance operatives. If so, relevant images with supporting factual statements will have to be produced by, at the latest, the last day for exchange of witness statements otherwise the defendant will have to obtain relief from sanctions that would otherwise apply preventing reliance on witness statements disclosed subsequently.

Similarly if the defendant wishes surveillance evidence to be reviewed by experts it will be important to ensure that is done before any deadline for service of expert evidence under case management directions or, again, the defendant will have to obtain relief from sanctions that will otherwise apply.

In the past the courts have accepted it is a legitimate tactic for the defendant to hold back production of surveillance evidence until the claimant has, especially where this is belated, complied with case management directions requiring service of details of the claim, for example witness statements or a schedule: *Uttley v Uttley*.[48]

The surveillance evidence should, however, only be retained for a reasonable period of time to achieve such purposes and should certainly not be used to 'ambush' the claimant. This reflects the continuing duty of disclosure, CPR 31.11 putting an obligation on parties to 'immediately notify every other party' on notice of further documents which are subject to disclosure in the proceedings. Accordingly, a defendant holding back disclosure of surveillance evidence may face problems when seeking to rely on such evidence if the claimant has complied with the case management timetable especially if the defendant is in default or has otherwise delayed.

Hence where a defendant failed to obtain surveillance evidence until after a trial had been adjourned this delay was relevant to the ultimate incidence of costs when, at the adjourned hearing, the claimant failed to beat a Part 36 offer: *Ford v GKR Construction Ltd*.[49]

---

[48] [2002] PIQR P12.
[49] [2000] 1 WLR 1397.

In *O'Leary v Tunnelcraft Ltd*[50] the defendant was refused permission to rely on surveillance evidence as failure to disclose that material until 31 days before trial amounted to an ambush and if it were admitted the lengthening of the trial would be contrary to the overriding objective.

Following revisions to the CPR in April 2013 the courts may be expected to take a tougher approach to late disclosure of evidence, particularly where this will require relief from any sanctions. In *Dass v Dass*[51] case management directions, given on 19 November 2010, directed that any further medical reports be filed and served by 27 May 2011. At a further case management hearing on 14 March 2013 the defendant was debarred from relying on expert evidence not already filed and served, although the reason for this was that the defendant had meanwhile arranged for surveillance and wanted that evidence to be taken into account by the medical experts whose reports were yet to be filed and served. An appeal against this ruling was dismissed with Haddon-Cave J observing:

> 'The court had made a court order; court orders are to be obeyed. If parties are unable to comply with court orders because of new developments, or for whatever reason, they must come back to the court and seek an extension of time or a fresh order. They cannot simply blithely ignore court orders as if they are a thing writ in water.'

The tactical considerations underpinning all of this made no difference, with Haddon-Cave J warning: 'Let this be a lesson that parties who deliberately refuse to comply with court orders for tactical reasons do so at their peril.' Consequently, older cases such as *Uttley* must, perhaps, now be viewed with some caution given the stricter regime applicable to compliance with court orders, generally, and sanctions, in particular.

Similarly, in *Hannon v Hillingdon Homes Ltd*[52] HHJ Thornton QC concluded that CPR 3.9 would be applicable where the defendant had not complied with directions in the timing of surveillance evidence, on which it was proposed to rely, being produced by way of inspection.

Consequently, older cases such as *Uttley* must, perhaps, now be viewed with some caution given the stricter regime applicable to compliance with court orders, generally, and sanctions, in particular.

5.6.3 Case management directions

Given the issues that can arise about the timing of disclosure and inspection of documents comprising surveillance evidence there are advantages in seeking a specific direction surveillance evidence be disclosed by a given date. The court may take the view this best serves the overriding objective as that is likely to be fair, as between the parties, and will certainly help to avoid satellite litigation and potentially disproportionate costs resolving problems that arise if no specific timetable is provided for.

---

50   [2009] EWHC 3438 (QB).
51   [2013] EWHC 2520 (QB).
52   [2013] EWHC 4335 (QB).

Such a direction will also help guard against difficulties that may arise with expert evidence should experts get to see evidence which the court then concludes should not be admitted (see **5.6.7.9**).

5.6.4   Privacy and admissibility

Article 8 ECHR is likely to engage in relation to surveillance evidence, providing a further dimension which may affect the admissibility of that evidence.

In general terms Art 8 is likely to be relevant where images were obtained in circumstances when there would usually be an expectation of privacy.

A number of cases have considered this issue.

- Secret filming by the police of defendants in the cell area of a magistrates' court has been held to be unlawful: *R v Loveridge*.[53]

- Even in a place to which the public has free access secret filming might be considered objectionable where it was not open to those who were the subject of the filming to take any action to prevent it: *R v Loveridge*.[54]

- The use of covert listening devices at a police station has also been held to violate the European Convention: *PG & JH v United Kingdom*.[55]

- Video footage of the claimant in her own home and in a day-care nursery attended by her child was held to be not admissible: *Rall v Hume*.[56]

- There may even be an expectation of privacy, though in part this depends on the purpose for which images are being taken, in what would generally be regarded as a public place: *Murray v Big Pictures (UK) Ltd*.[57]

Consequently, the court will need to balance the claimant's Art 8 rights with the countervailing right the defendant will no doubt rely upon under Art 6. Any interference with Art 8 rights will, on this basis, need to be proportionate.

A claimant who is subject to surveillance, in addition to reliance on the defendant's obligations on disclosure, may also acquire rights, including the right of subject access, under the Data Protection Act 1988.

5.6.5   Weight

The weight attached to surveillance evidence is likely to depend upon what the evidence itself illustrates and the significance attached to what is seen by witnesses, especially expert witnesses.

It is important to remember most claimants will have 'good days' and 'bad days'. That is why the totality of surveillance evidence needs to be disclosed. It is also important to

---

[53]   [2001] EWCA Crim 973, [2001] 2 Cr App R 591.
[54]   [2001] EWCA Crim 973, [2001] 2 Cr App R 591.
[55]   [2002] Crim LR 308, ECHR.
[56]   [2001] EWCA Civ 146, [2001] 3 All ER 248.
[57]   [2008] EWCA Civ 446.

remember the forensic context in which medico-legal appointments take place. Bell J noted in *Rogers v Little Haven Day Nursery Ltd*:[58]

> '... the exaggeration which I have described falls within the bounds of familiar and understandable attempts to make sure that doctors and lawyers do not underestimate a genuine condition, rather than indicating an outright attempt to mislead in order to increase the value of her claim beyond its true worth.'

Experts should always remember it is for the court, not experts, to decide whether a claimant is genuine or not, though clinical experience drawn on by medical experts may help inform the court in reaching a view.

5.6.6 Expert evidence

It may, occasionally, be appropriate for a claimant to seek permission to rely on expert evidence dealing with surveillance evidence relied on by the defendant.

Such evidence may be appropriate if there are doubts about the tactics employed by the surveillance operatives or issues about the integrity of the surveillance evidence disclosed. In such circumstances the court may be assisted, in determining those issues, by appropriate expert evidence.

In *Samson v Ali*[59] the court giving the claimant permission to rely on expert evidence from a video evidence consultant concluded there was sufficient expertise on the part of the proposed witness for expert opinion to be given and that this evidence would assist the court. Stadlen J held:

> 'This is an area in which a number of points have been made by Mr Simm on the video evidence. Some of those points, for example whether there are gaps in the evidence, are no doubt points which, through a painstaking analysis by counsel or by solicitors, could be arrived at by lawyers. As to those, it seems to me that it having been done by somebody who is experienced in that area can only save time. There are other aspects of it on which Mr Simm has expressed an opinion which it would be difficult for the court to form a view on without some assistance. It may be that it could. It may be that it could not. I have in mind in particular the suggestion that there is one aspect where the footage has been speeded up.'

Stadlen J went on to observe:

> '... if one compares the ability of a judge to draw inferences from a large amount of footage, both edited and unedited, on the one hand and someone who has spent many years in that area on the other, it seems to me that it may well be, and indeed is probably likely, that at the very least a great deal of time may be saved on those issues with the assistance of somebody like Mr Simm and beyond that it may well be that there are particular contentious aspects between the parties as to whether this was deliberately one-sided footage or not in which the evidence of somebody who has been involved in this area for so long may assist the court.'

Consequently, Stadlen J concluded:

---

[58] (Unreported) QBD, 30 July 1999.
[59] [2012] EWHC 4146 (QB).

'I do not have any doubt at all that this is material which the claimant ought to be entitled to deploy. It is a frequent practice that in a claim such as this insurers will engage private investigators to privately film the claimant with a view to trying to show that the claimant is deliberately lying or exaggerating the extent of her injuries, in particular, from the point of view of mobility. Where the insurer seeks to rely on video footage and the claimant wishes to challenge that video footage on the basis that it has been selectively filmed, is misleading or has left out bits that are helpful to the claimant, it seems to me that that is a central issue in the case and it does not lie in the mouth of the insurer to says that this is a collateral issue or likely to spawn collateral issues.'

5.6.7   Tactics with surveillance evidence

Defendants can adopt a very tactical approach to surveillance evidence, hoping to contradict the claimant's factual evidence and undermine the expert evidence on which the claimant relies, which often influences the manner and timing of disclosure. The clamant may need to take an equally tactical approach making proper use of the safeguards provided by the CPR and the general law.

5.6.7.1   *Ensuring disclosure is required by the defendant*

The nature of a video or DVD, as a document, will impact on the tactics to be adopted by the claimant on receipt of surveillance evidence from the defendant.

Because the video or DVD resulting from surveillance will be a document it is important, if surveillance evidence is a possibility, to ensure that the defendant is required to give disclosure, even if there are no other documents that would be obviously disclosable. Otherwise the defendant may be able to argue that the obligation to give timely disclosure of documents, including those relating to surveillance, has been dispensed with.

5.6.7.2   *Directions for disclosure of surveillance documents*

Although surveillance evidence is likely to be subject to disclosure it may be sensible to make express provision for any surveillance evidence to be disclosed by the date of lists of documents or, perhaps more typically, the last date for exchange of statements from witnesses of fact.

Such an approach gives the defendant the opportunity, if that is considered appropriate, to obtain and seek to rely on such evidence whilst avoiding the claimant being "ambushed", the court timetable being disrupted and experts finalising reports without reviewing surveillance evidence if, in the event, that is admissible.

A suitable direction would meet the concerns voiced by HHJ Thornton QC in *Hannon v Hillingdon Homes Ltd*[60] when he said:

'... it was clearly of particular importance for those managing the case preparation and the pre-trial steps on behalf of both parties to coordinate the various steps being taken and to maintain the timetable that had been crafted in order to give effect to those steps. This was because a balance would need to be struck between, on the one hand, maintaining the timetable and, on the other hand, the obtaining of evidence without the claimant being aware

---

[60]   [2013] EWHC 4335 (QB).

that it was being obtained, but with disclosure of that evidence taking place so that the claimant was not prejudiced. Moreover, the case manager for the time needed to be fully appraised of the situation so as to give effect to the overriding objective.'

5.6.7.3   Reviewing the surveillance evidence with the claimant

Surveillance evidence, like any documents or other evidence disclosed by the defendant, should be sent to the claimant for review and instructions.

It is rare, but not unknown, for the surveillance not to be of the claimant at all!

More frequently, the claimant's instructions can help put the events illustrated by the surveillance evidence into proper context. That, at its most general, may simply be that the surveillance was undertaken on a 'good day' for the claimant. The claimant may also, more specifically, be able to comment on events that have not been illustrated by the surveillance evidence, yet provide important context or help to show the evidence reveals only a very partial picture.

This information from the claimant will also assist in checking the provenance of the disclosed material and the possible existence of undisclosed surveillance evidence (see 5.6.7.5).

5.6.7.4   Challenging the evidence

If the authenticity of the video is not challenged the party relying on that evidence has a *prima facie* right to use it for the purposes of cross-examination, provided the evidence is likely to undermine the other party's case substantially and is not disclosed in circumstances amounting to trial by ambush: *Rall v Hume*.[61]

Consequently, the claimant may wish to serve a notice refusing to admit, requiring the defendant to prove the documents that comprise the surveillance evidence. Surveillance evidence, when not admitted, will usually be proved by evidence from surveillance operatives. However, any witness statement seeking to prove the authenticity of surveillance evidence is a statement that should be exchanged in accordance with case management directions, and otherwise cannot be relied on without permission of the court under the terms of CPR 32.10. This rule imposes a sanction and it may be difficult for a party in default to get relief from any such sanction imposed.

5.6.7.5   Seeking all surveillance evidence

The duties in relation to disclosure should require the whole document comprising the surveillance evidence, including any soundtrack, to be disclosed. Accordingly, on receipt of surveillance evidence, the claimant should ensure that full disclosure has taken place and may reserve the position on admissibility meanwhile.

In addition to requesting all unedited footage the claimant may also wish to seek disclosure of logs and records made by the surveillance operatives as these will help to establish when the claimant was under surveillance and assist in checking whether all

---

[61]   [2001] EWCA Civ 146.

footage, whether helpful to the defendant or not, has been disclosed (and indeed that the logs are consistent with the evidence disclosed and hence accurately record when the claimant was under surveillance).

Surveillance evidence will often include, within the images, dates and times of the recording. If not, a request should be made for the defendant to disclose copies with that information and, should this not be available, the defendant asked why not. These details will also facilitate cross-checking of images and logs as well as identifying gaps that might not otherwise be immediately apparent.

Following the review of surveillance evidence, including any further information provided by the defendant, consideration should also be given to making a formal request under Part 18 CPR to clarify matters such as when exactly surveillance was carried out, why there was any selective recording of images, why any editing was undertaken and any other matters that might usefully be the subject of further information.

5.6.7.6   Challenging admissibility

Surveillance evidence may be inadmissible if held to involve a disproportionate breach of Article 8 ECHR.

The defendant may also face difficulties in relying on surveillance evidence where the images, as documents, have not been disclosed at the appropriate stage. Disclosure should be given by the latest date provided for under case management directions, or if the images come into existence thereafter immediately so as to comply with the obligation on continuing disclosure imposed by the terms of CPR 31.11. If disclosure is not given at the appropriate stage the defendant faces the sanction of being unable to rely on the documents, under the terms of CPR 31.21. Where the surveillance evidence includes witness statements, to support or prove the images, that must be disclosed by the deadline for exchange of witness statements under case management directions, or the defendant faces the sanction imposed by the terms of CPR 32.10.

5.6.7.7   Regulatory issues

Surveillance evidence is likely to be personal data, relating to the claimant, which is subject to the terms of the Data Protection Act 1998, including the need for registration with the Information Commissioner of any organisation which processes that data.

It may, accordingly, be appropriate to check with the register kept by the Information Commissioner that any organisation retained to have undertaken surveillance has complied with the law. The register can be assessed at: https://ico.org.uk/for-organisations/register.

5.6.7.8   Obtaining expert evidence

If there are sufficient concerns about the surveillance evidence disclosed by the defendant consideration should be given to the need for expert evidence, on behalf of the claimant, analysing and explaining, for the benefit of the court, those concerns (see 5.6.6).

5.6.7.9 Ensuring admissibility is resolved before review by experts

Pending a decision on authenticity and admissibility, it will generally not be appropriate for surveillance to be viewed by experts involved in the case.

In *Jones v University of Warwick*[62] the Court of Appeal held that surveillance evidence should be admitted partly because the experts had already viewed that evidence and could not then be asked to give their evidence as if they had not seen it. While the instruction of fresh experts, who had not seen the surveillance evidence, was considered by the court that possibility was ruled out on the basis of the expense and delay involved.

However, in *Reynard v Exquisite Quisine Ltd*[63] the court required the experts, who had viewed a video the court ruled as inadmissible, to give evidence disregarding what those experts had seen in the video. The judge observed: 'The Defenders' agents had unfortunately, and unwisely, allowed their expert witnesses to study the video before making the motions to have the recording accepted into process and to amend the pleadings.'

In these circumstances it may be prudent, at an early stage, to warn the claimant's experts against reviewing any surveillance evidence until such issues of admissibility have been resolved. A potential danger that such a warning will guard against is the defendant sending surveillance documents direct to the experts with questions that reflect that surveillance, particularly where the evidence and accompanying questions are sent without disclosure to the claimant's representatives despite the requirement of para 4.2 of the Practice Direction to Part 35, which provides for any questions to an expert to be sent at the same time to the party who instructed that expert.

It may also be wise if the defendant is told, again at an early stage, surveillance evidence should not be provided to any experts, including the defendant's experts, until admissibility of such evidence has been confirmed. If that request is then disregarded by the defendant it may be more difficult to suggest the cost of fresh expert evidence would be disproportionate because that might then be a cost the defendant will have to bear in any event.

Ideally experts should be instructed to review the totality of the surveillance evidence, including all footage, as well as instructions from the claimant that put the evidence in context and, if appropriate, any expert evidence dealing with the surveillance itself.

5.6.7.10 Clarifying the defendant's case

The defendant may already have alleged fraud or dishonesty by the claimant, and rely on surveillance evidence in support of that case, or now seek permission to amend the defence to advance such allegations.

Because the very fact surveillance has been undertaken implies, at the very least, doubts about the claimant's integrity it is important, where there are no express allegations amounting to fraud or dishonesty, to clarify the nature of the defendant's case.

---

[62] [2003] EWCA 151.
[63] [2005] CSOH 146.

A look at the website of the organisation that has undertaken surveillance can often be revealing, some of those websites making express references to 'fraud' or 'dishonesty'. That, coupled with the implication that surveillance carries, may cause some embarrassment to the defendant if, in the event, the surveillance does not undermine the claimant's case and may even confirm the claimant's evidence. In such cases it is quite reasonable to seek express confirmation the claimant's character and integrity are not impugned. If that is not forthcoming it may be appropriate to remind the defendant that inappropriate allegations of fraud or dishonesty, perhaps even if only implicit, may be visited by indemnity costs and also that a claimant who obtains a judgment absolving that claimant of any impropriety may have gained something of value such that even if the damages did not exceed the amount offered by way of Part 36 offer that judgment would be regarded as being 'more advantageous' than the offer.

If a claimant does wish to advance a case based on fraud or dishonesty that should be pleaded (see **3.6.7.5**).

5.7   MEDICAL RECORDS

The confidential and potentially sensitive nature of medical records means that care should be taken when considering the extent to which disclosure and, and in certain circumstances, inspection of such documents is given.

The need for care is reflected in the description of medical records as 'sensitive personal data' under the Data Protection Act 1998, and the common law duty on those in possession of such records to keep them confidential.

Furthermore, Art 8 rights are likely to engage, meaning that any interference with that right will need to be proportionate: *MS v Sweden*.[64]

The government has also sought to reduce NHS bureaucracy by encouraging legal representatives to refrain from requesting records except where these are necessary.[65]

The RTA Protocol envisages that many claims within the scope of that protocol will be dealt with on the basis of medical reports being prepared without a review of medical records.

5.7.1   Disclosure of medical records

The first consideration is whether medical records are, in the particular case, disclosable at all.

Bearing in mind the fundamental need for disclosure of any particular document or category of document to be necessary CPR 31.6 confines, in any event, standard disclosure to documents that support or adversely affect a party's case.

---

[64]   (1999) 38 ECHR 313.
[65]   'Making a Difference: Reducing Burdens on General Practitioners' Cabinet Office 25 June 2002; 'Making a Difference: Reducing Burdens in Hospitals' Cabinet Office 31 July 2002.

While standard disclosure also includes documents that a party is required to disclose under a protocol it is important to note the PI Protocol does not provide for disclosure of the claimant's medical records, just for relevant records to be provided by the claimant's representative to the medical expert.

Whether disclosure of records will be necessary may depend on the nature and severity of the injury or the extent to which the fact, circumstances and cause of the injury are in issue. Hence in a claim involving issues of 'low velocity impact' specific entries relating to the alleged injury may be disclosable: *Kearsley v Klarfeld*.[66] Because the court spelt out the need for disclosure, though with irrelevant entries redacted, of records in such a case suggests that such disclosure should be regarded as an exception to the general rule, certainly in cases of modest injury, disclosure of records is not necessary.

The claimant's representative must still assess, in any particular case, whether the claimant's medical records are properly part of standard disclosure or, where this has been ordered, specific disclosure.

There can be difficulties in determining whether records are subject to standard, or indeed specific, disclosure and whether this is a matter that should be decided by the legal advisers or the medical experts. In many circumstances it will be the medical experts who are best placed to determine which records are relevant, in the sense of supporting or adversely affecting a party's case, given the familiarity of medical experts with such records and the overriding duty owed by all experts to the court.

In some circumstances, however, it will have to be the responsibility of legal representatives to determine the scope of disclosure in relation to medical records, particularly where the case involves complex legal issues to which those records directly relate.

Accordingly, provision of all potentially relevant records to the expert should ensure as well as an informed opinion based on the content of those records, any records of significance are identified by reference to relevant entries. However, the provision of all medical records to an expert should not, of itself, convert records that are not properly part of standard disclosure into documents that are disclosable. Even express reference to medical records in an expert's report will not, of itself, generate a right of inspection. That is because, although likely to be 'mentioned' for the purposes of CPR 31.14 those records should be regarded as part of the 'instructions' to the expert and hence subject to the terms of CPR 35.10(4): *Lucas v Barking, Havering and Redbridge Hospitals NHS Trust*.[67]

The RTA Protocol and EL/PL Protocol do help to clarify the situation by confirming an expert should attach relevant records to the report, though in this context that must surely mean relevant entries within the records.

5.7.2 Inspection of medical records

Even where records are disclosable it may be necessary to consider whether such records have to be made available for inspection.

---

[66] [2005] EWCA Civ 1510.
[67] [2003] EWCA Civ 1102 (see **5.2.4.3**).

That is because it may be disproportionate, in all the circumstances, to permit inspection of all medical records under CPR 31.3(2). The court clearly has power to control the way in which inspection is given where documents are sensitive: *Bennett v Compass Group UK*;[68] *Webster v Ridgeway Foundation School Governors*;[69] *Favor Easy Management Ltd v Wu*;[70] *Durham County Council v Dunn* (see **5.1.2.1.3**).[71]

5.7.3 Medical records as evidence

When considering the extent to which disclosure of records is necessary, and inspection proportionate, it is worth remembering the records may be of limited evidential value, at least so far as matters other than the treatment to which those records directly relate are concerned, and that certain procedural steps may be necessary if there is an issue about the accuracy of information contained within the records.

5.7.3.1 The evidential nature of medical records

In *Pettifer-Weeks v Everest Ltd*[72] HHJ Hampton observed: 'We are dealing with a general practitioner's notes ... intended only as a guideline to those who may come after that individual practitioner to apply further treatment for the individual patient.' Hence records may be valuable evidence about the diagnosis made at the time and treatment planned or given but those records are likely to be of less value in determining the background to the injury as that is likely to be hearsay evidence, which, at most, may establish inconsistency in the claimant's account that goes to credit.

This was recognised by the Court of Appeal in *Denton Hall Legal Services v Fifield*[73] where Buxton LJ noted:

> 'It is therefore necessary to remind ourselves of the evidential status of such material. What the doctor writes down as having been told him by the patient, as opposed to the opinion that he expresses on the basis of those statements, is not at that stage evidence of the making of the statement that he records. Rather where, as here, the record is said to contradict the evidence as to fact given by the patient, the record is of a previous inconsistent statement allegedly made by the patient. As such, the record itself is hearsay. It may however be proved as evidence that the patient did indeed speak as alleged in two ways. First, if the statement is put to the witness, she may admit to having made it. Alternatively, if she does not "distinctly" so admit the statement may be proved under section 4 of Lord Denman's Act 1865. Second, by section 6(5) of the Civil Evidence Act 1995 those provisions do not prevent the statement being proved as hearsay evidence under section 1 of that Act.
>
> If the court concludes that such inconsistent statement has been made, that goes only to the credibility of the witness; the statement itself cannot be treated itself as evidence of its contents. Authority is scarcely needed for so protean a proposition, but I would venture to mention the observations of Lord Esher MR in *North Australian v Goldsborough* [1893] 2 Ch 381 at p 386.'

---

68 [2002] EWCA Civ 642.
69 [2009] EWHC 1140 (QB).
70 [2010] EWCA Civ 1630.
71 [2012] EWCA Civ 1654 (see **5.7.3.5**).
72 (Unreported) Northampton County Court, 12 February 2013.
73 [2006] EWCA Civ 169.

Buxton LJ went on to outline the procedure which should be followed, prior to trial, if such issues, in relation to the content of the medical records, arise.

> 'To obviate such difficulties in future, and to ensure that factual issues in medical cases are economically and efficiently tried, the following procedure should be adopted. First, a party who seeks to contradict a factually pleaded case on the basis of medical records or reports should indicate that intention in advance, either by amendment of his pleadings or by informal notice. Then, the opposite party must indicate the extent to which they take objection to the accuracy of the records. When the area of dispute is identified, a decision will have to be taken as to whether the records need to be formally proved by either of the means referred to above. Thereby, not only will the ambit of the dispute be clarified in advance, but also it will be clear what interpretation is sought to be put on what my Lord has called somewhat Delphic records ...'

The failure to follow this procedure told against arguments advanced by the defendant in both *Pettifer-Weeks v Everest Ltd*[74] and *Cooper v Bright Horizons Family Solutions Ltd*.[75]

Where it is contended the records are relevant for the purpose of undermining the claimant's credit, by suggesting these contain previous inconsistent statements, it is worth noting that Buxton LJ recognised this is an issue as to credit only in *Denton Hall Legal Services*. Furthermore, it is also important to remember that documents going solely to credit are not part of standard disclosure: *Favor Easy Management Ltd v Wu* (see **5.1.1.3** and **5.5.5**).[76]

5.7.3.2 The evidential weight of medical records

Even if medical records are regarded as having some evidential value so far as the claimant's credit is concerned any inconsistencies will usually reflect the fact medical records are not completed primarily for forensic purposes. HHJ Hampton noted in *Pettifer-Weeks v Everest Ltd*:[77] 'No doubt when the general practitioner was making those notes he or she did not expect them to be dissected in the way that they have been some nearly four years after the event.'

Hence in *Bell v London Borough of Havering*[78] Jackson LJ observed:

> 'Anyone who has dealt with personal injury litigation over the years not infrequently encounters inaccuracies in records of what the patient said, not necessarily because the nurse or doctor got it wrong. The patient may be in a state of confusion or the doctor may be working, or nurse may be working, under pressure, and one has to view with some caution less significant inconsistencies.'

Similarly, in *Cooper v Bright Horizons Family Solutions Ltd*[79] David Pittaway QC held: 'In my view too much emphasis can sometimes be placed on short histories taken by medical attendants for purposes wholly unconnected with any subsequent litigation.'

---

74 (Unreported) Northampton County Court, 12 February 2013.
75 [2013] EWHC 2349 (QB).
76 [2010] EWCA Civ 1630.
77 (Unreported) Northampton County Court, 12 February 2013.
78 [2010] EWCA Civ 689.
79 [2013] EWHC 2349 (QB).

Consequently, the court may be ready to accept alleged inconsistencies carry no real evidential weight on the issue, if raised, of the claimant's credit. There may, of course, be cases where the inconsistency is such that the claimant's credit is called into question but so often the inconsistencies simply reflect the focus of the clinician on diagnosis of treatment rather than compiling a forensic record.

In *Hussain v Hussain*[80] the Court of Appeal questioned the weight attached to medical records, to support a finding of fraud, by the trial judge. Allowing the claimant's appeal Davies LJ held:

> '... I do not think the point about the medical records can have the effectively conclusive weight that the judge ascribed to it in support of a finding of, in effect, total adverse credibility and a conclusion of fraud on the part of the claimant.'

The defendant's point was that the relevant records contained no reference to the collision which was the subject matter of the claim. However, Davis LJ went on to observe:

> 'If anything, indeed, if there really was a fraudulently staged collision in which the claimant was complicit, then one perhaps might have thought that he would be careful to say to his doctor that he had been hurt in a road traffic collision, in order to enhance his claims.'

Consequently, Davis LJ considered, so far as the judge's conclusions which were adverse to the claimant had been based on omissions from the records, that:

"In my view, however, that was too slender a basis for concluding that the claimant's entire evidence relating to his non-complicity in the alleged fraud was not credible."

Accordingly, whilst entries in records about what the clinician recorded as being said by the claimant are not excluded simply because these parts of the records are hearsay this, coupled with the primary purpose of the records, inevitably has an effect on the weight attached to the records, for these purposes, as evidence.

5.7.4   Tactics with medical records

There are no absolute rules about when, and to what extent, the claimant's medical records should be subject to disclosure and inspection.

However, case-law in this area suggests some general guiding principles.

5.7.4.1   Pre-action disclosure

An order that the claimant give pre-action disclosure of medical records will generally be inappropriate: *OCS Group Ltd v Wells*.[81]

---

[80]   [2012] EWCA Civ 1367.
[81]   [2008] EWHC 919 (QB).

5.7.4.2 Medical experts

Relevant records should be made available to medical experts, whether instructed on behalf of the claimant, the defendant, or jointly.

The PI Protocol confirms the claimant's representative should provide such records to the experts the claimant instructs.

In *Dunn v British Coal Corporation*[82] the court considered circumstances in which disclosure of records to experts instructed by the defendant was appropriate.

- Where the claimant alleged a continuing loss of earnings and impaired earning capacity, general practitioner records and hospital records relating to the claimant were relevant, as the level of damages under this head could be affected by a pre-existing condition or some unrelated condition that might supervene to affect earning capacity before normal retirement.

- However, disclosure should be controlled by limiting inspection of records to the defendant's medical advisers in confidence, except in so far as it is necessary to refer to matters relevant to the litigation.

The defendant in that case only sought disclosure of records to medical advisors. Nevertheless, disclosure in this way would seem a proportionate approach consistent with the terms of the CPR introduced since the case was decided.

5.7.4.3 Fast track claims

In fast track cases, particularly lower value claims, it will not usually be necessary to give disclosure of medical records. Rather, it should suffice for the medical expert, usually a single expert in such cases, to review and deal with records when reporting. The overriding duty of the expert is to the court so that expert may be relied upon to draw relevant matters in the records to the attention of the court.

In *Rodgers v Bush*[83] the defendant had applied, in a fast track claim, for an order that unless and until the claimant's medical records were disclosed the action should be stayed. The application was refused by (as he then was) HHJ MacDuff QC.

- The overriding principle was that medical records need only be disclosed if there was something of relevance in them (for these purposes 'relevance' was approached on the basis of whether there was anything in those records which a medical advisor for the defendant would find of any use).

- Cases of modest value (typically under £5,000) had to be run with a sense of proportion and in such cases records should not be disclosed unless there was good reason to do so.

- The position may well have been different if the claim had been substantial as then then it might have been necessary for the records to be disclosed, for example to establish whether there was an underlying condition that might have led to the claimant being unable to work, and lose earnings, in any event.

- It was significant that the claimant's expert had reviewed the records and not found anything of relevance.

---

[82]   [1993] IRLR 396.
[83]   [1998] CLY 352.

5.7.4.4   Multi-track claims

If the claim is substantial there is a greater likelihood of the defendant having permission to rely on expert medical evidence, in which case any such expert should have access to the records: *Dunn v British Coal Corporation*.[84]

In such cases, whether or not the defendant has permission to rely on medical evidence, the defendant's legal representatives may seek copies of the claimant's medical records particularly if there may be entries in those records of relevance to legal issues such as limitation and causation. Such a request was considered in *Hipwood v Gloucester Health Authority*.[85]

- The court held that in cases involving a continuing disability and loss, 'relevant' records would normally include all medical records.
- Disclosure should be to the defendant's medical and legal advisors, as the combination of the two would be better able to gauge the relevance of records.
- Even in such cases, there may be particular entries or records that will not be relevant.
- If a dispute arose as to relevance, the court would have to look at the records or entries and determine whether they were disclosable.

That decision should not, however, be taken as a ruling such an order will generally be appropriate in a multi-track claim. First, the case involved disputes over liability and causation, as well as quantum. Secondly, the application was for non-party disclosure and the statutory provision then allowing for such an order (County Courts Act 1984, s 53) had no provision for disclosure only to medical advisors. Thirdly, and significantly, the decision was made before the implementation of the Human Rights Act and the need to ensure only a proportionate interference with Art 8 rights. Accordingly, changes in the law make the case distinguishable.

5.7.4.5   Controlling disclosure

Disclosure and inspection should usually be controlled by the claimant's solicitors and even when this is required the appropriate method of control may be by the claimant's representatives providing copies of records direct to any expert instructed by the defendant.

In *Bennett v Compass Group UK*[86] the claimant had agreed to provide records to the defendant for onward transmission to an expert the defendant had instructed but failed to provide authorities. The Court of Appeal confirmed a number of points relating to disclosure and inspection of medical records in these circumstances.

- The court had power to direct a party to give authority for disclosure of records.
- However, great care had to be taken both as to the circumstances in which orders of that kind should be made and also as to the terms in which they should be made.
  - Clarke LJ accepted that the defendant's solicitors would generally seek medical records by asking the claimant's solicitors to obtain and produce

---

84   [1993] IRLR 396.
85   [2002] EWCA Civ 642.
86   [2002] EWCA Civ 642.

them but an order allowing a defendant to obtain the records should only be made in exceptional circumstances, as a patient should retain control over his or her own records; any such order would have to be clearly and carefully drafted to ensure that the claimant's right to privacy was not infringed.

–   Chadwick LJ observed, after stressing that the courts should be very cautious before making orders of this kind in personal injury cases, that 'the normal and by far the most satisfactory course is for the medical records to be produced by the claimant's advisors for inspection and consideration by the defendant's expert'.

–   Pill LJ, in a dissenting judgment, concluded that the order was not one that could reasonably have been made by the district judge and observed that disclosure of records should be organised and managed by the claimant's solicitor to ensure proper protection of the claimant's interest in what was a sensitive area. He also relied on the PI Protocol stating that, as a general principle, the claimant's solicitors should organise access to relevant medical records and that the advice of the solicitor might also be required as to whether it was disproportionate to permit inspection of those records.

Consequently, it will rarely be appropriate for a claimant simply to provide the defendant with authorities to obtain records direct.

5.7.4.6   Questions to experts

It is sometimes argued on behalf of the defendant that disclosure of the claimant's medical records to the defendant's representatives is necessary for the purpose of formulating questions which will then be put to the claimant's medical expert.

This approach overlooks the purpose of questions, under Part 35, which are limited to 'clarification'. If a question cannot be formulated on the basis of the report itself that is not, logically, a matter of clarification.

Furthermore, the vital considerations of necessity, for disclosure, are proportionality, for inspection, must still be kept in mind. In *Catchpole v Young & Co's Brewery plc*[87] disclosure of the claimant's medical records was ordered, partly for the purpose of questions being put, though the judge recognised it was necessary to think long and hard before ordering such disclosure. Consequently, the judge concluded that in many cases it will be preferable for the defendant to put questions which relate to the records, or depend upon entries in the records, to the claimant's expert on the basis that the expert would deal with those questions by reviewing the records. That approach would help to guard against unnecessary disclosure and disproportionate inspection of records.

5.7.4.7   Applications for disclosure

Where an application is made for specific disclosure, pre-action disclosure or disclosure by a non-party, the court has discretion whether or not to grant the order.

Confidentiality and timing (a late application is less likely to succeed) will be factors in the exercise of this discretion. In *A v X and B (Non Party)*[88] the defendant made an

---

[87]   (Unreported) St Helen's County Court, 16 August 2004.
[88]   [2004] EWHC 447 (QB).

application for disclosure of medical records relating to the claimant's brother, on the basis that the claimant's condition would have occurred sooner or later for genetic reasons, irrespective of the relevant accident. Although accepting the relevance of those records, the court held that the making of an order was discretionary and it would only be in a very exceptional factual situation that confidential medical data relating to a non-party would be the subject of an order for disclosure. This was not such a case, as the burden of proof, on causation, remained on the claimant and disclosure of the brother's records was not necessary to dispose of the claim fairly or to save costs. Indeed, the court concluded that even if disclosure was necessary for a fair disposal of the claim, discretion would have been exercised against the defendant partly because of difficulties in preserving confidentiality and determining which records would be relevant and partly because the defendant only made the application at a late stage.

5.7.5 Summary

These CPR and case-law offer some guidance to practitioners when dealing with disclosure and inspection of medical records in personal injury claims, which can be summarised in the following principles:

- The claimant's representative should ensure that all medical records, or all relevant records, are reviewed by the medical experts instructed on behalf of the claimant.

- The claimant's representative should always be willing to allow inspection of all records by any other medical expert involved in the case.

- Disclosure of medical records in lower-value cases should, however, be resisted in order to respect the confidentiality of the records, save that it may be sometimes be appropriate to disclose relevant entries where these are of particular significance to an issue on the fact, circumstances or cause of the injuries.

- In higher-value cases there should be disclosure of medical records to the defendant's representatives only when this is strictly necessary, either because the defendant has no expert who can review the records or there are issues which require legal expertise to determine what records are relevant.

- Even when disclosure to and inspection by the defendant's representatives is appropriate the claimant may still be justified in arguing that some records are simply not relevant and should be redacted. Usually, however, this will only be necessary if those records are particularly sensitive (in such circumstances, it would not be appropriate simply for the records to be withheld; rather, the defendant's representatives should be advised that there are records which have been withheld and, in general terms, the reasons for that and, if necessary, relevance will have to be determined by the court on an application for inspection by the defendant).

5.8   ELECTRONIC DOCUMENTS

Documents are increasingly produced and/or retained in electronic format. As para 1 of Practice Direction 31B confirms the definition of 'document' in CPR 31.4 includes electronic documents.

Such documents are disclosable if part of standard or, if that is ordered by the court, specific disclosure.

The terms of Part 31 exclude personal injury claims, in both the fast track and the multi-track, from provisions that otherwise deal with the approach parties should take to electronic disclosure. Nevertheless, it can be important to remember the need for proper disclosure of electronic documents in personal injury clams where that is necessary.

5.8.1 General provisions

CPR 31.5(2)–(8) deals with disclosure in all multi-track claims except those which include a claim for personal injuries. These rules encourage the parties to agree the scope of disclosure before the first case management conference and make express reference to the use of the electronic documents questionnaire found in Practice Direction 31B. Practice Direction 31B recognises the complexities of dealing with disclosure of electronic documents and provides helpful guidance on a range of issues.

The court considered the practical application of these provisions in *Digicel (St Lucia) Ltd v Cable & Wireless plc.*[89]

In *Douglas v Hello ! Ltd*[90] it was held that the observations of Sir Robert Megarry in *Rockwell Machine Tool Co Ltd* applied to electronic messages in the same way as it applies to hard copies of documents.

5.8.2 Personal injury claims

While the provisions found in CPR 31.5(3)–(8) do not automatically apply in personal injury claims it is important to consider the need for disclosure of electronic documents, particularly in cases where liability is in issue.

To keep disclosure proportionate it may be helpful if the parties can reach agreement on the scope of electronic disclosure, which in turn will help define the nature of the search, by identifying the type of electronic documentation that is to be disclosed and any identifying features, for example reference to the claimant, the claimant's accident or injuries or other relevant factors.

5.9 NON-PARTY DISCLOSURE

Either the claimant or the defendant may wish to make use of the powers of the court to order a person who is not a party to the proceedings to give disclosure under CPR 31.17.

5.9.1 Procedure

To obtain an order for disclosure against a person who is not a party to the proceedings there will need to be an application notice and supporting evidence.

---

[89] [2008] EWHC 2522 (Ch).
[90] [2005] EWHC 55 (Ch).

The application should incorporate, or be accompanied by, a draft order specifying the documents or classes of document of which disclosure is sought.

The supporting evidence will need to explain why the documents sought are relevant and why disclosure is necessary to dispose fairly of the claim or to save costs.

5.9.2   Conditions

The court may only make an order if certain conditions are met, namely that:

- the documents must be likely to support the case of the applicant or adversely affect the case of another party; and
- disclosure must be necessary to dispose fairly of the claim or to save costs.

Furthermore, the power remains discretionary so that, applying the overriding objective, the court may still decline to make an order, even if these conditions are met *A v X and B (Non Party)*.[91] In other circumstances, if appropriate with relevant safeguards, the overriding objective will point the court in the direction of making an order: *Mitchell v News Group Newspapers Ltd*.[92]

5.9.3   Application by the claimant

The claimant may find it helpful to make use of the court's power to order non-party disclosure if, for example, documents are sought from a third party concerning the circumstances in which the injuries were suffered or to obtain earnings details from an employer of the claimant who is not directly involved in the proceedings.

Steps should be taken to secure disclosure on a voluntary basis before an application is considered. If, however, an application is necessary, it may be appropriate to establish (particularly where the documents relate to quantum) whether the defendant agrees with, and will support, such an application.

5.9.4   Application by the defendant

The defendant may wish to take advantage of the powers of the court to order non-party disclosure, eg for documents held by other parties relating to the claimant by way of general background information.

Often, before making an application, the defendant will invite the claimant to provide an authority for disclosure of such documents.

If the documents are relevant, and inspection would seem proportionate, it will be appropriate to advise the claimant that consent should be given; otherwise there is a risk that the defendant may obtain an order for costs against the claimant if an application has to be made.

---

91   [2004] EWHC 447 (QB).
92   [2014] EWHC 1885 (QB).

If, however, the documentation sought is not considered relevant, or the extent of the disclosure sought appears disproportionate, it would be reasonable to advise the claimant not to consent. Generally, however, the proceedings ought to be conducted with a degree of co-operation and, save for medical records, which have a particular sensitivity, it would be reasonable to allow the defendant access to documents held by another party that are likely to be relevant.

5.10 STATUTORY RIGHTS OF DISCLOSURE

There are statutory provisions that may be utilised, in addition to the powers conferred on the court by the CPR, to obtain disclosure of documents from the defendant and others.

5.10.1 Data Protection Act 1998

The Data Protection Act gives individuals, to whom relevant personal data relates, rights of access.

The Act implements the European Directive on this issue.

5.10.1.1 *Data*

This means information that:

- is being processed by means of equipment operating automatically in response to instructions given for that purpose;
- is recorded with the intention that it should be processed by means of such equipment;
- is recorded as part of a relevant filing system or with the intention that it should form part of a relevant filing system; or
- does not fall within the above but forms part of an 'accessible record'.

An 'accessible record' is defined by s 68 as including a health record and an educational record.

5.10.1.2 *Data controller*

This is a person who determines the purposes for which and the manner in which any personal data is processed.

5.10.1.3 *Personal data*

This means data relating to a living individual who can be identified:
- from the data; or
- from the data and other information which is in the possession of, or is likely to come into the possession of, the data controller.

5.10.1.4   Processing

This means obtaining, recording or holding information or data.

5.10.1.5   Rights

Personal data should be processed fairly and lawfully.

Section 7 entitles an individual to be informed of certain matters by any data controller.

- Whether personal data of which that individual is the data subject is being processed by or on behalf of that data controller.
- If that is the case, a description of the personal data of which that individual is the data subject, the purposes for which that data is processed and the recipients or classes of recipients to whom the data may be disclosed.
- To have communicated in an intelligible form the information constituting any personal data of which that individual is the data subject and any information available to the data controller as to the source of the data.
- Be informed by the data controller of the logic involved in decision-taking where the processing by automatic means of personal data of which that individual is the data subject is for the purposes of evaluating matters relating to the subject such as work performance, creditworthiness, reliability or conduct and where this is likely to constitute the sole basis for any decision significantly affecting the subject.

This is the right of 'subject access'.

An individual may also, in certain circumstances, give notice to a data controller restricting the ways in which data can be used, for example if the processing is causing substantial damage or substantial distress and this is unwarranted.

5.10.1.6   Enforcement rights

The Act applies to all organisations which hold or use personal data. Any such organisations must notify the Information Commissioner about the processing undertaken by that organisation and this information is placed on a public register.

The general requirement to process data fairly and lawfully means that individuals should be provided with information about the processing and identity of the data controller. In any event the register of data controllers can be checked to see whether a particular organisation is covered.

A subject access request can be made by writing to the data controller at the organisation holding data.

The organisation may ask for further information to confirm identity and locate the information required. The organisation may also ask for payment of a fee (usually up to £10 but up to £50 for health records that are not held in electronic form).

The Act allows organisations 40 calendar days to answer the request, starting from the date the request is received.

By s 7(9) a court can, on application, if satisfied a request has not been complied with order compliance with that request.

Section 13 gives an individual who suffers damage by reason of any contravention of the requirements of the Act by a data controller a right to compensation, including compensation for distress. It is, however, a defence to prove that the data controller had taken such care as in all the circumstances was reasonably required to comply with the relevant requirement of the Act.

Section 14 gives the court power to order a data controller to rectify, block, erase or destroy data which contains an expression of opinion that appears to the court to be based on inaccurate data.

The Commission may, in accordance with s 40, serve an enforcement notice requiring such steps as may be specified in the notice to be taken.

5.10.2   Access to Health Records Act 1990

This Act allows access to a health record, or any part of a health record, by application to the holder of the record.

The provisions of this Act have largely been superseded by the terms of the Data Protection Act 1998 but remain of relevance for obtaining access to the health records of a patient who has died.

5.10.3   Freedom of Information Act 2000

This Act allows access to information held by public authorities.

5.10.3.1   *The duty to confirm or deny*

Section 1 imposes a duty to confirm or deny on a public authority, if a request is made, as to whether information, of the description specified in the request, is held and, if it is, to have that information communicated.

Section 8 requires a request to:

- be in writing;
- state the name of the applicant and an address for correspondence; and
- describe the information requested.

A fee may be charged, if the public authority gives notice in writing of the amount within the time allowed for complying with the request, in accordance with the Freedom of Information and Data Protection (Appropriate Limit and Fees) Regulations 2004.[93] There are upper limits but, generally, the fee should reflect the total costs the authority reasonably expects to incur in relation to the request in terms of the costs of reproducing documents containing the information and posting or transmitting that information.

---

[93]   SI 2004/3244.

5.10.3.2   Exceptions

Section 17 allows a public authority to refuse the request provided, within the time for complying with that request, a notice is sent that:

* states the facts;
* specifies the exemption relied upon; and
* states why the exemption applies (if that is not otherwise apparent).

5.10.3.3   Public authority

Schedule 1 to the Act lists public authorities and this list includes:

* any government department;
* the armed forces;
* a local authority;
* a health authority or trust;
* any person providing medical and dental services under the National Health Service Act 1977.
* a police authority;
* the Health and Safety Executive;
* the Legal Services Commission.

5.11   BUNDLE OF DOCUMENTS

Disclosure is a good time to begin preparation of a bundle of documents, ultimately for use as a trial bundle, particularly if the documentation is extensive.

An organised, and even partially indexed, bundle will, as well as keeping the documents under control, facilitate access by those involved in the case, such as experts, to relevant documents and help with later preparations for trial.

5.11.1   Working bundle

Initially, as the case develops, it may be helpful to have a working bundle, to which documents are added as these become available.

5.11.2   Trial bundle

The final version of the working bundle can be utilised as a trial bundle.

Care is necessary on the agreement of documents contained within a trial bundle (see 5.1.2.7).

5.12   SANCTIONS

The sanctions provided by the CPR for failure to give disclosure of documents are limited, certainly in the context of a failure to give disclosure of documents adverse to the interests of the party required to give disclosure, meaning it will often be necessary to enforce case management directions rather than rely on the automatic sanctions.

5.12.1   Automatic sanctions

By CPR 31.21, a party may not rely on any document which that party fails to disclose or permit inspection of by the other party.

Proper disclosure and inspection of documents that support a party's case is essential and, in so far as the opponent fails to comply with relevant case management directions, the sanction provided for by CPR 31.21 will be effective. If the sanction imposed by CPR 31.21 applies relieve will be required, applying the approach in *Mitchell v News Group Newspapers Ltd*.[94]

This sanction, however, will not assist a claimant where the defendant fails to disclose documents that would either support the claimant's case or adversely affect the defendant's case. To ensure disclosure of such documents, enforcement of case management directions will be required.

5.12.1.1   When to rely on automatic sanctions

Properly dealing with both disclosure and inspection of documents which support a party's case are essential steps and in so far as the opponent fails to comply with relevant case management directions do this then the sanction provided for by CPR 31.21 will be effective.

If the sanction imposed by CPR 31.21 applies relief defendant fails to disclose and give inspection of relevant documents by the due date in case management directions relief from sanctions will be required, applying the approach in *Mitchell v News Group Newspapers Ltd*[95] as clarified by *Denton v T H White Ltd*.[96]

There may, of course, be documents which come into existence, or the control of the party, following the date by which disclosure has to be given under case management directions. A party should not, in these circumstances, be precluded from relying on such documents provided that party has properly complied with the duty of continuing disclosure. CPR 31.11(2) requiring that party to 'immediately notify every other party' when further documents to which the duty of disclosure extends, come to the notice of that party.

---

[94]   [2013] EWHC 2355 (QB).
[95]   [2013] EWHC 2355 (QB).
[96]   [2014] EWCA Civ 906.

5.12.1.2   When not to rely on automatic sanctions

The sanction provided for under CPR 31.21 will not assist a claimant where the defendant fails to disclose documents which would either support the claimant's case or adversely affect the defendant's case. To ensure disclosure of such documents enforcement of case management directions will be required.

5.12.2   Application to enforce directions for disclosure and inspection

Case management directions can be enforced in two ways.

5.12.2.1   General case management

An application, under the general case management powers of the court, can be made to enforce service of a list of documents. CPR 3.4(2) allows the court to strike out a statement of case if there has been a failure to comply with a court order. If the case management directions provide for the service of a list, the court may, in the event of default, be prepared to strike out a defence or at least make an unless order, giving the defendant a timescale to deal with disclosure, after which a striking-out of the defence may take effect in the event of continued default.

5.12.2.2   Specific disclosure or inspection

An application for specific disclosure or inspection can be made under CPR 31.12 in a number of situations.

- If disclosure has been given but it is considered that there remain documents disclosable under 'standard disclosure', or other documents which are relevant and ought to be disclosed, an order may be sought that specific documents, or classes of documents, be disclosed and, if need be, searched for.
- If documents have been disclosed but inspection has not been given, an order for specific inspection may be sought, which, in appropriate circumstances, allows a claim for privilege to be challenged.
- However, the making of an order is discretionary so, in deciding whether to make an order, the court will need to take account of the overriding objective, including proportionality, and also balance potentially conflicting rights under the European Convention.

5.12.3   Non-disclosure

In *Arrow Nominees Inc v Blackledge*[97] the court held that the object of the CPR on disclosure was to secure a fair trial in accordance with due process.

Hence, a party should not be deprived of the right to a proper trial as a penalty for disobedience of the Rules, even if such disobedience amounted to contempt for or defiance of the court if that object was ultimately secured by the late production of a document which had been withheld.

---

[97]   [2003] EWHC Ch 1516 ChD.

However, if that conduct put the fairness of the trial in jeopardy, so that any judgment would have to be regarded as unsafe, or where that conduct amounted to such an abuse of process that any further proceedings were rendered unsatisfactory and the court would be prevented from doing justice, then that litigant could be prevented from taking any further part in the proceedings or, where appropriate, have the proceedings determined against that party.

5.12.4 Destruction of documents

The destruction of documents was considered in *Douglas v Hello! Ltd*.[98] It was held that if documents are destroyed before the commencement of proceedings the question is whether there has been an attempt to pervert the course of justice, while if documents are destroyed after the issue of proceedings the question is whether a fair trial is still possible.

The related issue of destroying evidence, the approach to which could be applied by analogy when documents are destroyed, was considered in *Matthews v Herbert Collins* (see **5.3.1**).[99]

5.12.5 False disclosure statements

CPR 31.23 specifically provides that proceedings for contempt of court may be brought against a person if he makes, or causes to be made, a false disclosure statement without an honest belief in its truth.

In such circumstances the court might also exercise the power conferred by CPR 3.4 to strike the case of a party out given that a false disclosure statement will be a flagrant breach of the overriding objective and may render such a course of action just.

5.12.6 Admission of authenticity

The terms of CPR 32.19 may be regarded as imposing a sanction, namely the admission of authenticity unless notice requiring the document to be proved at trial is served within the stipulated time limit of seven days.

Whilst the court can extend time, under Part 3, if a sanction applies the party in default will need to obtain relief in accordance with CPR 3.9.

In *Nageh v David Game College Ltd*[100] the Court of Appeal confirmed that where the defence did not allege forgery and the defendant had failed to challenge the authenticity of the relevant document in accordance with CPR 32.19 the authenticity of that document could not be challenged, although the defendant was entitled to dispute its meaning and effect.

---

[98] (1990) *The Times*, 20 July.
[99] [2013] EWHC 2952 (QB) (see **5.3.1**).
[100] [2013] EWCA Civ 1340.

5.12.7   Agreement of content

If a party agrees a bundle of documents para 27.2 of the Practice Direction to Part 32 confirms that, unless the court otherwise orders or a party gives written notice of objection to the admissibility of particular documents, documents contained within the agreed bundles shall be admissible as evidence of their contents.

The phrase 'the court orders otherwise' is likely to be interpreted as imposing a sanction, so relief will be required if, having agreed a bundle there is then a challenge to the content of a document contained in that bundle: *Durrant v Chief Constable of Avon & Somerset;*[101] *Walsham Chalet Park Ltd v Tallington Lakes Ltd.*[102]

---

[101]   [2013] EWCA Civ 1624.
[102]   [2014] EWCA Civ 1607.

CHAPTER 6

FACTUAL EVIDENCE

6.1 INTRODUCTION

Most cases, and personal injury claims are no exception, will involve, and the outcome may well be determined by, matters of fact. Accordingly, factual evidence in support of the claim, and dealing effectively with the implementation of case management directions for exchange of that evidence, will be of critical importance to the claim.

Documents exchanged at the stage of disclosure if not before, will help establish, confirm or clarify some of the factual background. In some cases, in addition to the documents disclosed and witness statements exchanged, there may be other evidence of fact. Usually, however, it is witnesses whose evidence, initially in the form of witness statements exchanged in accordance with case management directions, that will be the principal evidence of fact and crucial to the eventual determination of most issues in the case.

Ultimately, as confirmed by CPR 32.2(1), the general rule is that any fact to be proved by a witness at trial must be by oral evidence. At trial the court is very likely to restrict such evidence to those witnesses who have made statements disclosed under case management directions, given the terms of CPR 32.10.

Accordingly, it is essential to obtain suitable directions from the court, for exchange of factual evidence, at the stage of initial case management and then to ensure that these are implemented by the relevant deadline so the oral evidence of those witnesses will be admissible at trial.

The rules relating to other factual evidence must, similarly, be complied with so that this, where necessary, will be admissible.

6.1.1 What is factual evidence?

Factual evidence includes:

- documents;
- the evidence of witnesses of fact; and
- other evidence of fact such as:
  - a plan, photograph or model (evidence of the kind specifically identified in CPR 33.6(1) which is not a document subject to disclosure, nor part of the evidence of a witness of fact nor contained in the evidence of an expert); or

–   investigative evidence, for example evidence of the kind considered in *Hoyle v Rogers*[1] (see **6.1.1.1**)).

Documents have been dealt with in Chapter 5 while expert evidence will covered in Chapter 7. This chapter considers factual evidence given by witnesses of fact and from other sources.

Factual evidence needs to be admissible, under the general law, and must also comply with the procedural requirements of the CPR.

When considering admissibility it is important to distinguish evidence of fact, which will be admissible and properly included in a witness statement, from analysis of documentary evidence, opinion evidence and legal argument. That is because CPR 32.4 describes a witness statement as 'a written statement signed by a person which contains the evidence which that person would be allowed to give orally'.

6.1.1.1   Witnesses of fact and documentary evidence

If there is factual evidence in the form of documents which are subject to disclosure those documents should be disclosed in accordance with case management directions by inclusion in the relevant list of documents, with any further documents that come into the possession of the party being disclosed immediately by supplemental list in accordance with CPR 31.11 and para 3.3 of the Practice Direction to Part 31, not introduced only at a later stage as part of the factual evidence (see **5.1.1.7**).

Witnesses of fact should not be developing legal arguments about the interpretation of documents. In some circumstances a witness may properly be able to put documentation into proper context and evidence of this kind may have 'narrative relevance': *Hoyle v Rogers*.[2] Generally, however, argument, submissions and/or expressions of opinion on documents will not be permitted. In *JD Wetherspoon plc v Harris*[3] the Chancellor of the High Court considered such comments by a witness of fact to be 'an abuse' and observed:

> '(The witness) would not be allowed at trial to give oral evidence which merely recites the relevant events, of which he does not have direct knowledge, by reference to documents he has read. Nor would he be permitted at trial to advance arguments and make submissions which might be expected of an advocate rather than a witness of fact. These points are made clear in paragraph 7 of Appendix 9 to the Chancery Guide (7th ed), which is as follows:
>
> > "A witness statement should simply cover those issues, but only those issues, on which the party serving the statement wishes that witness to give evidence in chief. Thus it is not, for example, the function of a witness statement to provide a commentary on the documents in the trial bundle, nor to set out quotations from such documents, nor to engage in matters of argument. Witness statements should not deal with other matters merely because they may arise in the course of the trial."'

---

1   [2014] EWCA Civ 257.
2   [2014] EWCA Civ 257.
3   [2013] EWHC 1088 (Ch).

6.1.1.2   Witness of fact and opinion evidence

Evidence given by witnesses of fact needs to be distinguished from expert evidence, as it is generally only experts who can give opinion evidence and because permission from the court will be required to rely on any expert evidence. Evidence from witnesses of fact, whilst subject to the general right of the court to control evidence (in CPR 32.1), can be relied on without specific permission from the court provided a statement of the witness has been disclosed in accordance with case management directions.

The distinction between factual and opinion evidence, and hence what is admissible and inadmissible from a witness of fact, is not always easy to discern.

6.1.1.2.1   Fact or opinion?

Factual evidence does not become expert evidence simply because the witness has a degree of expertise, rather the distinction turns upon the nature of the evidence to be given by that witness.

In *Kirkham v Euro Exide Corporation (CMP Batteries Ltd)*[4] the claimant wished to rely on evidence from the treating surgeon that, had it not been for the accident at work, he would not have advised the claimant to undergo surgery when he did. Whilst recognising the distinction between factual and expert evidence might not be immediately obvious the Court of Appeal confirmed the evidence of the treating surgeon was factual as he was simply saying what he would have advised the claimant to do, albeit in a hypothetical situation. The witness was not stating that the advice would necessarily have been correct or that most surgeons would have given that advice, which would have been matters of opinion and thus expert evidence. Consequently, there was no need for the court to determine whether permission should be given to rely on the evidence of the treating surgeon as it was factual, not expert, evidence.

The evidence of a medical practitioner was, once again, treated as factual evidence in *Rich v Hull & East Yorkshire Hospitals NHS Trust*.[5] The evidence of that witness concerned the meaning of the word 'likely' in treatment guidelines. The question for the court was whether, in context, the word 'likely' meant more likely than not or just that there was a material possibility. The witness was not giving an opinion on this point but stating his understanding, based on the factual background in which the guidelines were drawn up.

A case manager, if called to give evidence about the issues being dealt with for an injured person, was held clearly to be a witness of fact for such purposes: *Wright v Sullivan*.[6] It followed that there was no question of the case manager being jointly instructed as an expert.

---

[4]   [2007] EWCA Civ 66.
[5]   [2014] EWHC 1978 (QB).
[6]   [2005] EWCA Civ 656.

6.1.1.2.2   Inadmissible opinion

In *Hoyle v Rogers*[7] (a judgment which was upheld by the Court of Appeal[8]) Leggatt J explained why opinion is generally inadmissible from a witness of fact when he said:

> 'As a general rule, evidence that a person holds an opinion on a relevant matter is not admissible to prove that the opinion is true. A reason often given for this rule is that opinion evidence is irrelevant. But the admissibility of an opinion does not depend simply on whether it is likely to be reliable and therefore logically probative. The main justification for excluding opinion evidence lies not in its irrelevance but in the nature of the judicial role.
>
> A central part of a judge's task in a civil case is to evaluate the evidence adduced by the parties and to decide what conclusions may properly be drawn from that evidence. It is a cardinal principle, and an essential ingredient of the right to a fair trial before an impartial and independent tribunal, that in carrying out this task judges must form their own opinions by making their own evaluation of the evidence and must not defer to the opinion of anyone else. In the great case of Carter v Boehm (1766) 3 Burr 1905, 1917, in holding that the opinion of a broker was evidence to which the jury "ought not to pay the least regard" Lord Mansfield explained the reason as follows:
>
> > "It is an opinion which, if rightly formed, could only be drawn from the same premises from which the Court and jury were to determine the cause; and therefore it is improper and irrelevant in the mouth of a witness."'

The same approach was adopted by the Chancellor of the High Court in *JD Wetherspoon plc v Harris*[9] where, after finding attempts to interpret a document would be inadmissible evidence from a witness of fact, it was held that:

> 'Nor would (the witness) be permitted to give expert opinion evidence at the trial. A witness of fact may sometimes be able to give opinion evidence as part of his or her account of admissible factual evidence in order to provide a full and coherent explanation and account. That is what, it would appear, Master Bowles recognised when he refused the first Defendant's application to adduce expert evidence on market practice. It is what the first Defendant has done in his witness statements (The witness), however, has expressed his opinions on market practice by way of commentary on facts of which he has no direct knowledge and of which he cannot give direct evidence. In that respect he is purporting to act exactly like an expert witness giving opinion evidence. Permission for such expert evidence has, however, been expressly refused.'

Difficulties can arise where a witness of fact has expertise relevant to the issues in the case, distinguishing between admissible evidence of fact and non-admissible opinion evidence. In cases which involve an allegation of professional negligence it was recognised in *ES v Chesterfield & North Derbyshire Royal Hospital NHS Trust*[10] that:

> 'It is inevitable that a witness who happens to be a professional will give evidence of his actions based upon his or her professional experience and expertise ...'

Similarly in *DN v London Borough of Greenwich*[11] Brooke LJ held:

---

7   [2013] EWHC 1409 (QB).
8   [2014] EWCA Civ 257.
9   [2013] EWHC 1088 (Ch).
10 [2003] EWCA Civ 1284.
11 [2004] EWCA Civ 1659.

'It very often happens in professional negligence cases that a defendant will give evidence to a judge which constitutes the reason why he considers that his conduct did not fall below the standard of care reasonably to be expected of him. He may do this by reference to the professional literature that was reasonably available to him as a busy practitioner or by reference to the reasonable limits of his professional experience; or he may seek to rebut, as one professional man against another, the criticisms made of him by the claimant's expert(s). Such evidence is common, and it is certainly admissible.'

The lack of objectivity from a factual witness in these circumstances will affect the cogency of the evidence. Furthermore, whilst a witness of fact in a professional negligence claim can express his or her own view on standards in the context of why that witness acted as they did caution should be exercised before accepting more general observations, for example that this is how any other professional would have acted in the circumstances or the actions of the witness would be supported by most practitioners in that field of expertise. That is because comments of this kind go beyond opinion related directly to the facts although, inevitably, what is admissible will always be a matter of degree.

After noting there is 'relatively little authority on the extent to which witnesses, who are possessed of special expertise, can gloss their factual evidence with expert comment' Jackson J observed in *Multiplex Constructions (UK) Ltd v Cleveland Bridge UK Ltd*[12] that:

'Having regard to the guidance of the Court of Appeal and the established practice in TCC cases, I conclude that in construction litigation an engineer who is giving factual evidence may also proffer (a) statements of opinion which are reasonably related to the facts within his knowledge and (b) relevant comments based upon his own experience.'

Consequently, a professional person giving factual evidence ought to focus on the factual background known to that witness even if that is explained in terms of expertise and experience. The dividing line may be crossed if the witness tries to express an opinion on how the relevant standard of care should be set and whether that standard has been breached or if general observations are made about what those in the relevant profession might, or might not, consider appropriate.

6.1.1.2.3   Admissible opinion

There are, however, limits on the principle which excludes opinion being expressed by a witness of fact. This was also explained by Leggatt J in *Hoyle v Rogers*[13] when he observed:

'There are important limits to this principle. In particular, it is proper that a judge should have regard to the opinion of a person who is better placed to form that opinion than is the judge. The obvious example is the opinion of an expert on a subject involving specialised knowledge.

Even where the subject matter is not one in which the witness has any special expertise, a witness may be in a privileged position to express an opinion because of his or her observation of the relevant events. For example, a witness may from observation give evidence of a person's age or the speed at which a car was travelling. These are strictly matters of inference and therefore opinion, but they are inferences which the witness is

---

12   [2008] EWHC 2220 (TCC).
13   [2013] EWHC 1409 (QB).

peculiarly well placed to draw and cannot reasonably be expected to separate from the observed facts. Another example is evidence of what the witness would have done in a hypothetical situation – e.g. if a particular misrepresentation had not been made. Such a question is not one on which there is any observed fact of the matter – since by definition the situation did not occur – but a person may through self-knowledge not possessed by any third party be better able than others to form an opinion of what he or she would have done.

Unless, however, the person expressing an opinion is in a significantly better position than the court to evaluate the facts on which the opinion is based and to draw conclusions from those facts, evidence of the opinion itself is not admissible.'

These observations reflect the terms of s 2(2) Civil Evidence Act 1972, which provides that a witness, whether a witness of fact or an expert witness, is permitted to give 'a statement of opinion by him of any relevant matter on which he is not qualified to give expert evidence, if made as a way of conveying relevant facts personally perceived by him, is admissible as evidence of what he perceived.'

A number of cases illustrate, on this basis, the latitude given by the courts to witnesses of fact giving what, at face value, might be regarded as opinion evidence. That was recognised by Sir Mark Waller in *Lawrence v Kent County Council*[14] when he said:

'Furthermore time and again one sees references to the opinion of a factual witness in judgments in the authorities before us without any suggestion they are totally irrelevant. Thus in *Mills v Barnsley Metropolitan Borough Council* Steyn LJ refers to the unchallenged evidence of Mr Booth, the Council's Inspector, that if he had seen the missing corner of the brick he would not have regarded it as a problem and would have treated it as a minor defect … While the judge was not bound to accept Mr Booth's view as to the relative importance of the defect, it is not clear what inference he drew …. In *Uren v Corporate Leisure (UK) Ltd & Another* [2011] EWCA Civ 66 the Court of Appeal criticised the judge for thinking that "what spectators thought" about the dangerousness of a game was irrelevant and thought the judge was wrong to disregard the impressions of eye-witnesses. Perhaps the most striking case is that of *Dalton v Nottinghamshire County Council* [2011] EWCA Civ 776 where Tomlinson LJ, in dismissing an appeal without calling on the respondents, approved the judge having placed great reliance on the view of the Council's surveyor that a protrusion was dangerous.'

6.1.1.3   Witnesses of fact and legal argument

It is as inappropriate for a witness of fact to develop legal argument or make submissions on the law to the court as it is for that witness to interpret documentary evidence.

In *Alex Lawrie Factors Ltd v Morgan*[15] Brooke LJ, in the early days of the CPR, observed:

'The case is a very good warning of the grave dangers which may occur when lawyers put into witnesses' mouths, in the affidavits which they settle for them, sophisticated legal arguments which in effect represents the lawyer's arguments in the case to which the witnesses themselves would not be readily able to speak if cross-examined on their affidavits. Affidavits are there for the witness to say in his or her own words what the relevant evidence

---

[14]   [2012] EWCA Civ 493.
[15]   [2001] CP Rep 2, (1999) *The Times*, 18 August.

is and are not to be used as a vehicle for complex legal argument. Those considerations apply just as much to statements of truth under the Civil Procedure Rules as they do to affidavits.'

The point was made even more forcibly by HHJ Dean QC in *ED & F Man Liquid Products Ltd v Patel*[16] when he said:

'Witness statements are not the place for argument. It means you have to read everything twice. I am going to go through this statement. Paragraph 8 simply summarises what is in the documents. Paragraph 10 is a pure advocacy point. No witness would be allowed to say that in evidence. A lot of it is tendentious comment which is bound up with fact. I think this witness statement is an example of what a witness statement should not be whether in the Commercial Court or anything else. It is a tendentious advocate's document. I am minded to disallow the cost of it actually.

Look how long it goes on for. It goes on for 41 paragraphs. That is just a solicitor giving information on what his client has said. He expresses a reference to his client's belief which is not only irrelevant but inadmissible. I think that this is a statement of an enthusiastic solicitor who wishes he was an advocate. I am going to cut quite a lot off this. I do not think that is a proper statement at all. If you say that is legitimate under the Commercial Court's practice, you show me the rules of the Commercial Court which say that is so. There is far too much of this. It adds to the time of the hearing and it adds to the time of preparation.'

The same point was made yet again, this time by the Chancellor of the High Court, in *JD Wetherspoon plc v Harris*[17] when he held that a witness would not:

'... be permitted at trial to advance arguments and make submissions which might be expected of an advocate rather than a witness of fact. These points are made clear in paragraph 7 of Appendix 9 to the Chancery Guide (7th ed), which is as follows:

"A witness statement should simply cover those issues, but only those issues, on which the party serving the statement wishes that witness to give evidence in chief. Thus it is not, for example, the function of a witness statement to provide a commentary on the documents in the trial bundle, nor to set out quotations from such documents, nor to engage in matters of argument. Witness statements should not deal with other matters merely because they may arise in the course of the trial."'

This can be a particular problem with interim applications where practitioners needs to ensure, so far as possible, factual matters, relevant to the application, are dealt with by witness statements whilst legal argument and submissions are confined to case summaries or skeleton arguments.

6.1.1.4 *Witnesses of fact and conclusions on issues*

Even worse than witnesses of fact expressing an opinion or developing legal argument is the purported finding of fact or drawing of conclusions on any matters in issue, sometimes termed the 'ultimate issue', because that is a matter entirely within the province of the judge.

So, for example, it would not be appropriate for a witness to draw conclusions about what someone else must have thought or that, given the factual background, liability is established or a particular head of damages proved.

---

16   [2002] 1706 EWHC (QB).
17   [2013] EWHC 1088 (Ch).

In *Rock Nominees Ltd v RCO (Holdings) Plc*[18] Peter Smith J criticised much of the content in a witness statement on the basis 'the material there, consisting largely of assertions, expressions of opinion and usurpation of my role, should never have been there in the first place'.

In *Farrugia v Burtenshaw*[19] witnesses of fact, when dealing with matters relating to the claimant's care, expressed the opinion that what had been done provided the claimant with care that was reasonably required, when the claimant's care requirements was an issue for the court to decide.

6.1.1.5　Witnesses of fact and partiality

It is important any witness statement fairly reflects the totality of the evidence that witness can give and does not adopt a partisan approach. In *Nicholls v Ladbrokes Betting & Gambling Ltd*,[20] after observing 'the evidence which the defendant served in support of its defence was far from satisfactory', Jackson LJ held:

> 'Before parting with this case I wish to express my concern about the manner in which the defendant has conducted its defence. The defence of any personal injury case is a serious task, to be undertaken in a fair and responsible manner. It is inappropriate to serve witness statements which refute every allegation, whether right or wrong. It is also inappropriate for an expert witness to provide a partisan report which backs up his client at every turn.'

In the circumstances the defendant, although ultimately succeeding in the defence of the claim, suffered costs sanctions (see **6.7.3**).

6.1.2　What factual evidence does the claimant need?

When the defence is received part of the review which should then be undertaken of the claim, in readiness for case management, is an assessment of the issues to assess which of those will need to be proved by the claimant so that an assessment can be made of the evidence, including factual evidence, which will be required. It may also be necessary to assess assertions made by the defendant, to anticipate evidence the defendant may call and ensure evidence that will be needed in reply is available.

This process should involve an analysis of where the evidential burden of proof will rest and, once the issues the claimant will need to prove are identified, an assessment of the sources of factual evidence, bearing in mind the risks if a party fails to call a witness the court might expect to hear from.

6.1.2.1　Burden of proof

The burden of proof inevitably influences the factual evidence which the claimant will need.

18　[2003] EWHC 936 (Ch).
19　[2014] EWHC 1036 (QB).
20　[2013] EWCA Civ 1963.

The legal burden of proof always remains on the claimant. As Lord Pearson observed in *Henderson v Henry E Jenkins & Sons*:[21]

> 'In an action for negligence the plaintiff must allege, and has the burden of proving, that the accident was caused by negligence on the part of the defendants. That is the issue throughout the trial, and in giving judgment at the end of the trial the judge has to decide whether he is satisfied on a balance of probabilities that the accident was caused by negligence on the part of the defendants, and if he is not so satisfied the plaintiff's action fails. The formal burden of proof does not shift.'

However, when analysing the evidence required, it is important to recognise that what is sometimes termed the evidential burden may shift to the defendant.

In *Dawkins v Carnival Plc*[22] Pill LJ made reference to an article signed AT Denning (by the time of publication Denning J) entitled 'Presumptions and Burdens'[23] which, when dealing with evidential burdens, stated:

> 'The party on whom it rests must call evidence or take the consequences, which might not necessarily be adverse : for the place where the burden eventually comes to rest does not necessarily decide the issue : because at the end of the case the Court has to decide as a matter of fact whether the inference should be drawn or not. These presumptions and burdens are therefore *provisional* only. It is a mistake to raise these provisional presumptions into propositions having the force of law. They are recognised by the law but their force depends on ordinary good sense rather than on law.'

It may be necessary to anticipate factual evidence the defendant may rely upon so the claimant is ready to assert, on the basis of the claimant's own factual evidence, any positive case to help deal with the ultimate legal burden of proof. For example, in *Egan v Central Manchester and Manchester Children's University Hospitals NHS Trust*[24] Smith LJ, after recognising that under the Manual Handling Operations Regulations 1992 once it was shown there was a manual handling operation with a risk of injury the burden of proof was on the employer to prove the risk was reduced to the lowest level reasonably practicable:

> 'I accept of course, that, in practice, if a claimant wants to allege that there were steps which could and should have been taken and the employer says there were none, there will be an evidential burden on the claimant to advance those suggestions, even though the legal burden will remain on the employer.'

6.1.2.2 *Identifying witnesses*

Having identified all the issues which the claimant will need to prove, having regard to the legal burden of proof, all witnesses of fact, who may be able to help, should be identified and, as appropriate, approached to clarify whether or not relevant evidence can be given. If so, information from the witness should be gathered and a statement prepared.

---

[21]   [1970] AC 282.
[22]   [2011] EWCA Civ 1237.
[23]   (1945) 61 LQR 379.
[24]   [2008] EWCA Civ 1424.

6.1.2.3   Adverse inference

Irrespective of where the burden of proof lies a party must take care to ensure, unless there is good reason which can be given to the court, that party does call any witness who might be expected to deal with the issues. There is, otherwise, a risk that the court may draw an adverse inference from the absence of such evidence.

In *McQueen v Great Western Railway Company*,[25] Cockburn CJ held:

> 'If a prima facie case is made out, capable of being displaced, and if the party against whom it is established might by calling particular witnesses and producing particular evidence displace that prima facie case, and he omits to adduce that evidence, then the inference fairly arises, as a matter of inference for the jury and not as a matter of legal presumption, that the absence of that evidence is to be accounted for by the fact that even if it were adduced it would not disprove the prima facie case. But that always presupposes that a prima facie case has been established; and unless we can see our way clearly to the conclusion that a prima facie case has been established, the omission to call witnesses who might have been called on the part of the defendants amounts to nothing.'

This issue was also considered in *British Railways Board v Herrington*[26] where Lord Diplock said:

> 'As the appellants elected to call none of the persons who patrolled the line there is nothing to rebut the inference that they did not lack the common sense to realise the danger. A court is accordingly entitled to infer from the inaction of the appellants that one or more of their employees decided to allow the risk to continue of some child crossing the boundary and being injured or killed by the live rail rather than to incur the trivial trouble and expense of repairing the gap in the fence.'

More recently Lord Sumption observed in *Petrodol Resources Ltd v Prest*[27] that:

> 'The courts have tended to recoil from some of the fiercer parts of this statement, which appear to convert open-ended speculation into findings of fact. There must be a reasonable basis for some hypothesis in the evidence or the inherent probabilities, before a court can draw useful inferences from a party's failure to rebut it. For my part I would adopt, with a modification which I shall come to, the more balanced view expressed by Lord Lowry with the support of the rest of the committee in *R v Inland Revenue Commissioners, ex p TC Coombs & Co* [1991] 2 AC 283, 300:
>
> > "In our legal system generally, the silence of one party in face of the other party's evidence may convert that evidence into proof in relation to matters which are, or are likely to be, within the knowledge of the silent party and about which that party could be expected to give evidence. Thus, depending on the circumstances, a prima facie case may become a strong or even an overwhelming case. But, if the silent party's failure to give evidence (or to give the necessary evidence) can be credibly explained, even if not entirely justified, the effect of his silence in favour of the other party may be either reduced or nullified."'

In *Wisniewski v Central Manchester Health Authority*[28] Brooke LJ reviewed the relevant authorities and held:

---

[25]   (1874-5) LR 10 QB 569.
[26]   [1972] AC 877.
[27]   [2013] UKSC 34.
[28]   [1998] PIQR 324.

'From this line of authority I derive the following principles in the context of the present case:

(1)   In certain circumstances a court may be entitled to draw adverse inferences from the absence or silence of a witness who might be expected to have material evidence to give on an issue in an action.

(2)   If a court is willing to draw such inferences they may go to strengthen the evidence adduced on that issue by the other party or to weaken the evidence, if any, adduced by the party who might reasonably have been expected to call the witness.

(3)   There must, however, have been some evidence, however weak, adduced by the former on the matter in question before the court is entitled to draw the desired inference: in other words, there must be a case to answer on that issue.

(4)   If the reason for the witness's absence or silence satisfies the court then no such adverse inference may be drawn. If, on the other hand, there is some credible explanation given, even if it is not wholly satisfactory, the potentially detrimental effect of his/her absence or silence may be reduced or nullified.'

Following amendments to the CPR in 2013 it is increasingly likely a party may have to go to trial having been debarred from calling factual evidence which raises the question of how the court should view the evidence in such circumstances. In *Durrant v Chief Constable of Avon & Somerset Constabulary*[29] the defendant was not able to call some factual evidence at trial because a debarral order had previously been made. In these circumstances the judge held:

'The present case is unique in my experience, in that it is known to the court that there are witness statements, and that the Defendant would wish those statements to be in evidence and oral evidence given by their authors. There is no suggestion that the police officers who gave those witness statements were unwilling to attend to give evidence.

In my judgment it is therefore not appropriate to draw adverse inference against the individual police officers, or the Defendant, from the simple absence of statements or live evidence from those officers.'

An adverse inference may also be drawn if the defendant's conduct leads to the claimant not having evidence available, to deal with matters in issue, that might have been expected had the defendant acted more appropriately.

In *Armory v Delamirie*[30] a chimneysweep left a jewel, which had been found in a chimney, with a pawnbroker for valuation. The pawnbroker failed to return the jewel and the court held, when sued by the chimneysweep, he could not assert the absence of the jewel meant that the chimneysweep was unable to prove its value.

More recently in *Keefe v The Isle of Man Steam Packet Company Ltd*[31] the defendant breached the duty it had to measure noise levels in the workplace. When it was alleged there had been exposure to excessive noise levels the defendant was not allowed to rely on the absence of measurements in support of a contention that the claimant was unable to prove the claim. Noting this had been accepted law since *Armory* Longmore LJ held:

'If it is a defendant's duty to measure noise levels in places where his employees work and he does not do so, it hardly lies in his mouth to assert that the noise levels were not, in fact, excessive. In such circumstances the court should judge a claimant's evidence benevolently and the defendant's evidence critically. If a defendant fails to call witnesses at his disposal who could have evidence relevant to an issue in the case, that defendant runs the risk of

29   [2014] EWHC 2922 (QB).
30   (1721) 1 Strange 505.
31   [2010] EWCA Civ 683.

relevant adverse findings see British Railways Board v Herrington [1972] AC 877, 930G. Similarly a defendant who has, in breach of duty, made it difficult or impossible for a claimant to adduce relevant evidence must run the risk of adverse factual findings.'

6.1.3   Disclosure of factual evidence

Under the CPR factual evidence will usually be disclosed, ahead of trial, in accordance with the timetable given in case management directions.

CPR 32.4(2) requires the court to order disclosure of the evidence of witnesses of fact in the form of witness statements.

This reflects the general policy of openness in modern litigation so that, well ahead of trial, each party is aware of the case advanced by other parties. Accordingly, case management directions will invariably provide for the exchange of the statements of witnesses of fact, usually after disclosure but prior to completing exchange of expert evidence.

Disclosure of other factual evidence is dealt with by CPR 33.6.

6.1.4   Sequential for exchange of witness statements

The court has discretion as to the order in which witness statements are to be served. CPR 32.4(3)(a) expressly provides the court may give directions as to the order in which witness statements are to be served. However, this discretion, like any case management power, must be exercised to further the overriding objective.

Whilst the court will usually give directions for the simultaneous exchange of statements from witnesses of fact such exchange may be confined to a specific issue, might be sequential and could also make provision for subsequent exchange.

6.1.4.1   Issues

The court may direct exchange of witness statements, whether simultaneous or sequential, on a specific issue or issues only, for example where such issues are to be dealt with at a preliminary trial.

Directions for exchange of witness statements on other issues are, in these circumstances, likely to be deferred until such time as the preliminary issue has been decided.

6.1.4.2   Simultaneous exchange

Simultaneous, rather than sequential, exchange of witness statements will usually be appropriate as that is more likely to reflect the requirement in the overriding objective for the courts to ensure that the parties are on an equal footing.

Although that is not spelt out in Part 32 it is notable that para 3.9 of the Practice Direction to Part 28, dealing with fast track claims, and para 4.10 of the Practice

Direction to Part 29, the equivalent provision for multi-track claim, both stipulate that the 'general approach' will be 'to direct the disclosure of witness statements by way of simultaneous exchange'.

That suggests a case would need unusual features for it to be just that the court order sequential exchange.

6.1.4.3 Sequential exchange

Sequential exchange is likely to create a degree of inequality, because one party will have seen the evidence of the other before being committed to evidence already disclosed. Sequential exchange may, very occasionally, be appropriate, usually on issues of quantum only.

6.1.4.4 Subsequent exchange

The court might, in appropriate cases, give directions for exchange of witness statements coupled with a further direction for the subsequent exchange of any statements dealing with new matters arising from the evidence exchanged initially.

Recognising the potential difficulties in dealing with new matters, given the terms of CPR 32.10, this approach was canvassed by Turner J in *Karbhari v Ahmed*[32] where he observed:

> 'In this case there was nothing in the supplementary witness statement that could not and should not have been incorporated in the witness statement originally served. I ought, however, to sound a note of caution about the late service of witness statements generally.
>
> There will be other cases in which there are evidential developments which postdate the time at which earlier witness statements have been served. It is, by way of example only, by no means unusual in personal injury cases for updated witness statements to be served in order to cover a claimant's progress over the period since the original witness statements were served. This situation falls within the approach of the Court of Appeal in Mitchell at paragraph 41 which I repeat for ease of reference:
>
> > "Later developments in the course of the litigation process are likely to be a good reason if they show that the period for compliance originally imposed was unreasonable, although the period seemed to be reasonable at the time and could not realistically have been the subject of an appeal."
>
> In cases in which there is a realistic possibility that there will be evidential developments between the date upon which witness statements are to be served and the trial date this ought to be anticipated in the orders of the court. In such cases, the wisest course would be to seek to persuade the court to make two orders relating to the service of witness statements. The first would provide for a date which would give a realistic opportunity for all sides to comply with respect to matters which have arisen beforehand. A later backstop date could be ordered for the service of supplementary statements limited in content to matters which occurred, or were reasonably discoverable, only after the first date. This would have the advantage of obviating the need for further applications to the court and of giving the court the opportunity to exercise proportionate case management discipline in advance. In this way, in

---

[32] [2013] EWHC 4042 (QB).

the vast majority of cases the unanticipated last minute service of witness statements should become a thing of the past. I would expect the same to apply to expert reports.'

6.2   PREPARING WITNESS STATEMENTS FOR EXCHANGE

The evidence of each relevant witness must be put into a witness statement, in a format complying with the CPR, ready for exchange.

6.2.1   What is a witness statement?

CPR 32.4(1) defines a witness statement as a written statement, signed by a person, containing the evidence which that person would be allowed to give orally.

Consequently, evidence the witness would not be allowed to give orally, such as opinion or inadmissible hearsay, should be excluded from the witness statement, prepared for the purposes of exchange in accordance with case management directions and Part 32.

The importance of any witness statement complying with CPR 32.4 was emphasised by the Chancellor of the High Court in *JD Wetherspoon plc v Harris*.[33] The Chancellor, did, however, go on to observe that:

'I recognise, of course, that these rules as to witness statements and their contents are not rigid statutes. It is conceivable that in particular circumstances they may properly be relaxed in order to achieve the Overriding Objective in CPR r 1 of dealing with cases justly.'

The distinction between evidence of fact and opinion is also important because a factual witness should not generally give evidence on matters of opinion (see **6.1.1.2**).

6.2.2   Format

CPR 32.8 provides that a witness statement must comply with the requirements of the Practice Direction to Part 32.

Paragraphs 17 to 20 of the Practice Direction to Part 32 set out detailed requirements on the format of a witness statement for the purposes of the CPR.

- Paragraph 17 provides the witness statement should be headed with the title of the proceedings and, at the top right-hand corner of the first page, should state:
  - the party on whose behalf it is made;
  - the initials and surname of the witness;
  - the number of the statement in relation to that witness;
  - the identifying initials and number of each exhibit referred to;
  - the date on which the statement was made.
- Paragraph 18 stipulates that the witness statement must, if practicable, be in the own words of the witness and state:
  - the full name of the witness;
  - the address of the witness;
  - the occupation or description of the witness;
  - whether the witness is a party to the proceedings or the employee of such a party;

---

[33]   [2013] EWHC 1088 (Ch).

> – what evidence is made from the witness's own knowledge and what are matters of information or belief, stating the source of the latter;
> – and also set out how exhibits should be dealt with and referred to.

- Paragraph 19 requires a witness statement to:
  - be produced on A4 paper with a suitable margin;
  - be fully legible and typed on one side of the paper only;
  - be bound securely;
  - have pages numbered consecutively;
  - be divided into numbered paragraphs;
  - have all numbers, including dates, expressed in figures;
  - give the reference to any document mentioned either in the margin or in bold text in the body of the statement.

- Paragraph 20 confirms a witness statement is a document which must be verified by a Statement of Truth in accordance with Part 22, the appropriate statement being:

> 'I believe that the facts stated in this witness statement are true.'

It is important these requirements are met as CPR 32.8 specifically states that the witness statement must comply with this Practice Direction.

Although, strictly, relating to affidavits, paragraphs 11 to 14 of the Practice Direction to Part 32 explain how to deal with exhibits in a way equally applicable to witness statements.

All of these rules have added importance following the amendment to the overriding objective in April 2013 and the likelihood the court will be less tolerant of failure to comply with what might be regarded, erroneously, as purely technical matters.

6.2.3 Style and content

The requirement the statement be in the words of the witness means the statement should accurately reflect the evidence of that witness but the lawyer still has an important role in preparing the statement. Whilst using the words of the witness as raw material it is the lawyer's responsibility, if preparing a statement, to put that material into some order whether this be chronological, thematic or otherwise.

Whilst using the words of the witness as raw material it is the lawyer's responsibility, if preparing a statement, to put that material into some order whether this be chronological, thematic or otherwise.

It is essential, however, to retain the integrity of that raw material. That is so even if this results in a statement including the vernacular or even strong language. The importance of using, as accurately as possible, the words of the witness was illustrated, for example, in *Dorning v Rigby*[34] where Ward LJ, commenting on the claimant's statement, observed:

> 'that evidence has a ring of truth about it, the expletive springing to his lips, the initial stunned disbelief ...'

---

[34] [2007] EWCA Civ 1315.

The dangers of failing to keep to the words of the witness were highlighted in *Wreford-Smith v Airtours Holidays Ltd.*[35] This was, the trial judge concluded, just the sort of case in which it was essential the witness statement should be in the language and style of its maker if it was to be of any real value, yet the language appeared to be that of the solicitor not the witness. A further concern was that a number of statements, made by different witnesses, had many similarities in form and content. Those features caused the judge doubt about the reliability of the statements as reflecting the true memory of the witnesses. In the Court of Appeal Potter LJ endorsed those concerns and recognised the potential disservice to the client's case because of the impact all of this had on the assessment of credibility.

Similarly, it is generally inappropriate, in a witness statement, to use words, unless they are those of the witness, simply because such words may suit or support a legal argument being developed by a party. In *West Bromwich Albion Football Club v El-Safty*[36] the court noted an important aspect of one of the witness statements had 'in this respect ... been worded for (the witness)'.

In *A&E Television Networks LLC v Discovery Communications Europe Ltd*[37] Peter Smith J had some trenchant observations about the drafting of witness statements:

> 'This case demonstrates the need for solicitors preparing witness statements to curb their enthusiasm in seeking to obtain the best for their clients. It must not be forgotten that witness statements are merely a replacement for evidence which a witness previously used to give live in chief. It is intended to be the factual evidence of the witness in his own words. Too often witness statements are drafted by solicitors who put words in their mouth to achieve a better result.'

The judge stressed that statements should not be 'finessed' in this way.

In similar vein Gloster J observed in *Berezovsky v Abramovich*[38] that:

> 'Given the substantial resources of the parties, and the serious allegations of dishonesty, the case was heavily lawyered on both sides. That meant that no evidential stone was left unturned, unaddressed or unpolished. Those features, not surprisingly, resulted in shifts or changes in the parties' evidence or cases, as the lawyers microscopically examined each aspect of the evidence and acquired a greater in-depth understanding of the facts. It also led to some scepticism on the court's part as to whether the lengthy witness statements reflected more the industrious work product of the lawyers, than the actual evidence of the witnesses.'

There is an inevitable tension between the need for witness statements to be based on the actual words of the witness and the need, so far as possible, for all the evidence relied on to present a coherent picture reflecting the legal context within which the facts must be set.

Writing in the *Solicitors Journal* on 25 October 2002 Gordon Exall summed up how this tension might be reconciled:

---

35   [2004] EWCA Civ 453.
36   [2006] EWCA Civ 1299.
37   [2013] EWHC 109 (Ch).
38   [2013] EWHC 4348 (Ch).

'... the task of the statement is to convey information ... (and) ... best done when the witness recognises the statement as his own and the Court finds it easy to follow. Lawyers can legitimately help with presentation, but must be more cautious when dealing with content.'

Lawyers have professional duties, when taking statements, not to mislead the court by producing a statement which, whether because it creates the wrong impression or adopts incorrect assumptions. A breach of this requirement may attract professional sanctions (see 6.7.5).

6.2.4   Interviewing witnesses

Information from witnesses is best obtained at the earliest opportunity, when memories are less likely to have faded, even if the statements eventually exchanged are prepared at a later stage.

That information may be gathered, at least initially, by questionnaires. If statements are not prepared at that stage these questionnaires may be helpful in the event of any debate about how accurate the recollection of the witness was by the time of the formal statement.

An interview may be required, initially or subsequently, to clarify any details or if the subject matter is complex enough to require that.

When interviewing witnesses, it is important to allow sufficient time to get all relevant information. Whilst this may require some structure for the meeting it is essential the witness is allowed the opportunity to volunteer information. A skilled interviewer may be able to help the witness give accurate information by techniques such as assisting the witness in visualising the events and hence recall.

Witnesses should be advised about the purpose of any approach. Peter Smith J had observations about the proper way of dealing with witnesses in *A&E Television Networks LLC v Discovery Communications Europe Ltd*[39] when he said:

'... I do not think it is appropriate for a witness to have his statement taken from him when he does not realise that it is being taken from him for the purpose of giving evidence. That too is unfair. Further when such a person objects to giving evidence it cannot be appropriate in my view for that statement which has been taken down to be served up as a hearsay statement without reference to that potential witness (the more so when he has said he does not want to give evidence). Without the investigations in cross examination in this case none of the actual defectiveness of the hearsay statements would have come to light.'

The risk of gathering information from witnesses only at a late stage was illustrated in *Driver v The Painted House Trust*[40] where the claimant's key witness made a statement some two years after the accident and only signed her statement over four years after that accident. The judge observed: '... I am not satisfied that she has an accurate memory of the detail on what happened that night. That may be because she was not asked to remember detail until, at least on the face of it, two years after the event ...'.

---

39   [2013] EWHC 109 (Ch).
40   [2014] EWHC 1929 (QB).

6.2.5   Witness summaries

Where a party is required to serve a witness statement for use at trial but is unable to obtain one CPR 32.9(1) allows that party to apply for permission to serve a witness summary instead.

CPR 32.9(2) defines a witness summary as a summary of:

- the evidence, if known, which would otherwise be included in a witness statements; or
- if the evidence is not known, the matters about which the party serving the witness summary proposed to question the witness.

CPR 32.9(3) requires, unless the court otherwise orders, a witness summary to have the name and address of the intended witness.

Use of a witness summary may be appropriate when:

- the evidence of a witness is known, for example it is set out in a witness statement, but that statement is unsigned because the witness has not co-operated in signing the statement so, to this extent, the claimant has been 'unable' to obtain a witness statement; or
- the evidence to be given by the witness is not yet known, for example if the witness fails to respond to enquiries (in which case the summary should set out the matters about which the party serving the witness summary proposes to question the witness).

CPR 32.9(4) requires, unless the court orders otherwise, a witness summary to be served within the period in which a witness statement would have had to be served.

CPR 32.9(5) provides that, so far as practicable, a witness summary will follow the format of a witness statement, including the requirements set out in the Practice Direction to Part 32.

Consequently, if it is known there are witnesses the claimant may wish to rely on, but the claimant has been unable to either establish the evidence those witnesses can give or to obtain a signed statement, application for permission to rely on the witness statement should be made before the deadline, under case management directions, for exchange of witness statements and a witness summary, following as closely as possible the usual format for a witness statement, be served prior to that deadline as, if appropriate, extended by the court on application.

In *Scarlett v Grace*[41] Phillips J held that a party seeking permission to rely on a witness summary must establish that it had been unable to obtain a statement from the relevant witness as, generally, it was not satisfactory for the evidence of a witness not to be known prior to trial.

If a party proposes to rely on a witness summary, application for permission from the court needs to be made before the deadline, under case management directions, for

---

[41]   [2014] EWHC 2307 (QB).

exchange of witness statements otherwise there is likely to be non-compliance with any direction requiring exchange of a 'witness statement', given the definition in CPR 32.4 (see **6.2.1**).

6.3 DEALING WITH EXCHANGE OF WITNESS STATEMENTS

The implementation of many case management directions will not require any synchronisation between the parties. Each party will simply deal with the requisite step when ready to do so whilst ensuring this is no later than the final date for that step in the case management directions.

Where, however, case management directions provide for simultaneous exchange of witness statements, the need to ensure that mutuality requires either a degree of co-operation between the parties or some planning ahead, so that case management directions can be implemented within the timetable even in the absence of cooperation.

Accordingly, in addition to ensuring that the witnesses of fact have been identified and suitable witness statements prepared ready for exchange, it will be necessary to plan for exchange of evidence.

6.3.1 Planning

Once case management directions have been given it is worth trying to agree with the defendant arrangements for exchange of statements so that this takes place no later than the date given by the court timetable, and sooner if that is viable and agreed.

At this stage, therefore, the parties may agree that statements of witnesses of fact will be sent to the other, whether by DX, first-class post or otherwise, on a specified date within the timetable.

To guard against the absence of any agreement the claimant may wish to suggest, at this stage, that in default:

* statements of witnesses of fact the claimant intends to rely on will be placed in a sealed envelope;
* the envelope will be dispatched to arrive with the defendant no later than the last date, under the court timetable, for exchange;
* on condition the envelope remains unopened by the defendant until either statements have been dispatched to the claimant in return or confirmation given the defendant does not intend to rely on the evidence of any witnesses of fact whose evidence has not been disclosed in accordance with case management directions; and
* that the defendant, in the absence of either dispatching statements or confirming that none are to be relied on, will be deemed to have opened the envelope and received the claimant's witness statements by the due date in the court timetable.

The exact arrangements adopted for exchange will depend upon the nature of the case and the extent to which the parties are able to co-operate with each other.

6.3.2 Implementation

To ensure that statements are deemed served (in accordance with CPR 6.7) by the deadline in the timetable, it will be necessary either to send the statements in the post or DX two working days before that deadline or, if fax or other electronic method of service is available and appropriate, before 4.30 pm on the final day.

Given the sanction which will apply under CPR 32.10 if statements are not exchanged by the due date it may be wise to ensure statements are despatched, at the latest, a few days ahead of the deadline, adopting the procedure already outlined to ensure, so far as possible, exchange is simultaneous.

If the defendant indicates exchange will not be reciprocated then, unless and until there is a formal extension of time by agreement or court order, the claimant needs to work on the basis that steps to effect exchange within the extant timetable need to be taken. In *Fons HF v Corporal Ltd*[42] HHJ Pelling QC observed:

> 'The issue which arises, therefore, is whether and, if so, to what extent I should grant an extension of time for the filing of witness statements. I note that the order made by the district judge did not in terms provide for mutual exchange but simply provided that each party was to serve on every other party the witness statements on which the party serving the statements intended to rely. Thus, in truth, both parties are in breach of the order because it was the duty of the claimant to serve the witness statements or at the very least lodge them at court and either offer them for exchange or provide them to the defendants in escrow in a sealed envelope explaining to the court at the time why that step was taken.'

Whilst there is always a risk, when the parties have not expressly agreed a specific date for exchange, the claimant might be prejudiced in having disclosed statements by the due date and the defendant later serving statements to be relied upon the risk of this can be mitigated by sending statements in envelopes and given the greater focus, from April 2013, on the need to comply with the court timetable which may leave a defendant who fails to exchange with very real difficulties in obtaining relief from sanctions, especially if the claimant has exchanged.

Unless the parties have agreed arrangements for exchange it is important to minimise the risk of prejudice which could result from unilateral exchange, by the claimant disclosing witness statements, the defendant not reciprocating but still being permitted, at a later stage, to rely on statements by the court granting relief from the sanctions that would otherwise apply. Adopting the procedure set out already may help to control that risk.

In addition to witness statements the claimant will wish to send to the defendant witness summaries, where statements are not available, and evidence of experts where this is, or might be regarded as, factual evidence, especially if the claimant does not have permission to rely on the evidence of that witness as an expert.

6.3.3 Extension of time

If it becomes clear that exchange of witness statements cannot be completed by the relevant deadline, the parties may wish to agree a suitable extension of time.

---

[42] [2013] EWHC 1278 (Ch).

Because CPR 32.10 imposes a sanction, for failure to exchange witness statements by the due date, the terms of CPR 3.8(3) generally exclude the parties from agreeing an extension of time in accordance with CPR 2.11. Where, however, the extension is for no more than 28 days, and will not put at risk any hearing date, CPR 3.8(4) does permit prior written agreement between the parties for time to be extended, unless the court has ordered otherwise. Where a request to extend time within the scope of CPR 3.8(4) is made it will usually be appropriate to agree that request: *Denton v TH White Ltd.*[43]

Where the parties agree an extension of time it is essential, as ever, that agreement is made in writing by all parties: *Thomas v Home Office* (see **2.2.3.1**).[44]

Where the terms of CPR 3.8(4) do not apply, or agreement cannot be reached, application to extend time, before expiry of the deadline, is essential or sanctions will apply (see **6.7.1**).

6.4 REVIEW OF WITNESS STATEMENTS FOLLOWING EXCHANGE

Exchange of witness statements is an important stage in the case, when the claimant will be able to see whether or not the defendant has factual evidence which supports the defence. Accordingly, the evidence disclosed should be carefully reviewed and the need for any appropriate action assessed.

6.4.1 Admissibility

The defendant's witness statements should be reviewed to check the evidence contained in those statements will be admissible and that the general format of the statement complies with the CPR, particularly CPR 32.8 and the Practice Direction to Part 32, especially with the greater focus on compliance with the CPR and accompanying Practice Directions from April 2013.

- The statements must have been served within the timescale provided for in case management directions (unless an extension of time has been agreed or ordered by the court failing which the defendant will need to have obtained relief from sanctions).

- The format of the statements must comply with the requirements of CPR 32.4 and paragraphs 17 to 20 of the Practice Direction to Part 32, including a signed Statement of Truth (unless there is permission to rely on a witness summary).

- The statements should not contain any inadmissible evidence, for example hearsay (except to the extent allowed in civil proceedings), opinion (unless allowed as expert evidence or a way of conveying facts) or other non-factual content such as speculation on on the thoughts, motives or beliefs of others.

- The witness statement should not be dealing with factual matters outside the issues as defined by the Statements of Case. As with expert evidence which exceeds those parameters the court should be willing, under general case management powers, to strike out such parts of statements (see **6.7.2.1**).

---

[43] [2014] EWCA Civ 906.
[44] [2006] EWCA Civ 1355.

Where the defendant is entitled to rely on factual evidence which contains matters that might be regarded as expert opinion, or quasi-expert opinion, the claimant should consider whether permission should be sought to rely on expert evidence, or perhaps more than one expert, in the relevant discipline or ensuring experts from different disciplines cover, so far as possible, the same ground to help redress the balance (see 7.3.2.4.1).

6.4.2   Credibility

Evidence which is admissible should, where it conflicts with evidence on which the claimant relies, be assessed for the purposes of credibility, as that may influence further risk assessment of the case.

Credibility may not be easy to assess just on the written statement of a witness. Nevertheless, factors likely to be taken into account by a judge when assessing the credibility of a witness at a hearing can be at least partly discerned from the written statement of that witness. Accordingly, the approach which a court is likely to take towards credibility is worth bearing in mind when reviewing witness statements.

Guidance on the proper approach to the credibility of witnesses, often relied upon by the courts, was given by Lord Pearce in *Onassis v Vergottis*[45] where he said:

> '"Credibility" involves wider problems than mere 'demeanour' which is mostly concerned with whether the witness appears to be telling the truth as he now believes it to be. Credibility covers the following problems. First, is the witness a truthful or untruthful person? Secondly, is he, though a truthful person telling something less than the truth on this issue, or though an untruthful person, telling the truth on this issue? Thirdly, though he is a truthful person telling the truth as he sees it, did he register the intentions of the conversation correctly and, if so has his memory correctly retained them? Also, has his recollection been subsequently altered by unconscious bias or wishful thinking or by over much discussion of it with others? Witnesses, especially those who are emotional, who think that they are morally in the right, tend very easily and unconsciously to conjure up a legal right that did not exist. It is a truism, often used in accident cases, that with every day that passes the memory becomes fainter and the imagination becomes more active. ...And lastly, although the honest witness believes he heard or saw this or that, is it so improbable that it is on balance more likely that he was mistaken? On this point it is essential that the balance of probability is put correctly into the scales in weighing the credibility of a witness. And motive is one aspect of probability. All these problems compendiously are entailed when a Judge assesses the credibility of a witness; they are all part of one judicial process.'

As this passage recognises credibility is not, for these purposes, synonymous with honesty, a matter explored by Leggatt J in *Gestmin v Credit Suisse*[46] when he observed: 'Above all it is important to avoid the fallacy of supposing that, because a witness has confidence in his or her recollection and is honest, evidence based on that recollection provides any reliable guide to the truth.' Leggatt J went on to explain why an honest witness may give inaccurate evidence based on recollection when he said:

> 'While everyone knows that memory is fallible, I do not believe that the legal system has sufficiently absorbed the lessons of a century of psychological research into the nature of memory and the unreliability of eyewitness testimony. One of the most important lessons of such research is that in everyday life we are not aware of the extent to which our own and

---

[45]   [1968] 2 Lloyds Rep 403.
[46]   [2013] EWHC 3560 (Comm).

other people's memories are unreliable and believe our memories to be more faithful than they are. Two common (and related) errors are to suppose: (1) that the stronger and more vivid is our feeling or experience of recollection, the more likely the recollection is to be accurate; and (2) that the more confident another person is in their recollection, the more likely their recollection is to be accurate.

Underlying both these errors is a faulty model of memory as a mental record which is fixed at the time of experience of an event and then fades (more or less slowly) over time. In fact, psychological research has demonstrated that memories are fluid and malleable, being constantly rewritten whenever they are retrieved. This is true even of so-called 'flashbulb' memories, that is memories of experiencing or learning of a particularly shocking or traumatic event. (The very description 'flashbulb' memory is in fact misleading, reflecting as it does the misconception that memory operates like a camera or other device that makes a fixed record of an experience.) External information can intrude into a witness's memory, as can his or her own thoughts and beliefs, and both can cause dramatic changes in recollection. Events can come to be recalled as memories which did not happen at all or which happened to someone else (referred to in the literature as a failure of source memory).

Memory is especially unreliable when it comes to recalling past beliefs. Our memories of past beliefs are revised to make them more consistent with our present beliefs. Studies have also shown that memory is particularly vulnerable to interference and alteration when a person is presented with new information or suggestions about an event in circumstances where his or her memory of it is already weak due to the passage of time.

The process of civil litigation itself subjects the memories of witnesses to powerful biases. The nature of litigation is such that witnesses often have a stake in a particular version of events. This is obvious where the witness is a party or has a tie of loyalty (such as an employment relationship) to a party to the proceedings. Other, more subtle influences include allegiances created by the process of preparing a witness statement and of coming to court to give evidence for one side in the dispute. A desire to assist, or at least not to prejudice, the party who has called the witness or that party's lawyers, as well as a natural desire to give a good impression in a public forum, can be significant motivating forces.

Considerable interference with memory is also introduced in civil litigation by the procedure of preparing for trial. A witness is asked to make a statement, often (as in the present case) when a long time has already elapsed since the relevant events. The statement is usually drafted for the witness by a lawyer who is inevitably conscious of the significance for the issues in the case of what the witness does nor does not say. The statement is made after the witness's memory has been 'refreshed' by reading documents. The documents considered often include statements of case and other argumentative material as well as documents which the witness did not see at the time or which came into existence after the events which he or she is being asked to recall. The statement may go through several iterations before it is finalised. Then, usually months later, the witness will be asked to re-read his or her statement and review documents again before giving evidence in court. The effect of this process is to establish in the mind of the witness the matters recorded in his or her own statement and other written material, whether they be true or false, and to cause the witness's memory of events to be based increasingly on this material and later interpretations of it rather than on the original experience of the events.

It is not uncommon (and the present case was no exception) for witnesses to be asked in cross-examination if they understand the difference between recollection and reconstruction or whether their evidence is a genuine recollection or a reconstruction of events. Such questions are misguided in at least two ways. First, they erroneously presuppose that there is a clear distinction between recollection and reconstruction, when all remembering of distant events involves reconstructive processes. Second, such questions disregard the fact that such processes are largely unconscious and that the strength, vividness and apparent authenticity of memories is not a reliable measure of their truth.

In the light of these considerations, the best approach for a judge to adopt in the trial of a commercial case is, in my view, to place little if any reliance at all on witnesses' recollections of what was said in meetings and conversations, and to base factual findings on inferences drawn from the documentary evidence and known or probable facts. This does not mean that oral testimony serves no useful purpose – though its utility is often disproportionate to its length. But its value lies largely, as I see it, in the opportunity which cross-examination affords to subject the documentary record to critical scrutiny and to gauge the personality, motivations and working practices of a witness, rather than in testimony of what the witness recalls of particular conversations and events. Above all, it is important to avoid the fallacy of supposing that, because a witness has confidence in his or her recollection and is honest, evidence based on that recollection provides any reliable guide to the truth.'

The practitioner faced with the task of reviewing factual evidence, and trying to assess what conclusions a court may draw where there are disputed facts without the advantage of having heard the witnesses give evidence, might well follow the advice of Lord Gough in *Grace Shipping v Sharp & Co*[47] that veracity should be tested by 'reference to the objective facts and documents, to the witnesses' motives, and to the overall probabilities'.

Consequently, when there is a conflict between witnesses of fact the court, when deciding which evidence should be preferred, is likely to look at the statements from witnesses of fact in the context of the evidence as a whole, what might be termed 'triangulation'.

6.4.3   Excluding evidence?

CPR 32.2(3) allows the court to give directions:
*   identifying, or limiting the issues to which factual evidence may be directed;
*   identifying the witnesses who may be called or whose evidence may be read; or
*   limiting the length or format of witness statements.

In *MacLennan v Morgan Sindall (Infrastructure) Plc*[48] the scope and proper approach to this rule was considered by Green J who held: 'The power to prohibit the calling of witnesses sits towards the more extreme end of the Court's powers and hence is a power a judge will ordinarily consider after less intrusive measures have been considered and rejected.'

Whilst an order under CPR 32.3(3) would, if possible, be sought at the stage of case management it will not be too late to seek an order following exchange, although the court may consider, as the expense of the statements has then been incurred, it is now too late to make such an order.

6.4.4   Statements of Case

The Statements of Case ought to be reviewed, in the light of the factual evidence:
*   It is important the claimant has disclosed all available and necessary factual evidence to support those matters in the Particulars of Claim which will need to be

---

[47]   [1987] 1 Lloyds Rep 207.
[48]   [2013] EWHC 4044 (QB).

proved (though if the deadline for exchange of statements in the court timetable has now elapsed it may be difficult to introduce further evidence).

- The matters put in issue by the defence, so far as they need to be, should be supported by factual evidence the defendant has now disclosed.
- Any amendments, to reflect the issues emerging from the factual evidence, which may be necessary should be considered and, if appropriate, any permission to amend sought.

6.4.5   Advising the client

The client should be kept up to date following exchange of factual evidence, be sent copies of witness statements exchanged and instructions sought on any matters not already dealt with.

6.4.6   Further action

Further action, following a review of factual evidence after exchange, may include a number of steps.

- The defence should be reviewed to ensure the factual evidence does not seek to raise matters which have not been pleaded. If the factual evidence goes beyond the pleaded case the defendant should either seek permission to amend the defence or only be relying on factual evidence dealing with pleaded issues.
- If the factual evidence, once exchanged, is such that crucial aspects of the defence are not supported, and the claimant can now contend the defendant has no real prospect of defending the whole claim or any issue such as liability, an application for judgment, in accordance with Part 24, might be made.
- Where the claimant considers the factual evidence does not support the defence and that the defendant is unreasonably leaving matters in issue between the parties the claimant, whether or not making an application under Part 24, may wish to warn the defendant the claimant reserves the right to seek indemnity costs under Part 44.
- If the defendant's evidence does not deal adequately with all relevant matters the claimant may need to request further information under Part 18.
- Any issues concerning the format or admissibility of the factual evidence disclosed by the defendant should be raised at the earliest opportunity. If the claimant contends the defendant's witness statements contain inadmissible evidence the defendant should be invited to serve amended statements, without the inadmissible parts, and the claimant reserve the right to apply to the court, under the court's general case management powers found in Part 3, to strike out the inadmissible evidence or that the defendant be debarred from relying on evidence of witnesses of fact containing inadmissible evidence unless amended statements, without such evidence, be served.
- If the defendant will not remove potentially inadmissible evidence from witness statements, and no application to strike that evidence out is made, it may be necessary to write confirming the claimant's stance on that evidence and requesting that this be made clear to any reader of the trial bundle, so that the trial judge will be alerted to the potential issues on admissibility before considering the evidence in any depth.

- Part 36 offers, whether made or received, should be reconsidered in the light of the factual evidence and decisions made whether:
  - any offer made by the defendant, should now be accepted;
  - an offer, or further offer, should be made on liability by the claimant;
  - an offer, or further offer, should be made on any other issue by the claimant;
  - an offer, or further offer, in settlement of the whole claim should be made by the claimant;
  - any extant offer made by the claimant should be withdrawn or changed so as to be less advantageous to the defendant.

- If the defendant's factual evidence raises new points, which are properly part of that evidence, the claimant needs to consider whether any supplemental factual evidence should be relied upon, to deal with such matters, in which case the evidence will need to be obtained and disclosed. Furthermore, unless the defendant agrees, permission to rely on such evidence will have to be obtained from the court assuming this is served outside the timescale provided for under case management directions.

- Experts involved in the case, certainly if there are still reports of exchange, will need to review the factual evidence either to make further comments or finalise reports ready for exchange, in either case reflecting any further matters arising from the statements.

- If the defendant has not relied upon the evidence of any witnesses of fact the defendant might have been expected to call, and whose evidence would be likely to assist the court on matters in issue, it may be appropriate to warn the defendant, at this stage, the court will be invited, at trial, to draw an adverse inference from the absence of such evidence.

- The merits, in the light of the factual evidence should be reviewed and, if necessary, overall risk re-assessed.

6.4.7 Organising the file

Following exchange, it is important to keep the statements that have been exchanged readily identifiable, as these will be needed for inclusion in the trial bundle. Unless the statements exchanged are clearly identified, it may be difficult, subsequently, to distinguish these from earlier drafts. Accordingly, it may be helpful to put copies of the witness statements exchanged between the parties into a folder of court documents or a specific folder incorporating only statements as exchanged.

6.5 HEARSAY EVIDENCE

Hearsay evidence is defined, by CPR 33.1, as a statement made otherwise than by a person while giving oral evidence in proceedings which is tendered as evidence of the matters stated.

The Civil Evidence Act 1995 provides that evidence shall not be excluded, in civil proceedings, on the grounds that it is hearsay, but if the factual evidence includes any matters of hearsay, it is important to comply with the procedural requirements of Part 33.

6.5.1 Hearsay evidence given by a witness in oral evidence

CPR 33.2(1)(a) deals with a witness whose oral evidence will include matters of hearsay. That evidence will be admissible, provided the witness statement of that witness has been served in accordance with the case management directions. In other words, serving a witness statement containing hearsay evidence is sufficient notice that it is proposed to rely on that evidence to make this admissible under the Civil Evidence Act 1995.

It is important to remember the requirements of para 18 of the Practice Direction to Part 32, namely that the source of information should be given. In *Clarke v Marlborough Fine Art (London) Ltd*[49] Patten J held:

'... the provisions of paragraph 18.2 of the Practice Direction under CPR Part 32 are not concerned with evidence of primary fact. They are simply procedural provisions requiring the deponent to identify the source of the hearsay evidence he will give. They do not require that attribution to be based only on admissible evidence. They merely require it to be stated so that the party affected by the evidence knows who is the alleged source of the information.'

6.5.2 Hearsay evidence given by witness statement only

CPR 33.2(1)(b) and 33.2(2) deal with evidence which is hearsay simply because it is in written form only, and no oral evidence is to be given by the witness.

Here, when serving it, the party seeking to rely on the witness statement must:

* inform the other parties the witness is not being called to give oral evidence; and
* give reasons why the witness will not be called.

Subject to complying with these requirements, no separate Notice will be required and, again, the evidence will be admissible for the purposes of the Civil Evidence Act 1995.

6.5.3 Other hearsay evidence

In all other circumstances, the party seeking to rely on hearsay evidence must, to ensure this is admissible under the Civil Evidence Act 1995, serve a Notice which:

* identifies the hearsay evidence;
* states that the party serving the Notice proposes to rely on the hearsay evidence at trial; and
* gives the reasons why the witness will not be called.

Whilst, in these circumstances, there will be no witness statement, the Notice must, nevertheless, be served no later than the date given in the case management directions for service of witness statements.

6.6 OTHER FACTUAL EVIDENCE

In addition to disclosable documents which must be dealt with in accordance with Part 31, and the evidence of witnesses of fact to be dealt with in accordance with

---

[49] [2002] 1 WLR 1731.

Part 32, there may be other factual evidence. Such evidence must be dealt with in accordance with CPR 33.6 by the party who wishes to rely on it.

6.6.1　Factual evidence for Part 33

CPR 33.6 mentions specifically evidence such as a plan, photograph or model but any such evidence contained in a witness statement or an expert's report is specifically excluded from the evidence dealt with in this rule. Consequently, any plan, photograph or model which is part of a witness statement or an expert's report should be disclosed with the statement or report at the appropriate stage.

If a plan or photograph is a 'document', comprising part of standard disclosure or any specific disclosure ordered by the court, it should be disclosed at the appropriate stage. Photographs, by analogy with videos, are likely to be treated as documents.

Accordingly, the evidence to which CPR 33.6 applies will be limited to what might be termed 'real' evidence, as well as investigative evidence.

6.6.1.1　*Real evidence*

These are objects which are part of the factual background which the court may need to view as well as artefacts brought into being to assist the court in understanding and interpreting the other evidence.

6.6.1.2　*Investigative Evidence*

A prior investigation into the circumstances which subsequently led to proceedings may fall within the scope of CPR 33.6.

Investigations may have been carried out by the police, a local authority, the Health & Safety Exective or the Air Accident Investigation Branch of the Department of Transport.

This type of evidence is likely to contain a mixture of documentary evidence, factual evidence and opinion evidence. Admissibility is likely to be determined by relevance: *Hoyle v Rogers*.[50]

Where the investigation involves judicial findings that will, if those earlier findings have been made in civil proceedings, be excluded on the basis of relevance, as it is the responsibility of the judge trying the case to make findings on the evidence: *Hollington v Hewthorn*,[51] *Hoyle v Rogers*.[52] An exception to this general rule is that a conviction by a criminal court will be admissible as evidence in subsequent civil proceedings: s 11, Civil Evidence Act 1968.

Where evidence of this kind includes admissible opinion, because it is given by an expert, that evidence will not be within the scope of Part 35, and hence require express

---

[50]　[2014] EWCA Civ 257.
[51]　[1943] 1 KB 27.
[52]　[2014] EWCA Civ 257.

permission before it can be relied on by a party, because the purpose of Part 35 is to regulate the evidence of experts instructed by the parties: *Hoyle v Rogers*.[53]

The court retains the discretion to exclude such evidence under Part 32 but where the evidence appears to be relevant it is likely that evidence will be admitted so the trial judge can attach such importance to it as may be appropriate. Similarly, where such evidence is mixed opinion of fact it is likely all the evidence will be put to the trial judge who can disregard any evidence found to be inadmissible: *Hoyle v Rogers*.[54]

6.6.2 Procedural requirements of Part 33

Where a party intends to use factual evidence of the kind encompassed by the scope of CPR 33.6 notice, in accordance with that rule, must be given to the other parties or that evidence will not be receivable at a trial. The timing of the notice will depend upon the precise nature of the evidence.

Where the evidence is to be used as evidence of any fact then, unless part of the expert evidence, notice must be given no later than the latest date for serving witness statements.

Where the evidence forms part of the expert evidence notice must be given when the expert's report is served on the other party.

Where the evidence is being produced to the court for any reason other than as part of the factual or expert evidence, or is solely to disapprove an allegation made in a witness statement, notice must be given at least 21 days before the hearing at which it is proposed to put in the evidence.

Whenever notice is given, the party intending to rely on the evidence must give every other party an opportunity of inspecting that evidence and agreeing it.

6.6.3   Where evidence of this kind is capable of being included within the trial bundle and that bundle is agreed any documents contained in the bundle will be admissible as evidence of their contents in accordance with paragraph 27.2 of Practice Direction 32.

6.7   SANCTIONS

There are potentially very serious sanctions for non-compliance with the requirements in the CPR relating to exchange of factual evidence.

That is because any party, but particularly the claimant who usually has to discharge the burden of proof, is likely to be severely prejudiced if unable to rely on factual evidence, particularly witness statements.

Accordingly, sanctions which may apply to a party who defaults in the exchange of factual evidence under case management directions are potentially very significant. Great care is required to ensure case management directions are implemented and, if necessary,

---

[53]   [2014] EWCA Civ 257.
[54]   [2014] EWCA Civ 257.

any extension of time agreed or, where necessary, obtained from the court. If a sanction applies it may be difficult for the party in default to obtain relief.

There is, additionally, the risk of costs sanctions, where factual evidence that can be relied on does not meet the requirements of the CPR, personal sanctions against witnesses whose evidence is untrue and even professional sanctions against representatives if responsible for the court being misled by factual evidence.

6.7.1 Sanctions for failing to disclose factual evidence

Sanctions will apply, which may exclude otherwise admissible factual evidence, if a party does not comply with case management directions and/or the terms of the CPR.

6.7.1.1 Sanctions under Part 32

CPR 32.10 provides that if a witness statement (or a witness summary where this has been permitted) for use at trial is not served by the time specified in case management directions, the witness may not be called to give oral evidence unless the court gives permission.

Given that the evidence of a witness is to be proved by oral evidence at trial (CPR 32.2(1)(a)), this effectively prevents a party relying on the evidence of such a witness, unless the witness statement or, witness summary where permitted has been disclosed in accordance with the timescale provided for in the case management directions.

The significance, and immediacy, of this sanction was emphasised by the Court of Appeal in *Chartwell Estate Agents Ltd v Fergies Properties SA*[55] where Davis LJ held:

> '... the phrase "unless the court gives permission" as contained in CPR 32.10 cannot, in my view, be applied in a free-standing way, leaving the exercise of judicial discretion at large. In deciding whether to give permission, the court has to have regard to and give effect to other relevant rules such as CPR 3.1. It also seems to me inescapable that, for this purpose, the court must likewise give effect to CPR 3.8 and CPR 3.9: just because CPR 32.10 is demonstrably imposing a sanction in the event of failure to serve a witness statement within the time specified.

> I observe that in the notes to CPR 32.10 in the White Book (2014 ed.) it is suggested that:

> > "However, where before trial a party requests the court to exercise its powers under r.3.1(2)(a) to extend the time for serving their witness statements it could be argued that r.3.9 does not apply because at that stage the sanction imposed by r.32.10 has not had 'effect' within the meaning of r.3.8."

> I can see the argument on a narrow and literal approach to the wording. But in my view it is not correct: a broader reading is called for. Were it otherwise, an application to extend time for service of a witness statement made before trial could stand on a significantly different footing from an application for extension and relief from sanction made at trial when the witness is actually to be called. In my view, the sanction provided in CPR 32.10 is to be taken

---

as having effect once the time limit for serving the witness statement has expired. It would be contrary to the overall purpose of the rules, and could lead to arbitrariness, were it otherwise.'

If witness statements are not exchanged by the due date, it will be necessary for the party in default to seek relief from the sanction under CPR 3.9 (see **8.10.2**).

Where such a sanction applies the party in default may be unable to prove an issue, where the burden of proof is on that party, or may have an adverse inference drawn from the failure to call evidence even where the burden is on the other party (see **6.1.2.3**).

6.7.1.2   Sanctions under Part 33

CPR 33.6(3) provides that the evidence, covered by this rule, will be not receivable unless notice, in accordance with the time-limits and other requirements of the rule, has been given. Again, a party in default will need to seek relief from sanctions under CPR 3.9.

6.7.1.3   Relief from sanctions

CPR 3.8 confirms that if a sanction is imposed that will have effect unless the party in default applies for and obtains relief.

On an application for relief from any sanction the court will have to apply the terms of CPR 3.9 which, since April 2013, whilst still requiring the court to consider all the circumstances of the case require particular focus on two specific factors namely:

- the need for litigation to be conducted efficiently and at proportionate cost; and
- the need to enforce compliance with rules, Practice Directions and orders.

Despite the potentially draconian effect of a sanction which prevents a party from relying on factual evidence the courts are likely to approach relief, in the context of sanctions relating to factual evidence, in the same way as other sanctions in accordance with the guidance given by the Court of Appeal in *Mitchell v News Group Newspapers Ltd*[56] and *Denton v TH White Ltd.*[57]

A danger, with a mutual stage of the case such as exchange of witness statements, is that delay by one party might generate delay by other parties. That, however, is unlikely to justify non-compliance and hence parties must be ready to take steps to effect exchange even if that is approaching this on the basis of delivering statements in escrow as suggested in *Fons HF v Corporal Ltd*[58] (see **6.3.2**).

If statements have not been disclosed in accordance with case management directions, or notice in relation to other factual evidence is not given, it will be necessary for the party in default to seek permission from the court, by way of relief from sanctions, if that evidence is to be relied on.

---

[56]   [2013] EWHC 2355 (QB).
[57]   [2014] EWCA Civ 906.
[58]   [2013] EWHC 1278 (Ch).

Any such application will involve consideration by the court of the factors set out in CPR 3.9. Whilst the effect on the party in default, of being unable to rely on factual evidence, may incline the court to grant relief it is better to avoid depending on the discretion of the court, by ensuring that the timetable is complied with.

The court may, perhaps, be sympathetic where there is mutual default of this kind, not least because the relevant sanction may have a greater, perhaps disproportionate, effect on the claimant who, ultimately, has to prove the case as Davis LJ recognised in *Chartwell Estate Agents Ltd v Fergies Properties SA*:[59]

> 'In the present case, if relief from sanction were refused Chartwell's claim would in practice indeed come to an end. I do not think that circumstance can be entirely subordinated to the consideration that Chartwell might then have a prospective claim against its solicitors (which, ironically, would then potentially involve further satellite litigation). If, on the other hand, relief from sanction were granted, a fair trial could still be had, without any adjournment of the trial date being required and with no additional cost for the parties arising. And there was more. For one further particular factor, albeit to be coupled with the other factors listed by the judge, was the default of the defendants. There was designed to be simultaneous exchange on 22 November 2013: but the defendants themselves (as found) were not in fact ready to exchange on that date. They did not, for example, seek to lodge at court at that time their own witness statements. In fact, their witness statements were not even finalised as at 21 January 2014, they having participated in the debate on disclosure matters in the interim. They – as much as Chartwell – also needed relief from sanction if they were to rely at trial on their witnesses. They had made no application of their own. In the event, the application eventually issued by Chartwell had sought an order in this regard relating to both parties: an order the judge in the result made. It is not, in fact, difficult to deduce that the defendants ultimately never themselves filed their own application for relief just because of the calculation that if Chartwell, as claimant on whom the burden of proof lay, was knocked out from relying on any witness evidence it would not then matter to the defendants if they were likewise knocked out. (The calculation also no doubt would have been that if Chartwell obtained relief from sanction then the defendants inevitably would also.) That, when set also in the light of the intervening correspondence, would be a most unattractive result. Overall, the judge was, in my view, entitled to attach importance to the fault of the defendants.'

In other circumstances, however, the court may take an unforgiving approach: *M A Lloyd & Sons Ltd v PPC International Ltd*;[60] *Karbhari v Ahmed*.[61]

Difficulties can arise where one party contends new matters, which need to be dealt with by witness statements disclosed subsequently, arise from the factual evidence exchanged initially.

In *Karbhari v Ahmed*[62] the court recognised that this problem was anticipated in *Mitchell* on the basis that later developments might be good reason to grant relief from sanctions that would otherwise apply. In other circumstances sanctions may prohibit reliance on further factual evidence. A party wishing to guard against that may need to consider, at the stage of directions, an order making express provision for service of supplemental witness statements dealing with further matters (see **6.1.4.4**).

---

59   [2014] EWCA Civ 506.
60   [2014] EWHC 41 (QB).
61   [2013] EWHC 4042 (QB).
62   [2013] EWHC 4042 (QB).

The approach to granting relief from sanctions where the terms of CPR 32.10 have not been complied with might well inform any similar application where there has been non-compliance with the terms of Part 33 in relation to other factual evidence.

6.7.2 Strike out or exclusion of factual evidence

The court has the power to strike out inadmissible factual evidence and to exclude, in appropriate circumstances, factual evidence which would otherwise be admissible. These powers can be used as a form of sanction.

6.7.2.1 Strike out

CPR 32.4(1) provides that a witness statement should contain only admissible evidence.

Consequently, where a witness statement contains inadmissible evidence that may be regarded as an abuse and the court invited to exercise case management powers so as to strike out the statement or the inadmissible parts of that statement: *JD Wetherspoon plc v Harris*.[63]

Parts of a statement may be susceptible to being struck out where, for example, there is inadmissible opinion, as in *JD Wetherspoon plc v Harris*[64] and *Acamar Films Ltd v Microsoft Corporation*,[65] or reference to without prejudice communications, as in *Framlington Group Ltd v Barnetson*.[66]

Because the introduction of inadmissible evidence will be in breach of the terms of Part 32 the courts may apply, in the event of any application to strike out, the general approach found in CPR 3.9 given that this is reflected in the terms of Part 1 (see **8.10.2.5**).

The courts appear more ready to strike out the whole or parts of witness statements which contain inadmissible evidence than when dealing with a similar application to strike out part of an expert's report. That is, perhaps, because inadmissible evidence from witnesses of fact is usually more readily identifiable whilst with experts admissible evidence, including relevant opinion, often shades imperceptibly into what might be regarded as inadmissible evidence, hence procedural judges are often ready to leave the task of separating the admissible from the inadmissible to the trial judge.

6.7.2.2 Excluding evidence

CPR 32.2(3) allows the court to exclude factual evidence which would otherwise be admissible, though the court may be cautious about exercising this power: *MacLennan v Morgan Sindall (Infrastructure) Plc*[67] (see **6.4.3**).

---

63 [2013] EWHC 1088 (Ch).
64 [2013] EWHC 1088 (Ch).
65 [2012] EWHC 2164 (Ch).
66 [2007] EWCA Civ 502.
67 [2013] EWHC 4044 (QB).

6.7.3   Costs sanctions

Even if factual evidence is admissible the court may, in appropriate circumstances, impose costs sanctions on a party who fails to deal appropriately with that evidence.

The defendant's factual evidence was described as 'far from satisfactory' in *Nicholls v Ladbrokes Betting & Gambling Ltd*[68] which contributed to a decision the successful defendant have a 20% reduction in costs.

6.7.4   Sanctions on witnesses

Under the CPR a witness statement must contain a statement of truth.

This is self-evidently important and particularly so in an era when much evidence is given in written form and hence must be reliable.

In *Zurich Insurance Co Plc v Hayward*[69] Smith LJ noted:

> 'In the post CPR world, one aim of the rules is to encourage the parties to reach settlement of their disputes. This means that the statements or representations made at the pre-trial stage have taken on an even greater importance than they had under the old rules, where it was expected that their truthfulness and accuracy would probably be tested at trial. The importance of the truthfulness of pretrial statements is evidenced by the new requirement that a statement of case must be accompanied by a declaration of truth. The intention is that a party should be able to rely on (a) pre-trial statements in reaching settlement. Thus pre-trial statements play a vital role in the administration of civil justice.'

In the same vein Jackson LJ commented in *Nicholls v Ladbrokes Betting & Gambling Ltd*:[70]

> 'The fact remains, however, that the vast majority of personal injury actions settle before trial on the basis of the written evidence served. Therefore the written evidence matters, even if a party knows that it will abandon certain points in the event of a trial.'

CPR 32.14 expressly provides that proceedings for contempt of court may be brought against a person if he makes, or causes to be made, a false statement in a document verified by a statement of truth without an honest believe in its truth.

The meaning of this provision was explored in *Brighton & Hove Bus & Coach Co Ltd v Brooks*[71] where Richards LJ held:

> 'CPR 32.14 provides that proceedings for contempt of court may be brought, with the permission of the court, against any person if he makes or causes to be made a false statement in a document verified by a statement of truth without an honest belief in its truth. It has been held in that context that the applicant must prove beyond reasonable doubt, in respect of each statement relied on, (a) the falsity of the statement, (b) that the statement has, or if persisted in would be likely to have, interfered with the course of justice in some material respects, and (c) that at the time it was made, the maker of the statement had no

---

68   [2013] EWCA Civ 1963.
69   [2011] EWCA Civ 641.
70   [2013] EWCA Civ 1963.
71   [2011] EWHC 2504 (Admin).

honest belief in the truth of the statement and knew of its likelihood to interfere with the course of justice: see per Coulson J in *Walton v Kirk* [2009] EWHC 703 (QB), at [9].'

6.7.5   Sanctions on professionals

Professionals, engaged as the representatives of parties, need to be mindful of the duty not to mislead the court. There is a risk of misleading the court when drafting witness statements: *Brett v The Solicitors Regulation Authority.*[72]

---

[72]   [2014] EWHC 2974 (Admin).

CHAPTER 7

EXPERT EVIDENCE

7.1 INTRODUCTION

Dealing with expert evidence is a complex procedural stage in many personal injury claims because it extends:

- from the early investigation stages of the case, when the need for evidence to deal with the likely issues will be ascertained and at least some expert evidence usually obtained;

- through case management when permission to rely on expert evidence will need to be sought and directions given for the exchange of expert evidence not already disclosed;

- to listing when the court may need to determine whether oral expert evidence will be necessary at trial.

The breadth of procedural issues relating to expert evidence largely arises from the background to, and implementation of, the Civil Procedure Rules (the CPR).

The claimant's representative needs to understand this background, and the potential problems created for the claimant, so that all necessary expert evidence is obtained and can be relied upon.

7.1.1 Background to the CPR

Expert evidence was identified by Lord Woolf in 'Access to Justice – The Final Report' as a major factor causing costs and delay in civil claims. Paragraph 11 of the report stated:

> 'The basic premise of my new approach is that the expert's function is to assist the court. There should be no expert evidence at all unless it will help the court, and no more than one expert in any one speciality unless this is necessary for some real purpose.'

The CPR, consequently, made significant changes to the use of experts in civil proceedings.

Before expert evidence, even if otherwise admissible, may be relied on at all, permission from the court will be required.

Moreover, the intention underlying the CPR is that where expert evidence is necessary that should be given by one expert, who may be a single joint expert, in any particular discipline or any specific issue. Permission from the court is still necessary for such evidence to be relied upon even when given by a single expert.

If the court considers it necessary to do so permission may be given to rely on more than one expert in a particular discipline or dealing with a specific issue. In these circumstances relevant experts will usually be expected, following exchange of reports, to confer and prepare a joint statement. The joint statement should clarify whether there is any real disagreement on matters of opinion between the experts. Only where there is a range of expert opinion (usually identified by a joint statement) in a particular discipline or on a particular issue, should the court need to hear oral evidence from expert witnesses.

Underpinning the move towards the use of single experts, in each discipline or on a particular issue, is the emphasis in the CPR on the primary duty to the court, rather than the instructing party, on any expert giving evidence.

Accordingly, under the CPR, expert evidence will only be permitted where, as well as being admissible under the general law, that evidence is, for the purposes of the CPR, 'reasonably required to resolve the proceedings'. Moreover, wherever possible, there will be a single expert within each area of expertise.

All of this is reflected in the terms of Part 35 of the CPR, the Practice Direction accompanying Part 35 and, annexed to the Practice Direction, the Protocol for Instruction of Experts to Give Evidence in Civil Claims (the 'Expert Protocol'). The Expert Protocol has the express purpose of being intended to assist with the interpretation of both Part 35 and the associated Practice Direction.

7.1.2   The claimant's problem

This regime, admirable though its objectives of saving costs and delay are, contains real dangers for the claimant in a personal injury claim.

That is because the legal burden of proof is on the claimant to prove every aspect of the claim. Whilst, from time to time, the evidential burden may shift to the defendant it is, more often than not, the claimant who will need expert evidence to prove various elements of the claim, whether on liability or quantum.

When the evidential burden of proof rests, as it usually does, with the claimant, the ability to rely on expert opinion may be crucial.

On the issue of liability such evidence may be needed to help explain and interpret the factual background, or to assist in determining whether the relevant standard of care has been met in cases where the alleged breach concerns some special skill by identifying usual or accepted standards.

On quantum, expert opinion may be important to arm the court with the specialist knowledge necessary to understand the injuries and predict the future and options available to the claimant, so that damages can be accurately assessed.

Consequently, it will be important for the claimant to establish that the evidence on which it intends to rely will be admissible under the Civil Evidence Act 1972 or by establishing that the evidence is, in reality, factual rather than opinion.

If the expert evidence on which the claimant proposes to rely is admissible under the 1972 Act, the claimant, like any party, then has a further hurdle of persuading the court, by exercising case management powers in accordance with the terms of Part 35 in the context of the overriding objective, to give permission for that evidence to be relied on.

Without the court's permission, even if the evidence were admissible under the general law, the party seeking to rely on expert evidence will not be permitted to do so. For the claimant that may mean the legal burden of proof cannot be discharged either in establishing liability or in proving the extent of the injuries, loss and damage.

The new regime, introduced by the CPR, was illustrated by the court's approach to expert evidence on the issue of assessing a vehicle's pre-accident value, in *Bandegani v Norwich Union Fire Insurance Society Ltd*.[1]

In *Bandegani* at the arbitration hearing, held under the pre-CPR rules, the defendant insurer arrived at court with an expert and sought to rely on his evidence that, based on an inspection, the value of the vehicle should be put at £900. When the court ruled no account would be taken of that evidence the defendant submitted the claimant had failed to prove the case as the only evidence relied on was what he had paid for the car. That submission was, at first instance, accepted.

The Court of Appeal confirmed the judge had been wrong to conclude evidence of the price paid for the vehicle could not amount to evidence of its value. On the appropriateness of expert evidence to deal with such an issue Henry LJ held:

> 'I would say nothing to encourage the grant of such a permission in a case such as this for reasons of proportionality. There are published guides available in newsagents and used in the trade that give some indication as to the market price of second-hand cars which judges may find helpful. I suggest that, in the ordinary case, such guides would give better evidential value for money than the expensive calling of two live experts. When one is dealing with a modestly priced ordinary family car that seems to me to be clear.'

In the context of the case, therefore, the court was taking a pragmatic, and proportionate, approach to guard against the very problem of a defendant, perhaps with better resources or access to information, simply asserting that a claimant had not proved the case or an important element of that case without potentially expensive expert evidence.

In other circumstances, however, the courts have been perhaps too ready to effectively exclude evidence necessary to discharge the burden of proof on a particular issue. That is so even though it is understandable that case management powers may be used to exclude evidence which, whilst otherwise admissible, is there largely, if not exclusively, to bolster a case which could be established or refuted by other evidence.

---

[1]   Court of Appeal, 20 May 1999.

The focus of this problem is often at the stage of case management. It is not unknown for the claimant, at that stage, to be refused permission by the court to rely on expert evidence only for the court to find, at trial, that without such evidence an important aspect of the claim cannot be proved

A stark example of this problem is *Cassie v Ministry of Defence.*[2] The claimant sought to rely on the evidence of a psychologist but was refused permission by the procedural judge at the stage of case management. A paper application for permission to appeal that decision was subsequently refused. The trial judge, however, concluded that the claimant had failed to prove, on a balance of probabilities, the continuing symptoms had been caused by the relevant accident because '...it may well be that psychological factors are involved but I have no expert evidence which assists in determining whether they are or not'.

The Court of Appeal, dismissing the claimant's appeal, concluded the findings of the trial judge could not be impeached, and the problem lay with the case management directions which, of course, it was now too late to appeal. Laws LJ summed up the situation when he observed:

> 'Accordingly, though one has great sympathy with the claimant, the judge having roundly said that she lacked the very sort of evidence which he had earlier sought to have adduced, there is no step open to this court that can in any way shift or cure the matter.'

Brooke LJ added:

> 'I am uneasy as to whether substantive justice has in these circumstances been done.'

A similar issue arose, though in the context of an appeal against judgment in favour of the claimant where no expert evidence on the issue of liability had been relied on at trial, in *Ellis v William Cook Leeds Ltd.*[3] Here the defendant successfully objected at the stage of case management directions to the claimant having permission to rely on expert evidence dealing with issues relating to liability, pursued an appeal on grounds that included the argument 'there was no engineering or other sufficient evidence from which the judge could properly have found the accident occurred as he did'.

In the Court of Appeal May LJ observed:

> 'One difficulty with this case is that Mr Ellis remembers nothing of the accident itself, and although there were others working with him or in the vicinity, no one who gave evidence at the hearing before HHJ Langan QC in the County Court at Leeds in February 2007 actually saw the accident itself, or exactly how Mr Ellis was injured. So when HHJ Langan came to give his judgment on 10 February 2007, he had to reconstruct by inference from rather meagre direct evidence why and how the accident occurred. Furthermore, there was no engineering or other expert evidence to help the court, and I infer from references in the judge's judgment that he rather regretted that a District Judge had been persuaded by the defendants not to permit expert evidence. (Counsel), on behalf of the defendants, said this morning that the pleaded case did not require expert evidence, but I am not convinced that that is really right.'

In the context of the earlier skirmishes at the stage of case management May LJ added:

---

2   [2002] EWCA Civ 838.
3   [2007] EWCA Civ 1232.

'I further think that a defendant who successfully argues against having expert evidence in a case which truly needed it has to live with the appellate judicial product of evidence which is incomplete.'

In *Lougheed v On the Beach Ltd*[4] one of the key issues, in a claim arising out of an accident abroad, was local health and safety standards. The claimant's application for permission to rely on expert evidence dealing with local standards and regulations was dismissed, because at the stage it was made allowing such evidence would have resulted in vacation of the trial date. The claimant succeeded at trial but an appeal by the defendant was allowed, Tomlinson LJ observing, after noting it was preferable there be expert evidence on such matters, that:

'A claimant who chooses not to choose such evidence in a kind of this sort does so at his peril.'

These examples illustrate the very real problem a claimant may face when seeking permission to rely on expert evidence which, as the case develops, may turn out to be crucial in proving an important aspect of the claim, as well as the importance of identifying necessary evidence at an early stage and tactics the defendant may adopt at a case management hearing, to exclude such evidence.

7.1.3 The defendant's perspective

The cynical claimant might conclude the defendant, at least when dealing with the issue of reliance on expert evidence the claimant contends to be important, may be being disingenuous in ostensibly supporting the need to control evidence by the court when perhaps the real motive is to prevent the claimant from being able to call evidence that might support an important part of the case.

Consequently, the defendant, mindful of where the burden of proof will usually lie, may sometimes contend no expert evidence on a particular issue is required, despite firm assertions to the contrary from the claimant.

Conversely, from time to time, it is the defendant who faces the evidential problem usually encountered by the claimant, because the burden of proof on an issue rests with the defendant which it may be difficult to discharge without expert evidence. In these circumstances the defendant will not only need to perceive where the burden of proof lies, by the stage of case management, but also persuade the court permission to rely on such evidence should be given.

However, the more usual issue, from the defendant's perspective, is when expert evidence obtained by the claimant is not agreed and the defendant, conceding expert evidence on the relevant issue is required, wishes to obtain permission to rely on a corresponding expert in the same field.

Given that the court's duty to restrict expert evidence applies equally to confining expert evidence where necessary to a single expert on a particular issue, just as it does to exclude expert evidence altogether where not required, the claimant may, in these circumstances, wish to oppose the grant of such permission.

---

4   [2014] EWCA Civ 1538.

When this issue arises much, ultimately, will depend upon whether the original expert has been either jointly selected or jointly instructed and, even where unilateral instruction may not have been appropriate at the outset, whether the court would, nevertheless, benefit from the views of more than one expert.

It is certainly not the case that if permission to rely on an expert is given to one party the other party automatically has the right to duplicate that evidence, even where the case is allocated to the multi-track. That is because the intention, returning again to the principles underlying the CPR, is that expert evidence should only be allowed where reasonably required, which must mean being confined one expert, on any issue or in any expert field, wherever possible.

7.1.4   The claimant's solution

Given the potential problem for the claimant in seeking to show expert evidence is reasonably required, and the tactics that may be employed on behalf of the defendant, it is essential to anticipate, and help guard against, future difficulties concerning expert evidence from the outset.

That will require a careful analysis, when preparing the case plan, to identify matters that will inevitably require expert evidence. Appropriate steps can then be taken to limit that evidence to a single expert where appropriate. Subsequently it will be necessary to review the issues that emerge, as the case develops, to identify, in the light of other evidence available, where expert evidence may have become necessary and, conversely, no longer be essential.

All this will involve the claimant making effective use of both the Protocol and the CPR to help ensure that, ultimately, the court deals with the case justly (in other words in accordance with the overriding objective).

In practice all this will require a very careful analysis of the issues as the claim progresses, initially identifying key issues which the claimant will need to establish but then keeping these under review as they narrow or resolve and sometimes as further issues emerge.

In each case a critical question, for the party on whom the burden or proof lies, will be whether factual evidence is sufficient to prove the issue or if expert evidence is required, in which case that evidence will need to be admissible opinion and, moreover, the court will need to be persuaded to grant permission for it to be relied upon.

Consequently, it will be necessary, on behalf of the claimant, to keep a number of matters in mind when considering expert evidence from the outset, through investigation and case management up to and including listing and preparation for trial:

- At the outset the key issues the claimant will need to prove should, so far as possible, be identified. An assessment can then be made about available, or likely sources of, evidence and the extent to which, above and beyond factual evidence, expert evidence may be required because:
  - expert opinion is required to properly investigate and shape the case which will be put (for example claims involving allegations of professional negligence, claims where a reconstruction of events is based on interpretation of available factual evidence, claims where an inspection of the scene will be

required and claims in which technical issues will need explaining, all being the type of claim where opinion evidence is required to interpret available factual evidence; or

– the evidence required is essentially factual but best gathered, or presented, by an expert (such evidence may be the only way the claimant can introduce, and prove, factual issues necessary to establish the claim).

• Where the need for an expert is identified at this early stage considering whether that expert should be asked to give advice only, to help investigate and formulate the case, or expert evidence, in anticipation of that being an essential part of the evidence to be relied on.

• Where expert evidence is contemplated, as opposed to expert advice, recognising that:

– the evidence obtained will need to be admissible opinion evidence under the general law; and

– such evidence will have to be viewed by the court as 'reasonably required' for the purposes of Part 35 in the context of the particular claim.

• Whether there is any logical order, where more than one expert is required, for instruction, for example dealing with liability prior to quantum or, in relation to quantum only, identifying a lead expert or logical sequence (if the opinion of some experts will inevitably be dependent upon the views of others).

• Where expert evidence is identified, at the outset, as being appropriate whether the issue is such that unilateral instruction will be appropriate or, with a view to having a single expert on the issue if possible, utilising the machinery under the Protocol for joint selection or even contemplating, at the outset, joint instruction.

• Once expert evidence is received assessing, in the light of that, whether it will indeed be necessary to rely on such evidence and whether the evidence received suggests further expert opinion will be required (and if so, once again, whether this should be from a single expert or not).

• Identifying, presenting and seeking agreement of matters which, unless agreed, might require expert evidence, mindful that under both the Protocol and the CPR the defendant must respond to the claimant's case by identifying what is admitted and what is denied (with reasons for the latter).

• Identifying, on those matters that remain in issue, where the burden of proof rests as this may dictate which party needs expert evidence to help discharge that burden (even if the other party may then wish for permission to rely on corresponding evidence if expert evidence is allowed at all).

• Reviewing the evidence disclosed, or identified as likely to be disclosed, by the defendant on matters in issue to determine whether, even if factual, that will require evidence from an expert on behalf of the claimant (particularly if the defendant's evidence is what might be termed quasi-expert evidence which, without an expert, it may be difficult or impossible for the claimant to deal with).

• Dealing, ideally at the stage of initial case management, with getting permission to rely upon expert evidence with, where there is to be more than one expert in any particular field, directions for exchange. However, such permission can always be sought at a later stage and even if initially unsuccessful in getting permission further attempts may be made if there is a sufficient change of circumstances to justify this.

• Complying with any court timetable for exchange, to ensure admissibility of relevant evidence.

- Assessing the need for oral expert evidence in the light of joint statements, at the stage of listing.

Ultimately, the need for expert evidence is case sensitive and likely to depend upon the specific issues arising in the particular case and in the context of all the other evidence available to deal with such issues.

If, however, careful assessment is made, on a case by case basis and as that case develops, this should help avoid the trap, for the claimant, of either omitting to have, or being prevented from relying upon, expert evidence necessary to establish any important element of the claim.

7.1.5   Overview

Having considered expert evidence in the context of the CPR, and the possible difficulties this presents for the claimant, it is necessary to look at alternatives to expert evidence before considering, where expert evidence is likely to be required, problems concerning admissibility and the need for permission to rely on such evidence.

Those general principles can then be considered in the context of practical examples concerning the use of particular types of expert in personal injury claims.

Where there is more than one expert in a particular field, issues arise in relation to exchange of evidence, questions, joint statements and the need for oral evidence as well as the problems faced by a party who wishes to change experts which are reviewed.

Finally, there are sanctions which may be relevant to expert evidence.

7.2   PRELIMINARIES TO EXPERT EVIDENCE

Because of the additional hurdles, admissibility and permission which apply to expert evidence it is essential, when analysing the issues and evidence necessary to deal with these, to consider ways of narrowing the issues and dealing with those that remain without the need for reliance on experts where possible.

For the same reason it is important to determine whether evidence to be relied on is, in truth, expert or simply factual.

When expert evidence is considered necessary there may be a better prospect of being able to rely upon that evidence if the claimant can demonstrate to the court why it is required and that, where appropriate, steps have been taken to have, if possible, a single expert in any field of expertise. Those steps may well have been taken in accordance with the Practice Direction – Pre-action Conduct or the Protocol. Compliance, or otherwise, with the Protocol is, under Part 3 of the CPR, a relevant consideration for the court when deciding issues of case management, including whether to give permission for a party to rely on expert evidence, so that should generally be followed.

Consequently, getting the preliminaries to expert evidence right should help ensure permission to rely on such evidence, where still necessary to deal with the issues in the case, will be facilitated and reduced the risk that the claimant is left struggling, at trial, to prove key elements of the claim.

The Practice Direction – Pre-action Conduct deals, in general terms, with the approach a party should adopt, at the outset, towards expert evidence. Paragraph 9.4 provides that where the evidence of an expert is necessary the parties should consider how best to minimise expense, with further guidance on instructing experts being given in Annex C.

More specific advice on the correct approach to the use of experts is found in paragraph 6 of the Expert Protocol which suggests analysing, in relation to any proposed expert evidence, whether:

- it is relevant to a matter in dispute;
- it is reasonably required to resolve the proceedings;
- the expert has expertise relevant to the issues on which an opinion is sought;
- the expert has the experience, expertise and training appropriate to the value, complexity and importance of the case; and
- a single joint expert is appropriate.

All of these, and some other matters, will, therefore, be preliminaries to obtaining, and where appropriate relying upon, expert evidence.

7.2.1   The issues

The first task is to identify the issues, or likely issues, between the parties which the claimant will need to prove. The need for evidence to deal with those issues can then be addressed.

If the review of the case at the outset indicates issues on which expert evidence might be required it may, before even obtaining that evidence, be appropriate to see whether those issues can be narrowed.

Given the obligation under the Protocol, for the defendant to give reasons for any denial of liability and alternative version of events, efforts may be made pre-action to narrow the issues by detailing the claimant's case and pressing for a proper response from the defendant.

Once court proceedings have been commenced the terms of the CPR, and particularly the requirements of Part 16 on the content of the defence, may also help to identify, precisely, what matters are in issue and hence the evidence, including expert evidence, needed to deal with those issues.

Particulars of Claim may include matters which, if in dispute, might have to be proved by the claimant calling appropriate evidence, perhaps including expert evidence. However, if there are admissions or agreement by the defendant that may restrict the scope of the evidence, including expert evidence, necessary. In this way matters which are the subject of research, or even some expert advice, might end up being admitted provided the claimant's Statement of Case is drafted widely enough and the defendant sensibly narrows the issues.

In this context the suggestion in *Bandegani v Norwich Union Fire Insurance Society Ltd*[5] that, for example, the value of a vehicle be proved by the expedient of price guides rather than expert evidence, makes sense. The same approach might, of course, be applied to information obtained from a wealth of sources, particularly the internet, if identified and relied on early enough.

If the defendant puts the claimant to proof, in circumstances where the claimant considers there is an unreasonable failure to narrow the issues by admission, a Notice to Admit might be served as that will put the defendant at risk on costs of proving those facts, whatever the outcome of the claim, if the court considers the failure to admit was unreasonable.

Matters left or put in issue by the defendant will be a very relevant consideration as and when the court has to determine what expert evidence may be 'reasonably required to resolve the proceedings', not least because the overriding objective specifically refers to the nature of the issues. At that case management stage the onus will fall on the court to carefully scrutinise the issues and how these can be dealt with (see 7.3.2).

Where matters remain in issue these will need to be proved, by the party on whom the burden of proof rests, which will require evidence. Even information widely available, such as on the internet, will, in such circumstances, need to be proved and, particularly if this involves any element of subjective opinion, that may point towards the need for expert evidence.

It is also essential to keep in mind, on each remaining issue, where the burden of proof lies, as that may dictate whether or not a party wishes to obtain and then seek permission to rely upon expert evidence.

7.2.2 Expert or factual evidence?

The distinction between factual and expert evidence is significant because factual evidence will be admissible and may be relied on without express permission from the court, provided it is disclosed as part of the factual evidence in accordance with case management directions.

Because a witness may be regarded as an 'expert' that does not mean the evidence of such a witness will necessarily be 'expert evidence'.

The Civil Evidence Act 1972 allows any witness, including an expert, to give opinion evidence if that is a way of conveying relevant facts personally perceived. Use of an expert, to give evidence of this kind, can be useful where there is no other evidence of relevant factual background, perhaps describing detail at the scene of an accident, and involvement of an expert will not only be a useful way of introducing this evidence but will also bring the skill of that expert to bear on helping to identify the most salient features and helping to convey these in an effective way to the court.

---

[5] Court of Appeal, 20 May 1999.

Moreover, if a witness who happens to be an expert is giving simply factual evidence that is admissible as such even if given in the general context of expertise that witness has. For example, if a clinician is not dealing hypothetically with what that clinician would have done but explaining the reasons why treatment actually given was provided that would be factual, not expert opinion, see: *Kirkman v Euro Exide Corporation (CMP Batteries Ltd)*.[6]

However, even if evidence is factual the court still has power, under CPR 32.1, to exclude such evidence even though otherwise admissible. The exercise of this power, where an expert was proposing to give factual evidence, was illustrated in *Stevens v Gullis*[7] where, at first instance, the court concluded that an expert who failed to facilitate compliance with an unless order for joint statement should not be allowed to give expert opinion evidence. That was because the expert had apparently failed to understand his duties to the court and functions as an expert witness. The expert was not, however, to be precluded from giving evidence of fact.

In *Stevens* the court, at first instance, concluded that an expert who failed to facilitate compliance with an 'unless order' for joint statement should not be allowed to give expert evidence, as apparently failing to understand his duties to the court and functions as an expert witness, but would not be precluded from giving evidence of fact.

The Court of Appeal, upholding the ruling debarring the witness from giving expert evidence, held that the expert had, by his conduct, demonstrated no conception of the requirements placed on an expert under the CPR. That was not, however, the end of the matter for the reasons explained by Lord Woolf MR when he held:

> '... I consider it was a mistake to regard (the expert) as being in a position to give evidence as to fact although he could not give evidence as an expert. In this connection I draw attention to the period that had elapsed before (the expert) first inspected the site of the building work and also draw attention to the fact that other work had been carried out at the building site after the claimant withdrew from the contract. In my judgment it would be extraordinarily difficult, if not impossible, for (the expert) to give evidence as to fact without giving evidence as an expert. In any event, (the expert) was so discredited that it would be pointless for his evidence to be included on the hearing of the claim between the builder and the defendant. The court now has power to control evidence, even evidence as to fact, which is to be given in the course of the proceedings. In my view, it would have been more appropriate for the judge to have refused permission for (the expert) to give evidence as to fact.'

Consequently, it is necessary to assess whether the evidence on which the claimant proposes to rely is factual or expert in nature, to avoid unnecessary applications for permission to rely on evidence when that is not necessary, but what would otherwise be admissible factual evidence, if given by an expert witness, might still be excluded in circumstances such as occurred in *Stevens*.

7.2.3 Expert advice or expert evidence

There is an important distinction between expert advice and expert evidence, which may have a bearing on how any expert involved in the case is instructed.

---

6 [2007] EWCA Civ 66.
7 (2000) 1 All ER 527.

CPR 35.2 defines 'expert witness' as an expert who has been instructed to give or prepare evidence for the purpose of court proceedings. There is, accordingly, a distinction between an 'expert witness', as defined by the rule, and an 'expert' from whom advice, as opposed to evidence for court proceedings, might be sought.

An expert witness will be subject to Part 35 whereas an expert may advise a party on any matter without being subject to the terms of that rule. Consequently, such an advice will not need to be prepared in accordance with the terms of Part 35, as would a report prepared for potential use as evidence.

Consequently, it may be appropriate to seek initial advice from an expert, which will not need to be on a formal basis complying fully with the requirements of a report to be relied on as evidence, especially if some expert input is necessary to help establish the factual background, help identify the basis of the case on liability or simply assist in determining the merits.

Both an advice from an expert and an expert's report will be privileged (see **7.6.9**). Usually, even if the expert is later relied on and a report disclosed, any preliminary advices and reports will remain privileged. In *Jackson v Marley Davenport Ltd*[8] Longmore LJ held that:

> 'There can be no doubt that, if an expert makes a report for the purpose of a party's legal advisors being able to give legal advice to their client, or for discussion in a conference of a party's legal advisors, such a report is the subject matter of litigation privilege at the time it is made. It has come into existence for the purposes of litigation. It is common for drafts of expert reports to be circulated among a party's advisors before a final report is prepared for exchange with the other side. Such initial reports are privileged.'

Longmore LJ continued his judgment by observing:

> 'I cannot believe that the Civil Procedure Rules were intended to override that privilege. CPR 35.5 provides that expert evidence is to be given in a report unless the court directs otherwise. CPR 35.10 then changed the previous law by providing in sub-rule (3) that the expert's report must state the substance of all material (whether written or oral instructions) on the basis on which the report was written. By sub-rule (4) it is, moreover, expressly provided that these instructions shall not be privileged. But the reference in Rule 35.10 to "the expert's report" is, and must be, a reference to the expert's intended evidence, not to earlier and privileged drafts of what may or may not in due course become the expert's evidence.'

However, in *Edwards-Tubb v J D Weatherspoon plc*[9] the Court of Appeal concluded that where a conditional order for permission to rely on expert evidence was given, granting permission in return for the party concerned waiving privilege and producing the evidence of a discarded expert, not only the final report but also any earlier drafts would have to be disclosed. The court did, however, recognise the distinction between an expert and an expert witness and whilst endorsing the use of conditional orders where expert evidence was obtained through the mechanism of joint selection under the Protocol, where a party subsequently sought to rely on a different expert in the same field, emphasised that a way of avoiding such an order was to seek expert advice from such an expert.

---

8   [2004] EWCA Civ 1225.
9   [2011] EWCA Civ 136.

Furthermore, where a conditional order is made, the terms may require disclosure of draft reports (even though, applying *Jackson*, that would not occur when a party deploys, in the usual way, an expert's report) because in *Hajigeorgiou v Vasiliou*[10] Brooke LJ held:

> 'A question that was not considered in *Beck* is whether the condition of disclosure should relate only to the first expert's final report, or whether it should also relate to his or her earlier draft reports. In our view, it should not only apply to the first expert's "final" report, if by that is meant the report signed by the first expert as his or her report for disclosure. It should apply at least to the first expert's report(s) containing the substance of his or her opinion.'

Consequently, whilst the claimant may often wish to use the machinery for joint selection found in the Protocol, perhaps across a range of expert fields, if the relevant issue is such that the claimant may not necessarily wish to commit to the views of the first expert approached the advantages of joint selection may be outweighed by the disadvantages and an expert advice preferred, at least initially.

There is no reason why an expert, who provides advice as a preliminary, cannot then be instructed to prepare a report, for use in evidence, as an expert witness. However, the expert will have to then have proper regard to all the requirements of Part 35, which may require the advice to be re-written as a report.

If a party obtains preliminary expert advice in circumstances where joint selection or joint instruction, with a view to there being a single expert, may be appropriate, there is also no reason, in principle, why the expert who has advised should not be nominated. However, in such circumstances, it would seem appropriate for the party nominating to disclose the fact that the expert has already provided an advice.

The advice of an expert may suffice to help assess the merits of and formulate the case in a way that either allows the relevant issue to be agreed or presented in a way that permits any issues to be resolved by non-expert evidence. In those circumstances it will not be necessary for the initial advice to be supplemented, whether by the expert concerned or a different expert, with expert evidence.

7.2.4 Obtaining information from the defendant?

An alternative, or perhaps preliminary, to expert evidence is making use of the provision in CPR 35.9 that where a party has access to information which is not reasonably available to the other party the court may direct the party who has access to the information to prepare and file a document recording the information and serve a copy of that document on the other party.

This rule, seldom used in practice, was perhaps intended to help redress the imbalance between a well-resourced defendant, with ready access to relevant information that may include expert advice based on information available or acquired, and an individual claimant.

This intention would seem to be reflected by the terms of paragraph 4 of the Practice Direction to Part 35 which confirms any document to be served in accordance with

---

10 [2005] EWCA Civ 236.

CPR 35.9 must include sufficient details of all the facts, tests, experiments and assumptions which underlie any part of the information to enable the party on whom it is served to make, or to obtain, a proper interpretation of the information and an assessment of its significance.

Such information, if obtained under this rule, may have the effect of narrowing the issues or at least providing evidence of relevance to the court when determining the remaining issues which will obviate the need for expert evidence dealing specifically with such issues.

If the defendant is requested to provide such information voluntarily but declines to do so that may be a relevant factor, mindful of the specific provision in the overriding objective for there to be equality between the parties, if the court needs to consider whether the claimant reasonably requires permission to rely on expert evidence.

In *Humber Oil Terminal Trustee Ltd v Associated British Ports*[11] Morgan J held that the information sought under CPR 35.9 must at least be relevant to some issue which the court would be asked to try in the course of determining the case. Specifically, the judge held:

> 'That rule does not define the information which can be made the subject to an order. However, it is implicit that the information which is sought is, at least, relevant to an issue in the case.'

CPR 35.9 might be relied on, even though the report as a whole may be subject to privilege, where one party has had the opportunity of testing or experimenting with property that would be an exhibit at any final hearing or is a subject matter of the claim.

In *Carruthers v MP Fireworks Ltd*,[12] a claim involving a firework, the court gave the claimant permission to substitute one pyrotechnics expert for another on condition the report of the first expert be disclosed. Dismissing an appeal against this order Mr Recorder Moxon Browne QC held:

> 'If it fell to me to exercise my own discretion in this case, I would have taken the course followed by the Deputy District Judge, for the reasons given by him. In addition it is my view that where as in this case an expert has been instructed to perform tests on an exhibit (such as an exploded firework) open justice and fairness will usually demand that the results of those tests should be put before the other experts in the case, and before the Court. This will especially be so where there is a perception that those tests may have caused some physical alteration (albeit short of "destruction") to the exhibit in question. In such cases it is my view that justice will usually require the disclosure of the relevant report, whether or not its author is called to give evidence. In the present case the nature of the tests carried out by Mr Harriman, and their effect if any on the remains of the firework examined by him, are a secret in the hands of the claimant. I think that is unfair, and at the lowest gives rise to the perception of a potential injustice. That seems to me an additional reason for exercising a discretion in favour of ordering disclosure of Mr Harriman's report, as a condition of the claimant's permission to rely on a further report from Mr Miller.'

The making of such a conditional order has subsequently been confirmed as appropriate, at least in relation to experts jointly selected under the Protocol, in

---

[11]   [2011] EWHC 1184 (Ch).
[12]   (Unreported) Bristol County Court, 26 January 2007.

Edwards-Tubb v J D Weatherspoon plc[13] (the decision in Carruthers being specifically referred to and effectively endorsed by the Court of Appeal in that case).

Where there has been no joint selection under the Protocol the issue of privilege remains important and may make, in such circumstances, the terms of CPR 35.9 important for a party seeking relevant information, even if not the report or advice as a whole (on the grounds of privilege).

7.2.5 Expert evidence

It may be apparent, from the outset, that the claimant will need expert evidence. For example, in virtually every personal injury claim at least some expert medical evidence will be required. Sometimes it will be apparent, again from the outset, which medical specialism should be involved. In other cases only a provisional view can be formed or perhaps just a lead expert identified.

There may be cases where, again at the outset, it is apparent non-medical expert evidence will be necessary. In other cases that might be a provisional assessment, which ultimately will depend on the outcome of enquiries concerning liability and the terms of initial medical evidence dealing with quantum.

Where it is clear expert evidence will be required to deal with any issue, steps should be taken to obtain that evidence from an appropriate, and properly instructed, expert. Ideally, any such expert can give opinion evidence, in the framework of the relevant law, so that the court is assisted in determining the particular issue.

If the need for expert evidence, on any particular issue, remains a possibility, any such issues will need to be kept under review, as the claim progresses, remembering, if it is to be relied upon, such evidence will need to be admissible, under the general law, and that, additionally, the court will need to be persuaded that permission to rely on the evidence should be granted (see 7.3).

Case-law can do no more than indicate a court's view, on the particular facts of the individual case, whether expert evidence will be 'reasonably required', though some general conclusions can be drawn on the relevance of some types of expert evidence for particular issues (see 7.4).

Whenever expert evidence is considered necessary consideration should be given to the possibility of that being given by a single expert, whether jointly selected under the Protocol or jointly instructed.

7.2.6 Single expert

The Protocol and the CPR work together so as to facilitate and encourage the use, wherever possible, of a single expert in any relevant field.

---

[13]   [2011] EWCA Civ 136.

The use of a single expert will, in many cases, further the overriding objective and ensure that expert evidence is indeed limited to that which is reasonably required to resolve the proceedings.

Accordingly, if a case requires expert evidence on an issue it is necessary to consider how that may be given, if possible, by a single expert. This may be achieved either by using the mechanism, provided for in the Protocol, for joint selection or, if appropriate, by inviting the defendant to agree joint instruction.

However, as the Queen's Bench Guide recognises, a single expert will not always be appropriate and sometimes this can be recognised from the outset. To quote:

> 'In very many cases it is possible for the question of expert evidence to be dealt with by a single expert. Single experts are, for example, often appropriate to deal with questions of quantum in cases where primary issues are as to liability. Likewise, where expert evidence is required in order to acquaint the court with matters of expert fact, as opposed to opinion, a single expert will usually be appropriate. There remain, however, a body of cases where liability will turn upon expert opinion evidence and where it will be appropriate for the parties to instruct their own experts. For example, in cases where the issue for determination is as to whether a party acted in accordance with proper professional standards, it will often be of value to the court to hear the opinions of more than one expert as to the proper standard in order that the court becomes acquainted with the range of views existing upon the question and in order that the evidence can be tested in cross-examination.'

In such circumstances the claimant may prefer to unilaterally instruct an expert, even where the expert is being asked to provide a report as an expert witness rather than just an advice.

In other circumstances, however, the better course may be to establish if a single expert may be instructed, particularly pre-issue when the machinery for joint selection under the Protocol remains available. In fast-track cases the combination of the Protocol and terms of Part 35 may result in a nominated expert, to whom there is no objection, being the only expert allowed by the court on a particular issue.

Even if the case seems destined for the multi-track the nomination of experts under the Protocol may be a very relevant consideration for the court when deciding whether another expert in the same field is reasonably required for the purposes of Part 35, and might tell against permission being given unless there is some good reason for there to be a further such expert.

7.2.7   Permission and/or facilities?

Whilst a party will need the court's permission to rely on expert evidence, no such permission is necessary as a preliminary to obtaining expert evidence, or indeed expert advice (see 7.2.3).

An expert may be able to prepare a report, though more likely an advice, by just reviewing relevant documents. Where, however, a report is being prepared for use in court proceedings, that may be of limited value if it is more of a general thesis on the matters in issue rather than a guide which will assist the court based on a careful assessment of all the factual, documentary and real evidence relevant to the specific case.

If all matters to be dealt with by the expert can be covered by just a review of the documents, it may be possible to obtain the necessary expert evidence at an early stage, on behalf of the claimant, if the defendant provides disclosure in accordance with the Protocol or, if necessary, an order for pre-action disclosure obtained from the court.

If, however, the expert will need facilities, for example inspection of property to take account of what might broadly be termed the real evidence, in order to establish the background necessary to report fully, the party instructing the expert, unless able to provide those facilities or these are provided voluntarily, may wish to seek an order from the court, not for permission to obtain expert evidence as such but to ensure those facilities will be made available.

For example, a medical expert, certainly when asked to deal with condition and prognosis, will usually wish to examine the claimant. In *Jackson v MGN Ltd*[14] Neill LJ observed:

> 'I cannot, for my part, imagine any ordinary circumstances in which a medical witness should be invited to express an expert view about the condition of any person, without having any access to that person. There may be very exceptional cases, but it seems to me this is not such a case.'

Similarly in *Larby v Thurgood*[15] May J held:

> 'In a personal injury action, a medical consultant giving expert evidence will commonly be asked to say: (a) what injuries the plaintiff suffered at the time of the accident and what treatment he had, (b) what the plaintiff's disability or other state is at the time of trial, and (c) what in his opinion is the likely medical prognosis. The plaintiff's injuries and treatment at the time of the accident are very largely questions of fact. The consultant will habitually recite such facts having gleaned them from the plaintiff and from medical records. They are usually not in dispute. The plaintiff often gives evidence to prove his part of them in the course of the trial. The plaintiff's disability or other state at the time of the trial are again largely questions of fact. The consultant will usually give evidence to establish such facts based on his examination of the plaintiff and on his expert opinion about what his examination reveals. The likely medical prognosis is again a matter of expert opinion. It is accepted that in most cases a medical examination of the plaintiff is necessary to enable the consultant properly to form and express his opinion.'

Whilst the claimant can be expected to co-operate with arrangements for obtaining medical evidence which the claimant's own representatives are obtaining, the defendant is unlikely to be able to obtain a report, or at least a report based upon an examination, pre-issue of court proceedings without the claimant's agreement (see **1.8.8**) and thereafter only if the request for facilities is reasonable (see **7.2.7**).

Conversely, the claimant may wish to obtain expert evidence on liability which, ideally, will be based upon an inspection of the scene of the accident, machinery or other real evidence. That may require facilities from the defendant or perhaps a party who is not likely to be involved in any proceedings brought by the claimant.

The claimant will be in a stronger position, at least prior to issue of any court proceedings, in seeking such facilities, than the defendant would be in gaining facilities

---

14 Court of Appeal, 17 March 1994.
15 [1993] ICR 66.

to have the claimant examined by an expert. That is because CPR 25.5 allows the court to make a pre-action order allowing for inspection of property which is or may become the subject matter of the proceedings or be relevant to issues that will arise in such proceedings. It is also because whilst there may need to be some grounds for seeking facilities that will be, in the words of Dyson LJ in *Hajigeorgiou v Vasiliou*[16], a 'far cry' from a request for facilities to examine a claimant and the careful balancing exercise the court must then undertake when deciding whether what is inevitably an invasion of privacy ought to effectively be sanctioned (see **7.8.2**).

If the claimant cannot secure the facilities requested the relevant expert may, nevertheless, be asked to produce a preliminary report which might explain precisely what facilities are considered necessary and why, in terms of the potential benefits to the court of the evidence that would then allow the expert to give. This, in turn, may support any application to the court for an order under Part 25 whether pre-issue or at the stage of initial case management later.

In this context it may be important to emphasise to the court that allowing facilities to obtain expert evidence is not the same, at all, as giving permission to rely upon any evidence that may be obtained as a result of those facilities. Thus, it is important not to pre-judge whether the expert evidence which would be obtained if appropriate facilities are made available will be both admissible and reasonably required simply on the basis that the evidence is not available, and these issues cannot be assessed without it, as that allows a party to potentially dictate, by failing to co-operate, what expert evidence is ultimately before the court.

Whilst this discrepancy may seem potentially unjust it is important to remember that with expert evidence that might usually involve an examination of, or interview with, the claimant, there will usually be the joint selection of a mutually acceptable expert, in accordance with the Protocol, which should offset any disadvantage in not having any right to insist on facilities for an examination or interview at that stage. Indeed, the need for mutuality would suggest it is quite reasonable for the claimant to invite the defendant to agree joint selection of any experts who might carry out an inspection of property belonging to the defendant, or a third party, and certainly expect mutuality in the event the defendant unilaterally obtains evidence based on any such facilities. Ultimately, this is a question of the parties having a degree of equality, that being a specific factor identified in Part 1 of the CPR as helping to achieve the overriding objective.

Whilst a party may proceed to obtain expert evidence without permission, where facilities considered necessary for a definitive opinion are requested but refused, the absence of those facilities may become significant when that party seeks permission to rely upon the evidence obtained, because the available evidence may be of more limited value to the court which, in turn, may mean it is not 'reasonably required' for the purposes of Part 35. An example of the potential difficulties faced by a party in these circumstances is the ruling by HHJ Moir in *Hindmarch v Hasford*.[17]

In *Hindmarch* an application to rely on the evidence of an expert in a claim arising out of a road traffic accident was refused largely because the expert had not examined either vehicle involved in the incident, the judge concluding:

---

[16]   [2005] EWCA Civ 236.
[17]   (Unreported) Newcastle County Court, 8 April 2005.

'Having considered very carefully whether in the circumstances of this case the trial judge would be assisted by the admission of the report from (the expert), I have concluded that such assistance would be limited because of the limitation within the report itself and thus to incur the cost of allowing this report to be adduced in evidence and the costs of dealing with the further additional evidence which would be inevitable upon admission of this report would not be proportionate in the circumstances of this case, and having regard to the value of the claim.'

If, by the time the relevant request is made, facilities can no longer be given, due to changes made to the scene of the accident or disposal or destruction of relevant property, the more appropriate step may be to request details of any information or inspection available to the other party under the terms of CPR 35.9 (see 7.2.4).

If one party contends another party has failed to give facilities that are reasonably required pre-issue of court proceedings, this is likely to be a matter that will be raised at the stage of initial case management, the court having wide case management powers to ensure the case is dealt with justly which may include, directly or indirectly, ordering one party to provide appropriate facilities to another, not least because of the duty on the parties to help the court further the overriding objective.

7.3   ADMISSIBILITY AND RELIANCE

When expert evidence is considered necessary to establish any part of the claimant's case the issues of, first, admissibility and, secondly, obtaining permission to rely on such evidence will arise.

The first issue arises as opinion evidence is, generally, inadmissible. That is because such evidence may usurp the function of the court by interpreting other evidence, or even by suggesting conclusions on issues ultimately for determination by the court. There are, however, exceptions to the general rule which renders opinion evidence inadmissible which are found in the Civil Evidence Act 1972. Accordingly, any expert evidence to be relied on will need, as a starting point, to be admissible under the terms of the Act, namely 'opinion on any relevant matter on which (the witness) is qualified to give expert evidence'.

The second issue arises because, as the Act makes clear, the ability of a party to rely upon expert evidence also depends upon rules of the court, those rules now being the CPR. Consequently, expert opinion evidence, otherwise potentially admissible, may still be excluded under the CPR.

Accordingly, it is necessary for a party seeking to rely on expert evidence to show that this is potentially admissible within the terms of the Act and, if it is, to obtain, in accordance with the CPR, permission for that evidence to be relied upon.

7.3.1   Admissibility: Civil Evidence Act 1972

The terms of the Act will be the starting point in determining what is, when given by an expert, admissible opinion evidence.

The issue of admissibility only arises, of course, where a party seeks to rely on an expert to give evidence, as opposed to advice (see **7.2.3**), and where that evidence is opinion as opposed to factual (see **6.1.1.2** and **7.3.1.1**).

7.3.1.1   The Act

The terms of section 3(1) of the Act deal specifically with expert opinion evidence and provide:

> 'Subject to any rules of court made in pursuance of this Act, where a person is called as a witness in any civil proceedings, his opinion on any relevant matter on which he is qualified to give expert evidence shall be admissible in evidence.'

The terms of section 3(2) deal with opinion which is really a way of giving factual evidence and provide:

> 'It is hereby declared that where a person is called as a witness in any civil proceedings, a statement of opinion by him on any relevant matter on which he is not qualified to give expert evidence, if made as a way of conveying relevant facts personally perceived by him, is admissible as evidence of what he perceived.'

Consequently, both expert witnesses and witnesses of fact can give this type of 'opinion'. Such opinion is, in reality, a form of shorthand for detailed factual observations (which if the witness is an expert may be of a specialised nature shaped by the relevant expertise). Typical examples of such 'opinion' will be the speed of a vehicle, road or weather conditions and identification of an individual.

The term 'relevant matter', referred to in both section 3(1) and (2), is defined by section 3(3) as including an issue in the proceedings in question.

Factual evidence of this kind may be given by an expert who is purely, for these purposes, a witness of fact and, accordingly, can give evidence even if there is no permission to rely on expert evidence in the relevant field of expertise: *Blair-Ford v CRS Adventures Ltd*.[18]

7.3.1.2   What is admissible expert evidence?

The concept of what will amount to 'expert evidence', and hence potentially be admissible despite being opinion, has been explored in case-law.

In *Midland Bank Trust Co Ltd v Hett Stubbs & Kemp*,[19] a case involving alleged legal negligence, the court recognised three distinct categories of evidence in that context. Oliver J explained:

> 'The extent of the legal duty in any given situation must, I think, be a question of law for the court. Clearly, if there is some practice in a particular profession, some accepted standard of conduct which is laid down by a professional institute or sanctioned by common usage, evidence of that can and ought to be received. But evidence which really amounts to no more than an expression of opinion by a particular practitioner of what he thinks that he would

---

[18]   [2012] EWHC 1886 (QB).
[19]   [1979] Ch 384.

have done had he been placed, hypothetically and without the benefit of hindsight, in the position of the defendants, is of little assistance to the court; whilst evidence of the witnesses' view of what, as a matter of law, the solicitor's duty was in the particular circumstances of the case is, I should have thought, inadmissible, for that is the very question which it is the court's function to decide.'

The first category of evidence identified in that judgment, dealing with accepted standards of conduct, is clearly admissible expert evidence in such cases.

The second category, which whilst informed opinion is not based on any such standards, is of little value and hence likely to be inadmissible on this analysis.

The third category, essentially about whether the relevant duty has been breached, is clearly inadmissible as this is a matter for the court to determine.

That approach has been followed subsequently, for example in *Barings plc (In Liquidation) v Coopers & Lybrand (No 2)*.[20]

However, it was recognised by Neuberger J in *Liverpool Roman Catholic Archdiocese Trustees v Goldberg (No 2)*[21] that:

'... the state of the law is not clear and ... I do not think that it is possible to be absolutist about evidence of this nature being admissible or inadmissible in every case.'

Neuberger J, in the same judgment, went on to caution against too readily ruling expert evidence as inadmissible when he said:

'... in principle it seems to me that if there is real doubt as to whether or not expert evidence ought to be put in as admissible, the issue should be determined in favour of admissibility. If the court ruled out evidence which is subsequently transpires should have been admitted, then the trial is almost certainly likely to be an unfair trial if it is determined against the party who was seeking to put in the evidence. If, on the other hand, the court admits the evidence and it subsequently transpired that it should not have done so, it is much easier for the judge hearing the matter to put the evidence out of his mind or, if he has taken it into account, for the Court of Appeal to reconsider the case without the need for a retrial simply by discounting the effect of the expert evidence which the judge had wrongly taken into account.'

Admissible opinion, as well as being relevant to the issues, must be based upon relevant factual matters that are admitted or proved. Whilst such facts will often be established by other evidence, the expert may give factual evidence on matters where that expert has firsthand knowledge.

Furthermore, in giving an opinion, an expert is entitled to draw upon work done by others, including statistics, provided this is acknowledged in the report. Hence, when looking, broadly, at the extent to which evidence by an expert may be admissible, May J in *Larby v Thurgood*[22] observed:

---

20 [2001] PNLR 22 Ch D.
21 [2001] Lloyd's Rep PN 518.
22 [1993] ICR 66.

'The task of an expert witness in litigation is to express an opinion within his expert competence on matters susceptible to such an opinion relevant to the litigation. He expresses that opinion on facts agreed, proved or to be proved by evidence. In addition to expressing his opinion, he may himself give factual evidence of matters of which he has first hand knowledge. He cannot strictly give hearsay evidence of primary facts unless such evidence is admissible under the Civil Evidence Acts. Once the primary facts on which his opinion is based have been proved by admissible evidence, an expert is entitled to draw on the work of others as part of the process of arriving at his conclusion. The work of others can include statistical material lying within the field of the expert's expertise of the accuracy of which he has no personal knowledge, but which he has no reason to doubt: see *per* Kerr LJ in *R v Abadom*.[23] It is thus accepted and sensible practice for experts to give evidence of relevant published statistics.'

As a preliminary, of course, to identifying opinion evidence that may be admissible it is essential the witness concerned is 'qualified to give expert evidence', in other words a witness the court accepts as having appropriate and relevant expertise (see 7.3.2.3).

7.3.1.3   What is inadmissible opinion evidence?

Opinion evidence, even if given by a relevant expert, will still be excluded where that evidence attempts to usurp the function of the court, hence the inadmissibility of the third category of evidence identified by Oliver J in *Midland Bank Trust Co Ltd.*

Expert witnesses, like witnesses of fact, cannot give evidence reporting to determine those issues which are ultimately for determination by the court, such as liability or whether or not a particular head of damage is appropriate (or precisely what should be awarded under such a head).

Similarly, where the issue on which the expert proposes to give evidence which would effectively determine an ultimate issue that evidence should be excluded, for example evidence on the standard of the defendant's driving in *Liddell*.

Expert witnesses should also be precluded from giving evidence about the credibility of witnesses, as again this is a matter entirely for the court.

For example, in *Larby v Thurgood*[24] an application was made for the claim to be stayed unless the claimant agreed to be interviewed by an employment expert upon whom the defendant intended to rely. As May J observed the application could be summarised as 'a request to enable the employment consultant to assess the plaintiff as a person to be able to gauge such matters as his motivation, demeanour, appearance and experience so far as they are relevant to the job market'.

When refusing that application May J concluded issues of general suitability for employment and willingness and motivation to seek and undertake better paid employment were questions of fact to be determined by the court. That process of determination would not be assisted by expert opinion because the outcome would depend on an assessment of the credibility and perhaps truthfulness of the claimant.

---

[23]   [1983] 1 WLR 126.
[24]   [1993] ICR 66.

May J also concluded that the proposed evidence was in 'stark contrast' with the evidence of a medical expert who might describe, following examination, the claimant had a particular kind of fracture which, in the opinion of that expert, was likely to prevent the claimant pursuing particular activities.

Nevertheless, the same difficulty can sometimes arise with the evidence of an expert medical witness, although the court may be willing to accept evidence tending to go to credit where that is based on objective clinical findings. Accordingly, on the basis this reflects the application of expert knowledge to a collection of observations properly interpreted on the basis of that knowledge, a medical expert may be permitted to give evidence that there is 'no exaggeration' or, conversely, that there are 'inappropriate signs'. It must, however, always be for the court, ultimately, to determine issues such as the genuineness of the claimant along with the nature and extent of the injuries suffered. The determination of those issues may sometimes depend as much on the factual evidence as the expert evidence (see **7.14**).

If an expert gives opinion, which the court would otherwise be prepared to accept as evidence, suggesting conduct that would amount to fraud on the part of the claimant that must, of course, be part of the defendant's pleaded case. Consequently, the court should restrict expert evidence if that goes outside the issues as defined by the Statements of Case although the defendant may, in appropriate circumstances, be given the option of amending the defence to include the full scope of the expert evidence (see **7.15.3**).

More generally, opinion evidence should be excluded unless based on admissible facts, namely facts which are either admitted or ultimately proved (though experts can give a conditional opinion which will depend upon findings of fact to be made by the court).

When permission has been given to rely on expert evidence but it is contended that part of such evidence may be inadmissible the courts appear, generally, to consider admissibility is best left as an issue for the trial judge, rather than striking out any part of the evidence at the stage of case management.

7.3.2   Reliance: the Protocol and the CPR

Even where expert evidence is potentially admissible the terms of the Civil Evidence Act 1972 make such admissibility, and hence whether the evidence can be relied on, subject to rules of the court.

Those rules of the court are now found in the CPR which qualify the general right to rely on admissible expert evidence by imposing a further hurdle which involves exercise of the court's discretion in the grant of permission to rely on such evidence.

Consequently, whenever it is proposed to use the report of an expert as evidence it will be necessary to obtain permission from the court.

In deciding whether to give permission the court will, essentially, need to consider whether the expert evidence is 'reasonably required to resolve the proceedings', in accordance with CPR 35.1, in the general context of the need to deal with the particular case justly, under CPR 1.1.

Hence, in *ES v Chesterfield & North Derbyshire Royal Hospital NHS Trust*[25] Holman J observed:

> 'Masters and district judges have a heavy responsibility under the Civil Procedure Rules to control the type and number of experts in all cases, and must always be vigilant of their duty under Rule 35.1 to restrict expert evidence to that which is reasonably required to resolve the proceedings. But the approach cannot be mechanistic and must remain case specific, both by the terms of Rule 35.1 itself (which refers to "the proceedings") and by the overriding objective in Rule 1.'

Similarly, in *Field v Leeds City Council*[26] May LJ held:

> 'A judge managing the case under the Civil Procedure Rules has to be enabled to find out from the parties what the real issues in the case are. The parties have an explicit obligation under CPR Part 1(3) to help the court to further the overriding objective. This requires cooperation, not confrontation. Under the old procedure the parties would habitually have asked for blanket permission to call expert evidence under RSC Rule 36 or its county court equivalent, without properly having identified what issues really needed expert evidence. This all too often resulted in over numerous reports ... The CPR and its overriding objective aim to reduce or eliminate this disproportion.'

Consequently, within the general framework of the CPR, the court is likely to adopt a case sensitive approach, depending upon all the circumstances of the individual case, when deciding whether expert evidence, potentially admissible under the general law, should be the subject of an order giving a party permission to rely on that evidence.

Both the Protocol and the CPR have important provisions relating to the exercise, by the court, of the discretion to give permission for expert evidence to be relied on.

7.3.2.1 The Protocol

The Protocol seeks to create a framework for any proceedings that may follow in relation to expert evidence by helping to ensure that evidence is obtained from mutually acceptable experts, so reducing the risk of the need to duplicate reports.

Furthermore, the terms of the Protocol are, as CPR 3.1(4) confirms, of relevance to the exercise of the court's case management powers, which include the grant of permission to rely on expert evidence.

Paragraph 3.15 of the Protocol provides that a party, before instructing an expert, should give the other party a list of the name of one or more experts in the relevant speciality. If the other party does not object to an expert nominated then, under paragraph 3.19, that party will not be entitled to rely on corresponding expert evidence unless the first party agrees, the court so directs or the first party's report has been amended and the first party is not prepared to disclose the original report.

Consequently, whilst adopting the process of joint selection will not, of itself, make any expert evidence obtained admissible it will certainly not harm any argument that permission to rely on such evidence ought to be given. Indeed, in *Edwards-Tubb v J D*

---

[25] [2003] EWCA Civ 1284.
[26] CA (Lord Woolf MR, Waller LJ, May LJ) 8/12/99.

Weatherspoon plc[27] the Court of Appeal recognised the value, and potential assistance to the court, of any expert evidence obtained under the Protocol. Hughes LJ observed:

> 'An expert who has prepared a report for court is different from another witness. The expert's prime duty is unequivocally to the court.
>
> His report should say exactly the same whoever instructed him. Whatever the reason for subsequent disenchantment with expert A may be, once a party has embarked on the pre-action protocol procedure of co-operation in the selection of experts, there seems to me no justification for not disclosing a report obtained from an expert who has been put forward by that party as suitable for the case, has been accepted by the other party as suitable, and has reported. Thus although the instruction of a medical expert is a matter almost of course in most personal injury cases, it is appropriate for the court to exercise the control afforded by CPR 35.4 in order to maximise the information available to the court and to discourage expert shopping.'

Hence, it could be said any evidence obtained under the Protocol is likely to 'maximise the information available to the court' and has a value. The corresponding risk, as the judgment of Hughes LJ illustrates, is that once the selection of experts under the Protocol has been adopted the instructing party may have to voluntarily disclose any report obtained from a jointly selected expert, as a condition of getting permission to rely on an alternative expert, even if it is not proposed to rely on such evidence. Consequently, the claimant must always weigh up this potential disadvantage against the clear advantages of following the Protocol in selecting experts.

Whether or not the Protocol is followed it will be the CPR which governs, ultimately, the grant of permission by the court to rely on expert evidence.

7.3.2.2 The CPR

The CPR contain a number of specific provisions which have particular relevance to the granting, or refusal, of permission to rely on expert evidence:

- CPR 1.1: which will, as ever, be relevant and in the context of expert evidence is likely to require that the court try and assess what evidence ought to be permitted to deal with the case justly.
- CPR 1.3: which imposes a duty on the parties to help the court further the overriding objective.
- CPR 3.1(4): which provides that where the court gives directions it will take into account whether or not a party has complied with any relevant pre-action protocol and the Practice Direction – Pre-action Conduct.
- Paragraph 4.3 of the Practice Direction to Part 16: which requires the claimant, when relying on the evidence of a medical practitioner, to attach or serve with the Particulars of Claim a report from a medical practitioner about the personal injuries alleged in the claim.
- Paragraph 12.1 of the Practice Direction to Part 16: which requires the defendant, where the claimant has served a medical report with the Particulars of Claim, to:
  - state in the defence whether the report is agreed, disputed or neither agreed nor disputed (where the defendant has no knowledge of the matters contained in the report); and

---

27   [2011] EWCA Civ 136.

-     to attach to the defence any medical report obtained by the defendant on which it is intended to rely.

- CPR 35.1: which provides that expert evidence shall be restricted by the court to that which is reasonably required to resolve the proceedings.

- CPR 35.3: which provides that the overriding duty of an expert is to help the court on matters within his expertise, reflecting the need for experts not to be partisan.

- CPR 35.4: which prevents any party calling an expert, or putting in evidence an expert's report, without the court's permission.

- CPR 35.4(3A): which provides that where a claim has been allocated to the fast track, if permission is given for expert evidence, it will normally be given for evidence from only one expert on a particular issue.

- CPR 35.7: which allows the court to direct, when more than one party wishes to submit expert evidence on a particular issue, that evidence be given by a single joint expert (defined in 35.2(2) as an expert instructed to prepare a report for the court on behalf of two or more of the parties (including the claimant) to the proceedings).

The Practice Direction to Part 35 is also of importance, including as it does the Expert Protocol.

Whilst any decision on expert evidence will be case-specific some broad guidance, on the approach to case management of expert evidence, can be drawn from the terms of those rules which have particular relevance to this topic, specifically the requirement, in CPR 35.1, to restrict expert evidence but seen in the context of the overriding objective, as defined by CPR 1.1.

7.3.2.3   What is 'reasonably required' (Part 35)?

What is 'required' goes perhaps no further than confirming the evidence must be admissible, certainly inadmissible opinion would not be required to resolve the proceedings.

In *Liddell v Middleton*[28] the Court of Appeal, anticipating the implementation of the Civil Procedure Rules, was critical of the extent to which experts were then being used. Stuart-Smith LJ explained that:

> 'An expert is only qualified to give expert evidence on a relevant matter, if his knowledge and expertise relate to a matter which is outside the knowledge and experience of a layman.'

Stuart-Smith LJ went on to observe 'we do not have trial by expert' but 'trial by judge'.

Another way of approaching what will be 'reasonably required' is for the court, when deciding whether to give permission, to ask whether the evidence on which it is proposed to rely will assist the trial judge.

---

[28]   (1995).

Evans-Lombe J in *Barings plc (In Liquidation) v Coopers & Lybrand (No 2)*[29] and Patten J in *Clarke v Marlborough Fine Art (London) Ltd*[30] both approved the words of King CJ in the Australian case of *R v Bonython*[31] that:

> 'Before admitting the opinion of a witness into evidence as expert testimony, the Judge must consider and decide two questions. The first is whether the subject matter of the opinion falls within the class of subjects upon which expert testimony is permissible. This first question may be divided into two parts: (a) whether the subject matter of the opinion is such that a person without instruction or experience in the area of knowledge or human experience would be able to form a sound judgement on the matter without the assistance of witnesses possessing special knowledge or experience in the area, and (b) whether the subject matter of the opinion forms part of a body of knowledge or experience which is sufficiently organised or recognised to be accepted as a reliable body of knowledge or experience, a special acquaintance with which of the witness would render his opinion of assistance to the Court. The second question is whether the witness has acquired by study or experience sufficient knowledge of the subject to render his opinion of value in resolving the issue before the Court.'

Hence, in *Clarke v Marlborough Fine Art (London) Ltd*[32] when considering the first part of that first question Patten J framed the issue for the court in the following terms:

> 'I ... ask myself ... whether the evidence contained in (the expert's) report is likely to provide me with material assistance in determining the issues of liability in this action.'

Similarly, in *Hindmarch v Hasford*[33] HHJ Moir asked whether 'the trial judge would be assisted by the admission of the report'.

In both *Clarke* and *Hindmarch* the answer to this question resulted in the evidence being excluded. However, expert evidence was admitted, on the basis of this test, in *Bortniczak v Fresh-Pak Chilled Foods Ltd*[34] when HHJ Robinson held that, having read the report of the expert, the evidence was 'very definitely capable of assisting the judge'.

Similarly, when dealing with the procedural issue of whether to allow expert evidence in the somewhat unusual fields of phonetics and also field of vision/trajectory analysis, in *Mitchell v News Group Newspapers Ltd*,[35] Warby J concluded:

> 'Even if the evidence falls short of proving impossibility there is a real prospect it will assist in resolving the probabilities. It appears to be evidence that is potentially of value in resolving this important issue. It is reasonably required ...'

In the event, at trial, Mitting J did not find this expert evidence of assistance, but that only confirms a judge dealing with procedure should not pre-empt the approach to evidence which the trial judge may take.

Hence, expert evidence will not be 'reasonably required' if that evidence is unlikely to assist the court or where the expert would effectively be taking over the function of the

---

29 [2001] PNLR 22 Ch D.
30 [2002] EWHC 11 (Ch).
31 [1984] SASR 45.
32 [2002] EWHC 11 (Ch).
33 (Unreported) 8 April 2005, Newcastle County Court.
34 (Unreported) 8 July 2011, Sheffield County Court.
35 [2014] EWHC 3590 (QB).

judge and seeking to determine issues which the court alone must decide. That will be so where, for example the issue is one of law or when the court can reach a fully informed decision without hearing such evidence: see *Barings plc (In Liquidation) v Coopers & Lybrand (No 2)*.[36]

A careful analysis of whether or not evidence of an expert would be reasonably required was undertaken by Andrew Smith J in *Blair-Ford v CRS Adventures Ltd*.[37] The claimant was injured when participating in a 'welly wanging' event, which involved throwing a wellington boot as far as he could. Unfortunately, the claimant overbalanced, fell and suffered very serious injury. The claimant was refused permission to rely on the expert evidence of a biomechanical expert. The judge concluded the evidence was not reasonably required by considering each of the propositions it was contended the evidence would help to deal with in turn.

- The proposition that the force generated by propelling the boot backwards would cause the participant to be propelled forward was a statement of the obvious and not disputed by the defendant.

- The proposition the force might mean the participants could not instinctively prevent a somersault would also seem to be established simply by the fact of the injury having occurred as it did.

- The proposition that this risk would not be obvious to the participant did not appear to be within the realm of expertise of a biomechanical expert.

The claimant did, subsequently, successfully resist an application by the defendant to exclude the expert as a witness of fact: *Blair-Ford v CRS Adventures Ltd*.[38]

The addition of the adverb 'reasonably' suggests mere admissibility will not suffice and that the court, whilst seeking to restrict expert evidence, must do so in a way that allows the case to be dealt with justly, in accordance with the overriding objective.

7.3.2.4   What is just (CPR 1.1)?

Whether or not expert evidence is 'reasonably required' is likely to depend upon the particular factual background and issues to be decided by the court in any particular case. That decision will inevitably involve application of the factors identified in CPR 1.1 as relevant to achieving the overriding objective, in the context of the need for expert evidence, to the particular case.

The matrix of relevant matters, when deciding what will be most just, may involve any steps taken under the Protocol, the nature of the issues defined by the Statements of Case and the evidence available respectively to the parties, as well as where the burden of proof on any particular issue lies.

The same broad considerations will apply whether a single party is seeking permission to rely on expert evidence, the parties are seeking mutual permission or a party is, following the grant of earlier permission, seeking to duplicate evidence in a particular area of expertise or even to change experts.

---

[36] [2001] PNLR 22 Ch D.
[37] Unreported, 12 October 2011, QBD.
[38] [2012] EWHC 1886 (QB).

The factors identified in Part 1 may not always point in the same direction, so far as giving permission to rely on expert evidence is concerned, requiring the court to identify the most relevant factors in the particular case and where these point in terms of overall justice.

The courts have, in different cases, emphasised the various factors found in CPR 1.1, so it may be helpful to consider each of these in turn before looking at the broader issue of overall justice.

7.3.2.4.1 Ensuring that the parties are on an equal footing

Important considerations, in the factor of equality, may be where the burden of proof rests and the availability of other relevant evidence, to each party, which the party on whom the burden of proof rests is able to rely upon or has to deal with.

A particular difficulty for the claimant, which the court may wish to redress mindful of this aspect of the overriding objective, is when the defendant has available factual evidence of a kind that might be regarded as 'quasi-expert' in nature on an important issue the claimant has to prove.

This problem was illustrated by *ES v Chesterfield and North Derbyshire Royal Hospital NHS Trust*[39] where, even though the claimant already had permission to rely on an expert in the particular field, the need for the parties to be on an equal footing was seen as a crucial factor when considering whether permission for a second expert, in the same field, should be granted. That was because, in addition to an expert on whose evidence the defendant had been given permission to rely, the defendant intended to call, as witnesses of fact, two treating clinicians both of whom were consultants, one witness having been the consultant in charge of the treatment whilst the other had been a junior doctor but since promoted to a consultant post.

In these circumstances, giving judgment in the Court of Appeal, Brooke LJ noted:

> 'Anybody watching the trial would be bound to be impressed by the fact that there was only one consultant obstetrician giving evidence for the claimant, while there would be three giving evidence for the defendant hospital trust, and those three would cover a much wider spectrum of personal experience than the single expert permitted to the claimant. It is not as if the medical witness of fact for the defendants is a junior hospital doctor.'

Moreover, although witnesses of fact, without permission to give expert evidence, the court may be willing to allow such a witness, with a degree of expertise, to give what, usually, might be regarded as opinion on the basis that while such evidence may lack the objectivity of an independent expert that goes to cogency rather than admissibility: *DN v Greenwich London Borough*;[40] *ES v Chesterfield and North Derbyshire Royal Hospital NHS Trust.*[41]

Accordingly, in *ES* Brooke LJ went on to observe that, in this context, what expert evidence was 'reasonably required' was inevitably conditioned by the overriding objective when he concluded:

---

[39] [2003] EWCA Civ 1284.
[40] [2004] EWCA Civ 1659.
[41] [2003] EWCA Civ 1284.

'The governing rule, therefore, limits expert evidence to that which is reasonably required to resolve the proceedings in issue. What is reasonable in any particular context will inevitably be fact sensitive. It would be wrong to approach this question with the predetermined belief that to instruct more than one expert in the same discipline will always be excessive. In addition to considering the facts, the court will need to remind itself in any contentious case of the principles underlying the overriding objective in CPR 1.1. In the present context the most important of the considerations set out in CPR 1.1.(2) appear to be:

(a)   ensuring that the parties are on an equal footing;
(c)   dealing with the case in ways which are proportionate:
     (i)   to the amount of money involved;
     (ii)   to the importance of the case;
     (iii)   to the complexity of the issues;
     (iv)   to the financial position of each party.

While the other considerations listed in CPR 1.1(2) are always important, in a case like the present they are likely to be subordinated to the particular items I have listed.'

However, Brooke LJ went on to sound a note of caution when observing:

'Nothing in this judgment must be taken to give any sort of green light to the calling of two experts in a single discipline in any case which does not have exceptional features. On this appeal the presence of three consultants on the defendants' side constitutes such an exceptional feature.'

No doubt mindful of these comments, when faced with a similar application by the claimant to rely on more than one expert in the relevant field, Holroyde J, in *Beaumont v Ministry of Defence*,[42] held:

'My conclusion is that the circumstances of this case are not exceptional when compared with other actions of the same general nature. I, of course, fully understand the concern that if the claimant were to lose at trial there would, or might be an appearance of injustice, but the answer to that concern, in my judgment, is that there could only be an appearance of injustice if it were thought that weight of numbers is the decisive factor when the court is evaluating expert evidence. It is not the decisive factor. A trial judge will assess the evidence of the independent expert on each side and he or she will assess the evidence of Mr Forbes in the knowledge both that Mr Forbes was the treating doctor and that Mr Forbes is a man experienced in giving evidence in cases of this general kind.'

However, in *Heyward v Plymouth Hospital NHS Trust*,[43] although on the facts not allowing the claimant to call the proposed expert, the Court of Appeal recognised that where the factual witnesses of one party had some degree of expertise this might make it necessary for the other to be given permission to rely on expert evidence in reply, on the basis that scenario raised similar issues to those in *ES*.

Giving judgment Lord Phillips outlined the context:

'Drawing an analogy with that case, the anxiety as I understand it of those representing Mr Heyward is that the Trust may call as a witness of fact a witness in position to give expert evidence such as that which could be given by an occupational psychologist, and that that witness will state that he could not reasonably have foreseen or been expected to foresee that the working conditions to which Mr Heyward was subjected would result in his suffering psychiatric injury. An importance difference between Chesterfield and this case is that in Chesterfield the court knew what evidence of fact the defendants were going to adduce; we

---

[42]   [2009] EWHC 1258 (QB).
[43]   [2005] EWCA Civ 939.

do not. This is because the directions as to the exchange of evidence of fact were not complied with and a stay was subsequently ordered...'

Lord Phillips then explained the potential need for expert evidence when observing:

'There is a possibility, it seems to me – a remote possibility – that the Trust will rely on quasi-expert evidence of a type that needs to be rebutted by an occupational psychologist or physician. Should that happen, it will be, and always would have been, open to Mr Heyward to seek permission to call that additional evidence.'

Accordingly, where it is contended expert evidence is required to deal with factual evidence available to another party it is essential that allocation questionnaires are properly completed, so the court has an advance view on the likely nature of the factual evidence and hence the need for expert evidence at all on the relevant issue.

Usually, but not always, it will be the claimant who faces this type of difficulty, because of the burden of proof and also as the defendant is more likely to have available this type of, essentially factual, evidence. Examples might include: reliance on a defendant's health and safety official or worker with similar experience in a claim resulting from an accident at work (evidence of the kind relied on by the defendant in *Gravatom Engineering Systems Ltd v Parr*[44]); reliance on a police officer, in a claim arising out of a road traffic accident; reliance on any witness who has specialist qualifications (as occurred in *ES* and, potentially, in *Heyward*). Similar issues may arise where evidence of the kind considered in *Hoyle v Rogers*[45] is relied on by one party but not agreed by the other.

Similarly, if one party has information not available to the other then, unless volunteered or made the subject of an order made under CPR 35.9 (see **7.2.4**), the objective of equality may militate towards allowing the other permission to rely on expert evidence, if that is the most appropriate way of redressing this inequality of knowledge.

Consequently, the factor of equality will be very relevant in deciding whether any expert evidence at all is required on a particular issue on in a particular discipline.

The consideration of equality will also be relevant where there is already a single expert on a particular issue who expresses a particular view but one of the parties can demonstrate there is likely to be a range of opinion which, without further expert evidence, will not be available to the court (see **7.9.2.3**).

7.3.2.4.2 Saving expense

The objective of saving expense may be a factor in deciding whether to allow expert evidence at all, on a particular issue or in a particular discipline, but may perhaps be more relevant when determining whether it is appropriate for expert evidence to be duplicated or changed, particularly at a late stage.

---

[44] [2007] EWCA Civ 967.
[45] [2014] EWCA Civ 257.

7.3.2.4.3   Dealing with the case in ways which are proportionate

Proportionality may be relevant both when considering whether to permit expert evidence as well as when assessing the need for further experts on the same issue or in the same field.

It is, however, essential to remember that what is 'proportionate' is defined, in CPR 1.1(2)(c) of the CPR, not just in terms of the value but also the importance of the case, the complexity of the issues and the financial position of each party. A claim of modest value may, nevertheless, have complexities due to the matters put in issue by the defendant and, moreover, be a case where the defendant is better resourced (which may well have an impact on evidence available to deal with those issues which the claimant will need to prove).

Obviously, if a claim is substantial, that may more readily justify the need for expert evidence, and the extent of that evidence. However, bearing in mind the definition of 'proportionate', dealing with the case justly must mean the court properly and fairly addressing the issues on the basis of all necessary evidence. Thus it would be wrong simply to assess the need for expert evidence on value, including the track to which the case is allocated, though this is clearly a factor in that analysis.

In *Bandegani v Norwich Union Fire Insurance Society Ltd*[46] the Court of Appeal dealt specifically with the question of proportionality when ruling out expert evidence. Crucially, however, that was in the context of a case which would now be referred to the small claims track and in which the issue, to which the expert evidence related, could be fairly dealt with by other evidence readily available to both parties.

When dealing with quantum the range of expert evidence required will inevitably be linked to the severity of the injuries, and hence the value of the claim, so what is proportionate can properly be looked at largely if not entirely in terms of the amount at stake. With liability, however, the need for expert evidence will be governed by the background to the claim and matters put in issue by the defendant so proportionality will be linked more to the nature of the issues than simply the value of the case.

Accordingly, whilst proportionality is clearly a relevant factor in determining whether expert evidence is 'reasonably required', that does not mean expert evidence, if justice requires this, should be excluded because the claim is of modest value. Neuberger J cogently explained why this is so in *Layland v Fairview New Homes plc*[47] where he observed:

> 'A claimant with a small claim is entitled to the same treatment, in terms of substantive and procedural justice, as a claimant with a large claim. That is not inconsistent with the concept of proportionality. Proportionality involves the court ensuring that, subject always to the fundamental and overriding requirement that every case is disposed of justly, the resources, in terms of costs effort and time, devoted to a case are appropriate to what is at stage in that case. Hence the number of expert witnesses or the expert of disclosure directed by the court may be influenced by, interalia, the amount at stake. However, at least in my firm view, proportionality cannot be invoked to deprive a party of a direction, without which there would be a real risk of there not being a fair trial, or of some other injustice being

---

[46]   Court of Appeal, 20 May 1999.
[47]   [2002] EWHC 1350 (Ch).

perpetrated. It is right to add that, in some cases, particularly whether justice or fairness require a balancing exercise, proportionality itself will be a relevant factor in deciding what justice and fairness require.'

It may not be disproportionate, in the interest of equality, to permit a second expert, even if the case is of modest value, where that is necessary to ensure the court is aware of a range of opinion. Hence in *Carlson v Townsend*,[48] where the claimant elected not to rely on the report of a jointly selected expert who had reported initially, Simon Brown LJ observed:

'The defendant for her part would almost certainly, if she wished, be permitted to call an expert of her choice. The court would, after all, know that one expert at least, (the first expert), had reported less favourably to the claimant's cause than (the second expert).'

The likely usefulness of the expert evidence to the trial judge will also be a factor, in the general context of the issues arising and value of the case, when considering proportionality. Hence, in *Hindmarch v Hasford*[49] when considering an application to rely on the evidence of an expert in a claim arising out of a road traffic accident, HHJ Moir refused permission largely because the expert had not examined either vehicle involved in the incident. He concluded that any assistance to the trial judge would be limited and perhaps importantly, having regard to the modest value of the claim, the costs of allowing the report to be adduced, and dealing with further evidence which would then be inevitable, would not be proportionate.

7.3.2.4.4 *Ensuring the case is dealt with expeditiously and fairly*

Dealing with the case expeditiously will often be closely related to the factor of saving expense and may tell against, in particular, duplication or changing of experts.

The need for fairness reflects, in particular, the factors already considered concerning the need to put the parties on an equal footing and to deal with the case in a way that is proportionate to its importance and complexity.

7.3.2.4.5 *Allotting an appropriate share of the court's resources*

The court's resources will, clearly, not have been allotted appropriately if unnecessary expert evidence is permitted, as that is likely to lead to procedural skirmishes and, ultimately, a trial which is longer than it needs to be.

Conversely, however, a proper exploration of the need for expert evidence, on the issues arising in the particular case before the court, must surely be a proper use of court resources at the key stage, for these purposes, of case management. That, as a number of cases have observed, requires a case sensitive, rather than a mechanistic approach to determine what expert evidence is reasonably required (see **7.3.2**).

If the issue of expert evidence is not explored thoroughly at the stage of case management, the risk of satellite litigation, and consequent depletion of greater court resources at later stages, will be increased.

---

[48]   [2001] EWCA Civ 511.
[49]   (Unreported) Newcastle County Court, 8 April 2005.

These considerations apply equally to the primary question of whether expert evidence is required at all on a particular issue, or in a particular discipline, and the secondary question, which may arise when such evidence is required, as to whether there should be a further expert on the same issue or in the same field.

7.3.2.4.6 Compliance with rules, practice directions and orders

With this amendment to the terms of the overriding objective from April 2013 the court might be expected to give greater weight, when considering an application for permission to rely on expert evidence, to compliance with any court orders already made as well as compliance with any relevant Pre-Action Protocol and the terms of the Practice Direction – Pre-Action Conduct given that these have important provisions about steps the parties should often take to use a single expert where possible.

7.3.2.4.7 Overall justice

No single factor specifically identified in CPR 1.1 will necessarily be determinative in any particular case. Indeed, the court perhaps ought, after giving the individual factors identified in CPR 1.1 appropriate weight, then form a view about whether the outcome, to which those factors point, will deliver overall justice in the circumstances of the particular case.

Consequently, whilst needing to be mindful of the individual elements which make up the overriding objective, the court may still wish to look at the overall justice of the order that appears appropriate, on the basis of those individual factors, to see if such an order would be just. Hence, in *Cosgrove v Pattison*,[50] Neuberger J concluded:

> 'Standing back and looking at the justice between the parties, I ask myself two questions, do not represent a decisive test but they may be of some help. First if the appellants are not entitled to call (the expert) and they lose the case, will they have an understandable sense of grievance judged objectively? To my mind they would – an understandable if not an overwhelming, feeling. Secondly, if the appellants are entitled to call (the expert) and won, would the respondents have an understandable sense of grievance, judged objectively? I think it is inevitable that they would have a sense of grievance, because that is in the nature of litigation. But I do not think that to most people it would be a particularly understandable sense of grievance. In all the circumstances, it seems to me that this is an appeal which should be allowed, but allowed only on terms.'

This approach, in the context of giving permission to rely on expert evidence, appears to be equally applicable to a variety of situations including whether to allow permission for expert evidence at all, in a particular specialism or on a specific issue, whether a party should be allowed to rely on a further expert in the same field (perhaps as a result of dissatisfaction with a joint expert) and even whether a party should be allowed to change an expert (in a situation where permission to do so is required).

Hence, application of this test has been followed, and effectively approved, subsequently: *Stallwood v David;*[51] *Singh v CS O'Shea & Co Ltd*[52] (see **7.9.4.3**).

---

[50]   Chancery Division, 27 November 2000.
[51]   [2006] EWHC 2600 (QB).
[52]   [2009] EWHC 1251 (QB).

7.3.2.5   Timing

Whether expert evidence is 'reasonably required' may depend on the timing of the request made to the court for permission.

By the stage of initial case management, when permission will usually be sought, the issues, and evidence available to deal with those issues, will usually have been clarified by the content of the Statements of Case and, ideally, the allocation questionnaires.

Occasionally, however, that may not be so, in which case timing of the request may be important.

For example, in *Heyward v Plymouth Hospital NHS Trust*[53] the court was not willing to grant the claimant permission to rely on expert evidence not least because it was, at that stage, unclear whether the defendant would indeed be relying on factual evidence that the proposed expert intended to deal with.

Similarly, in *Arden v Malcom*,[54] when dealing with an application for permission to rely on expert evidence from a statistician on life expectancy, the court held that it was appropriate, at least initially, for questions to be put to the existing experts and meanwhile permission to rely on further expert evidence was not necessary for justice to be done.

Where the court concludes the time is not right to rule, one way or the other, on whether expert evidence, in a particular expert field or on a specific issue, is reasonably required, that issue may be raised again at a later stage, which may then be the appropriate time for the court to make a definitive ruling.

However, even where the court rules against the admission of expert evidence, that may not decide the matter once and for all. For example, if a party later obtains a report, which suggests such evidence is reasonably required, that may be a material change of circumstance allowing the court to vary the earlier order refusing permission, notwithstanding the absence of any appeal against such an order (see 8.3.3).

7.4   USE OF EXPERTS IN PERSONAL INJURY CLAIMS

General principles relating to the admissibility of, and permission to rely upon, expert evidence must be applied by the courts on a case-by-case basis. Accordingly, any attempt to identify hard and fast rules about the type of and circumstances in which reliance on expert evidence will be permitted by the court, is fraught with difficulty.

Nevertheless, some practical assistance can be drawn about the use of experts from those cases which have considered either the need for expert evidence in the individual circumstances of that case or have attempted to draw more general conclusions about the need for expert evidence in personal injury claims.

---

53   [2005] EWCA Civ 939.
54   [2007] EWHC 404 (QB).

For these purposes it may be most helpful to consider the use of experts dealing with primary liability by reference to different types of personal injury claim, whilst reviewing the use of experts to deal with quantum on the basis of those specialisms often relied upon to help prove typical heads of claim.

It is important to remember the very different approach necessary, from the claimant's perspective, to the use of experts when dealing with contributory negligence, because on that issue the evidential burden of proof will be on the defendant.

7.4.1   Primary liability

Factual evidence may often suffice for the court to make all the findings necessary to decide any issues relating to liability.

The court may, however, benefit from expert evidence on liability. Much will depend on the type of claim, the nature of the issues and the extent to which any expert evidence will be likely to assist the court in resolving those issues.

Where the evidential burden is on the claimant it may be important, for the claim to succeed at all, that permission to rely on such evidence is obtained.

The approach of the court to expert evidence on liability may depend very much on the nature of the claim, as that may have a bearing on the type of issues that will arise on liability if this is disputed and the likelihood such evidence will be of assistance.

7.4.1.1   Road traffic

In proceedings arising out of a road traffic accident an expert, although this will be essentially factual rather than opinion evidence, may be able to assist the court in understanding precise details about the scene of the accident.

Additionally, an expert may be able to provide helpful opinion evidence about the interpretation of post-accident real evidence noted at the scene and hence the possible circumstances of that accident.

However, in *Liddell v Middleton*[55] the Court of Appeal held that expert evidence dealing with liability in claims arising out of a road traffic accident will be the exception rather than the rule. Specifically, Stuart-Smith LJ held:

> 'In such cases the function of the expert is to furnish the judge with the necessary scientific criteria and assistance based upon his special skill and experience not possessed by ordinary laymen to enable the judge to interpret the factual evidence of the marks on the road, the damage or whatever it may be. What he is not entitled to do is to say in effect "I have considered the statements and/or evidence of the eye-witnesses in this case and I conclude from there evidence that the defendant was going at a certain speed, or that he could have seen the plaintiff at a certain point". These are facts for the trial judge to find based on the evidence that he accepts and such inferences that he draws from the primary facts found. Still less is the expert entitled to say that in his opinion the defendant should have sounded his horn, seen the plaintiff before he did or taken avoiding action and that in taking some action

---

55   [1995] PIQR P36.

or failing to take some other action, a party was guilty of negligence. These are matters for the court, on which the expert's opinion is wholly irrelevant and therefore inadmissible.... We do not have trial by expert in this country; we have trial by Judge.'

Even so, there are a number of circumstances in which an expert may well be able to assist the court in dealing with liability where the claim arises out of a road traffic accident. These include the following:

- If there are no witnesses capable of describing what happened and the circumstances of the accident have to be reconstructed solely from real evidence recorded on the scene at the time.

- Where deductions have to be drawn as to the speed of a vehicle, or the relative positions of the parties in the moments leading up to the impact, from evidence such as the post-accident position of damage to those vehicles or marks on the road.

- To introduce statistical evidence relevant to liability where the matters dealt with in that evidence are not agreed, for example average walking speeds of pedestrians in running-down cases.

- When there is a dispute on factual matters, such as road measurements or lines of sight, where an expert can give evidence to assist the court on facts personally perceived by that expert following a site inspection.

- If the claimant remembers nothing of, or cannot account for, the accident but contends it may have occurred in a way different to that alleged on the basis of available factual evidence (provided the interpretation of that evidence is susceptible to expert analysis in a way that would assist the court, and hence be admissible and required, not least to ensure equality between the parties).

Beyond receiving evidence on those matters there are real dangers for the court becoming too heavily dependant upon an opinion involving reconstruction, given that the accuracy of such an opinion may depend entirely upon the accident having occurred in a very precise way. In such circumstances the risk is that the expert will be permitted to decide issues which are really for the court to determine.

It is with this risk in mind that the courts have consistently recognised the dangers, with reconstruction of road traffic accidents, in placing too heavy a reliance even on admissible opinion. Wall J explained why in *Miller v C & G Coach Services Ltd*[56] when he observed:

> '...the expert evidence, competent as it was, could only provide parameters within which the case fell to be decided on its facts by the judge. In such circumstances, there is a tendency to treat such evidence as certain and determinative, whereas in reality, as both the judge and the experts themselves agreed, it provided at best a series of guidelines. It must be remembered that the whole incident, as I have already stated and which has been minutely examined over two days in the court below, and for a day in this court, was over in seconds.
>
> Accordingly, in my judgment, where events clearly happened so very quickly, and where measurements were not taken at the time, a metre here, and a second or even half a second there can make a substantial difference to outcome. The difficulty is always that the scientific evidence in a case such as this had to deal with precise mathematical calculations, even where

---

[56]   [2003] EWCA Civ 442.

variables are built in, whereas the judge's findings of fact are eye-witness dependent and imprecise, particularly in a case where, as here, there is no definitive contemporaneous evidence against which to judge it.'

The dividing line, often found in cases of this kind, between appropriate and inappropriate expert evidence was identified by Coulson J in *Stewart v Glaze*[57] where he said:

> 'Cases such as the present action often feature accident reconstruction experts. There is no doubt that their expertise can sometimes be of considerable assistance to the court. In the present case (both experts) provided some very helpful evidence on a variety of matters. But in the past, the courts have sometimes had cause to comment upon the accident reconstruction evidence exceeding its proper parameters, when the experts themselves have engaged in what was little more than an advocacy exercise with little or no expertise involved.'

The judge, later in his judgment, continued:

> 'In my judgment, it is the primary factual evidence which is of the greatest importance in a case of this kind. The expert evidence comprises a useful way in which that factual evidence, and the inferences to be drawn from it, can be tested. It is, however, very important to ensure that the expert evidence is not elevated into a fixed framework or formula, against which the defendant's actions are then to be rigidly judged with a mathematical precision.'

Because of the need to focus on introducing admissible evidence which will assist the court, rather than opinion which may risk usurping the court's function, case management directions, in such cases, may need to be very specific about the matters to be dealt with by the relevant experts.

In *Richardson v Butler*,[58] for example, the judgment at trial revealed how the parameters for expert evidence were set by the district judge at the case management stage. The directions provided that expert evidence on liability was limited to the following issues:

- evidence of the speed at which children run;
- evidence of driver reaction times;
- evidence of driver braking and stopping distances and times;
- evidence of the visibility of pedestrians in dipped headlights;
- a physical survey and photographs of the scene;
- evidence of the speed of the vehicle at impact as calculated from the pedestrian throw distance; and
- evidence to assist the Judge as to whether there was physical evidence which might indicate the claimant's direction of travel at impact.

These issues are typical of those which, while largely matters of factual evidence, are, perhaps, best put before the court by a witness with some understanding of what is likely to be most relevant coupled with knowledge of relevant statistics. Unless such statistics, along with relevant details of the locus, are agreed, by the stage of case management, that evidence may need to be introduced in this way.

---

[57]   [2009] EWHC 704 (QB).
[58]   [2010] EWHC 214 (QB).

The evidence given by experts in road traffic cases should, therefore, be a combination of factual evidence, based on an inspection of the locus and background research, coupled with appropriate opinion evidence, of the kind which keeps clear of issues which are solely for the court to decide with that opinion being given just to assist the court in the determination of those issues.

Defendants will often argue expert evidence on liability will not be required in a claim arising out of a road traffic accident. However, there is a category of road traffic accident where the defendant will sometimes contend expert evidence, even in a claim of modest value, is reasonably required; the so-called 'low velocity impact' claims.

In a low velocity case it is not unusual for the defendant to contend expert evidence will demonstrate no injury at all could have been sustained given the nature of the accident. Consequently, causation of any injury is denied, meaning the evidence relates to the issue of liability.

While the court will usually make a ruling on the existence, nature and extent of any injury by assessing the factual and expert medical evidence, the case management directions will, from time to time, allow expert evidence from, for example, an engineer on this issue of causation.

In *Casey v Cartwright*[59] the Court of Appeal gave guidance on the circumstances in which it would be appropriate for the court to allow permission to rely on expert evidence dealing with liability, more specifically causation, in low velocity impact cases. Whilst concluding it was not possible or desirable to produce an exhaustive list of the circumstances where such evidence would be appropriate, the court sought to restrict such cases to those where the defendant takes certain steps, to make clear such evidence is likely to be required from the outset.

Dyson LJ, giving the judgment of the court, identified the hurdles which a defendant should have to meet before the court will give permission to rely on such evidence in these cases.

> 'First, the timing of notification by the defendant that he intends to raise the causation issue. Unless the defendant notifies the claimant of his intention to raise the issue within three months of receipt of the letter of claim, permission to rely on expert evidence should usually be denied to the defendant. It is important that the issue be raised at an early stage so as to avoid causing delay to the prosecution of the proceedings. The period of three months is consistent with para 2.11 of the Pre-Action Protocol for Personal Injury Claims which provides that a defendant be given three months to investigate and respond to a claim before proceedings are issued.'

> 'Secondly, if there is a factual dispute, the resolution of which one way or the other is likely to resolve the causation issue, that is a factor which militates against the granting of permission to rely on expert evidence on the causation issue. In such a case, expert evidence is likely to serve little or no purpose.'

> 'Thirdly, there may be cases where the injury alleged and the damages claimed are so small and the nature of the expert evidence that the defendant wishes to adduce so extensive and complex that considerations of proportionality demand that permission to rely on the

---

[59] [2006] EWCA Civ 1280.

evidence should be refused. This must be left to the good sense of the judge. It does not detract from the general guidance given at para 32 above.'

Additionally, the Court of Appeal made the observation that, whilst single joint experts have an invaluable role to play in litigation, judges should be slow to direct expert evidence on causation in this type of claim be given by a single joint expert, because that causation issue was inevitably 'controversial'.

Whilst the type of expert evidence most frequently used, when permitted, in road traffic claims will be given by a forensic engineer, with relevant expertise, the issues in the case may sometimes require input from other types of expert, for example if there is an issue about weather conditions a meteorologist may be required. In *Ide v ATB Sales Ltd*,[60] a claim that might loosely be described as a road traffic accident, expert evidence from metallurgists was given to the court (see **7.4.1.5** below).

7.4.1.2 Employers' liability

It is notable that in *Liddell*, whilst expressing reservations about the use of experts where the case involved a road traffic accident, the court accepted that 'in industrial accidents an expert may well be needed to explain complicated machinery or to give evidence of practice and safety procedure'.

The word 'complicated' is perhaps important. The workings of some machinery may be straightforward and readily understandable by the court, at least if photographs, and perhaps a sketch or diagram, are available. Where, however, the working of a machine, or operation of a process, is less obvious or it is necessary to reconstruct how, using the equipment or process, the accident occurred, it is likely that the court will more readily regard expert evidence as being 'reasonably required'.

Accordingly, where the claim is based on employers' liability, or more generally any regulations relating to health and safety in the workplace, the court may be ready to conclude that expert evidence will assist the trial judge in resolving issues on, at least, primary, liability.

For example, when allowing an appeal against the refusal by a district judge to permit reliance on expert evidence describing the workings of a machine involved in the claimant's accident in *Bortniczak v Fresh-Pak Chilled Foods Ltd*[61] HHJ Robinson concluded there was no doubt the trial judge would be assisted by expert evidence 'going to the issues of whether it was possible to have so devised guarding on this machine, and whether the accident could have been avoided...'.

It is, however, once again important to distinguish between those cases where such evidence is necessary for the court to interpret the evidence, whether factual or real, and those where the court is well able to make all necessary findings without such assistance.

When expert opinion is required to help the court that evidence will not be confined to a description of the equipment or processes involved, helpful though that may be, but is likely to include opinion evidence in the sense of explaining technical points on the

---

[60] [2007] EWHC 1667 (QB).
[61] (Unreported) Sheffield County Court, 8 July 2011.

machinery or processes, and hence the context of the accident, as well as identifying measures that could have been taken to prevent an injury of the kind that has occurred.

Consequently, such evidence may only be true opinion in part as much of that evidence may be essentially factual in nature, based on observations of the expert. Even when an expert is giving evidence of fact that may still be the best way of introducing such evidence in a way that will assist the court in making findings necessary to determine liability.

None of this means that expert evidence will always be of assistance to the court in an employers' liability claim. For example, in *Hawkes v London Borough of Southwark*[62] the court concluded expert evidence was not required to determine, in a case brought under the Manual Handling Operations Regulations 1992, whether it was a one-man or two-man job to carry doors up a flight of stairs. That was because there was nothing of real expertise in assessing if that task required two men. Henry LJ explained:

'Before us, but not heralded either by respondent's notice nor the skeleton, the point was taken that this was not a case for expert evidence, and, on the authority of *Liddell v Middleton*[63] such evidence was irrelevant and inadmissible.

The complaint is that the "issue" as to which (the expert) was called to give expert evidence (whether there was a risk of injury in this task, and whether it was a one-man job or a two-man job) was a pure question of fact within the knowledge and experience of the lay-man.

I agree that it is hard to justify the employment of experts in this case. Looking at (the expert's) report, he gives the measurement and weight of the doors, and the measurement of the half-landing where the 180 degree turn had to be made. He advised the court that there was "little margin for error". He additionally said:

"It would not have taken a particularly detailed risk assessment of the task ... to reveal that it necessitated manually handling the doors up the winding flight of stairs.

Thereafter, even a simple assessment performed in accordance with Regulation 4 of the Manual Handling Operations Regulations, 1992 should have been sufficient to identify that doors of the material size and weight would require two people to carry them up the stairs in reasonably safety. Therefore, if the job had been adequately planned beforehand, Mr Hawkes should have been provided with assistance, at least for the duration of carrying all the doors from the van to their destinations.

It is therefore our opinion that Mr Hawkes' accident occurred as a result of a causal breach of Regulation 4(1) of the Manual Handling Operations Regulations, 1992 by his employer."

There is nothing of real expertise there. Though (the expert) had examined the task in question, he had not (understandably in my view) attempted himself to perform the task. I do not find this surprising, as if his evidence did not qualify as expert evidence before, having attempted the task once or twice would be unlikely to change that view of it.

In today's climate, I am not surprised that both sides came to the court with expert evidence. The "better safe than sorry" approach no doubt dictated this decision. It is to be hoped that

---

62 (Unreported) Court of Appeal, 20 February 1998.
63 [1995] PIQR P36.

the Access to Justice reforms will put this aspect of case management squarely in the hands of the judges to ensure that experts are only engaged or called when necessary.'

In other circumstances the courts have accepted the need for expert evidence to properly inform the findings which need to be made when dealing with a workplace injury.

Consequently, the initial task on behalf of the claimant, when deciding whether expert evidence on liability needs to be relied on in a claim where there is a dispute about breaches of workplace health and safety duties, is to assess exactly what is in issue, where the burden of proof rests and then whether expert opinion is likely to assist the court in dealing with those matters the claimant needs to prove.

Where, for example, the claimant seeks to establish liability by alleging the breach of a regulation which requires the defendant to avoid a 'danger', such as reg 11 of the Provision and Use of Work Equipment Regulations 1998, the court may expect the claimant to prove, if this is not admitted, that danger was reasonably foreseeable to the defendant. This is an issue which may require expert evidence for reasons explained by Smith LJ in *Allison v London Underground*[64] when she observed:

> '(Section 14 Factories Act 1961) was said to impose strict liability. However, it was not absolute in the sense that liability automatically followed if a worker was injured by a part of a machine which, by reason of the fact that an injury had occurred, could now be seen to have been dangerous. Liability only arose if the part was dangerous and whether it was dangerous depended on whether it was reasonably foreseeable that a person might be injured by it. What was reasonably foreseeable was not limited to what the employer actually foresaw; still less was it limited to what he had learned from past experience. At the trial of an action, the question of whether a part of a machine was dangerous was almost always a matter for expert evidence. If the judge was satisfied by expert evidence that the part of the machine was dangerous, then the employer ought to have known of it and it did not avail him to show that he had not realised that it was dangerous and had not thought it necessary (before the accident) to consult an expert on the subject. Once the claimant had shown that the part in question was dangerous, liability was strict in that it was no defence for the employer to show that it was not practicable for him to fence it.'

Until the ruling of the Supreme Court in *Baker v Quantum Clothing Group Ltd*[65] if the claimant relied on a regulation requiring a 'safe' outcome the fact the claimant was injured, whether or not this was reasonably foreseeable, was likely to suffice in establishing the worker had not been safe and hence was a breach of the relevant regulation by the defendant. In *Baker* the court held that, in the type of regulation relied on, the term 'safe' imported the concept of reasonable foreseeability. Accordingly, if there is an issue, where the claimant relies on a regulation requiring safety, about the reasonable foreseeability of injury then, applying the observations of Smith LJ in *Allison*, expert evidence may be necessary.

If, and this illustrates how much will depend on precisely what matters are in issue and where the evidential burden of proof lies, the defendant admits 'danger' the fact the claimant has been injured by that danger may relieve the claimant of the obligation to prove the precise mechanics of the accident, for which expert evidence might otherwise be necessary.

---

[64]   [2008] EWCA Civ 71.
[65]   [2011] UKSC 17.

Accordingly, in *McGowan v W & J R Watson Ltd*[66] Lord Macphail, on a claim based upon alleged breach of reg 11 of the Provision and Use of Work Equipment Regulations, rejected the defenders' argument it was for the pursuer to call expert evidence showing precisely how the accident occurred and that, without such evidence, a claim under reg 11 could not be established. That was because the judge decided the issue of liability on the straightforward basis that reg 11 identified an objective to be achieved and which had not been achieved. That decision was not overturned on appeal (*McGowan v W & J R Watson Ltd*[67]).

Another example of a statutory duty where the claimant may well not need expert evidence, because of the forensic approach taken to compliance with that duty, is where the relevant duty is to 'maintain'. In this context that word has been interpreted to mean a state of affairs rather than maintenance in the sense of servicing. Hence, when interpreting a statutory duty to maintain, Lord Morton of Henryton observed in *Galashiels Gas Co Ltd v Millar*[68] that:

> 'It ... imposes a heavy burden upon employers, but the object of this group of sections is to protect the workman. I think the sub-section must have been so worded in order to relieve the injured workman from the burden of proving that there was some particular step which the employers could have taken and did not take. This would often be a difficult matter, more especially if the cause of the failure of the mechanism to operate could not be ascertained. That statue renders the task of the injured workman easier by saying, "You need only prove that the mechanism failed to work efficiently and that this failure caused the accident".'

The same approach was taken when interpreting what is now reg 5 of the Provision and Use of Work Equipment Regulations 1998 in *Stark v Post Office*.[69]

Without the benefit of being able to rely on a duty of this nature, or when the claimant needs to establish some background to show the relevant duty is applicable at all, the absence of factual evidence from the claimant, or other witnesses, about the precise cause or circumstances of what happened may make expert evidence, helping the judge to reconstruct what occurred, from such evidence as there is, important as. That was recognised, for example, by the Court of Appeal in *Ellis v William Cook Leeds Ltd*[70] (see **7.1.2**).

Medical experts may sometimes be able to assist the court on matters relating to liability but, again, the issues must be carefully identified to ensure appropriate evidence, from relevant experts, is available to prove those matters the claimant must establish. For example, in *Arriva Trains Northern Ltd v Eaglen*[71] Longmore LJ observed:

> 'In the light of these findings the questions that had to be addressed were:
> (i)   Did (the claimant) suffer pain additional to that which would anyway have occurred as a result of his existing degenerative condition?
> (ii)   If so, was that caused by the configuration of the seat on which he was sitting while driving 158 trains?
> (iii)   If so, was it foreseeable that (the claimant's) heath would be affected by the seat in which he was driving?

---

[66]   [2005] CSOH 172.
[67]   [2006] CSIH 62.
[68]   [1949] AC 275.
[69]   CA (Civ Div) 2/3/2000.
[70]   [2007] EWCA Civ 1232.
[71]   [2009] EWCA Civ 352.

Medical expert evidence would help to resolve the first two of these questions, the third was a matter of ergonomic expertise.'

With statutory duties the evidential burden will be on the defendant to establish any statutory defence, hence it may be the defendant, rather than the claimant, who needs to adduce expert evidence where this will be necessary to establish any such assertion. That is because, as Lord Dyson confirmed in *Baker v Quantum Clothing Group*:[72]

'... if a defendant wishes to say that it was not reasonably practicable to make or keep a place of work safe, the burden is on him to do so; it is not on the claimant to prove that it *was* reasonably practicable.'

Hence in *McGowan*, despite submissions to the contrary, it was probably the defenders who would have needed expert evidence to establish all reasonably practicable measures, identified by reg 11 itself, had been taken to guard against injury from the 'danger'.

Similarly, when considering a case concerned with reg 12(5) of the Workplace (Health, Safety & Welfare) Regulations 1992 in *Broadfield v Meyrick Estate Management Ltd*[73] Hallett LJ, when dealing with the evidence about the issue as to whether a handrail would have obstructed the traffic route, held:

'... the judge was left to form his own impression from photographs. To my mind that is not good enough. The judge should not have been left in this position on such an important issue. I am not one to encourage the unnecessary use of experts, but to my mind much more was required by way of evidence and detailed analysis of an issue at the heart of the case, namely: whether a handrail would have obstructed the traffic route. For example, the judge might have been assisted by some proper measurements and information on the various forms of handrail now available. He could then form a sensible conclusion as to impossibility based on proper evidence. I would therefore uphold (counsel for the claimant's) complaint about the inadequacy of the evidence called to meet the statutory exception. To my mind the respondents failed to bring themselves within it on the evidence they called.'

Even where the evidential burden rests on the defendant there may be sufficient evidence to shift the burden back to the claimant who may then require expert evidence. Under the Manual Handling Operations Regulations 1992, for example, the burden of proof is on the defendant, if the claimant establishes injury occurred as a result of undertaking manual handling operations involving a risk of being injured, to prove all reasonably practicable steps were taken to reduce that risk: *Egan v Central Manchester NHS Trust*;[74] *Ghaith v Indesit Co UK Ltd*.[75]

Consequently, the starting point for the claimant, in such cases, is that there is no obligation to suggest or prove ways in which the risk could have been reduced. If, however, the defendant does contend, and support with evidence, all reasonably practicable steps were taken the claimant may well need to identify a measure which was reasonably practicable but the defendant failed to take, and that may need to be supported by expert evidence. In a claim brought in reliance on the Manual Handling Operations Regulations 1992 David Richards J observed in *Sloan v The Governors of Rastrick High School*[76] that:

---

72 [2011] UKSC 17.
73 [2011] EWCA Civ 1135.
74 [2008] EWCA Civ 1424.
75 [2012] EWCA Civ 642.
76 [2014] EWCA Civ 1063.

'The appellant led no expert evidence to the effect that the training provided to her and the other steps taken by the school to reduce any risk of injury were insufficient to reduce that risk to the lowest level reasonably practicable. There was of course no obligation on the appellant to do so but it means that the large number of criticisms made by counsel for the appellant in his skeleton argument in support of the appeal are no more than comment, although of course that would not prevent them from being well-founded.'

It remains to be seen whether the effect of the Enterprise and Regulatory Reform Act 2013, which will require most employers' liability claims to be based on the tort of negligence, will mean, if that involves the burden of proof resting more frequently on the claimant, a greater need for expert evidence in order to prove disputed issues.

The defendant, if contesting the need for expert evidence dealing with liability in a workplace claim, may suggest photographs will suffice to assist the court. Photographs will sometimes be enough but care is required, especially if those photographs are provided by the defendant, to ensure these provide adequate, and complete, information for the court.

Generally the interests of mutuality and equality will often make it appropriate, if the defendant has had facilities to obtain photographs, or similar evidence, for the claimant to be allowed reciprocal facilities. Indeed, where such facilities are granted it may often be an expert who is best placed to gather such evidence because, although factual in nature, an expert can give evidence on any relevant matters observed and, moreover, is well able to understand what would be the most relevant and helpful evidence to assist the court and hence ensure any photographs, plan or descriptive evidence fulfils that objective.

Consequently, even if opinion evidence, in the narrow sense, is unlikely to assist the court, that does not necessarily mean the claimant should be deprived the opportunity of having appropriate facilities to take photographs, measurements and gather other evidence, that requires an inspection of the locus, with the assistance of an expert.

The technical nature of the law relating to employers' liability, coupled with the forensic approach to statutory duties which recognises a shifting in the evidential burden of proof, makes this a particularly complex area of the law when deciding the claimant should obtain, and seek permission to rely upon, expert evidence dealing with liability. It may be appropriate to work through a series of questions when considering whether expert evidence on liability will be reasonably required in a claim of this kind.

- What are the precise statutory duties on which the claimant relies and will breach be established by factual evidence proving the general circumstances of the accident rather than the precise mechanics?
- Where is the burden of proof likely to rest, in particular will that shift to the defendant to establish a statutory defence?
- If the claimant does need to prove the precise circumstances or mechanics of the injury to establish breach of the relevant duty is expert evidence, dealing with the factual and real evidence, likely to assist the trial judge in determining that issue?

7.4.1.3 Occupiers' and public liability

In occupiers' liability claims, which inevitably depend upon an assessment of the safety of the premises, expert evidence may be required if the court will need guidance to help interpret the factual evidence, but not if the court is quite capable of doing so without such evidence.

In practice, drawing that distinction, especially at the crucial stage of case management and if the relevant evidence is not then available, can be a difficult task as observations made in a number of cases, with hindsight at trial or even on appeal, illustrate.

In *Nessa v Walsall MBC*,[77] a case involving a claimant who had fallen on a steep ramp leading from a car park to a public road, Mantell LJ held that:

> 'This was a case ... which called out for (expert) evidence, if not demanded it. The Judge was left with the very difficult task of making up his own mind about the dangerousness, or otherwise, of the slope without any assistance from an outside source.'

In *Lips v Older*[78] evidence was given by a surveyor who, after considering the scene of the accident, a low wall with a steep drop behind it, decided it was 'dangerous', moreover that any reasonably competent surveyor carrying out an acquisition survey would have been bound to advise the client of the possible consequences of leaving such a wall unguarded.

However, in *Searson v Brioland Ltd*,[79] a case involving a claimant who tripped over a small upstand in the doorway of a hotel, May LJ observed that:

> '... this was eminently a case for the judge to decide as a matter of broad general experience upon which, in the absence of a technical case from the defendants, really needed to go no further than some good photographs and the relevant dimensions.'

These comments of May LJ do, perhaps, illustrate the more typical approach to this kind of case where photographs of the scene, so that the court may form its own view, will be more appropriate than opinion evidence if the expert simply seeks to express a view on whether the premises were reasonably safe for the purposes of the Occupiers Liability Act 1957 (or 1984).

Consequently, in such claims, an expert may be appropriate if an opinion is required about, for example, good practice or the extent to which any guidelines or standards are applicable to the premises and, if so, what compliance would have meant in terms of safety. Additionally, as with road traffic accidents, where there is a dispute on facts relating to the scene of the accident an expert may assist the court by describing and explaining the scene, from the expert's own perception, following an inspection.

In other circumstances, however, whether the premises were unsafe is likely to be a matter for assessment by the court on the basis of just factual evidence.

---

[77] Court of Appeal, 18 December 2000.
[78] [2004] EWHC 1686 (QB).
[79] [2005] EWCA Civ 55.

A similar approach is likely to be adopted in public liability claims. For example, in *Perry v Harris*,[80] a case involving an accident when children were using a bouncy castle, the Court of Appeal held that:

> '... to a large extent a case of this nature properly turns on first impressions. The factual scenario is a simple one and the photographs give a very clear picture of the bouncy castle and the bungee run. The issue is whether a reasonably careful parent could have acted in the same way as the defendant. The case does not turn on expert evidence or special knowledge.'

However, the earlier part of the judgment in that very case illustrated this assessment of the evidence required by the court was perhaps not so straightforward given the observation that:

> 'The difficult task facing the judge was to decide what precautions the defendant should reasonably have taken to protect against risks to which she knew, or ought to have known, children playing on the castle would be exposed. The task was difficult because neither judges nor parents are likely to have everyday familiarity with bouncy castles or bungee runs or such risks as they pose.'

The need for expert evidence, even in such circumstances, may be avoided if there are, for example, British Standards which plainly apply and have not been met.

The extent to which such guidance can properly dictate liability was considered by Staughton LJ in *Green v Building Scene Ltd & Another*[81] where he said:

> 'But it is a fact that the stairs did not comply with the Building Regulations or the relevant British Standard. That is evidence which we must certainly take into account. It represents current professional opinion as to what is desirable in order that accidents should be avoided. But it is one thing to lay down regulations and standards, with that objective, and another to define what is reasonably safe in the circumstances of a particular case.'

Consequently, although reflecting 'the consensus of professional opinion and practical experience as to the sensible safely precautions' compliance, or otherwise, with such standards will not, of itself, determine whether the relevant premises were reasonably safe: *Ward v Ritz Hotel (London) Ltd*.[82]

Hence, in *Phee v Gordon*[83] evidence from experts on the design of golf courses was of assistance to the court in determining whether the premises where the accident occurred were 'reasonably safe' for the purposes of the Occupiers Liability Act 1957.

Accordingly, whilst the issue of breach is, ultimately, a matter solely for the court, that is a decision which may be influenced, and guided, by the extent to which any applicable standards have been complied with. The difficulty is that such standards are, themselves, inevitably technical matters where expert evidence (or at least preliminary expert advice) may be necessary to identify those of potential application. Moreover, if there is an issue about compliance with any such regulations that may require an element of expert evidence to help the court determine whether or not relevant standards had been met.

---

[80]   [2008] EWCA Civ 907.
[81]   [1994] PIQR P 251.
[82]   [1992] 1PIQR P 315.
[83]   [2011] CSOH 181.

7.4.1.4   Highways

Liability will turn on the application by the court of the test in *Mills v Barnsley Metropolitan Borough Council*[84] where Steyn LJ held that a claimant had to prove that:

> '...the highway was in such a condition that it was dangerous to traffic or pedestrians in the sense that, in the ordinary course of human affairs, danger may reasonably have been anticipated from its continued use by the public;...'

Very often, as when determining whether premises are unsafe for the purposes of the Occupiers Liability Act 1957, deciding liability on the application of the test in *Mills* will not require expert evidence.

Occasionally there may be need for a reconstruction, perhaps if the accident involved a rocking paving stone, or the court may be assisted by photographs or plans. Whilst this may not necessarily amount to expert opinion that evidence may need to be supported by factual observations most conveniently given by a person who has a degree of expertise, because that will facilitate the provision of relevant information to help the court decide key issues.

Usually it is factual evidence, whether or not this is provided with the benefit of some expertise, that may best assist the court when determining liability in a claim of this kind. Ideally such evidence will be photographs illustrating the scene of the accident.

In *Maguire v Lancashire County Council*[85] the claimant had expert evidence from a surveyor, who inspected the scene of the accident finding it 'unfit for purpose', whilst the defendant relied on corresponding evidence which expressed the view the scene was not 'dangerous'.

Reflecting on that evidence, along with the evidence of the claimant about the circumstances of the accident and the fact repairs were carried out by the defendant subsequently, Auld LJ noted that:

> 'It seems to me that of those factors the most critical is the picture of danger that springs out of the photographs ... showing the scene at the time of the accident.'

Interestingly, both experts appeared to express a view on the matter ultimately for the court, namely compliance, or otherwise, with the statutory duty imposed by section 41 of the Highways Act 1980. This illustrates how difficult it can be to draw a line between legitimate opinion and inadmissible evidence.

Another issue which may arise from time to time, and perhaps require expert opinion as well as an inspection, is whether the alleged danger does form part of the fabric of the highway. Expert evidence on this issue was relied on in *Thomas v Warwickshire County Council*.[86]

---

[84]   [1992] PIQR 291.
[85]   [2004] EWCA Civ 1637.
[86]   [2011] EWHC 772 (QB).

7.4.1.5 Consumer protection

In determining whether a product is 'defective' for the purposes of the Consumer Protection Act 1987, the court may well require expert evidence, not to decide the ultimate issue of whether the product was defective but to inform the court on relevant technical matters and standards and hence assist in the court's determination of that central issue as to whether the relevant product met the standard people were generally entitled to expect.

The nature of the expert evidence will inevitably vary, depending on the nature of the product and, sometimes, on the type of defect alleged.

For example, in *Tesco Stores Ltd v Pollard*[87] the claimant alleged a domestic product was defective because it was supplied with an ordinary screw top that was not as difficult for a child to open as it would have been if the British Standard torque measure had been complied with. This issue was dealt with by experts in the field or ergonomics.

In *Ide v ATB Sales Ltd*[88] one of the central issues of the case was whether a cycling accident had been caused by the handle bars of the bicycle failing due to a manufacturing defect. That issue was dealt with by expert metallurgists.

7.4.1.6 Animals

In this type of case the claimant may well rely on duties imposed by the Animals Act 1971. The Act is a complex piece of legislation which requires considerable care when formulating the precise nature of the claim. The evidence necessary for the claimant, including any expert evidence on liability, is likely to be determined by the particular provisions of the Act on which the claimant relies.

Where the claimant relies on the first limb of s 2(2)(b) of the Animals Act 1971, abnormal permanent characteristics, that will usually be established by factual evidence of those characteristics and that these were known to the keeper from previous incidents involving the animal.

Where, however, the claim is based on the second limb of s 2(2)(b), normal but temporary characteristics, expert evidence may be required because here the issue is not so much the behaviour of the particular animal but whether that is normal for the species.

Where the claimant relies on that second limb of s 2(2)(b), expert evidence may also be relevant to any issue concerning the keeper's knowledge of such characteristics, for the purposes of s 2(2)(c), as Dyson LJ explained in *Welsh v Stokes*[89] when he said:

> 'It is not in dispute that subsection (2)(c) requires it to be shown that the keeper knew that the particular animal which caused the damage had the characteristics found to satisfy subsection (2)(b). The only question is *how* that knowledge can be proved. (Counsel for the defendant) submits that it can only be proved by showing that the keeper knew that the particular animal had previously behaved in that way.

---

[87] [2006] EWCA Civ 393.
[88] [2007] EWHC 1667 (QB).
[89] [2007] EWCA Civ 796.

I do not agree. I do not see why a keeper's knowledge that a horse has the characteristic of normally behaving in a certain way in particular circumstances cannot be established by showing that the keeper knows that horses as a species normally behave in that way in those circumstances. Indeed, *Mirvahedy* shows that subsection (2)(b) may be satisfied where the characteristic is displayed by the animal in the same particular times or circumstances as by other animals of the same species. It is a general characteristic of horses to bolt in the particular circumstances of the facts of *Mirvahedy*, or to rear in the particular circumstances of the present case. It makes no sense to require a keeper, if aware of that general characteristic, to have some additional and more particular knowledge.

As regards Professor North's book, (counsel for the defendant) cites from pages 58–61. Professor North identifies a number of ways in which he says that the requirement of knowledge may be satisfied. These include proof that the animal has, to the knowledge of the keeper, actually caused this kind of damage before, that the animal has attempted to do the harm in question but, so far, without success, and proof that the keeper knows that the animal has a vicious characteristic even though it has not yet attempted to cause any injury.

But Professor North does not consider the particular issues raised by the second limb of subsection (2)(b) and, of course, did not have the benefit of the elucidation provided in *Mirvahedy*. Nor is there any discussion of the particular issue of whether knowledge of the characteristic found in the particular animal in particular circumstances can be acquired by knowledge that the characteristic is to be found generally in the particular circumstances in animals of the same species.'

Away from the Animals Act the need for expert evidence will depend upon the individual circumstances of the case and where the evidential burden of proof lies, as illustrated by *Wilson v Donaldson*.[90]

In *Wilson*, the claimant suffered injury as a result of the defendant's livestock straying onto the highway, the central issue on liability being whether the defendant should have done more to secure the livestock than provide, as the sole barrier between the cattle and the road, a stock gate which could be left open by walkers. The defendant argued the claimant could not prove the case without some expert evidence as to the practice of other farmers or the cost of making alternative precautions to secure cattle but the court held this argument was misplaced as:

'... upon the facts of this case, such evidence appears ... to have been unnecessary. Liability was established on the basis of common-sense consideration of the facts combined with the various admissions made by (the defendant).'

The court observed that if the case was to be contested on the basis of what was accepted farming practice then it was for the defendant to call expert evidence to support that assertion, reflecting that in each case it is important for every party to assess what needs to be proved and whether the court will be able to make relevant findings of fact unaided or may require some expert evidence to do so.

Wilson is also a reminder that it is for the claimant to prove the case, and where expert evidence on liability is appropriate but not called there is a real risk of the defendant asserting at trial the claimant is unable to prove the case and/or the court finding the claimant has indeed failed to prove the case.

---

[90]   [2004] EWCA Civ 972.

7.4.1.7 *Foreign accidents*

Liability for a foreign accident may depend upon local standards and whether these have been met: *Wilson v Best Travel Ltd.*[91]

These are issues which may well need to be dealt with by expert evidence. In *Lougheed v On The Beach Ltd*[92] Tomlinson LJ, after recognising evidence of relevant local practice or standards did not have to be given by an expert, observed:

> '...it is ordinarily preferable that evidence of these matters should be given in that way, not least because both the opponent party and the court has the protection and the reassurance of the standard form of declaration given by any person who seeks to give expert evidence.'

Tomlinson LJ continued by noting that:

> 'A Claimant who chooses not to adduce such evidence in a case of this sort does so at his peril.'

Care will be necessary to identify the most appropriate type of expert. That may be a lawyer in the relevant jurisdiction, though the court may prefer evidence from a practitioner in the relevant field of expertise who is based in, or familiar with, practice in the jurisdiction where the injuries were suffered, for example, *Japp v Virgin Holidays Ltd.*[93]

7.4.1.8 *Professional negligence*

A personal injury claim may involve allegations of professional negligence. If so, expert advice, to help assess the claim, and expert evidence, to help prove any matters remaining in issue, is likely to be required.

In *Sansom v Metcalfe Hambleton & Co*[94] Butler-Sloss LJ observed:

> '... a court should be slow to find a professionally qualified man guilty of a breach of his duty of skill and care towards a client (or third party) without evidence from those within the same profession as to the standard expected on the facts of the case and the failure of the professionally qualified man to measure up to that standard.'

Hence in a clinical negligence claim expert evidence on liability will invariably be required.

If the claim was originally one of clinical negligence or personal injury but, perhaps for limitation reasons, has become a professional negligence claim against former solicitors, expert evidence about the standard to be expected from a lawyer, for example issuing a claim form within the limitation period, is unlikely to be required as the court is likely to be able to form a view on the relevant standard, and whether this has been breached, without such evidence.

---

91   [1993] 1 All ER 353.
92   [2014] EWCA Civ 1538.
93   [2013] EWCA Civ 1371.
94   [1997] EWCA Civ 3019.

In such cases, however, the claimant may still need to introduce expert evidence, if that would have been required in the original claim, either to help establish liability (which in a subsequent professional negligence claim may translate into helping value the loss of chance) or the potential value.

7.4.2   Contributory negligence

The issue of contributory negligence, certainly so far as the claimant is concerned, is less likely to demand expert evidence than primary liability. That is partly because of the way the court is likely to assess whether there has been 'fault' on the part of the claimant, for the purposes of the Law Reform (Contributory Negligence) Act 1945, and partly because the burden of proof, when alleging contributory negligence, is on the defendant, often significant when assessing whether any fault was causative of the injuries suffered.

7.4.2.1   Fault

The question of whether there was any fault on the part of the claimant will often be a matter for the court to determine just by resolving any conflicts in the factual evidence and then by deciding, as a matter of law, whether the claimant's conduct, found or admitted, should be characterised as fault for the purposes of the 1945 Act.

Occasionally, expert evidence might be helpful to the court in determining factual issues, for example the use of forensic engineers to assist the court in deciding about the likelihood of a seat-belt having been in use where that is a disputed issue of fact. More frequently, however, this primary point of fault, where there is an issue of contributory negligence, can be resolved without expert evidence.

7.4.2.2   Causation

Even if there is fault on the part of the claimant the defendant must, to establish contributory negligence, prove that such fault either contributed directly to the injuries being suffered or that those injuries are more severe than they otherwise would have been.

On this aspect of any contributory negligence issue expert evidence may be essential. However, it is the defendant, on whom the burden of proof rests, that, without permission to rely on relevant expert evidence, may face difficulty in establishing causation even where there is clearly fault.

These difficulties are well illustrated by case-law considering contributory negligence where the claimant has failed to use a seat-belt or wear a cycle helmet.

The threshold for establishing contributory negligence in seat-belt cases was set out by the Court of Appeal in *Froom v Butcher*[95] where Lord Denning MR observed:

> 'Sometimes the evidence will show that the failure made no difference. The damage would have been the same, even if a seat-belt had been worn. In such case the damages should not be reduced at all. At other times the evidence will show that the failure made all the

---

[95]   [1976] 1 QB 286.

difference. The damage would have been prevented altogether if a seat-belt had been worn. In such cases I would suggest that the damages should be reduced by 25 per cent. But often enough the evidence will only show that the failure made a considerable difference. Some injuries to the head, for instance, would have been a good deal less severe if a seat-belt had been worn, but there would still have been some injury to the head. In such case I would suggest that the damages attributable to the failure to wear a seat-belt should be reduced by 15 per cent.'

This approach was endorsed in *Stanton v Collinson*[96] where the Court of Appeal upheld a first instance finding that without expert neurological evidence the defendant could not discharge the burden of proof in showing the failure to wear a seat-belt had made a 'considerable difference' let alone 'all the difference'. At first instance Cox J had found:

'....the claimant's failure to wear a seat-belt probably made a considerable difference; that is, although the claimant would still have suffered some injuries, that his injuries would have been a good deal less severe if he had worn a seat-belt, in which case his damages should be reduced by 15 per cent.'

The judge then continued:

'Given the well recognised vulnerability of the brain, the extent to which this different yet serious head injury would have given rise to less severe cognitive deficits than those he now suffers from is, in my judgment, a medical and probably a neurological question .... Yet the defendant has adduced no medical evidence in this case. Further, none of the medical evidence served with the Particulars of Claim, dealing only with condition and prognosis, has addressed this issue.'

The judge therefore concluded:

'I accept, of course, (the seat-belt expert's) extensive expertise and experience as a seat-belt specialist. However, leaving aside the lateness of the explanation now offered, I did not find it of assistance in resolving a question which, in my view can only properly be determined with the assistance of specialist medical evidence.'

Similarly, in *Smith v Finch*[97] the absence of neurological evidence meant the defendant was unable to prove causation, and hence contributory negligence, where the claimant had failed to wear a cycle helmet. Griffith Williams J observed:

'If a party seeks to persuade a court that an injury would not have occurred or would not have been so serious, only a medical practitioner can speak to that.'

The judge concluded:

'It follows that the state of the evidence is such that I am not persuaded by the defendant, on the balance of probabilities, that any of the injuries sustained by the claimant may have been reduced or prevented by the wearing of the helmet, even if the impact speed was a low enough speed for the helmet to have afforded protection.'

Consequently, at the stage of case management it may well be the defendant, rather than the claimant, who pushes the court for permission to rely on expert evidence dealing with causation in relation to allegations of contributory negligence. However, none of

---

[96] [2010] EWCA Civ 81.
[97] [2009] EWHC 53 (QB).

this means expert medical evidence will always be required to deal with issues of this kind. What expert evidence is 'reasonably required' will depend, as ever, on the particular facts and issues of the case. As Hughes LJ noted in *Stanton*:

> 'It does not follow that medical evidence is a necessity in every seat-belt case, or in every such case involving head (or even brain) injury. Each case will depend upon its facts and upon the state of the other evidence. Proportionality is also relevant: what is appropriate in a case with grave disabilities and large sums at stake may not be called for in one where the injury is relatively straightforward. A large part of the difficulty in the present case arose from the combination of the proposition in the joint report that serious head injury was likely even with a seat-belt, with the less than satisfactory evidence about what that meant. In other cases, if that difficulty did not arise, it may well be that skilled seat-belt engineers, if they agree about what kind of injury would have been occasioned if the belt had been worn, provide evidence which is sufficient for the judge to resolve the issue. However, any doubt about the appropriateness of medical evidence ought to be capable of avoidance in the great majority of cases if the case management process is operated in such a way as to ensure that it is clear to the parties well in advance of trial whether the causation aspect of contributory negligence is, or is not, in issue. The overriding objective in CPR 1, especially 1.4(2)(b) with 1.3 (the duty to help the court identify the issues), provides ample scope for ensuring that this happens.'

7.4.3   Quantum

Virtually every personal injury claim will require at least some expert evidence dealing with quantum. That will almost certainly include medical evidence and, in appropriate cases, may involve evidence from experts in other fields.

If, when assessing quantum, the court must apply foreign law expert evidence, although procedurally following the law of England and Wales, will need to assist the court in determining damages by applying relevant foreign law: *Wall v Mutuelle de Poitiers Assurances*.[98]

7.4.3.1   Medical evidence

Medical evidence is a vital ingredient in most personal injury claims. As Hughes LJ observed in *Edwards-Tubb v J D Weatherspoon plc*:[99]

> '... whilst a claimant in a personal injuries action could in theory proceed without medical evidence, and may do so in a simple case of transient injury easily provable, in a case such as the present some medical evidence is a practical necessity.'

Expert medical evidence dealing with quantum will be a mixture of factual observations and expert opinion. As May J observed in *Larby v Thurgood*:[100]

> 'In a personal injury action, a medical consultant giving expert evidence will commonly be asked to say: (a) what injuries the plaintiff suffered at the time of the accident and what treatment he had, (b) what the plaintiff's disability or other state is at the time of trial, and (c) what in his opinion is the likely medical prognosis. The plaintiff's injuries and treatment at the time of the accident are very largely questions of fact. The consultant will habitually recite such facts having gleaned them from the plaintiff and from medical records. They are

---

[98]   [2014] EWCA Civ 138.
[99]   [2011] EWCA Civ 136.
[100] [1993] ICR 66.

usually not in dispute. The plaintiff often gives evidence to prove his part of them in the course of the trial. The plaintiff's disability or other state at the time of the trial are again largely questions of fact. The consultant will usually give evidence to establish such facts based on his examination of the plaintiff and on his expert opinion about what his examination reveals. The likely medical prognosis is again a matter of expert opinion. It is accepted that in most cases a medical examination of the plaintiff is necessary to enable the consultant properly to form and express his opinion.'

Hence, in virtually every case an assessment of the injuries, from a collection of factual information including the history given and signs on examination, is a matter on which the claimant will need expert opinion to formulate the case, the defendant to assess the case and, if necessary, the court to determine the case. Moreover, the prognosis is inevitably a question of opinion, the expert drawing on experience to predict the future from what is known of the past, from the history, and the present, from examination.

These are all matters not within the knowledge of the ordinary layman and hence expert evidence will be required by the parties and the court.

This is all reflected in the terms of paragraph 4.3 of the Practice Direction to Part 16 which requires a claimant, relying on the evidence of a medical practitioner, to provide with the Particulars of Claim a report from a medical practitioner about the personal injuries alleged in the claim. Thus, the report with the Particulars of Claim does not have to be the medical evidence, and certainly not all the medical evidence, the claimant will later seek to rely upon, but in many cases that report will be the entirety of the claimant's expert evidence given that it is the medical expert who may best be able to cover the range of issues on which the court needs expert opinion dealing with the injuries.

Accordingly, efforts should be made, at the outset, to identify the most appropriate specialism so that the expert instructed will, if possible, be able to report on all aspects of the injuries.

If, however, the nature of the injuries are such that a medical expert in more than one specialism will be required, thought should be given as to whether all need to be instructed at the same time or if one is most suited to act as a lead expert.

The reason that in many personal injury cases the medical evidence will be the only expert evidence is because, in the light of the medical opinion, the claimant may well be able to formulate all aspects of the claim, the defendant may be able to assess those aspects of the claim and court, if necessary, may determine any issues remaining between the parties.

The skills of a medical expert will ensure, in most circumstances, that expert medical evidence is the best way of introducing what is essentially factual evidence on the presentation of the injuries. However, from time to time, other evidence may be just as, if not more, effective for these purposes. Photographs, for example, illustrating scarring or other cosmetic consequences of the injuries, may be important with either the claimant or the medical expert confirming these photographs illustrate the cosmetic appearance of the injuries as at the date such photographs were taken.

Indeed, it is the medical evidence which will often be the most important expert evidence, supporting not just the claim for pain, suffering and loss of amenity but also expenses and losses given that, at least indirectly, these will depend upon the nature and extent of the injuries. Hence, medical experts have a key role in personal injury litigation, perhaps also reflecting the particular standards, practices and ethics of medical professionals on which the courts rely to ensure a just outcome in many cases.

7.4.3.2 Employment evidence

Evidence from an expert on employment issues may sometimes be of assistance to the court when assessing future employment prospects and earnings, where the claimant has suffered an injury leaving significant residual complaints.

The court will, however, be used to assessing relevant heads of claim and, as ever, it is essential not to call expert evidence which, in effect, seeks to supplant the court's role by making findings. Accordingly, any such evidence might well be confined to specific items of information, or sometimes opinion where this will helpfully inform the decision of the court.

If the medical evidence indicates the claimant is, as a result of the injuries, 'disabled', the claim for future loss of earnings can be formulated and advanced on the basis of the methodology explained in the Ogden Tables. This is based on empirical evidence showing the likely effect of disability on working life. Consequently, that should relieve the claimant of the need to adduce evidence from an employment expert, which at one time might have been necessary, to support a claim based on a reduction in length of the claimant's working life. Indeed, the trend seems to be towards arguments by defendants that such evidence is reasonably required, when often it should not be and the grant of permission to rely on such evidence ought to be resisted on behalf of the claimant.

The reluctance of the courts to allow expert employment evidence was illustrated by the judgment in *Turner v Walsall Hospital NHS Trust*.[101]

Even if the medical evidence does not suggest the claimant is 'disabled' it is the medical evidence, where there are any residual consequences of the injuries, that may be the most relevant expert evidence in helping prove that there is a loss of earning capacity or disadvantage on the labour market.

7.4.3.3 Care evidence

A care report may be useful in the case of a claimant who, as a result of the injuries, has required a significant degree of care and attendance.

To an extent the need for, and amount of, care resulting from the injuries will be established by factual evidence. Where the claim for care is not significant the primary evidence to deal with this head of claim will be the witnesses of fact, most likely the claimant and those who have helped provide care.

However, there are cases in which the court is likely to be assisted by expert opinion on what care has been, and will be, reasonably required. Such evidence will be given on the basis of a detailed assessment of the claimant's situation and needs, with opinion on how those needs will best be met. That evidence may well include relevant statistics such as

---

[101] [2013] EWHC 1221 (QB).

rates of pay for those providing care, either to assess the cost of purchasing such care or to use as a benchmark for valuing care given gratuitously.

The need for such statistical information will not, of itself, justify the need for expert opinion as these may well be matters on which the court will be prepared to accept information in the public domain or as set out, for example, in PIBA 'Facts and Figures'. Even so the court will often accept the need for expert evidence dealing with care, for example *Garrington v Walsall Healthcare NHS Trust*.[102]

Whilst evidence about care needs will inevitably include matters of fact these can usefully be covered by any expert's report as Longmore LJ explained in *Wall v Mutuelle de Poitiers Assurances*[103] when he said:

> '... experts in personal injury cases will, not unusually, give evidence of matters of fact as well as of opinion. It will, for example, be necessary for the court to receive evidence of what care or what accommodation the claimant needs. This will be partly a matter of fact relating to the claimant's current condition and current accommodation and partly a matter of opinion relating to the current and future needs of the claimant with his current condition and his current accommodation. It is convenient for such evidence to be given in a single care report or a single accommodation report, as the case may be.'

Whether or not expert evidence dealing specifically with care is relied on it is important to remember that, along with many heads of claim, it will be the expert medical evidence which, as well as the factual evidence, will be of most importance. That is because the medical opinion inevitably underpins the claim for care as, fundamentally, the injuries will need to justify a claim for care before efforts are made to quantify the nature and extent of the care required (perhaps by expert evidence dealing specifically with this issue). As Underhill J explained in *Huntley v Simmonds*:[104]

> '... in a case of the present kind the care experts are doubly dependent on the input of others – that is, on the medical experts as regards the extent of the injury and the prospects of treatment and improvement, and on the claimant's family and support network for evidence of his capability and needs. On those I am in a good position to form my own views.'

There is a clear distinction between a care expert, whose role is to provide evidence for the court, and a case manager, whose responsibility is to the claimant alone as Brooke LJ explained in *Wright v Sullivan*[105] when he said:

> 'It seems to me inevitable that the clinical case manager should owe her duties to her patient alone. She must win the patient's trust and if possible her co-operation in what is being proposed, and while it will be in her patient's interests that she should receive a flow of suggestions from any other experts who have been instructed in the case, she must ultimately make decisions in the best interests of the patient and not be beholden to two different masters.'

Consequently, a case manager should be regarded as a witness of fact, not an expert. Moreover, there should be no question of a case manager being appointed jointly, in the

---

[102] (Unreported) 13 February 2015, QBD.
[103] [2014] EWCA Civ 138.
[104] [2009] EWHC 405 (QB).
[105] [2005] EWCA Civ 656.

manner of a joint expert, so preventing attendance at a conference with the claimant's legal advisors, or owing the same duty to the court as an expert preparing a report for use as evidence.

The distinction between the role of the case manager and the role of the care expert reflects the way in which the role of a clinical case manager has evolved. Brooke LJ explained in *Wright*:

> 'This practice started, we were told, in the United States, and has been developed in this country over the last ten years. For the purposes of this litigation it is sufficient to say that a clinical case manager may be appointed to assist a severely injured person whether or not litigation is pending against a third party tortfeasor. The expense may be borne by private funding or by a health authority or a local authority in an appropriate case.'

This approach does, however, mean that documentation produced by the case manager will be disclosable unless the dominant purpose is enough to attract litigation privilege.

7.4.3.4 *Accountancy and actuarial evidence*

The expert evidence of an accountant may be necessary, for example to help the claimant formulate, and the court assess, a claim for loss of earnings where the claimant is self-employed, in partnership or the proprietor of a business run through a limited company.

Accountancy evidence will, in other circumstances, not usually be required. Furthermore, when such evidence is relied on care will be necessary to ensure the report focuses on those matters where the court needs expert opinion, such as the extrapolation of earnings from the profits of the business or future projections of profit and income levels that it is considered could have been achieved had it not been for the injuries suffered.

Where such evidence is appropriate it may be helpful if this is provided in a way that can be utilised whatever findings of fact are made by the court, whether this be a formula to apply to those facts or figures applicable in a number of different factual scenarios as, for example, the expert evidence of this nature did in *XYZ v Portsmouth Hospitals NHS Trust*.[106]

Actuarial evidence may, occasionally, be necessary. However, in *Prigmore v Welbourne*[107] such evidence was held not to be required as the issue for determination did not turn on different actuarial views but a question of law, a matter for the Judge, as to which of those views should be preferred. This, again, illustrates it must be the court rather than the experts that determine the case.

7.4.3.5 *Statistical evidence*

Statistical evidence may be relevant to determine the life expectancy of the claimant. The issue as to whether such expert evidence is reasonably required will often turn on

---

[106] [2011] EWHC 243 (QB).
[107] [2003] EWHC 3259 (QB).

whether that evidence should be provided by experts dealing specifically with life expectancy or by the other medical experts already involved in the case.

In Arden v Malcom[108] Tugendhat J adopted the approach in Royal & Sun Alliance Insurance v T&N Limited[109] holding:

'In my judgment it is in the spirit in the decision of the Court of Appeal in *Royal v Victoria* that the clinician experts should be the normal and primary route through which such statistical evidence should be put before the court. It is only if there is disagreement between them on a statistical matter that the evidence of a statistician, such as Professor Strauss, ought normally to be required.'

However, if that primary route is explored, statistical evidence may then be regarded as required. In *Arden* Tugendhat J went on to observe:

'The real issue comes down to this. Should the court give permission to adduce a report from Professor Strauss at this stage, or should the statistical material to which he refers first be raised in the form of a question or direction to the existing experts, with the possibility of a report from Professor Strauss being left to be decided a future application, in the event that the question and directions route does not resolve the matter. Mr Purchas QC submits that this is not a practical way of proceeding, and that permission should first be given to rely on the report of Professor Strauss. I have regard to his great experience in cases such as this. It may be that in the end he will be proved right. But I am not convinced that giving permission now is necessary if justice is to be done.'

7.4.3.6 Occupational therapy evidence

If a care expert is appropriate the evidence of that expert, in some cases, may encompass any occupational therapy needs.

However, the claimant's requirements may be such that separate expert evidence, specifically on occupational therapy including needs and costings, may be reasonably required.

7.4.3.7 Speech and language evidence

The claimant may, as a result of the injuries which are the subject of the claim, have speech and language issues that an expert will need to deal with, including an assessment of the claimant's needs, details of treatment available and an opinion on future needs as well as the benefits this might bring and costings.

7.4.3.8 Accommodation evidence

If, as a result of the injuries the claimant will need to either adapt current accommodation or move to more suitable accommodation, expert evidence on this issue is likely to be required.

---

[108] [2007] EWHC 404 (QB).
[109] [2002] EWCA Civ 1964.

To inform the established method of calculating an accommodation claim, explained in *Roberts v Johnstone*[110] the expert may need to deal with a number of issues including the requirements of a suitable property, the availability and cost of such a property, the value of the claimant's current home, adaptations necessary (whether the claimant stays in present accommodation or moves) with costings and likely additional future running costs.

This is another issue where, even so, the opinion of medical experts remains important as the accommodation expert is concerned primarily with helping the court in assessing how this head of claim should be valued rather than whether the effect of the injuries is such that adaptations or new accommodation are appropriate.

7.4.3.9   Assistive technology evidence

The development of assisted technology has meant that even a seriously injured claimant can, with use of that technology, enjoy a degree of independence and quality of life.

Because of the technical and developing nature of the technology available, the court may benefit from the evidence of an expert outlining availability and cost of that technology though, once again, the need will be underpinned by the expert medical evidence.

7.4.3.10   Financial evidence

If a periodical payments order may be an appropriate way of dealing with at least part of the damages, expert evidence may well be required to help the claimant formulate, and the court assess, the award of damages in this way.

7.5   THE EXPERT

If there is to be expert evidence then, by definition, that must be evidence given by an 'expert'.

Defining an expert invites the anterior question of whether, for a person to be characterised as an expert at all, there must be an identifiable area of expertise.

Any person upon whom a party is given permission to rely as an expert will be allowed to give opinion evidence on relevant matters of expertise, but it is essential the expert understands the role and duties when giving evidence in civil proceedings or that party may still be prevented from relying on the evidence of the expert. Accordingly, not all potential experts will be suitable candidates for the role.

7.5.1   Who is an expert?

The court may start, in identifying an expert, by asking whether the opinion of a proposed expert 'forms part of a body of knowledge or experience which is sufficiently

---

[110]   [1989] QB 878.

organised or recognised to be accepted as a reliable body of knowledge or experience': *Clarke v Marlborough Fine Art (London) Ltd*[111] (see **7.3.2.3**).

Consequently, as a preliminary to assessing whether an individual has appropriate expertise, the court may expect there to be a discrete body of knowledge or experience which is sufficiently organised or recognised for those having such knowledge or experience to be properly characterised as experts.

In personal injury claims the courts are willing to recognise experts, on this basis, in a wide range of disciplines (see **7.4**).

There are, however, limits to how far the courts will go in treating a witness, however knowledgeable, as an expert if the relevant knowledge or experience cannot be regarded as being sufficiently organised. For example, in *Barings plc (In Liquidation) v Coopers & Lybrand (No 2)*[112] the court was not prepared to recognise 'banking management' as a recognised field of expertise and hence excluded evidence from a purported expert in that field.

An individual with requisite knowledge or experience in the relevant area, assuming that area is accepted by the court as being a reliable body of knowledge or experience, may, where there is an established system of qualification, be identified as an expert by having obtained the requisite qualifications acknowledged within the area itself as defining expertise. With medical experts, for example, the threshold for expertise might be taken to be entry on the register of medical practitioners kept by the GMC.

Given the wide range of potential disciplines in which expert evidence may be appropriate, the courts are likely to adopt a broad approach to how an individual expert is defined, for example by asking 'whether the witness has acquired by study or experience sufficient knowledge of the subject to render his opinion of value in resolving the issue before the court': *Clarke v Marlborough Fine Art (London) Ltd*[113] (see **7.3.2.3**).

There are areas of expertise which may, in a particular case, assist the court where there is no formal, or consistent, method of qualification. Consequently, the court may recognise informal qualifications of a proposed expert in such a field on the basis this might be acquired through experience on the ground.

Individual expertise will usually be established from content in the CV of the proposed expert.

7.5.2 Who is a suitable expert?

Expert evidence should only be given by a suitably qualified person, within a recognised field of knowledge or experience, on a relevant issue. Subject to a proposed expert meeting that basic criteria the most important consideration, as to the suitability of that expert, will be whether any such individual is aware of the overriding duty to help the court on matters within the expertise of that expert.

---

[111] [2002] EWHC 11 (Ch).
[112] [2001] PNLR 22 Ch D.
[113] [2002] EWHC 11 (Ch).

In *Field v Leeds City Council CA*[114] Waller LJ held:

> 'The question whether someone should be able to give expert evidence should depend on whether: (i) it can be demonstrated whether that person has relevant expertise in an area in issue in the case; and (ii) that it can be demonstrated that he or she is aware of their primary duty to the court if they give expert evidence.'

Provided the court has sufficient information to assess an expert's knowledge of the need for objectivity, and hence awareness of the primary duty to the court, it may even be appropriate for the employee of a party to give expert evidence as occurred in *Field*.

However, justice must be *seen* to be done, as well as be done, so a proposed expert who has a close personal relationship with the party seeking to rely on the expert evidence may be excluded on the grounds of public policy: *Liverpool Roman Catholic Archdiocesan Trust v Goldberg*.[115]

If an expert has shown a lack of understanding of the duties to the court, this may result in the expert's evidence being excluded even if permission to rely on such evidence was given at an earlier stage in the proceedings. That is because the expert's unsuitability may only emerge after exchange of evidence, when questions put to that expert are answered, or even at the stage of the experts preparing joint statements.

In these circumstances the court may exercise the power conferred by CPR 3.1(7), to vary case management directions, by revoking permission previously given to rely on the expert concerned. Such a ruling was upheld by the Court of Appeal in *Casey v Cartwright*[116] where the relevant expert had originally been the joint expert on orthopaedic issues in a claim concerned with injuries which the claimant alleged had occurred in a low speed road traffic accident. Dyson LJ noted:

> 'The judge's concern as to the suitability of Mr Williams was heightened by the answers he gave to the claimant's solicitors' questions. His answer "Whiplash injuries are uncommon in Singapore, New Zealand, Quebec, Greece, Russia and Lithuania. These countries either have no or restricted mechanisms of compensation". The judge said that this answer clearly demonstrated a lack of objectivity.'

Similarly, permission to rely on expert evidence was revoked where the expert failed to cooperate in arrangements for a joint statement, and generally to meet the standards which the court was entitled to expect of an expert: *Stevens v Gullis*[117] (see **7.11.2**).

Occasionally, a party might have grounds for regarding an expert as unsuitable on the basis of criticism made in earlier, unrelated, proceedings. Such criticism would need to be harsh enough to reflect what might be regarded as a wholesale disregard, by the expert, of the obligations imposed by Part 35. For example, in *Williams v Jervis*[118] the judge, when explaining why he was unable to place reliance on the evidence of the relevant expert, explained:

---

[114] (Lord Woolf MR, Waller LJ, May LJ) 8/12/99.
[115] [2001] 1 WLR 2337.
[116] [2006] EWCA Civ 1280.
[117] [2000] 1 All ER 527.
[118] [2008] EWHC 2346 (QB).

'... he approached the case with a set view of the claimant and looked at the claimant and her claimed symptomology through the prism of his own disbelief. From that unsatisfactory standpoint he unfortunately lost the focus of an expert witness and sought to argue a case. I am driven to the conclusion that I am unable to place reliance on (the expert's) evidence in this case.'

In such circumstances a party might have grounds for objecting to another party obtaining permission to rely on such an expert, perhaps before a report has even been written, on the basis of systemic failings of a kind wholly inconsistent with the terms of Part 35.

The Personal Injury Protocol provides a machinery, for joint selection with a view to there being a single expert on a particular issue, for excluding unacceptable experts, on the basis one party will nominate experts considered suitable and the other will identify any which are objected to. Whilst there may need to be some justification for objection to an expert nominated under the Protocol, that would not seem to require anything of the kind that might justify objection, on the grounds of suitability, at the stage when permission to rely on the evidence of the expert is being sought.

Where a party not only seeks permission to rely on the evidence of an expert but also facilities to obtain a report, for example with a medical expert, further consideration, in relation to the suitability of that expert, may sometimes arise, though the court will be reluctant to let one party prevent another relying on an otherwise suitable expert in this way (see **7.8.2.5**).

A party who wishes to call an expert where there is a potential conflict of interest should disclose details of that conflict at as early a stage in the proceedings as is possible: *Toth v Jarman*.[119] This is now reflected in paragraph 7 of the Expert Protocol and the risk of a conflict of interest is an issue that should always be raised with a potential expert at the outset.

Expertise, and hence suitability, will usually, though not always, require up to date knowledge and practice. Moses LJ explained why this is important in *R v Henderson: R v Butler; R v Olapado Oyediran*[120] when he said:

'Clinicians learn from each case in which they are engaged. Each case makes them think and as their experience develops so does their understanding. Continuing experience gives them the opportunity to adjust previously held opinions, to alter their views. They are best placed to recognise that that which is unknown one day may be acknowledged the next. Such clinical experience, demonstrated, for example, by Dr Peters in the case of Henderson, may provide a far more reliable source of evidence than that provided by those who have ceased to practise their expertise in a continuing clinical setting and have retired from such practice. Such experts are, usually, engaged only in reviewing the opinions of others. They have lost the opportunity, day by day, to learn and develop from continuing experience.'

Consequently, for example, the court may ask whether the opinion of a proposed expert 'forms part of a body of knowledge or experience which is sufficiently organised or recognised to be accepted as a reliable body of knowledge or experience': *Clarke v Marlborough Fine Art (London) Ltd*[121] (see **7.3.2.3**).

---

[119] [2006] EWCA Civ 1028.
[120] [2010] EWCA Crim 1269.
[121] [2002] EWHC 11 (Ch).

Where, however, professional standards are being judged it is usually essential to have an expert who was in practice at the relevant time, as it will be the standards of the day by which the court will need to judge the defendant's conduct.

7.5.3   Duties of an expert

A suitable expert witness will be one who understands, and meets, the duties of an expert under the CPR, which are drawn from Part 35, the accompanying Practice Direction and the Expert Protocol.

The nature of those responsibilities will depend upon whether the expert is giving advice to a party or preparing a report for use as evidence to be put before the court.

Paragraph 9 of the Expert Protocol confirms that an expert should promptly confirm whether or not any instructions are accepted and if and when any difficulties then arise.

7.5.3.1   *Advice*

Where the expert is giving advice only then the responsibility of the expert is towards that party.

Paragraph 5 of the Expert Protocol provides that:

*   The Protocol does not apply to an expert instructed to give advice the parties do not intend to adduce in litigation (whether such an expert is instructed before or after court proceedings are commenced).
*   However, the Protocol will apply if experts originally instructed to advise only are later instructed to give or prepare evidence.

7.5.3.2   *Evidence*

The duties of an expert under the CPR embody, in the court rules, guidance given in case-law prior to 1999, in particular the guidance given by Cresswell J in *The Ikarian Reefer*.[122]

Reflecting that approach, CPR 35.3 expressly provides that it is the duty of experts to help the court on matters within their expertise, a duty that overrides any obligation to the person from whom the expert has received instructions or by whom that expert will be paid.

Prior to the CPR, but following *The Ikarian Reefer*, Thorpe LJ observed in *Vernon v Bosley (No 1)*[123] that:

> 'The area of expertise in any case may be likened to a broad street with the plaintiff walking on one pavement and the defendant on the opposite one. Somehow, the expert must be ever mindful of the need to walk straight down the middle of the road and to resist the temptation to join the party from whom his instructions come on the pavement.'

---

[122] [1993] 2 Lloyds REP 68.
[123] [1997] 1 All ER 577.

More recently Hughes LJ, reflecting the sentiments now expressed by the CPR, observed in *Edwards-Tubb v J D Weatherspoon plc*[124] that:

> 'The expert's prime duty is unequivocally to the court. His report should say exactly the same whoever instructed him.'

When instructed as an expert witness, paragraph 2 of the Practice Directions to Part 35 makes it clear that:

- the paramount duty of the expert is to help the court on matters within the expertise of that expert, the evidence being uninfluenced by the pressures of litigation based on all material facts;
- the report should set out the substance of all facts and instructions material to the opinions expressed;
- where there is a range of opinion that range should be summarised;
- the report must be verified by a Statement of Truth;
- if, subsequently, the expert has a change of view on any material matter that change of view should be communicated to all parties without delay, and when appropriate to the court.

These duties are endorsed by the Expert Protocol which, at paragraph 5, confirms:

- the duty to help the court overrides any obligation to the person instructing or paying the expert;
- experts should be aware of the overriding objective, and are under an obligation to assist the court to deal with cases in accordance with the overriding objective;
- expert opinions should be independent defined as meaning 'the expert would express the same opinion if given the same instructions by an opposing party';
- experts should not engage in the role of advocate;
- opinions should be confined to matters material to the dispute and within the expertise of the expert;
- experts should take into account all material facts, the report setting out those facts and any literature or other material relied on;
- the report should indicate if an opinion is provisional, or qualified, or where the expert considers further information is required;
- an expert should inform those instructing that expert, without delay, of any change of opinion on a material matter and the reason for that change.

Under the terms of CPR 35.14, which reflects the direct responsibility owed to the court, an expert witness may always ask the court for directions. CPR 35.14, reflecting the direct responsibility owed by an expert witness to the court, may always ask the court for directions. That could be appropriate if, for example, an expert receives questions which are not considered compliant with the terms of CPR 35.6 or if the expert requires further information, particularly of the kind that might be covered by CPR 35.9. Paragraph 11 of the Expert Protocol explains how an expert should apply for directions from the court. That will be by letter, which should be copied to all parties, enclosing any relevant documentation explaining why directions are sought.

---

[124] [2011] EWCA Civ 136.

If the expert's report refers to articles, textbook entries or research studies these should, at the very least, be identified so as to be available for consideration by the other side: *DN v Greenwich London Borough*.[125] Case management directions may go further and expressly provide that any report be accompanied by copies of supporting literature of this kind.

The nature of the expert's duties are inconsistent with the expert acting as an advocate and an expert who does so may find this has a bearing on whether the evidence given is accepted by the Court: *Smith v Finch*;[126] *Williams v Jervis*.[127] Indeed, where an expert acts in this way that may even bring costs sanctions upon the party who relied on that expert (see **7.15.4**).

Nevertheless, an expert does have a duty of care to the party instructing that expert and may be liable in damages if that duty of care is not met: *Jones v Kaney*.[128]

7.5.4   Choosing an expert

The terms of the CPR make it important for any party, before instructing an expert who may be giving evidence, to identify both a relevant field of expertise and a proposed expert having requisite expertise within that field who is aware of the role and responsibilities applicable to experts under the CPR. Even then not all potential experts may be suitable.

Consequently, when identifying an expert, either for proposal to the defendant (for joint selection or joint instruction) or for unilateral instruction, a number of factors are likely to be relevant and various sources of information referred to.

- Once the field of expertise has been established, any proposed expert must meet the criteria for expertise within that field, which may require certain formal qualifications or for requisite experience to be demonstrated in other ways.
- Such experts might be identified from a number of sources including:
  - membership of professional organisations;
  - having provided evidence as an expert on similar issues in previous cases;
  - being included on a list of potential experts kept by the individual firm or external agencies such as APIL or AvMA;
  - recommendation by other experts;
  - recommendation by counsel;
  - recommendation by other solicitors; or
  - a search on the internet.
- Any such expert must understand, and be relied upon to act in accordance with, the responsibilities identified by the CPR.
- There should be no conflict of interest which would prevent the expert meeting the responsibilities identified by the CPR.
- Timescale for, and likely cost of, reporting may be relevant factors.
- If the expert is to be proposed for the purpose of joint selection or joint instruction, likely acceptability to the defendant may be a relevant consideration.

---

[125]   [2004] EWCA Civ 1659.
[126]   [2009] EWHC 53 (QB).
[127]   [2009] EWHC 1837 (QB).
[128]   [2011] UKSC 13.

- The claimant's approval to involve an expert in the case should always be sought and appropriate information given on any proposed experts so there is an opportunity for input.

7.5.5 The function of an expert

Ultimately, a suitable expert witness will fulfil, for the court, a function involving one or more of the following:

- to give expert assistance to the court on, for example, the laws of science or the working of a technical process or system; and/or
- to explain words or technical terms appearing on documents which have to be construed by the court; and/or
- to inform the court on the state of public knowledge with regard to relevant matters (for example statistics); and/or
- to give guidance on the usual practice and procedures adopted by professionals in relevant circumstances; and/or
- to assist the court on other matters within the particular expertise of the expert.

In addition to opinion on any of these matters an expert's evidence will also be admissible if made as a way of conveying relevant facts perceived personally by the expert (see **7.3.1.1**).

7.5.6 The expert's report

If an expert is giving advice to a party there is no format set out in the CPR for that advice.

If, however, the expert is writing a report, which may therefore be used as evidence, it will be necessary for that report to comply with the CPR:

- CPR 35.10 sets out general requirements for the content of an expert's report:
  - It must comply with the requirements set out in the Practice Direction to Part 35.
  - There must be a statement the expert understands and complies with the duty to the court.
  - The report must state the substance of all material instructions, whether written or oral.
- The Practice Direction to Part 35, referred to in CPR 35.10, sets out additional requirements:
  - Paragraph 2.1: Expert evidence should be the independent product of the expert uninfluenced by the pressures of litigation.
  - Paragraph 2.2: Experts should assist the court by providing objective, unbiased opinions on matters within their expertise, and should not assume the role of an advocate.
  - Paragraph 2.3: Experts should consider all material facts, including those which might detract from their opinions.
  - Paragraph 2.4: Experts should make it clear:
    - (a) when a question or issue falls outside their expertise; and
    - (b) when they are not able to reach a definite opinion, for example because they have insufficient information.

–   Paragraph 2.5: If, after producing a report, an expert's view changes on any
     material matter, such change of view should be communicated to all the
     parties without delay, and when appropriate to the court.
–   Paragraph 3.1: An expert's report should be addressed to the court and not
     to the party from whom the expert has received instructions.
–   Paragraph 3.2: An expert's report must:
     (a) give details of the expert's qualifications;
     (b) give details of any literature or other material which has been relied on
          in making the report;
     (c) contain a statement setting out the substance of all facts and
          instructions which are material to the opinions expressed in the report
          or upon which those opinions are based;
     (d) make clear which of the facts stated in the report are within the expert's
          own knowledge;
     (e) say who carried out any examination, measurement, test or experiment
          which the expert has used for the report, give the qualifications of that
          person, and say whether or not the test or experiment has been carried
          out under the expert's supervision;
     (f) where there is a range of opinion on the matters dealt with in the
          report:
          (i)   summarise the range of opinions; and
          (ii) give reasons for the expert's own opinion;
     (g) contain a summary of the conclusions reached;
     (h) if the expert is not able to give an opinion without qualification, state
          the qualification; and
     (i) contain a statement that the expert:
          (i)   understands their duty to the court, and has complied with that
                duty; and
          (ii) is aware of the requirements of Part 35, this Practice Direction
                and the Protocol for Instruction of Experts to give Evidence in
                Civil Claims.
–   Paragraph 3.3: sets out the precise terms of the Statement of Truth which
     must verify an expert's report.
• Paragraph 13 of the Expert Protocol confirms the Practice Direction, emphasising
   the Statement of Truth is mandatory and must not be modified. Additionally, this
   paragraph confirms some additional requirements for any expert to deal with:
   –   Details of qualifications should be given.
   –   Details of any tests of a scientific or technical nature carried out should be
        given.
   –   Reports of others should only be relied on or cited if they have been verified
        and details of those reports given.
   –   Questions of fact and opinion should be kept separate and discrete.
   –   The expert must distinguish between facts which are known to be true by the
        expert and those which are assumed.
   –   With facts, the expert must distinguish between those which are known to be
        true by the expert and those which are assumed.
   –   Where material facts were in dispute the expert should give separate opinions
        on each hypothesis and not express a view in favour of any disputed version
        of facts unless, as a result of particular expertise and experience, the expert
        considers one set of facts are improbable or less probable, in which case that
        view may be given with reasons.
   –   If the summary of the range of opinion is based on published sources experts
        should explain those sources, and if no available source the expert may need
        to express opinions on what is believed to be the range which other experts
        would arrive at if asked.

–   A summary of the expert's conclusions should be given, particularly if that will assist the court, at the outset, in establishing the direction in which the report will go.

Case-law has also endorsed the nature of the expert's duties in contested matters. In *Oldham MBC v GW, PW and KPW*[129] the judge emphasised that:

• experts need clear instructions and access to all relevant documents, not selected ones;

• the expert's report should set out the expert's analytical process, differentiate between facts, assumptions, deductions and note inconsistent or contradictory features of the case;

• the expert should identify the professional range of opinion and use a 'balance sheet' approach to their own opinion;

• the expert should volunteer where an opinion from other expertise is likely to assist the parties and the court; and

• the expert should not stray into the role of decision-maker.

7.6   CLAIMANT'S EXPERT

The need for expert evidence will inevitably depend upon the particular facts and issues of each case.

If the issues suggest evidence from an expert in a recognised field of expertise is likely to be required, to assist the court in making all necessary findings, and a suitable expert within that field can be identified, then tactical considerations will arise about the way such an expert should be involved in the case. Crucially, the claimant will need to assess whether any such expert should be instructed unilaterally, though perhaps following joint selection, or instructed jointly with the defendant.

Any expert upon whom the claimant may wish to rely will need to be properly instructed, the report admissible as evidence, permission obtained from the court for the claimant to rely on the expert's evidence and, if any further action by the expert will be necessary following disclosure of the report, that expert kept involved about progress with the case.

The instruction of an expert on behalf of the claimant will involve a number of stages, each requiring consideration of the most appropriate action in the particular matter.

7.6.1   Preliminaries

Considerations preliminary to the instruction of an expert are, of course, applicable whenever the claimant identifies the possible need for expert evidence.

These preliminaries will involve identifying the issues, the factual evidence that may be available, and will allow the court to resolve those issues without expert input, whether

---

129   [2007] EWHC 136 (Fam).

expert advice is, at least initially, more appropriate than expert evidence, what information might be obtained from the defendant and whether any facilities are required from the defendant (see 7.2.4).

7.6.2 Joint expert?

If expert evidence is required the next consideration will be whether, if *prior* to the issue of court proceedings, experts should be nominated with a view to joint selection or, if *after* issue of court proceedings, joint instruction contemplated.

Away from issues where it is almost inevitable each party will obtain expert evidence, where there is unlikely to be any benefit even in nomination, the claimant will have little to lose by nominating with a view to joint selection.

Joint instruction, following issue of court proceedings, is a much riskier strategy for the claimant, certainly on key areas of the claim, but may be appropriate (see 7.7).

7.6.3 Court permission?

Whilst permission of the court is necessary to use an expert's report as evidence, it is not necessary to gain the court's permission before obtaining a report from an expert, even if it is intended that permission to rely on that evidence will be sought once it is available.

In *Hajigeorgiou v Vasiliou*[130] Dyson LJ observed that:

> 'CPR 35.4 contains the rules which govern the court's power to restrict expert evidence. They do not refer to the "instruction" of experts. They provide that no party may "call" or "put in evidence an expert's report" without the court's permission.'

Accordingly, there is no restriction on use of experts purely on an 'advisory' or 'shadow' basis to help assess the strengths and weaknesses of a case and, as appropriate, to formulate how the claim is put. If a party intends to rely on such advice as evidence, permission from the court will then be required and the evidence of the expert need to be given in compliance with the CPR.

The risk, of not seeking advance approval from the court, is that, should it not be allowed, the costs of obtaining that evidence are unlikely to be recoverable. But set against this risk are a number of factors:

- It may be necessary to obtain the views of an expert before proceedings are commenced, hence permission cannot be sought from the court.
- The views of the expert may be used just for the purposes of advice, to shape the case, and in these circumstances even if the expert is not relied on as a witness there may be a good argument that the costs of that advice should be recovered as having been reasonably incurred.
- It may sometimes be difficult to persuade the court, in the abstract, that a report from a particular expert is likely to be reasonably required. If, however, the report

---

[130] [2005] EWCA Civ 236.

is already available, and can be read by the court, its probative value may be apparent and the party can more readily obtain permission to rely upon that evidence:

– In *Ahmed v Stanley A Coleman & Hill*[131] the court effectively accepted it was appropriate for a party to obtain a report and then seek permission to rely upon it. Indeed, the failure to obtain a report prior to the hearing when permission was sought told against the applicant and it was held to be too late, at the stage of an appeal, to seek to introduce a report not available at the initial hearing.

– Similarly, in *Austen v Oxford City Council*[132] the court recognised the difficulty faced by a party wishing to seek permission to call an expert when no report from that expert was immediately available.

– Consequently, where no report is available, and application for permission to rely on the proposed expert is refused, a party may decide to obtain a report from the relevant expert and renew the application once that report is available (see **8.3.3**).

Whilst the claimant does not need the court's permission, as a preliminary, to obtain expert evidence (although in some circumstances a court order may be required to get necessary facilities for that evidence to be obtained) it does remain necessary for the claimant to get permission from the court for any expert evidence to be relied upon.

7.6.4 Obtaining facilities

The court will, however, have a role in the obtaining of expert evidence if a party requires facilities for such purposes, for example if the defendant wishes for facilities to have the claimant examined or if the claimant wishes for facilities to inspect property belonging to the defendant or a non-party.

A practical problem may arise for the claimant if wishing to obtain, for example, expert evidence on liability that requires, as a preliminary, facilities to inspect property owned by the defendant or a third party and those facilities are not granted.

Whilst the claimant should, initially, seek facilities for an inspection in correspondence the court can, if necessary, make an order allowing inspection, and associated matters, under CPR 25.5 which may be dealt with pre-action or at the stage of case management direction.

The grant of such facilities should not depend, as it is a quite distinct issue, on whether, ultimately, expert evidence will be 'reasonably required' for the purposes of Part 35. That is because, until the evidence is available, the answer to this question may not be known. Moreover, if the defendant has carried out an inspection of the kind for which the claimant now seeks facilities, the terms of the overriding objective would normally suggest the claimant, in the interests of equality, have corresponding facilities. Allowing facilities to inspect a property does not raise the same issues as allowing the defendant facilities for the claimant to be examined, as explained by Dyson LJ in *Hajigeorgiou v Vasiliou*[133] (see **7.8.5.1**).

---

[131] [2002] EWCA Civ 935.
[132] (Unreported) QBD, Douglas Brown J 17/04/2002.
[133] [2005] EWCA Civ 236.

Irrespective of the need for permission, the parties ought to co-operate with eachother. In relation to experts, that would normally involve joint selection, under the Protocol, pre-issue or trying to agree joint instruction, following issue of proceedings.

7.6.5   Approaching the expert

When it is known the proposed expert is likely to be ready and able to act on appropriate terms, first contact may be a letter of instruction.

In other circumstances it may be more appropriate for the proposed expert to be sent a letter of approach summarising the scope of the proposed instructions, enquiring whether the expert can assist and, if so, seeking information on timescale and likely fee.

It may sometimes be necessary to send a letter of approach to more than one proposed expert in any particular field of expertise.

7.6.6   Instructing the expert

If it is known an expert is ready and able to act on appropriate terms, or a proposed expert has responded to a letter of approach confirming willingness to act on acceptable terms, a letter of instruction will need to be prepared.

The terms of the instructions to the expert will depend upon the nature of the case, and the issues to be dealt with, though general guidance is offered by paragraphs 7 and 8 of the Expert Protocol.

Typically, instructions to an expert will include some or all of the following matters:

- A request the expert advise promptly whether or not the instructions are accepted (unless an initial approach has been made and the expert has already confirmed a willingness to act).
- Confirmation of the particular party instructing the expert or that the instructions are on a joint basis (in which case those instructions should either confirm they are agreed, on behalf of both parties, or that each party will submit separate instructions).
- The identity of any other parties, or likely parties, to the proceedings or proposed proceedings.
- Whether the expert is being asked to provide advice or evidence.
- Where the expert is being asked to provide evidence it may be helpful to remind that expert of the consequent responsibilities by setting out, including copies in the instructions or expressly drawing the attention of the expert to Part 35 of the CPR, the accompanying Practice Direction, and the Expert Protocol.
- The relevant factual background (with alternative scenarios where applicable), any matters for the expert to investigate on that background, the legal context and issues to be dealt with.
- Specific matters on which the expert's opinion is sought, ideally questions for the expert to answer (though with expert evidence those answers will need to be admissible as opinion).

- Identifying all enclosures which should include relevant witness statements, documents forming part of standard disclosure and, if proceedings have been issued, the Statements of Case. Whilst the expert will need to refer to the instructions, the right of any other party to see such documents will turn upon the terms of CPR 31.14 and CPR 35.10 (see **5.2.4.3**).

- A request the expert provide with the report any relevant source material relied upon (so this is readily available to the parties).

- Whether or not proceedings have been issued (and if so details of the court and case number in the event the expert wishes to apply for directions as provided for under CPR 35.14).

- Any applicable time limits (including an estimate of future timescale for reporting which anticipates good case management).

- An estimate of the likely fee, or basis for calculating the fee, unless that has already been dealt with as a preliminary.

- A timescale for paying the expert's fees, again unless already agreed.

- A request for details of any conflict of interest there might be.

- Confirmation that, if necessary, the expert is willing, and can be available, to attend any trial to give oral evidence.

Whilst many experts may be familiar with these matters that will not always be so and it is good discipline to ensure each expert in every case is properly instructed: *Oldham MBC v GW, PW and KPW.*[134]

Indeed, the courts emphasise the responsibility of lawyers to ensure an expert is properly instructed and that caution should be exercised before criticising an expert unless it is clear any fault is that of the expert rather than the instructions: *Medimmune Ltd v Novarts Pharmaceuticals Ltd.*[135]

Given the terms of the Expert Protocol it may be appropriate, whether instructing unilaterally or jointly, to, amongst other matters, remind (if the expert is familiar with giving expert evidence in civil proceedings) or explain (if not) the terms of Part 35, the accompanying Practice Direction and the Expert Protocol.

7.6.7 Funding arrangements

An expert is entitled to be paid for time spent preparing a report and, if necessary, for giving evidence.

It is appropriate to ask, in advance, for details of the likely fee and also to seek agreement on timescale for payment as there is no objection, in principle, for agreeing that payment be deferred either to a specified date or event (such as conclusion of the claim).

However, it is not appropriate to enter into a fee arrangement with an expert which is dependant on the outcome of the case. Even so, the court retains a discretion to admit

---

[134] [2007] EWHC 136 (Fam).
[135] [2011] EWHC 1669 (Pat).

the evidence if it is clear that the expert has understood, and complied with, the paramount duty to help the court: *Davis v Stena Line Ltd*.[136]

Paragraph 7.6 of the Expert Protocol expressly prohibits conditional or contingency fees for experts, though paragraph 7.7 confirms an agreement to defer payment until conclusion of the case is permissible so long as the amount of the fee does not depend on the outcome of the case.

The Expert Protocol precludes an expert being paid on a contingency basis because of the risk of that generating a conflict, for the reasons explained by Lord Phillips MR in *R (Factortame) v Secretary of State for Transport (No 8)*[137] where he said:

> 'To give evidence on a contingency fee basis gives an expert, who would otherwise be independent, a significant financial interest in the outcome of the case. As a general proposition, such an interest is highly undesirable. In many cases the expert will be giving an authoritative opinion on issues that are critical to the outcome of the case. In such a situation the threat to his objectivity posed by a contingency fee agreement may carry greater dangers to the administration of justice than would the interest of an advocate or solicitor acting under a similar agreement. Accordingly, we consider that it will be in a very rare case indeed that the Court will be prepared to consent to an expert being instructed under a contingency fee agreement.'

7.6.8   Reviewing the report

When a report, intended for use as evidence, is received from an expert it is important to carefully review and check that report.

This review is likely to include checking a number of points:

- the format of the report complies with the CPR (and in particular CPR 35.9, paragraphs 2 and 3 of the Practice Direction to Part 35 and paragraph 13 of the Expert Protocol);
- the factual background is correctly stated;
- the opinion given and hence whether the claimant should be advised to rely upon the evidence or not;
- if, so far as it is proper to do so, any amendments to the report should be requested;
- if any matters require clarification.

A copy of the report should then go to the claimant. The claimant should also be asked to check the factual background and, of course, given advice on what the opinion means for the claim or relevant part of that claim.

Where, as a result of the review of the report or instructions from the claimant, an amendment seems appropriate, the guidance offered by paragraph 15.2 of the Expert Protocol should be followed. This provides that experts should not be asked to, and should not, amend, expand or alter reports in a manner that distorts the true opinion of the expert but may be invited to amend or expand reports to ensure accuracy, internal consistency, completeness and relevance to the issues and clarity.

---

[136] [2005] EWHC 420 (QB).
[137] [2002] EWCA Civ 932.

Where, ultimately, the claimant discloses the final version of the report, earlier drafts will remain privileged: *Jackson v Marley Davenport Ltd*.[138] Care is necessary where there are different versions of the report, to ensure only the report intended for disclosure is produced, otherwise privilege for earlier versions may be waived: *Gough v Mummery*.[139]

7.6.9 Relying on the report and privilege

When the report, amended appropriately if necessary, has been approved, and instructions have been obtained from the claimant confirming that the report is approved, reliance will be placed on that evidence, subject to court permission, by disclosing the report at the appropriate stage.

Meanwhile, unless and until he claimant deploys the report, privilege will attach to any report prepared solely on the instructions of the claimant, even where there has been joint selection under the Protocol: *Carlson v Townsend*.[140]

In *Causton v Mann Egerton (Johnsons) Ltd*[141] Roskill LJ observed:

> 'In my judgment it is not open to this court to order production of privileged documents against the wish of the party claiming privilege.'

Furthermore, as Hughes LJ explained in *Edwards-Tubb v J D Weatherspoon plc*:[142]

> 'The privilege belongs to the claimant and not to the doctor. His privilege to keep this document to himself is a substantive right in law. That privilege is a legal concept of considerable importance is demonstrated by a long succession of cases, of which *R v Derby Magistrates Court ex p B*[143] is perhaps the most striking. As that decision makes clear, there is no question of balancing privilege against other considerations of public interest; the balancing act has been accomplished many years ago and was resolved by preserving the right of privilege. A person in possession of a privileged document cannot be criticised for claiming the privilege and declining to waive it, nor can any adverse inference be drawn against him from his claim: *Wentworth v Lloyd*[144] and *Sayers v Clarke Walker*.[145] Thus in a case like the present, it is not permissible to infer at trial from the claimant's stand upon the privileged nature of Mr Jackson's report that that report was unfavourable to him.'

Once a report has been disclosed, privilege is waived and even if the party disclosing the report no longer seeks to rely upon it other parties may be permitted to do so under CPR 35.11: *Shepherd & Neame v EDF Energy Networks (SPN) Plc*[146] (see **7.9.4.5**).

A report may be disclosed before permission to rely on that evidence has been obtained, typically a medical report accompanying the Particulars of Claim will be disclosed prior to the claimant seeking permission to rely on that evidence at the stage of case management.

---

138 [2004] EWCA Civ 1225.
139 [2002] EWCA Civ 1573.
140 [2001] EWCA Civ 511.
141 [1974] 1 WLR 162.
142 [2011] EWCA Civ 136.
143 [1996] AC 487.
144 (1864) 10 HLC 589.
145 [2002] EWCA Civ 910.
146 [2008] EWHC 123 (TCC).

However, the claimant may wish to seek permission to rely on the evidence obtained on the basis of there being directions for disclosure at a later stage in the proceedings, perhaps by way of simultaneous exchange, so that only then will privilege be waived.

Permission from the court to rely on the evidence of an expert might sometimes only be obtained when the report of that evidence is already available. Even so, when to deploy that report will be a matter for the claimant, bearing in mind any time limits imposed by case management directions.

If, however, there has been joint selection of an expert under the Protocol and the claimant wishes to obtain permission to rely on a different expert, the court may make a conditional order requiring, in return for that permission, the claimant to voluntarily waive privilege and produce the original report (see 7.2.3).

CPR 35.10 confirms instructions set out in the report of the expert will not be privileged but, in relation to those instructions, the court will not order disclosure or permit any questioning in court, other than by the party who instructed the expert, unless satisfied there are reasonable grounds to consider the statement of instructions is inaccurate or incomplete. For these purposes the term 'instructions' is likely to be interpreted broadly: *Lucas v Barking, Havering and Redbridge Hospital NHS Trust.*[147]

7.6.10   Following disclosure of the report

Even after the expert evidence on which the claimant relies has been disclosed there are important obligations to keep in mind relating to that evidence.

7.6.10.1   *Updating the expert*

Paragraph 14 of the Expert Protocol confirms that experts should be advised, once reports have been prepared, whether, and if so when, such reports will be disclosed.

Consequently, as and when any report is disclosed, whether at the outset of proceedings or on exchange in accordance with case management directions, the relevant expert should be informed accordingly. Paragraph 7 of the Expert Protocol, as well as confirming experts should receive copies of relevant court orders, also provides for experts to be informed regularly about deadlines for all matters which concern those experts.

Paragraph 8 of the Practice Direction to Part 35 confirms copies of any court orders giving case management directions should be served on any expert affected by those directions.

Paragraph 19.2 of the Expert Protocol requires those instructing experts to ascertain availability of such experts before trial dates are fixed and to advise immediately if trial dates are vacated.

---

[147] [2003] EWCA Civ 1102.

7.6.10.2 *Change of opinion*

Cases can develop, following the preparation of an expert's report, hence paragraph 14 of the Expert Protocol provides that experts should be kept informed of any amendments to the Statements of Case and of any material change in the information otherwise available so that reports can be updated.

Furthermore, paragraph 15.4 of the Expert Protocol confirms that where an expert significantly alters an opinion as a result of new evidence, or because existing evidence has become unreliable, the report should be amended with reasons.

Where an expert has changed opinion the claimant must either rely on the amended opinion or abandon reliance on the expert altogether but may, in such circumstances, face difficulties obtaining permission to rely on an alternative expert (see **7.9.4.3**).

7.7 SINGLE (JOINT) EXPERTS

The intention of the CPR is that where expert evidence is required this should be given, if possible, by a single expert in a particular discipline or on a particular issue.

7.7.1 When will there be a single (non-joint) expert?

A single expert will often, though not necessarily, be a single joint expert which is defined by CPR 35.2 (1) as 'an expert instructed to prepare a report for the court on behalf of two or more of the parties (including the claimant) to the proceedings'.

There are a number of situations, however, when there is a single expert in a particular discipline or on a specific issue who is not a single joint expert:

- The claimant may rely on expert evidence where the defendant has never sought to rely on a corresponding expert, perhaps because the relevant expert was jointly selected under the Protocol or the defendant did not anticipate the court allowing permission to rely on a further expert in the same field (particularly in a fast track case).
- The defendant might not have been given facilities to obtain corresponding expert evidence and the court declines to grant a stay unless the claimant provides such facilities.
- The defendant does not obtain permission from the court to rely upon corresponding expert evidence (for example in a fast track case the court concluding the expert evidence should be confined to 'one expert').
- The defendant obtains, but chooses not to disclose and rely upon, corresponding expert evidence.
- The evidence obtained and disclosed by the claimant is agreed.

In all these situations the expert evidence, in the relevant field or on the particular issue, will effectively be that which the claimant has obtained and relied upon, whether or not using the mechanism of joint selection under the Protocol.

In other circumstances the single expert will be a joint expert and different arrangements have been made to obtain that evidence. There are important distinctions in the availability of an expert's report, and the ways in which parties can deal with such an expert, if the evidence is obtained jointly as opposed to unilaterally.

Before considering the instruction of and subsequent dealings with a joint expert it is important to note the difference between joint selection and joint instruction of experts, a distinction very relevant to issues of privilege and subsequent dealings with the expert concerned.

7.7.2   Joint selection and joint instruction of experts

There is a very important distinction between a single expert jointly selected, in accordance with the Protocol, and a single joint expert, jointly instructed by more than one party in accordance with the CPR.

In *Carlson v Townsend*[148] the Court of Appeal accepted this distinction and its significance. Simon Brown LJ observed:

> 'It seems to me one thing to provide, as the protocol undoubtedly does, for a practice whereby experts objectionable to one party are eliminated at the outset and with them an obvious barrier to the prospect of ultimately agreeing the expert evidence: quite another to hold that by giving the other side the opportunity to object to a proposed expert, a party is thereby waiving in advance the privilege which would otherwise attach to the report be obtained. In the Rules themselves, of course, there is express provision for the court to direct that evidence be given by a single joint expert ... there is plainly in these circumstances joint instruction of the expert with the result that both parties have (unless the court directs otherwise) an equal liability for his fees and an equal right to see his report. That, however, is not what happens when the protocol is followed ... jointly selected the expert in a real sense has been; jointly instructed, however, he is not.'

The procedure for jointly selecting experts is set out in the Protocol, reflecting the more general guidance given in the Practice Direction – Pre-action Conduct in Annex C, which, by definition, is only applicable prior to issue of court proceedings. However, that process for joint selection is not confined to medical experts, or even experts on quantum, but applicable to experts across the whole range of disciplines including experts who will deal with liability.

Once court proceedings have been issued, and the CPR holds sway, if there is to be a single expert that is likely to be an expert jointly instructed by the parties in accordance with CPR 35.7. Paragraph 7 of the Practice Direction to Part 35 gives further guidance on when a single expert would be appropriate in such circumstances.

7.7.2.1   *When to jointly select experts*

Prior to the issue of court proceedings the method for joint selection provided for under the Protocol should be used where it seems appropriate for there to be a single expert in a particular discipline or on a particular issue.

Joint selection of experts, at this stage, is appropriate for a number of reasons:

---

[148]   [2001] EWCA 511.

- That is what the Protocol and the Practice Direction – Pre-action Conduct envisage.

- The burden of proof is on the claimant who should, therefore, play the lead role in obtaining evidence necessary to discharge that burden.

- It will not be necessary for the instructions to be submitted jointly (with the disadvantage that the claimant thereby inevitably discloses the identity of the expert who has been selected out of those the defendant has not objected to).

- Privilege will attach to the report of a jointly selected expert, but not to the report of a jointly instructed expert: *Carlson v Townsend*.[149] Indeed, privilege will still attach to an initial report or draft report of an expert who has not been jointly instructed even after a final version of the report is disclosed: *Jackson v Marley Davenport Ltd*.[150]

- The claimant may hold a conference with the expert, without involving other parties, if the expert is jointly selected whilst all relevant parties ought generally to be present at a conference if the expert has been jointly instructed: *Peet v Mid-Kent Healthcare* Trust.[151]

Where there has been joint selection of an expert under the Protocol it is important to remember that if the claimant later seeks permission to rely on a different expert in the same field of expertise the court may well impose a condition that the report of the jointly selected expert be voluntarily disclosed: *Edwards-Tubb v J D Weatherspoon plc*.[152]

Consequently, and particularly if it seems unlikely the expert evidence on a particular issue or in a specific field will be confined to one such expert, the claimant may decide to unilaterally instruct an expert, if need be obtaining expert advice as a preliminary, rather than jointly select let alone jointly instruct that expert.

Neither the RTA Protocol nor the EL/PL Protocol provide for joint selection, or indeed joint instruction, of experts. If the claim remains within either Protocol there is no basis on which the defendant could seek corresponding evidence in the same field. To guard against a claim exiting the protocol, and an issue arising about experts having been neither jointly selected nor jointly instructed, the claimant may, in some cases entering either the RTA Protocol or the EL/PL Protocol, still wish to nominate experts, for the purposes of joint selection, adopting the procedure of the PI Protocol.

The claimant will be solely responsible for the expert's fee even when there has been joint selection (at least pending any subsequent order from the court as to costs).

The potentially broad scope of experts covered by the machinery for joint selection in the Protocol is reflected by the words of Lord Woolf MR in *Field v Leeds City Council CA*[153] when he said:

> 'Before I leave this case, I think it is right to say something of a more general nature. These cases have financial implications on local authorities and to the tenants which should not be ignored. The amounts which are in issue can be relatively small. Anything which reduces that

---

[149] [2001] EWCA Civ 511.
[150] [2004] EWCA CIV 1225.
[151] [2002] 1 WLR 210.
[152] [2011] EWCA Civ 136.
[153] (Lord Woolf MR, Waller LJ, May LJ) 8/12/99.

expense is to be warmly welcomed. The ideal way of disposing of issues such as that which arise in this case, is for one expert to be appointed by both sides. Clearly, someone in Mr Broadbent's position is not going to be acceptable by the other side. I would hope that procedures will be devised where claimants in cases such as this inform the authority of the expert whom they intend to engage so that the views of the authority can be taken into account. That could lead to single experts being appointed much more often than has happened in the past which is ideally to be desired.'

However, given the decision in *Edwards-Tubb* it may be necessary to exercise caution, and consider expert advice or unilateral instruction, particularly if the defendant will be aware of the identity of the expert concerned, perhaps because inspection facilities are required from the defendant.

7.7.2.2   *When to jointly instruct experts*

If one expert in a particular field, or on any issue, seems appropriate but court proceedings have been commenced prior to instruction of that expert, the parties will need to consider joint instruction.

Assuming the claimant is one of the parties providing instructions, the expert will be a single joint expert as defined by CPR 35.2(1).

Joint instruction, and hence evidence being given by a single joint expert, is a very different situation from that where there is just one expert, even if that expert has been jointly selected under the Protocol.

Key differences, from a jointly selected or unilaterally instructed expert, where there is joint instruction, include the following:

- Instructions will, ideally, be submitted to the expert on a joint basis, though if necessary one party can send the instructions and the other supplement those as appropriate or submit separate instructions: *Yorke v Katra*.[154] Where the instructions are not joint the terms of CPR 35.8 require each party submitting instructions to copy those instructions to other relevant parties.

- Privilege will not attach to the report, which will be sent out by the experts simultaneously to all instructing parties (in accordance with paragraph 17.14 of the Expert Protocol).

- If a conference with the expert is required, all instructing parties ought to be present, unless the parties have agreed otherwise in writing or the court has directed such a meeting may be held as confirmed by paragraph 17.12 Expert Protocol.

The restriction on one party dealing with a joint expert may extend further than meetings or conferences. In *Edwards v Bruce & Hyslop (Brucast) Ltd*[155] Coulson J observed:

'(The expert) can no more have communications with just one party about the substance of his report, in the absence of the other side, than a judge can have a conversation on the telephone with one party, and not the other, about the strengths and weaknesses of that party's case.'

---

[154] [2003] EWCA Civ 867.
[155] [2009] EWHC 2970 (QB).

The parties may have agreed that there should be a single joint expert on a particular issue but, if not, the court will, when giving permission to rely on expert evidence, want to consider whether that would be appropriate having regard to the guidance given in paragraph 7 of the Practice Direction to Part 35.

Paragraph 7, recognising some of the practical differences between joint selection and joint instruction, make some important provisions:

- Whether it is proportionate to have separate experts for each party on a particular issue with reference to:
  - the amount in dispute;
  - the importance to the parties; and
  - the complexity of the issue;
- Whether the instruction of a single joint expert is likely to assist the parties and the court to resolve the issue more speedily and in a more cost-effective way than separately instructed experts;
- Whether expert evidence is to be given on the issue of liability, causation or quantum;
- Whether the expert evidence falls within a substantially established area of knowledge which is unlikely to be in dispute or there is likely to be a range of expert opinion;
- Whether a party has already instructed an expert on the issue in question and whether or not that was done in compliance with any Practice Direction or relevant pre-action protocol;
- Whether questions put in accordance with rule 35.6 are likely to remove the need for the other party to instruct an expert if one party has already instructed an expert;
- Whether questions put to a single joint expert may not conclusively deal with all issues that may require testing prior to trial;
- Whether a conference may be required with the legal representatives, experts and other witnesses which may make instruction of a single joint expert impractical; and
- Whether a claim to privilege makes the instruction of any expert as a single joint expert inappropriate.

If the parties have, at an early stage, instructed their own experts, it may be disproportionate for the court to effectively require the parties to start again and instruct a single joint expert (particularly if the expert evidence already available suggests a range of opinions).

In a fast track case the court, whilst not imposing a single joint expert, may still limit the expert evidence on a particular issue to 'one expert' in accordance with CPR 35.4(3A) (and for these purposes it may be very relevant such an expert has been jointly selected even though not jointly instructed).

Paragraph 17.4 of the Expert Protocol confirms there is no objection, in principle, to an expert who has previously advised a party being proposed as a single joint expert, but other parties must be given information, by the party making the proposal, about that previous involvement. It may, once again, be relevant that any such expert was proposed for the purposes of joint selection.

Although joint instruction will normally be appropriate only once court proceedings have been commenced there may, nevertheless, be circumstances in which, prior to issue of court proceedings, joint instruction may be adopted by the parties. For example, paragraph 17.3 of the Expert Protocol confirms that where in the early stages of a dispute any examinations, investigations, tests, site inspections, experiments or the preparation of plans and photographs along with other similar preliminary expert tasks are necessary, the parties should consider instructing a single joint expert, to agree or narrow the issues, though it is recognised that may only be appropriate where such matters are not expected to be contentious. If matters are expected to be contentious, experts might still be offered by way of joint selection so that even if unilaterally instructed, there may be a greater likelihood of such evidence being agreed if necessary after questions.

An expert may be involved with the claimant for the purposes of treatment or rehabilitation, rather than primarily for forensic purposes, for example as a case manager. In such circumstances, even though appointed after litigation has been commenced and in circumstances such that the input of the expert may have some bearing on the way the litigation is conducted, joint instruction may well not be appropriate as the primary, if not sole, duty of the expert is towards the claimant as a patient: *Wright v Sullivan*.[156] Furthermore, joint instruction will prohibit a conference which took place solely with the claimant's legal advisors and that would be inconsistent with the nature of the expert's primary duty to the patient.

If the court has imposed, rather than the parties agreed, a single joint expert, difficulties may arise in agreeing the identity of the expert to be instructed. CPR 35.7 provides that, if necessary, the court will decide the identity of the expert either from a list prepared by the parties or in such other way as the court may direct. In practice, and this is a potential difficulty with single joint experts if the identity cannot be agreed, that may leave one party or the other dissatisfied. Hence, paragraph 17.5 of the Expert Protocol confirms the appointment of a single joint expert does not prevent parties instructing their own experts to advise but warns the costs of doing so may not be recoverable.

Accordingly, whether the route is joint selection or joint instruction, there may be a single expert in a particular field. However, just because there is a joint expert that will not necessarily prevent the involvement of a further expert in the same field if really necessary (see 7.9.2).

7.7.3 When will there be a single joint expert?

CPR 35.2(1) defines a single joint expert as 'an expert instructed to prepare a report for the court on behalf of two or more of the parties (including the claimant) to the proceedings'.

The circumstances in which there will be a single expert, rather than simply one expert, in a field of expertise or on a particular issue, will be when the parties have agreed to joint instruction or when the court, giving case management directions, has given permission for the parties to rely on a single joint expert (which will effectively mean an expert who must then be instructed, on a joint basis by those parties).

---

[156] [2005] EWCA Civ 656.

In either situation the prospect of a further expert, in the same field or dealing with the same issue, cannot be ruled out and a party may still be able to get appropriate permission from the court (see **7.9.2**).

7.7.4 The consequences of having a single expert

If there is a single expert, in any field or dealing with any issue, then, whether or not a single joint expert, there are a number of consequences.

Oral evidence, where there is a single expert, will be the exception rather than the rule. That is an important consideration if a party does not accept the opinion of a single expert (see **7.13.12**).

Whilst not bound to accept the opinion of an expert, even where there is a single expert, the court will need good reason to depart from the views of such an expert (see 7.14). This, again, is an important factor if a party does not agree the evidence of the expert concerned.

A party cannot convene a meeting or conference with the expert without involving other parties, unless all concerned agree or the court so directs.

7.7.5 Instructing a joint expert

The same considerations apply to instructing a joint expert as they do to the instruction of an expert unilaterally by the claimant.

However, given the terms of CPR 35.8, those instructions will either need to be agreed or copied to other parties.

CPR 35.8 also provides that the fee for a jointly instructed expert will usually be shared by the instructing parties, unless the court otherwise directs.

Paragraph 17.14 of the Expert Protocol confirms that any single joint expert should serve the report simultaneously on all instructing parties.

7.7.6 Reviewing a joint report

The report of a jointly instructed expert needs to be reviewed in exactly the same way as the report of an expert who has been unilaterally instructed by the claimant.

The report of a jointly instructed expert, however, will not be privileged and so even if the claimant chooses not to rely upon it that report will be available to any other instructing parties who may elect to rely on that evidence.

Where the claimant decides not to rely on the evidence of a jointly instructed expert, a decision must be made about whether to seek a further expert opinion on the same issue and whether, ultimately, permission to rely on such evidence is likely to be obtained (see **7.9.4.3**).

7.7.7   Updating a joint expert

There is still an obligation to keep an expert updated, even if a single joint expert, although that responsibility will rest on all instructing parties.

In practice, as there should be no need for a joint statement or oral evidence, this may be less of an issue then when an expert is instructed unilaterally.

Paragraph 17.12 of the Expert Protocol is a reminder that a single joint expert should not attend any meeting or conference which is not a joint one, unless all parties have agreed in writing or the court has directed such a meeting may be held.

7.8   DEFENDANT'S EXPERT EVIDENCE

The defendant, like the claimant, does not need permission to obtain expert evidence and, accordingly, may do so without any advance notice to the claimant or any attempt to agree arrangements for a single expert.

The terms of the Practice Direction – Pre-action Conduct do, however, apply equally to the defendant, as to the claimant, hence the defendant should not necessarily just instruct an expert unilaterally but consider, especially if the claimant has nominated, whether it is possible to have a single expert, whether joint or not, on any issue or in any relevant discipline.

Consequently, from the claimant's perspective, issues relating to the defendant obtaining expert evidence are most likely to arise in relation to the agreement of a single expert, whether jointly selected or jointly instructed, and where the defendant seeks facilities from the claimant to obtain such evidence, frequently a request that the claimant be examined by a medical expert instructed on behalf of just the defendant.

7.8.1   Preliminaries

Whilst the claimant's representatives can usually rely on the claimant to give facilities to obtain expert medical evidence, but may encounter difficulties arranging to inspect property belonging to the defendant or a third party, for the defendant the position is transposed.

If the defendant wishes to obtain expert medical evidence it is likely to involve the defendant seeking facilities to have the claimant examined, as an expert medical witness will usually want to base an opinion on such an examination as well as a review of the background from relevant documents.

Logically, the issue of such facilities will precede the question of whether permission to rely on the evidence produced should be granted, as the evidence may not be available unless and until facilities have been provided.

7.8.1.1 Pre-issue

Occasionally it may be appropriate for the claimant to offer the defendant facilities to obtain medical evidence pre-issue of court proceedings.

If, however, facilities are not given there is no basis for the defendant to apply to the court for any order in relation to the facilities requested and any such issue will need to be deferred until court proceedings have been commenced.

7.8.1.2 Post-issue

Following the issue of court proceedings the defendant will be in a stronger position to seek, if these are necessary, facilities to obtain expert evidence upon which permission to rely will be sought.

There is, however, no provision in the CPR, equivalent to that found in Part 25 allowing a claimant to inspect property, which provides a specific power for the court to order the claimant to give facilities for an examination.

Despite that it is not unusual to see court orders purporting to allow a defendant permission to obtain expert evidence, with the implication that should include the grant of such facilities by the claimant.

Despite the court's wide case management powers, case-law would suggest it will not be appropriate to direct that the claimant give facilities for the defendant to obtain a medical report (see **7.6.3**).

The court may, however, impose a stay on the claim, again in accordance with general case management powers, if the claimant acts unreasonably in refusing to give necessary facilities.

7.8.2 A stay

If the defendant seeks facilities for an expert to examine the claimant, or the court gives permission for the defendant to rely on expert evidence of a kind that would usually be based on an examination, a application for a stay is likely if the claimant declines to give the facilities requested.

In *Beck v Ministry of Defence*[157] the Court of Appeal considered such an application by the defendant for a stay under the CPR.

The circumstances of the application were slightly unusual in that the defendant wished for facilities to obtain a third opinion in the relevant discipline. That was because the claimant had obtained expert evidence from a psychiatrist following which the defendant was given facilities to obtain corresponding evidence from an expert in the same field. Subsequently, without disclosing that second report, the defendant indicated that report was not going to be relied on and requested facilities for the claimant to be examined by yet further psychiatrists.

---

[157] [2003] EWCA Civ 1043.

APIL Guide to Personal Injury Claims Procedure

When considering the application the court effectively approved the approach adopted prior to the introduction of the CPR, going back to *Edmeades v Thames Board Mills*[158] as applied in *Lane v Willis*.[159]

That pre-CPR approach reflected the fact that because the grant of any facilities would inevitably involve an invasion of the claimant's privacy, the party seeking such facilities had to show:

- these are reasonably required in the interests of justice; and
- if so, then whether any refusal to give those facilities is reasonable; and
- even if the refusal is unreasonable, that the case cannot properly be prepared without such facilities.

That approach seems consonant with the terms of Article 8 of the European Convention on Human Rights which permits only a proportionate interference with private life.

The burden is on the party seeking a stay to establish that is the appropriate order for the court to make.

This general approach raises a number of subsidiary points about the precise nature of the facilities requested.

7.8.2.1 Type of expert

The courts recognise that a medical expert, in accordance with usual medical practice, is likely to base any expert opinion on an examination as well as, of course, a proper history and review of relevant records (see **7.2.7**).

Away from medical experts the court may be more reluctant to expect the claimant to allow facilities for an examination or interview.

Hence in *Larby v Thurgood*[160] the court was not prepared to impose a stay when the claimant declined to give facilities to be interviewed by an employment expert.

Similarly, in *McMurray v Safeway Stores plc*[161] an application by the defenders in connection with a request the claimant give facilities to be examined and tested by a physical evaluation company was refused, the court recognising that with medically qualified practitioners the court could rely on training, professional qualifications, standards, practice and ethics to ensure 'a just determination of the cause'. Here, however, the tests would have been carried out by chartered physiotherapists and even though that meant standards would be guaranteed, and the investigations were endorsed by a consultant physician, the application was refused.

[1969] 2 QB 67.
[1972] 1 WLR 326.
[1993] ICR 66.
[2000] SLT 1033.

7.8.2.2   Examination by a medical expert

In *Beck* Lord Phillips MR observed that 'a claimant who brings proceedings for personal injury, whether physical or psychiatric, must accept that he is likely to have to submit to a medial examination by an expert instructed by the defendant'. However, these comments need to be seen in the context of the approval, in that case, of earlier case-law and also in the context of the European Convention on Human Rights, particularly Article 8 (though the right to privacy must be balanced against the corresponding right to a fair trial under Article 6).

Indeed, Simon Brown LJ, giving judgment in *Beck*, expressly approved the pre-CPR approach to this issue when he approved a passage from the leading judgment of Sachs LJ in *Lane* that:

> 'The principles upon which a court should, in aid of obtaining a medical examination of one of the parties to an action, act when deciding whether or not to take the somewhat strong course of staying the action if a medical examination is not afforded, are by now clear. An order for a medical examination of any party to an action has been well said to be an "invasion of personal liberty". Accordingly, it should only be granted when it is reasonable in the interests of justice so to order. When the refusal of a medical examination is alleged to be unreasonable, the onus lies on the party who says it is unreasonable and who applies for the order to show, upon the particular facts of the case, that he is unable properly to prepare his claim (or defence) without that examination. The onus lies firmly on the applicant ...'

This passage was also expressly approved by the Court of Appeal in *Smith v Ealing, Hammersmith and Hounslow Health Authority*[162] where, allowing an application for disclosure of medical records, the court concluded that would provide the defendant with relevant information for their case without the inevitable invasion of personal liberty occasioned by a psychiatric examination.

7.8.2.3   Tests and investigations

Reasonableness will depend, in part, on the facilities sought. In *Beck* the court noted that the proposed examination by a psychiatrist would not be intrusive or unpleasant, the judge at first instance noting features on the case diminishing the impact of this factor being:

> 'One is that it is a psychiatric examination; it is not one of those medical examinations which are either intimate or otherwise physically intrusive, nor one of those kinds of medical examination which, although mechanical, such as an MRI scan, are extremely unpleasant to experience. Second, this is not to be a medical examination of somebody who is, as it were, free of doctors. The claimant is unfortunately an ongoing psychiatric patient, who presumably sees practitioners regularly and, in any event, he is someone of whom a further examination closer to trial date might well be necessary.'

Similarly, in *Daniels* Lord Woolf MR noted that, 'this is not a case where it is suggested that the claimant would be unduly distressed, or anything of that nature, by the additional examination'.

The request may be viewed differently if the facilities are for extensive investigations, may be distressing to the claimant, or involve any kind of risk.

---

[162]   Court of Appeal, 1 May 1997.

Accordingly, it is quite proper to seek confirmation of exactly what facilities the defendant seeks and to ensure agreement is reached on exactly what will be involved. Hence, again in *Daniels*, Lord Woolf MR confirmed that, 'it was not unreasonable for the claimant's solicitors to say "if you want facilities to examine the claimant, please give us more information".'

In *McMurray* a relevant factor, in refusing the application, was, additionally, that the proposed testing could be painful and possibly detrimental to the pursuer.

X-rays always carry some risk, from the exposure to radiation, hence X-rays should usually only be arranged for sound clinical reasons and not just for medico-legal purposes. Indeed, it may be appropriate to seek an undertaking in respect of any damages caused: *Prescott v Bulldog Tools*.[163]

Some claimants experience difficulties with MRI scans. In *Laycock v Lagoe*[164] the court, although accepting the interest of justice required the MRI, concluded the claimant could show a substantial reason for not undertaking the test and declined to order a stay.

7.8.2.4   Parties

Where the defendant seeks facilities to examine a party whose health may be an issue but injuries suffered by that party are not the subject matter of the claim, for example a dependant in a fatal accident claim, the court may not be minded to order a stay: *Baugh v Delta Water Fittings Ltd*.[165]

7.8.2.5   Conditions

If the claimant is to give facilities for an examination it will be usual to agree conditions such as the prompt payment of reasonable travel expenses (and where the claimant has a significant disability it may be prudent to agree the nature of those arrangements, for example provision of a taxi).

In appropriate cases, for example an examination of the claimant at an early stage before liability is determined, it may be appropriate to agree what matters are to be discussed on the background, given that it will generally be undesirable for there to be a detailed discussion on such matters other than the basic facts relevant to the mechanics of the injury. Such conditions were considered appropriate in *Jackson v MGN Ltd*.[166]

The claimant will not generally be entitled to give facilities only on condition the identity of the doctor to be instructed by the defendant be agreed. In *Starr v National Coal Board*[167] the Court of Appeal concluded a claimant would need reasonable grounds for objecting to a particular doctor and have to be prepared to disclose those reasons to the court. Moreover, valid reasons are likely to be restricted to matters such as the doctor lacking proper qualification or being likely to conduct the examination and to make a

---

[163]   [1981] 3 All ER 869.
[164]   [1997] PIQR P518.
[165]   [1971] 1 WLR 1295.
[166]   Court of Appeal, 17 March 1994.
[167]   [1977] 1 WLR 63.

report unkindly or unfairly. Such matters should not be raised lightly though, from time to time, a way of avoiding such a problem would be for the defendant to offer the claimant a choice.

Different considerations may apply if the nominated expert is, for example, located a very considerable distance from the claimant, particularly if the claimant is badly injured, or has consulting rooms which would not be readily accessible to someone with injuries of the kind suffered by the claimant.

The court is unlikely to impose a condition that the claimant's doctor be present at the examination by the defendant's expert: *Hall v Avon Area Health Authority*.[168] It may well be reasonable, however, for the claimant to stipulate that there be a companion present.

Consequently, as well as ensuring the doctor concerned is identified, in case there are valid grounds for objection to the individual, enquiries should always be made about venue as well as proposed tests and investigations so that the reasonableness of the facilities requested, as a whole, can be considered and any appropriate terms and conditions agreed.

7.8.3   Request for facilities to obtain or for permission to rely upon expert evidence?

Before the introduction of the CPR, permission to rely on expert evidence was not required. Accordingly, whether or not there was more than one medical expert in a particular discipline would depend upon the claimant giving appropriate facilities or, if these were not given, whether the court was prepared to impose a stay unless and until such facilities were provided.

The requirement in the CPR that permission be obtained from the court to call any expert evidence, and that this only be given if such evidence is 'reasonably required', means that there is now usually a two stage process when dealing with medical evidence that the defendant may wish to rely on, where this corresponds to that already obtained.

The first stage is concerned with whether it is reasonable to expect that the claimant give facilities, where these are sought, to obtain such evidence.

Secondly, it will be necessary for the court to assess whether such evidence is 'reasonably required', so that permission to rely on it should be given.

In *Daniels v Walker*[169] Lord Woolf MR held that:

> '(The Judge) was clearly influenced by the fact that the way the case was presented the real issue was whether the defendant should be allowed to call an additional occupational therapist to give evidence. That was not the issue on which the Judge should have been focusing. He should have been focusing on whether the questioning should take place before the defendant had a report from his occupational therapist or whether the occupational therapist should be instructed by the defendant first and then put questions to (the claimant's expert) ...'

---

[168] [1980] 1 WLR 481.
[169] [2000] 1 WLR 1382.

He continued later in the judgment:

> 'If, having obtained a joint expert's report, a party, for reasons which are not fanciful, wishes to obtain further information before making a decision as to whether or not there is a particular part (or indeed the whole) of the experts report which he or she may wish to challenge, then they should, subject to the discretion of the court, be permitted to obtain that evidence.'

Then, later still in the judgment, he observed that:

> 'In the majority of cases, the sensible approach will not be to ask the court straight away to allow the dissatisfied party to call a second expert.'

If facilities to obtain expert evidence have already been given, the focus inevitably shifts to the question of whether permission to rely on that evidence should be allowed. However, *Beck* is a reminder that before permission to rely on evidence is granted, at least where such evidence requires facilities for a report to be prepared, it will be necessary for appropriate facilities to be given.

If such facilities have not been given, the court will need to consider whether it would be appropriate, in accordance with the established principles effectively adopted in *Beck*, to impose a stay unless and until such facilities are provided.

To do otherwise would be to condone an invasion of privacy not contemplated by the courts in 1972 and which certainly ought not to be accepted in the modern era of human rights legislation, despite the wide case management powers of the court under the CPR.

Hence, when a defendant wishes to rely on expert evidence corresponding to reports already disclosed by the claimant, at least unless the defendant's report is already available, it would not seem appropriate for the defendant simply to seek, at the stage of case management directions, permission to rely on the proposed expert evidence. Rather, in such circumstances, the defendant should request facilities to obtain the proposed evidence and, if those facilities are not granted, consider applying for a stay. Otherwise, unless it is clear the proposed evidence is 'reasonably required' the court may be eluding the two, in a sense distinct, issues.

Different considerations may apply where the expert evidence relates to an issue where a range of opinion seems likely or the court would, in any event, benefit from hearing from more than one expert in the field. In such circumstances the court may be willing to give permission to rely on further evidence without the report already being available, and to do so at the stage of dealing with a request for facilities, should that need arise.

7.8.4 Further facilities

A defendant may request further facilities to obtain a report either because it is not proposed to rely on the report of the expert originally instructed or because a report written by an expert, who is relied upon, needs to be updated.

The court is likely to view each of these situations quite differently.

7.8.4.1   Second expert

A defendant may request, and be granted, facilities to obtain a report but indicate the report then obtained is not to be relied on and make a request for yet further facilities to obtain another report from an expert in the same field.

In *Beck* the claimant refused to give the defendant facilities to obtain a third report (in addition to the claimant's own report and the undisclosed report already obtained by the defendant) from an expert in the same speciality.

The court held that, in these circumstances, if an order for a stay was made that would almost inevitably be conditional upon disclosure by the defendant of the existing report, in order to guard against the risk of 'expert shopping'. Ward LJ emphasised that:

> 'Expert shopping is to be discouraged, and a check against possible abuse is to require disclosure of the abandoned report as a condition to try again.'

The case management directions themselves did not prevent the defendant from changing experts but the court was prepared to impose a condition the existing report be disclosed as a preliminary to the defendant advancing any argument that a failure to give further facilities for an additional report on the part of the claimant would be unreasonable.

In *Hajigeorgiou v Vasiliou*[170] the claimant sought damages for breach of the defendant's covenant of quiet enjoyment in relation to premises intended to be used as a restaurant. Case management directions gave permission for the parties to rely on experts in the field of restaurant valuation and profitability. Such an expert, on behalf of the defendant, carried out an inspection of the premises following which the defendant sought permission to carry out a further inspection by a different expert in the same field of expertise.

The Court of Appeal observed that as the case management directions gave permission to rely on expert evidence by reference to a field of expertise it was open to either party to rely upon any expert falling within that field without having to go back to the court for further permission to do so. That was because Part 35 deals with permission to 'rely' upon expert evidence rather than, as it sometimes thought, permission to instruct experts or obtain evidence.

Accordingly, the key issue for the court was whether it was unreasonable for the defendant to seek facilities for a further inspection of the restaurant. On this point the Court of Appeal drew a sharp distinction between the facilities required for an inspection of premises and facilities for the examination of a claimant. Dyson LJ, on this point, observed:

> '... we consider that to impose such a requirement as a condition of giving (the new expert) permission to inspect the premises would have been unreasonable and disproportionate. The circumstances here are a far cry from a personal injury case where a second expert wishes to conduct a second medical examination on the claimant, and issues such as those discussed in *Lane v Willis*[171] arise.'

---

[170] [2005] EWCA Civ 236.
[171] [1972] 1 WLR 326.

This approach illustrates both the care necessary before the court sanctions an invasion of privacy, by imposing a stay unless facilities for an examination are given, and the greater willingness to allow, as the claimant may often seek, an inspection of property.

A further argument developed before the Court of Appeal in *Hajigeorgiou* was a direct attack on the decision in *Beck*, on the basis that it was inconsistent with the law of privilege and therefore wrong. The Court of Appeal rejected that argument, Dyson LJ concluding:

> 'The principle established in *Beck* is important. It is an example of the way in which the court will control the conduct of litigation in general, and the giving of expert evidence in particular. Expert shopping is undesirable and, wherever possible, the court will use its powers to prevent it. It needs to be emphasised that, if a party needs the permission of the court to rely on expert witness A in place of expert witness B, the court has the power to give permission on condition that A's report is disclosed to the other party or parties, and that such a condition will usually be imposed. In imposing such a condition, the court is not abrogating or emasculating legal professional privilege; it is merely saying that, if a party seeks the court's permission to rely on a substitute expert, it will be required to waive privilege in the first expert's report as a condition of being permitted to do so.'

Indeed, unlike the situation where a party chooses to deploy expert evidence, when earlier drafts will remain privileged, where a party must agree to waive privilege disclosure of all reports will be required. As Dyson LJ explained in *Hajigeorgiou*:

> 'A question that was not considered in *Beck* is whether the condition of disclosure should relate only to the first expert's final report, or whether it should be also relate to his or her earlier draft reports. In our view, it should not only apply to the first expert's "final" report, if by that is meant the report signed by the first expert as his or her report for disclosure. It should apply at least to the first expert's report(s) containing the substance of his or her opinion.'

The type of conditional order made in *Beck*, as endorsed in *Hajigeorgiou*, has since been endorsed as also appropriate in a situation where a party wishes to change experts after an expert jointly selected, under the Protocol, as reported: *Edwards-Tubb v JD Weatherspoon plc*.[172]

7.8.4.2 Supplemental report

A request for further facilities to obtain further expert evidence in a field where expert evidence has already been obtained and discarded should be contrasted with the request for further facilities simply to update the report of an expert whose earlier report has already been disclosed.

In these circumstances such a request is likely to be considered reasonable, assuming there was no settled prognosis at an earlier stage, further matters have arisen that require additional comment from the expert or there are other good reasons for wishing to update the earlier report.

---

[172] [2011] EWCA Civ 136.

7.8.5 Scope of any stay

Whilst, in appropriate circumstances, a stay on the action can be imposed if the claimant refuses to give reasonable facilities for the defendant to obtain expert evidence, that stay will not necessarily be on the whole claim. That is because, ultimately, the court must deal with the case justly and use case management powers to best achieve the overriding objective.

In *James v Baily Gibson & Co*[173] the claimant refused to cooperate with the defendant in giving facilities for expert evidence in the field of psychiatry to be obtained. May LJ, after noting the relevant issue could not be determined without psychiatric evidence, concluded the order under appeal had the affect of denying the claimant the opportunity of recovering damages on heads of claim unaffected by psychiatric evidence, hence an order staying the action as a whole was disproportionate. He went on:

> 'The court has under the Civil Procedure Rules a range of powers to manage cases to achieve the overriding objective of dealing with cases justly. These include in Rule 3 power to stay the whole or part of any proceedings, either generally or until a specified date or event.
>
> I consider that the court should use these powers in this case to achieve the just objective of enabling the claim to proceed on those issues which are unaffected by psychiatric evidence.'

On this basis damages were limited to a period of 15 months after the relevant accident because 12 months was the maximum period other experts reckoned to reflect the purely physical consequences of the relevant accident.

7.8.6 Permission

Whilst the defendant will not have needed permission to obtain expert evidence, as such, permission will be required to rely on any expert evidence, even if an issue has arisen as to whether facilities for that evidence to be obtained ought reasonably to have been given by the claimant.

7.9 SEEKING AND RESISTING PERMISSION

The terms of CPR 35.4 make court permission necessary before any party can rely upon expert evidence.

The court is likely to decide whether or not to grant such permission at the case management stage or on any specific application by a party seeking such an order.

The CPR restricts expert evidence to that which is 'reasonably required' and, where it is, the Protocol and the CPR work together so as to facilitate and encourage the use, wherever possible, of a single expert in any relevant field.

Consequently, the first issue for the court, when deciding whether to give permission, is whether expert evidence on the particular issue, or in the specific field, is required at all. This is often a problem for the claimant (see **7.1.2**).

---

[173] [2002] EWCA Civ 1690.

If expert evidence is required the court will then need to consider whether or not it is appropriate for that evidence to be given by a single expert (who may, or may not, be a 'single joint expert').

The use of a single expert will, in many cases, further the overriding objective and ensure that expert evidence is indeed limited to that which is reasonably required to resolve the proceedings.

There are, however, potential difficulties with the instruction of a single joint expert on those issues which are likely to be contentious. Accordingly, in a number of circumstances, the court may accept expert evidence from more than one expert in a particular discipline, or dealing with a particular issue, will be reasonably required.

Consequently, the instruction of a single expert in any particular discipline or an issue may often suffice. There are, however, circumstances in which it will be appropriate for there to be evidence from more than one expert in a particular field of expertise. That, usually, is an issue the defendant will have to face when seeking permission from the court though occasionally it may be the claimant who seeks to duplicate experts in the same field.

Subsequently, the court may be faced with issues about the grant of permission for a party to change experts in an area of expertise.

In all of these circumstances either party may wish to seek or oppose the grant of permission to rely on expert evidence.

7.9.1 Initial expert evidence

Issues about corresponding experts, and changing experts, will only arise if the court has, in the first instance, given permission to rely on expert evidence, on a particular issue or in a specific discipline, at all.

Whilst, from time to time, it may be the defendant who seeks permission to rely on evidence in a particular area of expertise it will usually, because that is where the burden of proof rests, be the claimant who seeks permission.

Mindful of the burden of proof, such an application may be met with a tactical response from the defendant seeking to resist the grant of permission (see **7.1.3**).

The claimant's representative must always be mindful of where the burden of proof lies on any issue and the problems which may occur at trial if appropriate expert evidence cannot be relied on, for example *Cassie v Ministry of Defence*[174] and *Ellis v William Cook Leeds Ltd*[175] (see **7.1.2**).

The claimant may be in a stronger position to seek permission if, from the outset, the analytical approach, in line with the Practice Direction – Pre-action Conduct and the Expert Protocol, has been adopted as that may help drive the court to the conclusion expert evidence is indeed 'reasonably required' to resolve the proceedings.

---

[174] [2002] EWCA Civ 838.
[175] [2007] EWCA Civ 1232.

This approach will have involved a number of stages as the claim has developed:

- Identifying issues, which may need to be dealt with by expert evidence, under the Protocol and perhaps in the Particulars of Claim. Unless such matters are admitted the claimant can rely on the need to prove these and expert evidence may be the only, or most proportionate, way of doing so.

- Inviting the defendant to agree matters in issue, informally or by serving Notice to Admit, if need be, on the express basis that may avoid expert evidence being required.

- Identifying whether the defendant has what might be termed quasi-expert evidence, which the claimant can only effectively respond to by calling an expert.

- Inviting the defendant to share information, available to the defendant but which the claimant could otherwise only obtain through instructing an expert:
  - CPR 35.9 provides that where a party has access to information which is not reasonably available to the other party, the court may direct the party who has access to the information to prepare and file a document recording the information and serve a copy of that document on the other party.
  - Paragraph 4 of the Practice Direction to Part 35 confirms any document to be served must include sufficient details of all the facts, tests, experiments and assumptions which underlie any part of the information to enable the party on whom it is served to make, or to obtain, a proper interpretation of the information and an assessment of its significance.

- Obtaining a draft expert's report with a view to showing the court how this contains evidence which is admissible, would be relevant and hence 'reasonably required'.

- Explaining, in a case summary, why the evidence is 'reasonably required', drawing together the steps taken from identification of the issues through to the ways in which the proposed evidence will assist the court in resolving those issues.

7.9.2   Corresponding expert evidence

If there is to be expert evidence on an issue or in a particular field of expertise each party may wish to rely on such an expert.

The parties may, from the outset, have taken the view that unilateral instruction of experts is appropriate. In these circumstances all parties are likely to agree expert evidence is appropriate and may well accept there will need to be corresponding experts.

There may, however, only be a single expert, at least initially, because only one party has unilaterally instructed an expert or, more likely, because there has been joint selection under the Protocol or even, perhaps, joint instruction. In these circumstances it will generally be the defendant who argues permission to rely on a corresponding expert, in the same field, or to deal with the same issue, is reasonably required.

7.9.2.1   *The general approach*

In *Daniels v Walker*[176] Lord Woolf MR held that:

---

[176]   [2000] 1 WLR 1382.

'... the correct approach is to regard the instruction of an expert jointly by the parties as the first step in obtaining expert evidence on a particular issue. It is to be hoped that in the majority of cases it will not only be the first step but the last step.'

In *Peet v Mid Kent Healthcare NHS Trust*[177] Lord Woolf CJ added:

'The starting point is: unless there is reason for not having a single expert, there should be only a single expert.'

In *ES v Chesterfield & North Derbyshire Royal Hospital NHS Trust*[178] the Court of Appeal approved the comments in the Final Report on Access to Justice that:

'There should be no expert evidence at all unless it will help the court, and no more than one expert in any speciality unless this is necessary for some real purpose when holding that ... it will only be in a really exceptional case that more than one expert in any particular speciality will be permitted.'

Despite the objective of there being a single expert, on any issue, where possible a number of circumstances may justify more than one such expert. Indeed, the Court of Appeal in *ES v Chesterfield & North Derbyshire Royal Hospital NHS Trust*[179] went on to comment that:

'It would be wrong to approach (the question of what is reasonably required to resolve the proceedings) with the predetermined belief that to instruct more than one expert in the same discipline will always be excessive.'

In some types of claim it is almost inevitable there will be a range of opinions, and if so it may be equally inevitable, from the outset, that it will be necessary for each party to obtain, and probably be given permission to rely on, expert evidence in relation to relevant issues.

In *Oxley v Penwarden*,[180] a clinical negligence case with a significant issue on causation, the Court of Appeal held that it was wrong to direct evidence be given by a single joint expert under CPR 35.7. Mantell LJ observed that:

'In my view, this was eminently a case where it was necessary for the parties to have the opportunity of investigating causation through an expert of their own choice and, further, to have the opportunity of calling that evidence before the court. It is inevitable in a case of this class that parties will find the greatest difficulty in agreeing on the appointment of a single expert. That burden would then be cast upon the court and would, in turn, lead to the Judge selecting an expert, if there be more than one school of thought on this issue, from one particular school of thought and that would effectively decide an essential question in the case without the opportunity for challenge.'

Even if not clear from the outset that more than one expert will be required it may become apparent, once there is the report of a single expert (even a joint expert), a further opinion is necessary, to help assess whether the court should hear from more than one expert on a particular issue. So, in *Daniels* Lord Woolf MR observed:

---

[177] [2002] 1 WLR 210.
[178] [2003] EWCA Civ 1284.
[179] [2003] EWCA Civ 1284.
[180] [2001] CPLR 1.

'Where a party sensibly agrees to a joint report ... the fact that a party has agreed to adopt that course does not prevent that party being allowed facilities to obtain a report from another expert, or, if appropriate, to rely on the evidence of another expert.'

However, Lord Woolf envisaged that this would have to be for reasons which were not 'fanciful'.

Subsequently, in *Peet* Lord Woolf CJ confirmed:

'... it is possible for the court still to permit a party to instruct his or her own expert and for that expert to be called at the hearing.'

In *Peet* Lord Woolf indicated that there would have to be 'good reason' for this course to be adopted.

Accordingly, it is important, whenever expert evidence from more than one expert in a particular field or on an issue is contemplated, to assess whether such evidence is likely to be 'reasonably required' for the purposes of CPR 35.1. That, in part, must be considered on the basis of the overriding objective which, in this context, will often mean balancing the objective of putting the parties on an equal footing with the requirement of saving expense and the overall need for proportionality.

Accordingly, whilst evidence from more than one expert in a particular field can be appropriate, it is important that the objectives of the CPR, in relation to costs and delay, are not thwarted by the unnecessary duplication of expert evidence.

7.9.2.2 *Proportionality*

The overriding objective of dealing with the case justly governs the court's approach to an application for permission to rely on a corresponding expert, just as it does when considering whether expert evidence is required on any issue at all (see **7.3.2.4.3**).

However, in the context of whether a second expert in a particular field is proportionate, Lord Woolf MR, in *Daniels v Walker*,[181] observed that:

'It may be said in a case where there is a modest amount involved that it would be disproportionate to obtain a second report in any circumstances. At most what should be allowed is merely to put a question to the expert who has already prepared a report.'

However, in *Layland v Fairview New Homes plc*[182] Neuberger J cautioned against the need for proportionality to override justice (see **7.3.2.4**).

'A claimant with a small claim is entitled to the same treatment, in terms of substantive and procedural justice, as a claimant with a large claim. That is not inconsistent with the concept of proportionality. Proportionality involves the court ensuring that, subject always to the fundamental and overriding requirement that every case is disposed of justly, the resources, in terms of cost effort and time, devoted to a case are appropriate to what is at stake in that case. Hence, the number of expert witnesses or the extent of disclosure directed by the court may be influenced by, inter alia, the amount at stake. However, at least in my firm view,

---

[181] [2000] 1 WLR 1382.
[182] [2002] EWHC 1350.

proportionality cannot be invoked to deprive a party of a direction, without which there would be a real risk of there not being a fair trial, or of some other injustice being perpetrated. It is right to add that, in some cases, particularly where justice or fairness require a balancing exercise, proportionality itself will be a relevant factor in deciding what justice and fairness require.'

Similarly, in *Edwards v Bruce & Hyslop (Brucast) Ltd*[183] Coulson J considered the advantages of having more than one expert, particularly if a single joint expert was to be called to give evidence, when he observed:

'By contrast, in a properly run case, if two experts meet, produce a CPR 35.12 statement identifying the matters they agree and the matters on which they disagree, and their subsequent written and oral evidence is limited to those matters on which they disagree, that leads to a much more focussed effort all round. It takes less court time, less preparation time, and is therefore ultimately less expensive.'

Accordingly, simply because a case is proceeding in the fast track that does not, of itself, preclude the use of more than one expert on a particular issue. CPR 35.4(3A) does, however, provide that where a claim is allocated to the fast track any permission for expert evidence will normally be given for only one expert on a particular issue. It is notable this rule uses the phrase 'one expert' rather than the term 'single joint expert', suggesting that in a fast track case the court may be willing to limit expert evidence in any particular field to an expert jointly selected under the Protocol.

Conversely, just because a case is suitable for the multi-track it does not follow that it will be proportionate to involve more than one expert in a particular speciality or to deal with a particular issue. In *Carlson v Townsend*[184] Brooke L J observed that:

'In a fast track case, the employment of a medical expert on each side, with all the ensuing disadvantages in time and cost that this entails, must be avoided wherever possible ... but even in "multi-track type claims" the overriding aim is still to achieve a settlement, wherever possible, in an economic and cost-effective manner. This is more likely to be attainable if the claimant's solicitor instructs an expert known to be acceptable to the other side.'

Proportionality is, in accordance with CPR 1.1, concerned with the issues in the case, not just the value, and in this context that makes any range of opinion on an issue particularly relevant.

7.9.2.3   Range of opinion

Perhaps the most important consideration, in assessing if more than one expert in a particular field is required, will be whether there is a range of expert opinion, amongst relevant experts, on the issues dealt with by that evidence.

There are certain issues, and certain types of claim, where it is likely more than one expert will be necessary to deal with a particular issue because a range of opinion is highly likely, if not inevitable. That is so, particularly when the issues relate to liability (both breach of duty and causation issues) and it is likely any evidence would need to be exchanged simultaneously at the appropriate stage in the proceedings. The

---

[183]   [2009] EWHC 2970 (QB).
[184]   [2001] EWCA Civ 511.

appropriateness of parties unilaterally instructing experts at the outset, in such circumstances, was accepted in *Oxley v Penwarden*.[185]

In other circumstances, especially when the evidence concerns quantum, it will be more appropriate, as envisaged in *Daniels*, to 'regard the instruction of an expert jointly by the parties as the first step in obtaining expert evidence on a particular issue'. Then, once that opinion is available, a decision can be made whether there are good reasons for seeking further expert evidence, in the same field, to help assess the extent of any range of opinion on the relevant issue.

If the evidence obtained indicates, or indeed surrounding circumstances suggest, a likely range of opinion, that will be a cogent reason why further expert evidence ought to be obtained as it must be the court, not the experts, who determine the case. In the same way that in *Liddell v Middleton*[186] the court stressed an expert should not make findings that are properly matters for the court, it would be inappropriate for the court to hear one expert, giving just one of a range of opinions, as that, too, would effectively allow the expert to determine the case.

Hence, in *Austen v Oxford City Council*[187] the Judge at first instance was held to have fallen into error when deciding to rely on the evidence of a single expert, despite other evidence to suggest a range of opinion, as '... the judge seems to have overlooked that he, not the (expert), had to decide whether the claimant was genuine'.

In *Kearsley v Klarfeld*[188] it was clear, even though the case was one of low value, that there was a considerable difference between the views of experts on the issues in the case and fairness therefore demanded permission for each party to call experts in the relevant specialisms.

However, the question as to whether a range of opinion is likely to exist has to be considered in the context of the overriding duty of the expert to the court, in accordance with CPR 35.3, and the specific requirements on the expert when preparing a report for evidence, in paragraph 2.2 of the Practice Direction to Part 35, that any range of opinion be identified and summarised. If the expert indicates there is no range of opinion there may need to be some cogent evidence or argument to explain why that view is wrong. In *Calden v Nunn*[189] the court, when refusing a late application for permission to rely on a second expert in a particular field, took particular note of this overriding duty of the expert to the court.

7.9.2.4 *Reasons for having a single expert*

The court may not need to hear from more than one expert in a particular field in a number of circumstances:

- There may have been joint selection in accordance with the Protocol or, indeed, joint instruction at a subsequent stage. In these circumstances, at least without some reason, giving permission to rely on a further expert might be seen as an

---

[185] [2001] CPLR 1.
[186] [1995] PIQR P36.
[187] (Unreported) 17 April 2002, Douglas Brown J, QBD.
[188] [EWCA] Civ 1510.
[189] [2003] EWCA Civ 200.

encouragement to engage in 'expert shopping' as deprecated in *Ahmed v Stanley A Coleman & Hill*,[190] *Hajigeorgiou v Vasiliou*[191] and *Edwards-Tubb v J D Weatherspoon plc*.[192]

- There may have been no likely range of opinion identified in the expert evidence already available, remembering the expert's duty to state any such range of opinion, as occurred in *Calden*.

- There may have been no points of disagreement identified in the evidence already disclosed, bearing in mind the requirements of Part 16 of the CPR and paragraph 12 of the Practice Direction to Part 16.

- No further report, suggesting there is a different view or range of opinion, may be available.

- No questions have been put to the relevant expert in order to clarify any issues. Such questions were envisaged as a usual preliminary to any decision on the need for further expert evidence in the same field by the court in *Daniels v Walker*.[193]

- It may not be proportionate, looking at the value of the case and issues dealt with by the expert, to have further evidence from an expert in the same field. In *Daniels* a factor, in allowing permission, was that the relevant expert evidence dealt with a substantial part of a high value claim.

Any of these factors would suggest corresponding expert evidence is not 'reasonably required' and that the case can be dealt with 'justly' with a single expert in any particular field or on a specific issue. In that sense it is proportionate to rely on just one relevant expert taking account of the issues and value.

In such circumstances a corresponding expert would not seem to be justified merely because one party does not like the opinion of the existing expert. Indeed, it will be inevitable from time to time, where the overriding duty of the expert is to the court not the parties, that there will be a reluctance to accept an expert's evidence. To allow a further expert, in these circumstances, would simply encourage a degree of 'expert shopping'.

7.9.2.5   Reasons for having a corresponding expert

The court may need to hear expert opinion from a second, or subsequent, expert in a particular field, or dealing with a specific issue, in a number of different circumstances:

- The expert evidence may relate to an issue where there is likely to be a range of opinion, or at least the court should be aware whether or not there is such a range, for example *Oxley v Penwarden*.[194]

- The expert who has reported already may indicate there is a likely range of opinion. In these circumstances, unless the report was exceptionally balanced, it is likely the expert will prefer one view and the court would need to know the extent to which other views might be supported by different opinion in order to reach a fair view on which opinion ought to be preferred.

- It may be clear from other reports available there is a different view or range of opinion.

---

[190]   [2002] EWCA Civ 935.
[191]   [2005] EWCA Civ 236.
[192]   [2011] EWCA Civ 136.
[193]   [2000] 1 WLR 1382.
[194]   [2001] CPLR 1.

- There may be a 'shadow' expert as in *Cosgrove v Pattison*[195] where Neuberger J held that:

  '... it does seem to me that if a new expert can be found who has a contrary view to the joint expert that is a reason for permitting that new expert to be called. It is certainly not a sufficient reason in every case, but if there are grounds for thinking that the joint expert may be wrong, because another expert takes a different view, that is certainly a factor which is to be born in mind.'

- There may be an expert in another field who nonetheless is able to give a valid opinion suggesting a range of views the Court ought to take into account. In *Austen v Oxford City Council*[196] the joint expert, a psychiatrist, disagreed fundamentally with an expert relied on by the claimant, a rheumatologist, as to the existence of fibromyalgia. Douglas Brown J held that this was sufficient to justify the claimant calling further evidence from another psychiatrist as:

  'Whilst it is true that each doctor approached the questions of issue from the point of view of his or her own discipline, there were areas of common controversy ... for example ... whether trauma could cause fibromyalgia. There was a clear difference of professional view on that ...'

- It seems clear, even if the evidence has not been disclosed, there is likely to be a range of opinion from the very fact there is expert evidence which has not been disclosed. In *Carlson v Townsend*,[197] where the report of a jointly selected expert was held to be privileged and thus not discloseable, Simon Brown LJ observed that the defendant was likely to be granted permission to rely on corresponding expert evidence if that were sought.

- The defence, in accordance with Part 16 of the CPR, may identify matters of disagreement with the expert evidence disclosed sufficient to justify further expert opinion on relevant issues even if that is not yet apparent from the only evidence then available on such topics.

- Questions have been put to the existing expert but it is not considered the answers adequately clarify the issues raised.

- There is a need to balance the weight of expert evidence between the parties. For example, in a clinical negligence case where there will inevitably be some overlap between the evidence of the treating doctor which will be partly factual and partly expert and to avoid the impression the claimant's single expert does not reflect a reasonable view: *ES v Chesterfield & North Derbyshire Royal Hospital NHS Trust*;[198] and/or

- It is proportionate to the issues arising and value of the case for further expert evidence to be obtained on the relevant issue. For example, in *Daniels* where the defendant wished to obtain the opinion of a further care expert and Lord Woolf MR noted that:

  '... in this case a substantial sum of money depended on the issue as to whether full-time or part-time carer was required.'

---

[195] (Unreported) 27 November 2010 (ChD).
[196] (Unreported) 17 April 2002, Douglas Brown J(QBD).
[197] [2001] EWCA Civ 511.
[198] [2003] EWCA Civ 1284.

Such factors suggest evidence from a corresponding, or further, expert in the same field as an existing expert will be 'reasonably required' for the court to deal with the case 'justly'. In such circumstances the need for further expert evidence could not properly be viewed as 'expert shopping'. In such circumstances, it would be proportionate for the court to give permission for additional expert evidence to be relied upon.

7.9.2.6   The sequence

With some issues, in some cases, it may be apparent, from the outset, each party will wish to unilaterally instruct experts, exemplified by the circumstances outlined in *Oxley v Penwarden*.[199]

In other circumstances the sequence will usually follow the guidance given by Lord Woolf MR in *Daniels v Walker*[200] where he explained:

> '... one starts ... from the position that, wherever possible, a joint report is obtained. If there is disagreement on that report, then there would be an issue as to whether to ask questions or whether to get your own expert's report. If questions to do not resolve the matter and a party, or both parties, obtain their own expert's reports, then that will result in a decision having to be reached as to what evidence should be called. That decision should not be taken until there has been a meeting between the experts involved. It may be that agreement could then be reached: it may be that agreement is reached as a result of asking the appropriate questions. It is only as a last resort that you accept that it is necessary for oral evidence to be given by the experts before the court. The expense of cross-examination of expert witnesses at the hearing, even in a substantial case, can be very expensive.'

Consequently, before the court decides whether more than one expert in a particular field is required it may be appropriate to explore:

- whether answers to questions will suffice;
- whether facilities to obtain further evidence are required (so that a report can be prepared and then assessed to see if the content is such that evidence from the expert is reasonably required);
- and even then whether, as a result of meeting, the experts are sufficiently agreed for oral evidence to be avoided.

7.9.3   Claimant's corresponding expert

On the basis it would be the claimant who obtains expert evidence, though often using the machinery of joint selection under the Protocol, it will usually be the defendant who seeks to rely on a corresponding expert in the same discipline, arguing more than one expert in that field is reasonably required. That will almost certainly be on the basis that the expert on whom the defendant wishes to rely expresses a materially different opinion to the claimant's expert.

But can the claimant, who already has evidence from an expert on a particular issue, ever be justified in seeking to rely on a corresponding expert, on the same issue, whose evidence essentially replicates, and hence supports, the evidence of the first expert?

---

[199] [2001] CPLR 1.
[200] [2000] 1 WLR 1382.

This question was considered in *ES v Chesterfield & North Derbyshire Royal Hospital NHS Trust*[201] where, exceptionally, permission to rely on the evidence of a corresponding expert was given to the claimant but, more typically, such permission will not be given as, for example, in *Beaumont v Ministry of Defence*[202] (see **7.3.2.4.1**).

Different considerations will apply where the claimant, who already relies on expert evidence in one specialism, seeks permission to rely on further expert evidence which may cover some of the same ground but is from an expert in a different discipline. That would not require the exceptional features found in *ES* and the question of permission will depend upon application of usual principles about what evidence was reasonably required (see **7.9.1**).

7.9.4 Changing experts

Where a party has obtained permission from the court to rely upon expert evidence, that party may subsequently wish to change the identity of the expert on whose evidence it is intended to rely.

That may, or may not, require further permission from the court.

7.9.4.1 No *further permission required*

Case management directions may give permission to rely on the evidence of a named expert. If so, the party who has such permission will need to seek permission afresh from the court if it is proposed to rely on a different expert, even if that new expert is in the same field of expertise as the original expert.

Case management directions may, however, give permission to rely on expert evidence by reference to a particular field of expertise. If an order in those terms is made a party can rely upon any expert in that field without the need for further permission from the court: *Hajigeorgiou v Vasiliou*.[203]

An issue, in these circumstances, may still arise if further facilities to obtain a report from the new expert are required and, if so, the court might impose a conditional order (see **7.2.3**).

Different considerations arise when an expert has been jointly selected under the Protocol when, even though no permission to rely on expert evidence will have been given at that stage, the court may still impose a conditional order, as and when permission is granted, requiring a party who has obtained, but does not intend to rely upon, the report of a jointly selected expert to voluntarily waive privilege and disclose that report (see **7.2.3**).

---

[201] [2003] EWCA Civ 1284.
[202] [2009] EWHC 1258 (QB).
[203] [2005] EWCA Civ 236.

7.9.4.2   Permission required

If case management directions name an expert, any party wishing to rely on a different expert, even within the same field of expertise, will need permission to do so: *Hajigeorgiou*.

Even if case management directions allow for expert evidence in a particular field, once the date for exchange of evidence has gone by a party will need permission from the court to change experts. That is because permission would then be necessary to rely on further evidence disclosed after that date, given the terms of CPR 35.13.

It is often after exchange of evidence that a party may wish to change experts, not least after experts have conferred and prepared a joint statement. A party is, in a sense, also seeking to change experts where it is no longer proposed to rely on the evidence of an expert instructed on a joint basis.

7.9.4.3   Unilaterally instructed expert

Where the parties have unilaterally instructed experts, so that there are corresponding experts in a particular field, the court is likely to direct that the experts confer and prepare a joint statement.

The joint statement may reveal that one of the experts has changed opinion, presenting a difficulty for the party relying on that expert if this is on an important aspect of the case.

If application for permission to rely on a different expert is made, by the party whose expert has modified the evidence given previously, the court has to reconcile the potential tension between the need to deal with the case justly and the intention, underpinning CPR 35.12, that an expert's meeting is likely to, and on occasions should, narrow the issues in a way that may leave one of the parties in a worse position.

This difficulty was addressed by Teare J in *Stallwood v David*[204] where he concluded:

> 'It follows, in my judgment, that where a court is asked for permission to adduce expert evidence from a third expert in circumstances where the applicant is dissatisfied with the opinion of his own expert following the experts' discussion, it should only do so where there is good reason to suppose that the applicant's first expert has agreed with the expert instructed by the other side or has modified his opinion for reasons which cannot properly or fairly support his revised opinion, such as those mentioned in the note in the White Book to which I have referred. It is likely that it will be a rare case in which such good reason can be shown. Where good reason is shown the court will have to consider whether, having regard to all the circumstances of the case and the overriding objective to deal with cases justly, it can properly be said that further expert evidence is "reasonably required to resolve the proceedings" (CPR 35.1).'

Whilst the claimant was not able to establish that permission should be given on these grounds the somewhat extraordinary interruptions, and conduct of the hearing, by the judge at first instance, resulted in the appeal being allowed, and permission to change

---

[204] [2006] EWHC 2600 (QB).

experts being given, on the basis that otherwise the claimant would have an understandable sense of grievance. Consequently, the judge adopted the test identified in *Cosgrove v Pattinson*[205] observing that:

> 'Although Neuberger J was dealing with a case in which a single joint expert had been instructed and I am not, the court must always have regard to the overriding objective to deal with the case justly and in that regard the approach of Neuberger J is apposite.'

However, giving a party permission to change experts after joint statements will be an exceptional course for the court to take, as the facts of *Stallwood* illustrate. More typically in *Singh v CS O'Shea & Co Ltd*[206] MacDuff J held:

> 'If an expert does change his opinion for no good reason or for a bad reason, that may be a matter to feed into the discretion enabling the judge to reach a different decision. Insofar as here the claimant would claim to have a sense of grievance that his expert has abandoned him, it has to be observed that the sense of grievance must be judged objectively.'

On the facts of that case any sense of grievance, judged objectively, would not have been understandable and permission was refused.

Similarly, in *Guntrip v Cheney Coaches Ltd*[207] the claimant was not given permission to change experts after a joint statement had been prepared. The Court of Appeal concluded that in the context of trial management it was good if an expert modified his opinion as that saved both time and costs.

The court may take a different approach where the claimant wishes to change experts before a joint statement has been prepared. In *Hort v Charles Trent Ltd*[208] the claimant lost confidence in the expert on whose evidence he had permission to rely. Initially the claimant was refused permission to substitute experts but on appeal permission was granted on the basis the claimant had already disclosed the evidence of the expert to be discarded and adopting the approach of Hughes LJ in *Edwards-Tubb v J D Weatherspoon plc*[209] that:

> '... I certainly accept that there may be perfectly good reasons for a party to wish to instruct a second expert. Those reasons may not always be that the report of the first expert is disappointingly favourable to the other side, and even when that is the reason the first expert is not necessarily right. That means that it will often, perhaps normally, be proper to allow a party the option, at his own expense, of seeking a second opinion. It would not usually be right simply to deny him permission to rely on expert B and thus force him to rely on expert A, in whom he has, for whatever reason, lost confidence.'

In these circumstances there was nothing unusual that justified what was regarded as an exceptional cause of preventing the claimant from the opportunity of putting his case more effectively.

In *BMF (Mansfield) Ltd v Galliford Try Constructions Ltd*[210] an elderly expert witness, in a long running case, wished to retire and, on condition that all of the retiring expert's

---

[205] (Unreported) 27 November, 2000 (ChD).
[206] [2009] EWHC 1251 (QB).
[207] [2012] EWCA Civ 392.
[208] [2012] EWHC 3966 (QB).
[209] [2011] EWCA Civ 136.
[210] [2013] EWHC 3183 (TCC).

reports were disclosed, permission to rely on fresh expert evidence was granted. In these circumstance the court held disclosure was not limited the expert's final report but could include other reports containing the substance of the expert's opinion. Disclosure of documentation falling short of a report, such as telephone attendance notes made by the solicitors instructing the expert as these were privileged and might not necessarily reflect the exact opinion of the expert, did not have to be disclosed. There would have to be a very strong case which suggested 'expert shopping' to justify a condition attendance notes of discussions with the expert be disclosed to avoid what would otherwise be a significant and unjustified invasion of privilege.

7.9.4.4   Jointly instructed expert

In *Kay v West Midlands Strategic Health Authority*[211] the court considered the approach to an application for permission to rely on a further expert in the same field of expertise as an expert who had been instructed on a joint basis.

Expert evidence had been obtained from a wide range of experts including expert evidence on assisted technology from a single joint expert.

The claimant subsequently obtained a further report, from another expert in this field, which suggested additional needs that would have added a significant sum to the claim.

HHJ MacDuff QC reviewed case-law under the CPR before concluding how the court should approach this issue.

The judge observed that in the early days of the CPR it was anticipated that where the parties had agreed a jointly instructed expert it would only be in rare circumstances a party would be allowed to rely on another expert in the same field.

That view was modified, to some extent, by the decision in *Daniels v Walker*.[212] That concerned an application for permission to rely on further care reports, after the instruction of a joint expert.

Daniels confirmed that there may be a two-stage process (allowing, where necessary, facilities to obtain a report followed by a determination of whether the evidence obtained could be relied upon) although the decision set down principles for both stages.

Subsequently, in *Cosgrove v Pattinson*[213] the court considered how to exercise discretion when deciding whether to allow a party its own report where there was a pre-existing joint report. Of importance was the need for overall justice, reflecting the overriding objective, defined in the sense of whether one party would be left with an understandable sense of grievance if permission was, or was not, given. This was considered to be a proper and powerful consideration but not determinative even in the largest of cases.

---

[211] (Unreported) Birmingham District Registry, 4 July 2007.
[212] [2000] 1 WLR 1382.
[213] (Unreported) 27 November, 2000 (ChD).

Then, in *Peet v Mid-Kent Healthcare Trust*[214] the court re-visited the decision in *Daniels* and it was held that the comments in *Peet* about the desirability of 'non medical' evidence being given by a single expert unless there was 'good reason' otherwise had to put *Daniels* in context, tempering the view that a party should have facilities for its own report provided the reason was not 'fanciful'. That was important to avoid a return to the pre-CPR days where there would often be polarisation between the views of the respective experts.

Although in *Peet* the court drew a distinction between 'medical' and 'non-medical' expert evidence the more appropriate distinction was held to be between fundamental expert evidence and peripheral expert evidence, whether medical or not. This was reflected by the general practice of the courts to allow a party its own expert evidence on issues that were central or fundamental to the case, involving questions of underlying principle, whereas in other circumstances a joint report would be more appropriate.

The judge then translated this case-law into principles for general application:

- Where the real and major dispute between the parties required expert evidence the court should allow each party to have its own evidence from the outset, certainly in large cases.
- Where there were areas, although there might be some contention, which did not involve matters of principle or fundamental dispute the parties should agree to a joint report and the court so order if they did not.
- These decisions should normally be made at an early case management hearing as the parties should, by then, be aware of what the case is really about.
- Once a joint report had been agreed or ordered the strong presumption was that the evidence would come from that expert save for exceptional circumstances, even if large sums turned upon that part of the evidence.
- Nevertheless, where justice demanded it, the court might allow each party to have its own expert. In deciding such an application the court must have regard to the overall justice, including the issue of grievance identified in *Cosgrove*.

Applying those principles to the facts of the case, the application for permission to rely on a further expert in the field of assisted technology was refused.

The judge indicated the sort of circumstances in which it would have been appropriate to exercise discretion, and allow a further expert, were:

- patent bias in favour of one party;
- the overlooking of some vital matter raised in the instructions to the expert;
- a demonstration of lack of expertise; and
- à failure to deal with the relevant issues.

7.9.4.5 *Using discarded expert evidence*

If a party changes experts, the report of the original expert may be available to the other parties. That may be because the report has been exchanged, in accordance with case management directions, at a time when the party disclosing that report still intended to

---

[214] [2002] 1 WLR 210.

rely upon the evidence. Alternatively, the court may have made a conditional order, when giving permission to rely on expert evidence, on terms that an undisclosed report be disclosed.

Where such evidence is available, CPR 35.11 provides that any party may use that expert's report as evidence at the trial.

Moreover, it is not necessary for the party seeking to rely on such a report to gain permission from the court to do so: *Gurney Consulting Engineers v Gleeds Health and Safety Ltd;*[215] *Shepherd & Neame v EDF Energy Networks (SPN) plc.*[216]

This rule seems likely to apply even when a party has disclosed a report without expressing any intention to rely upon it, for example when required to do so under the terms of a conditional order allowing a change of experts: *Edwards-Tubb v JD Weatherspoon plc.*[217]

Issues may arise about the need for any such evidence to be tested, raising questions of oral evidence. The potential difficulties were explored by Hughes LJ in *Edwards-Tubb* when he observed:

> 'CPR 35.11 provides:
>
>> "Where a party has disclosed an expert's report, any party may use that expert's report as evidence at the trial."
>
> Without more, that means that the party to whom the earlier expert report is disclosed can simply put it in evidence, and its author is not available to be tested. That will sometimes be perfectly appropriate. The report may contain a matter of fact which is incontestable, or an opinion which is perfectly possible for the judge to evaluate without seeing the author. But there may be some cases in which it is a disproportionate consequence. The party who is abandoning reliance on the report may have good reason, especially in a serious case, for needing to test or explore the strength of its contents. Whilst it is important not unnecessarily to expand the scope of litigation or of satellite disputes, courts should, I believe, be ready in occasional cases where the circumstances genuinely require it to entertain argument that such testing will be necessary. Where, in such a case, it is necessary to do so to do justice, the court should be ready to consider requiring of the party to whom such a report is disclosed that he call the expert if he wishes to rely on it. I agree that this may occasionally generate a further need for case management, but it seems to me a necessary precaution in some cases if the party to whom the report is disclosed is not to be presented with a potentially unfair tactical advantage.'

The result of that approach might be to add to the number of experts at trial, despite the clear intention of Part 35, and the CPR generally, to avoid that happening.

7.10   EXCHANGE OF EXPERT EVIDENCE

The general rule is that, as with witness statements, expert evidence should be exchanged simultaneously between the parties.

---

[215] [2006] EWHC 43 (TCC).
[216] [2008] EWHC 123 TCC.
[217] [2011] EWCA Civ 136.

There are, however, exceptions to this general rule so both sequential and simultaneous exchange of expert evidence is usual, the nature of that evidence being an important consideration in determining the appropriate method for exchange.

Case management directions, as well as providing for permission to rely on expert evidence, should set out a timetable for exchange of reports not already disclosed and further steps to be taken in relation to the expert evidence following exchange (see **4.6**).

7.10.1 Sequential exchange

Sequential exchange of expert evidence will take place in virtually every personal injury claim. That is because, if liability is admitted, expert evidence on quantum will usually be disclosed at that stage in accordance with the Protocol.

Moreover, even where liability is not admitted the terms of paragraph 4.3 of the Practice Direction to Part 16 require the claimant to serve at least one medical report with the particulars of claim (see **2.7.1**). As the Practice Direction refers to a report 'about the personal injuries', this provision does not require service, with the particulars of claim, of expert medical evidence dealing with liability: *Duce v Worcestershire Acute Hospitals NHS Trust*.[218]

If the defendant has obtained medical evidence prior to the issue of proceedings, the Practice Direction to Part 16 requires that reports to be relied on be served with the defence (see **3.6.5.1**).

The claimant may decide to serve with the Particulars of Claim, or sequentially disclose at any other stage, additional medical evidence, or other expert evidence on quantum, to see if these may be agreed or, at least, the defendant accept the evidence of a single expert in any of the relevant fields will suffice.

The court may order sequential exchange of expert evidence at the stage of case management, perhaps where that is necessary to allow other parties to understand the nature of the case or there seems a reasonable prospect this will allow evidence on the relevant issue to be given by one expert.

In many cases all the expert evidence will be exchanged sequentially, including those cases where the only expert evidence is a single medical report disclosed by the claimant. It is important, however, not to forget, because there are many such cases, the general rule that there be sequential exchange.

7.10.2 Simultaneous exchange

The reason for sequential exchange, away from those circumstances where sequential exchange is appropriate, is that this, in many situations, is likely to best achieve the overriding objective by ensuring no party has the advantage of seeing corresponding expert evidence from other parties before being committed to disclosure as Lawton LJ observed in *Kirkup v British Rail Engineering Ltd*:[219]

---

[218] [2014] EWCA Civ 249.
[219] [1983] 1 WLR 1165.

'In the majority of cases the probability is that it is convenient and just that there should be simultaneous disclosure of reports. The reason is obvious. In the case of expert opinions about a plaintiff's physical or mental condition the plaintiff is the subject-matter of the reports. The experts' opinions will be concerned with his condition and the consequences of such injury as he has received. The area of enquiry and possible disagreement is comparatively limited. Where the case arises because of an alleged dangerous machine or an unsafe system of work, once again the area of enquiry and dispute is limited. The experts on both sides look, for example, at a machine and say whether it has been properly fenced, and if one of them says it has not been he can say why, and if the other one says it has been he too can say why. In those cases there is normally no problem.'

Similarly, in *Naylor v Preston Area Health Authority*[220] Glidewell LJ held:

'We had some discussion as to whether the order should be for exchange or sequential disclosure of reports. In my view exchange should be the normal course to be ordered, though sequential disclosure may be appropriate in an exceptional case.'

In his judgment in that case Sir Frederick Lawton (as he had now become) reviewed the history of clinical negligence litigation, and the reasons why it had until then been thought generally inappropriate to direct exchange of expert evidence in such cases. After explaining this was because of the, in his view, mistaken understanding such cases normally involve disputed facts as to what actually occurred in the course of treatment (when in his experience the facts were normally well documented in the records and not usually in dispute) he concluded:

'I have no hesitation at all in saying that in most actions for medical negligence there should be a direction for the substance of expert medical reports to be exchanged. In some cases, however, there may be good reasons why they should not be exchanged. The particulars of negligence may be so vague that it would be unfair to the defendants to expect their experts to deal with them until such time as the plaintiff had disclosed, either by further particulars or by his own expert's reports, exactly what his case was. In such a case a sequential *976 direction for disclosure would be appropriate. An example of the kind of circumstance in which such a discretion was properly given is provided by *Kirkup v British Rail Engineering Ltd* [1983] 1 WLR 1165.'

These pre-CPR authorities were reviewed and, it would appear, approved by Brooke LJ in *O'Brien v Chief Constable of South Wales*.[221]

Meanwhile, in *Oxley v Penwarden*[222] when permitting each party to rely on expert evidence rather than imposing a single joint expert, the Court of Appeal implicitly accepted exchange should be simultaneous.

Simultaneous exchange will be usual where the parties have permission to rely on their own experts on the issue of liability or other issues where the court considers it appropriate for each party to unilaterally instruct an expert.

In general terms the more contentious the issue, the more likely it is simultaneous exchange will be appropriate. Hence, in addition to evidence dealing with liability it is not unusual to see the simultaneous exchange of expert evidence dealing with care.

---

[220] [1987] 1 WLR 958.
[221] [2003] EWCA Civ 1085.
[222] [2001] CPLR 1.

Even with issues that may be less controversial if each party is seeking to rely on expert evidence, the overriding objective would suggest that this should generally be exchanged simultaneously though sometimes sequential exchange will be provided for in the hope that the evidence can be confined to that of the first expert, if necessary after clarification by questions.

7.10.3   Preparing for exchange

Whenever expert evidence is disclosed, some preliminary steps will be necessary, particularly where the evidence is to be exchanged simultaneously, following disclosure and exchange of witness statements:

- Expert evidence, once disclosed, becomes part of the claimant's case and, accordingly should be approved by the claimant as a preliminary.
- The expert should be invited, so far as this is appropriate, under paragraph 15.2 of the Expert Protocol, to make any necessary amendments. Such amendments must not distort the true opinion of the expert but can be made to ensure accuracy, internal consistency, completeness, relevance to the issues and clarity.
- Where further Statements of Case have been exchanged, disclosure given and witness statements exchanged following preparation of the expert's report, it will usually be appropriate for the expert to finalise the report in readiness for exchange so that this can reflect any change of opinion as well as appropriate amendments. This will ensure compliance with the terms of paragraph 14 of the Expert Protocol.
- The expert should be advised, in accordance with paragraph 14 of the Expert Protocol, that the report is to be disclosed.

7.10.4   Procedure for exchange

Where there is to be simultaneous exchange, the procedure used for exchange of witness statements can be adopted (see 6.3.2).

Care is essential, on exchange, to make sure that where there are preliminary reports and a final version it is the correct version which is disclosed: *Gough v Mummery*.[223]

All relevant experts should be informed of the date of disclosure, in accordance with paragraph 14 of the Expert Protocol.

7.10.5   Consequences of exchange

The report of an expert commissioned for use, or potential use, in court proceedings will almost certainly be subject to legal professional privilege: *Causton v Mann Egerton (Johnsons) Ltd*.[224] Privilege still attaches to earlier drafts even if a final version of the expert's report is disclosed: *Jackson v Marley Davenport Ltd*.[225]

---

[223] [2002] EWCA Civ 1573.
[224] [1974] 1 WLR 162.
[225] [2004] EWCA Civ 1225.

To rely on that evidence it is necessary, above and beyond the evidence being admissible and permission having been obtained from the court to rely upon it, for the relevant party to waive privilege and produce the report no later than the date provided for under case management directions.

Once privilege has been waived it is lost for good and, in any event, CPR 35.11 expressly provides that other parties may use an expert's report disclosed, but not subsequently relied upon, by another party.

Privilege may be lost if, sometimes inadvertently, a party does enough to 'deploy' an expert's report. In *Dunlop Slazenger International Ltd v Joe Bloggs Sports Ltd*[226] the Court of Appeal quoted, with approval, the textbook Matthews and Malek:

> 'The key word here is "deploying". A mere reference to a privileged document in an affidavit does not of itself amount to a waiver of privilege, and this is so even if the document referred to is being relied on for some purpose, for reliance in itself is said not to be the test. Instead, the test is whether the contents of the document are being relied on, rather than its effect. The problem is acute in cases where the maker of an affidavit or witness statement has to give details of the source of his information and belief, in order to comply with the rules of admissibility of such affidavit or witness statement. Provided that the maker does not quote the contents, or summarise them, but simply refers to the document's effect, there is apparently no waiver of privilege. This benevolent view has not been extended to the case where the maker refers to the document in order to comply with the party's need to give full and frank disclosure, eg on a without notice (ex parte) application.'

In *ACD (Landscape Architects) Ltd v Overall*[227] Akenhead J reviewed the case-law in this area and drew from that a number of propositions:

- Unless there is a good reason otherwise, documents referred to in a witness statement submitted to be used in interlocutory or final court hearings must be disclosed by the party submitting the statement.

- One good reason is that the documents are privileged.

- Privilege will be waived where the otherwise privileged document is actually or effectively referred to in a witness statement and/or part of its contents are deployed for use actually or potentially in the interlocutory proceedings or in the final trial, as the case may be.

- A party which deploys part of the privileged document in a witness statement will, at least as a matter of general principle, be required to disclose the whole of the document because it is not just to allow a party by way of cherry picking to rely only on that part.

- The test of whether a document or part of it is being deployed is whether the contents of the document are being relied upon rather than the effect or impact of the document.

- Once having referred to the document or part of it in a witness statement, generally at least the court will presume that it is relevant, because the very fact that it is referred to in the statement demonstrates its relevance.

---

[226] [2003] EWCA 901.
[227] [2011] EWHC 3362 (TCC).

7.10.6 Defendant's expert evidence

Any expert evidence disclosed by the defendant must be carefully reviewed to deal with a number of points:

- To give opinion evidence at all the author of the report must be an 'expert' (see **7.5.1**).
- The opinion must be based on facts which are either admitted or can ultimately be proved.
- The opinion of the expert needs to be analysed to establish whether that is different, in any material respect, from the opinion of the corresponding evidence on which the claimant relies.
- The need for any questions should be identified and, if so, appropriate questions drafted.
- If there are corresponding experts, arrangements for a meeting and joint statement are likely to be required.
- The defendant's evidence needs to be sent, with any further appropriate advice, to the claimant.
- The admissibility of the evidence should be checked, including:
  - the report contains only admissible opinion relevant to the issues defined by the statements of case;
  - the identity of specialism of the expert, according to the terms on which permission was given, is allowed to give evidence under case management directions; and
  - the evidence has been disclosed within the timescale provided for in the court timetable (as varied).

7.10.7 Organisation

It is essential to have ready, and accurate, reference to statements and reports exchanged, particularly when there may be earlier, undisclosed, drafts.

Consequently, it is good practice to keep a bundle of documents, from an early stage in the litigation, updated as evidence is exchanged.

7.11 QUESTIONS AND ANSWERS

The CPR gave, for the first time, a formal method for putting questions to experts.

This procedure is part of the drive towards, where possible, there being a single expert in any relevant field of expertise, because the clarification of an opinion, by answers to questions, may often avoid the need for evidence from a corresponding expert in the same field. Even if there is more than one expert in a particular field, questions may help to avoid the need for oral evidence being given.

7.11.1 Questions

Questions to experts are dealt with by CPR 35.6.

7.11.1.1   Scope

Under the terms of CPR 35.6 such questions must:

* be proportionate;
* be put once only;
* be put within 28 days of service of the report; and
* be for the purpose only of clarification of the report.

The court is likely to view questions which may help clarify the expert opinion as useful. Accordingly, the court will most likely allow questions to be put more than once, will readily give directions that effectively extend time for questions to be put and also be likely to interpret what amounts to 'clarification' widely, on the basis answers from experts usefully assist, without binding, the court.

In *Mutch v Allen*[228] it was noted that if questions which could be put in cross-examination were not allowed under CPR 35.6 it might become necessary to call the expert to give oral evidence when that could otherwise be avoided. Furthermore, the overriding objective requires the court to be provided with all relevant matters in the most cost effective and expeditious way, with experts now contributing to the just disposal of disputes by making their expertise available to all.

Giving the judgment of the Court of Appeal in *Mutch* Simon Brown LJ noted:

'Moreover, as is observed in the footnotes at paragraph 35.6.1 of the White Book:

"This is a useful provision ... It enables a party to obtain clarification of a report prepared by an expert instructed by his opponent or to arrange for a point not covered in the report (but within his expertise) to be dealt with. In a given case, were it not possible to achieve such clarification or extension of a report, the court, for that reason alone, may feel obliged to direct that the expert witness should testify at trial."'

However, to be proportionate clarification of the expert's evidence any questions should relate to matters of opinion within the scope of the expert's report. It would not, for example, seem appropriate for a medical expert dealing with one aspect of condition and prognosis, at least without some good reason, to be questioned about other aspects of condition and prognosis or issues relating to liability.

Similarly, care is necessary in those cases where medical evidence served with the Particulars of Claim deals with condition and prognosis and further medical evidence (whether from the same expert or not) will be exchanged at a later stage to deal with issues on liability (whether breach of duty, causation or both). Simultaneous exchange of expert evidence on issues relating to liability will usually be the just way of dealing with the case. Accordingly, a requirement one party effectively give sequential exchange, by answering questions at an early stage, would seem inconsistent with the overriding objective which, ultimately, must influence the approach of the court as to whether answers should be given. Moreover, questions of such a broad nature might well be regarded as going beyond 'clarification' of the expert opinion, when that is confined to condition and prognosis, even with a broad definition being ascribed to this term.

---

[228] [2001] EWCA Civ 76.

It is, however, important to make effective use of the opportunity to put questions when there are various factual scenarios, but the evidence will be given in writing so the expert will not be available at court to deal with any matters not covered by the written report.

Hence in *Coopers Payen Ltd v Southampton Container Terminal Ltd*[229] the court stressed the importance of ascertaining the views of the expert on each scenario so the Judge could make a decision without the expert there. Clarke LJ observed that:

> 'It is, in my opinion, of the utmost importance that if at all possible all relevant questions should be put to experts, including a joint expert, together with all relevant assumptions of fact long before the trial in order to afford the parties the best chance of settlement and, failing settlement, the fairest and most efficient trial.'

Whilst questions will certainly be appropriate when put by a party with a view to avoiding the need for expert evidence in the particular field to be duplicated, it is less likely questions will be proportionate, as there is unlikely to be any saving in costs, if that party has already evinced an intention to rely on corresponding expert evidence in any event. Indeed, in these circumstances, detailed questions might be seen as unjust, if the effect will be to secure even more in the way of sequential exchange of information than has already taken place.

7.11.1.2   Disclosure

From time to time the defendant will contend that all medical records relating to the claimant need to be disclosed in order that questions can be put to an expert.

Unless documents are properly part of standard disclosure, the subject of an order for specific disclosure and properly subject to inspection the putting of questions, should not be used as a vehicle to inappropriately extend disclosure and inspection whether of medical records or other documents.

Furthermore, despite the likelihood that 'clarification' will be interpreted widely, disclosure of medical records would not seem necessary for questions to be put, particularly when the expert will have taken account of relevant records when reporting. Whilst the defendant may suggest that questions to the expert cannot be framed without the records, this argument has the difficulty that any questions which cannot be formulated just on reading the report ought not to be regarded as being for clarification only.

Furthermore, the provision in Part 35 for clarification can be contrasted with the terms of Part 18, where a party can seek further information as well as clarification, and that distinction seems relevant in this context.

7.11.1.3   Copying questions

Paragraph 6.1 of the Practice Direction to Part 35 requires a party, sending questions direct to an expert, to copy those questions to the solicitors acting for the other party.

---

[229]   (2003).

This is an important requirement and so in *Ahmed v Stanley A Coleman & Hill*[230] Brooke LJ observed that:

'The words of that Practice Direction mean what they say.'

Accordingly, when disclosing a report, it may be helpful to remind the defendant of the need for any questions to be copied so that there is an opportunity of challenging any questions that may be inappropriate and, of course, ensuring that answers are made available to all concerned as soon as these are given by the expert.

7.11.2   Answers

It seems implicit an expert who receives proportionate questions, put in time, for clarification purposes will provide answers within a reasonable timescale.

Where, in accordance with the Practice Direction to Part 35, the solicitors instructing that expert receive copies of questions and take the view these are inappropriate, whether because those questions are regarded as disproportionate, follow earlier questions, are served out of time or go beyond clarification, the expert may be advised of these views.

If an expert is placed in a position of any difficulty, given the overriding duty to the court, the expert may, of course, write to the court seeking directions in accordance with CPR 35.14.

The evidence of an expert who unreasonably fails to deal with questions might, ultimately, be excluded by the court, given the obligation on experts to comply with the requirements of the CPR: *Stevens v Gullis*.[231]

Paragraph 16.2 of the Expert Protocol confirms any answers given by an expert to questions become part of the expert's report. Accordingly, those answers (and if necessary to understand these then the questions as well) will need to be included with relevant reports in the bundle of documents prepared for trial. Copies of answers to questions should go, meanwhile, to the claimant for information and with any appropriate advice or comment.

7.12   EXPERT DISCUSSIONS AND JOINT STATEMENTS

Even where there is more than one expert in a particular field, the objective of saving costs means that those experts should only have to give oral evidence if, and to the extent that, there are real differences of expert opinion between those experts which the court will need to resolve.

Accordingly, CPR 35.12 allows the court to direct a discussion between experts, usually of like discipline, and for those experts to prepare a joint statement which identifies points of agreement and points of disagreement, with reasons for matters which are not agreed.

---

[230] [2002] EWCA Civ 935.
[231] [2000] 1 All ER 527.

The court will, in practice, usually give a direction that experts have a discussion and prepare a joint statement where permission is given to rely on the evidence of more than one expert in a particular field or on a specific issue.

Paragraph 9 of the Practice Direction to Part 35 and paragraph 18 of the Expert Protocol give further guidance on arrangements for expert discussions and joint statements.

7.12.1 Instructions

Any expert who needs to have discussions with a corresponding expert to prepare a joint statement will need further instructions. These are likely to include:

- up to date Statements of Case;
- all relevant documents;
- all relevant factual evidence exchanged;
- all relevant expert evidence exchanged including, of course, the reports of the corresponding expert;
- any questions and answers;
- any observations on the evidence of the corresponding expert; and
- (if applicable) an agenda.

7.12.2 Agenda

An agenda for the expert's discussions may be helpful, particularly in more complex cases. That is because an agenda may help to focus the discussions on points that will assist the court in determining the key legal issues.

The claimant's expert might usefully assist in preparing the agenda though, ultimately, this will be a matter for the lawyers.

Efforts should be made to agree any agenda with the defendant's representatives. If that is not possible it may be necessary to supply the experts with the agendas prepared by each party.

An agenda may usefully cover a range of matters:

- Objectives: a general reminder of the purpose of the discussions and the need for a joint statement.
- Legal principles: a reminder of the standard of proof, the approach of the court to causation and that the overriding duty of each expert is to the court.
- Factual alternatives: in a case where the court may make various findings of fact, a reminder that it would be helpful to have the views of the experts on, so far as possible, each such scenario. Experts should not, of course, be asked to deal with questions of fact otherwise.
- Questions: these should reflect what appear to be the key issues between the experts, by reference to the pleadings, if necessary identifying specific parts of each

report dealing with any such issues. Ideally, without an unduly rigid approach, closed questions will be framed. Questions designed to go to the credit of an expert should not be included.

- Timescale: a reminder of the timescale for preparing the joint statement.

Care is necessary to ensure issues are not re-opened by the use of inappropriate questions or agenda items.

Further guidance on agendas is given by paragraphs 18.5 and 18.6 of the Expert Protocol.

7.12.3   Discussion

The experts can generally be left to have the discussion, prior to preparing a joint statement, in the way that seems most appropriate, whether this be by telephone or face to face meeting.

Paragraph 18.3 of the Expert Protocol confirms the purpose of the discussion is to:

- identify and discuss the expert issues;
- reach agreed opinions on those issues and, if that is not possible, to narrow the issues;
- identify those issues on which they agree and disagree and summarise their reasons for disagreement on any issues; and
- identify what action, if any, may be taken to resolve any of the outstanding issues between the parties.

The role of the lawyers is likely to be limited, at this stage, to the giving of further instructions and attempting to agree an agenda, rather than participating in the expert discussions.

The decision in *Hubbard v Lambeth, Southwark & Lewisham Health Authority*[232] means that it will be rare for experts' discussions to be attended. That decision is reflection in paragraph 18.8 of the Expert Protocol which confirms lawyers may only be present, when the experts have a discussion, if all parties agree or the court so orders.

Paragraph 18.9 of the Expert Protocol confirms the content of discussions between experts shall not be referred to at trial unless the parties agree in accordance with CPR 34.12(4).

7.12.4   Joint statement

Paragraph 18.12 of the Expert Protocol confirms that, following the discussion between the experts a written statement should be prepared. Paragraph 18.11 provides that the joint statement should be signed and dated by the experts.

CPR 35.12(5) confirms any agreement reached between the experts will not bind the parties unless those parties have expressly agreed to be bound by such agreement.

---

[232] [2002] Lloyd's Rep 8.

However, paragraph 18.12 of the Expert Protocol notes that, given the overriding objective, the parties should give careful consideration before refusing to be bound by any such agreement reached.

Whilst the discussions between the experts will be privileged, any joint statement will not. Where the court has given a direction for joint statements any such document produced, even if prepared specifically for the purposes of facilitating negotiations, is likely to be admissible: *Aird v Prime Meridian Ltd*.[233]

Consequently, the joint statement may be used to cross-examine an expert: *Robin Ellis Ltd v Malwright Ltd*.[234]

The timetable for experts to discuss and prepare a joint statement is there to be obeyed: *DN v Greenwich London Borough*.[235] Indeed, there is a risk that the evidence of an expert will be excluded if that expert does not properly co-operate in discussions and the preparation of a joint statement: *Stevens v Gullis*.[236]

The joint statement will be filed at court, with pre-trial checklist, to assist the judge at the stage of listing, in particular in deciding whether oral expert evidence is required or if written evidence, in the form of the report supplemented by the joint statement, will suffice at trial.

7.12.5 Review

Any joint statement must be carefully reviewed as a number of matters will need to be considered:

- The extent of agreement and disagreement and how that affects the case generally.
- Any admission that should be given or sought.
- The need for further expert evidence in this or any other field.
- Proper application of the law, including the standard of proof, by the experts.
- That alternative factual scenarios have been adequately dealt with.
- Whether oral evidence is required.
- Whether any offers should be made, reviewed or withdrawn.

If any concessions or agreements significantly undermine any important aspects of the claimant's claim it will be necessary to consider whether there is any justification for seeking to change experts, even at this late stage. The court is unlikely to allow permission to change experts unless the sort of issue identified in *Stallwood v David*[237] arises (see **7.9.4.3**).

Any change of opinion reflected in the joint statement will carry the responsibility, confirmed by paragraph 15.5 of the Expert Protocol, that reasons for the change of opinion should be given.

---

[233] [2006] EWCA Civ1866.
[234] [1999] CPLR 286.
[235] [2004] EWCA Civ 1659.
[236] (2000) 1 All ER 527.
[237] [2006] EWHC 2600 (QB).

If a party, rather than simply seeking to substitute and expert in the same field who may be more amenable, can justify the need for further expert evidence, even if that expert will effectively act as a substitute, from a different specialist field, or perhaps more likely a more specific sub-specialism, permission might be more readily obtained from the court. This is especially true if a draft report is available, illustrating that there remains a range of opinion despite the concessions made by the first expert.

7.12.6   Advice

The joint statement, like any report from an expert, should go to the claimant for information purposes, accompanied by any advice that may be necessary in the light of that joint statement.

7.13   WRITTEN OR ORAL EVIDENCE

At the stage of listing the court will need to decide, if there has been no specific direction on this point previously, whether oral expert evidence will be necessary at any trial.

Without specific permission for oral evidence to be given, that evidence will be confined to written reports.

7.13.1   Written evidence

Written evidence will comprise all reports of the relevant expert in the format disclosed accompanied by any answers to questions which, under paragraph 16.2 of the Expert Protocol, are treated as part of the expert's evidence.

If there is a single expert in any field, or on any issue, it is most unlikely the court will wish to see that expert called to give oral evidence, so the expert evidence will be the written report of the expert. In *Peet v Mid Kent Healthcare NHS Trust*[238] Lord Woolf CJ held that:

> '....there should be no need for that report to be amplified or tested by cross-examination ... the assumption should be that the single joint expert's report is the evidence.'

Even where there are corresponding experts in the same field the general policy of the CPR is to avoid the need for oral evidence which should be seen as very much a last resort: *Daniels v Walker*.[239]

Paragraph 17.15 of the Expert Protocol confirms a single joint expert will not normally give oral evidence at trial.

---

[238]   [2001] EWCA Civ 1703.
[239]   [2000] 1 WLR 1382.

7.13.2   Oral evidence

Even with a single expert the parties may be allowed to require that the witness attend court to be cross-examined, for example if the report is produced late or the expert has not considered all the questions put: *Coopers Payen Ltd v Southampton Container Terminal Ltd.*[240]

Where there is more than one expert in a particular field of expertise, the joint statement will be a crucial document in determining whether oral evidence will be required.

If the joint statement indicates the experts are agreed it is most unlikely oral evidence would be necessary.

Conversely, if the joint statement suggests there are significant differences of opinion between the experts it is likely oral evidence will be necessary, as the trial judge will need to hear the experts give evidence, allow those experts to be cross-examined and form a view, on that basis, as to which opinion should be preferred: *Rengasamy v Homebase Ltd.*[241]

Occasionally the joint statement may suggest there are differences of expert opinion but these are of a limited nature and of a kind the court may well be able to resolve without hearing the experts so that written evidence will suffice.

The experts may purport to disagree in the joint statement but, in reality, the difference between them is a matter that can be resolved by the court determining factual issues so that, again, oral evidence may well not be necessary from those experts.

In *Kearsley v Klarfeld,*[242] there was a significant difference of opinion between the medical and other experts as to whether a low velocity impact could have caused the claimant to suffer the injuries alleged. The Court of Appeal upheld case management directions given by the Circuit Judge allowing oral expert evidence and overruling initial case management directions which had been based on the wrong assumption that the determination of such evidence was a paper exercise. The Court of Appeal confirmed that in these circumstances the expert witness had to be called in order to give oral evidence if justice was to be done.

A party who does not agree the opinion of a single expert must be cautious about the prospects of successfully challenging that evidence at trial.

The view that a trial judge would read the report of a single expert and only give such weight to it as was thought fit was described as 'bizarre' in *Austen v Oxford City Council.*[243] Rather, the court accepted cross-examination of that single expert would be necessary. Furthermore, in such circumstances, it was considered better still for further expert evidence to be called as:

> '... the restrictive cross-examination of (the expert), although of some value, is no substitute for the claimant's own expert ...'.

---

[240] [2003] EWCA Civ 1223.
[241] [2015] EWHC 68 (QB).
[242] [EWCA] Civ 1510.
[243] (Unreported) 17 April 2002, Douglas Brown J (QBD) (QBD).

Hence, whilst allowing a single expert to be called for the purpose of cross-examination, it was held that the calling of a further expert was preferable when the evidence of the single expert was significantly disputed.

If oral evidence is allowed an expert should not be permitted to depart substantially from the written report unless the Judge is satisfied no injustice will result in the circumstances of the particular case: *DN v Greenwich London Borough*.[244]

The Expert Protocol, at paragraph 19.1, confirms experts have an obligation to attend court if called upon to do so. Paragraph 19.3 confirms experts should normally attend court without the need for service of a witness order but recognises that, on occasion, service of a witness order may be required to ensure attendance.

7.13.3   Summary

Consequently, the circumstances in which written evidence and oral evidence will be appropriate, an important consideration at the stage of listing, can be summarised:

*   If there is a report from a single joint expert in any particular field that evidence should be given in written form, even if one of the parties does not agree the report.

*   Similarly, if there is a report from only one expert in a particular field, even if this is not a joint expert, written evidence should suffice, though the court may direct the expert attend the cross-examination.

*   If there is more than one expert in a particular field the court will still wish to confine the evidence to written reports if, as a result of the joint statement or otherwise, any difference of opinion is such that the trial Judge is likely to be able to resolve it without hearing oral evidence, for example if the difference between the experts really turns upon matters of fact that the court will need to determine.

*   If there is a clear difference of opinion, reflecting a range of expert opinion the court will have to reconcile, oral evidence is likely to be required.

*   The views of the expert on various factual scenarios should be sought, for reasons given in *Coopers Payen Ltd*. That will ensure the court is able to make a decision without the expert being at court to give further evidence.

7.14   THE FORENSIC APPROACH TO EXPERT EVIDENCE

The overriding principle governing the forensic approach to expert evidence was explained by Stuart-Smith in *Liddell v Middleton*[245] when he said:

> 'We do not have trial by expert in this country; we have trial by a judge'.

Consequently, even if there is only a single expert on a particular issue, or agreement between two or more experts in the same discipline, that does not bind the court to necessarily concur with the views expressed, although legitimate reasons will be required to depart from such views.

---

[244]   [2004] EWCA Civ 1659.
[245]   [1995] PIQR P36.

Where a single expert is the only witness on a topic or fact, whilst such evidence must be weighed against other evidence and subject to cross-examination, the court ought only to depart from that evidence in appropriate circumstances. Consequently, any party who does not accept the opinion of that expert will need either expert evidence to support a contrary view or relevant factual evidence to counter the expert: *Coopers Payen Ltd v Southampton Container Terminal Ltd*.[246]

Giving judgment in that case Lightman J noted:

> 'Where a single expert gives evidence on an issue of fact on which no direct evidence is called, for example as to valuation, then subject to the need to evaluate his evidence in the light of his answers in cross-examination his evidence is likely to prove compelling. Only in exceptional circumstances may the judge depart from it and then for a good reason which he must fully explain. But if his evidence is on an issue of fact on which direct evidence is given, for example the speed at which a vehicle was travelling at a particular time, the situation is somewhat different. If the evidence of a witness of fact on the issue is credible, the judge may be faced with what, if they stood alone, may be the compelling evidence of two witnesses in favour of two opposing and conflicting conclusions. There is no rule of law or practice in such a situation requiring the judge to favour or accept the evidence of the expert or the evidence of a witness of fact. The judge must consider whether he can reconcile the evidence of the expert witness with that of the witness of fact. If he cannot do so, he must consider whether there may be an explanation for the conflict of evidence or for a possible error by either witness, and in the light of all the circumstances make a considered choice which evidence to accept. The circumstances may be such as to require the judge to reach only one conclusion.'

On the facts of that case, where there was no surviving alternative explanation for the events in issue, the Court of Appeal concluded the trial judge could only properly have chosen to accept the evidence of the expert.

However, where there is a basis on the factual evidence to reject the opinion of an expert the court may do so even though the evidence is from a single expert and the court cannot even find any flaw in the logic of the expert in reaching conclusions which are at odds with the factual evidence. In *Armstrong v First York*[247] Brooke LJ held that:

> 'In my judgment there is no principle of law that an expert's evidence in an unusual field – doing his best, with his great experience, to reconstruct what happened to the parties based on the second hand material he received in this case – must be dispositive of liability in such a case a judge must be compelled to find that, in his view, palpably honest witnesses have come to court to deceive him in order to obtain damages, in this case, a small amount of damages, for a case they know to be a false one.'

Similarly, provided the credibility of the factual witnesses was tested by reference to objective facts proved independently of that evidence, for example by available expert evidence, the court could accept an account of an accident which depended upon this occurring as the result of an unexplained and undetected defect in a tool even when the single expert felt this explanation unlikely. In *Jakto Transport Ltd v Hall*[248] Smith LJ held:

---

[246] [2003] EWCA Civ 1223.
[247] [2005] EWCA Civ 277.
[248] [2005] EWCA Civ 1327.

'In summary, I accept that the judge did not approach the finding of facts as he should have done. He should have considered all the evidence, including that of the expert Mr Glenn before making any findings of fact, even provisional ones. However, on a proper analysis, the evidence of Mr Glenn, taken together with other relevant evidence about the absence of any accidents due to operator error, suggested that both potential explanations for the accident were unlikely, although both were possible. On a fresh analysis of all the evidence, giving due weight to the judge's impression of the witnesses, I am of the view that the accident was caused by a defect in the wrench for which the appellant was strictly liable under Regulation 5. I would dismiss the appeal.'

Similarly, even where the experts for both parties were, ultimately, agreed, the court was nevertheless entitled to reach a contrary conclusion as to whether the claimant was suffering from HAVS. In *Montracon Ltd v Whalley*[249] Chadwick LJ held:

'... diagnosis in these cases is more than usually dependent upon the claimant's description of his symptoms; and so more than usually dependent on the claimant's credibility.'

Consequently, Chadwick LJ continued:

'Whether the claimant was to be believed at the trial was not a question for the doctors: it was a question for the judge. The judge found the claimant to be a credible witness. He reached that conclusion after hearing the claimant's evidence tested by a careful and searching cross-examination. There is no basis upon which that conclusion can be challenged in this court.'

The court must strike a balance between applying commonsense without ignoring expert evidence where this is relevant.

In *Gravatom Engineering Systems Ltd v Parr*[250] Keene LJ observed:

'A judge in a civil case, like a jury in a criminal trial, is entitled, and indeed expected, to use his experience of the world and his common sense, and to apply judgment. That was what this judge was doing here.'

However, in *Smith v Hammond*[251] Moore-Bick LJ held the trial judge had been wrong to reject the evidence of an expert dealing with liability in a road traffic accident, that if the defendant had sounded his horn the accident would nevertheless have occurred. Holding:

'In my view the judge was wrong to reject (the expert's) evidence. He was not bound to accept it, of course, if he had good grounds for not doing so, but if he was going to reject it he should have given reasons for doing so other than simply saying that it did not accord with his own experience. It is tempting for judges when dealing with matters of everyday experience to regard their own perceptions and experience as more reliable than the opinions of those who seek to describe such matters in scientific terms, but the temptation should be resisted, if only because the layman's perception of matters of this kind may be well wide of the mark. The layman may think that he reacts to something instantaneously, but the scientist may be able to demonstrate that he does not.'

---

[249]   [2005] EWCA Civ 1383.
[250]   [2007] EWCA Civ 967.
[251]   [2010] EWCA Civ 725.

In *Tucker v Watt*[252] there was a joint orthopaedic expert who was not called to give oral evidence although a number of issues remained about the effect of the claimant's injuries, in particular whether the claimant's working capacity was restricted. On appeal the defendant challenged the finding of the trial judge that, on the basis of the orthopaedic evidence, the claimant did indeed have restricted working capacity, meaning she could only work a shorter working week. Waller LJ, drawing a distinction with *Coopers Payen Ltd v Southampton Container Terminal Ltd*[253] held:

'The position in this case seems to me to be stronger than in a case where the expert actually gives evidence. The defendant, or those representing him, chose to conduct this case on the basis that (the joint orthopaedic expert) should not be present, being aware when they so insisted that the claimant would give evidence, and would wish to challenge any conclusion being drawn from (the expert's) evidence, that she was simply exercising a choice as to her working practice. The court was persuaded that the defendant was entitled to take that position on the basis that it was the claimant's evidence which would be determinative and that it was unnecessary to have (the expert) there to deal with any points the claimant might wish to make. Once that stance had been successfully taken, it could not in fairness be open to the defendant to suggest that the court was bound by (the expert's) reports alone to draw the conclusion that the claimant was simply exercising a choice.'

Waller LJ concluded:

'It follows that the argument, that the judge was bound by expert opinion to hold that the claimant was simply exercising a choice, must fail. The judge had then to assess the evidence, including that of the claimant. It was, in my view, open to the judge on all the evidence to find as he did that the claimant had her working practices forced upon her by the accident.'

If there is conflicting expert evidence, part of the responsibility of the judge is to decide between and, when preferring the evidence of one expert over another, to give adequate reasons for so doing: *Uren v Corporate Leisure (UK) Ltd*.[254]

In *Faunch v O'Donoghue*[255] the Court of Appeal emphasised that a judge had been wrong to find an accident occurred in a way uncanvassed at the hearing and without giving the parties and experts an opportunity to address his findings.

The assessment of expert evidence may well depend upon the expert keeping in mind that the overriding duty is to the court rather than the party instructing that expert.

In *Stagecoach South Western Trains Ltd v Hind*[256] Coulson J was critical of the approach taken by an expert observing:

'Save in exceptional circumstances, experts should not embark on this kind of fact-finding exercise, particularly when they perform it so unprofessionally. Matters of fact are for witnesses of fact, not for experts. Because a formal claim had already been made against Ms Hind by this time, she should at the very least have been interviewed by a solicitor and been given the opportunity of checking the resulting notes of that interview. Neither of these things happened. Inevitably, therefore, these failures meant that I regarded the remainder of Mr Sheppard's evidence with considerable scepticism.'

---

[252] [2005] EWCA Civ 1420.
[253] [2003] EWCA Civ 1223.
[254] [2011] EWCA Civ 66.
[255] [2013] EWCA Civ 1698.
[256] [2014] EWHC 1891.

Coulson J also had observations about discrepancies between different versions of the expert's reports when he said:

> 'Mr Sheppard said that this trimming was for reasons of space. I regret that I am wholly unable to accept that explanation: indeed, I regard it as so absurd as to constitute further evidence that Mr Sheppard was not acting as an independent expert in accordance with CPR Part 35. It is plain that paragraph 7.5 of Mr Sheppard's first report was his honest belief, and, as we shall see, it is one that was in accordance with the authorities. But it was clearly detrimental to the claimant's case (because of the difficulty in pointing to anything which indicated that this apparently healthy tree was, in fact, potentially unsafe). I find that this was the reason why this important passage was omitted from the second report. It again confirmed my view that Mr Sheppard's expert evidence was unreliable.'

Experts regarded as partisan by the courts, for example through inappropriate attacks on the credibility of a party, may be criticised and have their evidence rejected as a result: *Williams v Jervis*;[257] *Ali v Caton*.[258]

Whilst experts are allowed to give opinion evidence, on relevant matters, evidence will be disregarded if it attempts to deal with matters that are for the judge to determine. For example, in *Garcia v Associated Newspapers Ltd*[259] Dingemans J held:

> 'Dr Gerada gave evidence about which respective version of events was most likely to be reliable. I have not taken that evidence into account, and Mr Browne was justified in stating that Dr Gerada's evidence on this point was not permissible expert evidence as it dealt with issues of fact, and not issues on which expert evidence was relevant.'

An expert, more generally, should always remain aware of the requirements set out in Part 35, and the related expert protocol, not merely reciting the requirements in the report without then applying these to the content. A failure to appreciate and apply the requirements of Part 35 may result in the court attaching little weight to the evidence of the expert: *Bacciottini v Gotellee & Goldsmith*.[260]

7.15 SANCTIONS

Expert evidence is a procedural stage where sanctions which apply automatically under the CPR will usually protect the position of the party who is not in default. This is because those sanctions, unless relief is given, are likely to exclude the defaulting party from relying on expert evidence affected by that default.

Sanctions, affecting expert evidence, may be incurred through the failure of a party to obtain permission for expert evidence to be relied upon, a failure to disclose evidence, where permission has been given, in accordance with the timetable and where an expert fails to comply with the obligations of the CPR.

---

[257] [2008] EWHC 2346 (QB).
[258] [2014] EWCA Civ 1313.
[259] [2014] EWHC 3137 (QB).
[260] [2014] EWHC 3527 (Ch).

7.15.1 Failure to obtain permission

The terms of CPR 35.4(1) mean that expert evidence can only be relied upon with the court's permission. Accordingly, to rely on expert evidence at all a party will need permission which will need to either identify the expert concerned or, at least, the relevant field of expertise. A party cannot rely on expert evidence outside the scope of the order, at least not without seeking further permission. Consequently, it is essential to obtain permission to rely on all necessary expert evidence, ideally at the stage of initial case management or, if necessary, in subsequent case management directions. There is, however, the risk that if application is made at a very late stage that may be refused, particularly if giving permission would prejudice a trial date or trial window.

In *Austen v Oxford City Council*[261] there was a joint report from an expert whose evidence the claimant did not accept. Despite this the claimant was not permitted to cross-examine the expert. On appeal, and despite the earlier failure to recognise the need for the evidence of the single expert to be challenged, it was ordered the claimant be permitted to cross-examine the expert. Furthermore, it was held that if application were to be made subsequently the court ought to look favourably on any application to adduce further expert evidence as '... the restrictive cross-examination of (the expert), although of some value, is no substitute for the claimant's own expert ...'.

However, in *Calden v Nunn*[262] a late application by the defendant for permission to rely on the evidence of a histopathologist, the claimant having previously obtained permission for the evidence of a histopathologist, was refused for a number of reasons:

- The claimant's solicitors had suggested, at an early stage, histopathology evidence would be desirable, but the defendant did not agree and so failed to adopt the approach recommended in *Daniels* by adopting, at least initially, a joint approach.

- This meant the defendant had failed to help further the overriding objective, as required by CPR 1.3.

- The court considered it appropriate to place emphasis on the sanctity of the trial window because, under CPR 1.1, there was a duty to ensure the case was dealt with expeditiously and fairly.

- That was a relevant consideration to the extent the defendant needed relief from sanctions under CPR 3.9.

- Account was also taken of the overriding duty owed by the expert, albeit an expert instructed by just one of the parties, to the court. That was held to offset any unfairness, in not being allowed to call evidence, to the defendant by refusing the application.

The dangers of not obtaining permission to rely on expert evidence, crucial to proving key issues in the case, are highlighted, so far as the claimant is concerned, by *Cassie v Ministry of Defence*[263] and *Ellis v William Cook Leeds Ltd*[264] (see **7.1.2**) and, so far as the defendant is concerned, by *Stanton v Collinson*[265] (see **7.4.2.2**).

---

[261] (Unreported) 17 April 2002, Douglas Brown J (QBD).
[262] [2003] EWCA Civ 200.
[263] [2002] EWCA Civ 838.
[264] [2007] EWCA 1232.
[265] [2010] EWCA Civ 81.

7.15.2   Failure to comply with the court timetable

Even where permission to rely on expert evidence has been given it remains necessary for the relevant expert evidence to be disclosed within the timescale provided for under case management directions.

This is because CPR 35.13 provides that a party who fails to disclose an expert's report may not use the report at the trial or call the expert to give evidence orally unless the court gives permission. Disclosure, for these purposes, is likely to be taken as requiring disclosure by the due date under case management directions.

A party in default may seek relief from the sanction but whether such relief is given will depend upon the court considering the terms of CPR 3.9 (see **8.10.2**).

In *Baron v Lovell*[266] the court ruled that:

- it did not matter that the direction for exchange of expert evidence was not in the terms of an 'unless' order, if the order was not complied with the party in default was 'at the mercy of the court';

- there was no need for the claimant to seek a debarring order, rather the onus was on the defendant to disclose the overdue report as promptly as possible; and

- in the circumstances of the case, the stage at which the report was disclosed would have delayed matters and so it was appropriate not to allow permission to rely on it.

However, in *RC Residuals v Linton Fuel Oils Ltd*,[267] although there was a failure to comply with an unless order relating to exchange of expert evidence, the court did grant relief from that sanction and allow the evidence to be relied upon as:

- non-compliance with a time limit was only by a matter of minutes;

- there was no intentional default; and

- the trial date could still be met.

Where the court has directed simultaneous exchange of expert evidence, for example with expert evidence on liability, the party who is not in default may have stronger grounds for resisting relief from sanctions, on the basis that the defaulting party will have secured sequential exchange and the potential advantage of having seen the expert evidence of the other party unilaterally which, of course, an order for simultaneous exchange is intended to prevent. Prejudice of this kind cannot simply be compensated in costs.

7.15.3   Failure to keep within the Statements of Case

If, when reporting, an expert deals with matters outside the scope of the Statements of Case the court can, unless the party relying on that evidence amends the Statement of Case, strike out relevant parts of the expert's report: *Upton McGougan Ltd v Bellway Homes Ltd*.[268]

---

[266] [2000] PIQR P20.
[267] [2002] EWCA Civ 911.
[268] [2009] EWHC 1449 (TCC).

Some issues, such as fraud, must, if they are to be advanced, be pleaded. Consequently, an expert's report should not contain allegations which amount to fraud unless that is, or becomes, part of the pleaded case: *Charnock v Rowan*.[269]

7.15.4   Failure to comply with expert's duties

Even if permission to rely on expert evidence is obtained, and the report disclosed within time, the court has a discretion to exclude that evidence if the expert fails to comply with the duties owed to the court, for example in relation to joint statements.

In *Stevens v Gullis*[270] a meeting of experts took place and, following that, a memorandum of agreement sent to one of the experts, who despite numerous reminders never responded satisfactorily.

That resulted in a further order, made in the terms of an unless order, that the expert comply fully with the requirements of Part 35, including paragraph 1.2 of the Practice Direction.

The expert failed to comply with the order and became debarred from giving evidence.

The Court of Appeal held the expert demonstrated by this conduct that he had no conception of the requirements placed upon an expert under the CPR where the expert is, in addition to the duty owed to the party instructing him, also under a duty to the court.

The court also held that it was important the requirements of the Practice Direction to Part 35 were complied with, as these are intended to focus the mind of the expert on his responsibilities in order that litigation may progress in accordance with the overriding objective.

Consequently, the expert was not allowed to give evidence, not even evidence of facts perceived by him, given that he had been discredited and given that the inspection on which that factual evidence was based had taken place some time after relevant events.

The conduct of an expert can, if sufficiently egregious, result in, where an adverse costs order is made against the party relying on that expert, a direction costs be assessed on the indemnity basis.

In *Williams v Jervis*[271] Roderick Evans J held:

> 'There remain the issues surrounding Dr Gross and Mr Hay without which Mr Grant frankly concedes an application for indemnity costs would not have been made. Both these doctors, in their conduct as expert witnesses, justify in the claimant's submission an order for indemnity costs. Each was the subject of severe criticism in the main judgment. Their conduct and the way they addressed their duties as expert witnesses fell well below what can properly be expected from expert witnesses and in my judgment can certainly be described as falling "outside the norm". It is not a question of the evidence of other witnesses being preferred to the evidence of these two doctors or of their merely performing poorly as witnesses during

---

[269]   [2012] EWCA Civ 2.
[270]   (2000) 1 All ER 527.
[271]   [2009] EWHC 1837 (QB).

the case. Nor is my assessment of them based on hindsight. The sad fact is that these two doctors did not address their responsibilities or conduct themselves properly as expert witnesses.'

'These two doctors supported that case and they gave strong evidence as to the lack of integrity in the claimant's case. However, in reaching the views they expressed they did not exercise the care which it was incumbent upon them to exercise and their approach to their duties was inadequately controlled and reality tested.'

'I have considered whether the Gross/Hay issues are such that an order for indemnity costs should be made for the case as a whole. I have come, not without hesitation, to the conclusion that the justice of the case can be met by an order that the claimant's remaining costs of the case be paid by the defendant but the claimant's costs attributable to dealing with the evidence of Dr Gross and Mr Hay be assessed on the indemnity basis. It is not practicable to make this order in terms of payment of a fixed sum or a proportion of the overall costs.'

An expert, subject to criticism by the court in sufficiently strong terms, may also face personal sanctions. For example, in *Hussein v William Hill Group*[272] the court reported medical experts involved in the case to the GMC. An expert owes a duty of care to the party relying on the evidence of that expert and no longer has immunity from proceedings where that duty is breached: *Jones v Kaney*.[273]

7.15.5   Failure to comply with the Protocol

Paragraph 9.4 of the Practice Direction – Pre-action Conduct confirms that where the evidence of an expert is necessary the parties should consider how best to minimise expense, further guidance being given in Annex C. That general approach is reflected, more specifically, in the procedure for joint selection found in the Protocol.

Paragraph 2.1 of the Practice Direction – Pre-action Conduct expressly confirms that this Practice Direction describes conduct normally expected of prospective parties, with paragraph 4.1 offering a reminder the court will take into account compliance when giving case management directions.

Furthermore, paragraph 4.6 expressly provides that the court can impose sanctions in relation to costs where the conduct described has not been adhered to.

---

[272] [2004] EWHC 208 (QB).
[273] [2011] UKSC 13.

CHAPTER 8

APPLICATIONS

8.1 INTRODUCTION

Application to the court for an interim order may be necessary, as the claim progresses, for a variety of reasons.

An order may have been sought pre-action or at an early stage following the issue of court proceedings but before case management directions and a timetable have been given.

At the case management stage specific application may have been made by a party, though this should only be necessary if a non-routine order is sought (see **4.3.2**).

Subsequently, once the court has given a timetable, application may be required to vary that timetable, enforce the directions given or to seek relief from any sanctions which have become applicable.

The procedure for making an application, even if pre-action, is found in Part 23 of the Civil Procedure Rules (the CPR) and the associated Practice Directions. It is paragraph 5 of the Practice Direction to Part 23 which confirms application for an order before the claim has commenced should be made under Part 23.

When running a personal injury claim it is important to be aware of when, how and why applications should be made as well as the best way of achieving the order sought and obtaining appropriate provision for costs.

Typically, an application will seek one or more of the following orders.

- A pre-action order for inspection of property, under CPR 25.5, or for disclosure, under either CPR 31.16 or 31.17, (see **2.1.1**).
- An order which is not part of routine case management, on the basis of the court's general powers of management provided for in CPR 3.1 or other powers conferred by various parts of the CPR (see **4.3.2**).
- A variation to the timetable, where that change is outside the scope of CPR 2.11 or CPR 3.8(4) so approval of the court is required, (see **8.3.1**).
- An order enforcing the timetable, relying on the court's general powers of case management in Part 3 (see **8.3.2**).
- An order varying or revoking earlier case management directions, on the basis of CPR 3.1(7) (see **4.6.7** and **8.3.3**).

- An order granting relief from sanctions, in accordance with CPR 3.8 and 3.9 (see **8.10.2**).

Applications, in many of these circumstances, are likely to seek from the court the exercise of general case management powers, towards achieving the overriding objective of dealing with the case justly in accordance with Part 1.

Issues about costs, specific to the application, are also likely to arise with interim orders.

Sanctions are relevant to applications, both in terms of the consequences for non-compliance with interim orders and because a party seeking relief from a sanction will need to make an application.

8.2   CASE MANAGEMENT POWERS

CPR 3.1 of the CPR identifies, in addition to those conferred by other rules and practice directions, a range of powers the court has available to manage cases.

Further important powers are those conferred by CPR 3.4, to strike out a Statement of Case in the circumstances identified in that rule, and by CPR 3.10, to remedy an error of procedure.

These case management powers will, as necessary, be used by the court when giving initial case management directions as well as when dealing with an application made by a party. Additionally, CPR 3.3 enables the court to exercise these powers, and make an order, of its own initiative.

The powers of most significance when the court is dealing with interim applications in personal injury claims need to be considered in turn.

8.2.1   Power to strike out

CPR 3.4(2) provides that the court may strike out a Statement of Case if it appears that:
- the Statement of Case discloses no reasonable grounds for bringing or defending the claim;
- the Statement of Case is an abuse of the court's process or is otherwise likely to obstruct the just disposal of the proceedings; or
- there has been a failure to comply with a rule, practice direction or court order.

When considering use of the power to strike out the court must have regard to Article 6 ECHR. As Lord Hope said in *Three Rivers DC v Bank of England (No 3)*:[1]

> 'The overriding objective of the CPR is to enable the court to deal with cases justly: rule 1.1. To adopt the language of article 6.1 of the European Convention for the Protection of Human Rights and Fundamental Freedoms with which this aim is consistent, the court must ensure that there is a fair trial. It must seek to give effect to the overriding objective when it exercises any power given to it by the Rules or interprets any rule: rule 1.2.'

---

[1]   [2001] UKHL 16.

8.2.1.1 No reasonable grounds or real prospects of success

Examples of Statements of Case which do not disclose reasonable grounds are given in paragraphs 1.4 to 1.6 of Practice Direction 3A.

There may be no reasonable grounds for bringing a claim if the Particulars of Claim disclose no, or insufficient facts. Similarly, a defence which is no more than a bare denial will not disclose reasonable grounds for defending the claim.

The Particulars of Claim, or as appropriate defence, may give a coherent account yet that may not, as a matter of law, amount to a valid claim or a valid defence.

In such circumstances the court, as this is consistent with the overriding objective, should strike out the claim or defence and that will not, of itself, be a breach of Article 6 ECHR.

The power conferred by CPR 3.4(2) overlaps with the power given by CPR 24.2 to enter summary judgment where there is no real prospect of succeeding on a claim or defence.

The court is likely to approach the question of whether there are 'reasonable grounds', under CPR 3.4, or a 'real prospect', whether under CPR 13.3 or CPR 24.2, on the same basis. In other words a real prospect of succeeding will amount to reasonable grounds.

However, whilst the burden of proof is on the defendant, to show good reason why a regular judgment should be set aside, on application under CPR 13.3, the burden of proof under both CPR 3.4 and CPR 34.2 is on the applicant. The respondent, whilst having to establish the case is better than merely arguable, does not have to go as far as showing that it will probably succeed at trial: *E D & F Man Liquid Products Ltd v Patel*[2] (see **3.9.4**).

8.2.1.2 Abuse of process

In *Aktas v Adeptus*[3] the Court of Appeal affirmed the pre-CPR approach that something more than non-compliance with court orders will be required before there is an abuse of process.

The court noted that when considering automatic strike out under CCR Ord 17, r.11(9) in *Gardner v Southwark London Borough Council (No 2)*[4] Sir Thomas Bingham MR had held:

> 'The object of the new procedural regime, as counsel for the defendants have urged, is quite plain. It has been described in earlier cases. It is intended to encourage the expeditious conduct of litigation and strongly to discourage delay. But, as it seems to me, a plaintiff who for reasons of negligence, dilatoriness, lethargy or mistake fails to apply for a hearing date before the guillotine date and so suffers the consequences of Ord. 17, r. 11(9), cannot be treated as if he were guilty of wilful or contumacious disobedience. The rules do not vary the

---

[2]   [2003] EWCA Civ 472.
[3]   [2010] EWCA Civ 1170.
[4]   [1996] 1 WLR 561.

ordinary rules which the court has habitually observed, and nothing short of a clear provision should, in my judgment, deprive a plaintiff of what is otherwise a potentially important right.'

Adopting this approach the court in *Aktas* concluded a second action, issued after the first action had not been served in time, did not amount to an abuse of process as the non-compliance with the rules, albeit carrying serious consequences for the future of that first action, was essentially a single error not amounting to 'wilful or contumacious disobedience'.

While successive civil actions from the same facts may amount to an abuse of process in *Johnson v Gore Wood & Co*[5] Lord Bingham explained a broad approach to this issue was necessary:

> 'I would not accept that it is necessary, before abuse may be found, to identify any additional element such as a collateral attack on a previous decision or some dishonesty, but where those elements are present the later proceedings will be much more obviously abusive, and there will rarely be a finding of abuse unless the later proceeding involves what the court regards as the unjust harassment of a party. It is, however, wrong to hold that because a matter could have been raised in earlier proceedings it should have been, so as to render the raising of it in later proceedings necessarily abusive. That is to adopt too dogmatic an approach to what should in my opinion be a broad, merits-based judgment which takes account of the public and private interests involved and also takes account of all the facts of the case, focusing attention on the crucial question whether, in all the circumstances, a party is misusing or abusing the process of the court by seeking to raise before it the issue which could have been raised before.'

Where earlier litigation has been compromised, rather than tried, it will be necessary to determine exactly what issues were raised, and hence whether these were compromised, before determining if any subsequent proceedings are an abuse of process: *Zurich Insurance Company plc v Hayward*.[6]

If a party's conduct means a fair trial is no longer possible the court may be willing to strike out a Statement of Case, as an abuse of process, because that is consistent with the overriding objective of dealing with the case justly: *Arrow Nominees Inc v Blackledge*.[7] Otherwise, even where the court is critical of the conduct concerned, it will be more appropriate for that criticism to sound in costs: *Woodhouse v Consignia plc*;[8] *Douglas v Hello! Ltd*.[9]

Exaggeration, even when deliberate, will not amount to an abuse of process which justifies striking out the whole claim where the claimant is able to prove at least some aspects of that claim: *Shah v Ul Haq*;[10] *Summers v Fairclough Homes Ltd*.[11] Quite different considerations arise where an insured brings a claim directly against an insurer, where such exaggeration will defeat the claim as a whole, because of the duty of good faith that exists between insurer and insured.

---

5   [2002] 2 AC 1.
6   [2011] EWCA Civ 641.
7   (2000) *The Times*, 7 July.
8   [2002] EWCA Civ 275.
9   [2003] EWHC 55 (Ch).
10   [2009] EWCA Civ 542.
11   [2010] EWCA Civ 1300.

8.2.1.3 Non-compliance

The proper approach of the court to an application to strike out for non-compliance with a rule, practice direction or court order was considered soon after the introduction of the CPR in *Biguzzi v Rank Leisure*.[12]

This case involved delay on the part of both parties but an application was made by the defendant to strike out the action. The court held that under the CPR the keeping of time-limits was important and that was reflected in the power to strike out a Statement of Case conferred by CPR 3.4.

However, the court recognised that the fact this power existed did not mean that it should be exercised in every case. The CPR, in a stricter regulatory environment, provided alternative, and more flexible, remedies to the draconian step of striking the case out.

On the facts, where there was a lack of expedition by both parties and it was still possible to have a fair trial, the claim was not struck out.

Similarly, in *Asian Sky Television plc v Bayer Rosin*[13] Clarke LJ stated that, when deciding what was the judge order to make, consideration should be given to the question whether striking out the Statement of Case would be disproportionate and that there would need to be 'flagrant' abuse before the court struck out an action where a fair trial was still possible.

This approach was affirmed in *Marstons Plc v Charman*[14] when it was observed that, whilst that accepting delays in complying with court orders could not be tolerated, courts should not abuse the case management powers available under the CPR, by striking out claims, when a proportionate use of a more flexible case management power would be more appropriate.

Use of case management powers in a proportionate way, reflecting the seriousness of conduct involving the defaulting party, was again confirmed in *Aktas v Adepta*[15] which also described *Biguzzi* as one of the most important early decisions on the CPR.

If, however, there has been non-compliance with an order which specifies the consequences of such a failure, typically an unless order, the court, whilst retaining the power to give relief from sanctions, is likely to take a more robust view of that non-compliance (see 8.2.2).

Moreover, even without there being conduct amounting to abuse or breach of an unless order the court may, if ultimately this is the just thing to do, exercise the power to strike out for non-compliance: *Hayden v Charlton*.[16]

---

12   [1999] 1 WLR 1926.
13   [2001] EWCA Civ 1792.
14   [2009] EWCA Civ 719.
15   [2010] EWCA Civ 1170.
16   [2011] EWCA Civ 791.

If the terms of an unless order have not been complied with, and the consequence of non-compliance is specified as striking out, that order will take effect automatically on elapse of the time limit given in the order, without the need for further application for an order expressly striking out (see **8.3.2.2**).

In other circumstances if a party wishes to seek an order striking out for non-compliance application for an order made in accordance with CPR 3.4(2), will be necessary.

Following revision to the CPR in April 2013 the court may, when considering whether to strike out or impose some other sanction, adopt the approach, directly applicable to CPR 3.9, set out in *Denton v TH White Ltd*,[17] as explained in *Walsham Chalet Park Ltd v Tallington Lakes Ltd*,[18] (see **8.10.2.5**).

8.2.2   Power to specify the consequences of non-compliance

CPR 3.1(3)(b) confirms that whenever the court makes an order it may also specify the consequences of failing to comply with that order.

Before the introduction of the CPR, when there were no automatic sanctions, a party wishing to enforce an order against another party would often need to seek a further order. That further order would specify the consequence of continued default in compliance with the earlier order normally being framed in terms of, and being known by, an 'unless order'.

Whilst the introduction of automatic sanctions, under the CPR, removed the need, in many circumstances, for such order the CPR still confers power on the court to make an order specifying the consequences of non-compliance. Given that the court may well not impose the draconian sanction of strike out where an order which does not expressly identify the consequences of default has not been complied with, unless orders still have an important part to play under the CPR.

The nature, purpose and likely consequences of unless orders was considered, pre-CPR, in *Hytec Information Systems Ltd v Coventry City Council*[19] where Ward LJ summarised the position:

> '(1) An unless order is an order of last resort. It is not made unless there is a history of failure to comply with other orders. It is the party's last chance to put his case in order. (2) Because that was his last chance, a failure to comply will ordinarily result in the sanction being imposed. (3) This sanction is a necessary forensic weapon which the broader interests of the administration of justice require to be deployed unless the most compelling reason is advanced to exempt his failure. (4) It seems axiomatic that if a party intentionally or deliberately (if the synonym is preferred), flouts the order then he can expect no mercy. (5) A sufficient exoneration will almost inevitably require that he satisfies the court that something beyond his control has caused his failure to comply with the order. (6) The judge exercises his judicial discretion in deciding whether or not to excuse. A discretion judicially exercised on the facts and circumstances of each case on its own merits depends on the circumstances of that case; at the core is service to justice. (7) The interests of justice require that justice be shown to the injured party for the procedural inefficiencies caused the twin scourges of delay and wasted costs. The public interest in the administration of justice to contain those two

---

17   [2014] EWCA Civ 906.
18   [2014] EWCA Civ 1607.
19   [1997] 1 WLR 1666.

blights upon it also weigh very heavily. Any injustice to the defaulting party, though never to be ignored, comes a long way behind the other two.'

Following the introduction of the CPR the approach in *Hytec Information Systems Ltd* was confirmed as remaining applicable in *Marcan Shipping (London) Ltd v Kefalas*[20] where Moore-Bick LJ noted:

'A well-recognised way of imposing a degree of discipline on a dilatory litigant is to make what is known as an "unless" order by which a conditional sanction is attached to an order requiring performance of a specified act by a particular date or within a particular period. Although the CPR have given the court greater powers to control proceedings and a greater responsibility for ensuring that they are conducted fairly and efficiently, for reasons which will become clear in due course I do not think that there is a significant difference between the approach to this problem adopted under the former Rules of the Supreme Court and that which is now embodied in the CPR.'

However, the Court of Appeal also stressed that before making conditional orders, particularly orders striking out Statements of Case, the judge should consider carefully whether the sanction being imposed was appropriate in all the circumstances of the case given that such an order is a powerful weapon and should not, therefore, be deployed unless the consequences could be justified. Moore-Bick LJ summarised the position by observing:

'... before making conditional orders, particularly orders for the striking out of statements of case or the dismissal of claims or counterclaims, the judge should consider carefully whether the sanction being imposed is appropriate in all the circumstances of the case. Of course, it is impossible to foresee the nature and effect of every possible breach and the party in default can always apply for relief, but a conditional order striking out a statement of case or dismissing the claim or counterclaim is one of the most powerful weapons in the court's case management armoury and should not be deployed unless its consequences can be justified. I find it difficult to imagine circumstances in which such an order could properly be made for ... "good housekeeping purposes".'

Given that the court may expect precise compliance with the terms of an unless order this can be a very effective tactical step for the party who obtains such an order but potentially dangerous for the party against whom the order is made.

Accordingly, very careful consideration, about the ability to comply, is required before agreeing to such an order. If necessary, when opposing an application for an unless order, the court should be reminded of the restraint that should be deployed before making such an order.

The need for the court to be realistic when setting a timetable was emphasised by Lord Dyson MR giving judgment in *Denton v T H White Ltd*[21] when he said:

'We should also make clear that the culture of compliance that the new rules are intended to promote requires that judges ensure that the directions that they give are realistic and achievable. It is no use imposing a tight timetable that can be seen at the outset to be unattainable. The court must have regard to the realities of litigation in making orders in the first place. Judges should also have in mind, when making directions, where the Rules provide for automatic sanctions in the case of default. Likewise, the parties should be aware

---

[20] [2007] EWCA Civ 463.
[21] [2014] EWCA Civ 906.

of these consequences when they are agreeing directions. "Unless" orders should be reserved for situations in which they are truly required: these are usually so as to enable the litigation to proceed efficiently and at proportionate cost.'

In *Pannone LLP v Aardvark Digital Ltd*[22] the Court of Appeal described the decision of the claimant's solicitors to agree an unless order in 'drastic terms', where there was no breach of an earlier order and giving a very short timescale to comply, as 'foolhardy'.

Usually, where an unless order has been made and not complied with, it is to be expected the condition imposed by the court will be effective. Hence, where the claimant breached an unless order by deleting data from computers before delivering them up for inspection the claim was struck out as the court was not prepared to assist a litigant in fighting a case on limited material he chose to make available and suppressing other evidence: *Ryback v Langbar International Ltd*.[23] Similarly, a claim for special damages (though not the whole claim) was struck out when the claimant failed to comply with an unless order requiring service of a schedule: *Tomer v Atlantic Cleaning Service Ltd*.[24]

8.2.3   Power to impose a condition

CPR 3.1(3)(a) allows the court to impose a condition when making an order.

Additionally, CPR 3.1(5) allows the court to direct that the party in default make a payment into court, as an alternative to an order striking out the claim.

However, these powers should not generally be exercised just because a rule, Practice Direction or Protocol has not been complied with: *Biguzzi v Rank Leisure*.[25]

Consequently, the court declined to exercise the power requiring the party in default to make a payment into court, when extending time for service of witness statements, because the proper penalty, for non-compliance, was generally the requirement to seek relief from sanctions and any further penalty would only be appropriate if there was, for example, a history of repeated breaches of the timetable: *Mealey Horgan plc v Horgan*.[26]

Essentially, CPR 3.1(3) allows the court to attach a condition to a specific order granting relief, as the price of doing so, rather than imposing conditions when making an order of any kind: *Hushcroft v P&O Ferries Ltd*.[27]

Furthermore, a party should only be subject to such an order if seen to be regularly flouting proper court procedures or otherwise demonstrating a want of good faith, good faith for that purposes consisting of a will to litigate a genuine claim or defence as economically or expeditiously as possible in accordance with the overriding objective: *Olatawura v Abiloye*.[28]

---

[22]   [2011] EWCA Civ 803.
[23]   [2010] EWHC 2015 (Ch).
[24]   [2008] EWHC 1653 (QB).
[25]   [1999] 1 WLR 1926.
[26]   (1999) *The Times*, 6 July .
[27]   [2010] EWCA Civ 1483.
[28]   [2002] EWCA Civ 998.

Accordingly, these provisions should not be used as a way, for example, of circumventing the requirements of Part 25, concerning the need for security for costs.

Use of the power to impose a condition when making an order, under CPR 3.1(3), has also been exercised when the court would not have power simply to order the party, on whom the condition is imposed, to take a particular step. For example, in *Edwards-Tubb v J D Weatherspoon plc*[29] whilst the claimant could not be ordered to disclose an expert's report to which privilege attached, the court did feel able to impose a term, by making that grant of permission conditional upon waiving privilege and disclosing the report of an expert jointly selected under the Pre-action Protocol for Personal Injury Claims.

8.2.4   Power to extend or shorten time

CPR 3.1(2)(a) confirms the court may extend or shorten the time for compliance with any rule, practice direction or court order.

In some situations, however, this general power to extend or shorten time is not available to the court or must be exercised having regard to particular circumstances.

8.2.4.1   *Exclusion of the general power*

Where aspects of the CPR are self-contained, making specific provision for circumstances in which time should be extended, the court will have to work within that code rather than exercising, in accordance with the overriding objective, the more general power conferred by CPR 3.1.

Notably both CPR 7.6, dealing with extension of time for service of the claim form, and Part 36 operates in this way.

CPR 3.1(2)(a) expressly provides that the power to extend time is available even if the application for an extension is made after the time for compliance has expired. At that stage it is likely a sanction will have taken effect which, strictly, requires an application for relief under CPR 3.8.

However, if the party in default only applies for an extension of time, without additionally seeking relief from sanctions, the court may regard the power to extend time as not being restricted by the terms of CPR 3.8 and will, if it is appropriate to do so, extend time on the court's own initiative: *Marcan Shipping (London) Ltd v Kefalas*;[30] *Pannone LLP v Aardvark Digital Ltd*.[31]

8.2.4.2   *Extending time of consent orders*

It was pointed out by Lord Denning MR in *Siebe Gorman & Co Ltd v Pneupac Ltd*[32] that there is an ambiguity in expressing an order to be made 'by consent' when he said:

---

[29]   [2011] EWCA Civ 136.
[30]   [2007] EWCA Civ 463.
[31]   [2011] EWCA Civ 803.
[32]   [1982] 1 WLR 185.

'There are two meanings to the words "by consent". That was observed by Lord Greene MR in *Chandless-Chandless v Nicholson*.[33] One meaning is this: the words "by consent" may evidence a real contract between the parties. In such a case the court will only interfere with such an order on the same grounds as it would with any other contract. The other meaning is this: the words "by consent" may mean "the parties hereto not objecting". In such a case there is no real contract between the parties. The order can be altered or varied by the court in the same circumstances as any other order that is made by the court without the consent of the parties. In every case it is necessary to discover which meaning is used. Does the order evidence a real contract between the parties? Or does it only evidence an order made without objection?'

In *Pannone LLP v Aardvark Digital Ltd*[34] the Court of Appeal concluded that distinction, though it may have been relevant under earlier rules, was now of no significance when considering the power of the court under CPR 3.1(2)(a), although the fact of the earlier agreement was important when deciding whether to exercise the power to extend time.

8.2.4.3   *Extending time of unless orders*

Even if the timescale to be varied is enshrined in an unless order, and that timescale has elapsed, the court still has power to extend time, see *RC Residuals Ltd v Linton Fuel Oils Ltd*.[35]

However, if time for compliance with the order has already elapsed the sanction will apply automatically and the court must decide whether it would be appropriate to give relief from that sanction. A relevant consideration, to be taken into account when deciding whether to give relief, will be the fact that the time limit was subject to an unless order which may tell against relief being given.

Accordingly, the power of the court to extend time is not excluded simply because the relevant order was expressed as an unless order, even when that order was made by consent.

8.2.4.4   *Extending time of deemed orders*

Where a costs order has been deemed to have been made, for example under CPR 44.12, the court cannot, by seeking to extend time under CPR 3.1(2)(a), circumvent the effect of that order: *Walker Residential v Davis*;[36] *Lahey v Pirelli Tyres Ltd*.[37]

By CPR 44.12 there will be a deemed costs order:

•   under CPR 36.10(1), in favour of the claimant, when a Part 36 offer is accepted within the relevant period;

•   under CPR 38.6 in favour of the defendant, when the claimant discontinues; and

---

[33]   [1942] 2 KB 321, 324.
[34]   [2011] EWCA Civ 803.
[35]   [2002] EWCA Civ 911.
[36]   [2005] EWHC 3483 (Ch).
[37]   [2007] EWCA Civ 91.

- under CPR 3.7 in favour of the defendant, when the claim is struck out for non-payment of fees (at the stage of either allocation or listing after the claimant fails to comply with notice from the court requiring payment of the fee under CPR 3.7(2).

By CPR 44.13(1A)(a) there will be a deemed costs order for applicant's costs in the case when the court makes an order granting permission to appeal or where an order follows an application without notice and that order does not mention costs. However, here the court does have power to vary such an order under the terms of CPR 44.13 (1B).

8.2.5   Power to vary or revoke orders

CPR 3.1(7) provides that the power of the court to make an order includes a power to vary or revoke the order.

This rule, at first sight, would appear to confirm a very wide power on the court, at least when dealing with case management directions, to overturn earlier orders without the need for an appeal. However, there are constraints on this power as Patten J explained in *Lloyds Investment (Scandinavia) Ltd v Christen Ager-Hanssen*[38] when he said:

'Although this is not intended to be an exhaustive definition of the circumstances in which the power under CPR Part 3.1(7) is exercisable, it seems to me that, for the High Court to revisit one of its earlier orders, the applicant must either show some material change of circumstances or that the judge who made the earlier order was misled in some way, whether innocently or otherwise, as to the correct factual position before him.'

'If all that is sought is a reconsideration of the order on the basis of the same material, then that can only be done, in my judgment, in the context of an appeal. Similarly it is not, I think, open to a party to the earlier application to seek in effect to re-argue that application by relying on submissions in evidence which were available to him at the time of the earlier hearing, but which, for whatever reason, he or his legal representatives chose not to employ.'

These views were confirmed by the Court of Appeal in *Collier v Williams*[39] where the court confirmed:

'We endorse that approach. We agree that the power given CPR 3.1(7) cannot be used simply as an equivalent to an appeal against an order with which the applicant is dissatisfied. The circumstances outlined by Patten J are the only ones in which the power to revoke or vary an order already made should be exercised under 3.1(7).'

Moreover, this power is applicable only to case management decisions and not to final orders. In *Roult v North West Strategic Health Authority*[40] the Court of Appeal held:

'But it does not follow that wherever one or other of the two assertions mentioned (erroneous information and subsequent event) can be made, then any party can return to the trial judge and ask him to reopen any decision. In particular, it does not follow, I have no doubt, where the judge's order is a final one disposing of the case, whether in whole or in part.'

---

[38]   [2003] EWHC 1470 (Ch).
[39]   [2006] EWCA Civ 20.
[40]   [2010] 1 WLR 487.

In *Kojima v HSBC Bank plc*[41] Briggs J explained that this was because once the court had finally determined the case, or part of the case, the considerations identified in *Lloyds Investments (Scandanavia) Ltd* would generally be displaced by the larger, if not overriding, public interest in finality (subject only to any right of appeal).

Additionally, in *Kojima* the court concluded there was no difference, for these purposes, between a final order on the merits, after trial, and final order by way of judgment on admissions, as the latter was still a judgment on the merits even without the panoply of a trial.

The same principle should be applicable to a final order reflecting agreement reached between the parties.

> A court has no general power to vary the terms of an agreement set out in the schedule to a Tomlin order, except insofar as the circumstances give rise to a power so to do as a matter of the general law of contract: Community Care North East v Durham County Council.[42]
>
> Where the agreement is enshrined in an order made by the court 'must be very careful in exercising a discretion to vary the terms of an order which represents a contract between the parties' and should aim to ensure that 'a bargain freely made should be upheld': Arden LJ in *Weston v Dayman*.[43] Hence in *Pannone LLP v Aardvark Digital Ltd*[44] Tomlinson LJ held:
>
>> 'Assuming that there is a power so to do, where the settlement is embodied in an order of the court, it can rarely be appropriate for the court to intervene further than to the extent to which the contract can, by its own terms or pursuant to general contractual principles, be modified or discharged in the light of changed circumstances.'

Whilst these cases concerned agreements to settle the substantive dispute the fact of consent will still be of relevance when the court decides whether to vary an interim order. Tomlinson LJ explained the position in *Pannone LLP*:

> 'In my view the weight to be given to the consideration that an order is agreed will vary according to the nature of the order and thus the agreement. Where the agreement is the compromise of a substantive dispute or the settlement of proceedings, that factor will have very great and perhaps ordinarily decisive weight, as it did in *Weston v Dayman*, which was not in any event concerned with an application to extend time. Where, however, the agreement is no more than a procedural accommodation in relation to case management, the weight to be accorded to the fact of the parties' agreement as to the consequences of non-compliance whilst still real and substantial will nonetheless ordinarily be correspondingly less, and rarely decisive.'

Consequently, a variation of time, particularly timescale provided for in an interim order, is likely to be granted more readily by the court than the term of an order dealing with a substantive issue, given the need to uphold bargains freely made, even where such a provision is contained in an interim order.

---

41 [2011] EWHC 611 (Ch).
42 [2010] EWHC 959 (QB).
43 [2006] EWCA Civ 1165.
44 [2011] EWCA Civ 803.

The Court of Appeal reviewed the proper approach to CPR 3.1(7) in *Tibbles v SIG Plc*[45] where Rix LJ held:

> 'The cases all warn against an attempt at an exhaustive definition of the circumstances in which a principled exercise of the discretion may arise. Subject to that, however, the jurisprudence has laid down firm guidance as to the primary circumstances in which the discretion may, as a matter of principle, be appropriately exercised, namely normally only (a) where there has been a material change of circumstances since the order was made, or (b) where the facts on which the original decision was made were (innocently or otherwise) misstated.'

The power conferred by CPR 3.1(7) will also be inapplicable where there has been a deemed order (see **8.2.4.4**).

8.2.6 Power to rectify an error of procedure

CPR 3.10 confirms that where there has been an error of procedure, that does not invalidate any step taken in the proceedings unless the court so orders and the court may, in any event, make an order to remedy the error.

This power is not likely to save a party who has failed to take a step altogether, such as failing to make any attempt to serve the claim form within time, but might be successfully relied upon if a timely step has been taken, yet this involves a procedural error: *Steele v Mooney*;[46] *Phillips v Symes*[47] (see **2.10.7**).

Similarly, timely issue of proceedings but in the wrong format or venue might be corrected under the scope of CPR 3.10: *Cala Homes (South) Ltd v Chichester District Council*.[48]

8.2.7 Power to order a costs budget

This express power allows the court to direct the filing and exchanging of costs budgets, even when these would not otherwise be required.

8.2.8 Power to hold a hearing by telephone

CPR 3.1(2)(d) expressly provides for a hearing to be dealt with by telephone or, indeed, any other method of direct oral communication.

This power is likely to be exercised when the court lists hearings suitable for being dealt with in this way (see **8.6.2**).

8.2.9 Power to make orders on the court's own initiative

The court may, under Part 3, make an order of its own initiative.

---

[45] [2012] EWCA Civ 518.
[46] [2005] EWCA Civ 96.
[47] [2008] UKHL 1.
[48] *The Times*, 15 October 1999.

If the court exercises this power any order made must contain, to comply with CPR 3.3(5), notice of the right to vary or set aside that order under CPR 3.3(5).

8.2.10   Power to manage cases generally

CPR 3.1(2)(m) has a catch-all provision that the court may take any other step or make any other order for the purpose of managing the case.

This provision, seen in the context of CPR 3.1 as a whole, would appear to confer an unfettered discretion on the court in the exercise of case management powers. However, in practice the exercise of those powers will be governed by a number of considerations.

Most importantly the court, when exercising case management powers, should have in mind the overriding objective (see **2.2.1**). Indeed, CPR 3.1(2)(m) specifically confirms that the wide powers conferred are to further the overriding objective.

Additionally, CPR 3.1(4), which uses the word 'will', makes it mandatory for the court to take into account, when exercising case management powers to give directions, whether a party has complied with the Practice Direction – Pre-action Conduct and any relevant protocol.

Furthermore, the court must have regard to any specific provisions in the part of the CPR being relied on at the hearing of an application. For example, if seeking relief from sanctions the court must have regard to the factors identified in CPR 3.9.

Consequently, when making or responding to an application seeking the exercise of case management powers the parties will wish to bring to the attention of the court not only the terms of any specific rule under consideration but, more generally, relevant aspects of the overriding objective as well as compliance, or otherwise, with the Practice Direction Pre-action Conduct and any relevant protocol.

The weight attached to any particular factor will need to be determined by the court when dealing with the particular application but, to approach the application correctly as a matter of law, the court will need to have regard to all relevant circumstances where these are identified in the CPR.

8.3   THE TIMETABLE AND APPLICATIONS

Case management directions given by the court, at the stage of allocation as subsequently varied if appropriate, will have set out a timetable which takes the claim up to listing or a further case management conference.

It is important to keep, if possible, to the overall timetable given by the court up to listing or further review, even if there have been variations to the dates for particular stages meanwhile. That is because the pre-trial checklist, filed at the end of the timetable set by case management directions, is intended to simply confirm that timetable has been completed.

Accordingly, an application may be necessary to enforce case management directions, so that the case progresses in accordance with the timetable.

During the timetable, however, circumstances may change which may have a bearing on the directions already given. This may require an application to bring the matter back before the court for a change to the timetable or even to vary, or revoke, the directions previously given.

It is important to recognise that the claimant will not always need to make an application in the event of a variation to the timetable becoming necessary or there being default by the defendant in complying with case management directions. That is because some variations to the timetable may be agreed between the parties, without needing a court order, and also because, depending on the nature of the default, the claimant may be able to rely on the sanctions applied to the defendant automatically by the CPR.

If the claimant is unable to keep to the timetable or is in default of case management directions a decision, once again, will have to be made whether an application is necessary either to vary the timetable or seek relief from sanctions.

8.3.1 Changing the timetable

If the timetable set out by the court, when giving case management directions, needs to be changed it may not always be necessary to make an application for a further order varying that timetable.

8.3.1.1 *When an application is not required*

CPR 2.11 provides a general rule that the time specified to do any act may be varied by the written agreement of the parties.

If the parties agree the court timetable needs to be varied it will suffice for that agreement to be recorded in writing without the need for a court order. However, the 'written agreement' must conform with the definition of this phrase given in *Thomas v Home Office*[49] (see **2.2.3.1**).

8.3.1.2 *When an application is required*

If variation of the timetable is considered necessary by one of the parties but not agreed by other parties, an application will be necessary. In these circumstances it is preferable for the application to be made prior to default in compliance with the timetable as, otherwise, any sanction will automatically apply and the party in default will then also, strictly, need relief from that sanction (see **8.10.2**).

In any both CPR 28.4 which deals with fast track claims and CPR 29.5 which deals with multi-track claims, provides that certain dates in the timetable cannot be varied without application to, and approval by, the court. These are the dates for:

- a case management conference;
- a pre-trial review;

---

[49]   [2006] EWCA Civ 1355.

- the return of a pre-trial checklist;
- the trial; and
- the trial period.

Furthermore, even if any of these dates are not specifically varied, approval of the court will be required if a variation to the timetable would inevitably make it necessary to change any such date.

The terms of CPR 2.11 are limited by the provisions of CPR 3.8(3) which provide that where a rule, practice direction or court order requires a party to do something within a specified time, and also specifies the consequence of failure to comply, the time for doing the act in question may not be extended by agreement between the parties. This provision is now, however, subject to the terms of CPR 3.8(4) which allows the parties to agree, in many circumstances, an extension of time for up to 28 days. In *Denton v TH White Ltd*[50] the Court of Appeal encouraged parties to readily agree extensions of time requested under this rule. It is important to note, however, this requires 'written agreement', which is likely to be interpreted as it was *Thomas v Home Office*[51] (see **2.2.3.1**).

A number of important rules, which relate to the timetable, do specify the consequence of failure to comply including CPR 31.21, which deals with the failure to give disclosure or inspection, CPR 32.10 which deals with the failure to serve witness statements by the due date, and CPR 35.13, which deals with failure to disclose expert evidence.

There is, of course, nothing to stop the parties agreeing a consent order, varying the timetable, which can be submitted to the court for approval (and once made the exercise of the court's power to extend time will modify the timetable).

The court may, in most circumstances, make an order extending time under CPR 3.1(2)(a) (see **8.2.4**).

8.3.1.3   Dealing with changes to the timetable

If the timetable is revised, by agreement between the parties or court order, it is important, just as when directions are given by the court initially, important to take a number of steps.

- Diary entries to ensure, so far as possible, the timetable, as now revised, is complied with.
- Arrangements for implementation of directions should, so far as necessary, be agreed with the defendant.
- The client should be advised of the revised timetable.

8.3.2   Enforcing the timetable

One or more of the parties may not comply with the timetable given by the court as the case progresses.

---

[50] [2014] EWCA Civ 906.
[51] [2006] EWCA Civ 1355.

Whilst at some key stages, such as filing the allocation questionnaire or pre-trial checklist, the court will deal with default by making an order of its own initiative it will usually be necessary, where a further order is required for enforcement of the timetable, for a party to make application.

That application will seek an order, to deal with the default, under the general, and wide-ranging, case management powers of the court conferred by Part 3 (see **4.3**).

When assessing if an application, concerning the timetable, should be made there are a number of preliminary considerations.

8.3.2.1 Is there a failure to comply?

Before deciding whether to rely on sanctions or make application it is first necessary to assess whether the opponent has failed to comply with a court order.

The court will wish to be satisfied, particularly if dealing with an alleged breach of an unless order, the terms of the order were sufficiently precise, so it is clear whether or not those terms have been complied with.

Difficulties can arise if it is alleged there has been default by a party in complying with the letter, but not the spirit, of the order. For example, if it is suggested there is non-compliance because, whilst a party has given disclosure, the list of documents is inadequate or that further information has been provided but is incomplete.

The court may accept an order has been complied with if what has been provided is given in good faith and is not illusory: *Scottish & Newcastle plc v Raguz*[52] (applying *Realkredit Danmark A/S v York Montague Ltd*[53]).

If, however, the question is whether the terms of an unless order have been complied with the court may expect there to be, subject only to the de minimus exception, full compliance with the precise terms of the order: *Jani-King (GB) Ltd v Prodger.*[54]

If there has been a failure to comply with a court order a decision must be made whether simply to rely on sanctions which may now apply or to make an application.

8.3.2.2 Do sanctions already apply?

The CPR contain a number of instances where sanctions will apply automatically. Several of these deal with key stages in a personal injury claim.

- By CPR 31.21 a party may not rely on a document if that party fails to disclose or permit inspection of the document.

- By CPR 32.10 a party who fails to disclose witness statements in accordance with case management directions will be prevented from relying on that evidence unless the court gives permission to do so.

---

[52] [2004] EWHC 1835 (Ch).
[53] [1999] CPLR 272.
[54] [2007] EWHC 712 (QB).

- By CPR 35.13 a party who fails to disclose an expert's report may not use the report at trial, or call the expert to give evidence orally, unless the court gives permission to do so. This rule reinforces CPR 35.4 but is likely also to prohibit a party who already has permission to rely on expert evidence doing so outside the scope of that permission, for example if the report is not disclosed by the due date in the timetable.
- By CPR 44.3B a party who fails to promptly provide information about a funding arrangement, in accordance with the Costs Practice Direction, will be unable to recover additional liabilities.

CPR 3.8(1) confirms that any sanction for failing to comply with the rule, practice direction or court order takes effect unless the party in default applies for and obtains relief from sanctions.

If the court has made an order specifying the consequence of failure to comply, such an order will take effect automatically, without the need for a further court order, in the event of the terms not being complied with. Hence, where an unless order is not complied with the terms will take effect without the need for a further court order. Hence, if the sanction, for non-compliance with the order, is striking out a Statement of Case that will occur without the need for an application under CPR 3.4(2). All the other party needs to do is make a request for judgment in such terms as that party is entitled to. The right to proceed straight to a request for judgment in this way was explained by Moore-Bick LJ in *Marcan Shipping (London) Ltd v Kefalas*[55] where he said:

> 'Rule 3.1(3)(b) expressly gives the court the power when making an order to specify the consequences of failure to comply with its terms and rule 3.8(1) expressly provides that where a party has failed to comply with an order any sanction imposed by the order has effect unless the party in default applies for and obtains relief from the sanction. This makes it clear, in my view, that no further order is required to render the sanction effective; on the contrary, the onus is on the defaulting party to take steps to obtain relief. Moreover, in case there should be any doubt about the effect of a failure to comply with an order of this kind paragraph 1.9 of the Practice Direction supplementing Part 3 states that:
>
>> "where a rule, practice direction or order states 'shall be struck out or dismissed' or 'will be struck out or dismissed' this means that the striking out or dismissal will be automatic and that no further order of the court is required."
>
> If it is thought that the party seeking to take advantage of the default must apply to the court in order to render the sanction effective, in my view that is wrong. The sanction takes effect without further order and the statement of case is struck out; it follows, therefore, that it is unnecessary and inappropriate to make an application under rule 3.5(5) or rule 3.4(2)(c) for an order to that effect. If, however, the party seeking to take advantage of the failure to comply wishes to obtain judgment in his favour, he must, except in those cases covered by rule 3.5(2), make an application to the court to enable it to determine whether he is entitled to judgment as a result and, if so, in what form. In such cases the operation of the sanction does not lie in the discretion of the court; only if there is an application under rule 3.8 is the court required to consider whether, in all the circumstances, it is just to make an order granting relief from the consequences that would otherwise follow.'

---

[55] [2007] EWCA Civ 463.

8.3.2.3   Should applicable sanctions be relied on?

Where non-compliance with case management directions will attract automatic sanctions the party in default will have to apply for relief from those sanctions, which will otherwise apply unless and until relief is given by the court. This, effectively, relieves the party who is not in default from having to make an application for an order where an appropriate sanction applies automatically.

Nevertheless, and for the avoidance of doubt, the party relying on any automatic sanction may wish to confirm as much to the party in default with a reminder that any application for relief from such sanction should now be made promptly.

If a sanction applies application is required, by CPR 3.8, for relief from that sanction. When the application is heard the court must consider all the circumstances, including the factors set out in CPR 3.9, in deciding whether to grant relief (see **8.10.2**).

8.3.2.4   Should an application be made?

In certain circumstances it may be necessary to enforce case management directions, particularly where the claimant needs the defendant to comply with the directions in order to obtain relevant information.

There are several stages in a personal injury claim where such information is likely to be required:

- Disclosure and/or inspection (where the defendant's failure to give full disclosure may result in documents, helpful to the claimant's case, not becoming available).

- Service of a counter schedule (where the claimant needs the counter schedule in order to fully understand the defendant's case, and perhaps the evidence necessary to deal with the issues, and/or assess any offer made by the defendant).

- A response to a Request for Further Information (in order to fully understand the defendant's case, and again the evidence that may need to be called to deal with the real issues).

Such an application will normally be made under CPR 3.4 on the basis of the failure to comply with a rule, Practice Direction or court order.

Under CPR 3.4 the court may strike out a Statement of Case. If a defence is struck out the defendant will then be at risk of an application for judgment (in default of a defence).

However, the court is more likely to use the general powers of management, set out in CPR 3.1, in an effort to keep the case, so far as possible, on track towards trial and to make an order appropriate to the nature of the breach: *Biguzzi v Rank Leisure plc*,[56] as approved in *Marstons Plc v Charman*[57] and *Aktas v Adepta*.[58]

---

[56]   [1999] 1 WLR 1926.
[57]   [2009] EWCA Civ 719.
[58]   [2010] EWCA Civ 1170.

Accordingly, if such an application is required, the claimant may wish, in that application, to seek an order which is proportionate to the default.

For example, if the defendant has failed to serve a counter schedule, it may be appropriate to seek an order, or unless order, that the defendant be deemed to admit the claimant's schedule.

However, in some circumstances the court may be willing to make an order, or conditional unless order, striking out a Statement of Case, for example on failure to give disclosure. That is because disclosure is such a crucial part of the court process.

8.3.2.5 Tactics

Before making an application to enforce case management directions, the defendant should usually be given an opportunity of putting matters right within a reasonable timescale. That reflects the overriding objective, found in Part 1, and the need for the parties to co-operate in furthering that objective. If, however, outstanding matters are not swiftly dealt with an application should then be made promptly.

Giving the defendant an opportunity to put matters right first may, if no explanation or corrective action has been taken, support a request that any application then made be considered by the court without a hearing.

Additionally, where the defendant fails to take appropriate steps after advance warning, about the intention to make an application, has been given this will support an argument that costs have been incurred as a result of the defendant's default and that, accordingly, the costs of the application should be paid by the defendant in any event.

Conversely, if application is made by the defendant without affording the claimant a reasonable opportunity of putting matters right that may support an argument that, particularly if outstanding matters are then dealt with promptly, costs should not necessarily follow.

A further tactical consideration, if the defendant makes an application, is whether a cross-application is required to deal with any matters where it may be contended the defendant is in default. Given that the court should, under Part 3, deal with as many matters as possible on one occasion, any such application ought to be listed with the defendant's application. Such a step may effectively make the hearing a matter of general case management, where costs are more likely to be in the case.

8.3.3 Varying or revoking case management directions

Rather than merely adjusting timescale, or seeking to enforce that timescale, a party may wish to vary the substance of directions comprising part of the timetable, or even revoke certain directions given altogether.

In these circumstances it will be necessary to rely on CPR 3.1(7). This power, in practice, is not as broad as might first appear from the rule itself (see **8.2.4**).

This provision can usefully be relied on where there has been a material change of circumstances since the earlier order and can be of particular significance on the question of permission to rely on expert evidence. If directions originally make no provision for permission to rely on expert evidence in a particular field, even if the court expressly rejected a request by one or other party for such permission, the subsequent availability of an expert's report, which appears to be reasonably required for the purposes of Part 35, is likely to amount to a relevant change of circumstances such that the court can vary the earlier directions and now give the party seeking to rely on that evidence permission to do so: *Fox v Foundation Piling Group Ltd*.[59] The outcome of such an application may well be different if the party concerned had the evidence available at the time but chose not to deploy it at the earlier hearing: *Kojima v HSBC Bank plc*.[60]

The Court of Appeal reviewed the proper approach to CPR 3.1(7) in Tibbles v-SIG Plc[61] where Rix LJ held:

> 'The cases all warn against an attempt at an exhaustive definition of the circumstances in which a principled exercise of the discretion may arise. Subject to that, however, the jurisprudence has laid down firm guidance as to the primary circumstances in which the discretion may, as a matter of principle, be appropriately exercised, namely normally only (a) where there has been a material change of circumstances since the order was made, or (b) where the facts on which the original decision was made were (innocently or otherwise) misstated.'

8.4 MAKING AN APPLICATION

The claimant may need to make application for an interim order, whether to change the timetable, enforce case management directions or vary those directions.

If so, appropriate advice needs to be given and instructions, to make such an application, sought.

8.4.1 When to apply

As soon as it is clear a court order on any aspect of the case is required an application ought to be made, as required by paragraph 2.7 of Practice Direction 23A.

Consequently, if there is a variation to the timetable which needs approval of the court it is important, given the responsibility of the parties to help the court manage the case, to bring the matter back before the court at the earliest opportunity. CPR 23.5 confirms an application is deemed to have been made when it is received by the court.

Part of the court's duty to manage cases, with which the parties should assist, involves dealing with as many aspects of the case as possible on the same occasion. Accordingly, when a hearing, at which the court may deal with any aspect of case management, has already been scheduled the parties should consider the need, and if appropriate make

---

[59] (Unreported) 2 October 2008, Sheffield County Court.
[60] [2011] EWHC 611 (Ch).
[61] [2012] EWCA Civ 518.

application, for any orders considered necessary that are not already the subject of specific application and cannot properly be regarded as incidental routine case management.

In such circumstances the court should be invited to list the further application for hearing at the date already fixed, in accordance with paragraph 2.8 of Practice Direction 23A. If time does not permit service of an application notice both the court and the other parties should at least be advised of the nature of the application and the reason for it. Oral application can then made at the hearing, in accordance with paragraph 2.10 of Practice Direction 23A.

Whilst a party should not have to make formal application for an order which is part of routine case management, and which is sought at a scheduled case management hearing, both the opponent and the court ought to be made aware of the intention to seek such an order. That can be done by filing and serving a draft order.

All these steps will help the court fully manage the case at any hearing.

8.4.2   Where to apply

When an application notice is required that should be made to the court where the claim was started unless:

- the claim has been transferred to another court; or
- the parties have been notified of a fixed date for the trial at another court.

In either case, the application should then be made to that other court.

An application for a pre-action order should be made to the court where it is likely the claim, to which the application relates, will be started, unless there is good reason to do otherwise.

8.4.3   How to apply

If an application is required, the court has power to dispense with some or all of the formal requirements. Generally, however, an application will require the necessary documents to comply with the procedure set out in Part 23, accompanied by the appropriate fee.

8.4.3.1   Application notice

The notice, for which form N244 may be used, will need to comply with CPR 23.6 and paragraph 2.1 of Practice Direction 23A:

- The notice must give relevant details of the claim to which it relates, including the title, reference number and full name of the applicant.
- The order the applicant seeks must be identified, though this may be by way of reference to an attached draft. That order is likely to seek appropriate use of the court's case management powers (see **4.3**).

- The notice must state, briefly, why the order is sought. Further matters, in support of the application, may be set out later in the notice or by separate evidence in support.

- Appropriate provision for the costs of the application should be sought from the range of orders the court may make when dealing with costs at an interim hearing (see **8.9.2**).

- There must be, in the notice, either a request for a hearing (if appropriate by telephone) or that the application be considered by the court without a hearing (see **8.6.1.1** and **8.6.2**).

- A time estimate for the hearing, which needs to be as realistic as possible, should be given.

- The notice should identify the party or parties on whom it should be served (though this will not be applicable if the court is requested to consider the application without a hearing). If the applicant is not already a party an address for service, including a postcode, must be given.

- The level of judge appropriate for dealing with the application should be indicated. With an interim order this will usually be a district judge but some applications, for example concerning the trial in a multi-track case, may need to be made to the trial judge.

- The notice should indicate whether the evidence to be relied on will be the existing Statements of Case, a witness statement or evidence in the application notice itself. If evidence is contained in the notice itself that will need, in accordance with Part 22, to be verified by a Statement of Truth.

- The notice will need to be signed and dated.

8.4.3.2   Draft order

If the terms of the draft order sought from the court are reasonably brief, details can be given in the application notice itself. Otherwise a separate draft of the order sought should be prepared to accompany that application notice.

Paragraph 6.12 of Practice Direction 23A provides a draft order must be filed and served if an application is made in a multi-track case, or in any other case if the court so directs.

Consequently, notice from the court, confirming when the application is to be heard, needs to be carefully checked to clarify whether this directs filing of a draft order prior to the hearing.

8.4.3.3   Case summary

Paragraph 6.12 of Practice Direction 23A requires there to be a case summary where an application is made in a multi-track case. A case summary will also be required if the court so directs in any other case.

Once again, notice of hearing must be carefully checked to establish whether the court has directed filing of a case summary.

Because issues may have clarified or narrowed between issue and hearing of the application a case summary might usefully be prepared, if required, as that hearing date approaches.

8.4.3.4   Evidence

The application will usually be supported by some evidence, even if that is a brief explanation of the background to and reasons for the application set out in the notice itself.

The application may be supported by a witness statement which, in accordance with CPR 32.6, will be the general format of evidence given at any hearing other than a trial. Any such statement will need to comply with the requirements of Part 32 concerning witness statements (see **6.2**).

Some provisions in the CPR specifically require an application to be supported by evidence, notably applications for an interim remedy, unless the court orders otherwise, under the terms of CPR 25.3(2).

Paragraph 9.3 of Practice Direction 23A confirms, so far as timescale for service of evidence in support of an application is concerned, that:

> 'Where it is intended to rely on evidence which is not contained in the application itself, the evidence, if it has not already been served, should be served with the application.'

Evidence, in support of an application, should deal with relevant factual matters but not legal argument (see **6.1.1.3**).

8.4.3.5   Skeleton argument

If legal argument needs to be set out it is, rather than dealing with by witness statement, preferable to have a skeleton argument (unless the argument can be contained within a case summary).

8.4.3.6   Costs statement

If the party making the application seeks the costs in any event a statement of those costs, for summary assessment, will usually be required.

The costs statement may be prepared at the stage of issuing the application but, as it will not then be clear exactly what work is likely to be required, the party applying to court may prefer to prepare the statement later, remembering that this must be served at least 24 hours prior to the hearing of the application.

If the court is invited to consider the application and make an order without a hearing this can include provision for costs, including that such costs be paid in any event, but it seems doubtful those costs can be assessed, as there will have been no hearing for the purposes of paragraph 13.2 of the Costs Practice Direction.

If costs, for whatever reason, will not be assessed at the hearing there is no point preparing a costs statement (see **8.9.1** and **8.9.3**).

8.4.3.7 Fee

A court fee will be payable on the issue of the application. The amount of that fee will depend upon whether the court is invited to deal with the application by a hearing (whether telephone or in person) or without a hearing (which will include orders the court is invited to make by consent).

8.4.4 Serving the application

Unless the court agrees to a request that the application be considered without a hearing the application notice, and accompanying documentation, need to be served on any respondent, in accordance with CPR 23.4(1).

Like all documents served in the proceedings, other than the claim form, service is governed by CPR 6.20 to 6.29.

The application must be served as soon as possible but, in any event, at least three days prior to the hearing (or five days if there is to be a telephone hearing) as required by CPR 23.7 and paragraph 4 of Practice Direction 23A.

CPR 23.7 also requires that the application notice, when served, be accompanied by any written evidence in support as well as any draft order attached to the application.

The applicant may also wish to prepare and file at court a certificate of service (to guard against non-appearance by the respondent).

8.4.5 Tactics

The claimant needs to strike a balance between making application, where this is necessary to properly progress the case, and avoiding unnecessary risk of an adverse, discrete, costs order given that when matters are argued about as part of general case management, costs are more likely to be in the case. Assuming the claimant succeeds, overall, that will facilitate recovery of costs associated with case management, even when the claimant has not obtained, or succeeded in resisting, all the directions sought.

Conversely, if a specific application is made and the defendant ordered to pay the costs, is likely these will be assessed, and hence payable, as the case progresses and irrespective of the eventual outcome.

8.5 RECEIVING AN APPLICATION

The rules which apply to the making of an application by the claimant apply equally to any application made by the defendant.

Whenever the defendant issues an application the claimant needs to carefully consider how best to deal with that application.

8.5.1   Agreement?

On receipt the application should be carefully considered to assess what the defendant seeks and if, or to what extent, this may be capable of agreement.

The claimant needs to be advised of the application and instruction sought on whether, and if so to what extent, terms might be agreed.

The order sought must be one which the rules and/or the substantive law allow. If not, it may be appropriate to make this clear to the defendant on receipt of the application.

If the order sought can be agreed it may be sensible to confirm as much to the defendant as soon as possible, before further costs are incurred, so that a consent order can be agreed and submitted to the court.

If it is accepted the defendant may be entitled to an order on the application, but not necessarily in the terms sought, appropriate proposals should be put to the defendant, again at the earliest opportunity. It may be useful to make any such proposals 'without prejudice except as to costs' so that the efforts made to try to and agree the matter can be referred to at the hearing, if necessary, in connection with the costs of that hearing.

The claimant should be advised of the application made and, where necessary, instructions sought on the response which is to be made.

Care should be exercised, to ensure the terms can be fully complied with in the timescale agreed, before consenting to an unless order, given the risk that the court may then be reluctant to vary the timescale (see **8.2.2**).

8.5.2   Arrangements for the hearing

The notice of hearing should be checked to establish whether that hearing is to take place in person at court or by telephone.

If the hearing has been listed to take place in person, given that the majority of interim applications can now be dealt with by telephone, it may be appropriate to seek the defendant's agreement for a request that the court re-list for a telephone hearing. The guidance given in Practice Direction 23A helpfully indicates hearings which will normally be suitable to be dealt with by telephone.

If the hearing is listed to be dealt with by telephone it will be necessary to check which party is to make the necessary arrangements with a telephone provider. If those arrangements are to be made by the defendant, details of the claimant's representative, and contact telephone number, will need to be supplied.

If it is proposed to instruct counsel to deal with the hearing then counsel's availability ought to be checked and, although strictly not required, it may be courteous to inform the defendant that counsel is to represent the claimant. Similarly, if this may have a bearing on whether counsel is instructed to appear for the claimant, it may be appropriate to check with the defendant's solicitors whether counsel is to be briefed for the defendant. Should counsel be involved that does not prevent the hearing being dealt with by telephone if it is otherwise appropriate to do so.

Whatever the format of the hearing, the time estimate should be checked and both the defendant and the court notified, straightaway, if it seems likely the time allowed will not suffice.

Diary entries should be made to ensure that details of the hearing date are duly noted.

8.5.3 Cross-application

If the claimant wishes to seek any order, consequent upon or independent of the defendant's application, both the court and the defendant should, at the very least, be notified as to the terms of the order to be sought and careful consideration should be given as to the need for a cross-application to be issued.

An application notice, made as a cross-application, may be sent to the court with a request this is listed for hearing at the same time as the defendant's application (if necessary by that application being re-listed to an occasion when suitable time can be allowed by the court).

8.5.4 Evidence

The evidence in support of the application needs to be considered, as part of a general assessment of the tactics to adopt.

If there are further matters the claimant wishes to put before the court, either in reply or to seek some other order, it is likely evidence will need to be filed and served in response to the defendant's evidence so steps should be taken to deal with that as soon as possible.

8.5.5 Costs

The terms sought by the defendant as to costs of the application will need to be considered. If an order can be agreed it may be the claimant will have to concede costs although, in some circumstances, it may be appropriate to agree an order, in or along the lines sought, but only on suitable terms as to costs.

If the claimant intends to seek an order for costs against the defendant on the hearing of the application, for example when resisting the application outright, a costs statement, for summary assessment, will need to be prepared ready for filing and service at least 24 hours before the hearing of the application.

8.5.6 Tactics

The claimant needs to be wary of the defendant making specific application for matters that should be treated as routine case management, not requiring an application. That is because the costs of these may follow the event rather than being costs in the case which will often be to the detriment of the claimant.

It may be useful, at the outset, to invite the defendant not to make application on what are essentially case management issues, at least not without giving the claimant an opportunity, first, to confirm that no specific application will be necessary.

The claimant may also wish to invite the defendant to give notice, at the time, of any application which the court is invited to consider, and make an order on, without a hearing so that the claimant does have an opportunity to make representations if such an order is not considered appropriate rather than having to rely on an application to set aside made after the event.

8.6   HOW THE COURT DEALS WITH APPLICATIONS

When an application is made the court may consider it without a hearing or deal with that application at a hearing, which may be in person or by telephone.

When deciding how to deal with the application the court may be influenced, though this will not be decisive, by how the party making the application has requested, in the application notice, it be dealt with.

8.6.1   Without a hearing

CPR 23.8 provides that the court may deal with an application, and make an order, without a hearing.

The court may consider an application without a hearing in a number of circumstances.

8.6.1.1   When a hearing is not appropriate

An application may be dealt with, whether or not all parties agree, without a hearing if the court is satisfied a hearing is not appropriate.

Accordingly, when a party makes an application completed with a request that it be considered without a hearing, the court will need to decide, as a preliminary to dealing with the application, whether a hearing is appropriate.

Guidance was given by the Court of Appeal in *Collier v Williams*[62] as to the circumstances in which it will be 'appropriate' for the court to make an order without a hearing, when requested to do so by the party making that application.

Giving the judgment of the court Dyson LJ observed:

> 'First, generally speaking, there are huge benefits in disposing of routine applications without a hearing. The need to conduct litigation efficiently and proportionately requires that, so far as practicable, applications should be disposed of without a hearing. Routine case management decisions are obvious candidates for such treatment.'

However, later in the same judgment a note of caution was also sounded:

---

[62]   [2006] EWCA Civ 20.

'On receipt of a without notice application with a request for the matter to be disposed of on paper, the court should consider whether it is appropriate to dispose of the matter without a hearing. In our view, there is a danger in dealing with important applications on paper.'

This warning was affirmed by Ward LJ in in *Vernon v Spoudeas*[63] where a further difficulty was highlighted; but when the court makes an order without a hearing it is unlikely reasons will be given, yet reasons are likely to be important if the order is significant in the proceedings.

The same sentiments were expressed by Leggatt J in *Evans v Royal Wolverhampton Hospitals NHS Foundation Trust*.[64]

If the court does think it is appropriate to consider the application without a hearing evidence may, nevertheless, be called for and directions given accordingly. After that the application may proceed without a hearing, by paragraph 2.4, Practice Direction 23A, or the court may then list the application for a hearing, by paragraph 2.5, Practice Direction 23A.

If the court considers a hearing will be appropriate it is likely the matter will be listed without further assessment of the merits, or otherwise, of the application.

If the court decides it is appropriate to consider the application without a hearing then, following that consideration, an order, whether allowing or refusing that application, will be made and sent out to the parties. Such an order made without a hearing must contain a statement of the right, under CPR 23.10, to make application for it to set aside or vary the order.

In *Collier* the Court of Appeal confirmed the right to set aside or vary the order is available equally to the party seeking the order, if the application is refused in whole or in part, or to the other party, should the application be allowed in whole or in part. However, to avoid repeated applications the court also held that any such an application should be dealt with at a hearing, rather than on paper, and if then dismissed any further application on the same point should be struck out as an abuse of process, unless based on substantially different material from the earlier application.

8.6.1.2 *By agreement of the parties*

If the party making an application requests this to be considered at a hearing, or without a hearing, but the court concludes this would not be appropriate, the parties may, nevertheless, then agree to it being considered without a hearing, perhaps on the basis of written submissions.

However, with the availability of telephone hearings it would be rare for a contested application, unless it is an application where the court accedes to a request that no hearing is appropriate, for that matter to be dealt with in this way.

---

[63]   [2010] EWCA Civ 666.
[64]   [2014] EWHC 3185 (QB).

8.6.1.3   Consent orders

The court may always make an order, without a hearing, on the basis the parties consent to the terms.

Where there is such agreement the parties are likely to want the court to make an order without the need for a hearing, to save costs. Indeed, paragraph 10.5, Practice Direction 23A reminds the parties of the need to inform the court immediately in the event of agreement being reached ahead of a hearing date.

The parties should file a signed draft order, expressed as being 'By Consent', to comply with CPR 40.6. The signature on the order must be by the legal representative for each of the parties to whom the order relates, or by the party if acting in person. Alternatively, where all parties affected by an order have written to the court consenting to the terms of a draft already filed, the court will treat the draft as having been signed in accordance with CPR 40.6 (under the terms of paragraph 10.2, Practice Direction 23A).

The court will also need any relevant material to confirm it is appropriate to make an order in the terms proposed. For these purposes a letter will suffice as confirmed by paragraph 10.4, Practice Direction 23A. Clearly, the court must have power to make the order agreed but, beyond that, the court may need to exercise care before declining to endorse an agreement freely reached between the parties which will inevitably have involved an element of give and take.

In *Noel v Becker*[65] the parties, during the course of a hearing, agreed terms and prepared a written order setting out those terms. The judge refused to make an order in the agreed form, making an order in different terms. The Court of Appeal allowed an appeal. Davies LJ observed:

> 'These terms were scheduled to the consent order and I do not think that the judge was concerned to approve them or disapprove them. There is nothing in the order which the court was asked to make which is outside the jurisdiction of the court and, without more ado, I would say that the County Court judge fell into error here and ought to have made the order agreed on between the parties.'

Where an order is agreed under which costs are to be paid by one party to the other the parties will need, as well as agreeing the substance of the order, to fix a figure for those costs, as required by paragraph 13.4, Costs Practice Direction. That means where the costs order provides for costs of the application to be paid by one party to another party 'in any event'. In other circumstances, where costs will be dealt with at the end of the case, it will suffice to have the agreement reached for the incidence of costs without quantifying the amount.

Parties do need to be mindful that consenting to an order may, in appropriate circumstances, generate a binding compromise which may limit the power of the court to subsequently vary that order (see **8.2.4.2**).

---

[65]   [1971] 1 WLR 355.

8.6.2 Hearing by telephone

The court has power to deal with an application by telephone under CPR 3.1(2)(d) and is likely (subject to the exceptions in paragraph 6.3) to exercise that power in accordance with paragraph 6.2, Practice Direction 23A namely for:

- allocation hearings;
- listing hearings; and
- interim applications, case management conferences and pre-trial reviews with a time estimate of no more than one hour.

The court may direct a telephone hearing of its own initiative but also at the request of the parties, hence paragraph 6.6, Practice Direction 23A confirms a party applying for an interim order should indicate on the application notice if the court is requested to deal with that application by a telephone hearing.

If the court directs a telephone hearing it will be necessary to make appropriate arrangements and preparations (see **4.5.3.2** and **4.5.3.3**).

A warning about the inappropriate use of telephone hearings, for more complex matters, was given by HHJ Richardson QC in *Hockley v North Lincolnshire and Goole NHS Foundation Trusts.*[66]

8.6.3 Hearing in person

Hearings in person should usually be reserved for those hearings which are not straightforward enough for the court to determine without a hearing and which do not fall within the parameters of paragraph 6.2 of Practice Direction 23A and hence are not suitable for hearing by telephone.

That is because hearings in person are likely to incur greater costs than other ways of dealing with applications and, accordingly, should be confined to those applications where such a hearing is essential.

8.6.4 Tactics on dealing with applications

Consideration of an application by the court without a hearing is likely to be the most expeditious way of obtaining an order where, for example, the defendant has failed to comply with the court rules, or a court order, without explanation or, where necessary, any application for relief from sanctions. Accordingly, in such circumstances, the claimant may wish, in the application notice, to request that the court deal with the application without a hearing. It may be useful to explain the reasons for requesting that an application be considered without a hearing in the notice itself or the supporting evidence.

Conversely, to guard against the defendant making an inappropriate request, without any notice to the claimant, for an application to be considered without a hearing, it may be appropriate, at the outset, to request that the defendant at least notify the claimant ahead of any application (see **8.5.6**).

---

[66] (Unreported) Kingston upon Hull County Court 19 September 2014.

Telephone hearings are a very effective way of controlling costs as:

- Travelling and waiting time at court will be avoided.
- Hearings usually run to time (or if not the parties can be stood down and usefully deal with other matters whilst awaiting the start of the hearing).
- The format tends to restrict prolix oral submissions.

8.7 HEARING OF APPLICATIONS

Unless an application is considered, and the order made, without a hearing parties will receive notice of the date and time fixed for the court to deal with that application. This notice will include any directions for the hearing to be dealt with by telephone.

Meanwhile, the parties have the opportunity to try to agree the terms of an order the court can be invited to make, though if that is not possible it will be necessary to prepare for the hearing.

8.7.1 Agreement of an order

The parties may be able to narrow the issues or even reach agreement on the terms of an order the court can be invited to make.

Where agreement is reached a draft order may be prepared and sent to the court, prior to the hearing, for approval. If approved that should avoid the need for a hearing.

8.7.2 Preparation for the hearing

If there is to be a hearing, whether by telephone or in person, it is important to carefully prepare for that hearing. This may involve a number of steps:

- Preparing submissions which, if it will be helpful for the court to have these summarised in written form in support of submissions made orally at the hearing, may be put in a skeleton argument.
- Preparing, if necessary, an amended draft order incorporating calendar dates. Paragraph 12.1 of Practice Direction 23A provides that there should be a draft of the order sought except for the simplest case. If the parties have reached at least partial agreement it may be helpful if the draft denotes those parts of the order which are agreed and those which remain in issue (perhaps indicating the alternatives proposed). The court may have a draft order from each party but a single document will be easier to work from at the hearing.
- Filing, where this is required and has not already been done, evidence which is necessary in support of the application.
- Preparing and filing, if necessary or if so directed by the court, a case summary.
- Additionally, or alternatively, a skeleton argument may be appropriate, to set out any legal submissions relied on either to support or resist the order sought in the application.
- Preparing and filing, if necessary, an indexed and paginated bundle to allow ease of reference to all documents at the hearing (which will be particularly important if the hearing is to be dealt with by telephone).

- Preparing a costs statement, if it will be appropriate to seek summary assessment of costs relating to the application at the hearing (see **8.9.3**).

Practice about filing documents by email varies between courts and different judges. However, where email may be used this can be particularly useful for filing draft orders as, in the right format, the judge can then use the draft to readily prepare any order made.

8.7.3 Presentation of the application

At the hearing of the application the applicant will usually be invited by the court to make submissions in support of the application. The other party will then be invited to respond and, if necessary, to deal with any points arising out of that response, the applicant allowed to reply.

Any application, like a case management conference, may be utilised by the court to deal with general case management issues. Accordingly, it is essential the application is presented by someone who is sufficiently familiar with, and has authority to deal with, any matters which may arise.

8.7.4 Deciding the application

After considering oral, and if appropriate written, submissions the judge will decide the application, give reasons and set out the terms of the order.

It is also necessary for the judge to give reasons, sufficient for the parties to understand why the order has been made, see *English v Emery Reimbold & Strick Ltd*.[67] This is a further reason why it may not be appropriate for the court to consider a contentious application without a hearing as Ward LJ explained in *Vernon v Spoudeas*[68] (see **8.6.1.1**).

8.8 DEALING WITH INTERIM ORDERS

When the court makes an interim order the claimant will need to abide by, and implement, the terms of the order, apply to set the order aside (if this option is available) or consider an appeal.

In some circumstances, rather than appealing a case management decision, the claimant may decide to await developments with a view to making further application, at a later stage, to vary or revoke directions given.

8.8.1 Implementation

If the terms of the order are accepted, so no application will be made to set aside or appeal the order as appropriate, steps will be necessary to ensure implementation of the order:

---

[67] [2002] EWCA Civ 605.
[68] [2010] EWCA Civ 666.

- Relevant dates should be diarised to ensure compliance.

- Anyone affected by the order ought to be notified, particularly experts who should be sent a copy of the order to comply with paragraph 8 of the Practice Direction to Part 35.

- The claimant should be advised of the order and any consequences this has on further steps to be taken or the timetable for the case.

- Any action required by the defendant, including payment of costs assessed, should be diarised.

- If an adverse costs order has been made against the claimant steps must be taken to deal with payments of those costs by the due date and also to advise the claimant both of that order and the reasons for it (see **8.9.6**).

8.8.2   Re-listing

CPR 23.11 confirms the court can proceed with an application should one of the parties fail to attend, but may decide to re-list.

To guard against the risk of non-appearance at the hearing it is useful to have filed a certificate of service, relating to the application notice, or at least have available details of the steps taken to serve the application. Additionally, where the hearing is dealt with by telephone, it can be useful to have confirmation of the arrangements made with the defendant and provider for that hearing.

8.8.3   Applying to set aside

Should an order be made without a hearing, or on the court's own initiative, the claimant may prefer, if the terms of the order are not accepted, to make application for that order to be set aside or varied. If so, application will need to be made within seven days from receipt of the order. There may, in such circumstances, be a concurrent right of appeal but the better course may be to apply to set aside under Part 3: *Vernon v Spoudeas*.[69]

8.8.4   Appealing

An interim order, like a final order, may be appealed.

Part 52 deals with the rules relating to permission, time limits, routes, documents and hearings of appeals (see **10.12**).

If the interim order is a case management decision, involving an exercise of the powers conferred by CPR 3.1(2), paragraph 4.5 of the Practice Direction to Part 52 stipulates that the Appeal Court must, in addition to other factors, take into account whether the issue arising is of sufficient significance to justify the costs of the appeal, whether the procedural consequences of an appeal outweigh the significance of the case management decision and whether it would be more convenient to determine the issue at or after trial.

---

[69]   [2010] EWCA Civ 666.

8.8.5   Applying to vary or revoke directions

Mindful of the court's power to vary or revoke case management directions under CPR 3.1(7) a party, rather than seeking to appeal an order, may elect to subsequently apply for variation or revocation, perhaps once further evidence is available on the basis this amounts to a material change of circumstance (see **8.2.4** and **8.3.3**).

8.9   COSTS OF APPLICATIONS

If an application is required it is important this seeks provision for, and the order made deals with, the costs of that application.

That is because, under CPR 44.13(1)(a), unless provision for costs is made no costs will generally be recoverable in relation to that order, so any such costs will not simply be part of the costs of the case picked up by any final order as to costs. However, CPR 44.13(1A)(c) does provide that where an order is made on application without notice, and does not mention costs, it will be deemed to include an order for the applicant's costs in the case.

The terms of the costs order made on the hearing of an application will also be important given that, unless later specifically varied or set aside, the terms of that order will prevail over any general order for costs made at the end of the proceedings.

Accordingly, the claimant's representatives must keep in mind the need for any order made in response to an application to make appropriate provision for costs, even if this is just that costs be in the case (as costs in the case will be picked up by any final costs order made and be recoverable provided the claimant succeeds overall).

If costs follow the outcome of the application, rather than the case as a whole, those costs will usually be assessed and become payable, unless the court otherwise directs, within 14 days. This can be a useful way of recovering costs as the matter progresses from the defendant but, equally, may result in adverse costs orders against the claimant which have to be met as the case progresses.

It is necessary to be aware of the range of orders the court can make for the costs of an application, both when drafting the application so that appropriate provision is sought and, of course, when dealing with the hearing. It is also necessary to be aware of how, in appropriate circumstances, any costs of the application may be assessed on a summary basis.

8.9.1   The court's discretion as to costs

When the court exercises discretion as to the appropriate order, if any, to make as to costs on the hearing of an interim application, a number of provisions may be of relevance.

8.9.1.1   Costs Practice Direction

Paragraph 8.3 of the Costs Practice Direction confirms the court may make an order about costs at any stage in a case.

This paragraph goes on to emphasise that, in particular, the court may make an order about costs when it deals with any application, makes any order or holds any hearing. That order about costs may relate to the costs of that application, order or hearing.

8.9.1.2   Part 44

Accordingly, when dealing with an interim matter the court has the general discretion conferred by CPR 44.3(1) as to whether to order costs be paid by one party to another party.

When this discretion is exercised the general rule, set out in CPR 44.3(2), is that the unsuccessful party will be ordered to pay the costs of the successful party. This rule applies just as much to an interim hearing as it does to a final hearing.

However, an interim hearing will often be an inevitable part of the litigation, particularly when it concerns case management issues, and the unsuccessful, and indeed successful, party will not be known until the conclusion of the case as a whole. In such circumstances costs will usually be in the case.

Costs are more likely to follow the event, at an interim hearing, if that hearing, or the application leading to the hearing, could have been avoided had it not been for the conduct of a party whether this be in failing to comply with court orders or the CPR.

Costs may also follow the event where the application, rather than general issues of case management, deals with a discrete issue which the court decides one way or the other. In that situation it is usually straightforward to determine, on that application, who has been the successful party and, accordingly, generally entitled to the costs of the application.

The court may, of course, make a different order and the factors relevant to the exercise of discretion, and range of costs orders, found in CPR 44.3 may be relevant for these purposes. However, at an interim hearing the court is likely, rather than making one of the orders provided for in CPR 44.3(6), to adopt one of the costs orders which paragraph 8.5 of the Costs Practice Direction describes as commonly made in proceedings before trial (see **8.9.2**).

8.9.1.3   Part 48

Part 48 deals with costs in a number of special circumstances.

CPR 48.1 deals specifically with pre-action applications where the general rule is that the person against whom the order is made will be entitled to the costs. However, the court may make a different order and a very relevant factor, for these purposes, is the extent to which parties have complied with any relevant pre-action protocol.

Consequently, where a defendant fails to give disclosure under the Protocol the claimant, when making a pre-action application, has good grounds for seeking the costs (see **2.11.2.7**).

8.9.1.4 Practice Direction – Pre-action Conduct and protocols

Compliance with this Practice Direction may be a relevant consideration in relation to both the incidence of costs and the basis for assessment of such costs.

CPR 44.3(5)(a) identifies the extent to which parties followed the Practice Direction – Pre-action Conduct or any relevant pre-action protocol as conduct which, in turn, is a relevant factor for the court to take into account when deciding what, if any, order to make about costs.

Similarly, CPR 3.1(4) provides that the court will take into account, when giving directions, whether or not a party has complied with the Practice Direction – Pre-action Conduct and any relevant pre-action protocol.

8.9.1.5 Part 36 and 'Calderbank' offers

If a party has made a Part 36 offer, this is unlikely to result in the consequences found in CPR 36.14 applying at an interim hearing, unless that does result in judgment.

Furthermore, where the costs of an application are ordered to be paid in any event the fact the party against whom the order is made has put forward a Part 36 offer is not likely, of itself, to prevent an interim adverse costs order. However, such a offer may be relevant to costs where the court determines a preliminary issue at an interim hearing.

In *HSS Hire Services Group PLC v (1) BMB Builders Merchants Ltd (2) Grafton Group (UK) PLC*[70] the Court of Appeal held that where preliminary points have been decided by a court at first instance but there is a Part 36 offer of settlement, and quantum is still unknown, the best person ultimately to rule on costs will be the trial judge.

However, in *Kew v Bettamix*[71] there was a preliminary trial on the issue of limitation. The claimant succeeded, in part, on this issue and was ordered to pay the defendant's costs on the unsuccessful issue, despite the claimant having made a Part 36 offer of settlement.

The approach in *HSS Hire Services Group PLC* has subsequently been followed by the Court of Appeal in *RTS Flexible Systems Ltd v Morkerei Alois Müller GmbH & Co KG*.[72]

At face value it does seem curious if a claimant who has made a Part 36 offer of outright settlement and is unsuccessful on a preliminary issue should be ordered to pay the costs of that issue there and then whilst a defendant, in essentially the same situation, can defer determination of the costs issue until such time as the outcome of the case as a whole is known.

---

[70] [2005] EWCA Civ 626.
[71] [2006] EWCA Civ 1535.
[72] [2009] EWCA Civ 26.

In these circumstances a party who has made a Part 36 offer of settlement can, at the very least, argue that the costs of a preliminary issue, which goes against that party, might not be determined until all aspects of the case are concluded. If, however, the relevant issue is a discrete one, which can readily to be seen to have added to the overall costs of the case, the court may feel able to make a costs ruling there and then, notwithstanding the offer of outright settlement.

Where costs are to be in the case then, of course, the ultimate incidence of those costs may be determined by a Part 36 offer. Occasionally a defendant, who has admitted liability, may complain that the effect of an order for costs in the case is that the defendant will end up bearing those costs in any event. However, that is not necessarily so because a defendant can always obtain costs protection by making an adequate Part 36 offer. The failure to do so should not effectively protect the defendant on costs.

Whilst CPR 36.13(2) prohibits the fact of a Part 36 offer having been made being communicated to the trial judge, or any judge allocated in advance to conduct the trial, there is no such prohibition so far as any procedural judge, likely to be determining interim applications, is concerned.

CPR 44.3(4)(c) and paragraph 8.4 of the Costs Practice Direction confirm that the court should have regard to any admissible offer to settle, which is not an offer to which the costs consequences under Part 36 apply, when deciding what order to make about costs. Consequently, an offer made 'without prejudice except as to costs' concerning the application itself may be very relevant to the incidence of costs association with that application. Part 36 offers are, under the terms of CPR 36.13(1) treated as being 'without prejudice except as to costs'. The term will also encompass a 'Calderbank' offer but not a wholly without prejudice offer (see **11.2.2** and **11.2.3**).

8.9.2   Costs orders

There are a number of different orders that may be made by the court, in relation to costs, on the hearing of an application. These are usefully summarised in paragraph 8.5 of the Costs Practice Direction.

8.9.2.1   *Claimant's costs/costs in any event*

This means the claimant will recover the costs of the application, or relevant part of the proceedings, whatever the final outcome and consequent costs orders. Accordingly, such an order would only usually be appropriate when those costs were incurred because of some default on the part of the defendant.

Summary assessment of those costs, if these cannot be agreed, will usually be appropriate and so a statement of costs should be prepared for the hearing of the application.

8.9.2.2   *Defendant's costs/costs in any event*

This means the defendant will recover the costs of the application, or relevant part of the proceedings, whatever the final outcome and consequent costs orders. Again, such an order would only usually be appropriate when those costs were incurred because of some default, this time on the part of the claimant.

Summary assessment of those costs, if these cannot be agreed, will usually be appropriate and so a statement of costs should be prepared for the hearing of the application.

8.9.2.3 Claimant's costs in the case/application

This means the claimant will recover the costs of the application, or part of the proceedings, if successful in obtaining an order for costs at the end of the proceedings. Such an order may be appropriate when the court does not feel able to go as far as providing the claimant should have the costs in any event but there is perhaps some element of fault on the part of the defendant which led to the costs being incurred.

The court will not, when such an order is made, need to determine the amount of those costs and so no statement of costs will be necessary for the hearing.

8.9.2.4 Defendant's costs in the case/application

This means the defendant will recover the costs of the application, or part of the proceedings, if successful in obtaining an order for costs at the end of the proceedings. As with the claimant's costs in the case such an order may be appropriate if there is an element of fault, this time on the part of the claimant.

The court will not, when such an order is made, need to determine the amount of those costs and so no statement of costs will be necessary for the hearing.

8.9.2.5 Costs in the case/application

This means whichever party obtains an order at the end of the proceedings will be entitled to the costs of the application or part of the proceedings to which the order relates. That will be the usual order when the application was necessary or the involvement of the court required. So, any hearing dealing, essentially, with case management will normally result in an order for costs in the case even if one party or other might be regarded as having been unsuccessful in seeking particular directions.

The court will not, when such an order is made, need to determine the amount of those costs and so no statement of costs will be necessary for the hearing.

The proper approach to costs which are ordered to be costs in the case, when dealing with those costs at the conclusion of the claim, was considered by Warby J in *Ontulmus v Collett* [73] when it was held that such costs should be approached on the following basis:

> 'A simpler and better criterion is to hand for a case like this, which is to have regard to when in the proceedings the relevant costs were incurred and which party has obtained an order for costs in relation to that phase of the proceedings. As a starting point I would suggest that acceptance of a Part 36 offer, which will ordinarily lead to an order for the costs up to the

---

[73]   [2014] EWHC 4117 (QB).

relevant date, should also carry with it any costs incurred within that period which are the subject of an order for costs in the case. Equally, if an offer is accepted "out of time" and an order is made, in the ordinary way, for the offeree to pay costs since the expiry of the relevant period that order should carry with it any costs incurred in that period which are the subject of an order for costs in the case.'

8.9.2.6   Costs reserved

This means the decision about costs of the application or part of the proceedings is deferred. The court may later make a ruling in relation to those costs but if no later order is made the costs will be treated as costs in the case.

This is a useful alternative to an order for costs in the case, or indeed any other order as to costs, where it is not yet clear what order may be appropriate or the issue of costs cannot readily be agreed and the parties are content for the issue to be deferred.

The court will not, when such an order is made, need to determine the amount of those costs and so no statement of costs will be necessary for the hearing.

8.9.2.7   Costs thrown away

This may be provided for when, for example, a judgment or order is set aside allowing the party in whose favour the order is made to the costs incurred as a consequence which might include dealing with any hearing at which the order set aside was made, the hearing when the setting aside order was made and any steps taken to enforce an order meanwhile.

Summary assessment of those costs, if these cannot be agreed, will usually be appropriate and so a statement of costs necessary for the hearing of the application.

8.9.2.8   Costs of and caused by

This may be provided for an application to amend a Statement of Case allowing the party in whose favour the order is made to the costs of dealing with the application and any consequential amendment for that party's own Statement of Case.

Summary assessment of those costs, if these cannot be agreed, will usually be appropriate and so a statement of costs necessary for the hearing of the application.

It may, however, be difficult for the court, at this stage, to assess the extent of the costs incurred, as at the date of the order, and consequently whilst making a costs order it may decide detailed assessment is necessary: *Chadwick v Hollingsworth (No 2)*;[74] *Millburn-Snell v Evans*.[75]

---

[74]   [2010] EWHC 2718 (QB).
[75]   [2011] EWCA Civ 577.

8.9.2.9   Costs here and below

Such an order may be made at the hearing of an appeal, allowing the party in whose favour the order is made not only to the costs of the appeal but also the costs of the proceedings in any lower court.

Costs of an appeal may well be appropriate for summary assessment. Costs incurred in the lower court may, or may not, be appropriate for summary assessment. If detailed assessment of any costs is appropriate the court may conclude that detailed assessment of all costs will be appropriate.

Accordingly, depending on the circumstances, it may, or may not, be appropriate to have a statement of costs prepared for the hearing of an appeal.

8.9.2.10   No order as to costs/each party to pay own costs

This expressly provides for what would occur in the event of there being no reference to costs, namely that no party can recover the costs of the application, or part of the proceedings, as part of the overall costs of the claim.

8.9.3   Assessment of interim costs

CPR 44.7 provides that where the court orders a party to pay costs to another party it may either make a summary assessment of the costs or order detailed assessment. Consequently, if costs are to be in the case, or there is no order for costs, summary assessment will not be appropriate as there will be no order for a party to 'pay costs to another party'.

However, paragraph 9.1 of the Costs Practice Direction states the general rule is that the court should make a summary assessment of costs:

* at the conclusion of any hearing which has lasted not more than one day (which will include most interim applications);
* unless there is good reason not to do so, for example insufficient time to carry out a summary assessment;
* provided that a summary assessment will not be made if the receiving part is:
  – an assisted person (paragraph 13.9); or
  – a child or patient, unless the solicitors waive the right to recover further costs, (paragraph 13.11).

An example of a 'good reason not to do so', other than lack of time, will be when it is impossible to determine, at the time of the interim hearing, what costs are attributable to the order and hence properly assessed as payable.

In *Chadwick v Hollingsworth (No 2)*[76] a judge was held to have erred in principle when ordering the claimant to pay the costs of proceedings up to the date of amended Particulars of Claim. That was because it was not possible to summarily conclude the whole of the costs of the proceedings were wasted, because some of the steps taken might ultimately result in the claim succeeding.

---

[76]   [2010] EWHC 2718 (QB).

Similarly, in *Millburn-Snell v Evans*[77] when proceedings were a nullity but a new properly constituted claim was likely to be brought, steps in the first claim could be treated as effective in that new claim. Consequently, whilst some further costs would be incurred, that would not justify the claimant simply being ordered to pay all the costs of the claim which had proved to be a nullity. The similar approach might be applicable where, for example, a claimant issues a second action because of a failure to serve earlier proceedings.

Summary assessment would not seem appropriate where the court considers the application without a hearing, even if one party is ordered to pay the costs of another party irrespective of the final outcome, as there has been no 'hearing' for the purposes of paragraph 13.2, Costs Practice Direction. Indeed, only the judge who hears the case is in a position to make a summary assessment of the costs of that case, otherwise the issue of costs will need to be dealt with by a costs judge: *Mahmood v Penrose*.[78]

When a party is ordered to pay the costs of an application to another party, without summary assessment, those costs will need to be the subject of a detailed assessment at the end of the case, when the costs are dealt with generally.

Whenever assessment takes place that may be on the standard basis or, if appropriate, on the indemnity basis (see **12.2.6**).

8.9.4   Costs statement

Accordingly, where the costs of an interim hearing are sought in any event, the party wishing to recover those costs should file and serve a costs statement not later than 24 hours before the time fixed for the hearing, in accordance with paragraph 13.5(4) of the Costs Practice Direction.

If the costs statement has not been filed and served more than 24 hours before the hearing, the court is likely to impose a penalty. Unless served very late the court may only reduce, rather than disallow completely, the costs: *MacDonald v Taree Holdings Ltd*.[79]

A costs statement will not be required if the applicant seeks an order that costs be in the case (including the claimant's or defendant's costs in the case) or no order for costs, given that assessment will only be appropriate under CPR 44.7 where the court orders a party to pay costs to another party.

Section 13.5 sets out the requirements of the costs statement which should follow, as closely as possible, form N260.

If it is necessary to give further background that can be set out in a supplemental statement although at an interim hearing this background may be readily apparent to the court from the other documentation filed.

---

[77]   [2011] EWCA Civ 577.
[78]   [2002] EWCA Civ 457.
[79]   [2001] CPLR 439.

8.9.5 Base costs and additional liabilities

At the stage of an application in the proceedings the court will only be able to assess base costs, as any additional liability cannot be assessed until the conclusion of the proceedings in accordance with CPR 44.3A(1) and paragraph 9.2, Costs Practice Direction.

Accordingly, the costs statement prepared for the hearing of an application should not include details of the additional liabilities. For the avoidance of doubt it may be sensible to confirm that the statement concerns base costs only.

Additional liabilities, including any success fee on costs assessed at an interim stage, can be dealt with at the conclusion of the claim.

8.9.6 Adverse costs orders

If the court makes a costs order against a legally represented party, who is not present when the order is made, that party's solicitor must notify the client in writing of the costs order within seven days of receiving notice of that order under the terms of CPR 44.2(1).

Furthermore, paragraph 7.2, Costs Practice Direction requires an explanation to be given to the client as to how that order came to be made.

It is important to be mindful of these requirements if the court makes such an order.

8.9.7 Timescale for payment of costs

If an order for costs is made, even if the proceedings are continuing, those costs, unless the court otherwise orders, are payable within 14 days of the order by CPR 44.8.

However, the court may be willing to otherwise order. For example, if a party would be unable to meet the costs order and might, as a result, be deprived of the opportunity of pursuing or defending the claim, the overriding objective might suggest deferring payment for those costs. If the paying party already has an adverse costs order against the receiving party, but these have yet to be assessed, or is about to seek an interim payment, these might also be grounds for seeking postponement of the order.

If the court orders detailed assessment then, unless also making an order for a payment on account of those costs under CPR 44.3(8), no costs will be payable until that assessment has been conducted, usually at the end of the case.

8.9.8 Enforcement

If costs are assessed and payable forthwith, or a payment on account of costs is to be subject to a detailed assessment ordered, the receiving party can enforce the order, by any available means of enforcing the court judgment, once the timescale for payment has elapsed.

Enforcement of costs, in this way, may present difficulties, if the defendant, against whom such an order has been made, is, whilst insured, not able to meet those costs, rendering enforcement impracticable. In such circumstances, on further application, the court may be prepared to make an appropriate order under CPR 3.4, perhaps debarring the defendant unless the order for payment of costs is complied with. The advantage of such an order is that the sanction would then impact on the defendant's insurers and hence be likely to prompt a payment even if enforcement steps could not be taken direct against those insurers.

The court may, however, be concerned about making an order which could deprive a party of the opportunity to pursue or defend a claim as a result of impecuniosity, though the onus may be on that party to explain why the order could not be met.

An unless order, in relation to an outstanding costs order, was made, under the general case management powers of the court, in *Khatib v Ramco International*.[80]

8.10   SANCTIONS

In the context of applications, sanctions are relevant both to interim orders, where such an order effectively imposes the sanction, and when relief is sought from any applicable sanction, as that will generally require an application.

Accordingly, it is necessary to consider when sanctions will apply and, when they do, how to seek, or resist, an application for the grant of relief.

8.10.1   When sanctions apply

CPR 3.8 provides that where a party has failed to comply with a rule, Practice Direction or court order, any sanction for failure to comply imposed by the rule, Practice Direction or court order has effect, unless the party in default applies for, and obtains, relief from the sanction.

Accordingly, if the court has made an order, sanctions will apply automatically in default. Additionally, the CPR provide for some automatic sanctions which will be applicable for default in complying with certain standard case management directions.

Some sanctions provided automatically by the rules are of particular significance in personal injury claims:

- CPR 31.21 which prevents a party from relying on a document which is not disclosed or which that party fails to permit inspection of, unless the court gives permission.
- CPR 32.10 which prevents a party relying on oral factual evidence unless a witness statement or witness summary is served for the intended witness within the time specified by the court under case management directions.
- CPR 35.13 which prevents a party who fails to disclose an expert's report from using the report at trial, or calling the expert to give evidence orally, unless the court gives permission.

---

[80]   [2011] EWCA Civ 605.

- CPR 44.3B which prevents a party who has failed to provide appropriate information about a funding arrangement, at the appropriate stage, from recovering additional liabilities.

Additionally, where the court makes an order which specifies the consequences of non-compliance, that consequence will take effect automatically, for example striking out of a Statement of Case (see **8.2.2**).

CPR 3.8(3) provides that where a rule, practice direction or court order requires a party to do something within a specified time and specifies the consequences of failure to comply the timescale cannot be extended simply by agreement between the parties making a further court order necessary (see **8.3.1.2**). However, CPR 3.8(4) allows, unless the court orders otherwise, the time for doing any act identified by the terms of CPR 3.8(3) to be extended by prior written agreement of the parties for up to a maximum of 28 days provided any such extension does not put at risk a hearing date. Where such agreement is reached it will be important that this is the written agreement of all relevant parties: *Thomas v Home Office*.[81]

CPR 3.8 is not applicable simply because a party fails to comply with a rule, practice direction or order where no sanction is specified for the breach or where application for an extension of time is made before any sanction takes effect: *Hallam Estates Ltd v Baker*.[82]

Costs might be seen as a sanction but CPR 3.8(2) confirms that relief from an order in relation to costs can only be obtained by appealing that order.

8.10.2 Relief from sanctions

Relief from sanctions is governed by the terms of CPR 3.9. This rule was amended significantly in April 2013 so that, rather than incorporating a lengthy checklist, it now provides:

> 'On an application for relief from any sanction imposed for a failure to comply with any rule, practice direction or court order, the court will consider all the circumstances of the case, so as to enable it to deal justly with the application, including the need –
> (a)   for litigation to be conducted efficiently and at proportionate cost; and
> (b)   to enforce compliance with rules, practice directions and orders.'

This significant change was heralded by the judgment of Jackson LJ in *Fred Perry (Holdings) Ltd v Brands Plaza Trading Ltd*[83] when he said:

> 'There is a concern that relief against sanctions is being granted too readily at the present time. Such a culture of delay and non-compliance is injurious to the civil justice system and to litigants generally. The Rule Committee has recently approved a proposal that the present rule 3.9(1) be deleted and the following be substituted ...'

After setting out the terms of the new rule and that this was expected to come into force on 1 April 2013 Jackson LJ continued:

---

81   [2006] EWCA Civ 1355.
82   [2014] EWCA Civ 661.
83   [2012] EWCA Civ 224.

'After that date litigants who substantially disregard court orders or the requirements of the Civil Procedure Rules will receive significantly less indulgence than hitherto. As I say, that rule amendment lies in the future. In the present case, on the rules as they stand, relief from sanction must be refused.'

In the early days of the CPR Brooke LJ had observed in *Sayers v Clarke-Walker*[84] that:

'The philosophy underpinning CPR Part 3 is that rules, court orders and practice directions are there to be obeyed. If a sanction is imposed in the event of non-compliance, the defaulting party has to seek relief from the sanction on an application made under CPR 3.8 and in that event the court will consider all the matters listed in CPR 3.9 so far as relevant.'

Accordingly, if a party incurs a sanction it will be for that party to make an application for relief. From April 2013 the court must approach any such application on the basis of the new version of CPR 3.9. As this still makes reference to 'all the circumstances of the case' it may be that some aspects of the checklist found in the former version of the rule will remain relevant, though the court would only have to have regard to those factors and not have to go through the exercise of considering each and every item of that former checklist.

Consequently, it is worth reviewing the approach taken to the former version of CPR 3.9 before considering the forensic approach that has been adopted under the 2013 version of that rule.

8.10.2.1   Former CPR 3.9

When considering whether to exercise the general discretion to give relief from any sanction, the court had to consider all relevant circumstances with nine particular factors being set out. These were identified in a list which was contained with the rule, namely:

- the interests of the administration of justice;
- whether the application for relief has been made promptly;
- whether the failure to comply is intentional;
- whether there is a good explanation for the failure;
- the extent to which the party in default has complied with other rules, Practice Directions, court Orders and any relevant pre-action Protocol;
- whether the failure to comply was caused by the party or his legal representative;
- whether the trial date or the likely trial date can still be met if relief is granted;
- the effect that the failure to comply had on each party;
- the effect that the granting of relief would have on each party.

8.10.2.1.1   General approach

Granting relief from sanctions is an exercise of the court's general powers of the case management conferred by CPR 3.1. The court has a complete discretion subject to taking into account all relevant circumstances including those set out in CPR 3.9 and, of course, having regard to the overriding objective.

---

[84]   [2002] EWCA Civ 645.

Given the wide ranging powers of management set out in CPR 3.1(2) the court, when deciding whether to give relief from sanctions, does not just have to simply refuse or accede to the application but may choose to make an order which provides a proportionate response to the circumstances that have given rise to the imposition of the sanction. This may result in only partial relief being granted.

The same principles will apply even where the sanction has not been imposed automatically, under the Civil Procedure Rules, but as a result of non-compliance with a court order, including an unless order or a consent order.

Identifying factors likely to be relevant, in the way provided for in CPR 3.9, encouraged a form of structured decision making and, accordingly, such factors had to be considered systematically by the judge determining the application: *Bansal v Cheema*.[85] However, it was not necessary for the court to adopt an over-formalistic approach, provided all relevant factors have properly been taken in to account: *Khatib v Ramco International*.[86]

Every factor identified in CPR 3.9 was not be relevant in any particular case, equally as the rule required the court to consider all relevant circumstances there may be other factors which did need to be taken into account. Hence, the fact that a party had a sanction imposed by an unless order is relevant, though not decisive, in determining whether to grant relief: *CICB Mellon Trust Co v Stolzenberg*.[87] Similarly, the fact the party in default consented to the order will be relevant but not decisive: *Pannone LLP v Aardvark Digital Ltd*.[88]

A number of cases, decided since the introduction of the CPR but prior to April 2013, have illustrated the significance of particular factors when exercising discretion to grant, or refuse, relief from sanctions under the former version of CPR 3.9. All of these may now be regarded as having been superseded by subsequent authority although, because of the need to have regard to all the circumstances of the case, it is possible some may still be considered of relevant in particular situations.

8.10.2.1.2   The interests of the administration of justice

In *Tarn Insurance Services Ltd v Kirby*[89] the claimant obtained a freezing injunction against the defendant which provided for disclosure of assets in default of which the defendant would be debarred from defending. The defendant failed to comply but sought relief from sanctions.

The judge, at first instance, found the defendant in breach of the order but gave additional time on the basis there was a real prospect of successfully defending the proceedings and the effect on the claimant was 'relatively slight'.

The Court of Appeal concluded the judge had failed to give proper weight to what was the deliberate breach of an unless order, an important point for the administration of justice, observing:

---

[85]   (Unreported) 2 March 2002.
[86]   [2011] EWCA Civ 605.
[87]   [2004] EWCA 287.
[88]   [2011] EWCA Civ 803.
[89]   [2009] EWCA Civ 19.

'CPR 3.9(1) requires the court to consider all the circumstances of the case; including, in particular, the matters listed under that rule. The first of those matters is "the interests of the administration of justice". The interests of the administration of justice require that the court, when considering whether to relieve from sanction imposed by an unless order, should have regard to the circumstances in which the unless order itself was made.'

The error of the judge was, in effect, to re-visit the merits of the court, having previously made an unless order. Rather, the focus should have been on whether, in the circumstances known at the time of the application for relief, it remained appropriate for the sanction to take effect.

The interests of justice, which include requiring a party to comply with an order of the court made with a view to achieving a fair trial, mean that refusing to grant relief will not contravene Article 6 of the ECHR, provided the refusal was proportionate: *Monson v Azeez*.[90]

8.10.2.1.3   *Whether the failure to comply was intentional*

In *Tarn Insurance Services Ltd v Kirby*[91] an important factor, in refusing to grant relief, was the deliberate breach of an unless order.

In *CIBC Mellon Trust Co v Stolzenberg*[92] judgment was entered after a failure to comply with unless orders after which application was made to set judgment aside and to seek relief from sanctions.

The court held the fact a fair trial was possible did not mean that relief from sanctions should necessarily follow.

Applying the overriding objective, on the basis of the deliberate non-compliance with unless orders, the first instance decision refusing the application to set judgment aside and to give relief from sanctions was upheld.

However, in *RC Residuals Ltd v Linton Fuel Oils Ltd*[93] the claimant failed to comply, albeit by a matter of minutes, with the terms of an unless order which set out the time limit for service of an expert's report.

Whilst acknowledging the importance of ensuring parties complied precisely with the terms of unless orders, the court considered the objective sought by the earlier order was an important consideration. Here the non-compliance with the order would not thwart that objective as the trial date could still be met.

In these circumstances, and importantly given that there was no intentional default (indeed the claimant had tried hard to comply with the order), the failure was not a substantial one and relief was granted.

---

90 [2009] EWCA Civ 202.
91 [2009] EWCA Civ 19.
92 [2004] EWCA 287.
93 [2002] EWCA Civ 911.

Similarly, in *Pannone LLP v Aardvark Digital Ltd*[94] where real efforts were made to comply with the order it was appropriate to grant relief.

8.10.2.1.4   Whether there is a good explanation for the failure

This is a relevant factor for the court in deciding whether to grant relief but not necessarily a decisive factor and certainly not a pre-requisite to the allowing of an application for relief.

In *Supperstone v Hurst*[95] Floyd J suggested:

> 'I agree that relief and sanctions should not be granted lightly and any party who fails to comply with CPR runs a significant risk that he will be refused relief. Thus, if a party does not have a good explanation, or the other side is prejudiced by his failure, relief from sanctions will usually be refused. It is vitally important to the administration of justice that the rules of procedure are observed.'

Subsequently Master O'Hare noted in *Robinson-Tait v Cataldo*[96] (Costs) that the comments of Floyd J had to be seen in context, and did not mean a good explanation for the default was a necessary preliminary, when he held:

> 'However, I do accept that the quality of an explanation on the one hand and the degree of prejudice suffered by the opposing party on the other can be determinative factors. In those very rare cases in which the applicant can show a good explanation for his failure, relief against sanctions is likely to follow. However, in cases in which the opposing party can show real and substantial prejudice, relief against sanctions is much less likely to be given, even if the applicant can show a good explanation for his failure.'

In *Robinson-Tait*, where the claimant sought relief from sanctions to recover additional liabilities, relief was granted as the failures to comply with the Costs Practice Direction, in giving details about the funding arrangements, were of a minor nature that had no substantial effect on the defendants about which they were entitled to complain.

8.10.2.1.5   Whether the failure to comply was caused by the party or the legal representative

In certain circumstances it may be hard to discern whether the fault is truly attributable to the party or the legal representative. In *Training in Compliance Ltd v Dewse*[97] Peter Gibson LJ explained:

> 'Of course, if there is evidence put before the court that a party was not consulted and did not give his consent to what the legal representatives had done in his name, the court may have regard to that as a fact, though it does not follow that it would necessarily, or even probably, lead to a limited order against the legal representatives. It seems to me that, in general, the action or inaction of a party's legal representatives must be treated under the Civil Procedure Rules as the action or inaction of the party himself. So far as the other party is concerned, it matters not what input the party has made into what the legal representatives have done or have not done. The other party is affected in the same way; and dealing with a case justly involves dealing with the other party justly. It would not in general be desirable

---

94   [2011] EWCA Civ 803.
95   [2008] EWHC 735 (Ch).
96   [2010] EWHC 90166.
97   [2001] CP Rep 46.

that the time of the court should be taken up in considering separately the conduct of the legal representatives from that which the party himself must be treated as knowing, or encouraging, or permitting.'

However, where the fault clearly lies with the legal representative this may well be a factor supporting the grant of relief not least because the courts recognise a professional negligence claim is not necessarily an adequate way of an innocent party obtaining proper redress. In *Welsh v Parnianzadeh*[98] Mance LJ observed:

> 'A claimant who is reduced to a claim which would perforce be on a percentage basis for loss of a chance against her legal advisers is not only suffering a real loss in the sense of being caused further delay and expense, but is also suffering a real reduction in the value of her claim.'

Similarly, in *Hansom v E Rex Makin & Co*[99] it was held that if fault lay with the legal representative that was a factor which weighed in favour of the application for relief from sanctions.

8.10.2.1.6   Unless orders

Although not specifically identified as a factor in CPR 3.9 it is clear that if the order leading to the sanction was an unless order this will be a relevant circumstance when deciding whether to grant relief.

In *CIBC Mellon Trust Co v Stolzenberg*[100] the court concluded the fact an unless order had been made was inevitably an additional factor to consider and the gravity of that non-compliance was increased where this resulted from a conscious decision not to comply. The court approved the observation of Ward LJ in *Hytec Information Systems Ltd v Coventry City Council*[101] that, '... if a party intentionally or deliberately...flouts the order, he can expect no mercy'.

8.10.2.1.7   Consent orders

Similarly, although not expressly referred to in CPR 3.9, the fact the order breached was made by consent will be a relevant factors: *Pannone LLP v Aardvark Digital Ltd*.[102]

8.10.2.1.8   The effect of failure to comply and granting of relief

In *Bansal v Cheema*[103] the claimant failed to comply with a direction for exchange of witness statements and, accordingly, had to seek relief from the sanction imposed by CPR 32.10.

The court, stressing the need for a systematic consideration of each factor listed in CPR 3.9, granted relief. Crucially the delay in disclosing witness statements had not had any serious effect on the defendant whereas if relief had not been granted the defendant

---

[98]   [2004] EWCA Civ 1832.
[99]   [2003] EWCA Civ 1801.
[100] [2004] EWCA 287.
[101] [1997] 1 WLR 1666.
[102] [2011] EWCA Civ 803.
[103] (Unreported) 2 March 2002.

would have gained an unsolicited windfall while the claimant would suffer the catastrophic effect of having the action struck out.

The minor effect of the failures in *Robinson-Tait v Cataldo*[104] (Costs) were of significance in the granting of relief, even in the absence of a good explanation for those failures.

8.10.2.1.9   The overriding objective

The court must, as ever, have regard to the overriding objective when deciding whether or not to grant relief from sanctions. In other words will it, ultimately, be just to grant or refuse relief.

In *Welsh v Parnianzadeh*[105] Mance LJ observed:

'…one should stand back and look at the whole position and ask whether a fair trial is still possible and what the interests of justice require in the circumstances. We should not count numbers, but we should ask ourselves whether striking out would be proportionate, bearing in mind whether a fair trial would be possible.'

This echoed the observations Mance LJ had previously made in *Hansom v E Rex Makin & Co*[106] where he said:

'…at the end of the day, the right approach is to stand back and assess the significance and weight of all relevant circumstances overall, rather than to engage in some form of "head-counting" of circumstances.'

This approach was followed in *CIBC Mellon Trust Co v Stolzenberg*[107] where the court emphasised the outcome of an application for relief from sanctions is not ascertained simply by adding up the 'score' of factors in favour or against the grant of relief and deciding the matter according to the tally. Arden LJ explained:

'The dictum of Mance LJ makes it clear that although the court must go through each of the matters in the list in CPR 3.9 as a separate and distinct exercise the result is not ascertained by adding up the "score" of either side on each point. If that were the right method, there would be a danger of double-counting. The object of CPR 3.9 is to ensure that all the right questions are asked. That produces "structured decision-making". In addition to going through the subparagraph of CPR 3.9, the court must ask itself if there are any other circumstances that need to be taken into account. However, having done all this, the court is then also required to stand back and form a judgment to the aggregate of the relevant circumstances that have been identified in going through the list to see whether it is in accordance with the overriding objective in the CPR to lift the sanction. This overall "look see" is simply the overriding objective in action.'

Having undertaken this exercise justice may require partial, rather than full, relief from sanctions as *Price v Price*[108] illustrates.

---

[104] [2010] EWHC 90166.
[105] [2004] EWCA Civ 1832.
[106] [2003] EWCA Civ 1801.
[107] [2004] EWCA 287.
[108] [2003] EWCA Civ 888.

The claimant issued and served a claim form, applying to the court for an extension of time for service of Particulars of Claim. The claim form indicated, for the first time, this was a far more substantial claim than had previously been indicated.

The real delay appeared to have occurred because the claimant had been undertaking what might be termed 'expert shopping'. At the time of the application, evidence to substantiate the claim formulated was still not available.

The court recognised the tension between the interests of the administration of justice and the effect of granting relief, suggesting the balance best be struck by adopting a proportionate response to the failure which had led to the imposition of sanctions.

That meant looking objectively at the extent to which the defendant would be prejudiced, if the case was allowed to continue, and then considering whether, and the extent to which, the claimant's cumulative default caused that prejudice. It could then be decided whether it was a disproportionate response to stop the case or whether a more proportionate response could be fashioned.

In this case, with a considerable history of default, the court concluded the application for relief should be refused unless suitable conditions could be imposed under the general case management powers of the court found in CPR 3.1.

Here such conditions could be imposed to ensure a proportionate response; that avoided giving the defendant a windfall by preventing the claimant from proceeding altogether but did not unduly relax the disciplinary framework created by the CPR.

Accordingly, a condition was imposed on the grant of relief, that no claim could be made for damages other than what might have been substantiated by medical evidence available at the time the Particulars of Claim should have been served.

The real determinative factor, in deciding whether to grant relief, was held to be the effect of granting relief on each party.

The court also concluded that this approach was entirely consistent with the Article 6 right to a fair trial.

8.10.2.2   Current CPR 3.9

The proper approach to an application for relief from sanctions under the version of CPR 3.9 introduced in April 2013 was considered by the Court of Appeal in *Mitchell v News Group Newspapers Ltd*[109] and then again in *Denton v TH White Ltd*.[110]

In *Denton* the Court of Appeal analysed the terms of CPR 3.9 noting that contained three elements, which were not to be confused with the three stages which the court went on to suggest be adopted when considering an application for relief from sanctions.

The elements of CPR 3.9 were identified as the following.

---

[109] [2013] EWCA Civ 1537.
[110] [2014] EWCA Civ 906.

- First, the rule states when it engages, which is the failure to comply with any rule, practice direction or court order. Hence the first task of the court is to identify the breach which triggers the operation of the rule in the first place.

- Secondly, where the rule engages, the court must consider all the circumstances of the case to deal justly with the application.

- Thirdly, that exercise of discretion expressly requires a consideration of factors (a) and (b).

The Court of Appeal then moved on to give guidance about the proper approach by first instance judges to these elements. For these purposes the Court of Appeal recommended the judge should address the application in three stages.

- The first stage is to identify and assess the seriousness and significance of the failure which engages CPR 3.9 and if that is neither serious nor significant the court would be unlikely to need to spend much time on the second and third stages.

- The second stage is to consider why the default occurred.

- The third stage is to evaluate 'all the circumstances of the case' including factors (a) and (b).

Recognising that 'hard-pressed first instance judges need a clear exposition of how the provisions in rule 3.9(1) should be given effect' the majority judgment dealt with each of the three stages so that judges could 'avoid the need in future to resort to the earlier authorities'.

8.10.2.2.1   The first stage

Recognising the word 'trivial' as given rise to some difficulty in future this first stage should be considered by deciding whether the breach has been serious of significant.

A breach which is not significant or immaterial, provided this is understood as including the effect on liability generally and not only the litigation in which the application is made, is one which neither imperils future hearing dates nor otherwise disrupts the conduct of the litigation.

There are, however, also breaches which are serious but not, in the sense that word is defined for these purposes, significant, for example the failure to pay court fees.

The significance or seriousness of a breach should not, at this first stage, involve unrelated failures in the past (although these may be relevant to the third stage).

If a judge concludes, at this first stage, a breach is not serious or significant then relief from sanctions will usually be granted and it will usually be unnecessary to spend much time on the second stage or third stage (though these will have greater importance if the breach is serious or significant).

8.10.2.2.2   The second stage

The court should consider why the default occurred, particularly where the breach is serious or significant.

The judgment in *Mitchell* gives some examples of good and bad reasons:

- Good reasons are: the party or his solicitor suffering a debilitating illness or being involved in an accident; later developments in the course of the litigation which show the period for compliance originally imposed was unreasonable (but could not realistically have been appealed at the time).
- Bad reasons are: overlooking a deadline.

8.10.2.2.3   *The third stage*

Even if there is a serious or significant breach without good reason relief from sanctions may still be granted as CPR 3.9 requires that, in every case, the court consider 'all the circumstances of the case so as to enable it to deal justly with the application'.

For these purposes factors (a) and (b) may not be of paramount importance but are of particular importance and should be given particular weight at this third stage when all the circumstances of the case are considered, as that is why these are singled out for mention in the rule (otherwise it is hard to see why they would have been singled out given that they are mentioned in the overriding objective and so would be taken into account in any event.

The majority judgment summed up how these factors should be applied in this third stage by observing:

> 'Factor (a) makes it clear that the court must consider the effect of the breach in every case. If the breach has prevented the court or the parties from conducting the litigation (or other litigation) efficiently and at proportionate cost, that will be a factor weighing in favour of refusing relief. Factor (b) emphasises the importance of complying with rules, practice directions and orders. This aspect received insufficient attention in the past. The court must always bear in mind the need for compliance with rules, practice directions and orders, because the old lax culture of non-compliance is no longer tolerated.'

At this third stage, therefore, the more serious or significant a breach the less likely it is that relief will be granted unless there is good reason. Relief is likely to be granted where the breach is not serious or significant or, even if it is, where there is good reason for what happened.

The promptness of the application for relief is one of the relevant circumstances to be weighed in the balance in this third stage.

Similarly, other breaches of the rules, practice directions or court orders by the parties may also be taken into account as part of the circumstances in this third stage.

8.10.2.2.4   *General guidance*

The Court of Appeal also offered some general guidance about the approach parties should take to application for relief from sanctions when observing:

> 'We think we should make it plain that it is wholly inappropriate for litigants or their lawyers to take advantage of mistakes made by opposing parties in the hope that relief from sanctions will be denied and that they will obtain a windfall strike out or other litigation advantage. In a case where (a) the failure can be seen to be neither serious nor significant, (b) where a good

reason is demonstrated, or (c) where it is otherwise obvious that relief from sanctions is appropriate, parties should agree that relief from sanctions be granted without the need for further costs to be expended in satellite litigation. The parties should in any event be ready to agree limited but reasonable extensions of time up to 28 days as envisaged by the new rule 3.8(4).'

The judgment continued:

'The court will be more ready in the future to penalise opportunism. The duty of care owed by a legal representative to his client takes account of the fact that litigants are required to help the court to further the overriding objective. Representatives should bear this important obligation to the court in mind when considering whether to advise their clients to adopt an uncooperative attitude in unreasonably refusing to agree extensions of time and in unreasonably opposing applications for relief from sanctions. It is as unacceptable for a party to try to take advantage of a minor inadvertent error, as it is for rules, orders and practice directions to be breached in the first place. Heavy costs sanctions should, therefore, be imposed on parties who behave unreasonably in refusing to agree extensions of time or unreasonably oppose applications for relief from sanctions. An order to pay the costs of the application under rule 3.9 may not always be sufficient. The court can, in an appropriate case, also record in its order that the opposition to the relief application was unreasonable conduct to be taken into account under CPR rule 44.11 when costs are dealt with at the end of the case. If the offending party ultimately wins, the court may make a substantial reduction in its costs recovery on grounds of conduct under rule 44.11. If the offending party ultimately loses, then its conduct may be a good reason to order it to pay indemnity costs. Such an order would free the winning party from the operation of CPR rule 3.18 in relation to its costs budget.'

Guidance was also given in relation to case management, to avoid problems occurring in the first place, when the Court of Appeal said:

'We should also make clear that the culture of compliance that the new rules are intended to promote requires that judges ensure that the directions that they give are realistic and achievable. It is no use imposing a tight timetable that can be seen at the outset to be unattainable. The court must have regard to the realities of litigation in making orders in the first place. Judges should also have in mind, when making directions, where the Rules provide for automatic sanctions in the case of default. Likewise, the parties should be aware of these consequences when they are agreeing directions. "Unless" orders should be reserved for situations in which they are truly required: these are usually so as to enable the litigation to proceed efficiently and at proportionate cost.'

8.10.2.3 Supreme Court

The Supreme Court, following *Denton*, considered the approach to sanctions in *Prince Abdulaziz v Apex Global Management Ltd*[111] where, endorsing the approach taken by the Court of Appeal, Lord Neuberger said:

'The importance of litigants obeying orders of court is self-evident. Once a court order is disobeyed, the imposition of a sanction is almost always inevitable if court orders are to continue to enjoy the respect which they ought to have. And, if persistence in the disobedience would lead to an unfair trial, it seems, at least in the absence of special circumstances, hard to quarrel with a sanction which prevents the party in breach from presenting (in the case of a claimant) or resisting (in the case of a defendant) the claim. And, if the disobedience continues notwithstanding the imposition of a sanction, the enforcement

---

[111] [2014] UKSC 64.

of the sanction is almost inevitable, essentially for the same reasons. Of course, in a particular case, the court may be persuaded by special factors to reconsider the original order, or the imposition or enforcement of the sanction.'

8.10.2.4   *Evidence*

CPR 3.9(2) requires an application for relief from sanctions to be supported by evidence. As the application is likely to be at a hearing other than the trial, that evidence will be in the form of a witness statement in accordance with CPR 32.6.

Given the need for the court to consider the factors relevant to CPR 3.9, it is helpful if the evidence can deal with each of these factors in the context of the particular case and the circumstances leading to the application.

The party opposing the application may do likewise, again in the form of a witness statement dealing with the same factors, but from the perspective of that party.

8.10.2.5   Broader application of CPR 3.9

Because the terms of CPR 3.9 are replicated in the overriding objective, found in Part 1, the approach recommended by the Court of Appeal in Denton has resonance away from applications relating directly to relief from sanctions, as the Court of Appeal made clear in *Walsham Chalet Park Ltd v Tallington Lakes Ltd*.[112]

This approach will also be relevant where there is what might be termed an implied sanction: *Robert v Momentum Services Ltd*;[113] *Altomart Ltd v Salford Estates (No 2) Ltd*.[114]

Where, however, no sanction applies, for example if where a party applies to extend time before expiration of the deadline (even when if that is not heard until after the deadline expires) the court will not be approaching the application on the basis of CPR 3.9 but solely on the basis of the overriding objective in Part 1: *Robert v Momentum Services Ltd*;[115] *Hallam Estates Ltd v Baker*.[116]

---

[112] [2014] EWCA Civ 1607.
[113] [2003] EWCA Civ 299
[114] [2014] EWCA Civ 1408.
[115] [2003] EWCA Civ 299.
[116] [2014] EWCA Civ 661.

CHAPTER 9

PRE-TRIAL CHECKLISTS

9.1 INTRODUCTION

The pre-trial checklist will often, certainly in fast track cases which have run in accordance with initial directions, be the only stage after allocation at which the court is involved in case management.

The date given by the court in case management directions for the filing of checklists is an important milestone. That is because this is a date which cannot be varied just by agreement of the parties but only with the approval of the court.

In many cases after the filing of checklists the court will, where the case is ready for hearing, list for trial and give any further directions on the papers. This reflects the definition of active case management which includes dealing with the case without the need for the parties to attend court in accordance with CPR 1.4(1)(j).

However, some cases may require a case management hearing or pre-trial review to determine further directions required and to make arrangements for trial.

9.2 CHECKLISTS AND LISTING

The title, and change of name from listing questionnaire to pre-trial checklist, reflects the proper role of the checklist with listing of the case for trial.

9.2.1 Purpose of the checklist

Whilst the allocation questionnaire is designed to help the court with case management the pre-trial checklist should be exactly that: a check that all directions have been complied with and confirmation the case is ready for trial.

9.2.2 Date for filing the checklist

If it becomes impossible to keep to the timetable for filing the checklists, the court's approval to vary the timetable should be sought at the earliest opportunity.

Case management directions given at the stage of allocation will usually stipulate a date by which the pre-trial checklists are to be filed. That is a date which must be observed, as any variation will require approval by the court. Accordingly, it is important to keep the case moving through the directions given, keeping to that timetable so far as possible, with the deadline for pre-trial checklists in mind.

If it becomes impossible to keep to the timetable for filing the checklists the court's approval, to vary the timetable, should be sought at the earliest opportunity, given the obligation on the parties to assist the court in the managing of the case and the need for the court's agreement to put back the date for checklists.

If the parties are agreed the date should be varied a consent order might be submitted, though the court is likely to need an explanation of the reasons why the parties seek the extension. Otherwise an application notice, made in accordance with Part 23, will be necessary.

9.2.3   Pre-trial review

In complex claims, typically allocated to the multi-track, it may be appropriate for the court to hold a (further) case management conference or pre-trial review at, or prior to, the stage of listing.

Indeed, the court may direct, at the stage of initial case management, that there be a further case management conference, before or shortly after the filing of pre-trial checklists. If, in the event, no hearing is required at that stage the court may, on receipt of checklists, simply list the case. Equally, the court may, on receipt of pre-trial checklists, decide to hold a pre-trial review, even if this was not previously envisaged as being necessary.

A pre-trial review will normally be conducted in some courts by a district judge managing the case or by the trial judge listed to hear the case. If that hearing is in person, rather than by telephone, the parties may choose to be represented by the trial advocates who, as the purpose of the review is to provide a further opportunity for settlement, should have instructions and authority to negotiate a settlement if possible.

At any such hearing the judge is likely to check earlier case management directions have been complied with, give any further directions for outstanding matters, consider the extent to which evidence can be agreed, assess the need for oral expert evidence in the light of joint statements and consider any trial timetable together with the effect of this on the time estimate.

9.2.4   Listing

The court is likely, certainly in most fast track cases, to list the case following receipt of pre-trial checklists, within the existing trial window.

The court is likely to be reluctant to see a trial window, and certainly a trial date, vacated unless that is essential to deal with the case justly.

9.3   STOCKTAKE

Completion of the checklist is a good opportunity to take stock of the case generally.

This review should ensure that the checklist will be properly completed and, more generally, that the case is ready for trial. That is important when a hearing may be fixed for a date that is not long after the time at which the checklist is submitted.

9.3.1 Issues and statements of case

The stocktake is likely to include a general review of the issues, in the context of the statements of case, which may involve, amongst other matters, the following questions:

- What are the real issues that have emerged following exchange of evidence?
- Do the statements of case need amending or updating to reflect those issues?
- Are there any outstanding requests for further information?
- Have, if these have been ordered or are otherwise necessary, up-to-date schedules and counter schedules been served?

9.3.2 Disclosure and inspection

The stocktake will, having reviewed the issues, look at disclosure and inspection on the basis of those issues and may well involve the following questions:

- Have all earlier orders for disclosure and inspection been complied with by the claimant?
- Has the defendant complied with case management directions in relation to disclosure and any request for inspection of documents?
- Is there, or does there need to be, any request for further disclosure or inspection?

9.3.3 Evidence

The stocktake will also assess the evidence, both factual and expert, which will involve checking a number of matters:

- Have witness statements been exchanged?
- Is any further evidence from witnesses of fact required and, if so, is permission to rely on that required?
- Does the defendant's factual evidence support the defence? If not, can judgment be sought on any issue?
- Has expert evidence been exchanged?
- Is the expert evidence complete or is anything further required?
- Have questions to experts been put/answered?
- Have, where there is more than one expert in a field, experts conferred and joint statements been prepared?
- Has permission already been given for the claimant to rely on all relevant experts at least in written form?
- Is oral evidence required from any expert witness?
  - Written evidence will usually suffice where:
    (i) the evidence is agreed;
    (ii) there is not more than one expert in a particular field unless there is good reason for that expert to attend for cross-examination. The assumption should be that the expert's report is the evidence of that

expert and any amplification or cross-examination should be restricted as far as possible: *Peet v Mid-Kent Healthcare NHS Trust;*[1]

(iii) there is more than one expert in a particular field, and there remain points of disagreement between those experts, but those differences do not result from differences of expert opinion or any such differences can, nevertheless, be resolved by the Trial Judge without having to hear oral evidence from the experts concerned.

– Oral evidence will be required where there is a significant difference of opinion between experts in the same field, usually a difference on matters within the expertise of the experts, so that the trial judge does need to hear oral evidence, and the witnesses be cross-examined, in order to determine which opinion should be preferred, for example *Rengasamy v Homebase Ltd.*[2]

9.3.4   Schedules

Schedules will often be exchanged, at least if these are updated, shortly before listing.

The claimant's own schedule should be checked to ensure all claims, as now valued on the basis of the evidence relied on, are included, because the court is likely to restrict the claimant to sums claimed when awarding damages: *Ilkiw v Samuels;*[3] *Davison v Leitch* (see **2.8.3**).[4]

The claimant should ensure the defendant has complied with any directions for service of a counter schedule. That means not just a document purporting to be a counter schedule but a document which properly identifies the issues and puts forward any figures on behalf of the defendant.

The defendant should not be allowed to use the counter schedule as an opportunity to introduce documents, factual evidence or expert evidence which has not been disclosed previously by the due date under case management directions (given the automatic sanctions applicable under the terms of CPR 31.21, 32.10 and 35.13).

9.3.5   Negotiations

The stocktake is a good time to review negotiations and the prospect of settlement.

That is likely to prompt some questions:

• Does the strength of the case on liability and/or quantum need to be reviewed?

• Is there any outstanding request for clarification of a Part 36 offer that needs to be dealt with or chased up?

• Should any offer made by the defendant, which remains open for acceptance, be reconsidered?

• Should the claimant make any, or any further, offer on liability or quantum?

• Should the claimant withdraw or change any existing Part 36 offer?

---

[1]   [2001] EWCA Civ 1703.
[2]   (Unreported) 23 January, 2015 (QBD).
[3]   [1963] 1 WLR 991.
[4]   [2013] EWHC 3092 (QB).

If the defendant is reluctant to engage in ADR it may be appropriate to give a reminder of the importance attached to this topic by the Court of Appeal in *PGF II SA v OMFS Company Ltd*,[5] given the potential costs consequences if the defendant persists in rejecting ADR.

9.3.6 Case management directions

The stock take should also check the status of earlier case management directions:

- Have, in addition to the above, all other case management directions been complied with?
- Do there need to be any variations to the timetable/further Orders?
- Is there any change to the time estimate for the trial?

9.3.7 Availability

Whilst it is likely witnesses will have been advised, at the stage of initial case management directions, of the trial window a further check will need to be made at this stage so that the pre-trial checklist will give accurate, up to date, information on availability of those witnesses who will need to attend the trial.

If counsel is already involved in the case it will also be essential to check counsel's current availability for the trial window.

9.4 THE CLAIMANT'S CHECKLIST

Following review, the checklist should be completed, filed and served. The checklist will need to be accompanied by some further documentation, depending on the type of case and the circumstances.

9.4.1 Format

The checklist is in Form N170.

9.4.2 Application

Ideally, the checklist should be confirmation that all directions have been complied with and the case is ready for trial.

If not, an explanation will be required and, most likely, the checklist will need to be accompanied by an application, made in accordance with Part 23, seeking appropriate further directions.

An application will require:

- an Application Notice in Form N244;
- a draft of the Order sought (either in the application notice or as a separate draft);

---

5   [2013] EWCA Civ 1288.

- evidence in support (either on the application notice or, in accordance with CPR 32.6, by witness statement).

If an application is required simply because the defendant is in default of case management directions, it is worth remembering, especially as the trial window may be approaching, the power of the court to deal with an application without a hearing and that the aim of the court should be to try and preserve the trial window and any trial date.

9.4.3   Costs estimates and budgets

For pre-April 2013 cases an estimate of costs should accompany the checklist, in accordance with the former s 6.4(2), Costs Practice Direction.

Once again that estimate must include base costs and disbursements but need not give details of any additional liabilities.

It is particularly important to get the estimate as accurate as possible, especially if the estimate previously given at the stage of allocation no longer properly reflects the likely costs the claimant will seek from the defendant if successful.

In a case where a costs management order has been made this is a key stage to review the budget and ensure that remains sufficient to cover the work necessary to conclude the claim.

9.4.4   Proposed timetable

If the case has been allocated to the multi-track, a proposed trial timetable will need to accompany the checklist.

The timetable will break down the overall time estimate for trial, so as to suggest how that time may be allocated.

For example, the timetable may include time for:
- pre-reading;
- opening;
- witnesses of fact;
- expert evidence;
- closing arguments;
- judgment;
- costs and consequential matters.

In many cases no specific time for pre-reading needs to be allowed, but if there is a significant amount of material for the judge it may be helpful to do so.

The time allotted for witnesses of fact will, usually, be for the purpose of cross-examination and re-examination only. That is because, in accordance with CPR 32.5, the witness statements should stand as evidence-in-chief.

Under CPR 35.5 expert evidence will normally be given in writing. Hence it may not be necessary to make specific provision for this in the trial timetable, unless the volume of evidence is significant and time has not been allocated for any pre-reading. Appropriate time must, of course, be allowed if any expert evidence is to be given orally.

9.4.5 Case summary

If an application is required a witness statement, which will effectively summarise the case and explain why further directions are necessary, will be required.

It may be necessary, in other circumstances, to file a case summary so that the court is aware of any further issues relating to case management which will need to be dealt with.

If all case management directions have been complied with but further directions are necessary an application may not be required but a case summary might still be appropriate to explain why, for example, it is considered that oral expert evidence is required.

Sometimes, case management directions may provide that a case summary accompanies the checklist in any event. Accordingly, the earlier case management directions should be checked to ensure that such provision is made.

9.4.6 Other documents

The checklist must be accompanied by any other documents which the court has directed be filed with that checklist. Earlier directions should be reviewed accordingly to see if, for example, these direct witness statements and/or experts' reports to be filed.

Even if there is no specific direction to file such documents it will be appropriate to file any evidence, not already lodged, the court may need in order to properly manage the case at this stage. For example, if there is more than one expert in any field the joint statement should be filed, so that the court can assess whether oral evidence will be necessary or if reading the written reports should suffice for the trial judge.

9.4.7 Filing and service

As well as filing the checklist with accompanying documentation by the due date, the checklist will also need to be served on the defendant and might also be sent to the claimant.

Paragraph 6.1(4) of the Practice Direction to Part 28 (fast track claims) and paragraph 8.1(5) of the Practice Direction to Part 29 (multi-track claims) encourage the parties to exchange copies of the checklists so as to avoid the court being given conflicting or incomplete information. Furthermore, as part of the general duty to help the court manage the case, the parties ought to co-operate by exchanging information and, if further directions are required, try and agree these.

In accordance with s 6.4(2) of the Costs Practice Direction the costs estimate accompanying the questionnaire must be served on the defendant. Paragraph 6.4(1) also requires a copy of the estimate to be sent to the claimant. There is no obligation to send the claimant a copy of the checklist but this may, nevertheless, be provided.

9.5   THE DEFENDANT'S CHECKLIST

As the parties are encouraged to exchange checklists, and must serve costs estimates at this stage, it is important to ensure the defendant's checklist, along with any accompanying documentation, is obtained and reviewed.

If the defendant does not supply the checklist, and related documents, copies may be sought from the court. That request, if necessary, will also establish whether appropriate documents have been filed and, if not, alert the court to the need for further action.

9.5.1   Reviewing the checklist

A review of the checklist should help to ensure that the court is not given conflicting or incomplete information, or at least allow the information to be clarified. That review should also ensure that any issues between the parties, relating to further case management and listing, can be identified. In particular, the defendant's checklist should be reviewed for:

- expert evidence: to check whether there is agreement on the evidence, and the format of that evidence, to go before the court at trial;
- time estimate: so that, so far as possible, the court can work to an agreed time estimate;
- availability: as, if there are obvious problems with availability during the trial window, it will be better to address those sooner rather than later.

9.5.2   Defendant's costs

With a pre-April 2013 case the checklist should be accompanied by a costs estimate, again for the purposes of the Costs Practice Direction.

The same considerations applicable to the review of the estimate given by the defendant at the stage of allocation apply to the review of this estimate.

If a costs management order has been made the claimant will have already formed a view on the potential costs liability to the defendant and it will, of course, be for the defendant to seek any necessary review, if that should be required, to the budget.

9.5.3   Defendant's timetable

If the defendant has provided a trial timetable it may be possible to reach agreement both on the overall time the trial is likely to take and, perhaps, a schedule for the witnesses who will need to give oral evidence.

9.6 ACTION FOLLOWING FURTHER CASE MANAGEMENT DIRECTIONS

The court will, either following the filing of checklists or at the hearing of an application for the pre-trial review, give further directions, including a date for trial.

9.6.1 Further directions

The directions that the court will give on listing are dealt with by paragraph 7 of the Practice Direction to Part 28 (for fast track claims) and paragraph 9 of the Practice Direction to Part 29 (for multi-track claims).

The directions may include:

- the trial date, with place of trial and time estimate;
- provision about evidence, especially expert evidence and whether any is to be given orally;
- the trial timetable;
- preparation of a trial bundle;
- any other matters needed to prepare the case for trial, often including a direction that there be a case summary filed with the bundle.

An example of an order that may be given at this stage is set out in the Appendix to Part 28.

The order will usually contain the important reminder to the parties that the court is to be informed immediately if the claim is settled, whether or not it is then possible to file a draft consent Order giving effect to the agreement.

9.6.2 Diarising

Diary entries will be required on receipt of the further court order:

- dates for dealing with any further case-management directions will need to be diarised and appropriate steps actioned by the due date; and
- for the trial date itself with, perhaps, advance entries for final reviews including the filing of any case summary, any costs statement and the bundle

9.6.3 Further action

Further action is likely to be required at this stage to get the case ready for trial.

- The client should be brought up to date on the timetable, including trial date and location.
- All witnesses, including experts, who will need to attend the trial to give oral evidence need to be notified of the date and location, and given advance notice of any intention to serve witness orders (see **10.4**).
- Agreement should be reached, so far as possible, with the defendant on how any outstanding matters should be dealt with.

- If counsel is to deal with the trial an opportunity to review the case now should be afforded while there is time to deal with any further matters that may arise.

- The index to the trial bundle should be prepared, at least in draft form, so this can be sent to the defendant and efforts made to get the bundle agreed.

- Consideration must be given to the arrangements for preparing any case summary, either by drafting this or including a request for a summary to be settled in the instructions to counsel.

The sooner these steps are taken after listing the better given the trial date may be no more than a few weeks ahead.

9.7   SANCTIONS

It is essential that the claimant promptly files the pre-trial checklist, accompanied by the appropriate fee, or the claim is at risk of being struck out.

If the defendant does not file a pre-trial checklist, the general approach of the court is indicated by paragraphs 6.4 of the Practice Direction to Part 28 and 8.3 of the Practice Direction to Part 29. The court should, in a fast track case, give directions and fix a trial date, while in a multi-track case, the court is more likely to fix a hearing when directions will be given and a trial date fixed.

Alternatively, the court may exercise its general powers of case management by directing that, in the event of continued default, the claim and/or defence will be struck out.

Appropriate and prompt action should be taken by the court in the event of default in filing a checklist by the defendant. However, to avoid any unnecessary delay, it is appropriate to press the defendant for sight of the questionnaire and, if this is not produced, to seek a copy from the court. That should ensure that prompt action is taken in the event of default.

If relief from sanctions is sought the court will apply the terms of CPR 3.9 when considering that application (see **8.10.2**).

CHAPTER 10

TRIAL

10.1 INTRODUCTION

A case which has been prepared using the relevant protocols, and following the CPR, should be ready, at the stage of listing, for trial. The issues will have been identified at an early stage, relevant documents made available and evidence, both factual and expert, exchanged.

With a properly run case the final preparations for trial should be, to a large extent, building on the work already done. Even so there will be important further work necessary at this stage to finalise the case and help ensure the trial runs smoothly.

However, if the protocols and the CPR have not been properly followed the task of preparing for trial will be much more onerous as it may require, belatedly, identifying the issues and trying to obtain, and then get permission to rely upon, relevant evidence.

It is at this stage the litigator recognises the benefits of preparing a case, from the outset, on the basis it may go to trial. With a well prepared case the focus should now be just on preparing trial bundles, organising witnesses and briefing counsel.

10.2 TRIAL BUNDLE

The court will need a trial bundle so directions given following the filing of pre-trial checklists will normally provide for there to be a bundle.

Putting together the bundle is a vital stage of preparation for trial and should be seen as the starting point for the presentation of the claimant's case to the court. That is because the trial judge is likely to start by pre-reading the trial bundle. First impressions are important, so care should be taken in the content, organisation and format of the bundle.

10.2.1 Claimant's duty

CPR 39.5 requires the claimant, unless the court orders otherwise to file a trial bundle:
- containing documents required by a relevant Practice Direction (namely paragraph 3.2 of the Practice Direction to Part 39) and the terms of any specific court order;
- not more than 7 days, and not less than 3 days, before the start of the trial.

Accordingly, although the parties should attempt, where possible, to agree the bundle, responsibility for preparing and filing, that bundle rests solely with the claimant's representatives. That is why it is important, no later than the time the case is listed for hearing, to take the steps necessary for this obligation to be met.

10.2.2   Content

The bundle should include all relevant documents and have these, so far as possible, in an order which will allow the judge to identify the key issues and readily review the evidence dealing with these.

Paragraph 3.2 of the Practice Direction to Part 39 confirms that the bundle should include copies of a number of key documents:

- Case summary.
- Chronology (if appropriate).
- Claim form and statements of case (including requests for and further information given).
- Witness statements.
- Experts' reports (with any questions, answers and joint statements).
- Court orders giving directions.
- Notices relating to the evidence, for example:
  - notice of intention to rely on hearsay evidence under CPR 32.2;
  - notice of intention to rely on evidence (such as a plan, photograph or model) under CPR 33.6.
- Other necessary documents which, in a personal injury claim, may include:
  - the schedule of expenses and losses and the counter schedule;
  - source documents;
  - lists of documents;
  - documents relating to funding (for example notice of funding or notice of issue);
  - pre-action correspondence (if issues may arise at trial on matters relating to the protocols).

Whilst copy documents should be used for the bundle all originals should be available for the court at trial, in accordance with paragraph 3.3 of the Practice Direction to Part 39.

Care should be taken to ensure inadmissible documentation is not included. A judge is not, however, prevented from reading inadmissible material, as what the judge decides to pre-read is a matter for the judge: *Barings Plc v Coopers & Lybrand*.[1]

If the trial judge reads material such as a Part 36 offer on an issue yet to be determined, it may be necessary, depending on the circumstances, for the judge to withdraw from the case. Withdrawal of the judge could have costs consequences if that resulted in an adjournment of the trial: *Garratt v Saxby*.[2]

---

[1]   [2001] EWCA Civ 1163, [2001] All ER (D) 269 (Jul).
[2]   (Practice Note) [2004] EWCA Civ 341, [2004] 1 WLR 2152.

10.2.3 Indexation, tabulation and pagination

Having organised the content and the order of that content, the bundle itself should be arranged so that it is easily manageable, and the content readily identifiable.

This will mean proper indexation, tabulation and pagination.

10.2.3.1 Indexation

The index should describe each individual document, or category of document, perhaps grouped under broad subject headings. The index should also identify relevant page numbers for each document or category of document.

10.2.3.2 Tabulation

Dividers can be used to separate the bundle into relevant parts corresponding with the subject headings of the index. This is of particular assistance in making a larger bundle more manageable and relevant documents readily accessible.

10.2.3.3 Pagination

The bundle should be fully and accurately paginated in a way that:

- is numerically consistent;
- is easily identifiable on each document, for example putting the page number centre bottom of each page;
- accords with the index.

10.2.4 Format

Once the content has been identified and organised the bundle should be completed by presenting it in proper format for the court, in accordance with paragraph 3.6 of the Practice Direction to Part 39.

Use of a ring binder or lever arch file, which on the front clearly denotes the case to which the bundle relates, is an ideal format.

User unfriendly problems, which will otherwise spoil the effect of a well organised bundle, must be avoided, for example:

- if there are pages missing, illegible or out of sequence;
- if the ring binders are damaged, the pages are otherwise difficult to turn or there are other problems which prevent easy use of the bundle; or
- if the pagination is out of sequence or there is no consistency in the way individual documents are numbered.

If the best quality copies that can be produced of documents remain partly illegible a legible copy should be typed out and put immediately behind that document, in accordance with the requirements of paragraph 3.8 of the Practice Direction to Part 39.

10.2.5   Responsibility

Ultimately, as confirmed by paragraph 3.4 of the Practice Direction to Part 39, the lawyer running the case must accept responsibility ensuring the bundle is in a format that will be of assistance to the court and will best present the claimant's case.

Accordingly, whilst preparation of copy bundles will often be delegated, the lawyer ought to ensure that:

• relevant documents for the bundle are identified;

• the order of the bundle is thought out;

• the index is properly drafted; and

• all those involved in the task are fully aware of the importance of a properly prepared bundle at the trial.

10.2.6   Agreement

Although responsibility for preparing and filing the bundle rests solely with the claimant, paragraph 3.9 of the Practice Direction to Part 39 encourages the parties to agree the contents of the trial bundle where possible.

Accordingly, at the earliest opportunity, a copy of the draft index should be submitted to the defendant with a request that, if possible, this be agreed. Whilst it will not be possible to do this until exchange of evidence has been completed the bundle ought to be largely ready, and the index submitted to the defendant, at or soon after the time the case is listed for hearing.

If the bundle is agreed all documents included will be admissible at trial as evidence of their contents, in accordance with paragraph 27 of the Practice Direction to Part 32, unless otherwise ordered by the court or a party gives written notice of objection to a particular document.

If it is not possible to agree the bundle then:

• the parties should prepare a summary of the points on which they are unable to agree; and

• the parties should still try to agree that the documents included may be treated as evidence of the facts stated in them (this, if the facts are not already admissible by agreement of the bundle, can be important in reducing the evidence necessary to prove those facts as, for example, with a police accident report).

Accordingly, the defendant should be expected, if the bundle is not agreed when the index is submitted, to identify at least those documents which are agreed, any documents which the defendant objects to being included in the bundle and any further documents the defendant would wish to see included. If there are any further such documents the claimant will need to give written notice of objection should those added to the bundle not be agreed.

10.2.7   Filing and service

As required by CPR 39.5 the bundle should be filed at court not more than seven days and not less than three days before the start of the trial. The bundle will usually be filed in duplicate, one for the trial judge and one for use by witnesses.

Paragraph 3.10 of the Practice Direction to Part 39 also requires the party filing the bundle to supply identical bundles to other parties, so necessary copies should be made and sent.

Additionally, copies of the bundle are likely to be required by counsel, if appearing for the claimant, and it may assist the claimant to have, at the stage the bundle is filed, a complete copy to give ample time for review of the content prior to the day of the trial.

10.3   CASE SUMMARY

A case summary, which in practice may involve skeleton arguments from each party, setting out their respective positions, will usually be appropriate at the stage of trial.

10.3.1   When required

A case summary is not required unless provided for in case management directions. However, directions given following pre-trial checklists will usually provide for a case summary to be filed.

Even if no such direction is given it may be useful if a case summary is provided. A summary should assist the trial judge in identifying the key issues to be determined by the court, the evidence to deal with those issues and the principal submissions of the parties.

10.3.2   Format

A case summary prepared for trial will usually need to contain:
- a synopsis of the case;
- the issues on liability, if liability is disputed;
- the issues on quantum;
- the key evidence dealing with the issues identified.

The case summary should be cross-referenced to relevant parts of or page numbers in the bundle.

10.3.3   Length

If a direction for a case summary is given, this will often specify the maximum length, perhaps just 500 words.

It is a useful discipline to ensure that the issues are distilled into the required number of words, and a reminder that a case summary, like a skeleton argument, should be exactly that.

10.3.4   Drafting

Where counsel is dealing with the trial it will usually be appropriate for counsel, as trial advocate, to prepare a case summary and/or any skeleton argument.

10.3.5   Skeleton arguments

Whilst not generally required for a personal injury claim tried in the county court, skeleton arguments may be of use to the trial judge. The case summary will, ideally, be a joint document whilst skeleton arguments will reflect the case of the party preparing the skeleton.

Skeleton arguments may, therefore, supplement a case summary or be relied on in place of a case summary.

10.4   WITNESS ORDERS

Whenever oral evidence is to be given at trial, the use of witness orders should be considered.

10.4.1   When to use

To guard against the risk of a witness failing to attend court it is, in principle, always prudent to arrange for the issue of a witness order.

However, in practice, a different approach is often adopted as between witnesses of fact and expert witnesses.

With witnesses of fact, service of a witness order is usually the safest, and most appropriate, course.

With experts it is generally best to check whether the expert prefers to receive a witness order or not. Some experts do wish to be served with a witness order, as that deals with conflicts between different trials that the expert may be involved in. However, other experts object to being served with a witness order and, in such circumstances, it is usually preferable to rely on the professional responsibility of the expert to attend court.

10.4.2   Service

The witness order must be served on the witness. This may be done by the court directly or by the claimant's solicitors. Service by the court will, usually, be quickest and most straightforward.

10.4.3   Format

The witness order will be in Form N20, which should be completed to indicate whether the court or the claimant is to serve the order.

The witness order must be accompanied by conduct money, which will be reasonable travel expenses together with the current subsistence allowance.

If a case settles it is important to tell any witness, especially one who has received a witness order, that it will no longer be necessary to attend the hearing.

10.5   COUNSEL

Ahead of the trial, a decision needs to be made whether counsel is to be instructed to deal with that hearing. If so, further steps will need to be taken.

10.5.1   Advice

Counsel to be briefed for the trial may well have been involved in the case previously but, in any event at this stage, now need the opportunity of reviewing the papers and advising.

The matters counsel will need to advise upon, or provide an up to date advice on, are likely, at this stage, to include:

- the statements of case, to ensure that these are in order;
- the evidence, to ensure this is complete and admissible;
- liability, if this remains an issue;
- quantum;
- settlement (including changing, withdrawing or accepting any Part 36 offers);
- overall merits;
- the time estimate, to ensure that this will suffice; and
- the format and content of the bundle and case summary.

10.5.2   Funding

Counsel's role may relate to, and will be affected by, funding issues.

If the claimant is pursuing the claim under a conditional fee agreement enquiries will need to be made to check that counsel is willing to enter a conditional fee agreement or, at least, continue acting under a conditional fee agreement up to and including the trial.

Where the claimant is publicly funded it may be necessary to get the funding extended to trial which, in turn, is likely to depend upon counsel advising this is appropriate.

10.5.3   Attendance on counsel

If counsel is dealing with the trial it may be appropriate to provide attendance at court.

When deciding whether it is appropriate for counsel to be attended it may be helpful to refer to guidance given in the *Law Society Gazette* of 12 April 2001 which suggested the circumstances when counsel should be attended by instructing solicitors at court:

- Counsel should be attended in any multi-track case.
- Attendance on counsel will normally be dispensed with in a fast-track case (and a small claims track case), except where:
  - the case is more complex than a typical fast track case;
  - the determination of costs at the conclusion of proceedings requires the presence of the solicitor; or
  - one of the parties in the case is a child.
- Counsel should be attended if the client is unable to understand the proceedings or give adequate instructions to counsel because of inadequate knowledge of English, mental illness or other mental or physical disability.
- Counsel should be attended if counsel is representing more than one party.
- Counsel should be attended if the client is likely to disrupt the proceedings if counsel were to appear alone.
- Counsel should be attended if there are any issues likely to arise which question the client's character or the solicitor's conduct of the case.
- Counsel should be attended if there is any other exceptional circumstance which makes this desirable.

This guidance may be particularly relevant when the court considers, in a fast track case, the reasonableness of any costs claimed for attending the trial advocate.

10.5.4   The brief

If counsel is representing the claimant at trial, a brief will need to be delivered. Counsel will, ideally, have previously advised on the evidence. Even so the brief should be delivered in time for counsel to undertake a final review prior to trial and have ample opportunity to prepare for the hearing.

Matters that the brief ought to include or deal with are:

- provision of a fully indexed and paginated trial bundle, ideally agreed with the defendant;
- provision of any other relevant documentation for counsel's use;
- confirmation of the evidence to be called;
- a summary of the status on negotiations including any Part 36 or 'Calderbank' offers;
- instructions as to settlement and any specific terms to be included in that event (perhaps set out in a draft order);
- instructions in relation to costs; and
- where it is proposed that counsel should appear unattended, informing counsel accordingly.

Delivery of the brief commits to counsel's brief fee. That does not mean delivery should be delayed to the last moment but does allow the claimant to indicate to the defendant, especially where negotiations are taking place, that after a certain date, sufficiently ahead of trial, the brief will be delivered. This gives the defendant a reasonable opportunity, if sensible terms of settlement can be agreed meanwhile, to avoid what may be unnecessary cost. Any such time limit needs to ensure the brief if received by counsel in sufficient time for the papers to be reviewed and the case fully prepared for trial.

10.6 ADVISING THE CLIENT

It is important to keep the client fully advised at this stage of the case.

Many claimants are, understandably, concerned about the prospect of having to attend court and give evidence. The client needs to be notified as a hearing date has been fixed but may be reassured if that is accompanied by an explanation about the general format of the hearing and a reminder that negotiations towards settlement may still take place as well as that, if a realistic assessment of the situation, a settlement might still be achieved.

If the case does reach a settlement the client should be informed promptly of the terms agreed and given confirmation that attendance at court will no longer be required unless this is necessary, for example for the court to approve settlement.

10.7 FINAL REVIEWS

Final reviews should be made, ideally, not less than 21 days before trial and again not less than 7 days before trial.

These will ensure that all outstanding matters are dealt with and the case is fully prepared for a hearing.

10.7.1 The 21-day review

No later than 21 days before trial a number of matters will need to be checked.

- Have all case management directions been complied with by both parties?
- Are the statements of case in order?
- Is all the evidence in order and disclosed, and, where necessary, permission to rely on such evidence obtained from the court and any notice of intention to rely on hearsay evidence given?
- Has a bundle of documents been prepared and the index sent to the defendant for agreement?
- Has everyone involved been notified of the hearing and any witness orders been obtained and served?
- Are appropriate funding arrangements in place for trial?
- Should the claimant make, change or withdraw any offer to settle?
- Should the claimant re-consider acceptance of any extant Part 36 offer, or other offer which remains open, made by the defendant?

•Does any notice that reliance is to be placed on a plan, photograph or model not comprising part of the factual or expert evidence need to be served?

- Does a costs statement need to be prepared for the summary assessment of costs?

10.7.2 The 7-day review

No later than 7 days before trial a number of further matters will need to be checked:

- Is the bundle of documents agreed and in any event ready for filing?
- Has everyone involved in the case confirmed that they are aware of the hearing and will attend?
- Is everyone aware of where the trial will take place?
- Is everyone aware of the time they need to attend court?
- Have any outstanding funding arrangements now been made?
- Has a brief been delivered?
- Have arrangements been made for counsel to be attended, if attendance on counsel is appropriate?
- Has any costs statement required been prepared ready for filing and service?
- Has a case summary and/or skeleton argument been prepared ready for filing and service?
- Have all attempts at ADR now been exhausted and, once again, should any extant Part 36 offer be accepted, changed or withdrawn?

10.8 JUDGMENT BY THE COURT

If it is not possible for the parties to reach agreement on all outstanding matters the court will need to determine the remaining issues and give judgment accordingly.

10.8.1 Terms

The terms of the judgment will need to deal with any relevant issues which may include the following.

- Liability, and any apportionment.
- The amount of damages awarded under each head of claim.
- The amount of interest awarded on each head of damages allowed.
- The extent to which any CRU deduction is allowed against relevant heads of damage awarded (as required by s 15 of the Social Security (Recovery of Benefits) Act 1997.
- The incidence of costs and how any costs are to be assessed (see **10.9**).
- Timescale for payment of damages and (where already assessed or a payment on account pending detailed assessment is ordered) of costs.
- Grant or refusal of permission to appeal (where permission has been sought) and the destination of any such appeal for the purposes of CPR 40.2(4) and paragraph 4.3A of the Practice Direction to Part 52.

It may be helpful to provide counsel with a draft order, with blanks where appropriate, for use in the event of the judge finding in favour of the claimant or terms being agreed.

10.8.2   Reasons

Where the court has to determine issues the parties are entitled to adequate reasons: *English v Emery Reimbold & Strick Ltd.*[3]

For information purposes, and certainly in the event of an appeal, a transcript of the judgment should be obtained. It is for this reason the CPR provides for hearings to be recorded.

10.8.3   Action

Following trial further action will be necessary whatever the outcome of the hearing.

- The terms of the judgment should be reported to the client, with details of any sums payable and timescale.
- Any further witness expenses should be met and the witnesses advised of the outcome of the case.
- Experts should be advised of the outcome, if applicable thanked for attending the hearing and any further or outstanding expenses met.
- Counsel's clerk should have confirmation of the outcome and an up to date fee note should be requested.
- Any deadline for payment imposed by the court should be diarised so that payment can be chased up and enforced if necessary.

If permission to appeal has been granted, or is to be sought, the timescale for serving appellant's notice should be diarised.

10.9   COSTS AT TRIAL

The claimant will wish to obtain, if possible, an order at trial that the costs of the action be paid by the defendant. If such an order is obtained the court may, under CPR 44.6, either make a summary assessment or order a detailed assessment of those costs. The general rule, provided by s 9.1 of the Costs Practice Direction, is that the court should in appropriate circumstances make a summary assessment.

Accordingly, part of the preparation for trial will be to determine which method of assessing costs is likely and ensuring that, if likely to be appropriate, costs can be dealt with by summary assessment.

10.9.1   Range of costs orders

CPR 44.2(1) confirms that the court has a general discretion as to costs, including whether to order one party to pay the costs of another party.

---

[3]   [2002] EWCA Civ 605.

CPR 44.2(2) goes on to provide that where the court does decide to make an order about costs the general rule is that the unsuccessful will be ordered to pay the costs of the successful party. The court may, however, make a different order and for these purposes should have regard to all the circumstances. CPR 44.4(3) identifies some particular circumstances the court should take into account including conduct, the extent of success and 'any payment into court or admissible offer to settle made a party which is drawn to the court's attention, and which is not an offer to which costs consequences under Part 36 apply' (see **12.2.4.3**).

If the court does exercise discretion, and make an order for costs, that may be simply for one party to pay the costs of the other. However, there are a range of costs orders, set out in CPR 44.2(6), the court may make to reflect the particular circumstances of each case.

This ability of the court to make what might be termed a special costs order is significant where there has been a trial because the paying party has the opportunity of seeking to minimise the potential effect of an adverse costs order by inviting the court to reflect the terms of CPR 44.2(6) by directing payment of only:

- a proportion of costs;
- a stated amount of costs;
- costs from or until a certainly date only;
- costs incurred before proceedings have begun;
- costs relating to particular steps taken in the proceedings;
- costs relating to a distinct part of the proceedings; or
- interest on costs from or until a certain date.

The court may also direct, under CPR 44.3(1) that any costs payable by one party to another party be assessed on the standard basis or indemnity basis (see **12.2.6**). Any trial is an opportunity for the receiving party to make submissions on the basis for assessment.

Under CPR 44.4(2) the court, when deciding the amount of costs, will give effect to any costs orders which have already been made. Consequently, any final order dealing with costs will not override earlier orders unless expressly providing to the contrary. For these purposes any orders for costs in the case are likely to follow the ultimate incidence of costs as at the date when such order was made: *Ontulmus v Collett*.[4]

Where costs are payable by one party to another those may, in appropriate circumstances, be the subject of a summary assessment but otherwise will have to go to detailed assessment.

10.9.2   Summary assessment

Summary assessment of costs should take place:

- at the conclusion of the trial of a case which has been dealt with on the fast track (where the order will deal with the costs of the whole claim); and

---

[4]   [2014] EWHC 4117 (QB).

- at the conclusion of any other hearing which has lasted not more than one day (where the order will deal only with the costs of the application or matter to which the hearing relates unless that hearing disposes of the whole claim).

However, there will be no summary assessment of costs if there is good reason not to do so. For example, where the paying party shows substantial grounds for disputing the sum claimed, that cannot be dealt with summarily or there is insufficient time to carry to out a summary assessment (and even a summary assessment will require the court to focus on the detailed breakdown of costs rather than simply applying a judicial tariff: *Flowers (I–800) Inc v Phonenames Ltd*;[5] *Morgan v Spirit Group Ltd*).[6]

There will also be no summary assessment of costs if the receiving party is an assisted person (unless the solicitors waive the right to recover further costs) a child or a protected party.

If there may be a summary assessment a costs statement should be filed and served not later than 2 days before the hearing, in accordance with s 9.5 of the Costs Practice Direction.

If the costs statement has not been filed and served more than two days before the hearing the court may impose a penalty. However, unless the statement is served very late the court may well only reduce, rather than disallow completely, the costs: *MacDonald v Taree Holdings Ltd*.[7]

Section 9.5 sets out the requirements of the costs statement which should follow, as closely as possible, form N260. That form essentially just sets out hourly rates, times spent and details of disbursements, with the sums claimed for costs. This is very limited information for the court where there may be a number of factors relevant to the proper assessment of costs and the requirement to make an assessment which means the court cannot simply apply a tariff.

Accordingly, the claimant may wish to accompany the statement of costs with further background information which, whilst not in the format of a full bill of costs, helps to explain, by reference to the relevant factors in CPR 44.5, why the claimant contends the work done, and hence costs claimed, are reasonable and, if appropriate, necessary and proportionate.

The costs statement should not, of course, give details of any recoverable additional liabilities, as it must be served prior to the hearing. However, if the claimant intends to seek additional liabilities as part of the costs of the claim then, in accordance with the former s 14.9 of the Costs Practice Direction, there should be prepared, for use at the conclusion of the hearing, a bundle which includes a copy of:

- every notice of funding arrangement filed;
- every estimate and statement of costs filed;
- the risk assessment prepared at the time any relevant funding arrangement was entered into and on the basis of which the amount of the additional liability was fixed.

---

5 [2001] EWCA Civ 721, [2001] 2 Costs LR 286.
6 [2011] EWCA Civ 68.
7 [2001] CPLR 439.

Summary assessment ought only to be undertaken by the judge who has dealt with the hearing and, accordingly, already has a good idea of the issues that arose and factors relevant to assessment (reflecting the wording of paragraph 9.2 of the Costs Practice Direction which anticipates summary assessment only at the conclusion of a 'trial' or 'hearing' and paragraph 13.8 which refers to assessment by the 'same judge' who dealt with that trial or hearing). The practice of judges conducting a summary assessment when no such hearing has taken place received disapproval in *Thenga v Quinn*.[8]

Unless the court orders otherwise any costs order where the amount of costs is stated, which will include a summary assessment, will, in accordance with CPR 44.8, be payable within 14 days.

10.9.3   Detailed assessment

Except where summary assessment is appropriate the court should, if making a costs order, direct a detailed assessment.

If there is any doubt about whether it is appropriate, or viable, to carry out a summary assessment the parties may wish to agree how costs should be dealt with, particularly if that saves the cost of preparing what might otherwise be unnecessary costs statements.

Counsel, or other trial advocate, should be instructed of any circumstances making detailed, as opposed to summary, assessment of costs appropriate.

If there is to be a detailed assessment it will usually be appropriate for the receiving party to request the court to make a payment on account of costs under CPR 44.2(8) (see **12.2.11.1**). For these purposes costs estimates given by the parties may be of assistance to the court in deciding the proper level of a payment on account of costs.

10.9.4   Interest on costs

CPR 44.2(6)(g) provides that the court may make an order for payment of interest on costs from or until a certain date, including a date before judgment.

Where the receiving party has had to fund costs the court may be ready to award interest on those costs from a date prior to judgment: *Bim Kemi AB v Blackburn Chemicals Ltd*.[9] Similarly, where the receiving party had a 'resounding victory', interest on costs was allowed back to the date proceedings were commenced: J *Murphy & Sons Ltd v Johnston Precast Ltd*[10] and *Nova Production Ltd v Mazooma Games Ltd*.[11]

Interest on costs from the date of judgment, rather than assessment of those costs, was allowed even where the receiving party had funded the litigation with the benefit of an interest free loan: *Fattal v Walbrook Trustees (Jersey) Ltd*.[12] First instance decisions have suggested a different approach should be taken where the claim has been funded by a conditional fee agreement but it seems curious that this approach draws a distinction

---

8   [2009] EWCA Civ 151.
9   [2003] EWCA Civ 889.
10   [2008] EWHC 3104 (TCC).
11   [2006] EWHC 189 (Ch).
12   [2009] EWHC 1674 (Ch).

between those cases where judgment is entered by agreement or by the court and those where there is a deemed costs order, for example on acceptance of a Part 36 offer within the relevant period (as in those circumstances CPR 44.9(4) specifically provides interest under the Judgments Act will run from the date on which the event gave rise to the entitlement to costs occurred).

10.9.5 Instructions on costs

Counsel, or other trial advocate, will need sufficient instructions to deal with issues likely to arise on costs. A separate brief, dealing specifically with costs, may be necessary.

It will be essential counsel is made aware of any factors that may be relevant to the exercise of the court's discretion on costs. These are likely to include the following matters.

- Any factors relevant to determining who has 'won' and hence likely to benefit from the usual costs order.
- Any information likely to be relevant for the court in deciding whether it is appropriate to depart from the general rule, the unsuccessful party pay the costs of the successful party, or to make one of the special costs orders provided for in CPR 44.3(6).
- Any Part 36 offers made by the defendant, given the term of CPR 36.14(1)(a).
- Any Part 36 offers made by the claimant, given that under CPR 36.14(1)(b) if judgment is at least as advantageous to the claimant as such an offer the court must, unless it would be unjust to do so, award the claimant:
    - indemnity costs;
    - enhanced interest on costs;
    - enhanced interest on damages; and (for offers made on or after 1 April 2013);
    - an additional amount.
- Any admissible offer which does not have Part 36 consequences that may be drawn to the court's attention under CPR 44.3(4)(c), though such an offer should be just one of the circumstances the court takes into account rather than simply having the consequences the offer would have had if made under Part 36: *Widlake v BAA plc*.[13]

Counsel, or other trial advocate, is likely to require the following documents in the event of a summary assessment:

- The claimant's costs statement (and in the event of a claim for recoverable additional liabilities the supplemental bundle).
- Further background information, and perhaps documentation for filing with the court, to explain any particular features of the case and hence why it is contended the costs claimed are reasonable, and if appropriate necessary and proportionate.
- Details of any Part 36 offers, or other offers which may carry costs consequences under Part 44.
- The defendant's costs statement with comments on the sums claimed including the appropriateness of:
    - hourly rates applied;

---

[13] [2009] EWCA Civ 1256.

- – time spent;
- – any additional liabilities claimed; and
- – disbursements.
- Any reasons why, in the event the defendant is successful, costs should not follow the event or that there should be a special costs order.

10.10   FINANCIAL ADVICE

Where the court enters judgment for the claimant, or terms of settlement are agreed, advice on various financial matters may be necessary.

It is important the client is at least made aware of the potential need for such advice. If the client then wishes for that advice this may involve referral to the firm's private client department or to a specialist firm providing appropriate services.

10.10.1   Wills

The client should be reminded of the need to make, or update, a will particularly if the level of damages may generate or increase potential liability to Inheritance Tax.

10.10.2   Personal injury trusts

A personal injury trust is an important mechanism for helping to preserve damages where the client is now receiving, or may become entitled to, means-tested state benefits.

10.10.3   Pre-nuptial agreements

If the client might marry, or re-marry, in the future there is now the opportunity to enter a pre-nuptial agreement which may help guard against damages becoming part of the matrimonial assets, particularly if those are likely to be needed for matters such as care or accommodation in the future.

10.11   ENFORCEMENT

When the court has entered judgment, after trial or by agreement, that judgment can, if necessary, be enforced by the claimant.

In personal injury litigation it may be more difficult, than some other types of claim, to get to the stage of judgment but it is then less likely problems will be experienced in recovering any monies due, as the defendant will usually be insured and the insurer will generally make reasonably prompt payment.

However, from time to time, it may be necessary to enforce a judgment and the involvement of an insurer can sometimes make this more complex.

10.11.1 Pre-issue

If a claim is settled before issue of court proceedings, provided the terms have been recorded clearly enough, that will constitute a binding contract. In such circumstances the claimant may issue proceedings for breach of contract with the advantage that this should not allow any issues on liability to be opened.

Otherwise, if court proceedings have not yet been commenced, it would be necessary for the claimant to start proceedings but with the risk matters may then be put in issue by the defendant. Nevertheless, the claimant may be able to rely on any relevant pre-action admissions, if necessary by application for judgment.

Once judgment has been entered the claim can, if necessary, be enforced like any other post-issue settlement.

10.11.2 Post-issue

If the claimant has a judgment that may be enforced by any of the usual methods.

The difficulty is that this has to be enforced against the nominal defendant who may not have any, or any significant, assets. However, if the defendant is able to meet the debt, either because the defendant has substantial assets or the debt is relatively modest, it may be appropriate, and more straightforward, simply to enforce the judgment directly against the defendant.

Enforcement is only possible if the claimant has a judgment rather than a 'Tomlin' order (see **11.7.2.3**).

10.11.3 Third Parties (Rights Against Insurers) Act 1930

Where the defendant is insured, and not able to meet the judgment, the Act confers additional rights on the claimant.

Essentially, the Act allows the claimant to enforce the judgment against the relevant insurer in certain circumstances. However, as a preliminary, it will be necessary for the claimant to obtain a bankruptcy order, against an individual defendant, or an order for liquidation, if the defendant is a limited company.

Thereafter, the claimant can start further court proceedings, direct against the insurer, under the 1930 Act.

If the claimant wishes to rely on the Act it will be necessary for the defendant to have complied with relevant terms of the policy, as the claimant effectively stands in the defendant's shoes. As the claimant may not be aware of the precise terms of the policy it may be appropriate, throughout, to keep the insurer involved and ask if there are any terms of the contract the claimant should be made aware of so as to ensure compliance.

In a claim arising out of a road traffic accident proceedings may have been issued at the outset, against the insurer, in accordance with the European Communities (Rights

Against Insurers) Regulations 2002. Where the insurer is a party to the claim any judgment can be enforced direct in the usual way.

10.11.4   Rights against other non-parties

If a non-party has effectively controlled the litigation there is the prospect of seeking a costs order against any such party which, in turn, may allow for enforcement of a judgment not otherwise recoverable (see **12.4.5**).

10.11.5   Interest

If the claimant obtains, or agrees, judgment, that should include interest, at appropriate rates, on damages to the date of trial or settlement.

The judgment will usually provide a timescale for payment and provided payment is made within that time no further interest should accrue.

If payment of sums due is not made promptly the claimant is likely to seek interest under the Judgments Act, certainly if enforcement is necessary, down to the date of payment.

10.12   APPEALS

A party who is dissatisfied with a decision of the court, whether an interim or final order, may wish to appeal.

Part 52 of the CPR deals with the right to appeal, applicable time limits, procedure for and destination of appeals.

The same rules apply to appeals against both interim and final orders, though there is an additional hurdle for a party who wishes to appeal a case management decision.

10.12.1   Appeal or application?

A party who is not satisfied with a decision of the court will usually need to appeal that decision.

However, there are two situations, which arise quite frequently, when rather than appealing the order the party should make an application in accordance with Part 23.

- Where a party wishes to set aside or vary an order which has been made without a hearing, in accordance with CPR 3.3 or CPR 23.8 (in such circumstances there may also be a concurrent right of appeal but the better course may be to apply under Part 3: *Vernon v Spoudeas*).[14]

- Where a party, as a result of a change in circumstances, wishes the court to exercise the power conferred by CPR 3.1(7) to vary case management directions. This power cannot be used to challenge a final order and it is unlikely the court will exercise the power otherwise unless there has been a material change in circumstances.

---

[14]   [2010] EWCA Civ 666.

10.12.2   Permission

CPR 52.3(1) requires, in most circumstances, that permission to appeal be given as a preliminary to any appeal.

An application for permission to appeal may, under CPR 52.3(2), be made to the court at which the decision to be appealed was made or to the relevant appeal court.

If the court making the decision to be appealed refused permission, a further application for permission to appeal may be made to the relevant appeal court.

If the relevant appeal court, without a hearing, refuses permission to appeal, the person seeking permission to appeal may request the decision to be reconsidered at a hearing (save where the court of appeal refuses permission to appeal without a hearing and orders that the person seeking permission may not request the decision to be reconsidered at a hearing.

CPR 52.3(6) provides that permission to appeal may only be given where:
• the court considers that the appeal would have a real prospect of success; or
• there is some other compelling reason why the appeal should be heard.

Where a party wishes to pursue a second appeal, CPR 52.13 provides that permission for such an appeal will not be granted by the Court of Appeal unless:
• the appeal would raise an important point of principle or practice; or
• there is some other compelling reach for the Court of Appeal to hear it.

Additionally, if the appeal concerns a case management decision (matters such as disclosure, witness statements, experts reports and timetable as described by CPR 3.1(2)) there is the additional hurdle, imposed by paragraph 4.5 of the Practice Direction to Part 52, that the appeal court must take into account whether the issue is of sufficient significance to justify the costs of the appeal, whether the procedural consequences of an appeal outweigh the significance of the case management decision and whether it would be more convenient to determine the issue at or after trial.

Where the earlier decisions reflect an error of law that should, of itself, be a compelling reason, for example *Threlfall v Hull City Council*.[15]

Where permission to appeal is required that must, in accordance with CPR 52.4, be requested in the appellant's notice.

Where permission to appeal is given on terms, a party unhappy with those terms must either abandon the prospective appeal, accept the terms or treat the conditional permission as a refusal of permission to appeal and make a fresh application to the appellate court: *R v Secretary of State for the Home Department*.[16] What that party cannot do is use the permission which has been given as an opportunity to appeal to the appellate court against some or all of the terms applied by the lower court.

---

[15]   [2010] EWCA Civ 1147.
[16]   [2011] EWCA Civ 269.

10.12.3   Time limit

CPR 52.4 provides that the appellant's notice (including the request for permission to appeal where this is required) must be filed at the relevant appeal court within 21 days after the date of the decision the appellant wishes to appeal (unless the court being appealed stipulates a longer or shorter period).

The appellant's notice must also be served on each respondent as soon as practicable and in any event not later than seven days after it is filed.

However, CPR 52.6 does allow an application to vary the time limit. If an extension of time is necessary an application should also be included in the appellant's notice and reasons for the request given.

10.12.4   Routes

Paragraph 2.A of the Practice Direction to Part 52 sets out the routes of appeal which depend upon the level of judge making the decision and whether that is an interim or a final decision.

• Appeals from decisions made by the district judge of a county court will be heard by a circuit judge.

• Appeals from decisions made by the district judge of the High Court will be heard by a High Court judge.

• Appeals from decisions made by a circuit judge will be heard by the High Court judge.

• Appeals from decisions of a High Court judge will be heard by the Court of Appeal.

• However, if the decision to be appealed is a final decision in a Part 7 claim allocated to the multi-track the appeal will always be heard by the Court of Appeal.

A 'final decision' is a decision of a court that would finally determine (subject to any possible appeal or detailed assessment of costs) the entire proceedings whichever way the court decided the issues before it.

Case management decisions, granting or refusing interim relief, summary judgment and the striking out of a claim are not final decisions for this purpose.

A decision will be treated as a final decision for these purposes where it is made at the conclusion of part of a hearing or trial which has been split into parts and would, if it had been made at the conclusion of that hearing or trial, have been a final decision, for example judgment on liability where that has been tried as a preliminary issue.

Helpful guidance, in the early days of the CPR, on routes of appeal was given by the Court of Appeal in *Tanfern Ltd v Cameron-MacDonald*.[17]

---

[17]   [2000] 1 WLR 1311.

Where a party applies for permission to appeal at a hearing where the relevant decision was made, paragraph 4.3A of the Practice Direction to Part 52 requires the judge to state:

- whether or not the decision is final;
- whether an appeal lies from the decision and, if so, to which appeal court;
- whether the court gives permission to appeal; and
- if not, the appropriate appeal court to which any further application for permission may be made.

This obligation is also reflected in CPR 40.2(4) compliance with which should be a matter of course: *Chadwick v Hollingsworth*.[18]

10.12.5 Documents

To comply with Part 52, and the accompanying Practice Direction, the appellant will need the following documents:

- Appellant's notice in Form N161 (incorporating, if required, application for permission to appeal and/or application for an extension of time).
- Grounds of appeal.
- A copy of the order under appeal (as sealed by the court).
- A transcript of the judgment. Paragraph 6.1 of the Practice Direction to Part 39 requires judgments to be recorded, unless the judge directs otherwise, reflecting the importance under the CPR of decisions given at first instance and hence the need for any appeal court to be able to read a reliable version of the judgment being reviewed: *Tanfern Ltd v Cameron-MacDonald*.[19] Paragraph 5.12 of the Practice Direction to Part 52 gives guidance on what will be a suitable record of the judgment for the purposes of an appeal.
- A copy of any order giving or refusing permission to appeal (including reasons given by the judge).
- A skeleton argument (guidance on the format of which is given by paragraph 5.10 of the Practice Direction to Part 52).
- Any other documents required by paragraph 5.6 of the Practice Direction to Part 52.
- A certificate signed by the appellant's solicitor, counsel or other representative to the effect that he has read and understood the requirement, in paragraph 5.6 of the Practice Direction to Part 52, that all documents extraneous to the issues to be considered on the application or appeal must be excluded.

Not all the required documents may be available to the appellant within the applicable time limit. Accordingly, paragraph 5.7 of the Practice Direction to Part 52 confirms that where it is not possible to file all relevant documents the appellant must indicate the documents that have not yet been filed, the reasons why and an estimate of when these will be filed. Consequently, if any documents are missing that should not delay filing and service of the appellant's notice.

---

18 [2010] EWCA Civ 1210.
19 [2000] 1 WLR 1311.

If necessary, the appellant will need to file the appellant's notice on the basis that the further documentation will follow once available and, if required to do so, make an application for an appropriate extension of time.

Once all relevant documents, at least for the application for permission to appeal, are available these will need to be put into a bundle that ought to contain any relevant background documents so that, whilst as concise as possible, the bundle does, in effect, have the material which the appeal court will need to refer to when deciding whether it is appropriate to give permission to appeal.

Details of Part 36 offers, unless relevant to the substantive issues in the appeal, should not be included in the appeal bundles.

If the respondent to the appeal files a respondent's notice or relies on any skeleton argument these documents should also be included in the bundle ready for the hearing of the appeal.

Paragraph 15.4 of the Practice Direction to Part 52 provides specific guidance for the preparation of bundles of documents for use by the Court of Appeal. Although strictly not applicable to other appeals the guidance given may be of assistance when preparing bundles in other circumstances.

10.12.6   Listing

Following the appellant's notice, where permission to appeal has already been given, or once the appellate court has given permission to appeal, the appeal hearing will need to be listed.

In an appeal to the Court of Appeal the parties will be requested to provide further information, in an appeal questionnaire, and will also be expected to liaise over listing.

Away from the Court of Appeal it is likely the Appellate Court will, after checking details of availability, simply list the appeal.

Prior to the hearing of the appeal the appeal bundle will usually need to be updated, particularly if the bundle was originally prepared for an application for permission to appeal.

10.12.7   Hearing

CPR 52.11 provides that an appeal will, except in certain limited circumstances, be a review of the decision of the lower court and not a re-hearing.

An appeal will be allowed where the decision of the lower court was:
* wrong: which is likely to mean the court:
  – erred in law;
  – erred in fact;
  – erred in the exercise of discretion; or
* unjust: because of a serious procedural or other irregularity.

A review, rather than a re-hearing, inevitably restricts the circumstances, at least when the appeal is on issues of fact or the exercise of discretion, when the decision under appeal can be said to be 'wrong'.

What would be wrong inevitably depends upon upon the subject matter of the appeal. In *EI Dupont De Nemours & Co v ST Dupont*[20] May LJ recognised that:

> 'There will also be a spectrum of appropriate respect depending on the nature of the decision of the lower Court which is challenged. At one end of the spectrum will be decisions of primary fact reached after an evaluation of oral evidence where credibility is in issue and purely discretionary decisions. Further along the spectrum will be multi-factorial decisions often depending on inferences and an analysis of documentary material.'

To be unjust the procedural or other irregularity detected must be a serious one and that irregularity must have caused the decision to be unjust: *Tanfern Ltd v Cameron-MacDonald*.[21]

10.12.7.1 Error of law

If the appeal raises a point of law the appellate court can readily say the decision is wrong if, as a matter of law, that is so. Hence, Ward LJ observed in *Scout Association v Barnes*[22] that:

> 'It is, in my view, trite that a judgment of this sort is a value judgment where there is a right answer and a wrong answer: it is not a question of an exercise of discretion where there is a band of reasonable choice to be made.'

It can sometimes be difficult to distinguish what is an issue of law and what is an issue of fact. That difficulty is compounded by the Court of Appeal having a role in ensuring consistency, Sir Mark Waller explained, after reviewing case-law the proper approach to appeals on fact or inference, in *Lawrence v Kent County Council*[23] that:

> '... time and again one finds the Court of Appeal reviewing whether the judge was right to impose a duty on the facts as found by him. Nothing said by Clarke LJ or Lord Mance was in our view intended to alter the approach of an appellate court to this type of case, and since part of a Court of Appeal's function is to strive for consistency, it is important that it retains this degree of oversight.'

On this basis Sir Mark Waller went on to observe:

> 'Of course the court must have regard to the advantage the judge had in hearing the evidence and the whole case; and much as it does in considering the exercise of a discretion it will examine whether the findings of primary fact are justified; whether the judge relied on evidence which was not admissible or placed too great a reliance on evidence; and whether a judge misdirected himself. But even if there is no misdirection the appellate court is entitled to assess for itself whether on those facts an inference or finding of dangerousness, to an extent which imposes a duty on the Council, was justified.'

---

[20] [2003] EWCA Civ 1368.
[21] [2000] 1 WLR 1311.
[22] [2010] EWCA Civ 1476.
[23] [2012] EWCA Civ 493.

With an error of law the appeal court will usually be in a position to determine the appeal, by applying the law correctly, without the need for a re-trial. If, however, the error of law reflects a failure to make findings of all relevant facts, a re-trial may be inevitable.

10.12.7.2 Error of fact

An appellate court will be reluctant to interfere with findings of fact.

In *Thomas v Thomas*[24] Lord Thankerton explained:

> 'Where a question of fact has been tried by a judge without a jury, and there is no question of misdirection of himself by the judge, an appellate court which is disposed to come to a different conclusion on the printed evidence should not do so unless it is satisfied that any advantage enjoyed by the trial judge by reason of having seen and heard the witnesses could not be sufficient to explain or justify the trial judge's conclusion.'

More recently in *Assicurazioni Generali SpA v Arab Insurance Group*[25] Ward LJ observed:

> 'The Court of Appeal can only interfere if the decision of the lower court was wrong and in deciding whether or not findings of fact were wrong, we take a retrospective look at the case and do not decide it afresh untrammelled by the judge's conclusion.
>
> The trial judge's view inevitably imposes a restraint upon the appellate court, the weight of which varies from case to case. Two factors lead us to be cautious about interfering. First, the appellate court recognises that judging the witness is a more complex task than merely judging the transcript. Each may have its intellectual component but the former can also crucially rely on intuition. That gives the trial judge the advantage over us in assessing a witness's demeanour, so often a vital factor in deciding where the truth lies. Secondly, judging is an art not a science. So the more complex the question, the more likely it is that different judges will come to different conclusions and the harder it is to determine right from wrong. Borrowing language from other jurisprudence, the trial judge is entitled to "a margin of appreciation".
>
> Bearing these matters in mind, the appeal court conducting a review of the trial judge's decision will not conclude that the decision was wrong simply because it is not the decision the appeal judge would have made had he or she been called upon to make it in the court below. Something more is required than personal unease and something less than perversity has to be established. The best formulation for the ground in between where a range of adverbs may be used –"clearly", "plainly", "blatantly", "palpably" wrong, is an adaptation of what Lord Fraser of Tullybelton said in *G v G* [1985] 2 All ER 225 at 229, [1985] 1 WLR 647 at 652, admittedly dealing with the different task of exercising a discretion. Adopting his approach, I would pose the test for deciding whether a finding of fact was against the evidence to be whether that finding by the trial judge exceeded the generous ambit within which reasonable disagreement about the conclusion to be drawn from the evidence is possible.'

This approach was subsequently affirmed in *McGraddie v McGraddie*[26] and *Liquidator of Letham Grange Development Co Ltd v Foxworth Investments Ltd*.[27]

---

[24] [1947] SC (HL) 45.
[25] (BSc) [2002] EWCA Civ 1642.
[26] [2013] UKSC 58.
[27] [2014] UKSC 41

Where the error is said to relate to an inference drawn from primary facts the appeal court may be more ready to review the decision of a trial judge as the court dealing with the appeal will often be in as good a position as the trial judge to drawn appropriate inferences.

Hence, for example, an appeal was allowed where the trial judge had made findings, based on the factual evidence, the Court of Appeal regarded as 'fallacious': *Davies v Pay*.[28]

There must, of course, be a proper evidential basis, in factual findings, for the decision ultimately reached or that decision will be 'wrong'.

The appeal court may be able to determine the appeal but if the appeal has to be allowed because of inadequate findings of fact it may be necessary to order a re-trial.

10.12.7.3 Error of evaluation

An error in properly evaluating the evidence has similarities to an error of fact, or at least drawing inferences from findings of primary fact, and also an error of law, but is a distinct basis for an appeal.

There will be an appealable error of evaluation where, for example, the judge fails to adopt the correct forensic approach to dealing with conflicting evidence whilst keeping the balance of probabilities in mind.

Accordingly, after observing the judgment did 'not read like a judgment which depends on a finding of credibility' in *Eyres v Atkinsons Kitchens and Bedrooms Ltd*[29] Wards LJ held:

> '... it is essential that all the circumstances of the case have to be analysed carefully to see where the balance of probabilities lay, and indeed whether he could be satisfied on the balance of probability at all. The judge takes account of all the circumstances of the case but in his conclusion he does not analyse them and balance one possibility against the other. It is an essential analysis.'

Similarly, in *Uren v Corporate Leisure (UK) Ltd*[30] Smith LJ concluded that she could not be satisfied the trial judge 'reach a sound and tenable conclusion' which meant the judgment could not stand.

In *Hussain v Hussain*[31] a finding of fraud against the claimant was overturned by the Court of Appeal with Davis LJ noting:

> 'This case is of a kind which depended entirely on the judge's assessment and evaluation of the relevant evidence (which was primarily, though by no means solely, oral) and the conclusion to be drawn from the facts as found. For this purpose it is well-established that an appeal court simply does not have the advantages of the trial judge, who will have observed the witnesses give evidence, will have been able to assess their demeanour and, generally, will

---

[28]   [2010] EWCA Civ 752.
[29]   [2007] EWCA Civ 365.
[30]   [2011] EWCA Civ 66.
[31]   [2012] EWCA Civ 1367.

have the "feel" of the case. Since the Court of Appeal does not have these advantages, the trial judge's assessment of the witnesses will naturally carry significant weight.'

However, after reviewing the evidence underlying the judgment being appealed Davis LJ concluded:

'I do of course remind myself of the advantages that a trial judge has and remind myself that it is not enough for an appellate court to feel unease at a trial judge's factual findings and conclusions. But in my view the two matters identified in paragraph 21 of the judgment – being the sole identified bases for the finding of fraudulent involvement on the part of the claimant – were not sufficiently cogent to justify an inference of fraudulent complicity on the part of the claimant in a staged collision.'

The advantage of the trial judge, respected by appeal courts when reviewing findings of fact, is also an important factor when dealing with appeals alleging an error in the evaluation of those factual findings for the reasons explained by Lord Hoffmann in *Piglowska v Piglowski*[32] when, after referring to the earlier authority of *G v G*[33] he said:

'This passage has been cited and approved many times but some of its implications need to be explained. First, the appellate court must bear in mind the advantage which the first instance judge had in seeing the parties and the other witnesses. This is well understood on questions of credibility and findings of primary fact. But it goes further than that. It applies also to the judge's evaluation of those facts. If I may quote what I said in *Biogen Inc. v Medeva Plc.* [1997] RPC 1, 45:

"The need for appellate caution in reversing the trial judge's evaluation of the facts is based upon much more solid grounds than professional courtesy. It is because specific findings of fact, even by the most meticulous judge, are inherently an incomplete statement of the impression which was made upon him by the primary evidence. His expressed findings are always surrounded by a penumbra of imprecision as to emphasis, relative weight, minor qualification and nuance ... of which time and language do not permit exact expression, but which may play an important part in the judge's overall evaluation."

The second point follows from the first. The exigencies of daily court room life are such that reasons for judgment will always be capable of having been better expressed. This is particularly true of an unreserved judgment such as the judge gave in this case but also of a reserved judgment based upon notes, such as was given by the district judge. These reasons should be read on the assumption that, unless he has demonstrated the contrary, the judge knew how he should perform his functions and which matters he should take into account... An appellate court should resist the temptation to subvert the principle that they should not substitute their own discretion for that of the judge by a narrow textual analysis which enables them to claim that he misdirected himself.'

An appeal court will usually be able, on the basis of a revised evaluation of the facts, to decide whether or not the appeal should be allowed.

Robust but fair case management decisions may uphold sanctions, as in *Durrant v Chief Constable of Avon Somerset*,[34] or grant relief from sanctions, as in *Chartwell Estate Agents Ltd v Fergies Properties SA*.[35]

---

[32]   [1999] 1 WLR 1360.
[33]   [1985] 1 WLR 647.
[34]   [2013] EWCA Civ 1624.
[35]   [2014] EWCA Civ 506.

Where the evaluation concerns questions such as proportionality under the European Convention on Human Rights specific guidance, in relation to appeals, was given by the Supreme Court when giving judgment *In the Matter of B (a Child)*[36] where Lord Neuberger held:

> 'An appellate judge may conclude that the trial judge's conclusion on proportionality was (i) the only possible view, (ii) a view which she considers was right, (iii) a view on which she has doubts, but on balance considers was right, (iv) a view which she cannot say was right or wrong, (v) a view on which she has doubts, but on balance considers was wrong, (vi) a view which she considers was wrong, or (vii) a view which is unsupportable. The appeal must be dismissed if the appellate judge's view is in category (i) to (iv) and allowed if it is in category (vi) or (vii).'

There is likely to be an error in evaluation if the reasoning of the judgment under appeal does not support the conclusion or cannot be discerned, for example *Jackson v Murray*.[37]

10.12.7.4 *Error of discretion*

In *Lawrence v Kent County Council*[38] Sir Mark Waller recognised that:

> 'Albeit at times there may seem to be similarities between appeals from the exercise of a discretion and appeals on fact or inference to be drawn from facts, they are not the same, and the right approach or the ability of a Court of Appeal to interfere depends on the circumstances of particular cases.'

In *G v G*[39] Lord Fraser of Tullybelton held:

> 'It is comparatively seldom that the Court of Appeal, even if it would itself have preferred a different answer, can say that the judge's decision was wrong, and unless it can say so, it will leave his decision undisturbed.'

Lord Fraser went on to observe, in words subsequently adopted by Brooke LJ in *Tanfern Ltd v Cameron-MacDonald*[40], that:

> 'Certainly it would not be useful to inquire whether different shades of meaning are intended to be conveyed by words such as "blatant error" used by the President in the present case, and words such as "clearly wrong", "plainly wrong", or simply "wrong" used by other judges in other cases. All these various expressions were used in order to emphasise the point that the appellate court should only interfere when they consider that the judge of the first instance has not merely preferred an imperfect solution which is different from an alternative imperfect solution which the Court of Appeal might or would have adopted, but has exceeded the generous ambit within which a reasonable disagreement is possible.'

Assessment of quantum, unless there is an error or law, is effectively regarded as an exercise of discretion. Hence in *Housecroft v Burnett*[41] O'Connor LJ held:

---

36   [2012] EWCA Civ 1475.
37   [2015] UKSC 5.
38   [2012] EWCA Civ 493.
39   [1985] 1 WLR 647.
40   [2000] 1 WLR 1311.
41   [1986] 1 All ER 332.

'This Court does not interfere with an award under this head (pain, suffering and loss of amenity) unless it is manifestly too high or too low or it can be shown that the judge has erred in principle in relation to some element that goes to make up the award.'

An example of error of principle, resulting in an award which was wrong, in assessing quantum is *Santos v Eaton Square Garage Ltd*.[42] The trial judge aggregated awards of damages, reflecting the various injuries the claimant suffered for pain, suffering and loss of amenity. The injuries were not, however, entirely discrete and so it was wrong simply to aggregate in this way as the different injuries had largely contributed to the same pain, suffering and loss of amenity.

Similarly, orders as to costs are likely to be characterised as an exercise of discretion and hence the observation of Chadwick in LJ in *Summit Property Ltd v Pitmans (a firm)*[43] that:

'The first question for this court is not whether it would have made the order which the judge made. The first question is whether this court is satisfied that this basis upon which the judge reached the conclusion he did has been shown to be flawed. It is only if that question is answered in the affirmative that this court can properly interfere with the exercise of the judge of the discretion entrusted to him. It is only then that this court will go on to consider what order it will make in the exercise of its own discretion.'

An issue which will be, in the absence of an error of law, essentially a question of discretion is the assessment of the extent of any contributory negligence.

If the court has made a finding of contributory negligence, where there should be no such deduction, or failed to make a finding of contributory negligence where that is appropriate, this will be an error of law. If, however, the court has correctly decided there should be a finding of contributory negligence an appellate court will not generally interfere with the assessment of the extent to which it is just and equitable to reduce damages to reflect the finding.

However, where any dispute on the proper apportionment reflects a finding of which party was more to blame the exercise of discretion will more readily become an issue of law. As Hale LJ observed in *Eagle v Chambers*:[44]

'We also accept that this court is always reluctant to interfere with the trial judge's judgment of what apportionment between the parties is "just and equitable" under the 1945 Act. But a finding as to which, if either, of the parties was the more responsible for the damage is different from a finding as to the precise extent of a less than 50% contribution. There is a qualitative difference between a finding of 60% contribution and a finding of 40% which is not so apparent in the quantitative difference between 40% and 20%.'

The judgment of Hale LJ was approved by the Supreme Court in *Jackson v Murray*[45] where Lord Reed confirmed:

'The question, therefore, is whether the court below went wrong. In the absence of an identifiable error, such as an error of law, or the taking into account of an irrelevant matter, or the failure to take account of a relevant matter, it is only a difference of view as to the

---

[42]   [2007] EWCA Civ 225.
[43]   [2001] EWCA Civ 2020.
[44]   [2003] EWCA Civ 1107.
[45]   [2015] UKSC 5.

apportionment of responsibility which exceeds the ambit of reasonable disagreement that warrants the conclusion that the court below has gone wrong. In other words, in the absence of an identifiable error, the appellate court must be satisfied that the apportionment made by the court below was not one which was reasonably open to it.'

Lord Reed added:

'The need for the appellate court to be satisfied, in the absence of an identifiable error, that the apportionment made by the court below was outside the range of reasonable determinations is reflected in the fact that apportionments are not altered by appellate courts merely on the basis of a disagreement as to the precise figure.'

Lord Woolf MR summed up the approach to errors of discretion in *AEI Rediffusion Music Ltd v Phonographic Performers Ltd*[46] when he said:

'Before the court can interfere it must be shown that the judge has either erred in principle in his approach or has left out of account or has taken into account some feature that he should, or should not, have considered, or that his decision was wholly wrong because the court is forced to the conclusion that he has not balanced the various factors fairly in the scale.'

Appeals against case management decisions often raise arguments based on error of discretion. In *Royal Sun Alliance Insurance plc v T & N Ltd*[47] Chadwick LJ held:

'... this Court should not interfere with case management decisions made by a judge who has applied the correct principles, and who has taken into account the matters which should be taken into account and left out of account matters which are irrelevant, unless satisfied that the decision is so plainly wrong that it must be regarded as outside the generous ambit of the discretion entrusted to the judge. '

This approach has been endorsed in a number of subsequent judgments including *Mannion v Ginty*[48] where Lewison LJ said:

'... it has been said more than once in this court, it is vital for the Court of Appeal to uphold robust fair case management decisions made by first instance judges.'

Where there has been an error of discretion the appellate court will usually be able to determine the appeal, inevitably in such circumstances that will be by reviewing the decision, on the basis of all relevant matters whilst excluding irrelevant factors, and exercising discretion afresh which may not necessarily result in a different outcome.

10.12.7.5 Procedural Irregularity

An appeal may be allowed because the decision is unjust because of a serious procedural or other irregularity.

This may cover a variety of issues, but frequently a failure to give adequate reasons for the decision.

---

[46] [1999] 1 WLR 1507.
[47] [2002] EWCA Civ 1964.
[48] [2012] EWCA Civ 1667.

In *English v Emery Reimbold & Strick Ltd*[49] the Court of Appeal emphasised why a trial judge must give adequate reasons:

- Reasons are necessary in order to render practicable the exercise of any right of appeal.

- Justice must be seen to be done.

- It must be apparent both to the parties and to the public why one party has won and the other has lost.

- The giving of reasons provides a necessary discipline for judges and it contributes to the setting of precedents for the future.

Whilst a judge does not have to deal with every argument presented the judge must make plain the principles on which he has acted and the reasons which lead him to his decision.

The judge should also give reasons, where this is inevitably a part of the decision making process, why certain evidence is preferred or rejected, including evidence of experts: *Uren v Corporate Leisure (UK) Ltd.*[50]

10.12.7.6   Bias, delay and other conduct

If the issue of judicial bias, delay or other conduct arises that may give grounds for allowing an appeal on the basis or irregularity.

The issue of bias was explored by the Court of Appeal in *Locabail (UK) Ltd v Bayfield Properties Ltd*[51] where the court concluded:

> 'It would be dangerous and futile to attempt to define or list the factors which may or may not give rise to a real danger of bias. Everything will depend on the facts, which may include the nature of the issue to be decided. We cannot, however, conceive of circumstances in which an objection could be soundly based on the religion, ethnic or national origin, gender, age, class, means or sexual orientation of the judge. Nor, at any rate ordinarily, could an objection be soundly based on the judge's social or educational or service or employment background or history, nor that of any member of the judge's family; or previous political associations; or membership of social or sporting or charitable bodies; or Masonic associations; or previous judicial decisions; or extra-curricular utterances (whether in text books, lectures, speeches, articles, interviews, reports or responses to consultation papers); or previous receipt of instructions to act for or against any party, solicitor or advocate engaged in a case before him; or membership of the same Inn, circuit, local Law Society or chambers.'

> 'By contrast, a real danger of bias might well be thought to arise if there were personal friendship or animosity between the judge and any member of the public involved in the case; or if the judge were closely acquainted with any member of the public involved in the case, particularly if the credibility of that individual could be significant in the decision of the case; or if, in a case where the credibility of any individual were an issue to be decided by the judge, he had in a previous case rejected the evidence of that person in such outspoken terms as to throw doubt on his ability to approach such person's evidence with an open mind on any later occasion; or if on any question at issue in the proceedings before him the judge had expressed views, particularly in the course of the hearing, in such extreme and unbalanced terms as to throw doubt on his ability to try the issue with an objective judicial mind...'

---

49   [2002] EWCA Civ 605.
50   [2011] EWCA Civ 66.
51   [2000] QB 451.

'In most cases, we think, the answer, one way or the other, will be obvious. But if in any case there is real ground for doubt, that doubt should be resolved in favour of recusal. We repeat: every application must be decided on the facts and circumstances of the individual case. The greater the passage of time between the event relied on as showing a danger of bias and the case in which the objection is raised, the weaker (other things being equal) the objection will be.'

The House of Lords subsequently confirmed in *Magill v Porter*[52] the appropriate test when considering apparent bias is as follows:

'The question is whether the fair-minded and informed observer, having considered the facts, would conclude that there was a real possibility that the tribunal was biased.'

Consequently, an inappropriate remark, even if intended as a joke, may suffice to generate a real risk of apparent bias: *El Farargy v El Farargy*.[53]

There may also be a real risk of apparent bias if the judge uses words which suggest the premature formation of a concluded view which is adverse to one of the parties: *Steadman-Byrne v Amjad*.[54] Moreover, the judge must retain an objective judicial mind throughout the hearing: *Co-Operative Group Ltd v International Computers Ltd*.[55]

A tenuous connection between a judge and a party is not going to meet the test of apparent bias: *Baker v Quantum Clothing Group*.[56] If, however, there is a real risk then recusal is likely to be appropriate on the basis the additional cost and delay is outweighed by the imperative of judicial impartiality: *Morrison v AWG Group Ltd*.[57]

If there may be a conflict of interest it is prudent for the judge to advise the parties of that at the outset. Where this occurs any party wishing to object should do so promptly: *Baker v Quantum Clothing Group*.[58] A party may, nevertheless, elect to proceed but it is essential a free and informed choice, based on all relevant information, is made and if not a re-trial may be necessary even many years later: *Smith v Kvaerner Cementation Foundations Ltd*.[59]

Delay between trial and judgment may be a relevant factor in the event of an appeal. In *Bond v Dunster Properties Ltd*[60] Arden LJ recognised the timescale for delivery of a judgment would vary, from case to case, but the 'usual period' was taken to be three months. However, Arden LJ went on to observe:

'Findings of fact are not automatically to be set aside because a judgment was seriously delayed. As in any appeal on fact, the court has to ask whether the judge was plainly wrong. This high test takes account of the fact that trial judges normally have a special advantage in fact-finding, derived from their having seen the witnesses give their evidence. However there is an additional test in the case of a seriously delayed judgment. If the reviewing court finds that the judge's recollection of the evidence is at fault on any material point, then (unless the

---

52 [2001] UKHL 67.
53 [2007] EWCA Civ 1149.
54 [2007] EWCA Civ 625.
55 [2003] EWCA Civ 1955.
56 [2009] EWCA Civ 566.
57 [2006] EWCA Civ 6.
58 [2009] EWCA Civ 566.
59 [2006] EWCA Civ 242.
60 [2011] EWCA Civ 455.

error could not be due to the delay in the delivery of judgment) it will order a retrial if, having regard to the diminished importance in those circumstances of the special advantage of the trial judge in the interpretation of evidence, it cannot be satisfied that the judge came to the right conclusion. This is the keystone of the additional standard of review on appeal against findings of fact in this situation.'

Lord Carswell giving the opinion of the Board in the Privy Council case of *Boodhoo v A-G of Trinidad and Tobago*[61] explained that *Goose v Wilson Sandiford*[62] provided an example where:

'delay may have so adversely affected the quality of the decision that it cannot be allowed to stand. It may be established that the judge's ability to deal properly with the issues has been compromised by the passage of time, for example if his recollection of important matters is no longer sufficiently clear or notes have been mislaid.'

A six-month delay in delivering judgment was held not to have affected the judge's findings of fact or law in *Langsam v Beachcroft LLP*.[63]

Other conduct, for example intemperate judicial behaviour if sufficiently egregious, may amount to a serious procedural irregularity.

In *The Mayor and Burgesses of the London Borough of Southwark v Kofi-Adu*[64] Jonathan Parker LJ, giving the judgment of the Court of Appeal, held:

'It is important to stress at the outset that, within the bounds set by the Civil Procedure Rules, a first instance judge is entitled to a wide degree of latitude in the way in which he conducts proceedings in his court. However, that latitude is not unlimited. Ultimately, the process must always be the servant of the judicial function of dealing with cases justly (see the overriding objective expressed in CPR 1.1).'

The Court of Appeal went on, however, to quote Lord Denning MR in *Jones v National Coal Board*[65] who, after explaining the judge is not 'a mere umpire to answer the question "How's that?"' said:

'His object, after all, is to find out the truth, and to do justice according to law; and in the daily pursuit of it the advocate plays an honourable and necessary role. Was it not Lord Eldon LC who said in a notable passage that 'truth is best discovered by powerful statements on both sides of the question'? ... And Lord Greene MR who explained that justice is best done by a judge who holds the balance between the contending parties without himself taking part in their disputations? If a judge, said Lord Greene, should himself conduct the examination of witnesses, "he, so to speak, descends into the arena and is liable to have his vision clouded by the dust of conflict".'

Concluding the manner in which the judge conducted the trial lead to a failure on his part to discharge his judicial function the Court of Appeal held:

'In the instant case we are left in no doubt that the judge's constant (and frequently contentious) interventions during the oral evidence, examples of which we have given earlier

---

[61]   [2004] 1 WLR 1689.
[62]   [1998] TLR 85.
[63]   [2012] EWCA Civ 1230.
[64]   [2006] EWCA Civ 281.
[65]   [1957] 2 QB 55.

in this judgment, served to cloud his vision and his judgment to the point where he was unable to subject the oral evidence to proper scrutiny and evaluation.'

Giving judgment *In the Matter of A (children)*[66] Aikens LJ held:

'The transcript of the hearing makes embarrassing reading and I hope that Judge Dodds will read it for himself and be ashamed of his behaviour on that particular occasion. Appointment as a judge, at whatever level, is not a license for intemperate language or for being gratuitously rude to advocates and others appearing before you. Judge Dodds' behaviour on that occasion was beyond what is permissible. It meant that there was a serious procedural irregularity. That particular hearing was not fair.'

Where a decision is held to be irregular the remission for a re-hearing is likely to be inevitable.

10.12.7.7 Fraud

Unless a decision can be appealed on the grounds it is 'wrong' or 'unjust' that decision will be final, though fraud by one of the parties will leave the judgment open to challenge.

In *Owens v Noble*[67] the Court of Appeal confirmed that even after judgment where cogent evidence suggesting fraud emerged the aggrieved party was not restricted to commencing a separate action, seeking damages for fraud, but could seek to re-open the original hearing, though in such circumstances the likelihood is that any appeal court will remit the matter for re-trial.

10.12.8   Part 36 and ADR

CPR 36.3 provides that a Part 36 offer made in the first instance proceedings will not have cost consequences in an appeal.

Accordingly, in the event of an appeal it is essential to re-assess the merits of the issue being appealed, or perhaps the case generally, and make any further appropriate Part 36 offer either to settle the claim as a whole or an issue including any specific issue arising in the appeal.

Part 36 offers made or received in the first instance proceedings need to be reviewed as the order being appealed may have a bearing on the overall merits of the case and hence whether any offer received should now be accepted or an offer which has been made withdrawn or changed. If, of course, the appeal follows a trial, permission of the court would now be required to accept any such offer under the terms of CPR 36.9(3)(d).

Although Part 36 offers prior to the appeal are largely superseded for costs purposes it would still be inappropriate to refer the appeal court to any Part 36 offers unless these relate to the substantive issues in the appeal.

---

[66]   [2015] EWCA Civ 133.
[67]   [2010] EWCA Civ 284.

In the Court of Appeal the parties are likely to be offered the assistance of the mediation scheme run specifically for such appeal cases.

10.12.9   Evidence

Parties will not be allowed to introduce new evidence where this could, and should, have been put before the lower court: *Ladd v Marshall*.[68]

10.12.10   Funding

The claimant's funding arrangements need to be reviewed, in the event of an appeal, to ensure that the costs associated with the appeal are covered or that any necessary steps to implement further funding are taken.

10.12.11   Costs

The successful party in the appeal is likely to seek the costs of the appeal and, if unsuccessful in the court below, an order for costs 'here and below'.

If the hearing does not take longer than one day the court is likely to carry out a summary assessment of costs and the parties should be ready for that.

10.12.12   Following an appeal

Following a successful appeal, against a final order, exactly the same action will be appropriate as if the claimant had succeeded both in relation to costs and consequential orders.

---

[68]   [1954] 1 WLR 1489.

CHAPTER 11

SETTLEMENT

11.1   INTRODUCTION

The Practice Direction – Pre-action Conduct and the protocols encourage the parties, from the earliest stage of a claim, to reach settlement and help to provide a framework for achieving that objective.

The CPR also encourages settlement by providing, in appropriate circumstances, potential benefits and sanctions which are likely to act as an incentive, for both claimant and defendant, to make reasonable offers to settle. Those provisions, unusually for the CPR, apply to the time before, as well as after, court proceedings are commenced.

It is, accordingly, important that practitioners keep in mind, from the outset, ways of achieving a settlement of the claim or at least reaching agreement on issues that may help save costs even if there remain matters which will have to be decided by the court.

11.1.1   Ways of achieving settlement

There are various ways the parties may seek to resolve the dispute, or narrow the issues, without needing a ruling by the court.

Any option chosen as a means of resolving the dispute, or narrowing the issues, is likely to involve the making of offers. A party may wish to make offers in a way which can carry costs and other consequences, because that may help focus the minds of all concerned on the need to engage with ADR rather than leaving matters for the court to decide.

11.1.2   Advice and instructions

The claimant should be advised, at an early stage, about the opportunities for resolving the claim, without the need for determination by the court, including the potential cost and other consequences of formal offers to settle, particularly under Part 36, whether made to or received from the defendant.

The need for that information to be provided, to all parties, is endorsed by the scope of the Directions Questionnaire, which specifically asks for confirmation such advice has been given.

Before making or accepting an offer to settle instructions must be obtained from the claimant, on the basis of clear advice about the consequences of reaching agreement, in the context of any likely decision from the court on the claim as a whole or the relevant issue.

11.1.2.1   General advice

The claimant should be warned about the potential cost implications of a formal offer, particularly under Part 36, made by the defendant, so those consequences are not a surprise as and when any such offer is made.

The claimant also needs to be advised about the opportunity for, and possible means of, ADR, so an informed decision can be reached about how best to approach settlement. Specific advice should be given about the costs and other consequences of Part 36 offers, especially when the benefits for a claimant, should judgment be at least as advantageous as the claimant's own Part 36 offer, include an 'additional amount' which, in most personal injury claims, will be a 10% uplift on all damages. That may require careful advice on the tactics and timing of offers taking account of the particular circumstances, including merits and potential value, of the individual claim.

11.1.2.2   Advice on offers received

Accordingly, whenever an offer is received the claimant should be advised:

- that acceptance of the offer is recommended; or
- that acceptance of the offer is not recommended (and the terms of any counter -offer recommended); or
- that it is not possible to advise whether or not the offer should be accepted (identifying what information, whether further evidence or clarification, will be necessary to give more definitive advice and, ideally, when that is likely to become available); and
- of any potential costs implications resulting from the offer, whether accepted or not accepted; and
- of any other relevant terms in the offer, including any time limits which apply to acceptance or the application of costs consequences.

11.1.2.3   Advice on offers made

Similarly, whenever an offer to settle is made the claimant should be reminded:

- of the terms and hence the scope of the agreement which will be reached if that offer is accepted, specifically if acceptance will conclude a final binding compromise of the claim as a whole or a particular issue; and
- of the timescale during which the offer will remain open for acceptance and, particularly with a Part 36 offer, of the need to change or withdraw that offer in the event it no longer represents an acceptable settlement; and
- of any potential costs consequences in the event of the offer being accepted and not being accepted.

11.1.2.4 *Other advice and action*

It may also be helpful, whenever an offer is made or received, to advise, or remind, the claimant that in the event of a final hearing there should be no mention to the trial judge of any offers made without prejudice.

ATE or BTE insurers should be kept advised of offers, particularly offers from the defendant which carry a risk on costs.

Counsel, particularly if acting under a conditional fee agreement, will also need to be kept advised of any negotiations taking place.

11.1.3 Objectives

Damages will usually be an integral part of personal injury and clinical negligence claims but there may be other objectives, important to the client, which need to be taken into account when formulating offers, particularly offers intended to achieve an outright settlement of the claim.

When considering settlement it is necessary to think about how the client's objectives can best be communicated to the opponent and the extent to which use should be made of the CPR, and particularly provisions which give offers potential costs and other consequences, to help achieve those objectives.

11.1.4 Good faith and mistakes

Good faith is essential when trying to negotiate settlement of the claim or reach agreement of an issue with the opponent.

Legal representatives owe duties to their respective clients but also have a duty to help the court further the overriding objective of dealing with the case justly and towards the administration of justice.

On a more practical level it is more likely the dispute can be resolved, or the issues narrowed, if there is a degree of trust, and mutual respect, in the way negotiations are conducted.

In *Ernst & Young v Butte Mining plc*[1] Walker J observed:

> '... solicitors do not owe each other duties to be friendly (so far as that goes beyond politeness) or to be chivalrous or sportsmanlike (so far as that goes beyond being fair). Nevertheless, even in the most hostile litigation (indeed especially in the most hostile litigation) solicitors must be scrupulously fair and not take unfair advantage of obvious mistakes ...'

Similarly, a party should not seek to mislead another party about negotiations, for example by indicating that if certain terms were proposed these would be accepted, and

---

[1] [1996] 1 WLR 1605.

then turning them down, or stating that a proposal is a final offer when it is known it will not to be. As Nelson J explained in *Thames Trains Ltd v Adams*:[2]

> 'A solicitor's overriding duty is to his or her client. The Solicitors Rules, which are statutory, impose a duty of good faith upon the solicitor so that he must act towards other solicitors with frankness and good faith consistent with his or her overriding duty to the client.'

Further difficulties can arise where it might be said one party has caused or allowed another party to make a mistake. Sometimes there is a duty of candour, for example *The Stolt Loyalty*.[3] Generally, however, one party to litigation is not bound to correct mistakes made by another. As the Chancellor of the High Court explained in *Bethell Construction Ltd v Deloitte and Touche*:[4]

> 'It is well established that whether or not a party is bound by an estoppel of any description depends on his own acts. Generally silence will not ground an estoppel. But if there is a duty to act or speak then a failure to do so may give rise to an estoppel. A duty to speak may arise from the circumstance that a failure to do so may render false an express statement which may be literally true ...'

There is greater scope for problems of this kind in discussions or face to face negotiations, hence the need for these to take place after proper preparation and with the appropriate authority or instructions having been obtained from the relevant party.

Where one party makes a mistake which ought to be obvious, as such, to another party that may be sufficient to prevent an agreement being reached; but in other circumstances the making of a mistake in negotiations will not preclude a binding settlement (see 11.5.7.7.7).

11.1.5   Clarity and interpretation

Care is necessary to ensure clarity whenever making, changing, withdrawing or accepting offers to settle.

Use of Part 36, when making offers to settle, is a useful shorthand for incorporating terms such as timescale for payment and provisions as to costs which otherwise need to be dealt with expressly. Part 36 operates, however, as a self-contained code: (*Gibbon v Manchester City Council*[5]). Accordingly, it is important to remember that if a party chooses to make an offer intended to have the consequences of that rule those consequences are understood: *Onay v Brown*[6]) The certainty afforded by the machinery provided for in Part 36 when making offers does, therefore, need to be seen in that context.

If a party chooses to make a non-Part 36 offer it is essential to remember, when making or considering such an offer, the need for terms, which would be imported under the scope of Part 36, to be stated expressly.

---

2   [2006] EWHC 3291 (QB).
3   [1993] 2 LlLR 281.
4   [2011] EWCA Civ 1321.
5   [2010] EWCA Civ 726.
6   [2009] EWCA Civ 775.

If the parties have not achieved the necessary degree of clarity the court may need to interpret the dealings between them to identify what, if any, terms have been agreed. If that becomes necessary the court may adopt the general approach to interpretation of contractual documents applied in *Investors Compensation Scheme Ltd v West Bromwich Building Society (No 1)*,[7] as in *C v D*.[8] If, however, the court concludes there is simply a failure to comply with the rules on form and content found in Part 36 there may be no contract to construe by applying these principles: *Shaw v Merthyr Tydfil County Borough*.[9]

Where, however, an offer makes any reference to Part 36 that may be a factor which the court takes into account if called upon to make sense of the parties' dealings: *C v D*[10] (see **11.5.5.1.1**).

11.1.6 Finality

If agreement is reached that is likely to be a binding compromise of the claim as a whole or of the relevant issue which, except where it can be set aside under the general law, will be final (see **11.7.3**).

The extent to which future claims are compromised is likely to depend upon the subject matter and scope of the dispute in which terms are reached, and the matters which are in the contemplation of the parties at the time of agreement: *Zurich Insurance Company Plc v Hayward*;[11] *Naeem v Bank of Credit & Commerce International*.[12]

Where a binding compromise is reached on the issue of liability that is very different to an admission> Thehe binding nature of any agreement reached leaves no scope for the court to set that agreement aside applying just the overriding objective or the rules relating to withdrawal of admissions: *Burden v Harrods Ltd*[13] (see **1.7.2.4.1**).

11.1.7 Costs

Agreement on costs ought to be part of any terms reached. Accordingly, where the parties seek to agree terms for the claim as a whole that will usually need to include provision for costs.

If the parties make use of Part 36 the terms of that rule will either stipulate certain costs consequences or provide guidance to the court on what will usually be the appropriate terms as to costs.

Away from Part 36 express agreement on costs will be required as part of the terms reached. Whilst the court might be willing to make a ruling on the issue of costs, when terms have otherwise been agreed, a judge may instead treat the agreement as final on the basis that, in the absence of any agreement on this issue, there is to be no order for costs (see **11.5.7.7.1**).

---

7 [1998] 1 WLR 896.
8 [2011] EWCA Civ 646.
9 [2014] EWCA Civ 1678.
10 [2011] EWCA Civ 646.
11 [2011] EWCA Civ 641.
12 [2001] UKHL 8.
13 [2005] EWHC 410 (QB).

If there have been interim costs orders it is important to remember, when negotiating, these will remain extant, under the terms of CPR 44.4(2), unless there is express provision to the contrary in the terms of any final agreement reached. It may, sometimes, be appropriate to make such provision, even if limited to an agreement such an order will not be enforced.

The potential costs of the claim are also an important consideration in efforts made towards settlement. The parties may simply, and laudably, wish to save costs by settling the claim, or at least narrowing the issues, at the earliest opportunity. Sometimes, however, one party may wish to focus the mind of the other party by making an offer which carries the potential consequence of shifting the risk, or some of the risk, on costs to that party.

the need to focus minds through potential costs consequences will be a major consideration for the offeror where the offeree is being intransigent.

A defendant who faces a claimant unwilling to negotiate reasonable terms has the opportunity, particularly under Part 36, of putting the claimant at risk on the costs incurred after an offer is made.

From the claimant's perspective the opportunity of putting the defendant at additional risk on costs may be important in a claim of modest value where, because of the way the defendant runs the case or the nature of the issues, there is the risk, if the claim ultimately succeeds, the costs incurred will be viewed as disproportionate. Hence securing an assessment of those costs on the indemnity basis, applicable where the claimant equals or betters the claimant's own Part 36 offer, may be an important objective when considering offers to settle.

If an offer is to carry potential costs consequences that offer will have to be, at the very least, admissible, so that it may be taken into account as and when the court exercises discretion as to costs in accordance with Part 44. However, the offer may well need to comply with the terms of Part 36 if it is to give the offeror a real prospect of achieving the costs consequences sought, and will certainly need to comply with that rule if the offeror wishes the costs consequences provided for to be automatic, subject to those not being 'unjust'.

11.2   ADMISSIBILITY OF OFFERS

The admissibility of offers, or other efforts to achieve settlement, at any hearing when the court determines costs is an important consideration. That is because if evidence of steps taken to settle the claim, or narrow the issues, is inadmissible any such steps cannot carry costs consequences.

A party may wish to openly narrow the issues, with a view to saving costs or showing willingness to compromise, and later be able to rely on those steps when the question of costs is considered by the court. Usually, however, a party making an offer, or approach to narrow the issues, will not want the other party to draw such steps to the attention of the court and have the opportunity of arguing these amount to an admission.

Consequently, a party making an offer will usually wish to do so in a way that can be relied upon later, if necessary, in connection with costs but cannot be used by the other party meanwhile as an admission. An offer intended to be used in this way must be put expressly on these terms, as the court will generally regard any efforts towards compromise as inadmissible.

Accordingly, when offers, or other approaches, are both made and received it is important to be clear about whether, and if so to what extent, these will be admissible on the substantive issues and/or in relation to costs.

11.2.1 Open communications

Correspondence exchanged or other dealings between the parties will, generally, be on an open basis and, as such, any party may refer the court to these.

If, however, dealings between the parties amount, in reality, to negotiations towards settlement these are likely to be treated by the court as having been made wholly 'without prejudice'. If any dealings between the parties are not expressly stated to be 'without prejudice' that does not, of itself, mean those dealings will be admissible, as what amounts to a 'without prejudice' communication depends upon substance rather than form: *Belt v Basildon & Thurrock NHS Trust*.[14]

For these reasons it is important to distinguish an offer from an admission, as illustrated by *Belt* (see **1.7.2.2**). Consequently, an admission, such as an admission of liability under the Protocol, ought to be made on an open basis, as that is simply a concession to narrow the issues, rather than an attempt at a negotiated compromise.

There may be matters a party wishes to refer to in open correspondence, even though these may amount to an admission, so there is no doubt, as and when the question of costs is dealt with, appropriate concessions or efforts had been made. A party may, similarly, wish to make an open offer though it may be wise, in such circumstances, to expressly state the correspondence is intended to be open.

In *Ali v Stagecoach*[15] the defendant sent, by open letter, a cheque, described as an interim payment, of £3,200. At trial the claimant was awarded damages of £1,750. On the basis of the letter making the interim payment the trial judge concluded he was entitled to take the defendant's letter into account as an equivalent to an offer and, as the claimant had to make a repayment to the defendant, to conclude that he was the losing party. Consequently, an adverse costs order was made against the claimant from 21 days after the date of the letter making the interim payment.

The Court of Appeal, allowing the claimant's appeal, held that the letter was not the equivalent of an offer for the purposes of Part 44 as it carried no offer as to the costs incurred up to the date of the offer and, in the words of Longmore LJ:

> 'An offer is intended to achieve finality if it is accepted. This was not an offer which was capable of being accepted and thus achieve finality.'

---

[14] [2004] EWHC 783 (QB).
[15] [2011] EWCA Civ 1494.

However, because the letter was an open letter the judge had been entitled to consider it but was wrong by giving it the weight he did. Given that, at the end of the day, the claimant had to pay the defendant money the appropriate order as to costs was that there should be no order as to the costs of the trial.

11.2.2   Without Prejudice' communications

Negotiations may expressly take place on a 'without prejudice' basis or, because that was the substance of the negotiations, treated as such by the court.

It is a long established principle that parties who negotiate on a wholly 'without prejudice' basis do so on the understanding that what is said cannot be used against them, even on the question of costs: *Walker v Wilsher*.[16]

The exclusion of 'without prejudice' negotiations is, strictly, a rule of evidence. Accordingly, unlike a right of privilege which can be waived by the party claiming that right, both parties will have to waive rights of non-disclosure in relation to 'without prejudice' negotiations for these to become admissible. The reason for this was explained by Fox LJ in *Cutts v Head*[17] when he said:

> '... whilst the ordinary meaning of 'Without prejudice' is without prejudice to the position of the offeror if his offer is refused, it is not competent to one party to impose such terms on the other in respect of a document which, by its nature, is capable of being used to the disadvantage of that other. The expression must be read as creating a situation of mutuality which enables both sides to take advantage of the 'Without prejudice' protection. The juridical basis of that must, I think in part derive from an implied agreement between the parties and in part from public policy.'

In *Reed Executive plc v Reed Business Information Ltd*[18] the Court of Appeal held that the rule in *Walker* had survived the introduction of CPR. That is because, whilst there are some exceptions to the general rule of non-admissibility of 'without prejudice' negotiations, reference to those dealings when it comes to the question of costs is not amongst those exceptions in the CPR. Consequently, the court concluded that parties could not be compelled to disclose details of 'without prejudice' negotiations, concerning use of ADR, despite the potential relevance of this to the incidence of costs.

The court also noted that whilst CPR 44.3 identifies matters to be taken into account when determining costs this rule expressly refers to an 'admissible offer', by implication assuming some offers are inadmissible.

Whilst the court recognised the significance attached to ADR in *Halsey v Milton Keynes General NHS Trust*[19] that decision was, in *Reed Executive plc*, held not to abrogate the rule in *Walker* and indeed assumed that the rule still applied. Although there was reference in *Halsey* to the court considering 'all the circumstances' it was held in *Reed Executive plc* that this should be read as meaning 'all admissible circumstances'.

---

[16]   (1889) 23 QBD 335.
[17]   [1984] 1 Ch 290.
[18]   [2004] EWCA Civ 887.
[19]   [2004] EWCA Civ 576.

Furthermore, in *Halsey*, the court had encouraged the use of directions in relation to ADR, which may require a party to justify a refusal to engage in ADR without affecting admissibility. That encouragement would not have been necessary if any party could simply rely on efforts made towards ADR, even if wholly 'without prejudice'.

The decision in *Walker* remaining good law, after the introduction of the CPR, was held not to be damaging from the point of view of encouraging ADR, given that everyone should be taken to know the rules which allow offers to be made 'without prejudice except as to costs' (see **11.2.3**).

In *Reed Executive plc* the court also held that it would not be appropriate to draw any adverse inference from one party objecting to the court reviewing details of 'without prejudice' negotiations, even though the other party would be willing for the court to do so.

Similarly, and on the same basis, it was held that an offer made at a confidential settlement conference was not admissible in *Jackson v Ministry of Defence*.[20]

It is in these circumstances that any party sending a communication will be wise to state expressly if it is intended to be 'without prejudice'. The recipient, where the status of the communication is not made clear, may wish to seek clarification whether or not such correspondence is intended to be open.

Being clear about the status of offers should help avoid arguments on admissibility at a later stage, particularly concerning costs, given that wholly without prejudice communications may not be referred to by the court even on costs, unless the parties agree.

The dangers of a recipient agreeing to potentially inadmissible material on negotiations going before the court on the issue of costs is illustrated by *French v Groupama Insurance Company Ltd*.[21] In that case the claimant agreed to the court looking at letters which were, on the basis of *Reed Executive plc*, inadmissible but used, at least at first instance, to found an adverse costs order against the claimant. Even on appeal, whilst the adverse order was set aside, the claimant did not recover costs from the defendant as a result of those offers.

The inadmissibility of 'without prejudice' communications will protect a party who might be seen as making an admission from this being utilised by the other party on the substantive issues. That does, however, preclude reliance on such efforts made towards settlement in connection with costs. Accordingly, when it is intended communications are not to be referred to at all it is appropriate for these to be on a wholly 'without prejudice' basis, but if reference may need to be made to those communications in connection with costs something more will be required.

Where the issue for the court is whether a binding compromise has been concluded even 'without prejudice' communications are admissible, as these will be the evidence

---

necessary to determine the issue before the court: *Tomlin v Standard Telephones and Cables Ltd*;[22] *RTS Flexible Systems Ltd v Molkerei Alois Müller Gmbh & Company KG (UK Productions)*.[23]

The relevant communication must, however, take place in the context of a dispute for the reasons explained by Lewison LJ in *Avonwick Holdings Ltd v Webinvest Ltd*[24] when he said, after observing there are two bases for the operation of the without prejudice rule namely public policy and contract, that:

> 'However, in order for that head of public policy to be engaged there must be a dispute. The concept of dispute is given a wide scope so that an opening shot of negotiations may fall within the policy even though the other party has not rejected the offer.'

11.2.3   Without prejudice except as to costs' communications

A party who makes efforts towards narrowing the issues or settlement may wish to refer, without wanting to run the risk of making an open admission that could be used on the substantive issues, to those efforts as and when the question of costs has to be determined by the court.

There is a useful exception to the general rule excluding wholly 'without prejudice' communications which applies when the relevant communication is expressly stated as being made 'without prejudice except as to costs': *Cutts v Head*.[25]

Accordingly, if an offer is made without prejudice but may need to be relied upon in connection with costs it is important to make clear it is sent 'without prejudice except as to costs'. Such an offer, by reference to the family law case which considered this topic, is often known as a 'Calderbank' offer.

If, however, the proposal is not expressly stated to be made 'without prejudice except as to costs' the rule in Walker will prevail as even the relevance of ADR to costs in modern litigation does not affect the long standing rule excluding admissibility of wholly 'without prejudice' negotiations: *Reed Executive plc v Reed Business Information Ltd*.[26]

A Calderbank offer, as an admissible offer, will be a factor for the court when deciding what order, if any, to make about costs, as it is specifically identified as relevant for these purposes by the terms of CPR 44.3(4)(c) which provides:

> 'The court must have regard to any payment into court or admissible offer to settle made by a party which is drawn to the court's attention and which is not an offer to which costs consequences under part 36 apply.'

There must, for these purposes, be an offer, that is something intended to achieve finality. Accordingly, a letter which made an interim payment was not an 'offer' and therefore not relevant for the purposes of CPR 44.3(4)(c).[27]

---

22   [1969] 3 All ER.
23   [2010] UKSC 14.
24   [2014] EWCA Civ 1436.
25   [1984] 2 WLR 349, applying *Calderbank v Calderbank* [1976] Fam 93.
26   [2004] EWCA Civ 887.
27   *Ali v Stagecoach* [2011] EWCA Civ 1494.

11.2.4   Part 36 offers

CPR 36.13(1) expressly provides that a Part 36 offer will be treated as having been made 'without prejudice except as to costs'. Accordingly, a party who has made a Part 36 offer can chose to waive privilege and refer the court to the offer, usually in connection with costs, except where the rule itself specifically prohibits that.

CPR 36.13(2) prohibits communication of the fact a Part 36 offer has been made at all, let alone the amount, to the trial judge or any judge allocated in advance to conduct the trial unless and until:

- the case has been decided;
- proceedings have been stayed under CPR 36.11 following acceptance of a Part 36 offer; or
- the offeror and offeree agree in writing otherwise.

The terms of this rule present particular difficulties where the court tries a preliminary issue, such as liability. The reference in the rule to the 'trial judge', and the prohibition on communication of information 'until the case has been decided', has been interpreted to mean that even Part 36 offers just on the issue tried must not be disclosed to the court. Hence it may be impossible for the court to decide costs following determination of issues at a preliminary trial, at least if any Part 36 offers have been made: *AB v CD*;[28] *Ted Baker plc v Axa Insurance UK plc*;[29] *Beasley v Alexander*[30]

Where no Part 36 offers have been made the rule does not prevent that fact being communicated to the court. In *Ted Baker plc v Axa Insurance UK plc*[31] the judge observed that would lead to an inference, where no such information was given to the court, there had been a Part 36 offer (which would undermine the prohibition in the rule). However, in *Beasley v Alexander*[32] the parties accepted it was reasonable and appropriate for the court to be told when there had not been any Part 36 offers, because in the absence of any such offers there was unlikely to be any basis for the party against whom an adverse costs order would be made objecting to the court dealing with costs there and then.

CPR 36.13(2) does not prevent a judge, other than the trial judge, dealing with a procedural matter being referred to a relevant Part 36 offer by the offeror, nor even the judge trying a preliminary issue being referred to an offer made 'without prejudice except as to cost' by the offeror. Consequently, if reference to an offer may be necessary at the conclusion of a preliminary trial it may be necessary, whether or not a Part 36 offer is made, for the offeror to make a non-Part 36 offer which may be in the same terms as a Part 36 offer (though such an offer may not carry the same costs consequences as a Part 36 offer and hence may not be an adequate substitute for these purposes).

Similarly, CPR 52.12(1) prohibits disclosure of the fact a Part 36 offer has been made to the judge of an appeal court determining an application for permission to appeal or an

---

[28]   [2011] EWHC 602.
[29]   [2012] EWHC 1779.
[30]   [2012] EWHC 2715 (QB).
[31]   [2012] EWHC 1779.
[32]   [2012] EWHC 2715 (QB).

appeal until all questions other than costs have been determined, except where the Part 36 offer is relevant to the substance of the appeal.

Despite the terms of CPR 36.13(1) it may still be safest to expressly state on any correspondence containing a Part 36 offer that this is made 'without prejudice except as to costs'. That will avoid any difficulties on admissibility if there are arguments about whether the offer is a Part 36 offer, and thus covered by the terms of CPR 36.13(1).

11.2.5   Tactics on admissibility

Care is necessary when making offers: that, when this is intended, any such offer is expressly stated to be 'without prejudice; that any offer which is intended to be a Part 36 offer complies with the terms of that rule on form and content; and that offers made outside Part 36, which may need to be referred to in relation to costs, are expressly made 'without prejudice except as to costs'.

Care is also necessary on the part of the offeree particularly if the status of the offer, so far as admissibility is concerned, has not been made clear. In such circumstances it may be necessary to clarify the nature of the offer, to limit the opponent's opportunity of later seeking to capitalise on any ambiguity.

- If a proposal is simply made 'without prejudice' that will generally be clear enough unless, for example, the proposal is really an admission which ought to be made on an open basis, for example on liability under the Protocol.

- If the proposal has ostensibly been made openly, but the substance would appear to be 'without prejudice', it may well be appropriate to clarify whether the maker views that proposal as being wholly 'without prejudice', so that the opponent is not able to argue later that negotiations which truly are 'without prejudice' should be produced to the court in connection with costs.

11.3   ALTERNATIVE DISPUTE RESOLUTION ('ADR')

ADR is defined in the glossary to the CPR, and paragraph 3.1(3) of the Practice Direction – Pre-action Conduct, as the 'collective description of methods of resolving disputes otherwise than through the normal trial process'.

Methods of ADR available to the parties, as confirmed by paragraph 8.2 of the Practice Direction – Pre-action Conduct, include:
- negotiation;
- early neutral evaluation;
- arbitration; and
- mediation.

ADR, by any of these means, should be considered from the earliest opportunity, so that resolution of matters by the court is very much a last resort.

In personal injury claims the methods of ADR most likely to be adopted will be negotiation (whether by correspondence, telephone conversation or meeting) and, from time to time, mediation.

Where the defendant is a public body it is worth noting that the Government gave, on 23 March 2001, a pledge to engage in ADR. All public bodies, including NHS Trusts, should be covered by the scope of that pledge.

11.3.1 Negotiation

Most claims are ultimately resolved through the negotiation process. A negotiated settlement has the advantage of achieving what all parties are likely to regard as being an acceptable outcome.

Negotiation has been recognised by the court, reflecting the terms of the CPR, as a form of ADR: *Corenso (UK) Ltd v D Burnden Group plc*.[33] Accordingly, entry into negotiations should meet the obligation on the parties to embrace ADR.

Negotiation may take place in a number of different ways. The method of negotiation may depend upon the stage of the claim reached as well as the wishes, and to some extent tactics adopted, of the parties.

11.3.1.1 Correspondence

The parties may exchange offers in correspondence, and certainly will need to do so if the offers are intended to be relied upon for costs purposes, whether under Part 36 or Part 44.

Negotiations will often take place by correspondence during the earlier stages of a case, when the parties are defining the parameters of the dispute.

Written offers, as well as being effective for cost purposes if drafted correctly, have the advantage of clarity.

11.3.1.2 Discussions

Discussions, perhaps over the telephone, may often follow the exchange of written offers. Sometimes, however, the parties may wish to have a discussion at the outset.

Such a discussion can be useful for sounding out the opponent, to see what prospect there is of negotiations taking place at all, or with a view to seeing if any gap between the positions taken by the parties in correspondence can readily be bridged.

Care is always necessary before engaging in discussions, especially at an early stage before each party has a full understanding of the other's position, as there is a risk of making, or being drawn into, unguarded comments which may prove damaging.

If a party wishes that an offer made orally should carry potential cost consequences it will be necessary for that offer to be repeated in writing.

---

[33] [2003] EWHC 1805 (QB).

11.3.1.3   Joint settlement meeting

A formal meeting, convened for the purpose of trying to achieve a settlement, can be a very effective method of negotiation as it will focus the minds of all concerned on settlement.

Careful planning is appropriate so far as the timing, venue and format of the meeting are concerned, as well as giving thought to tactical considerations.

11.3.1.3.1   Timing

A joint settlement meeting will typically take place at a relatively late stage in the claim, often as the trial date is approaching.

Whilst there is much to be said for convening a meeting at the earliest opportunity, to save costs, it is usually necessary, if the meeting is to have a realistic prospect of resulting in a settlement, for the case to be significantly advanced so that each party knows both the strengths and weaknesses of the party' own case and the case of the opponent.

It will be also be not unusual for the parties to have exchanged offers at an earlier stage, and where negotiation by those means is capable of achieving a settlement it will have done so. Where offers have been exchanged there is some sense in exploring the prospect of settlement by further exchange of offers, any meeting being timed for the stage at which each party is aware of the gap that still needs to be bridged if a settlement is to be reached.

11.3.1.3.2   Venue

The venue for the meeting will often be the office of the claimant's solicitors or chambers of counsel for the claimant.

The location for the meeting needs to have appropriate facilities, comprising a room for the use of each party together with a separate room where the parties can meet for the purpose of negotiations.

Joint settlement meetings can take time so it is also helpful for any venue to have facilities for refreshments to be provided.

11.3.1.3.3   Documents

It is helpful if, by the time of the meeting, there is, in effect, a trial bundle available, so that all parties are working from the same documentation.

11.3.1.3.4   Role of the claimant

The claimant may wish to be at the settlement conference and certainly will need to be available to give instructions by telephone.

Beyond giving instructions thought needs to be given about the extent to which the claimant will play an active role. It is helpful for many claimants to feel in control of the process but, equally, it is important to guard against giving the defendant an advance opportunity to cross-examine, even if done informally.

11.3.1.3.5   Preliminaries

When agreeing to a joint settlement meeting there are some preliminary points which it may be worth agreeing with the defendant. These might be some or all of the following.

- Commitment by the parties to move from any previous offer or stance towards the position of the other.
- The meeting will be on a wholly without prejudice basis.
- The scope of the issues to be negotiated, whether this be a particular issue such as liability, the claim as a whole or both.
- Agreement that any offers made should be held open for a specified, if short, period of time after the meeting for consideration (for example the end of the next working day.
- If there any pre-conditions in relation to costs, such as any agreement to settle the whole claim being on the basis that the claimant's costs will be met by the defendant.
- Confirmation, unless otherwise appropriate, the meeting will deal only with the substantive issues, and not extend to negotiations about the amount of costs or, indeed, involving any costs inclusive offers.
- Agreement, in principle, for a payment on account of the claimant's costs if settlement is reached.
- Confirmation those attending will have, or will be in a position to obtain, authority to settle the claim or agree relevant issues.

11.3.1.3.6   Agreement

If agreement is reached that should be recorded in writing, by a consent court order if proceedings have been commenced.

It may be helpful to have a draft order ready for use, which deals with all the issues that will need to be covered.

11.3.1.4   Costs

The costs of negotiations, in whatever form, should be treated as part of the costs of the claim.

11.3.2   Early neutral evaluation

This method of ADR, like mediation, involves a neutral third party who, rather than simply facilitating negotiations, will deliver an evaluation, usually non-binding, of the merits on the stance of each party.

If the outcome of the claim depends upon, for example, a matter of expert opinion a neutral expert could adopt the role of evaluator but, generally, this form of ADR is not used in personal injury claims.

If it is proposed there be ADR by early neutral evaluation it will be important to agree suitable terms. These may include some or all of the following:

- who pays for the evaluation (and whether the cost is treated as part of the costs of the claim).

- who will do the evaluation.

- the extent to which the parties will set out their respective cases in Statements of Case (or drafts) and will support this by factual and expert evidence and documents.

- whether either or both parties will be bound by the evaluation (or not as the case may be).

- whether the evaluation is just on the substantive claim or will include any issues relating to costs (if these will effectively follow the outcome).

11.3.3   Arbitration

This method of ADR also involves a neutral third party, but acting as an arbitrator with authority to decide issues in a way that will bind the parties.

Arbitration is not a common form of ADR in personal injury claims, being more suited to commercial disputes.

Agreement of terms by the parties for an arbitration, which may involve very similar considerations to those preceding any early neutral evaluation, will be important, including terms as to costs of the arbitration and whether that will be treated as part of the costs of the claim which then follow the event.

11.3.4   Mediation

A neutral mediator may help facilitate negotiations, even without that role involving any evaluation of the strength of each party's case let alone authority to make decisions which will bind those parties.

Occasionally mediation might, in a personal injury claim, be a useful way of getting negotiations under way, or finalised, if one party or other is reluctant to do so and the input of a mediator might act as a catalyst.

Mediation can be particularly helpful if negotiations have stalled or one party is unwilling to engage in negotiation at all. The courts have consistently recognised the advantages of mediation in these circumstances.

In *Burchell v Bullard*[34] Ward LJ stated that:

> 'The defendants behaved unreasonably in believing, if they did, that their case was so watertight that they need not engage in attempts to settle.'

In *Daniels v The Commissioner of Police of the Metropolis*[35] Ward LJ added that:

---

[34]   [2005] EWCA Civ 358.
[35]   [2006] EWCA 1622 (QB).

'Mediation) does have an extraordinary knack of producing compromise, even where the parties appear, at the start, to be intractably opposed.'

Ward LJ subsequently endorsed, in very strong terms, the need for parties to consider mediation in appropriate cases when in *Egan v Motor Services (Bath) Ltd*[36] he said:

'Mediation can do more for the parties than negotiation... It is not a sign of weakness to suggest. It is a hallmark of commonsense. Mediation is a perfectly proper adjunct to litigation. The skills are now well developed. The results are astonishingly good. Try it more often.'

Ward LJ emphasised all these points when observing in *Ghaith v Indesit Co UK Ltd*[37] that:

'The opening bids in a mediation are likely to remain as belligerently far apart as they were in correspondence but no one should underestimate the new dynamic that an experienced mediator brings to the round table. He has a canny knack of transforming the intractable into the possible. That is the art of good mediation and that is why mediation should not be spurned when it is offered.'

Although in the specific context of a neighbour dispute, both Ward LJ and Jackson LJ again endorsed the advantages of mediation in *Faidi v Elliot Corporation*.[38] Ward LJ observed:

'Not all neighbours are from hell. They may simply occupy the land of bigotry. There may be no escape from hell but the boundaries of bigotry can with tact be changed by the cutting edge of reasonableness skilfully applied by a trained mediator. Give and take is often better than all or nothing.'

Jackson LJ, in relation to the huge costs incurred by taking this case to the Court of Appeal, commented:

'If the parties were driven by concern for the well being of lawyers, they could have given half that sum to the Solicitors Benevolent Association and then resolved their dispute for a modest fraction of the monies left over.'

Sir Alan Ward, as he had now become, also had observations about the importance of mediation, including cases involving litigants in person, in *Wright v Michael Wright (Supplies) Ltd*[39] when after noting that it had not been possible 'to shift intransigent parties off the trial track onto the parallel track of mediation', that:

'Both tracks are intended to meet the modern day demands of civil justice. The *raison d'être* (or do I simply mean excuse?) of the Ministry of Justice for withdrawing legal aid from swathes of litigation is that mediation is a proper alternative which should be tried and exhausted before finally resorting to a trial of the issues. I heartily agree with the aspiration and there are many judgments of mine saying so. But the rationale remains a pious hope when parties are unwilling even to try mediation.'

---

[36] [2007] EWCA Civ 1002.
[37] [2012] EWCA Civ 642.
[38] [2012] EWCA Civ 287.
[39] [2013] EWCA Civ 234.

It is notable that the Court of Appeal has a dedicated mediation service available to help parties resolve appeals that might otherwise have to be heard.

Many of the same practical considerations apply to a mediation as they do to a joint settlement meeting.

The costs of a mediation may, like costs of negotiation, be treated as part of the costs of the claim and hence be recoverable by the party in whose favour a costs order is ultimately made even where a mediation takes place, as part of efforts to comply with a pre-action protocol, prior to issue of court proceedings: *Roundstone Nurseries Ltd v Stephenson Holdings Ltd*.[40] It is preferable, however, that where additional costs of involving a mediator are to be incurred the parties expressly agree, if this be the case, the cost will be treated as part of the costs of the claim.

11.3.5 Costs sanctions

ADR is concerned with achieving a resolution of the claim rather than, necessarily, focusing the mind of the opponent through potential costs sanctions. The latter will require offers for the purposes of Part 36 or Part 44.

Accordingly, offers made in the course of oral negotiations or a mediation should be repeated, as a formal offer made for the purposes of Part 36 or Part 44, if a party wishes to stand by that offer and for it to carry potential costs consequences.

Care will be necessary to ensure it is possible to identify whether or not any subsequent judgment is more advantageous, or at least as advantageous, as the terms of that offer.

Where a party fails to engage in ADR and is, in a sense, later vindicated by obtaining judgment costs sanctions may, nevertheless, apply (see **12.2.4.1**).

11.4 TACTICS

Tactics inevitably play a part in selecting the appropriate method and means of ADR at any particular stage of the case.

Tactics may also dictate which party initiates ADR.

Appropriate tactics, for the particular case, are likely to be influenced by events in the particular case, as it develops, but some considerations will be of general application when considering tactics with ADR.

11.4.1 General tactics

Both parties ought to be considering, from the outset, how a settlement may be facilitated. However, in most personal injury and clinical negligence claims it is reasonable to expect, once sufficient information has been given by the claimant, that

---

[40] [2009] EWHC 1431 (TCC).

the defendant will put forward some proposals, certainly if the defendant is, ultimately, likely to be found liable to pay damages to the claimant.

This view is endorsed by the terms of the PI Protocol which, where liability has been admitted and the claimant thus disclosed details on quantum, effectively requires an opening offer from the defendant (see **1.7.2.1**).

Judicial support for this approach can be found, for example, in *Day* v *Day*[41] where Ward LJ observed:

> 'In my judgment the valuable use of payments into Court and Part 36 offers to settle place an onus, in the first place, on the defendant.'

Similarly, in *Hall* v *Stone*[42] Waller LJ observed:

> '... both parties could have made realistic Part 36 offers 'without prejudice as to costs' but the greater responsibility for failing to do so falls on the defendant's insurers.'

That is so even if the defendant considers the claimant is exaggerating. In *Widlake v BAA Ltd*[43] Ward LJ noted:

> 'Defendants are, therefore, used to having to cope with false or exaggerated claims. Defendants have a means of protecting themselves. Part 36 is that shield.'

Any opening proposals may be for outright settlement of the claim though, where that is not possible, offers to narrow the issues, for example on liability, might be expected.

Both the RTA Protocol and the EL/PL Protocol, exceptionally, do require an opening offer from the claimant as part of the settlement pack (see **1.14.4.7.6**).

A party may prefer to establish whether the other party is, whatever the formal stance on the issues, willing to engage in ADR and, if so, what terms are thought appropriate before committing to any offers. There may also be some advantage in establishing what the opponent is proposing before committing to an offer.

Conversely, there may be advantages in 'anchoring' the negotiations by an opening bid, as that may help to set the parameters for any subsequent negotiations.

Moreover, the benefits specifically conferred on a claimant, who obtains judgment in terms at least as advantageous as the claimant's own offer, may, in a number of circumstances, encourage the claimant to engage in ADR by making Part 36 offers whatever the stance of the defendant. As Hildyard J observed in *The Procter & Gamble Company v Svenska Cellulosa Aktiebolaget SCA* :[44]

> 'Thus, CPR 36.10 and 36.14 are carefully crafted particularly to incentivise a claimant to make a Part 36 offer. It seems that the rationale for this is that whereas a claimant in a money claim can ordinarily expect to recover his costs if he succeeds to any material extent, and so

---

41 [2006] EWCA Civ 415.
42 [2007] EWCA Civ 1354.
43 [2009] EWCA Civ 1256.
44 [2012] EWHC 2839 (Ch).

needs to be specially incentivised to make an offer, a defendant plainly has every incentive already, being to stop the claimant incurring more of the costs for which if the defendant loses he is likely to be required to pay: and see *per* Simon Brown LJ in *Victor Kermit Kiam II v MGN Ltd* [2002] EWCA Civ 66 at paragraph 8.'

11.4.2   Should the claimant make an opening offer?

If no opening proposals are made by the defendant the claimant may wish to put forward proposals at an early stage, and certainly before court proceedings are issued. Such proposals may result in agreement being reached, but if not show willingness on the part of the claimant to try and resolve matters. That should also act as an encouragement to the defendant in trying to find a way of resolving the claim.

In some circumstances any opening offer by the claimant might be for outright settlement of the whole claim but it may be more appropriate to make an offer on liability only.

11.4.2.1   *The whole claim?*

If the claimant expects to succeed in the claim the defendant may well be expected to open negotiations, as that gives the claimant the advantage of seeing what value the defendant puts on the claim as a whole or a relevant issue.

There can be dangers in making early offers to settle the whole claim, particularly when the claim may be substantial but cannot yet be accurately valued. In these circumstances the potential advantages to the claimant under Part 36 may not outweigh the risks of making such an offer although there may, of course, be other good reasons to try and achieve a settlement of the whole claim at an early stage.

Although there are some disadvantages in the claimant making an opening offer, it may important, particularly if the claim is of relatively modest value, for it to be made clear to the defendant, before further significant costs are involved, the claim would not be expensive to settle at that stage.

If the defendant declines to make any proposals that suggests further work is likely to be proportionate to the issues and importance of the case, even if less so to the value.

Moreover, if the claimant succeeds, and obtains judgment at least as advantageous as the claimant's own Part 36 offer, the costs consequences provided for in the rule should result in the claimant having costs assessed on the indemnity basis. To the extent costs are assessed on the indemnity basis they do not have to be proportionate, often a crucial consideration in the recovery of proper costs in a claim of modest value.

11.4.2.2   *Liability?*

An offer on the issue of liability by the claimant ought to be at least considered in every case where primary liability is not admitted.

For the claimant to get maximum potential benefit the need for such an offer should be considered at the stage of a decision on liability under the Protocol and certainly before court proceedings are issued.

Most defended cases carry at least some litigation risk to the claimant so that a nominal discount on the issue of liability, such as the 5% offered by the claimant in *Huck v Robson*,[45] can quite properly been recommended once it is known liability is in dispute. At that stage the claimant, whilst able to make such an offer on liability, may not have the information necessary to make an offer to settle the whole claim, or at least an offer which puts the defendant at significant risk.

If a claim is defended in circumstances where there cannot really be said to be any litigation risk to the claimant, rather the defendant is just being intransigent on the issue of liability, it may be more appropriate for the claimant to warn of the possible costs consequences under Part 44. However, it is important to be mindful that an order for indemnity costs under Part 44 will not follow unless there has been something out of the ordinary. Consequently, to recover costs assessed on the indemnity basis the claimant will usually need to make a Part 36 offer and obtain judgment at least as advantageous as that offer.

If a trial has involved the issue of liability, even though both liability and quantum have to be determined, the approach in *Huck* ought to apply and the claimant secure the benefits conferred by CPR 36.14 if a judgment is obtained, even though the only relevant offer from the claimant concerns liability: *Black* v *Doncaster & Bassetlaw Hospitals NHS Foundation Trust*.[46]

11.4.3   Counter offers?

The need to engage with ADR will normally require the party receiving an offer to make a response, ideally by a counter offer. Hence the observation of Longmore LJ in *Painting v University of Oxford*[47] that:

> '... it is relevant that Mrs Painting herself made no attempt to negotiate, made no offer of her own and made no response to the offers of the University. That would not have mattered in pre-CPR days but, to my mind, that now matters very much. Negotiation is supposed to be a two–way street, and a claimant who makes no attempt to negotiate can expect, and should expect, the Courts to take that into account when making the appropriate order as to costs.'

On the same theme Smith LJ in *Hall v Stone*[48] observed:

> 'In these days where both sides are expected to conduct themselves in a reasonable way and to seek agreement where possible, it may be right to penalise a party to some degree for failing to accept a reasonable offer or for failing to come back with a counter offer.'

Similarly, after endorsing the need for a defendant to make a Part 36 offer to gain greater security of costs protection, in *Widlake v BAA Ltd*[49] Ward LJ went on to conclude:

---

45   [2002] EWCA Civ 398.
46   (Unreported) Sheffield County Court, 20 April 2009.
47   [2005] EWCA Civ 161.
48   [2007] EWCA Civ 1354.
49   [2009] EWCA Civ 1256.

'Part 36 now also affects a claimant. Whilst not obliged to make a counter -offer, in this day and age of encouraging settlement, claimants who do not do so run the risk that their refusal will impact upon the costs they may otherwise be entitled to recover.'

Although in those cases the court was concerned with the failure of the claimant to enter negotiations the same approach could be adopted, in appropriate circumstances, to a defendant. To suffer costs penalties, however, a successful defendant will need to have been unreasonable by refusing to engage in ADR: *Halsey v Milton Keynes*;[50] and *PGF II SA v OMFS Company 1 Ltd*.[51]

The failure to engage in ADR may sometimes be relevant in determining whether the outcome is 'more advantageous' than a Part 36 offer, and may explain how the outcome in *Carver v BAA Plc*[52] contrasted with the costs orders in both *Morgan v UPS*[53] and *Fox v Foundation Piling Ltd*.[54] Since the introduction of CPR 36.14(1A) this factor, certainly when dealing with monetary offers, may not be a relevant consideration.

The claimant may not, however, be able to make a realistic counter -offer, at least to settle the whole claim. In those circumstances the same caution should be exercised when considering a counter -offer as it would be when deciding whether to make an opening offer of outright settlement.

The court will be reluctant to speculate, when considering costs, about what would have happened if offers which were not made had in fact been made. Hence, in *Straker v Tudor Rose*,[55] Waller LJ observed:

'In my view it does not come well from a defendant who has paid money into Court to argue that if a claimant had been more reasonable he would have offered more. An investigation as to how negotiations would have gone is precisely the form of investigation which should be avoided. In a case about money a defendant has the remedy in his own hands where a claimant is being intransigent. He can pay into Court the maximum sum he is prepared to pay.'

Similarly in *Sonmez v Kebabery Wholesale Ltd*[56] the claimant, who maintained there should be no deduction for contributory negligence in the face of an offer of 75% on liability for the defendant, was not penalised for failing to make a counter offer when judgment was entered for 80% on liability, although this was 'not without hesitation' on the part of the Court of Appeal. The court adopted, essentially, the approach taken in *Straker*; that the defendant has the means to obtain protection from costs against an intransigent claimant by making an adequate offer.

11.4.4   Best offer?

A decision needs to be made, whether this is an opening offer or counter -offer, if the claimant should start with the best offer which will be made or open with an offer which leaves scope for further negotiation.

---

[50]   [2004] EWCA Civ 576.
[51]   [2013] EWCA Civ 1288.
[52]   [2008] EWCA Civ 412.
[53]   [2008] EWCA Civ 1476.
[54]   [2011] EWCA Civ 790.
[55]   [2007] EWCA Civ 368.
[56]   [2009] EWCA Civ 1386.

Usually it is to be expected the parties will start at, or towards, the best position of that party so that further negotiation is likely to take place.

Sometimes, however, there is scope for making a 'once and for all' offer and that should normally be accepted at face value. Indeed, cases such as *Straker v Tudor Rose*[57] suggest it is reasonable for a party to assume an offer made by the opponent is the best offer that will be made, as otherwise the court ends up speculating about what would have happened if further offers, which were not in fact made, had been put forward.

In a case of modest value there is a lot to be said for the claimant making the best offer at an early stage, even if not straightaway. That is because, with less at stake, it is all the more important to avoid issues on proportionality by obtaining an order for indemnity costs which will be unlikely unless an appropriate Part 36 offer has been made.

With, however, increasing focus on ADR the courts may not look kindly on a party who makes a final offer and then refuses to engage in ADR, even when the offer is made under Part 36. That is because offers, including Part 36 offers, will often not be a reflection of the valuation on the claim made by the party, not least when the offer is made on behalf of a defendant. As Briggs LJ observed in *PGF II SA v OMFS Company 1 Ltd*:[58]

> '... it is in my view simply wrong to regard a Part 36 offer, without any supporting explanation for its basis, as a living demonstration of a party's belief in the strength of its case. As I have said, defendants' Part 36 offers are frequently made at a level below that which the defendant fears having to pay at trial, in the hope that the claimant's appetite for, or ability to undertake, costs risk will encourage it to settle for less than its claim is worth. 46. Nor do Part 36 offers necessarily or even usually represent the parties' respective bottom lines.'

11.4.5 Extension of time?

If a party receives an offer when inadequate information is available to properly assess that offer the decision in *Matthews v Metal Improvements Co Inc*[59] suggests the appropriate step is to explain the situation and ask that time for acceptance of the offer, and if a Part 36 offer the 'relevant period', be extended. If such a request is made, and refused, that may be relevant in determining whether it is just that the usual adverse costs consequences should follow in the event of subsequent late acceptance of that offer by the offeree.

That approach was effectively endorsed in Lumb v Hampsey[60] though, as the facts of that case illustrate, there may sometimes be a danger highlighting a potential weakness of the claimant's position given the ability of the defendant to simply withdraw an offer to settle.

---

57   [2007] EWCA Civ 368.
58   [2013] EWCA Civ 1288.
59   [2007] EWCA Civ 215.
60   [2011] EWHC 2808 (QB).

It is not, however, essential to seek an extension of time if, in all the circumstances, it would be unjust for the cost consequences provided for in Part 36 to follow: *SG v Hewitt*.[61]

11.4.6   Clarification?

A request for clarification, as well as providing helpful information to assist in understanding the offer may bring, at least if the offer is made under Part 36 and the clarification is reasonably required, additional time, until that clarification is provided, before costs consequences will apply: *Colour Quest Ltd v Total Downstream UK plc*.[62]

Away from Part 36 there is no formal rule providing for clarification of offers but, equally, no specific costs consequences of the kind provided for under Part 36. Even so a request for clarification may be relevant to the exercise of discretion on costs under Part 44 including, importantly, whether it was reasonable to expect any time-limited offer should have been accepted within the stipulated period and hence be of significance to costs subsequently incurred: *Trustees of Stokes Pension Fund v Western Power Distribution (South West) plc*.[63]

11.4.7   Use of Part 36 or Part 44?

There are some tactical considerations which may influence the decision whether an offer is made under Part 36, with the potential to carry the cost consequences found in that rule, or made as an 'admissible offer to settle', without the specific costs consequences of Part 36 but relevant to the exercise of the court's general discretion on costs under Part 44.

If a claim is being dealt with under the RTA Protocol an offer which is to carry consequences on costs in stage 3 must be made under Section II of Part 36, but otherwise, as CPR 36.1(2) confirms:

> 'Nothing in this Section prevents a party making an offer to settle in whatever way he chooses, but if the offer is not made in accordance with rule 36.2, it will not have the consequences specified in rules 36.10, 36.11 and 36.14.'

The costs consequences of Part 36 may be more significant for the claimant, and hence influence the decision to make use of Part 36, than the defendant.

11.4.7.1   By the defendant

For a defendant the principal differences between the costs consequences under CPR 36.14(2) and Part 44 are that if the claimant fails to obtain judgment at least as advantageous as a Part 36 offer by the defendant:

- there is a presumption the costs consequences of CPR 36.14(2), that the defendant is entitled to costs from the date the relevant period in the offer expired, will apply unless that would be 'unjust'; and

---

61   [2012] EWCA Civ 1053.
62   [2009] EWHC 823 (Comm).
63   [2005] EWCA Civ 854.

- the defendant is entitled to interest on those costs, again unless that would be 'unjust'.

Under Part 44, where the claimant fails to better an offer made by the defendant, the court must to have regard to all the circumstances, not simply whether it would be 'unjust' for the claimant to pay the defendant's costs after the offer, when deciding what order to make as to costs: *Widlake v BAA Ltd;*[64] *Fox v Foundation Piling Ltd,*[65] *Saigol v Thorney Ltd,*[66] *Coward v Phaestos Ltd.*[67]

When making a Part 36 offer it is important the defendant recognises that should the offer be accepted within the relevant period CPR 36.10(1) will apply, namely that the defendant will pay the claimant's costs. Indeed, where a Part 36 offer is accepted after the relevant period there is, in effect, a presumption the defendant will pay the claimant's costs up to the expiry of the relevant period even if there is also a presumption the claimant will pay the defendant's costs thereafter. Whilst the Court has a discretion this should mean, even with late acceptance, the claimant recovering costs, without exercise of the discretion under Part 44 to make a partial costs order: *Jopling v Leavesley.*[68]

Nevertheless, it is only Part 36 that will give the defendant a degree of certainty of the costs consequences in the event the claimant fails to obtain a judgment more advantageous than the terms of the defendant's offer. That is the benefit the defendant secures, by making use of Part 36, in return for the potential burden of costs consequences in the event of acceptance. There are, even so, some circumstances in which the court may look more sympathetically on a non-Part 36 offer by the defendant so far as costs consequences are concerned (see **12.2.2.2**).

11.4.7.2 By the claimant

For the claimant CPR 36.10 is a useful provision as it avoids the need to spell out the costs consequences which will follow if the offer is accepted. If an offer is not made under Part 36 it will be necessary for the costs consequences to be expressly provided for.

For the claimant the distinction between the costs consequences of CPR 36.14(3) and Part 44 is likely to be significant.

That is because CPR 36.14(3) provides that where judgment against the defendant is at least as advantageous to the claimant as the claimant's own Part 36 offer then, unless this would be 'unjust', the claimant is entitled, after the expiry of the relevant period in the offer, to indemnity costs and enhanced interest on both those costs and damages as well as an additional amount.

Under Part 44, however, the award of indemnity costs will usually be regarded as a penalty, hence it will be necessary for the claimant to show that the defendant has acted

---

[64] [2009] EWCA Civ 1256.
[65] [2011] EWCA Civ 790.
[66] [2014] EWCA Civ 556.
[67] [2014] EWCA Civ 1256.
[68] CA (Civ Div) 24/07/2013.

unreasonably in a way that takes the case out of the norm: *F & C Alternative Investments (Holdings) Ltd v Barthelemy*[69] (see **12.2.6**).

Similarly, the court has a discretion on awarding interest but is unlikely, simply because the defendant has failed to accept an offer, to allow enhanced interest.

Furthermore, there is no basis for an 'additional amount', whether damages or costs, to be allowed away from Part 36.

Consequently, for the claimant, tactics may dictate the use of Part 36 unless the offer needs to be time limited, and in particular open for less than 21 days, and is made with a focus on settlement rather than potential costs consequences. In these circumstances the claimant may be best advised to forego the potential benefits of a Part 36 offer because these are outweighed by the potential advantages of achieving a settlement of the claim by use of an offer containing a short time limit. Such an offer may, of course, be expressed to expire within the relevant period of a Part 36 offer made by the defendant, forcing a decision from the defendant on the claimant's offer before the claimant is required to make a decision on the defendant's offer.

Mindful of the difference in costs consequences, particularly for the claimant, practical considerations, which may dictate tactics on the format of the offer, are whether the offeror is content for the costs consequences, particularly those found in CPR 36.10, to apply and, significantly, whether the offeror is willing to keep the offer open, at least until it is expressly withdrawn or changed, or wishes to make a time limited offer, as an offer may be made under Part 36 or may be time limited but cannot be both: *C v D*.[70]

Consequently, there may be occasions when the claimant will wish to forego the potential benefits of a Part 36 on costs because those are outweighed by the need for a Part 36 offer to have a period of at least 21 days when it remains open for acceptance or because a Part 36 offer will have to be expressly withdrawn or changed even after that 21 days.

11.4.8   Agreeing issues?

The making of offers to settle will often be dictated by tactics concerned with the need to gain some protection on costs, for the claimant especially in cases of modest value, and hence focus the mind of the opponent on the need to achieve settlement or agreement of an issue.

In some circumstances, however, tactics will be governed by the wish to achieve agreement, and hence a binding compromise, of the case as a whole or on a particular issue.

---

[69]   [2012] EWCA Civ 843.
[70]   [2011] EWCA Civ 646.

11.4.8.1 *Liability*

In a case where there is a real dispute on primary liability there are advantages to the claimant in reaching agreement on that issue as that will remove the risk of losing outright, and having to factor that risk into negotiations for settlement of the claim as a whole.

Where the only issue is contributory negligence there is much less pressure on the claimant to agree the issue of liability, even where a Part 36 offer has been made on that issue, as there is no risk of the claim failing altogether. Obviously, there are advantages in reaching agreement if a good deal can be struck on the proper apportionment to reflect contributory negligence. However, it is important to remember, in a case where there is no or little risk on primary liability, that commitment to a particular apportionment will then inevitably impact on negotiations concerning quantum.

Hence, if the claimant should succeed on primary liability, but perhaps with a discount to reflect contributory negligence, the claimant may be better to hold back from agreeing the issue so as to keep this open for negotiation unless the offer is sufficiently attractive, compared with the likely outcome on this issue, so that it is better for it to be agreed there and then.

If there are arguments on contributory negligence in a case where there is also a genuine dispute on primary liability, the claimant is likely to be in a better position for future negotiations on quantum if the issue of liability is resolved, as it is then no longer becomes necessary to factor in the risk of outright loss on top of any factor to reflect the risk of an apportionment reflecting contributory negligence.

Even when the defendant has made a Part 36 offer on liability there is often no significant costs risk, unless the case is going to trial of liability as a preliminary issue, as the key consideration on whether any judgment is 'more advantageous' will be whether the claimant ultimately recovers more than the damages offered (though there may be some risk on the costs of liability only if the court makes a finding on liability which is not more advantageous to the claimant than the defendant's offer on that issue).

11.4.8.2 *Damages for pain, suffering and loss of amenity*

It is very important to remember that the term 'damages for pain, suffering and loss of amenity' is not synonymous with the term 'general damages'. That is because general damages include not only damages for pain, suffering and loss of amenity but other heads of claim, such as loss of congenial employment, as well as all future losses and expenses. Accordingly, precision when exchanging offers is critical.

Situations in which agreement of such an issue might be desirable would be when a very favourable offer is made or, perhaps, there is some risk a defendant would seek to resile from an admission on liability and it may be advantageous to have a binding agreement even if that is for only part of the claim, such as damages for pain, suffering and loss of amenity (as unless quantum is agreed subject to liability a binding compromise will have been reached on the issue concerned).

Care should, however, be taken before agreeing this issue in isolation when other issues have yet to be resolved because, as with liability, this can narrow the options for further negotiations to settle the claim as a whole.

The claimant is unlikely to face any significant costs risk, even from a Part 36 offer on damages for pain, suffering and loss of amenity, unless that is an issue the court has to determine, the outcome is not more advantageous to the claimant than the offer and the nature of the issue is such that significant, identifiable costs have been incurred on it.

11.4.8.3   Expenses and losses

Similar considerations apply when considering whether to agree heads of claim for expenses and losses.

Where there are relatively small items there may be something to be said for agreeing these as, again assuming that is not subject to liability, a binding compromise will then have been reached on each item agreed.

The claimant may not, however, be under pressure to agree individual items of expenses and losses at an early stage, on the basis that even if the defendant offers what later proves to be a reasonable sum for individual heads of claim these may still be capable of agreement at a later stage without necessarily committing the claimant to specific figures too soon.

Once again any costs risk, even from a Part 36 offer, is not likely to be significant unless the court makes a ruling on the relevant head of claim and it is an issue that has incurred identifiable costs.

11.4.8.4   Global quantum

Reaching agreement on global quantum, particularly in a claim of relatively modest value where liability needs to be resolved (but a split trial dealing with liability as a preliminary issue cannot be justified on the basis of proportionality) can be a useful, way of saving time at trial but is not without potential problems.

Care must be taken, of course, to ensure any agreement properly reflects the value of the claim on full liability. Where the claimant has made a Part 36 offer any agreement should exclude interest, or at least the element of enhanced interest that may be awarded under CPR 36.14 if any judgment is at least as advantageous to the claimant as the claimant's own offer.

If the claimant has made a Part 36 offer to settle the whole claim, particularly if that reflects perceived risks on liability, it may be unwise, tactically, to agree a figure for quantum which is lower than the terms of that Part 36 offer, given that if the claimant succeeds on liability judgment might well be in terms that are at least as advantageous as the offer and hence likely to trigger the benefits conferred by CPR 36.14. Conversely, if a figure slightly in excess of the claimant's offer can be agreed then the claimant will have a very strong argument those benefits should be conferred in the event the claim succeeds on liability and judgment for the agreed sum is entered.

11.4.9 Method of ADR?

Negotiation, by whatever means seems most suitable, will usually be the appropriate starting point on behalf of the claimant, tactically, for ADR.

If negotiation does not prove successful other methods of ADR might be proposed to the defendant. If negotiations never get going, or break down, mediation may be the most appropriate next stage as that may even resolve a dispute that had seemed to be intractable.

The claimant may face a defendant who, without initiating or even responding to efforts at negotiation, will suggest moving directly to another form of ADR such as mediation or early neutral evaluation. If so, as well as needing to agree some practical preliminaries (see 11.3) it is necessary to assess whether, tactically, that is the appropriate method of ADR for the claimant at the stage it is suggested. That is because it is, particularly in a more complex case, necessary to attempt settlement at a stage when evidence necessary to properly assess the claim, or relevant issue, has been obtained and, perhaps, exchanged. The claimant may also wish to have the parameters of any mediation effectively defined by an exchange of offers. The risk, of course, for a defendant who is not minded to make any formal offer is that simply proposing the parties engage in ADR is unlikely to carry specific costs consequences (although the risk to the claimant on costs cannot be ruled out altogether).

Consequently, advice should be given to the claimant, and instructions sought, at the earliest opportunity on all available methods of ADR and the tactics considered appropriate to adopt.

The advice given may be influenced by the extent to which any efforts at ADR may have costs consequences if efforts at ADR are not reciprocated or what later prove to have been reasonable offers to settle are not accepted. Consequently, the provisions of the CPR, on the costs consequences of offers to settle, need to be kept in mind when offering advice.

11.4.10 Advice

It is the responsibility of the claimant's lawyer to offer advice on the options for ADR and what, tactically, seems most appropriate while it is for the claimant to make an informed decision, based on that advice, what instructions to give on ADR, much may depend on the claimant weighing up risks and benefits and also whether the claimant wishes to see the claim resolved swiftly, perhaps for less damages than might be recoverable, or hold out for the maximum compensation likely to be available.

This advice is also, of course, essential so that the directions questionnaire can be completed to confirm it has been given.

It is particularly important, following the introduction of the 'additional amount' as a potential benefit to a claimant obtaining judgment 'at least as advantageous' as the claimant's own Part 36 offer to be made aware of this potential benefit as, for some claimants, that may be an important factor in reaching a decision on the approach that is to be taken towards ADR.

It is also important the claimant understands the essentials of a Part 36 offer, made or received, particularly that such an offer remains 'on the table' and hence can usually be accepted, unless and until changed or withdrawn, so the claimant is both aware of the option to accept a defendant's offer late and the need to change or withdraw any claimant offer which no longer represents an acceptable settlement to the claimant.

The claimant also needs advice on relevant differences between Part 36 and non-Part 36 offers, again with particular reference to acceptance where an offer made outside Part 36 imposes a time limit, after which it cannot be accepted, as well as the consequence of making a counter offer, namely that the offer received is then no longer open for acceptance.

Where instructions are received to make a Part 36 offer it is essential that advice is implemented, by making an offer that does comply with the rule and hence is effective to action the claimant's instructions.

A broader consideration, and again the claimant needs advice on the appropriate tactics, is whether, particularly in a higher value case, it is appropriate to attempt quantification, at a relatively early stage, for the purposes of making an offer or better to await a stage at which the issues are clearer and, perhaps, negotiations can take place at a face-to-face meeting.

There is also a need to ensure that the claimant understands the perceived advantages and disadvantages of ADR at any particular stage of the claim. There is the potentially significant benefit, under Part 36, of a 10% uplift on damages but, equally, the possible disadvantage of making offers before the defendant's stance is known.

The advice given to the claimant inevitably reflects tactical considerations including the need to assess, at any stage, whether the objective of an offer is principally settlement or takes account of the broader considerations involving potential costs and other benefits provided for under Part 36.

11.4.11   Using the CPR

The party engaging in ADR may wish to do so in a way that has the potential to deploy relevant terms of the CPR, so that costs consequences may follow if the other party does not respond reasonably by narrowing the issues or settling the claim as a whole.

Both Part 36 and Part 44 will be of relevance when considering ADR in the form of negotiations by offers to settle and, in particular, the potential costs consequences of such offers.

Each rule operates quite differently from the other so tactical considerations may, therefore, play an important part in deciding whether to make an offer to settle under Part 36 or for the purposes of Part 44.

11.4.11.1   *Part 36*

Part 36 provides for very specific consequences of offers to settle made in accordance with the terms of the rule itself.

CPR 36.1(2) expressly recognises that offers to settle may be made in whatever way a party chooses, so an offer to settle does not have to be made under Part 36. If not made in accordance with Part 36 an offer may still be relevant to costs, under the terms of Part 44. Accordingly, a party who does not wish the offer to carry all the consequences of Part 36 should not make reference to that rule when formulating the offer, but to do so in a way that means the offer may be relevant as to costs under Part 44.

In *Gibbon v Manchester City Council*[71] Moore-Bick LJ explained that Part 36 was a self-contained code so it was important a party choosing to make an offer under the rule was fully aware of the consequences when he observed:

> 'It can be seen from Part 36 as a whole ... that it contains a carefully structured and highly prescriptive set of rules dealing with formal offers to settle proceedings which have specific consequences in relation to costs...'

Moore-Bick LJ went onto conclude:

> 'In my view, Part 36 ... is to be read and understood according to its terms without importing other rules derived from the general law, save where that was clearly intended.'

11.4.11.2   Part 44

CPR 4.3 confirms the Court has a discretion as to whether one party should be ordered to pay the costs of anot4her party.

CPR 44.3(4) requires the Court to have regard to all the circumstances in deciding what, if any, order to make about costs but goes on to identify some specific factors of relevance.

Consequently, an offer which is not made under Part 36, but is expressed to be made 'without prejudice except as to costs', a 'Calderbank' offer, will be a matter the court should take into account, when making an order about costs, because CPR 44.3(4)(c) identifies a relevant factor as being an 'admissible offer to settle ... which is not an offer to which costs consequences under Part 36 apply'.

Not every offer made outside Part 36 will, however, be an 'admissible offer' for the purposes of Part 44 (see **11.2.2**).

11.4.11.3   Differences between Part 36 and non-Part 36 offers

Because Part 36 is a self-contained code the general law of contract, particularly in relation to offer and acceptance, does not apply where it is inconsistent with the terms of the rule itself.

Away from Part 36 negotiations are subject, in all respects, to the general law of contract and of particular relevance for these purposes is the common law on offer and acceptance.

---

[71]   [2010] EWCA Civ 726.

Another crucial difference between a Part 36 offer and a non-Part 36 offer is, even with an 'admissible offer' which can be taken into account under Part 44, the respective costs consequences of such offers.

It is essential to be clear about whether a offer made or received is a Part 36 offer.

11.4.11.3.1   Acceptance

Because the general law of contract applies to non-Part 36 offers such an offer cannot be accepted in the event of:

* withdrawal (even if withdrawn within the timescale for which the offer is expressed to be open: *Scammell v Dicker*;[72]
* rejection (which will include any response by the offeree which is construed as a counter -offer);
* lapse of time (once any express condition as to time has elapsed or, if no such condition is imposed, once a reasonable timescale for acceptance has expired);
* occurrence of an express condition in the offer;
* death; or
* supervening personal or corporate incapacity.

Subject to CPR 36.9(3) a Part 36 offer may be accepted at any time unless withdrawn or changed.

Furthermore, Part 36 contains terms, automatically applicable in the event of acceptance, dealing with timescale for payment and interest, which will need to be the subject of express agreement outside Part 36.

11.4.11.3.2   Timescale for payment

Part 36 provides a specific timescale for payment of sums due following acceptance (14 days in accordance with CPR 36.11 (6)).

A non-Part 36 offer ought to expressly state the timescale for payment, in the event of agreement, failing which that is likely to be, with all the uncertainties that gives, a 'reasonable time'.

11.4.11.3.3   Costs consequences

Part 36 sets out specific terms as to costs which will automatically apply on acceptance while, once again, if an offer is not made under Part 36 suitable terms as to costs will need to be the subject of express agreement.

Part 36 offers also carry, in certain circumstances, specific costs consequences in the event of non-acceptance. Under Part 44 the costs consequences of an admissible offer will depend upon all the circumstances of the individual case, not just a comparison of the offer with any judgment.

---

[72]   Court of Appeal, 21 December 2000.

11.5   PART 36 OFFERS

An offer to settle can, with a view to attracting the costs consequences found in the rule, be made in accordance with Part 36.

Part 36 provides a formal framework for negotiations which supplements the general law of offer and acceptance, operating as a self-contained code where the terms of the rule prevail over the general law: *Gibbon v Manchester City Council*.[73]

Part 36 also avoids the need to make express provision, as part of the offer, on a range of matters including interest, timescale for payment and costs.

11.5.1   History

Before the advent of the CPR in 1999, whilst both claimant and defendant might make offers, it was usually only a defendant's offer, in the form of a payment into court, which had costs consequences. Those consequences were to shift the risk on costs to a claimant who, though successful, failed to beat the defendant's payment in.

Both parties could make offers 'without prejudice except as to costs' (a 'Calderbank' offer). Such an offer might have costs consequences but would not generally carry such consequences if made by a defendant who could have, but did not, make a payment into court.

Part 36 also avoids the need to make express provision, as part of the offer, on a range of matters including interest, timescale for payment and costs.

11.5.1.1   *The original Part 36*

The original version of Part 36, introduced with the CPR in 1999, preserved the payment into court, now in the form of a Part 36 payment, which was still required from a defendant in a money claim if the costs benefits of the new rule, reflecting in the CPR costs consequences of a payment into court under the earlier regime, were sought.

Part 36 also introduced the new concept of a Part 36 offer. Such an offer might be made by a defendant in response to a non-monetary claim, as well as prior to issue of court proceedings in a money claim, and, significantly, by a claimant. For the first time, therefore, a claimant might secure benefits if the defendant failed to better, under the terms of the original rule by judgment at trial, such an offer. These benefits were indemnity costs and enhanced interest and, unlike the approach away from Part 36, not awarded to penalise conduct but there for the specific purpose of incentivising the claimant to make a reasonable offer.

The potential use of Calderbank offers, by both claimant and defendant, was preserved by the terms of CPR 44.3(4) (since April 2013, CPR 44.2(4)).

---

[73]   [2010] EWCA Civ 726.

11.5.1.2   Amendments to Part 36 in 2007

Following case-law, which had blurred the distinction between the costs consequences of a Part 36 payment and a Part 36 offer by the defendant, Part 36 was substantially amended in 2007.

The amended version of Part 36 was introduced on 6 April 2007 by the Civil Procedure (Amendment No 3) Rules 2006.

These amendments attempted to harmonise, where possible, the way the rule applied to claimants and defendants. Hence both claimants and defendants could now make Part 36 offers and the concept of the 'relevant period' was introduced, being the timescale the offer could not be changed or withdrawn without court permission and within which, if accepted, the rule provided for the defendant to become automatically liable to pay the claimant's costs.

It was these changes, as later case-law emphasised, that highlighted how Part 36 would operate as a self-contained code meaning, for example, that the significance of the relevant period was confined to the opportunity of changing or withdrawing an offer without court permission and to costs, where the offer is accepted within that timescale. Consequently, the relevant period was not intended to operate as a time limit for acceptance of the offer so that, again as case-law has since confirmed, Part 36 offers remain 'on the table' unless and until expressly changed or withdrawn in accordance with the terms of the rule itself.

A consequential amendment was also made to the terms of CPR 44.3(4)(c), confirming an offer was not relevant under that rule if the costs consequences under Part 36 applied to that offer.

11.5.1.3   Amendments to Part 36 in 2010

In April 2010, with the introduction of the RTA Protocol, Part 36 was amended again by being divided into two sections.

> Section I now contains the earlier Part 36, namely rules 36.1 to 36.15.
> Section II deals with offers to settle for the purposes of the RTA Protocol, comprising rules 36.16 to 36.22.

The two sections are quite distinct. CPR 36.1 confirms Section I does not apply to an offer to settle to which Section II applies, while CPR 36.16(1) confirms that where Section II applies Section I does not apply.

11.5.1.4   Amendments to Part 36 in 2011

A further important amendment was made to Part 36 with effect from 1 October 2011.

The Civil Procedure (Amendment No 2) Rules 2011 provided that after CPR 36.14(1) there would be inserted:

'1A) For the purposes of (1), in relation to any money claim or money element of a claim, 'more advantageous' means better in money terms by any amount, however small, and 'at least as advantageous' shall be construed accordingly.'

This provision effectively reversed *Carver v BAA plc*,[74] at least so far as offers made on or after 1 October 2011 are concerned.

11.5.1.5 Amendments to Part 36 in 2013

Further changes were made to Part 36 in 2013.

The Civil Procedure (Amendment) Rules 2013 provide for the insertion of additional sub paragraph in CPR 36.14(3) which, when that rule applies, provides for the claimant to have, as well as indemnity costs and enhanced interest, an 'additional amount' not exceeding £75,000.

The additional amount is calculated by applying the prescribed percentage to the amount which is, where the claim is or includes a money claim, the sum awarded to the claimant by the court or, where the claim is only a non-monetary claim, the sum awarded to the claimant by the court in respect of costs.

The prescribed percentage is calculated as follows:

Amount awarded by the court	Prescribed percentage
Up to £500,000	10% of the amount awarded;
Above £500,000 up to £1,000,000	10% of the first £500,000 and 5% of any amount above that figure'

This amendment does not, however, apply in relation to a claimant's Part 36 offer which was made before 1 April 2013. Consequently, a claimant who wishes to have all the benefits now conferred by CPR 36.14(3) may wish to repeat an earlier Part 36 offer (see 11.5.4.9).

11.5.2 The Forensic approach to Part 36

The correct forensic approach, certainly in the form the rule has taken since 2007, is dictated by that rule being drafted, as Moore-Bick LJ observed in *Gibbon v Manchester City Council*,[75] as a 'self-contained code'.

In *Gibbon* Moore-Bick LJ went on to explain:

'Basic concepts of offer and acceptance clearly underpin Part 36, but that is inevitable given that it contains a voluntary procedure under which either party may take the initiative to bring about a consensual resolution of the dispute. Such concepts are part of the landscape in which everyone conducts their daily life. It does not follow, however, that Part 36 should be understood as incorporating all the rules of law governing the formation of contracts, some

---

[74] [2008] EWCA Civ 412.
[75] [2010] EWCA Civ 726.

of which are quite technical in nature. Indeed, it is not desirable that it should do so. Certainty is as much to be commended in procedural as in substantive law, especially, perhaps, in a procedural code which must be understood and followed by ordinary citizens who wish to conduct their own litigation. In my view, Part 36 was drafted with these considerations in mind and is to be read and understood according to its terms without importing other rules derived from the general law, save where that was clearly intended.'

The Court of Appeal emphasised that the significance of the relevant period, a concept introduced with the 2007 amendment, was limited to the restriction on changing or withdrawing the offer during that time, at least without court permission, and the costs consequences that followed in the event of acceptance within that period. After the relevant period the offer, nevertheless, remained open for acceptance unless and until changed or withdrawn (even if the general law of contract would provide otherwise).

Consequently, it is to the terms of the rule itself that, at least in the first instance, the practitioner must look when deciding whether the rule is available for the purposes of an offer, making an offer intended to have the consequences of Part 36, reviewing and considering the consequences of an offer which refers to the rule, when withdrawing or changing such an offer and when wishing to accept a Part 36 offer.

11.5.3   The scope of Part 36 offers

The current version of Part 36 makes clear that an offer, under the rule, can be made at any stage of a claim, including before the commencement of proceedings and in an appeal. CPR 36.2(d) recognises an offer may relate to the whole of the claim, part of the claim or an issue in the claim. It is, of course, a requirement to state what the offer does relate to.

11.5.3.1   Pre-issue offers

CPR 36.3(2)(a) confirms a Part 36 may be made at any time, including before the commencement of proceedings. This avoids some of the issues about the effectiveness of pre-issue offers, under the original version of the rule, explored in *Huck v Robson*.[76]

The availability of Part 36, and applicability of the consequences found in the rule, even before court proceedings have been commenced was confirmed in *Thompson v Bruce*[77] and *Solomon v Cromwell Group plc*.[78]

11.5.3.2   Post-issue offers

An offer is, of course, effective when court proceedings have been commenced given that such an offer may be made at 'any time'.

11.5.3.3   Offers in appeals

CPR 36.3(2)(b) confirms a Part 36 offer may be made in appeal proceedings. That is important as CPR 36.3(4) provides a Part 36 offer will only have Part 36 costs

---

[76]   [2002] EWCA Civ 398.
[77]   (Unreported) 28 June, 2011 (QBD).
[78]   [2011] EWCA Civ 1584.

consequences in relation to the costs of the proceedings in respect of which it is made and not in relation to the costs of any appeal from the final decision in those proceedings.

If appeal proceedings are subject to the CPR then a Part 36 offer may be made even if that would not have been possible in the original proceedings to which the appeal relates: *Blue Sphere Global Ltd v Revenue & Customs Commissioners*.[79]

11.5.3.4 Offers in costs proceedings

The phrase 'any time' might be considered wide enough to encompass, after the substantive claim has been dealt with, offers in costs proceedings. Use of Part 36 at that stage was not ruled out when the topic was considered by the Court of Appeal in *Howell v Lees-Millais*.[80]

Where detailed assessment proceedings are commenced after 1 April 2013, CPR 47.21(4) expressly provides that the provisions of Part 36 will, with appropriate modifications, apply to the costs of those detailed assessment proceedings.

11.5.3.5 Offers on the whole of the claim

An offer to settle the whole claim will, at least in a case where the remedy sought by the claimant is damages, be just an offer to pay, or accept, a specified sum of money.

Such an offer may, however, have other conditions attached. If any such condition is inconsistent with the terms of Part 36, for example specifying costs consequences which do not accord with the rule, that may have the effect of rendering the offer ineffective for the purposes of Part 36 (see **11.5.5.1**). In other circumstances there may still be an effective Part 36 offer but if the terms, above and beyond the payment of damages, are not sufficiently clear there may not be sufficient agreement in the event of purported acceptance (see **11.5.7.7.1**).

Where valid conditions are attached to a Part 36 offer, or where the claim is about more than money but only money offers have been made to settle the claim as a whole that may be relevant when comparing the judgment with the offer to establish whether it is 'more advantageous' or 'at least as advantageous': *Smith v Trafford Housing Trust (Costs)*.[81]

Whilst offers will often relate to the whole of the claim these may relate only to 'part of a claim' or 'an issue in the claim'.

Where an offer to settle the whole claim is accepted within the relevant period there is a deemed costs order in favour of the claimant under CPR 36.10(1): *Lahey v Pirelli Tyres Ltd*.[82]

[79] [2010] EWCA Civ 517.
[80] [2011] EWCA Civ 786.
[81] [2012] EWHC 3320 (Ch)
[82] [2007] EWCA Civ 91.

11.5.3.6 Offers on part of the claim

An offer may be made on just part of the claim. It is important to distinguish an offer on part of the claim from an offer made on an issue in the claim as these carry different costs consequences.

CPR 36.10(2) provides that where a defendant's Part 36 offer relates to part only of the claim and on acceptance within the relevant period the claimant abandons the balance of the claim the claimant will be entitled to the costs of the proceedings unless the court orders otherwise. Consequently, the court has a discretion and there is no deemed costs order of the kind provided for under CPR 36.10(1): *E Ivor Hughes Education Foundation v Leach*.[83]

11.5.3.7 Offers on an issue in the claim

Any identifiable issue may, potentially, be the subject of a Part 36 offer.

CPR 36.2(5) expressly provides that an offeror may make a Part 36 offer solely in relation to liability, which can be very effective for claimants: *Huck v Robson*.[84]

An offer on an issue in the claim is not an offer on part of the claim hence if accepted within the relevant period there is a deemed costs order under CPR 36.10(1): *Onay v Brown*;[85] *Sutherland v Turnbull*.[86]

11.5.4 Making a Part 36 offer

When making a Part 36 offer a number of provisions within the rule will be relevant given that a 'Part 36 offer' is defined in CPR 36.2 as 'An offer to settle which is made in accordance with this rule'.

11.5.4.1 General requirements for form and content

The general requirements as to the form and content of a Part 36 offer are found in CPR 36.2(2), which provides that such an offer must:

(i)   be in writing (CPR 36.2(2)(a));

(ii)   state on its face that it is intended to have the consequences of Section I of CPR 36 (CPR 36.2 (2)(b));

(iii) specify a period of not less than 21 days within which the defendant will be liable for the claimant's costs in accordance with CPR 36.10 if the offer is accepted (CPR 36.2(2)(c));

(iv)   state whether it relates to the whole of the claim or to part of it or to an issue that arises in it and if so to which part or issue (CPR 36.2(2)(d)); and

(v)   state whether it takes into account any counterclaim (CPR 36.2(2)(e)).

---

[83]   [2005] EWHC 1317 (Ch)..

[84]   [2002] EWCA Civ 39.

[85]   [2009] EWCA Civ 775.

[86]   [2010] EWHC 2699 (QB).

Use of the word 'must' makes compliance with these rules on form and content essential.

11.5.4.1.1 In writing

A Part 36 offer must be in writing.

11.5.4.1.2 Intended consequences

In *Shaw v Merthyr Tydfil County Borough*[87] the Court of Appeal held that omission of the requirement to state the intended consequences of the offer meant that, despite express reference to the rule, there had not been a valid Part 36 offer. Maurice Kay LJ held:

> 'In these circumstances, as a matter of form, the offer did not satisfy the mandatory requirements of Part 36. Accordingly it was not a Part 36 offer, even though the letter described it as one.'

In adopting this approach the Court of Appeal relied upon the description of Part 36 as 'a self-contained code' by Moore-Bick LJ in *Gibbon v Manchester City Council*[88] and the observation that CPR 36.2(2) stipulates 'mandatory requirements' in *PHI Group Ltd v Robert West Consulting Ltd*.[89]

In *PHI Group Ltd* the offer, though stating it was intended to have the consequences of Part 36, failed to refer, specifically, to section I of the rule. The Court of Appeal held, however, that did not mean the offer failed to meet the requirements as to form and content for that reason, because there was nothing in section II that could have been of relevance to the offer and hence no doubt about which section of Part 36 was intended to apply.

11.5.4.1.3 The relevant period

The period stated in the offer, to comply with CPR 36.2(2)(c), is defined by CPR 36.3(1)(c) as 'the relevant period'.

It is this requirement of form and content which, in practice, appears to have caused parties the most difficulty when making Part 36 offers.

Where an offer is made less than 21 days before trial the relevant period will be the period up to the end of the trial or such other period as the court has determined. Thus, the rule itself provides a specific exception to the usually applicable minimum of 21 days, as defined in CPR 36.2. Moreover, this provision is the exception to the general rule that the court has no discretion to dispense with the rules on form and content found in CPR 36.2. That allows the court to stipulate a relevant period of less than 21 days, so a late offer may be effective against the costs of trial. The court may also, if demanded by the justice of the case, make such an order even before the offer has been made: *Matharoo v Medway NHS Foundation Trust*.[90]

---

[87] [2014] EWCA Civ 1678.
[88] [2010] EWCA Civ 726.
[89] [2012] EWCA Civ 588.
[90] [2013] EWHC 818 (QB).

Where a late offer is made the offeree will still need permission from the court to accept once the trial has started but, if permission is given, the deemed costs order under CPR 36.10(1) will be applicable as acceptance will then have been within the relevant period.

Save for the exception provided for in CPR 36.3(1)(c), when an offer is made not less than 21 days before trial, the requirement for a relevant period of at least 21 days, in accordance with CPR 36.2(2)(c), is obligatory. Hence, in practice it has been this requirement to specify a period of not less than 21 days, within which the defendant will be liable for the claimant's costs in accordance with rule 36.10 if the offer is accepted, that has proved most problematic. Particular difficulties have been caused by offerors adopting the pre-2007 terms of the rule by expressing the offer to remain open for 21 days as illustrated by comparing the outcome in *C v D*[91] *Thewlis v Groupama Insurance Co Ltd*[92] (whilst the decision in *Thewlis* has been criticised it was affirmed as correct by the Court of Appeal in and *Shaw v Merthyr Tydfil County*).[93]

While the court will try to give effect to an offer which described itself as a Part 36 offer, as *C v D*[94] illustrates, that does not allow the court to circumvent the mandatory requirement for the offer to contain a relevant period of not less than 21 days.

Hence in *PHI Group Ltd v Robert West Consulting Ltd*,[95] where the offer was expressed as being intended to have the consequences of Part 36 but as to time simply stated 'our client would, be grateful if your client's response to this offer could be provided within the next 7 days', Lloyd LJ emphasised, as that offer letter failed to specify a period of not less than 21 days, that:

> 'The judge considered that this was fatal, and I agree with him.'

Lloyd LJ did go on to observe:

> 'it is ... not part of the mandatory requirements of the rule, once the period has been specified, to state expressly that this is the period 'within which the defendant will be liable for the claimant's costs in accordance with rule 36.10 if the offer is accepted'. But this letter did not specify any period for the purposes of the rule.'

Whilst the offer in that case also failed to refer, specifically, to Section I of Part 36, as now required by CPR 36.2, that, of itself, would not have meant the offer failed to meet the requirements as to form and content, because there was nothing in Section II which could have been of relevance to the offer and hence no doubt about which section of Part 36 was intended to apply.

If, however, a relevant period of at least 21 days is identified in the offer it will not be necessary, to comply with CPR 36.2(2)(c), for the offeror to spell out the precise costs consequences which would follow, on acceptance, under CPR 36.10: *Proctor & Gamble Company v Svenska Cellulosa Aktiebolaget SCA*.[96] There are, indeed, potential risks for

---

[91]   [2011] EWCA Civ 646.
[92]   [2010] EWHC 3 (TCC).
[93]   [2014] EWCA Civ 1678.
[94]   EWCA Civ 646.
[95]   [2012] EWCA Civ 588.
[96]   [2012] EWHC 2839 (Ch).

an offeror who does set out details of costs if that amounts to imposing a term of the offer: *Shepherds Investments Ltd v Walters*[97] (see **11.5.1.1**).

11.5.4.1.4   *Whole, part or issue*

The offer must be clear about what is relates to.

11.5.4.1.5   *Counterclaim*

CPR 36.2(2)(e) requires a Part 36 offer to state whether it takes into account any counterclaim.

Accordingly, a Part 36 offer can be effective to conclude both claim and counterclaim if accepted on that basis.

However, the defendant who might wish to make a Part 36 offer faces the potential difficulty that, if accepted within the relevant period, CPR 36.10 will normally result in a deemed costs order in favour of the claimant.

Hence, in *AF v BG*[98] the defendant sent a letter to the claimant, headed as a Part 36 offer, indicating there was a counterclaim, though not yet pleaded, and offering to settle both claim and counterclaim on the basis of a payment to the defendant.

Although sent by the defendant that letter was expressly stated as intending to have the consequences of a *claimant's* offer to settle under Part 36.

Even though the counterclaim had not yet been pleaded that was held to be a genuine claim and, of course, Part 36 allows for offers under the rule to be made before court proceedings are commenced.

The offer made clear it was on a net basis and hence CPR 36.3(4), with its reference to 'the proceedings in respect of which (the Part 36 offer) is made', applied to both claim and counterclaim. Accordingly, where CPR 36.10(1) spoke of 'the costs of the proceedings' it would mean the costs of both the counterclaim and the claim.

Additionally, the court noted that Part 20, which includes counterclaims, provides 'an additional claim should be treated as if it were a claim for the purposes of these rules ...'. Nothing in Part 20, the court held, excepted Part 36 from that provision.

Accordingly, the offer was an effective Part 36 offer such that on acceptance the claimant would have become liable to pay the defendant the costs not only of asserting the proposed counterclaim but also of defending the original claim.

Furthermore, if the offer was not accepted, and judgment was ultimately at least as advantageous to the defendant as the terms of the offer, the court would, unless unjust, confer the benefits outlined in CPR 36.14(3) on the defendant.

---

[97]   [2007] EWCA Civ 292.
[98]   [2009] EWCA Civ 757.

11.5.4.1.6   *The importance of form and content*

The importance of the rules on form and content was again stressed by the Court of Appeal in *F & C Alternative Investments (Holdings) Ltd v Barthelemy*[99] where Davis LJ held:

> '... there is no reason or justification, in my view, for indirectly extending Part 36 beyond its expressed ambit. Indeed to do so would tend to undermine the requirements of Part 36 ... Part 36 is highly prescriptive with regard to both procedures and sanctions.'

Davis LJ also observed:

> 'Perhaps there can be de minimis errors or obvious slips which mislead no one: but the general rule, in my opinion, is that for an offer to be a Part 36 offer it must strictly comply with the requirements.'

CPR 36.2(4) provides that, in appropriate circumstances, further provisions relating to form and content will apply namely: CPR 36.5 (future pecuniary loss); CPR 36.5 (provisional damages); and CPR 36.15 (CRU).

11.5.4.2   *Future pecuniary loss*

CPR 36.2(4) requires, in appropriate cases, a Part 36 offer to contain the information provided for under CPR 36.5.

CPR 36.5 applies in a claim for damages for personal injury where there is a claim for future pecuniary loss.

A Part 36 offer where CPR 36.5 applies must state the amount of any offer to pay the whole or any part of any damages in the form of a lump sum and must state what part of the offer relates to any damages for future pecuniary loss to be paid or accepted in the form of periodical payments specifying:

(1)   the amount and duration of the periodical payment; and

(2)   the amount of any payments for substantial capital purchases and when they are to be made; and

(3)   that each amount is to vary by reference to the retail prices index (or to some other named index or that it is not to vary by reference to any index).

The offer must also state either that any damages which take the form periodical payments will be funded in a way which ensures that the continuity of payment is reasonably secure in accordance with s 2(4) of the Damages Act 1996 or how such damages are to be paid and how the continuing of their payment is to be secured.

11.5.4.3   *Provisional damages*

CPR 36.2(4) requires the offer when CPR 36.6 applies to contain the information identified in that rule.

---

[99]   [2012] EWCA Civ 843.

CPR 36.6 applies in a claim for damages for personal injury where an offeror makes a Part 36 offer in respect of a claim which includes a claim for provisional damages.

In such cases the Part 36 offer must specify whether or not the offeror is proposing that the settlement shall include an award of provisional damages. If the offer is to agree the making of an award for provisional damages the Part 36 offer must also state:

(1) that the sum offered is in satisfaction of the claim for damages on the assumption that the injured person will not develop the disease or suffer the type of deterioration specified in the offer;

(2) that the offer is subject to the condition that the claimant must make any claim for further damages within a limited period; and

(3) what that period is.

11.5.4.4 CRU

CPR 36.2(4) requires a Part 36 offer, where CPR 36.15 applies, to contain the information referred to in that rule.

CPR 36.15 applies where a payment to a claimant, following acceptance of a Part 36 offer, would be a compensation payment as defined by the Social Security (Recovery of Benefits) Act 1997.

CPR 36.15(3) requires a defendant (though not a claimant) who makes a Part 36 offer, acceptance of which will be a compensation payment under the 1997 Act, to state either:

- that the offer is made without regard to any liability for recoverable benefits; or
- that it is intended to include any deductible benefits in which case CPR 36.15(6) requires the offer to state:
    - the amount of gross compensation;
    - the name and amount of any deductible benefit by which that gross amount is reduced; and
    - the net amount after deduction of the amount of benefit.

Additionally, CPR 36.15(5) requires the offeror to apply for a certificate of recoverable benefits before making the offer. If when the offer is made the certificate has not been received the information in 36.15(6) must be given within 7 days of receiving the certificate.

If the defendant makes an offer without regard to any liability for recoverable benefits there is the potential advantage for the defendant of retaining any recoverable benefits refunded in the event of an appeal following conclusion of the case but the disadvantage of not offsetting deductible benefits.

This rule reflects guidance given by the Court of Appeal, when considering the earlier version of the rule, in *Williams v Devon County Council*.[100] That case emphasised the importance of providing relevant CRU information, observing that a failure to do so might render the offer ineffective for the purposes of Part 36.

---

[100] [2003] EWCA Civ 365.

11.5.4.5   Interest

When making a Part 36 offer the total sum needs to make allowance for interest as CPR 36.3(3) provides that the offer will be treated as inclusive of all interest until the end of the relevant period.

11.5.4.6   Offers on issues

A party may choose to make a Part 36 offer for just part of the claim or an issue in the claim.

CPR 36.2(5) expressly provides that a Part 36 offer may be made solely in relation to liability. An offer on this issue can be a useful tactical step for the claimant.

That is because an offer on liability will be treated as an offer on an 'issue' in the claim rather than for 'part', which has significance so far as the deemed costs order is concerned in the event of acceptance within the relevant period: *Onay v Brown*;[101] *Somnez v Kebabery* Wholesale Ltd.[102]

Because negligence is a composite concept, involving a duty of care which has been breached causing damage that the law recognises as not being too remote, an admission or offer on 'liability' necessarily involves both breach of duty and causation. As Lord Hoffmann observed in *Kuwait Airways Corporation v Iraqi Airways Company*:[103]

> 'One cannot separate questions of liability from questions of causation. They are inextricably connected. One is never simply liable: one is always liable for something....'

Where causation is not an all or nothing issue but may affect the extent of the adverse outcome it may be difficult to assess the impact of accepting an offer on liability framed, in the conventional way, as a percentage figure. Nevertheless, this may be a matter for the defendant to raise by way of requesting clarification.

Where a Part 36 offer expressly identifies, when there is an issue as to causation, the injuries for which damages are offered, perhaps on a percentage of liability basis, that will be an issue rather than part of the claim, in other words if an offer framed in that way is accepted that will conclude a final agreement which does not allow claims for the other injuries to be pursued: *Sutherland v Turnbull*.[104]

11.5.4.7   Making multiple offers

In the conjoined appeals of *Gibbon v Manchester City Council*[105] and *LG Blower Specialist Bricklayer Ltd v Reeves*[106] the Court of Appeal confirmed, in Gibbon, a further Part 36 offer would not amount to implied withdrawal of an earlier Part 36 offer and, in *LG Blower Specialist Bricklayer Ltd*, that a subsequent Part 36 offer would not automatically change a previous Part 36 offer.

---

[101]   [2009] EWCA Civ 775.
[102]   [2009] EWCA Civ 1386.
[103]   [2002] UKHL 19.
[104]   [2010] EWHC 2699 (QB).
[105]   [2010] EWCA Civ 726.
[106]   [2010] EWCA Civ 726.

Consequently, offers on different issues will remain extant, unless and until withdrawn or changed, despite further offers being made. Even if the offer on an issue corresponds to an offer to settle the whole claim this will not extinguish the offer to settle the whole claim, as that whole claim remains live: *Mahmood v Elmi*.[107]

In *LG Blower Specialist Bricklayer Ltd* the court concluded a party might make several Part 36 offers, even on the same issue or to settle the whole claim, which remained open for acceptance at any one time. That was held to reflect both the language and purpose of Part 36.

Accordingly, there is no reason why a party should not make more than one offer at a time and leave it to the other to decide which, if any, offer to accept. If, however, the offeror does not want an earlier offer to remain open for acceptance it is essential that offer is either withdrawn (see **11.5.6.1**) or changed (see **11.5.6.2**).

On this basis a claimant who wishes to obtain the prospect of recovering an 'additional amount' on a pre-April 2013 offer, but without losing the potential costs consequences of the earlier offer, may wish to repeat that earlier offer on or after 1 April 2013 while leaving the earlier offer extant.

11.5.4.8 *Making offers with multiple defendants*

With multiple defendants the claimant's approach to making offers will depend upon whether those defendants are joint tortfeasors (or perhaps more frequently separate tortfeasors who are responsible for the same damage) or separate tortfeasors responsible for separate damage.

If the defendants are alleged to be responsible for the same damage, whether or not joint tortfeasors, the claimant should be able to make a Part 36 offer in the same terms to each of those defendants, given that the value of the claim against every defendant will be identical (any apportionment being an issue between those defendants). If only one of the defendants accepts the offer the claimant will need to argue that the 'costs of the proceedings', for the purposes of CPR 36.10, include costs of joining some or all of the other defendants.

If separate damage has been caused by defendants who are not joint tortfeasors the claimant may need to value the claim against each defendant and make Part 36 offers to each reflecting that assessment. The claimant should make clear any such offer is to settle only the issue of the claim against that defendant rather than the claim as a whole so that, if accepted, the claimant is able to pursue claims against other defendants. If such an offer is accepted the 'costs of the proceedings' for the purposes of CPR 36.10 will only be the costs of proceeding against that defendant (though there will inevitably be some common costs some of which would have been incurred in any event and which can therefore be recovered): *Haynes v Department for Business Innovation & Skills*.[108]

Should the claimant not be able to value the separate claims against each defendant, but can value the claim overall, there is nothing to stop the claimant making an offer on that basis because, if accepted, adequate damages will have been recovered. Such an offer is

---

[107] [2010] EWHC 1933 (QB).
[108] [2014] EWHC 643 (QB).

less likely to have the potential of attracting the costs consequences found in CPR 36.14, against an individual defendant, but the focus of the claimant may be more on resolving the claim than trying to secure those benefits.

11.5.4.9   Service

CPR 36.7 confirms a Part 36 offer is made when served.

CPR 6.20 to 6.29, found in s.III of Part 6, deal with service of documents other than the claim form and so apply to the making of a Part 36 offer. CPR 6.20 sets out available methods of service, CPR 6.26 confirms the deemed date of service, according to the method adopted, whilst CPR 6.23 deals with, at least once the claim form has been served, the requirement for any party to the proceedings to give an address for service (see **2.10.11**).

Additionally, paragraph 1.2 of the Practice Direction to Part 36 confirms that where there is a legal representative a Part 36 offer must be served on that representative. This may be particularly relevant pre-issue of court proceedings. If, at that stage, a party is legally represented any Part 36 offer must be sent to that legal representative. There is, however, no requirement, as there is prior to service of the claim form, for the address of that legal representative to be given as the address for service.

The rules relating to service are important under Part 36 as it may be critical for a party to establish the fact and/or precise timing of a Part 36 offer being made, changed or withdrawn.

The relationship between Part 6 and Part 36 was illustrated in *Sutton Jigsaw Transport Ltd v Croydon London Borough Council*.[109]

The defendant made a Part 36 offer that was not withdrawn after the 21 day period referred to in the offer had elapsed.

At court, on the first day of the trial, the claimant sought to orally accept the offer.

The defendant stated that oral acceptance was insufficient under Part 36 following which the claimant handed over a handwritten note purporting to accept the offer.

The defendant then promptly sent a fax to the office of the claimant's solicitors withdrawing the offer.

The judge held that Part 36 provided a mechanism by which parties were able to settle claims and provided clear rules, being in effect a code to ensure the parties were on a level playing field.

CPR 36.9(1) provided that a Part 36 offer was accepted by serving written notice on the offeror. While CPR 6.22(2)(a) did allow for personal service of documents an exception was where a party had given an address for service. The defendant had given the address of the solicitors acting as the address for service.

---

[109] [2013] EWHC 874 (QB).

The judge concluded that to dispense with service or retrospectively order substituted service would give the claimant an unfair advantage over the defendant who had complied with the rules. Consequently, there had been no valid acceptance of the offer prior to that offer being withdrawn.

Where it would be just to do so, having regard to the overriding objective, the court may, exercising the case management power to extend or shorten timescale under CPR 3.1(2)(a), extend or abridge the 'relevant period' as, for example, occurred in *Matharoo v Medway NHS Foundation Trust*.[110]

11.5.4.10 How to make a Part 36 offer

Problems in complying with the rules as to form and content under Part 36 can be avoided if Practice Form N242A is used when making offers.

Use of form N242A is encouraged by the terms of paragraph 1.1 of Practice Direction 36A, which expressly refers to that form. There has also been judicial encouragement to utilise this form, HHJ Platt observing in *Shah v Elliott*[111] that:

> 'If this sad story has any moral it is first that the use of form N242A will enable insurers and solicitors to make offers which enjoy the protection of Part 36 and to concentrate the mind so that offers do have the foreseeable consequences which are intended.'

Any covering letter, and indeed any letter containing what is intended to be a Part 36 offer, should be headed as a Part 36 offer and, to err on the side of caution, also expressed to be 'without prejudice except as to costs'.

The offer must be duly served on the offeree, in accordance with Part 6 to ensure it is 'made' for the purposes of CPR 36.7.

11.5.4.11 Failure to comply with form and content

CPR 36.1(2) provides that if an offer is not made in accordance with CPR 36.2 it will not have the consequences specified in CPR 36.10, 36.11 and 36.14.

That may be significant for a claimant who wishes to rely on an offer made as being effective under Part 36. In particular:

- if the claimant seeks to rely on the costs provisions found in CPR 36.10 in the event of acceptance within the relevant period; and/or
- if the claimant needs to rely on other provisions contained within Part 36 such as timescale for payment; and/or
  if the claimant later obtains judgment against the defendant in terms that are at least as advantageous to the claimant as the offer and the claimant wishes to obtain the benefits conferred by CPR 36.14(3).

---

[110] [2013] EWHC 818 (QB).
[111] [2011] EW Misc 8.

A claimant who seeks to rely on an offer to secure the benefits conferred by CPR 36.14(3) is likely to have the efficacy of that offer challenged if it does not meet the rules on form and content: *Shaw v Merthyr Tydfil County Borough*.[112]

The rules on form and content, and hence whether an offer is an effective Part 36 offer, will also be significant if any party wishes to accept an offer made by another party once the relevant period has expired, as such acceptance will usually be effective where Part 36 applies but otherwise the general law of contract will determine whether or not an agreement has been reached (see **11.4.10.3.1**). Paradoxically, in such circumstances, it may be the offeror arguing the offer did not have the intended consequence!

Where an offer is made by a defendant the effectiveness of that offer, for the purposes of Part 36, may be important if the claimant fails to obtain judgment which is at least as advantageous as that offer and the defendant seeks the benefits conferred by CPR 36.14(2).

Consequently, the rules on form and content of Part 36 offers are just as important to the claimant at the stage of reviewing an offer received as they are when making an offer.

11.5.5 Reviewing a Part 36 offer

The rules about form and content of Part 36 offers are as important to the offeree as the offeror because the offeree needs to know whether or not the offer is subject to the provisions of Part 36 for a number of reasons.

First, if an offer is subject to the terms of Part 36 this will give the claimant the potential benefits of the deemed costs order in CPR 36.10, if accepted within the relevant period, and the possibility of late acceptance along with a degree of certainty on the costs consequences in that eventuality, even where acceptance would not be permitted under the general law of contract (unless the offer is changed or withdrawn meanwhile).

Secondly, if there has been an effective Part 36 offer the offeree faces the potential detriment of the adverse consequences provided for in CPR 36.14.

Consequently, the first consideration for the offeree is to assess the status of an offer which purports to be made under Part 36. If the offer is indeed a Part 36 offer then, depending on the circumstances, some other tactical considerations may arise.

11.5.5.1 Status of the offer

CPR 36.1(2) is, just as when making a Part 36 offer, an important provision when reviewing what is expressed to be a Part 36 offer, given that if the offer is not made in accordance with CPR 36.2 it will not have the consequences specified in CPR 36.10, 36.11 and 36.14. Depending on the circumstances the offeree may, or may not, wish for those rules to apply to that offer.

---

[112] [2014] EWCA Civ 1678.

When reviewing a Part 36 offer made by a defendant it is important to remember the requirements of CPR 36.2, given the terms of CPR 36.2(4) will, where applicable, include those specified in CPR 36.5 (periodical payments), CPR 36.6 (provisional damages) and CPR 36.15 (CRU).

Moreover, if an offer to settle is not made under Part 36 the general law of contract will be applicable, which may restrict the ability of the offeree to accept the offer.

The offeree may, ultimately, have to form a view, in order to give advice, whether or not a court is likely to regard the offer as effective under Part 36.

Particular difficulties can arise when an offer which refers to Part 36 does not comply fully with the requirements about form and content or contains express provisions which are inconsistent with fundamental precepts of the rule.

The pre-2007 version of Part 36 contained a provision that an offer not made in accordance with the rule could have the consequences specified in that rule but only if the court so ordered. There is no equivalent provision in the current version of the rule reflecting, certainly since the 2007 changes, the prescriptive and self-contained nature of Part 36.

In *Huntley v* Simmons[113] the judge, recognising the change made to Part 36 in 2007, concluded the appropriate way of dealing with the problem of technical non-compliance with the rules on form and content was to exercise the general discretion as to costs under CPR 44.3(4)(c), so that the relevant offer was held to have exactly the same costs consequences as if it had been 'Part 36-compliant'. This approach, however, has since been expressly disapproved by the Court of Appeal in *F & C Alternative Investments (Holdings) Ltd v Barthelemy*.[114]

There has also been a view that even if the formal requirements of Part 36 are not complied with the court may regard an offer as effective under that rule if the parties treated the offer as complying: *J Murphy & Sons Ltd v Johnston Precast Ltd*;[115] *Howell v Lees-Millais*.[116]This view adopts the approach in *Hertsmere Primary Care Trust v Rabindra-Anandh*[117] that the parties are under a duty to co-operate in furthering the overriding objective, was followed; in this context meaning that any technical point on non-compliance should be notified promptly by the offeree to the offeror.

Hence, in *Seeff v Ho*[118] when an issue arose as to whether an offer complied with the terms of Part 36 the court held it was relevant, when determining this point, that the offeror had requested, at the time the offer had made, the offeree indicate if the offer was considered to be defective in any way or non-compliant with Part 36 and the offeree, at that stage, failed to do so.

---

[113] [2009] EWHC 406 (QB).
[114] [2012] EWCA Civ 843.
[115] [2008] EWHC 3104 (TCC).
[116] [2011] EWCA Civ 786.
[117] [2005] EWHC 320.
[118] [2011] EWCA Civ 401.

In *Haynes v Department for Business Innovation and Skills*[119] the judge went as far as stating that, whilst an offer had probably not complied with the terms of Part 36, because no point had been taken by the offeree at the time on form and content any non-compliance was waived.

The dangers of departing too far from the requirements of a system designed to confer costs benefits were explained by Devlin J in *Martin French v Kingswood Hill*,[120] when he observed:

> '... a payment into court is simply an offer to dispose of the claim on terms. If the defendant were free to formulate the terms himself, he could make his offer in whatever form he liked. But if he seeks to effect his compromise under the rules which permit a payment into court, he must make his offer according to the rules.'

Reflecting this approach the Court of Appeal have emphasised the need to comply with the rules on form and content if an offer is to carry the consequences provided for in Part 36: *PHI Group Ltd v Robert West Consulting Ltd*;[121] *F & C Alternative Investments (Holdings) Ltd v Barthelemy*.[122] Consequently, there must be some question about the weight that can properly be attached to how the parties treat offers made although this may remain a relevant consideration where there are ambiguities.

The leading authority on the approach the court should take to Part 36 remains *Gibbon v Manchester City Council*,[123] where, after noting Part 36 contains highly prescriptive rules, Moore-Bick LJ concluded:

> 'parties are not bound to make use of the mechanism provided by Part 36, but if they wish to take advantage of the particular consequences for costs and other matters that flow from making a Part 36 offer, in relation to which the court's discretion is much more confined, they must follow its requirements.'

Moreover, the Court of Appeal has also cautioned against eliding the concepts of taking an offer into account for costs purposes, under Part 44, and applying the cost consequences found in Part 36. In *French v Groupama Insurance Company Ltd*[124] Rix LJ held:

> 'the question remains not merely whether the withdrawn offer be *taken into account* but whether *Part 36 consequences* should ordinarily flow where a Part 36 offer has been withdrawn...'

In *Carillion v PHI Group*[125] an offer was expressed to be made under Part 36 but contained no express 'relevant period', simply inviting a response within 7 days if possible. That offer was held to be ineffective for non-compliance with the terms of CPR 36.2(2). Akenhead J held:

> 'The first exercise in this case therefore is to determine whether or not, on a proper reading of the letter of 5 February 2010, it was a Part 36 offer which complied with the provisions of

---

[119] [2014] EWHC 643 (QB).
[120] [1961] QB 96.
[121] [2012] EWCA Civ 588.
[122] [2012] EWCA Civ 843.
[123] [2010] EWCA Civ 726.
[124] [2011] EWCA Civ 1119.
[125] [2011] EWHC 1581 (TCC).

Part 36. I have formed the view that it did not comply for the simple reason that it did not, as prescriptively required by Part 36, 'specify a period of not less than 21 days within which [RWC would] be liable in accordance with rule 36.10 if the offer is accepted'. Although Paragraph 4.5 of the letter said that the offer was "made under Part 36…and the offer is intended to have the consequences of Part 36 …", this does not, in my judgement, begin to comply with the prescriptive requirements of Rule 36.2. A Court should be cautious about seeking to introduce purely contractual interpretation and construction principles into the exercise of determining whether an offer is compliant with Part 36.'

This approach was upheld, on appeal, by the Court of Appeal where the case went under the name *PHI Group Ltd v Robert West Consulting Ltd*.[126]

The same strict approach was taken, this time to an offer by the claimant, in *F & C Alternative Investments (Holdings) Ltd v Barthelemy*.[127] The Court of Appeal took the opportunity of expressly disapproving *Huntley v Simmons*.[128]

On occasions it will, paradoxically, be the offeror who contends that an offer, even where that offer was expressed as being intended to have the consequences of the rule, was not an offer that complied with Part 36. That may happen because the offeree seeks to accept the offer at a time when a non-Part 36 offer would no longer be open (as in C) or because the offeror does not fully appreciate costs consequences (as in *Onay v Brown*[129] and *Harper v Hussain*[130]).

This is a further reason why the offeree, when reviewing what purports to be a Part 36 offer, should carefully consider compliance with the rules as to form and content to guard against the offeror seeking to have the potential costs benefit of the offer under Part 36 whilst also, possibly, having scope to argue the offer should not carry the consequential burden if that should later suit.

Generally, even if not intended by the offeror, the consequences provided for under the rule will follow if the offer is effective under Part 36. That is for the reasons given by Carnwath LJ in *Onay* when he observed:

'The moral of this story is that someone who writes a letter headed "Part 36 offer", and which is stated as "intended to have the consequences of that rule", should make sure that he knows what those consequences are. I agree with my Lord that those consequences in a case such as this are clearly set out in 36.2(2) and 36.10(1). If the party writing the letter does not want those consequences to apply, he should put his offer in some other way, as is expressly permitted by rule 36.2.

it seems to me important, in the interest of certainty, that, when the Part 36 jurisdiction is expressly invoked, the court should generally take that as face value, and as far as possible give effect to the consequences as envisaged by the rules.'

Similarly, in *Mahmood v Elmi*[131] Cox J noted:

[126] [2012] EWCA Civ 588.
[127] [2012] EWCA Civ 843.
[128] [2009] EWHC 406 (QB).
[129] [2009] EWCA Civ 775.
[130] (Unreported) Birmingham County Court, 19 March 2008.
[131] [2010] EWHC 1933 (QB).

> 'Ultimately, if the parties before the Court choose to use the machinery prescribed by the CPR in order to settle their disputes, then they must be taken to submit to the consequences.'

A failure to comply with one of the rules on form and content, or inclusion of a provision inconsistent with the terms of Part 36, may result in that offer being ineffective for the purposes of the rule. However, a mere reference to Part 36 may suffice to imply into the offer any specific requirements of form and content not expressly stated, at least where other express terms are not inconsistent with the rule, so that the offer is made effective under Part 36. As Rix LJ emphasised in *C v D*:[132]

> '... an offer presented as a Part 36 offer and otherwise complying with its form will not readily be interpreted in a way which would prevent it from being a Part 36 offer; and that if an offeror wishes to bring his Part 36 offer to an end, so that it cannot be accepted, then he must serve a formal notice of withdrawal.
>
> Any ambiguity in an offer purporting to be a Part 36 offer should be construed so far as reasonably possible as complying with Part 36.'

Although not fatal to raising the argument at a later stage it is preferable, in the event the offeree contends an offer does not comply with Part 36, for that point to be raised as soon as possible after the offer is made.

Nevertheless, it may not be until the stage when costs are being considered the offeree will seek to argue the relevant offer was not compliant with Part 36.

Whilst even a reference to Part 36 may be significant, if the court has to determine whether the offer is effective under the rule, and the court will try to give effect to the stated of intention, sometimes the terms of the offer are simply inconsistent with the fundamental aspect of the rule and hence it cannot properly be characterised as a Part 36 offer at all. It is significant that in *C* Rix LJ emphasised the need for a purported Part 36 offer to be 'complying with its form'.

Case-law has identified some specific instances in which an offer, however it describes itself, will not be an effective Part 36 offer.

11.5.5.1.1   Time-limited offers

An offer, given the terms and purposes of the rule, cannot be both a time-limited and a Part 36 offer.

In *C v D*[133] the crucial terms of the offer read:

> 'the offer will be open for 21 days from the date of this letter (the "Relevant Period").'

The offeree purported to accept the offer well after the 21 days had elapsed and, in determining whether there had been a valid acceptance of the offer, the court had to decide whether an offer could be both time-limited and made under Part 36, but if not which type of offer this was.

---

[132]   [2011] EWCA Civ 646.
[133]   [2011] EWCA Civ 646.

At first instance the judge explained why time-limited offers and Part 36 offers were mutually exclusive when he said:

> 'The policy of Part 36 can thus be identified, under this argument, as being to encourage a defendant to accept a reasonable Part 36 offer from the claimant but so that, if the offer is not kept open, by being withdrawn or changed detrimentally, the sanction ceases to apply. The successful offeror can take the benefit of the provisions only, as the quid pro quo, if he has left it open to the offeree to accept ...'

The judge went on to rule:

> 'In my judgment, a time-limited offer, as I have described it, is not capable of being a Part 36 offer. I consider that the structure of Part 36 in general and the provisions of rule 36.2(2) and rule 36.14(6) in particular, establish that an offer must be capable of acceptance unless and until withdrawn by service of a notice within rule 36.9(2), although an offer may also be changed; but if its terms are less advantageous, the costs sanctions under rule 36.14(6) do not apply.'

That approach echoed the comments of Moore-Bick LJ in *Gibbon* where he explained why there were good reasons for the idea that a Part 36 offer should remain 'on the table' to carry the costs consequences found in the rule when he said:

> 'The rules state clearly how a Part 36 offer may be made, how it may be varied and how it may be withdrawn. They do not provide for it to lapse or become incapable of acceptance on being rejected by the offeree. That would be the case at common law, but it is inconsistent with the concepts underlying Part 36, which proceeds on the footing that the offer is on the table and available for acceptance until the offeror himself chooses to withdraw it. There are good reasons for that. An offer which appears unattractive when made, and which is therefore rejected, may become more attractive as the proceedings progress and the parties reassess the strength of their respective cases. A defendant who chooses to leave his offer on the table may tempt the claimant into accepting it, with the benefit to himself of the consequences for costs of an offer made at an early stage. Part 36 allows a defendant (or for that matter a claimant) to decide whether to leave his offer open for acceptance or to withdraw it and make another offer later. To import into Part 36 the common law rule that an offer lapses on rejection by the offeree would undermine this important element of the scheme. It could give rise to disputes about whether the offer had been rejected in any given case so as render it incapable of acceptance.'

On appeal the Court of Appeal agreed with the analysis of the trial judge that a time-limited offer could not also be a Part 36 offer. On this point Stanley Burnton LJ observed:

> 'Any ambiguity in an offer purporting to be a Part 36 offer should be construed so far as reasonably possible as complying with Part 36. Once it is accepted that a time-limited offer does not comply with Part 36, one must approach the interpretation of the offer in this case on the basis that the party making the offer, and the party receiving it, appreciated that fact.'

Consequently, the Court of Appeal then had to decide whether the judge had also been correct in finding the offer, as framed, was time-limited and hence not effective under Part 36. On this point Rix LJ observed:

> 'It is common ground that the offer was intended to be made and understood as a Part 36 offer. It is disputed, however, what the meaning of 'open for 21 days' means in that context. The claimant submits that it means that the offer lapses at the end of 21 days (in this case on

31 December 2009), ie that the offer is not open for acceptance after 21 days. The defendant submits that it means that the offer is open for 21 days as an expression of the relevant period but that after those 21 days it may be withdrawn.'

On this point the Court of Appeal concluded that, on proper interpretation of the offer, it was validly made under Part 36. That was because, crucially, the period of 21 days was defined as the 'relevant period'. Given that the significance of this phrase, under the rule, is simply to define the timescale within which, if accepted, the claimant will secure the benefit of the deemed costs order set out in CPR 36.10, the court was able to conclude that the offer was not time-limited and therefore a valid Part 36 offer.

Rix LJ explained:

'In the context of Part 36, it seems to me to be entirely feasible and reasonable to read the words "open for 21 days" as meaning that it will not be withdrawn within those 21 days. Part 36 permits withdrawal within the 21 day relevant period, but only with the permission of the court. It seems to me that 'open for 21 days' is an obvious way of saying that there will be no attempt to withdraw within those 21 days. It is also a warning that after the expiry of those 21 days, a withdrawal of the offer is on the cards. Such a construction would save the Part 36 offer as a Part 36 offer and would also give to both parties the clarity and certainty which both Part 36 itself, and the offer letter with its reference to "open for 21 days", aspire to.'

In *Epsom College v Pierse Contracting Southern* Ltd[134] the relevant offer, whilst expressed to remain open for acceptance for 21 days, made reference to the 'expiry' of that offer. This, like the phrase 'relevant period', was held to pick up the language of Part 36 itself and, as such, the offer was a valid Part 36 offer.

In *Thewlis v Groupama Insurance Co Ltd*,[135] however, the relevant offer made no such reference to terminology found in the current, 2007, version of Part 36. Rather, the relevant letter stated that the offer was:

'... made pursuant to Part 36 of the CPR and remains open for acceptance for a period of 21 days, from your receipt of this offer letter, thereafter it can only be accepted if we agree the liability for costs or the court gives permission.'

Even though this wording reflected the terms of Part 36, until amended in 2007, it was held to be a time-limited offer, and therefore not an effective Part 36 offer. In reaching that conclusion the judge noted that in C Moore-Bick LJ had pointed out that an ambiguous offer which referred to Part 36 must still 'otherwise comply with its form'.

Identification of a relevant period is essential if an offer is to comply with the rules as to form and content found in Part 36. In *PHI Group Ltd v Robert West Consulting Ltd*[136] Lloyd LJ explained when reference to a specific period, such as such as 21 days, might comply with the terms of Part 36 and when that might amount to a time-limited offer which would not, therefore, be a Part 36 offer. He held:

'If an offer letter were to specify a period of 21 days, but not to follow the language of the relevant paragraph of the rule, the question might arise as to whether that was in itself a sufficient compliance with rule 36.2(2)(c). I have mentioned above in summary terms the

---

[134] [2011] EWCA Civ 1449.
[135] [2010] EWHC 3 (TCC).
[136] [2012] EWCA Civ 588.

phrases used in Onay v Brown and in C v D. Rix LJ said in C v.D at paragraph 56: 'A point may perhaps have been taken that the offer did not comply with rule 36.2(2)(c). But no such point has been taken, and the judge was satisfied that the rule had been complied with.' In *Epsom College v Pierse Contracting Southern Limited* [2011] EWCA Civ 1449 the offer stated 'This offer will remain open for acceptance 21 days ...' without reference to a relevant period. The present point was not in issue, only the C v D point about what 'open for acceptance' meant. It was in that context that Rix LJ said (at paragraph 66) that there was no sufficient difference of language to take the case outside the rationale of C v.D.'

The decision in *Thewlis* was upheld by the Court of Appeal in *Shaw v Merthyr Tydfil County Borough*[137] where, once again, what purported to be a Part 36 offer was stated to be 'open for a period of 21 days from the date of receipt' without defining this as the relevant period, although the basis given for the decision was that the offer also failed to expressly state that it was intended to have the consequences of Part 36 (see **11.5.4.1.2**).

11.5.5.1.2   Costs-inclusive offers and offers excluding costs

An offer which was made inclusive of costs was held not to be a valid Part 36 offer, under the earlier version of the rule, in *Mitchell v James*.[138] That is principally because the costs consequences provided for under Part 36 are inconsistent with a term as to costs being part of an offer made under that rule. In *Mitchell* Peter Gibson LJ concluded that:

> 'a term as to costs is not within the scope of a Part 36 offer. That does not of course mean that a claimant cannot make an offer which includes a term as to costs; the court will have regard to that in exercising its usual discretion in relation to inter partes costs at the end of the case. As r. 36.1(2) states, nothing in Part 36 prevents a party making an offer to settle in whatever way he chooses. However, nothing in r.36(1)(2) permits a party to include a term as to costs as part of a Part 36 offer for the purpose of obtaining an order for costs on an indemnity basis.'

Under the 2007 version of the rule an offer stated to be inclusive of costs was held not to comply with Part 36 in *L G Blower Specialist Bricklayer Ltd v Reeves*.[139]

In *French v Groupama Insurance Company Ltd*[140] the Court of Appeal, similarly, concluded an offer expressed to be inclusive of costs could not be a Part 36 offer, approving *Mitchell*.

The same approach, from the courts, seems likely if the usual costs provisions found in Part 36 are otherwise excluded. For example, an offer which is purported to be made under Part 36 but proposes terms that there be no order as to costs or that costs be dealt with other than by assessment on the standard basis, that would inconsistent with the terms of CPR 36.10 and hence be inconsistent with that fundamental aspect of the rule. Hence in *Howell v Lees-Millais*[141] Lord Neuberger MR observed, on an offer which contained terms as to costs, that:

> 'I would agree that the letter was not a Part 36 offer, because it could not, by its very terms, comply with CPR 36.10(1). That rule states that, subject to certain irrelevant exceptions,

---

[137] [2014] EWCA Civ 1678.
[138] [2002] EWCA Civ 997.
[139] [2010] EWCA Civ 726.
[140] [2011] EWCA Civ 1119.
[141] [2011] EWCA Civ 786.

'where a Part 36 offer is accepted within the relevant period [i.e. the 21 days referred to in the April 2009 letter] the claimant will be entitled to the costs of the proceedings up to the date on which notice of acceptance was served on the offeror.' The April 2009 letter specifically excluded the offeree from recovering all her costs, as it gave her the option of recovering only a proportion of her costs or a fixed sum in respect of her costs.'

In *Shah v Elliot*[142] an offer referring to Part 36 provided for payment of predictable costs. During the 'relevant period' of that offer proceedings were issued. That offer was held to be ineffective under Part 36 given that, following issue, the terms as to costs were less favourable than those the claimant would have then been entitled to under CPR 36.10.

Where, however, predictable costs are applicable, because the offer is for less than £10,000 in a claim arising out of a road traffic accident where court proceedings have not yet been issued, an offer expressed to be made under Part 36 will, if accepted, result in the claimant receiving predictable costs in accordance with CPR 45.7: *Solomon v Cromwell Group Plc*.[143]

In *Hall v Stone*[144] the defendant contended that it had not been appropriate to make a Part 36 offer because, if accepted, this would have given the claimant an entitlement to assessed costs when the defendant wished to argue costs should be restricted to those applicable on small claims track, because of the amounts for which the claims were ultimately settled. The Court of Appeal, rejecting this argument, observed that, in such circumstances, the defendant could have made a Calderbank offer at any stage, even before proceedings began, which could have included a proposal for costs reflecting those arguments.

In *Summers v Fairclough Homes Ltd*[145] the Supreme Court suggested a Calderbank offer might also be appropriate in cases involving exaggeration of the type found in that claim. Again such an offer could make provision for costs as part of the terms.

Some provision for costs, though what that needs to be may depend upon the particular circumstances as both *Hall* and *Summers* illustrate, may be an integral part of any offer to settle because, as Longmore LJ recognised in *Ali v Stage Coach*,[146] an offer should be intended to achieve finality if accepted and, certainly if an offer to settle the whole claim, finality will require an agreement as to costs.

If the defendant does make a costs-inclusive offer it will usually be reasonable for the claimant to ask that this be broken down between damages and costs except, perhaps, where a figure for damages has already been identified or agreed. Indeed, without such a breakdown it may be very difficult, if not impossible, to identify whether the offer was more advantageous to the claimant than the judgment eventually obtained.

There is not even any requirement, in the rules on form and content found in CPR 36.2(2), for the offeror to provide details of costs when making a Part 36 offer, a

---

[142] [2011] EW Misc 8.
[143] [2011] EWCA Civ 1584.
[144] [2007] EWCA Civ 1354.
[145] [2012] UKSC 26.
[146] [2011] EWCA Civ 1494.

point recognised in *Mehjoo v Harben Barker*.[147] This again reflects the principle that Part 36 offers are concerned with the substantive issues rather than costs.

It may, indeed, be dangerous for an offeror to even give a breakdown of costs, certainly if there is any risk of that being regarded as part of the offer. In *Shepherds Investments Ltd v Walters*[148] the claimant sent a letter headed 'Part 36 Settlement Offer' which stated:

> 'Accordingly, in an attempt to dispose of this dispute, our clients will accept a payment of Ł1.00 inclusive of interest in full and final settlement of all their claims under claim number HC04C02668. If this offer is accepted our clients will be entitled to their costs to the date of acceptance. Accordingly, the offer is that our clients will settle for Ł1 plus their costs. In accordance with CPR 36.14, for the purposes of assisting the Defendants in clarifying the basis of our clients' offer, we confirm that our clients' costs to date are Ł99,230.00 (inclusive of VAT).'

The first instance the judge concluded that this was not a valid Part 36 offer as it included a term as to costs, applying *Mitchell v James*.[149]

Although not deciding this point, as that was not necessary to determine the appeal, the Court of Appeal considered it was 'reasonably arguable' the claimant had made a valid Part 36 offer on the basis the figure given for costs was not a term of the offer but an item of additional information. That was expressed only as a view rather than a ruling on the first instance judgment.

11.5.5.1.3 'Total capitulation' offers

A defendant might propose the claimant simply discontinue the claim (although such an offer might well be ineffective in any event if, as is likely, it seeks to exclude the provisions of CPR 36.10 that the defendant pay the claimant's costs if the offer is accepted within the relevant period).

A claimant might offer to accept 100% on liability (with a view to arguing later that judgment in such terms is 'at least as advantageous' as the offer for the purposes of CPR 36.14(1A)).

The effectiveness of which might be regarded as a 'total capitulation' offer, for the purposes of Part 36, was considered in *AB v CD*[150] where Henderson J held:

> 'The concept of an 'offer to settle' is nowhere defined in Part 36. I think it clear, however, that a request to a defendant to submit to judgment for the entirety of the relief sought by the claimant cannot be an 'offer to settle' within the meaning of Part 36. If it were otherwise, any claimant could obtain the favourable consequences of a successful Part 36 offer, including the award of indemnity costs, by the simple expedient of making an 'offer' which required total capitulation by the defendant. In my judgment the offer must contain some genuine element of concession on the part of the claimant, to which a significant value can be attached in the context of the litigation. The basic policy of Part 36 is to encourage the sensible settlement of claims before trial, or even before the issue of proceedings (see rule 36.3(2)(a) which provides that a Part 36 offer may be made at any time, including before the commencement of

---

[147] [2013] EWHC 1669 (QB).
[148] [2007] EWCA Civ 292.
[149] [2002] EWCA Civ 997.
[150] [2011] EWHC 602 (Ch).

proceedings). The concept of a settlement must, by its very nature, involve an element of give and take. A so-called 'settlement' which was all take and no give would in my view be a contradiction in terms.'

The words 'significant value' should, perhaps, be viewed with caution given the guidance now provided for comparing offer and judgment in CPR 36.14(1A). Additionally, and certainly in the context of an appeal, there is support for the view a party may make an offer, effective under Part 36, for exactly that which the party is entitled to: *Blue Sphere Global Ltd v Revenue & Customs Commissioners.*[151]

Consequently, a better way for the court to approach such an offer might perhaps be to conclude that it would be 'unjust' for the consequences found in CPR 36.14 to apply. That was very much the approach taken by the Court of Appeal in *Huck v Robson* when contrasting an offer of 95% on liability, which was held to be effective under Part 36, and a notional offer of 99.9%, which the court appeared to doubt would be effective for costs purposes under the rule.

Tuckey LJ observed:

'I would however add that if it was self-evident that the offer made was merely a tactical step designed to secure the benefit of the incentives provided by the Rule (e.g. an offer to settle for 99.9% of the full value of the claim) I would agree with Jonathan Parker L.J. that the judge would have a discretion to refuse indemnity costs. But that cannot be said of the offer made in this case, which I think did provide the Defendant with a real opportunity for settlement even though it did not represent any possible apportionment of liability. I would therefore allow this appeal.'

Earlier in his judgment Tuckey LJ had noted:

'I do not think that the court is required to measure the offer against the likely outcome in a case such as this. In this type of litigation a Claimant with a strong case will often be prepared to accept a discount from the full value of the claim to reflect the uncertainties of litigation. Such offers are not usually based on the likely apportionment of liability but merely reflect the reality that most claimants prefer certainty to the ordeal of a trial and uncertainty about its outcome. If such a discount is offered and rejected there is nothing unjust in allowing the claimant to receive the incentives to which he or she is entitled under the Rules. On the contrary, I would say that this is a just result.'

In that passage Tuckey LJ was making exactly the same point subsequently made, though then in the context of a defendant's offer, by Briggs LJ in *PGF II SA v OMFS Company 1 Ltd*[152] that:

'... defendant's Part 36 offers are frequently made at a level below that which the defendant fears having to pay at trial, in the hope that the claimant's appetite for, or ability to undertake, costs risk will encourage it to settle for less than its claim is worth.'

In *Wharton v Bancroft*[153] Norris J recognised that the concept of what amounts to a purely tactical step, in effect seeking total capitulation, was not easy to apply when he observed:

---

[151] [2010] EWCA Civ 517.
[152] [2013] EWCA Civ 1288.
[153] [2012] EWHC 91 (Ch).

'All Part 36 offers are tactical in the sense that they are designed to take advantage of the incentives provided by Part 36.'

11.5.5.1.4   Offers without adequate CRU information

Because the terms of CPR 36.15 are prescriptive, and by CPR 36.2 incorporated into the rules relating to form and content, a failure by the defendant to comply with the requirements of this rule may also mean, whether or not the offer is expressed as intending to have the consequences of Part 36, the terms of CPR 36.10, 36.11 and 36.14 will not apply.

In *Williams v Devon County Council*[154] the Court of Appeal, when considering the pre-2007 version of Part 36, expressed doubt as to the efficacy of an offer purportedly made under Part 36 if relevant CRU information was not provided.

Despite the subsequent introduction of CPR 36.15, in 2007, it is still not unusual to see offers that fail to comply with the terms of that rule. For example, offers made 'net of CRU', hence failing to identify whether the gross offer does or does not include any deductible benefits, or 'gross of CRU', hence failing to identify the information required by CPR 36.15(6) and the net offer after allowing for any deductible benefits.

11.5.5.1.5   Other ineffective offers

The failure in other circumstances to comply with the rules on form and content, or the imposition of an express term inconsistent with a fundamental precept of the rule, is likely to render an offer ineffective under Part 36.

11.5.5.2   Clarification

CPR 36.8 provides that the offeree may, within 7 days of a Part 36 offer being made, request the offeror to clarify that offer.

If clarification is not provided the offeree may apply to the Court for an order the clarification be given. Furthermore, the absence of clarification might be relevant when the court determines whether it is 'unjust' for the usual costs consequences to apply in relation to that offer. The court may decide the costs implications in Part 36, even if otherwise applicable, should not take effect until such time as clarification is given: *Colour Quest Ltd v Total Downstream UK plc.*[155]

It would seem appropriate, at the very least, for there to be clarification of matters required by the terms of Part 36 itself such as, in an offer that includes deductible benefits, the information identified in CPR 36.15(6) are not given: *Williams v Devon County Council.*[156]

There is no definitive definition of the appropriate scope of a request for clarification though guidance can be drawn from the provisions of the CPR and case-law.

---

[154]   [2003] EWCA Civ 365.
[155]   [2009] EWHC 823 (Comm).
[156]   [2003] EWCA Civ 365.

In *R v Secretary of State for Transport ex-parte Factortame* Limited[157]the court held that a party might ask for clarification in order to understand the basis of an offer but could not interrogate the other party as to the thinking behind the making of the offer, for example what view was taken on the chances of success for the purposes of the offer. However, the court also held that, distinct from the issue of clarification, was the question whether documents or other information should have been provided by the offeror to apply proper consideration of the offer and, if not, the justice of Part 36 costs consequences applying to the offer.

In *Johnson v Deer*[158] it was held that, to further the aim of the overriding objective of dealing with the case justly and expeditiously, it was appropriate to order clarification, in a personal injury claim, so that the defendant had to specify either the approximate division of the offer between general and special damages or the approximate percentage on liability on which the offer was based.

Nevertheless, the overriding objective, and the general philosophy of the CPR, encourages the parties to assist each other. That would suggest, generally, clarification ought to be given, or at least appropriate information provided to allow proper evaluation of the offer. Paragraph 3.21 of the Protocol appears to endorse this view and confirms that general approach should apply pre-action.

Evidence which will allow the recipient to properly judge the offer should normally be disclosed: *Ford v GKR Construction Ltd.*[159] Accordingly, clarification of such matters might to be allowed.

The judgment will be compared with any relevant offer on a 'like for like' basis, so interest will need to be taken into account: *Blackham v Entrepose UK*.[160] Accordingly, that will mean excluding further interest, between the date of offer and date of judgment, so it may be necessary to seek clarification of the interest element of any offer which excludes interest (though under CPR 36.3(3) interest is deemed to be included unless expressly excluded).

If clarification is not given the offeree may either:

- apply to the court for an order there be clarification under CPR 36.8(2); or
- reserve the right to argue, if necessary at a later stage, it would be unjust, for the purposes of CPR 36.14 for the offer to carry the costs consequences found in that rule in the absence of the clarification requested.

If a court order is obtained that will determine the need for clarification though a party may prefer not to run the risk that the court will rule against clarification and rely on the opportunity to argue, at a later stage if necessary, costs consequences under Part 36 would be unjust without the clarification, even though no order was made that it be provided.

It would not seem necessary for a party to obtain an order for clarification before arguing, if necessary at a later stage, it would be unjust, with particular reference to the

---

[157] [2002] EWCA Civ 932.
[158] [2001] CLY 619.
[159] [2000] 1 WLR 1397.
[160] [2004] EWCA Civ 1109.

information available to the parties for the purposes of CPR 36.14(4)(c), for the usual costs consequences under CPR 36.14 to apply. In *Mehjoo v Harben Barker*[161] Silber J observed:

> 'I should also add that CPR 36.8 states that a party may request the offeror to clarify the offer. So before a party is able to say that it would be unjust for a Part 36 order to be made against it because it had failed to comply with an obligation to make information available, the party should have invoked Part 36.8. That is, after all, the procedure designed to deal with cases where there is a need for clarification.'

11.5.5.3   Multiple defendants

Care is necessary when reviewing a Part 36 offer if there are multiple defendants.

If a Part 36 offer is made by all the defendants that may be accepted without the need for court permission (unless that permission is required for any of the other reason identified in CPR 36.9(3)).

Where, however, a Part 36 offer is made by one or more, but not all, of a number of defendants the claimant must be more cautious.

- CPR 36.12(2) provides that if the defendants are sued jointly or in the alternative the claimant may accept the offer only if the claim is discontinued against those defendants who have not made the offer and those defendants give written consent to the acceptance of the offer.
- CPR 36.12(3) provides that if the claimant alleges the defendants have a several liability the claimant may accept the offer and continue with the claims against the other defendants if entitled to do so.
- CPR 36.12(4) requires the claimant, in all other cases, to apply to the court for an order permitting acceptance of the Part 36 offer.

Consequently, when this is not made clear at the time of the offer, the claimant may wish to seek confirmation that the offer is made on behalf of all defendants and, if not, to try and agree terms, in relation to the costs of those other defendants, as a preliminary to acceptance. If that is not done the claimant may be at risk in relation to the costs of the other defendants by simply accepting the offer: *Messih v McMillan Williams*.[162]

The claimant may, alternatively, apply to the court for an order in accordance with CPR 36.12(4) permitting acceptance of the Part 36 offer but may wish, in these circumstances, to make clear any agreement to accept the offer is conditional upon appropriate provision as to costs.

11.5.5.4   Single sum of money

CPR 36.4 requires a Part 36 offer by a defendant to pay a sum of money in settlement of a claim be an offer to pay a single sum of money (unless the offer includes periodical payments and/or provisional damages).

---

[161] [2013] EWHC 1669 (QB).
[162] [2010] EWCA Civ 844.

The offeree does, however, have the option of treating the offer as effective under Part 36 by accepting the offer. Sometimes the disadvantage to a claimant, of not receiving damages as a single sum of money, may be outweighed by the advantages of Part 36, in particular the costs consequences where a Part 36 offer is accepted within the relevant period.

11.5.5.5   Decision

When reviewing a Part 36 offer it is important to assess whether a decision can be made, at that stage, to recommend either acceptance or a counter offer.

If a decision cannot be reached because further information is required from the defendant it may be appropriate to seek clarification (see **11.4.6** and **11.5.5.2**).

If no decision can be reached on the offer either because information, other than from the defendant, or further developments need to be awaited it may be appropriate to explain to the defendant and seek an extension of time (see **11.4.5**).

These matters may be relevant if the claimant subsequently fails to obtain judgment which is 'more advantageous' than the offer: *SG v Hewitt*.[163]

Should the offer be withdrawn a relevant consideration, in relation to costs, is likely to be whether it was reasonable, on the information available at the time, to have accepted the offer during the time it was open: *Rehill v Rider Holdings Ltd*.[164]

If the claimant does not indicate any difficulty in reaching a decision on the offer at the time, and particularly if the claimant makes a counter offer, an argument that the offer could not be properly assessed when made is likely to be unsuccessful: *Ivison v Northern Lincolnshire & Goole Hospitals NHS Foundation Trust*.[165]

11.5.5.6   Format

The offeror will, ideally, have used form N242A or, at least, given in any letter making the offer all the information in that form. If that is not done the offeree will need to carefully review the offer and, if there is any ambiguity, indicate whether the offer is treated as a Part 36 offer and if not, certainly where the offer refers expressly to Part 36, explaining the reasons for that stance.

If the status of the offer is unclear the offeree might also be invited to clarify any issues, and perhaps to re-make the offer using form N242A if that has not already been done, to avoid any ambiguity and, perhaps, issues arising in the future as to the status of the offer.

---

[163] [2012] EWCA Civ 1053.
[164] [2014] EWCA Civ 42.
[165] (Unreported) York County Court, 14 February 2014.

11.5.6   Withdrawing or changing a Part 36 offer

CPR 36.3(5) restricts an offeror from withdrawing or changing the terms of an offer, to be less advantageous to the offeree, prior to expiry of the 'relevant period' unless the court gives permission. Paragraph 2.2 of the Practice Direction to Part 36 confirms application for such an order must be made in accordance with Part 23 CPR.

The 'relevant period' is the period specified in the offer within which the defendant will be liable for the claimant's costs if the offer is accepted or, if the offer is made less than 21 days before trial, the period up to the end of the trial or such other period as the court determines.

Where, within the relevant period, the offeror wishes to withdraw or change the offer and the offeree wishes to accept the offer the offeror will need evidence showing a sufficient change of circumstances if the court is to conclude that it will be just to permit withdrawal of the offer or a change which makes that offer less advantageous to the offeree. In *Evans v Royal Wolverhampton Hospitals NHS Foundation Trust*[166] Leggatt J held:

> 'The test to be applied when the court is considering whether to give a party permission to withdraw a Part 36 offer is whether there has been a sufficient change of circumstances to make it just to permit the party to withdraw its offer. That test was set out by the Court of Appeal in relation to payments into court in Cumper v Pothecary [1941] 2 KB 58 at 70. The Court of Appeal gave as examples of such circumstances "the discovery of further evidence which puts a wholly different complexion on the case ... or a change in the legal outlook brought about by a new judicial decision..." This test was adopted in relation to Part 36 payments by the Court of Appeal in Flynn v Scougall [2004] 1 WLR 3069, 3079 at para 39. I see no reason why the test should be different in relation to a Part 36 offer and, as mentioned earlier, the defendant's application to withdraw its Part 36 offer was made on the basis that this is the applicable test.'

Once the relevant period has elapsed then, unless accepted meanwhile, the offeree may either withdraw the offer or change the offer so that it is less advantageous to the offeree without needing permission from the court.

It is, accordingly, important that the offeree understands the risk that an offer, once made, may not remain open for acceptance because that offer may be withdrawn or changed by the offeror unless accepted meanwhile.

11.5.6.1   *Withdrawing a Part 36 offer*

CPR 36.3(6) allows the offeror, after expiry of the relevant period and provided the offeree has not previously served notice of acceptance, to withdraw the offer without permission of the court.

CPR 36.3(7) requires the withdrawal of a Part 36 offer to be effected by serving a 'written notice' on the offeree. There is no practice form for use when withdrawing an

---

[166]   [2014] EWHC 3185 (QB).

offer (unlike when making an offer) but the Court of Appeal in *Gibbon v Manchester City Council*[167] gave some guidance on what will be required to effectively withdraw a Part 36 offer. Moore-Bick LJ observed:

> 'Rule 36.3(7) provides that an offer is withdrawn by serving written notice on the offeree. In my view that leaves no room for the concept of implied withdrawal; it requires express notice in writing in terms which bring home to the offeree that the offer has been withdrawn. If justification for that requirement is sought, it can be found once again in the need for clarity and certainty in the operation of the Part 36 procedure. Although the rule does not prescribe any particular form of notice, in order to avoid uncertainty it should include an express reference to the date of the offer and its terms, together with some words making it clear that it is withdrawn.'

The need to 'bring home to the offeree that the offer has been withdrawn' suggests use of words in the notice such as 'withdrawn' or 'withdrawal'.

However, provided an offeror serves something in writing which would be understood by any reasonable offeree as withdrawing a Part 36 offer that should suffice: *Super Group Plc v Just Enough Software Corp Inc*.[168] In that case withdrawal was held to be effective by writing in the following terms:

> '...our client made every effort to settle this matter, which was simply ignored by yourselves and your client which offers are, needless to say, withdrawn.'

Excluding the concept of an implied withdrawal means that, for example, the making of a further Part 36 offer will not, of itself, amount to a withdrawal of an earlier Part 36 offer. On the facts in *Gibbon* a letter from the claimant's solicitors, rejecting the defendant's offer, was not only irrelevant, in the sense that rejection itself could not affect the status of the Part 36 offer, but could not amount to notice of withdrawal of the kind required by CPR 36.3(7).

The requirement to serve written notice of withdrawal, under CPR 36.6(7), and to do so after expiry of the relevant period, in accordance with CPR 36.6(6), prevents a party expressing a Part 36 offer in a way that prospectively, and automatically, withdraws the offer at the end of the relevant period. Depending on the precise words used such a term seems likely to either to be ineffective (so that there will be an extant Part 36 offer unless and until it is withdrawn or changed) or to create a time-limited offer (which by definition is not a Part 36 offer at all).

CPR 36.9(2) provides that once notice of withdrawal has been served the offer may no longer be accepted.

It is important to note that CPR 36.14(6) confirms that the costs consequences otherwise provided for in that rule do not apply to a Part 36 offer that has been withdrawn, or changed so that its terms are less advantageous to the offeree (provided the offeree has beaten that less advantageous offer).

---

[167] [2010] EWCA Civ 726.
[168] [2014] EWHC 3260 (Comm).

11.5.6.2   *Changing a Part 36 offer*

CPR 36.3(5) also restricts an offeror from changing the terms of an offer, to be less advantageous to the offeree, prior to the expiry of the 'relevant period' unless the court gives permission.

CPR 36.6(6) confirms that once the relevant period has expired, provided the offeree has not previously served notice of acceptance, the offeror may then change the offer, so the terms are less advantageous to the offeree, without permission of the court.

An offer must be changed, in accordance with CPR 36.3(7), by giving written notice of the change of terms to the offeree.

There is, once again, no scope for impliedly changing an offer, whether by making a subsequent Part 36 offer in different terms or otherwise. In *LG Blower Specialist Bricklayer Ltd v Reeves*[169] (the conjoined appeal in *Gibbon*) Moore-Bick LJ explained:

> 'Although at first sight it may seem anomalous that a party should be able to make several offers in different terms, all of which may at any one time be capable of acceptance, that does in my view reflect both the language and the purpose of Part 36. As to the language, Part 36 is quite clear as to the manner in which offers may be made, varied and withdrawn. It does not provide that only one offer may be available for acceptance at any one time; nor does it provide that a later offer is to be treated as a varying or revoking a previous offer and it would be inconsistent with the recognition of Part 36 as a self-contained code to read provisions of that kind into it.'

Hence Moore-Bick LJ concluded:

> 'There is no reason why a party should not make more than one offer and leave it to the other to decide which, if any, to accept. Or, if he wishes, he may change the terms of the original offer which then continues to stand in its varied form as from the date it was originally made. I accept that in some cases there could be argument about whether a later offer was intended to vary an earlier offer or to stand alongside it. The solution, however, is for parties and their legal advisers to follow the requirements of the Rules carefully and make their intentions clear. If they do so, problems of that kind should not arise.'

Consequently, an offeror who wishes to change an offer would be wise to use, in the written notice to the offeree, words such as 'change' or 'changed'. Additionally, for the avoidance of any doubt, the offeror may wish to expressly identify both the offer which is being changed and precisely how that offer has been changed. That might be by serving an amended version of the original N242A denoting the changes (assuming that form has been used to make the original offer). However, as when an offer is being withdrawn, there is no specific form of written notice and the test is likely to be whether a reasonable offeree would understand the notice given as changing the relevant offer: *Super Group Plc v Just Enough Software Corp Inc* (QBD 27 June 2014). In *Burrett v Mencap Ltd*[170] the court held the following wording was effective to change a Part 36 offer:

> 'We hereby change the terms of our client's Part 36 offer dated 19th of July pursuant to CPR 36.3(6).'

---

[169]   [2010] EWCA Civ 726.
[170]   (Unreported) Northampton County Court, 14 May 2014.

Once a Part 36 offer has been changed it is treated as though the offer had been made in its new form, hence there is no new relevant period, or window, for the offeree to accept the offer without penalty on costs: *Burrett v Mencap Ltd* (above).

11.5.6.3   Tactics on withdrawing or changing a Part 36 offer

Practical and tactical considerations will determine whether the offeror withdraws a Part 36 offer, changes a Part 36 offer or makes a further Part 36 offer.

11.5.6.3.1   When to withdraw an offer

When the offeror considers an earlier offer is now too advantageous to the offeror but cannot identify terms that would be acceptable, the safest course will be to withdraw the earlier offer despite the loss of potential costs consequences under CPR 36.14.

11.5.6.3.2   When to change an offer

When the offeror considers an earlier offer is now too advantageous to the offeror but can identify new terms which would be appropriate for agreeing the relevant issue or the claim as a whole, there may be advantages in changing the earlier offer rather than withdrawing any such offer and making a new offer.

That is because when a Part 36 offer is changed the original offer retains potential costs consequences, for the purposes of CPR 36.14, at a later stage (though it will then be necessary to compare the offer as changed with the judgment entered given the terms of CPR 36.14(6)).

Hence an offer, once changed, effectively continues to stand for the purposes of Part 36, though in its varied form, as from the date it was originally made.

Changing an earlier offer in this way will be crucial, if the terms are now less advantageous to the offeree, otherwise that offeree may simply accept the earlier offer.

11.5.6.3.3   When to make a new offer

The ability to make more than one Part 36 offer at any time allows the offeror, rather than withdrawing or changing an offer, just to make a new offer.

Where the offeror chooses to make a new offer that, in the absence of any implied withdrawal or change of earlier offers, will leave any earlier offers open for acceptance (subject to the terms of CPR 36.9(3)).

That does not present any difficulty where the new offer is more advantageous to the offeree, as will often be the case. Indeed, in such circumstances, it would not be appropriate, or necessary, to either change or withdraw the earlier offer, as the offeror will wish to retain any potential costs consequences of such an offer. Furthermore, even if the offeree decided to accept such an offer, which seems most unlikely, that would not prejudice the offeror.

The making of a new offer by the offeror, which is more advantageous to the offeree, does not impliedly withdraw any earlier offer hence any such offer will retain the potential for costs consequences under CPR 36.14. As Cox J explained in *Mahmood v Elmi*:[171]

> 'The automatic costs provisions in CPR 36.14 will apply whenever one party, whether claimant or defendant, fails to 'beat' a Part 36 offer made by the other, so long as the offer was made at least 21 days before trial and has not been withdrawn. There is no exception provided within the Part 36 regime for a party who chooses to make more than one offer.
>
> This regime also reflects what I understand to be common practice. Were it otherwise, a defendant who makes a Part 36 offer before proceedings are issued would be protected in costs only if he made no subsequent offers. There would be no incentive for him to make a further offer, as the trial date approached, because he would thereby be deprived of all the costs protection he had acquired until then. This would hardly encourage or promote the sensible and realistic settlement of cases, in accordance with the aim of the CPR, once litigation has commenced.'

For these reasons Cox J concluded that HHJ Holman in *Whitstance v Valgrove Ltd*[172] was wrong to hold a subsequent Part 36 offer effectively replaces an earlier Part 36 offer with the result that the earlier offer is withdrawn and cannot be accepted.

11.5.6.4 How to withdraw or change a Part 36 offer

The rules require written notice to either withdraw or change an offer. Moreover, the absence of a practice form makes clarity on the part of the offeror essential (see **11.5.6.1** and **11.5.6.2**).

The written notice must be served on the offeree. Once again, as when making a Part 36 offer, service will need to be in accordance with Part 6 (see **2.10.11**).

The correct method of service, at the appropriate address for service, may be critical if the offeror seeks to withdraw or change an offer before the offeree can serve notice of acceptance as occurred, for example, in *Sutton Jigsaw Transport Ltd v Croydon London Borough Council*.[173]

11.5.7 Accepting a Part 36 offer

There are a number of issues which may arise at the stage of the offeree wishing to accept a Part 36 offer.

11.5.7.1 When permission to accept is required

CPR 36.9(3) provides that the permission of the court is required to accept a Part 36 offer only where:

- the claimant wishes to accept a Part 36 offer made by one or more, but not all, of a number of defendants unless:

---

[171] [2010] EWHC 1933 (QB).
[172] (unreported) (17 September 2009, Manchester County Court).
[173] [2013] EWHC 874 (QB).

- in accordance with CPR 36.12(2), the defendants are sued jointly or in the alternative, the claimant discontinues the claim against those defendants who have not made the offer and those defendants give written consent to the acceptance of the offer; or
- in accordance with CPR 36.12(3), the claimant alleges the defendants have a several liability, in which case the claimant may accept the offer and continue with the claims against all other defendants if entitled to do so; or

- the offer includes deductible benefits, the 'relevant period' has expired and further deductible benefits have been paid since the date of the offer; or
- the court needs to apportion money in a fatal claim; or
- the trial has started.

Additionally, CPR 21.10 provides that where a claim is made by or on behalf of a child or protected party or against a child or protected party, no settlement will be valid, so far as it relates to the claim by or against the child or protected party, without the approval of the court.

Different considerations may be applicable depending on the circumstances in which permission from the court is required to accept a Part 36 offer.

11.5.7.1.1   Multiple defendants

Where the claimant wishes to accept a Part 36 offer made by one or more, but not all, of a number of defendants the court, if granting permission, may need to reflect, if the costs are not agreed, what seems appropriate on the basis of general principles applicable to cases where there are successful defendants and unsuccessful defendants (see **12.2.2**).

Subject to that costs point if the offer is 'on the table' it would seem likely permission to accept will be given.

11.5.7.1.2   CRU

If the claimant is accepting an offer inclusive of deductible benefits, where further benefits have been paid since the offer, the court may wish to consider granting permission in a way that does not prejudice the defendant. Subject to that consideration then, once again, it would seem appropriate to allow acceptance of an offer which remains 'on the table'.

11.5.7.1.3   Fatal claims

In a fatal claim the court will apportion damages in a way that protects, and reflects, the interests of all concerned.

Once again where the offer is 'on the table' it seems likely the court will give permission.

11.5.7.1.4   During the trial

Where a party wishes to accept an offer after the trial has started the court is likely to be more reluctant, than in the other situations covered by CPR 36.9(3) to give permission for acceptance even though that offer remains 'on the table'.

That is because the complexion of, and risks associated with, a case can quickly change as soon as a trial starts.

A trial is likely to have 'started' for the purposes of Part 36 at the same point as, under Part 45, the 100% success fee, where success fees are fixed under the rule, is triggered. For these purposes there is no distinction between the commencement of a hearing and the commencement of a contested hearing: *Amin v Mullings*.[174] Even if the final hearing only opens for the purpose of one party seeking an adjournment this is likely to be regarded as the commencement of the 'trial': *Liozou v Gordon*.[175]

Once a trial has started the offeree will need permission from the court to accept a Part 36 offer.

In *Sampla v Rushmoor Borough Council*[176] the principal issue was whether a Part 36 offer could be accepted after the trial had started.

The judge noted there was no implied term an offer could not be accepted once the trial had started, as that would inconsistent with the terms of CPR 36.9(3) which makes plain the court can give permission to accept an offer after the trial has started.

The judge held that whenever exercising the discretion to give permission to accept an offer once the trial had started the relevant test was that set out in *Flynn v Scougall*,[177] namely whether there had been a sufficient change of circumstances such that it would now be just to refuse permission.

A change in the perception of the parties on the likely outcome of the trial would be a material change of circumstance. However, it was not necessary for there to be a 'knock out blow' (for example the cross-examination of the claimant revealing a 'somewhat murky background' in *Proetta v Times Newspapers*.[178] As Coulson J observed in *Sampla*:

> 'There will always be cases, indeed they may be in the majority, where the individual events during the trial are not particularly dramatic or of themselves determinative of the eventual result, but where, as a result of an accumulation of small things – an unexpected answer here, an admission there, a judicial intervention that might not have been expected – the tide of battle during the days of the hearing flows resolutely one way.'

In *Nulty v Milton Keynes Borough Council*[179] the judge observed, similarly, that a Part 36 offer is directed to a contingency, namely the outcome of the trial. Consequently, once the trial starts the contingency has started to happen hence a case may go disastrously wrong for one party right from the outset or a judge may make observations indicating a fairly strong provisional view has been formed on the merits. In such circumstances, the judge concluded, a court would usually refuse permission to then accept an offer.

---

[174] [2011] EWHC 278 (QB).
[175] [2012] EWHC 90221 (Costs).
[176] [2008] EWHC 2616 (TCC).
[177] [2004] 1 WLR 3069.
[178] [1991] 1 WLR 337).
[179] [2012] EWHC 730 (QB).

In *Wilson v Ministry of Defence*[180] the words 'the trial had started' in CPR 36.9(3)(d) were held to include the trial of any preliminary issue. Consequently, where a Part 36 offer to settle the whole claim was made prior to the trial of a preliminary issue the offeree could not accept, at least in the absence of permission from the court, that offer once the trial of a preliminary issue had commenced.

Once such a trial has started, let alone concluded, it is likely a 'knock out blow' will occur. In any event, once the trial has ended but before judgment is handed down CPR 36.9(5) prevents a Part 36 offer being accepted unless this is agreed by the parties (and without that agreement the court no longer has discretion to allow acceptance). Once judgment has been given that will, of itself, prevent acceptance of a relevant Part 36 offer (see **11.5.7.7.4**).

In such circumstances the offeror may be in the unusual position of having made a Part 36 offer which can no longer be accepted but, as not withdrawn, continues to have potential costs consequences. Ultimately, so far as costs are concerned, much may depend on whether the offeree subsequently makes an appropriate offer to settle and it is possible more than one party could be in a position to argue judgment is entered on terms 'more advantageous' or 'at least as advantageous' as a Part 36 offer as occurred, for example, in *Pankhurst v White & MIB*[181] (see **11.5.7.7.4**).

11.5.7.1.5 After the trial

Once the trial has ended but prior to judgment being handed down CPR 36.9(5) prevents a Part 36 offer being accepted at all, unless the parties agree. Once judgment has been handed down, and even when a draft judgment has been circulated, it is unlikely a Part 36 offer could be accepted (see **11.5.7.7.4**)

11.5.7.1.6 Approval

Although CPR 21.10(2) infers agreement will be reached before approval is sought, given the approach in cases such as *Drinkall v Whitwood*[182] it would seem that there is no valid acceptance, which would amount to a binding compromise, until the court has approved the proposed settlement. This may be significant if the offeror, as in *Drinkall*, withdraws, or changes so that it is less advantageous to the offeree, the offer meanwhile.

11.5.7.1.7 Exercise of discretion for permission

The need for permission, where CPR 36.9(3) applies, clearly gives the court a discretion as to whether permission should be granted.

Usually on an application under sub-paragraphs (a), (b) or (c) of CPR 36.9(3) it seems likely, as already noted, the court will follow the approach in *Gibbon*, namely that a Part 36 offer should be treated as 'on the table' until changed or withdrawn, and hence be open for acceptance.

---

[180] (unreported) 23 April 2013, Winchester County Court.
[181] [2010] EWCA Civ 1445.
[182] [2003] EWCA Civ 1547.

However, if there has been a 'knock-out blow' or a sufficient change of circumstances (applying the test in *Flynn* from the days when permission to accept a payment into court late was required), so that it would be just to refuse permission to accept, even before trial, the court might so rule. That would be applying, by analogy, the test for changing or withdrawing a Part 36 offer within the relevant period identified in *Evans v Royal Wolverhampton Hospitals NHS Foundation Trust*.[183] Ultimately, as ever, exercise of discretion will be shaped by the overriding objective.

11.5.7.2 *When permission to accept is not required*

If the court's permission to accept an offer is not required then, unless notice of withdrawal has been served, an offer, if changed in that amended form, may be accepted at any time, whether or not the 'relevant period' has expired.

Even if a claim has been stayed an extant Part 36 offer can be accepted during the currency of that stay: *Hadaway v Raza*.[184]

A number of cases have illustrated how there may be valid acceptance of a Part 36 offer after that offer has been rejected or a considerable amount of time has elapsed, so the offer could not have been accepted outside of Part 36 under the general law of contract, including: *J Murphy & Sons Ltd v Johnston Precast Ltd*;[185] *Fitzpatrick Contractors Ltd v Tyco Fire & Integrated Solutions (UK) Ltd No 3*;[186] *Gibbon v Manchester City Council*;[187] *Mahmood v Elmi*;[188] and *Lumb v Hampsey*.[189]

For reasons explained by Moore-Bick LJ in *Gibbon* the general law of contract will not apply to Part 36 offers so as to restrict the ability of the offeree to accept an offer, unless and until that offer has been changed or withdrawn, but it seems likely the court retains a discretion which allows some principles from the law of contract to be applied by analogy (see **11.5.7.7.8**).

11.5.7.3 *Acceptance with multiple defendants*

Difficulties can arise where one of a number of defendants makes a Part 36 offer which is then accepted by the claimant, in reliance on CPR 36.12, without court permission or the claimant otherwise reaches terms with one defendant which involves discontinuing against any other defendants.

In *Messih v McMillan Williams*[190] the claimant settled the claim with one defendant and then discontinued against the other defendant. The issue of the costs of that other defendant then arose. At first instance, the claimant was successful in an application that the other defendant should not recover costs. The Court of Appeal, reversing that decision, concluded that there must be some reason to make it just to depart from the

---

183   [2014] EWHC 3185 (QB).
184   (Unreported) Central London County, 12 May 2011).
185   [2008] EWHC 3104 (TCC).
186   [2009] EWHC 274 (TCC).
187   [2010] EWCA Civ 726.
188   [2010] EWHC 1933 (QB).
189   [2011] EWHC 2808 (QB).
190   [2010] EWCA Civ 844.

normal rule, found in CPR 38.6, that a claimant who discontinues a claim should pay the costs of the defendant concerned (see **11.9**).

If several defendants make a collective offer this problem will not arise. Otherwise, however, the claimant may need to seek agreement the offer is made on behalf of all the defendants, or aim to agree terms in relation to the costs of those other defendants, as a preliminary to acceptance.

In personal injury claims where there is more than one defendant those defendants may be joint tortfeasors, or more likely separate tortfeasors but responsible for the same damage, so there is a reasonable prospect those defendants will confer and make a joint offer, combined offers or an offer by one defendant which acknowledges responsibility for costs of other defendants in the event of acceptance.

11.5.7.4   Acceptance with multiple offers

The decision in *Gibbon* confirms that where the offeror has made a number of Part 36 offers then, unless earlier offers are expressly withdrawn or changed, the offeree may choose which offer to accept. That is so even if an offer to settle an issue in the claim happens to coincide with an offer to settle the whole claim: *Mahmood v Elmi*.[191]

Where, however, an offer to settle the whole claim is accepted that has the effect of extinguishing the claim preventing the offeree then accepting any other offers that may have been extant up to that point. In Mahmood it was argued that an earlier offer should be treated as impliedly withdrawn when a subsequent offer was made because, for example, if a defendant offered £10,000 and then made an offer of £15,000 the claimant could otherwise accept both and recover £25,000. Rejecting that argument Cox J held:

> 'Once the claimant has accepted the second offer of £15,000.00 he has agreed to settle the whole of his claim for that sum. His cause of action would thereby be extinguished, and it would no longer be open to him to accept an earlier offer in respect of what would then be a non-existent claim.'

If, however, the offers do not all deal with the whole of the claim, or identical issues in the claim, they can be accepted individually, as occurred in *Mahmood*.

11.5.7.5   Acceptance after earlier rejection

Whilst CPR 36.9(2) expressly states that a different offer by the offeree (in other words a counter -offer) will not preclude acceptance of a Part 36 offer case-law confirms that this is just an example of how Part 36 operates differently to offers made outside the rule. In *Gibbon v Manchester City Council* the Court of Appeal emphasised the general law of contract, relating to offer and acceptance, does not apply where inconsistent with the terms of Part 36. Moore-Bick LJ ruled:

> 'Rule 36.9(2) is quite clear: a Part 36 offer may be accepted at any time unless the offeror has withdrawn the offer by serving notice of withdrawal on the offeree. Moreover, it may be accepted whether or not the offeree has subsequently made a different offer, a provision which is contrary to the general position at common law. The rules state clearly how a

---

[191] [2010] EWHC 1933 (QB).

Part 36 offer may be made, how it may be varied and how it may be withdrawn. They do not provide for it to lapse or become incapable of acceptance on being rejected by the offeree. That would be the case at common law, but it is inconsistent with the concepts underlying Part 36, which proceeds on the footing that the offer is on the table and available for acceptance until the offeror himself chooses to withdraw it.'

The Court of Appeal's answer to the central issue in *Gibbon*, that Part 36 offers are subject to the self-contained code found in the rule itself rather than the general law of offer and acceptance, draws a sharp distinction between offers to settle made under Part 36 and other offers to settle. That distinction is crucial to the acceptance of offers, as well as the costs consequences of those offers, with Part 36 offers, unlike non-Part 36 offers, remaining 'on the table' for acceptance unless and until withdrawn or changed (subject to the need for court permission only where the terms of CPR 36.9(3) apply).

Accordingly, the judgment in *Gibbon* endorses the approach previously taken by the courts towards Part 36, and before that payments into court, as being statutory schemes not simply based on the law of contract: *Flynn v Scougall*.[192]

Whilst rejection of a Part 36 offer will not have any bearing on the ability of the offeree to later accept that offer, unless withdrawn or changed by the offeror meanwhile, the fact of rejection may be very relevant if the claimant, having accepted the offer after expiry of the relevant period, seeks to argue that the usual costs consequences provided for by CPR 36.10 (5) would be 'unjust'. That is because, in such circumstances, the court may more readily conclude the claimant viewed the offer as inadequate rather than being unable, on the information then available, to reach a decision on whether to accept that offer within the relevant period.[193]

11.5.7.6 How to accept a Part 36 offer

CPR 36.9(1) provides that a Part 36 offer is accepted by serving written notice of acceptance on the offeror.

There is no practice form for the acceptance of a Part 36 offer so, just as when withdrawing or changing an offer, precision is important. The offeree may be wise to use words such as 'accept' or 'accepted'.

Particular care is required by the offeree if there is more than one Part 36 offer from the offeree open for acceptance at the relevant time (given that a further Part 36 offer will not be taken, of itself, to withdraw or change an earlier offer: *LG Blower Specialist Bricklayer Ltd v Reeves*.[194] In these circumstances the offeree should clearly identify the offer which is being accepted.

Even if there is only a single Part 36 offer open at the time the offeree wishes to accept precision is essential. If the intentions of the offeror are not made clear it may be necessary for the court to determine whether there has been acceptance or a counter offer, which may lead on to the further question of whether the original offeror has then accepted that counter offer.

---

[192] [2004] EWCA Civ 873.
[193] *S G v Hewitt* [2012] EWCA Civ 1053.
[194] [2010] EWCA Civ 726.

It may be prudent for the offeree to recite the terms of the offer being accepted to avoid any ambiguity and the risk of the court finding that, rather than accepting the offer as a whole, the offeree is offering to agree an issue or a part of the claim as, for example, occurred in *Rosario v Nadell Patisserie Ltd.*[195]

The requirement to serve notice of acceptance means that, once more, the terms of Part 6 are significant (see **2.10.11**). Acceptance must be served by a prescribed method at the appropriate address for service. Failure to comply with the requirements of Part 6 may give the offeror the opportunity of changing or withdrawing the offer, if appropriate notice is duly served first, before the offeree has served notice of acceptance as occurred, for example, in *Sutton Jigsaw Transport Ltd v Croydon London Borough Council.*[196]

11.5.7.7   Ineffective acceptance

Despite the terms of CPR 36.9(2), that a Part 36 offer may be accepted at any time unless the offeror serves notice of withdrawal, and the relatively limited circumstances in which permission to accept will be required under CPR 36.9(3) there remain a number of circumstances in which purported acceptance of an apparently extant Part 36 offer will be ineffective.

11.5.7.7.1   Agreement or agreement to agree?

For there to be effective acceptance there must be an agreement, rather than merely an agreement to agree.

An agreement will require a consensus between the parties on all necessary terms. Part 36, once again, will assist the parties in reaching agreement because, by definition, both offer and acceptance will have been in writing. Moreover, reference to Part 36 will carry with it a number of important consequences provided for under the rule, even if not expressly spelt out by the parties, which should ensure agreement is implied, if not expressly spelt out, on all terms which are likely to be material.

For an agreement, rather than an agreement to agree, there will need to be a sufficient consensus coupled with an intention to create legal relations. Consequently, the court may have to analyse the dealings between the parties, even where Part 36 has been invoked in the course of those dealings, if there is a dispute about whether the parties have reached the stage of concluding an agreement (see **11.6.4**).

11.5.7.7.2   Acceptance or counter offer?

An offeree, even when purporting to accept an offer, who adds terms or otherwise suggests there is not a consensus between the parties may be treated as having made a counter offer.

Where a counter offer, even implicitly, is made questions may then arise as to whether the original offeror has, by subsequent dealings, accepted that counter offer.

---

[195] [2010] EWHC 1886 (QB).
[196] [2013] EWHC 874 (QB).

These difficulties were considered in *Rosario v Nadell Patisserie Ltd*[197] where the acceptance of an offer by specific reference just to the sum proposed, rather than the offer as a whole, was held to be a counter offer that in turn was later accepted by the original offeror.

Similarly, in *Mahmood v Elmi*[198] the defendant's response to the claimant's unequivocal offer to settle the whole claim for Ł2,100, that 'we agree your figure of Ł2,100 for general damages', was a counter offer which, in turn, the claimant accepted to agree that issue. This, however, left the claimant's offer to settle the whole claim, even thought this was for the same sum of Ł2,100, extant, allowing the defendant to later accept this figure in settlement of the whole claim.

In *Howell v Lees-Millais*[199] the purported acceptance of a Part 36 offer after the trial had started was held to be a counter offer which, though not accepted, was of potential relevance to costs under Part 44 CPR.

11.5.7.7.3   Acceptance after strike out?

Where a claim has been struck out any Part 36 offer can no longer be accepted, even if relief from sanctions is subsequently given and the action reinstated, as the claim had in substance then been brought to an end. As Kenneth Parker J explained in *Joyce v West Bus Coach Services Ltd*:[200]

> 'The reason why the dismissal of the claim or the entry of judgment precludes the acceptance of a Part 36 offer is that on dismissal or entry of judgment the claim is to all intents and purposes at an end.'

Given that the offer would not have been withdrawn it would, unusually, still seem to have the potential for carrying costs consequences under CPR 36.14, on judgment, even though not available for acceptance and hence 'on the table'.

11.5.7.7.4   Acceptance after discontinuance?

Approving and adopting the approach in *Joyce* service of Notice of Discontinuance was held to preclude subsequent acceptance of a Part 36 offer in *Super Group Plc v Just Enough Software Corp Inc*.[201]

11.5.7.7.5   Acceptance after judgment?

For the same reason that it would be inappropriate for a Part 36 offer to be accepted after strike out, the unsuccessful party will not be able to accept a Part 36 offer, made by the successful party, following judgment.

If an issue, such as liability, is dealt with at a preliminary trial judgment on that issue would, on this basis, prevent subsequent acceptance of the offer even though the claim, as a whole, remains extant. Whilst decided under the pre-2007 version of Part 36 it is

---

[197]   [2010] EWHC 1886 (QB).
[198]   [2010] EWHC 1933 (QB).
[199]   [2011] EWCA Civ 786.
[200]   [2012] EWHC 404 (QB).
[201]   [2014] EWHC 3260 (Comm).

likely, on these general principles, any court considering the current version of the rule would follow the decision to this effect in *Pankhurst v White & MIB*.[202]

Once again, as such an offer would not have been withdrawn, there seems no reason why it could not continue to carry costs consequences though, as in *Pankhurst*, there might, ultimately, be offers by both parties which, to them, are more advantageous or at least as advantageous as the judgment entered. Under the current version of Part 36 the court may need to resolve that tension by deciding the extent to which costs consequences in favour of each party, on judgment, would be 'unjust' for the purposes of CPR 36.14(2) or (3).

Where there has been a trial the terms of CPR 36.9(5) prevent acceptance of a Part 36 offer before judgment is handed down, unless the parties otherwise agree. This rule does not deal with the situation where there has been a hearing which will be determinative of the claim, or a relevant issue, but that hearing is not a trial. The offeror needs to be mindful that the offeree may be able to accept during, and even after, such a hearing and hence weigh up the advantages and disadvantages of withdrawing or changing the relevant offer. Once a draft judgment has been circulated, purported acceptance of a Part 36 offer by the offeree, to pre-empt the formal handing down of that judgment, might amount to a contempt of court given that paragraph 2.4 (b) of Practice Direction 40E provides that no action is to be taken in response to a draft judgment before it is handed down, and paragraph 2.8 expressly provides that any breach of paragraph 2.4 may be treated as a contempt of court.

11.5.7.7.6   Compromise

If the parties reach agreement on the claim as a whole then as Cox J observed in *Mahmood v Elmi*:[203]

> 'His cause of action would thereby be extinguished, and it would no longer be open to him to accept an earlier offer in respect of what would then be a non-existent claim.'

11.5.7.7.7   Protocol offer

Where an offer has been made under section II Part 36, while a case is in the relevant Protocol, that offer, again because of the prescriptive nature of the rule, may not remain open for acceptance if and when the claim exits that Protocol: *Bostan v Royal Mail Group plc*.[204]

If a claim reams within the relevant protocol, and proceeds to stage 3, the offer was held to remain open for acceptance in *Purcell v McGarry*.[205]

Section II Part 36 does not contain provisions equivalent to S.I concerning the ability of the offeree to accept an offer in circumstances when that would not be permitted at common law. It remains to be seen whether the courts take the view S.II should, in any event, be interpreted in the same way as S.I or if, in the absence of express provision in the relevant part of the rule, the general law of contract will apply. This is a particular

---

[202] [2010] EWHC 311 (QB).
[203] [2010] EWHC 1933 (QB).
[204] (Unreported) Bradford County Court 11 June 2012.
[205] (Unreported) Liverpool County Court, 7 December 2013.

issue following the amendments to Part 36 in 2013 which deem certain offers to be 'protocol offers' with the potential to carry costs consequences after the claim has left the relevant protocol without, necessarily, that offer remaining 'on the table' in the way usually expected of a Part 36 offer.

11.5.7.7.8 General discretion and mistake

It does seem that the court has a residual general discretion, for use in appropriate circumstances, to control whether acceptance of a Part 36 offer is effective: *Warren v Random House Group Ltd.*[206]

That discretion might be used, for example, where the offeror makes what must have been to the offeree an obvious mistake in the offer.

Hence, in *OT Africa Line Ltd v Vickers plc*[207] Mance J proceeded on the basis that a party who had made a mistake between pounds and dollars in a figure offered in settlement would not be bound if they could show that the other party, or those acting for that party, either knew or ought reasonably to have known, that there had been such a mistake but otherwise there was nothing inequitable in holding the other party to the apparent bargain.

Where, however, there is nothing to alert the offeree to an obvious mistake it is likely that acceptance of the offer will create a binding compromise which the court will recognise.

Accordingly, in *Milton v Schlegal (2006) Ltd*[208] the defendant made a Part 36 offer of £4,300. After acceptance by the claimant it was contended by the defendant that there had been a typographical error as the offer should have been £1,200. The court held there was nothing on the face of the offer to suggest a typographical error, such as an extra zero, and there were no special circumstances so different from those contemplated or intended at the time the offer was made, that it would be appropriate to give permission for the offer to be withdrawn despite purported acceptance. There was, therefore, a binding settlement.

This approach followed that taken in *Hilton International v Martin-Smith*[209] where there was held to be valid acceptance of an offer which was regarded as unequivocal with no evidence the offeree either knew or should have known the offeror had made a mistake.

The same principles ought to apply if the offeree makes what must have been to the offeror an obvious mistake when accepting an offer though, again, the court may have regard to the overriding objective in determining whether or not such a mistake invalidates acceptance: *Draper v Newport.*[210]

---

[206] [2008] EWCA Civ 834.
[207] [1996] 1 Lloyds Law Reports 700.
[208] (Cambridge County Court 31 October 2008).
[209] (QBD 5 October 2000)
[210] (Unreported) Birkenhead County Court, 3 September 2014.

Whilst the overriding objective is clearly of the upmost importance when the court is determining issues of procedure it is not usually regarded as sufficient to override the substantive law (see, for example, the approach in *Burden v Harrods Ltd* (above).

When distinguishing an obvious mistake, which would prevent valid acceptance, from a mistaken offer that nevertheless can give rise to a binding compromise the court may also take account of the duties of legal representatives in this context (see **11.1.4**).

The court will, however, apply the overriding objective and, even when a mistake has been made, this may push the court towards concluding there has been a valid acceptance: *Barrett v Nutman*.[211]

In addition to mistake the general law of contract may also apply to vitiate a purported agreement on grounds such as misrepresentation, duress, undue influence and illegality (as well as capacity where approval has not been sought).

11.5.7.8   Action following acceptance

When a Part 36 offer is accepted paragraph 3.1 of Practice Direction 36A requires notice of acceptance to be both served on the offeree and filed with the court where the case is proceeding.

This is important to ensure the court is aware of the extent to which the issues have been narrowed, or the claim as a whole resolved, and also in the event of the defendant failing to honour the agreement, so that further steps can then be taken promptly.

Accordingly, whether it is the claimant accepting the defendant's offer, or vice versa, the claimant may wish to ensure this part of the Practice Direction is complied with by filing relevant documentation at court. Moreover, because the acceptance will not always spell out the precise terms of the offer it will generally be necessary to file both the offer and the acceptance at court. Obviously, this provision is only applicable when court proceedings have been issued.

Additionally, there are two situations in which, on acceptance of a Part 36 offer, a further step will be necessary:

(1)   If an offeree accepts a Part 36 offer which includes payment of any part of the damages in the form of periodical payments the claimant must, in accordance with CPR 36.5(7), within 7 days of the date of acceptance apply to the court for an order there be an award of damages in the form of periodical payments under CPR 41.8.

(2)   If the offeree accepts a Part 36 offer which provides for an award of provisional damages the claimant, to comply with CPR 36.6(5), must within 7 days of the date of acceptance apply to the court for an order for an award of provisional damages under CPR 41.2.

---

[211]   (Unreported) Liverpool County Court, 20 June 2014.

11.5.7.9   *Effect of acceptance*

CPR 36.11 provides that if a Part 36 offer is accepted the claim will be stayed, if the relevant offer relates to part only of the claim then the claim will be stayed as to that part on the terms of the offer.

Any stay arising under CPR 36.11 does not affect the power of the court to enforce the terms of a Part 36 offer or to deal with any question of costs relating to the proceedings. Furthermore, if approval of the court is required before a settlement can be binding, any stay which would otherwise arise on acceptance of a Part 36 offer will take effect only when that approval has been given.

In *Jolly v Harsco Infrastructure Services Ltd*[212] the view was expressed that the stay imposed by CPR 36.11 prevented judgment being entered, which may have some significance for the costs consequences in the event of acceptance of a claimant's Part 36 offer by the defendant after expiry of the relevant period (see **12.2.3.3.2**), although CPR 36.11(7) expressly provides that where a sum accepted is not paid within the appropriate timescale judgment may be entered (see **11.5.7.10**).

A different approach to the entry of judgment was, however, taken in *Ontulmus v Collett*[213] where the judge recognised the entry of judgment was consonant with CPR 36.11(7).

CPR 36.10 deals with the costs consequences on acceptance of a Part 36 offer.

11.5.7.10   *Timescale for payment*

CPR 36.11(6) requires the defendant, once a Part 36 offer to pay a single sum of money has been accepted, unless the parties agree otherwise in writing, to make payment of that sum within 14 days.

Where the offer included deductible benefits the sum payable will be the net figure. If there is an appeal against the amount of recoverable benefits, following the conclusion of the claim, a further sum may then be payable to the claimant (see **11.7.4**).

If payment of the full sum due is not made within 14 days the offeree may, under CPR 36.11(7), enter judgment for the unpaid sum. Whilst this rule talks only of the offeree making application the court may well entertain a request made by the claimant as offeror (when the defendant has accepted the claimant's Part 36 offer) to save the costs of an application that would otherwise be necessary, under Part 23, for judgment.

CPR 36.11(7) has no requirement for an application as it just provides that judgment be entered. Accordingly, a letter to the court should suffice, without any fee being payable, provided the relevant documentation evidencing the agreement has, in accordance with Practice Direction 36A, already been filed (and if not it will need to be filed with the request).

---

[212] [2012] EWHC 3086 (QB).
[213] [2014] EWHC 4117 (QB).

If such a request is made the claimant may also wish to request that the judgment expressly record any deemed costs order to which the claimant is entitled, on acceptance of the offer, under CPR 36.10.

If a Part 36 offer is accepted before court proceedings have been commenced this procedure will not be open to the claimant who may, therefore, need to issue a Part 7 claim form seeking a declaration a binding compromise has been concluded on the basis of a Part 36 offer that has been accepted. If, however, any agreed damages are paid, the only issue being costs, a Part 8 claim may be the appropriate way of dealing with those costs.

In *Cave v Bulley Davey*[214] it was held that the terms of CPR 36.11(6) required payment of the accepted sum in full by the due date even when the claimant had accepted the relevant offer outside the relevant period and it was agreed there would be liability on the part of the claimant for costs from the end of the relevant period down to the date of acceptance. That was because the terms of the rule gave no right to set off costs against damages in these circumstances.

11.5.7.11   Enforcement

Once the claimant has judgment, that may be enforced by any available and appropriate method.

11.5.7.12   Indemnity

Until 2007, when most offers to settle by a defendant required a payment into court, the claimant could be confident of receiving relevant funds on acceptance, as the monies would then be paid out of court.

It is now implicit that a party making a Part 36 offer is good for the money and will honour any agreement made by prompt payment. Where an insurer is involved on behalf of the defendant the claimant might have earlier sought confirmation that the insurer will indemnify the claimant and may, at the stage of any Part 36 offer, wish to make clear that reliance will be placed on that insurer providing an indemnity and hence making prompt payment if the offer is accepted. That should help to mitigate the risk of having to take enforcement proceedings against the defendant following acceptance.

11.6   NON-PART 36 OFFERS

A party may, as CPR 36.1(2) acknowledges, make an offer to settle in any way that party chooses.

Consequently, an offer to settle may never be intended to have the consequences of Part 36. An offer might, occasionally, have been intended to have the consequences of Part 36 but fail to do so because the provisions as to form and content in that rule have not been complied with.

---

[214]   [2013] EWHC 4246 (QB).

If an offer is not made in accordance with CPR 36.2 it will not, however, have the consequences specified in CPR 36.10, 36.11 and 36.14.

That offer may, nevertheless, have been put in a way that makes it an effective and admissible offer to settle, albeit in the form of a Calderbank offer, and hence with potential costs consequences under Part 44.

If an offer is neither a Part 36 offer nor an admissible offer to settle it may still allow the parties to reach agreement but should not carry any costs consequences, as neither Part 36 nor Part 44 will apply (see **11.2.2**).

Away from Part 36 the general law of contract will apply to negotiations between the parties. Consequently, it is important to have that law in mind when making, reviewing, withdrawing or changing and accepting such an offer.

11.6.1 Making a non-Part 36 offer

If a party does not wish an offer to be made under Part 36 there should be no mention of that rule, given the risk the court will seek to interpret any offer making such a reference as being an effective Part 36 offer with all the consequences that follow from that.

Because Part 36 is convenient shorthand for a number of matters any offer not made under that rule will need to be clear about exactly what is proposed. That will require express provisions as to whether or not interest is included, whether the offer is made without regard to CRU or inclusive of CRU (in which case a breakdown of the kind required by Part 36 may also be necessary), timescale for acceptance, timescale for payment of any sums due in the event of acceptance and, as there are no deemed provisions of the kind found in Part 36, what is proposed so far as costs are concerned.

If an offer may need to be relied upon so far as costs are concerned the letter should expressly be sent 'without prejudice except as to costs' (see **11.2.3**).

11.6.2 Reviewing a non-Part 36 offer

Although a Part 36 offer does, potentially, carry greater costs risk for a claimant it does, equally, confer a number of potential benefits including the ability to accept, usually, at any time until the offer is withdrawn or changed together with certainty as to the costs implications on acceptance as well as timescale for payment.

Accordingly, if a non-Part 44 offer is received in circumstances where a Part 36 offer would usually be appropriate the defendant might be reminded of the option to make a Part 36 offer and, particularly if there is any ambiguity in the terms of the offer made, invited to utilise Part 36 in the interests of certainty. In such circumstances the defendant might also be reminded that, should it not be accepted, the offer will not automatically carry the consequences provided for under Part 36 where any judgment does not prove 'more advantageous' to the claimant.

A further important consideration, if an offer is not made under Part 36, will be the application of the general law of contract. Accordingly, such an offer cannot be accepted in the event of:

- withdrawal (even if expressed as being open for a fixed timescale);
- rejection (which will include any response construed as a counter-offer);
- lapse of time;
- occurrence of an express condition in the offer;
- death; or
- supervening personal or corporate incapacity.

The claimant will have to make a decision within any time limit imposed about whether to accept the offer. Moreover, care must be exercised before making any counter -offer, if the claimant might wish to ultimately accept the offer made, given that a counter -offer will amount to a rejection ruling out any automatic right to accept the offer subsequently. In such circumstances the claimant may need to cautiously explore the prospect of any further negotiations without either rejecting the offer or even going as far as making a counter -offer.

Any non-Part 36 offer will need, as well as dealing with the substantive issues, to cover costs. Unlike a Part 36 offer there are no automatic costs consequences on agreement of substantive issues so express provision will be required and, without that, there is a risk the court will conclude any agreement makes no provision for costs. Accordingly, Unless the offer is clear in this respect the terms may need to be clarified.

The offer will also need to be clear about timescale for payment of any monies due on acceptance.

If a non-Part 36 offer does not expressly state for how long it is to remain open the offeree may wish to seek confirmation whether the offer is time-limited and, if so, what that time-limit is. The potential uncertainty, pending determination by the court of how long the offer remained open in such circumstances, was illustrated in *Wakefield v Ford*.[215]

Where a time-limit is imposed an important consideration on costs, at a later stage, may be whether it was reasonable for the offeree to make a decision on that offer within the applicable timescale. Consequently, if there is any reason why the offeree is unable to do so, because clarification is required or otherwise, it may be wise to inform the offeror accordingly within that timescale.

Away from Part 36 there is no right to clarification, as such, but it is reasonable for a party to ask for clarification where that is necessary to understand the precise terms of the offer. Failure to give reasonable clarification may be relevant to the costs consequences of the offer, including whether a decision to accept should have been made within the timescale for which any time-limited offer is open (see **11.5.5.5**).

---

[215] [2009] EWHC 122 (QB).

11.6.3 Withdrawing or changing a non-Part 36 offer

The restrictions found in Part 36 on withdrawing or changing offers, at least within the relevant period, do not apply to non-Part 36 offers. Rather the general law of contract will apply.

11.6.4 Accepting a non-Part 36 offer

The general law of contract, once again, will apply so far as acceptance of an offer is concerned. Consequently, specific requirements in Part 36 for effective acceptance of such an offer may not be essential, as what will be required depends upon the law of contract as applied to the circumstances in which the relevant offer was made.

If any ambiguity remains about the terms of the offer the offeree may wish to spell out the terms it is understood are being agreed on acceptance (though this carries the risk of the acceptance being regarded as a counter -offer with all the consequences that has outside of Part 36 on the right to accept the offer subsequently).

Whilst there is no requirement to notify the court, as there is under Part 36, on the acceptance of a non-Part 36 offer it is important parties bear in mind the duty to help the court further the overriding objective which will mean, particularly if any hearings are approaching, the court being informed promptly of any developments likely to affect the use of court resources, which will include hearing time.

It is important that any agreement reflects a clear intention to create legal relations or there is a risk that acceptance will not be effective to conclude a binding agreement: *RTS Flexible Systems Ltd* v *Molkerei Alois Müller Gmbh & Company KG (UK Productions)*.[216] Relevant principles, derived from this and other authorities, are usefully summarised by Males J in *Air Studios (Lyndhurst) Ltd v Lombard North Central plc*[217] in the following terms:

> 'In deciding whether the parties have reached agreement, the whole course of the parties' negotiations must be considered and an objective test must be applied: *Chitty on Contracts*, 31st edition (2012), Vol 1, paras 2-028 and 2–029. Once the parties have to all outward appearances agreed in the same terms on the same subject matter, usually by a process of offer and acceptance, a contract will have been formed. The subjective reservations of one party do not prevent the formation of a binding contract. Further, it is perfectly possible for the parties to conclude a binding contract, even though it is understood between them that a formal document recording or even adding to the terms agreed will need to be executed subsequently. Whether they do intend to be bound in such circumstances, or only as and when the formal document is executed, depends on an objective appraisal of their words and conduct.
>
> These principles are well established. They were summarised, for example, by Lord Clarke giving the judgement of the Supreme Court in *RTS Flexible Systems Ltd. V Molkerei Alois Muller GmbH* [2010] UKSC 13, [2010] 1 WLR 735 at [45]:
>
> > 'The general principles are not in doubt. Whether there was a binding contract between the parties and if so, upon what terms depends upon what they have agreed. It depends not upon their subjective state of mind, but upon a consideration of what

---

[216] [2010] UKSC 14.
[217] [2012] EWHC 3162 (QB).

was communicated between them by words or conduct, and whether that leads objectively to a conclusion that they intended to create legal relations and had agreed upon all the terms which they regarded or the law requires as essential for the formation of legally binding relations. Even if certain terms of economic or other significance have not been finalised, an objective appraisal of their words and conduct may lead to the conclusion that they did not intend agreement of such terms to be a precondition to a concluded and legally binding agreement.'

Lord Clarke went on at [49] to set out the well known summary of the relevant principles by Lloyd LJ in *Pagnan SpA v Feed Products Ltd.* [1987] 2 Lloyd's Rep 601 at at 619, adding that the same principles apply where the question is whether a contract was concluded in correspondence as well as by oral communications and conduct:

'(1) In order to determine whether a contract has been concluded in the course of correspondence, one must first look to the correspondence as a whole ...

(2) Even if the parties have reached agreement on all the terms of the proposed contract, nevertheless they may intend that the contract shall not become binding until some further condition has been fulfilled. That is the ordinary 'subject to contract' case.

(3) Alternatively, they may intend that the contract shall not become binding until some further term or terms have been agreed ...

(4) Conversely, the parties may intend to be bound forthwith even though there are further terms still to be agreed or some further formality to be fulfilled ...

(5) If the parties fail to reach agreement on such further terms, the existing contract is not invalidated unless the failure to reach agreement on such further terms renders the contract as a whole unworkable or void for uncertainty.

(6) It is sometimes said that the parties must agree on the essential terms and it is only matters of detail which can be left over. This may be misleading, since the word 'essential' in that context is ambiguous. If by 'essential' one means a term without which the contract cannot be enforced then the statement is true: the law cannot enforce an incomplete contract. If by 'essential' one means a term which the parties have agreed to be essential for the formation of a binding contract, then the statement is tautologous. If by 'essential' one means only a term which the Court regards as important as opposed to a term which the Court regards as less important or a matter of detail, the statement is untrue. It is for the parties to decide whether they wish to be bound and if so, by what terms, whether important or unimportant. It is the parties who are, in the memorable phrase coined by the Judge [at page 611] 'the masters of their contractual fate'. Of course the more important the term is the less likely it is that the parties will have left it for future decision. But there is no legal obstacle which stands in the way of the parties agreeing to be bound now while deferring important matters to be agreed later. It happens every day when parties enter into so called "heads of agreement".'

The fourth of these principles was already well established by the time of Parker J's judgment in *Von Hatzfeld-Wildenburg v Alexander*.[218] Parker J said:[219]

'It appears to be well settled by the authorities that if the documents or letters relied on as constituting a contract contemplate the execution of a further contract between the parties, it is a question of construction whether the execution of the further contract is a condition or term of the bargain or whether it is a mere expression of the desire of the parties as to the manner in which the transaction already agreed to will in fact go through. In the former case, there is no enforceable contract either because the condition is unfulfilled or because the law does not recognise a contract to enter into a contract. In the latter case, there is a binding contract and the reference to the more formal document may be ignored.

---

[218] [1912] 1 Ch 284 at 288.
[219] Ibid at 288.

I refer also to the helpful summary by Andrew Smith J in *Bear Stearns Bank plc v Forum Global Equity Ltd.* [2007] EWHC 1576 (Comm) at [171]:

> "The proper approach is, I think, to ask how a reasonable man, versed in the business, would have understood the exchanges between the parties. Nor is there any legal reason that the parties should not conclude a contract while intending later to reduce their contract to writing and expecting that the written document should contain more detailed definition of the parties' commitment than had previously been agreed."

More recently, this principle was applied by the Court of Appeal in *Immingham Storage Company Ltd. v Clear Plc* [2011] EWCA Civ 89, 135 Con LR 224. The facts there were particularly compelling in favour of a conclusion that the parties intended to be bound notwithstanding the contemplation that a formal contract would be signed in due course. The parties had reached express agreement in writing as to the application of one party's standard terms and conditions; certain subjects (board approval and tank availability) which had previously been stipulated had been lifted; the defendant had been expressly assured of the availability of the tank space in question and that it could now proceed to source its product; and the reference to a formal contract to be sent was stated to be in confirmation of what had been agreed. Giving the judgment of the court, David Richards J at [19] and [25] contrasted these factors with a case where agreement was stated to be subject to contract or subject to execution of a formal agreement and observed that they pointed overwhelmingly to an intention to create a contract. He added:

> "Set against those factors, the provision that a 'formal contract will then follow in due course' does not indicate that the claimant's acceptance of the signed quotation will be no more than an agreement subject to contract."

Of course, these facts were merely an example, albeit a particularly strong one, of a case falling on one side of the line. Each case will depend on its own facts.

> Because the existence of a binding agreement needs to be determined objectively and does not depend on the parties' subjective state of mind, evidence from the parties about what they intended by or understood from their written communications is of little or no relevance. There was a certain amount of such evidence from the witnesses on both sides in this case, despite the fact that the objective nature of the question was common ground, but such evidence was of no real assistance when all of the parties' relevant exchanges were in writing. The evidence was, however, relevant in informing me of the background against which the parties' negotiations took place.'

Moreover, away from Part 36 there are no deeming provisions dealing with a range of matters which, accordingly, will need to be the subject of express agreement. If court proceedings have been commenced it will be best to record all those terms in a consent order.

Matters that should be covered by agreement will include the following.

- What is the total sum payable (and does that include interest)?
- What, if any, deductions are to be made, for example CRU and/or interim payments?
- The timescale for payment.
- Payment of Costs (as whilst Part 36 makes provision for costs in the event of agreement on the substantive issues there is no corresponding implication away from Part 36 and in the absence of agreement the court may conclude either that there is no agreement or there is an agreement with no provision for costs to be paid by one party to another).

- What will happen with any pending proceedings, for example a stay or a judgment reflecting the terms agreed.

In the event of any subsequent dispute about the scope of the agreement reached an application may be made for judgment reflecting the agreement and for these purposes the court can be referred to correspondence that would otherwise be privileged (see **11.2.2**).

If the parties have reached agreement the court may proceed to enter judgment reflecting that agreement: *Ontulmus v Collett*.[220]

The general law of contract will apply to vitiate any agreement on grounds such as misrepresentation, mistake, duress, undue influence and illegality as well as, where applicable, capacity.

11.6.5   Enforcement

Where agreement has been reached, but not honoured, the claimant may sue on the agreement but may prefer to issue proceedings as a personal injury claim and seek a declaration that a binding compromise has been reached. The latter course has the advantage of allowing the court to determine any issue that may arise as to whether or not a compromise has been reached and may also, depending on the figures involved, prevent arguments about allocation to the small claims track.

11.7   REACHING SETTLEMENT

The objective of all forms of ADR, utilising Part 36 where appropriate, is to reach agreement on any issue, and, if possible, outright settlement of the claim.

If settlement is reached action will be required, that action depending upon the extent to which agreement is reached and the means by which that agreement has been achieved.

11.7.1   Agreement of an issue

A number of steps may be appropriate when agreement is reached on an issue, particularly if that issue is liability:

- The terms reached should be recorded, precisely, in writing:
  - If court proceedings have been issued those terms should be reflected in a court order.
  - If court proceedings have not been issued those terms should be recorded in correspondence.
- If agreement is reached on the issue of liability, where there is an apportionment, it is preferable to record that the claimant will ultimately receive the agreed percentage of damages and interest later assessed or agreed (to reduce the risk of the defendant asserting any apportionment amounts to an admission by the claimant which might found or support a counterclaim).

---

[220]   [2014] EWHC 4117 (QB).

- If a child or protected party is involved in the claim, the court's approval of the agreement should be sought either by application in existing proceedings or issue of a Part 8 claim for the purpose of seeking approval, as until approval is given there will be no binding agreement: *Drinkall v Whitwood*.[221]

- The claimant should be advised of the agreement reached and the implications of that agreement.

- The claim will need to be reviewed, in the light of the agreement reached, to identify further action now required or the extent to which the agreement modifies any pending matters or earlier case management directions (in which case further directions will need to be agreed or given by the court).

- If agreement is reached by acceptance of a Part 36 offer, notice of acceptance must be filed with the court where the case is proceeding in accordance with Practice Direction 36A.

- If there is any hearing date affected by the agreement, such as a date for trial of liability as a preliminary issue:
  - The court should be notified forthwith of the agreement reached, even if a draft order is not yet available.
  - All witnesses should be informed that attendance at court should not now be required.
  - Counsel's clerk, if counsel is booked or briefed, should be notified.

Once judgment has been entered on an issue such as liability the defendant can no longer seek to withdraw any admission on which that judgment is based but would have to have grounds for setting the judgment aside (see **4.3.1.4**).

11.7.2 Agreement of the whole claim

Some action will always be appropriate whenever the claim as a whole is settled. Further action may be required if court proceedings have been commenced and if settlement is reached on the basis of a Part 36 offer being accepted.

11.7.2.1 General action

A number of steps will always be appropriate on settlement of the whole claim.

- Confirmation should be given to the claimant that the case is concluded and a reminder given of the sums payable and timescale applicable for payment.

- Witnesses should be informed the case is concluded.

- Experts should also be informed the case is concluded, confirmation sought of any further fees and, as they are usually interested in such information, told the terms of settlement reached.

- Counsel's clerk, if counsel has been involved in the case, should also be informed the case has settled and an up to date fee note obtained.

- ATE or BTE insurers will usually require notification the claim has settled.

---

[221] [2003] EWCA Civ 1547, [2004] 4 All ER 378, [2004] 1 WLR 462.

11.7.2.2   If court proceedings have not been issued

The terms of settlement reached should be clearly set out in correspondence which the parties agree reflects the compromise reached.

Those terms will need to cover all substantive issues and costs (see **1.13**).

11.7.2.3   If court proceedings have been issued

When settlement is reached after court proceedings have been issued further action will be necessary.

- If a hearing date has been fixed, the court should be notified forthwith of the settlement, even if a draft order is to be filed and that is not yet available.
- If agreement is reached by acceptance of a Part 36 offer, the notice of acceptance must be filed, in any event, with the court where the case is proceeding in accordance with Practice Direction 36A.
- The need for a court order recording the terms of settlement reached should be considered.
- Where the claim has settled on acceptance of a Part 36 offer within the relevant period that, of itself, deals with the matters that might otherwise need to be covered by the court order, in particular CPR 36.10(1) deals with costs.
- If the claim settles other than by acceptance of a Part 36 offer within the relevant period (and even where that happens but there are terms reached above and beyond those covered by Part 36) there will need to be a court order.
- If there is to be a court order that may be dealt with in one of two ways.
  - There may be a 'Tomlin' order, which stays the action on the basis of the terms agreed. The disadvantage, for the claimant, is that if the terms are not complied with it will be necessary to apply back to the court for the stay to be lifted and further steps taken.
  - There may, alternatively, be an order, in the form of a judgment, setting out the terms agreed. The advantage, for the claimant, is that this is then an order which can, if necessary, be enforced, by any available means of enforcement, in the event of non-compliance.

Given the advantages of a judgment this will usually be the better way of concluding settlement though if, for example, the defendant is an individual for whom an adverse judgment might present future credit difficulties it may be more considerate to agree to there being a 'Tomlin' order.

If an order is required this will need to deal with a number of matters:

- To record any apportionment of liability (which, as with judgment on this issue only, is best done by stating the percentage of damages the claimant is to receive with further figures in the order being net of that percentage).
- To record the total sum payable and how this breaks down between:
  - Any monies paid into court.
  - Any CRU deduction or, where the terms of settlement are without regard to CRU, that the sum payable is net of CRU.
  - Any interim payments, whether or not made out of monies already paid into court.

- Any balance payable.
- Timescale for payment.
    - All interest up to the date of agreement being paid out to the defendant's solicitors.
    - All interest thereafter being paid to the claimant's solicitors.
- Costs, including the basis for assessment and any provision for a payment on account of costs in accordance with CPR 44.2(8). The order should also deal, if appropriate, with any variation to earlier costs orders (if it is agreed, for example, any interim costs order adverse to the claimant will be modified as otherwise those will stand, given the terms of CPR 44.4(2), despite the terms of any final order providing generally for the costs of the claim).
- Confirmation the terms represent full and final settlement of the claim, and if necessary any counter claim.

11.7.3   Finality?

Agreement between the parties, once reached, will amount to a binding compromise which, likely any contract, may be vitiated but only on grounds such as misrepresentation, mistake, duress, undue influence or illegality.

Moreover, once a judgment has been entered there will need to be grounds, of that kind, for setting the judgment aside.

If a judgment may have been obtained because of fraud by one party the other party may, rather than having to appeal, be allowed to make application to have that judgment set aside: *Owens v Noble*.[222] If, however, the matter raised, to support an application to set judgment aside, was an issue that was then compromised as part of the original settlement this may rule out any such application: *Zurich Insurance Co Plc v Hayward*.[223]

In these circumstances, if the claim has been compromised on acceptance of a Part 36 offer, such circumstances might well give grounds for seeking to have the stay lifted.

11.7.4   CRU

If there is an appeal against the amount of recoverable benefits, following the conclusion of the claim, the party to whom any refund is payable will be determined by the nature of the offer.

- If the defendant has made a gross offer including deductible benefits then these are part of the offer and if the appeal is allowed they are refundable to the claimant: *Hilton International v Martin-Smith*.[224]
- If, however, the offer is made without regard to benefits then any refund will be due to the defendant.

---

[222]   *Owens v Noble* [2010] EWCA Civ 284
[223]   [2011] EWCA Civ 641, [2012] 1 WLR 1962, [2012] 1 All ER 302.
[224]   (Unreported) 5 October 2000 (QBD).

11.8   APPROVAL OF A SETTLEMENT

If a child or protected party is involved in the claim some additional steps will be necessary on agreement of an issue or settlement of the whole claim.

Even if just an issue is agreed, in such circumstances, it is preferable to seek approval of that agreement from the court as there will be no binding agreement until such approval is given: *Drinkall v Whitwood*.[225]

Approval prior to issue of court proceedings can still be sought, by making specific application for that purpose.

11.8.1   Pre-issue approval

Approval is sought by issuing a Part 8 claim form for the specific purpose of seeking the court's approval of the settlement. The procedure that follows issue of the claim form will be similar to that which applies when approval is sought in proceedings which are already under way.

11.8.2   Post-issue approval

Application for approval should be made in accordance with Part 23 (see **8.4**).

However, if a trial date has been arranged, and settlement is achieved very close to that date, the hearing may be used for the purposes of seeking approval. In these circumstances the court should to be notified that the parties have agreed a settlement which the court will be invited to approve. The disadvantage of using the trial date in this way is that it may still be necessary to prepare for trial, and be ready to deal with a hearing, in the event the court does not approve the settlement. Accordingly, whenever possible, it is preferable to make specific application for approval and for a hearing dealing just with that application.

11.8.3   Documentation for an approval hearing

It is important the documentation for the court is fully prepared ready for the hearing of an application seeking approval of a settlement. In addition to the Part 8 claim form, in a pre-issue settlement, or application notice, otherwise, it is likely the court will need a number of documents

(a)   Factual evidence in the form of witness statements setting out the background.

(b)   All medical evidence relied on.

(c)   An up to date Schedule of Expenses and Losses.

(d)   Advice from counsel or a specialist solicitor (unless it is a case of very modest value in which case a statement from the lawyer with conduct of the file or case summary identifying the reasons why the settlement is recommended may suffice) together with, unless sufficiently set out in the advice, the instructions to prepare the advice.

---

[225] [2003] EWCA Civ 1547.

(e) A case summary (unless relevant matters are dealt with sufficiently in counsel's advice) confirming:
   (i) whether and to what extent the defendant admits liability;
   (ii) the age and occupation (if any) of the child or patient;
   (iii) the circumstances of the accident and, where there is an issue on liability, attaching any Police Report or Inquest Depositions with details of any prosecution brought.

(f) The approval of the proposed settlement by the litigation friend.

(g) A draft of the order sought, generally following form N292.

(h) CFO form 320, dealing with any payment out and arrangements for investment of the balance.

11.8.4 The hearing

The court will consider the papers and decide whether to approve the settlement, if so making an order in, or along the lines of, the draft with directions for any payment out and investment of the balance.

The court would usually wish the claimant, and litigation friend, to be present and so attendance should be arranged.

11.8.5 Professional responsibility

It is important, despite the requirement that the court's approval be obtained, usual care is taken in assessing the appropriateness of any settlement as the fact the court has given approval will not preclude an action for professional negligence if the settlement was one a reasonably competent practitioner would not have recommended: *Griffin v Kingsmill*.[226]

11.8.6 Investment

The court is likely to direct investment of damages on behalf of the claimant.

The court may be willing to order a payment out of court, straightaway, to the litigation friend either for the benefit of the claimant, where some specific need is identified, or, in appropriate cases, to reimburse the litigation friend for expenses and losses incurred by that person.

Further requests for a payment out will usually be arranged by the litigation friend who may apply directly to the court as and when appropriate.

11.9 DISCONTINUANCE

Discontinuance may be appropriate if, as the case progresses, risk is re-assessed and it appears the claim no longer has sufficient merit.

---

[226] [2001] EWCA Civ 934.

Before court proceedings are issued the claimant will, usually, be able to discontinue without any adverse costs consequences, even if the defendant has had to do a considerable amount of work complying with the Protocol: *McGlinn v Walsham Contractors Ltd.*[227]

Following issue of court proceedings discontinuance is effected by filing and serving a Notice of Discontinuance in form N279. However, care must be exercised before discontinuing the claim, following issue, as, under CPR 38.6 and CPR 44.12(1), a costs order will be deemed to have been made, on the standard basis, in favour of the party against whom the claim has been discontinued.

Application may be made to the court for permission to discontinue without adverse costs consequences, which will require an application under Part 23 rather than filing and serving notice of discontinuance. Whilst the court has power to make such an order the general approach is likely to be that where the claim is discontinued costs consequences should follow: *Messih v McMillan Williams.*[228]

In *Teasdale v HSBC Bank* plc[229] Moore-Bick LJ approved the formulation of principles, drawn from earlier case-law, by the judge at first instance who had summarized these as follows:

> '(1) when a claimant discontinues the proceedings, there is a presumption by reason of CPR 38.6 that the defendant should recover his costs; the burden is on the claimant to show a good reason for departing from that position;
>
> (2) the fact that the claimant would or might well have succeeded at trial is not itself a sufficient reason for doing so;
>
> (3) however, if it is plain that the claim would have failed, that is an additional factor in favour of applying the presumption;
>
> (4) the mere fact that the claimant's decision to discontinue may have been motivated by practical, pragmatic or financial reasons as opposed to a lack of confidence in the merits of the case will not suffice to displace the presumption;
>
> (5) if the claimant is to succeed in displacing the presumption he will usually need to show a change of circumstances to which he has not himself contributed;
>
> (6) however, no change in circumstances is likely to suffice unless it has been brought about by some form of unreasonable conduct on the part of the defendant which in all the circumstances provides a good reason for departing from the rule.'

These principles were also applied in *Nelson's Yard Management Co v Eziefula*[230] where the Court of Appeal emphasised that if there was no trial it was not the function of a court considering costs to decide whether the claim would have succeeded but rather whether the unreasonableness of the defendant's conduct provided good reason to depart from the terms of CPR 38.6(1) a relevant factor, when considering the unreasonableness of a defendant's conduct, was compliance with the spirit of any

---

[227] [2005] EWHC 1419 (TCC).
[228] [2010] EWCA Civ 844.
[229] [2011] EWCA Civ 354.
[230] [2013] EWCA Civ 235.

applicable Pre-action Protocol and where there had been non-compliance to consider dis-applying the default rule found in CPR 38.6(1). Even so the claimant, once a defence had been served, should have applied to have it struck out or for summary judgment. Hence, the proper order was for the defendant to pay the claimant's costs to the date of the defence and that, thereafter, there be no order for costs.

Accordingly, before discontinuing, it is important to consider the costs implications and either reach agreement with the defendant there should be no order for costs, and conclude the case by consent order rather than notice of discontinuance, or ensure the step of discontinuance is approved by the claimant and any relevant ATE or BTE insurer.

Where Notice of Discontinuance was served in error the court was held to have power to set aside the notice under CPR 3.10 in *Toplain Ltd v Orange Retail Ltd*.[231]

11.10 SANCTIONS

A party who fails to engage in ADR may well face, even if indirectly, costs sanctions.

A defendant who fails to make an adequate offer, even if the claimant exaggerates the claim, is likely, if the claimant recovers any damages, to face an adverse costs order. As Ward LJ observed in *Widlake v BAA Ltd*:[232]

> 'The basic rule is that the claimant gets his (or her) costs if the defendant fails to make a good enough Part 36 ...'.

A claimant recovering costs on the standard basis is unlikely to make a full recovery of costs and hence the incentive of indemnity costs which, usually, will only be recovered if the claimant obtains judgment in terms 'at least as advantageous' as the claimant's own Part 36 offer (see **12.2.3.4**).

Where the defendant does engage in ADR the claimant may be at some risk on costs, even if successful, in the event of a failure to reciprocate. In *Painting v University of Oxford*[233] Longmore LJ held that:

> 'Negotiation is supposed to be a two-way street, and a claimant who makes no attempt to negotiate can expect, and should expect, the courts to take that into account when making the appropriate order as to costs.'

Similarly, as Ward LJ also observed in *Widlake*:

> 'Part 36 now also affects a claimant. Whilst not obliged to make a counter-offer, in this day and age of encouraging settlement, claimants who do not do so run the risk that their refusal will impact upon the costs they may otherwise be entitled to recover.'

In the same way a successful defendant may be at risk on costs if that party has rebuffed efforts made by the claimant to engage the parties in ADR.

---

231 [2012] EWHC 4254 (Ch).
232 [2010] EWCA Civ 1256.
233 [2005] EWCA Civ 161.

Whilst rejection of an offer by the defendant, who goes on to succeed in defending the claim, would not be likely, of itself, to attract adverse costs consequences the failure to engage in ADR at all may do so.

Hence, if the claimant has made offers which are not reciprocated by the defendant, and it seems clear the defendant will not engage in ADR by negotiation, the claimant may wish to suggest mediation. It should be no answer for the defendant to argue that mediation is pointless because no offers will be made, as that is simply reflective of an entrenched attitude which is exactly the approach mediation is intended to tackle. Ward LJ has had some interesting observations to make about the efficacy of mediation, in such circumstances, when giving judgment in a number of cases (see **11.10**).

In these circumstances the defendant's stance may have costs consequences even if the claim is unsuccessful: *Halsey v Milton Keynes*[234] and *Burchell v Bullard*[235] where Ward LJ observed:

> 'The defendants behaved unreasonably in believing, if they did, that their case was so watertight that they need not engage in attempts to settle.'

If there is a refusal to mediate there must have been a reasonable prospect any mediation would have been successful for that refusal to have costs implications. If so, such a stance may be relevant not just when the defendant succeeds outright but where, for example, the claimant accepts a Part 36 offer after the relevant period and an issue arises as to the defendant's entitlement to costs thereafter: *PGFII SA v OMFS Co.*[236]

In Halsey the Court of Appeal concluded it would not be appropriate that unwilling parties be obliged to refer disputes to mediation but in *Wright v Michael Wright (Supplies) Ltd*[237] Sir Alan Ward suggested the court should consider imposing a stay where there was an unreasonable refusal to engage in ADR (see **4.3.1.14**).

Furthermore, the failure to engage in ADR is increasingly viewed by the courts as contrary to the overriding objective and a matter which may have a bearing on the appropriate costs order. In *PGF II SA v OMFS Co 1 Ltd*[238] the Court of Appeal stressed the importance of ADR, in the context of the overriding objective, and emphasised the risk on costs, even for a successful party, where there was inadequate engagement with ADR. Briggs LJ held:

> '... the constraints which now affect the provision of state resources for the conduct of civil litigation (and which appear likely to do so for the foreseeable future) call for an ever-increasing focus upon means of ensuring that court time, both for trial and for case management, is proportionately directed towards those disputes which really need it, with an ever-increasing responsibility thrown upon the parties to civil litigation to engage in ADR, wherever that offers a reasonable prospect of producing a just settlement at proportionate cost. Just as it risks a waste of the court's resources to have to try a case which could have been justly settled, earlier and at a fraction of the cost by ADR, so it is a waste of its resources to have to manage the parties towards ADR by robust encouragement, where they could and should have engaged with each other in considering its suitability, without the need for the court's active intervention.'

---

[234] [2004] EWCA Civ 576.
[235] [2005] EWCA Civ 358.
[236] [2012] EWHC 83 (TCC), [2012] 3 Costs LO 404.
[237] [2013] EWCA Civ 234.
[238] [2013] EWCA Civ 1288.

Concluding that a successful party who had, it was held unreasonably, refused to explore ADR by mediation Briggs LJ concluded:

> 'The court's task in encouraging the more proportionate conduct of civil litigation is so important in current economic circumstances that it is appropriate to emphasise that message by a sanction which, even if a little more vigorous than I would have preferred, nonetheless operates pour encourager les autres.'

Consequently, the litigant who wishes to avoid, at least metaphorically, the fate of Admiral Byng, as satirised by Voltaire, would do well to heed this warning.

CHAPTER 12

CONCLUDING THE CLAIM

12.1 INTRODUCTION

Until the court has given judgment, or the parties have agreed terms of settlement, on all substantive issues the procedural focus will have been on making best use of relevant protocols and the Civil Procedure Rules (the CPR) to help identify the issues and then deal with these in the most effective way.

Once the substantive issues have been resolved, further action, on a number of matters, will be necessary to conclude all aspects of the claim.

It is particularly important that the parties agree, or the court determine, issues relating to costs at the conclusion of the substantive claim. If the defendant is to pay damages, or give any other remedy sought, the claimant will usually wish for payment of costs to be a term of any agreement or judgment. However, an offer to settle made by the defendant, depending upon its potential for costs consequences, may influence the agreement or court order made on the costs of the claim.

Unless these are fixed or agreed, the claimant may need to take steps to have any costs, which the court has ordered the defendant to pay, assessed. And an offer to settle by the claimant may, if that offer carries costs consequences, have an impact on the basis for assessment of costs as well as the rate of interest and, from April 2013, the amount of damages.

The claimant may also need to take action to recover any damages and costs payable by the defendant, if these remain unpaid.

If the claim is unsuccessful there will still be matters which need to be dealt with, including issues relating to the defendant's costs.

Consideration, particularly where the claimant is receiving a substantial sum in damages, also needs to be given to the future. Appropriate information and, if requested, advice for the client, should be provided about potential future issues and steps that may be required to deal with these. That may necessitate some private client work being carried out on conclusion of the claim.

Each of these topics needs to be considered, and appropriate steps taken, before the claim is finally concluded.

12.2 COSTS

At the conclusion of the claim, in addition to dealing with the substantive matters, any issues relating to the costs of the claim will need to be resolved.

A claimant who has successfully recovered damages, or any other remedy, will wish to see provision for the payment of costs by the defendant either as part of any agreement reached or the court ruling, unless settlement is achieved in circumstances where an order for costs is deemed to have been made in favour of the claimant.

Furthermore, unless these are fixed, the claimant will need to have any costs payable under the agreement reached or judgment given assessed by the court, or reach agreement on the figure payable, so that there is a specific sum identified which, if unpaid, will allow action for the recovery of that sum, just like any unpaid damages.

12.2.1 Deemed costs orders

In certain very specific circumstances the CPR provide, even without express agreement, for costs to be paid by one party to another party and, where court proceedings have been issued, that there will be a deemed costs order to this effect.

Where there is a deemed costs order, that may exclude the court's general discretion as to costs and, in effect, automatically entitle a party with the benefit of that deemed order to recover costs.

12.2.1.1 *Deemed order in favour of the claimant*

CPR 44.12(1) (from April 2013, CPR 44.9(1)) confirms that where a Part 36 offer is accepted within the relevant period, so CPR 36.10(1) or (2) applies, a costs order, in favour of the claimant, will be deemed to have been made on the standard basis.

CPR 36.10(1) provides that unless the offer relates to part only of the claim or is made less than 21 days before the start of trial, that where a Part 36 offer is accepted within the relevant period the claimant will be entitled to the costs of the proceedings up to the date on which notice of acceptance is served on the offeror.

CPR 36.10(2) deals with a Part 36 offer which relates to part only of the claim and applies when, within the relevant period, the claimant both accepts the offer and abandons the balance of the claim. In those circumstances the claimant will, unless the court orders otherwise, be entitled to the costs of the proceedings up to the date of serving notice of acceptance. It is significant that CPR 36.10(2), unlike CPR 36.10(1), includes the words 'unless the court orders otherwise' giving the court a discretion, although in default of such an order the deemed order under Part 44 will take effect.

Whilst the costs order is stated to apply up to the date of serving notice of acceptance, the deemed costs order, like any costs order, will cover costs of implementation (see 12.3.6).

CPR 36.10(3) confirms that, if not agreed, any costs to which the claimant is entitled under CPR 36.10(1) or (2) will, if not agreed, be assessed on the standard basis.

Where the claimant thus becomes entitled to costs to be assessed, that will generate the right to seek a payment on account of those costs under CPR 44.3(8) (from April 2013, CPR 44.2(8)) (see **12.2.11.1**).[1]

If proceedings have not been issued, when the Part 36 offer is accepted, the terms of CPR 36.10(1) and (2) will still apply but, in the absence of a court action, there can be no deemed order under Part 44. Consequently, if the CPR contain a specific provision about how costs should be assessed, such as section II of Part 45, then that specific provision will apply rather than there being a detailed assessment (which otherwise would be appropriate under the terms of CPR 36.10(3)).[2]

From April 2013 the CPR makes clear, as CPR 44.9(2) will specifically confirm, that there will be no deemed costs order where a Part 36 offer is accepted before the commencement of proceedings.

Where there is a deemed costs order, Part 44 confirms that interest payable under the Judgments Act 1838 or County Courts Act 1984 on the costs deemed to have been ordered shall begin to run from the date on which the event giving rise to the entitlement to costs occurred.

CPR 36.2(d) requires any Part 36 offer to state whether it relates to the whole of the claim or to part of it or to an issue that arises in it (and if so to which part or issue). The nature of the offer, as defined by this rule, will determine the precise costs consequences that follow where it is accepted within the relevant period.

12.2.1.1.1 Offer on the whole of the claim

An offer made to settle the whole of the claim will, if accepted within the relevant period, carry the costs consequences of CPR 36.10(1), which unlike CPR 36.10(2) contains no discretion for the court to order otherwise.

Furthermore, once a costs order has, in these circumstances, been deemed to have been made it cannot be varied or set aside.[3]

In both *Walker* and *Lahey* the defendant repeated an earlier Part 36 offer but because those new offers were accepted within the relevant period the claimant, in each case, secured the benefit of the automatic costs consequences provided for under CPR 36.10(1), which prevailed over the potential costs implications of the earlier offers.

Despite circumstances, such as an earlier offer, which might otherwise be relevant in determining costs the court cannot, certainly where there is a deemed costs order under CPR 44.12(1), exercise that discretion and make an order as to costs of the kind identified in CPR 44.3(6) (from April 2013 CPR 44.2(6)). That is because the power conferred by CPR 3.1(7), to vary an earlier order, does not apply to a deemed order. As Dyson LJ observed in *Lahey*:

---

1   *Barnsley v Noble* (unreported) 7 March, 2012 (ChD).
2   *Solomon v Cromwell Group plc* [2011] EWCA Civ 1584 (see **11.5.5.1.2**).
3   *Walker Residential Ltd v Davis* [2005] EWHC 3483 (Ch); *Lahey v Pirelli Tyres Ltd* [2007] EWCA Civ 91; *Letts v Royal Sun Alliance Plc* [2012] EWHC 875 (QB).

'The ability of the court to vary an existing order is given by rule 3.7(7): "a power of the court under these Rules to make an order includes a power to vary or revoke the order". But we agreed with what Park J said in *Walker Residential Ltd v Davis & Another* [2005] EWHC 3483 (Ch) at paragraph 49: the power to vary or revoke an order given by rule 3.1(7) is only exercisable in relation to an order that the court has previously made, and not to an order that is deemed to be made by operation of the rules.'

In the light of subsequent authority[4] if a case is settled prior to the issue of court proceedings there will be no deemed costs order, and hence no entitlement to assessed costs rather than any applicable fixed costs. Equally, however, there will then be no proceedings which would be an appropriate forum for the court to make any order under Part 44 restricting the costs otherwise recoverable by the claimant on acceptance of a Part 36 offer within the relevant period.

The claimant may, occasionally, be faced with a Part 36 offer from the defendant which equals, or is more advantageous to the claimant, than an earlier Part 36 offer by the claimant. In these circumstances, if the claimant wishes to seek indemnity costs and interest, it will be important to make application for judgment rather than simply accept the defendant's offer. That is because on acceptance the deemed costs order, including provision for assessment on the standard basis, will prevail over the potential costs implications arising from the earlier offer.[5]

12.2.1.1.2   Offer on part only of the claim

If a Part 36 offer relates to part only of the claim, CPR 36.10(2) provides that if, at the time of serving notice of acceptance within the relevant period the balance of the claim is abandoned, then the claimant will be entitled to the costs of the proceedings.

This rule, however, specifically allows the court to order otherwise, hence giving a discretion as to costs not found in CPR 36.10(1).

In *E Ivor Hughes Educational Foundation v Leach*[6] the claimant sought damages of over £610,000, yet accepted a Part 36 payment of just £5,000 made in respect of part of the claim whilst abandoning the rest of the claim. The claimant was ordered to pay the defendant's costs because, CPR 36.10(2) applying, the court had a discretion to order that the default position under the rule, that the defendant pay the claimant's costs, should not apply. That discretion would not have been available had the offer not been for part of the claim and the terms of CPR 36.10(1) applied.

If the court does not order otherwise at the time, there will be a deemed costs order in favour of the claimant under CPR 36.10(2) and, again, once that order has been deemed to have been made it cannot be set aside under CPR 3.1(7).

The need for the claimant to expressly abandon the balance of the claim, when accepting an offer on part only of the claim, was emphasised in *Sutherland v Turnbull*[7] where the court held that simply accepting an offer for part of the claim would not suffice, a separate act of abandonment being essential under the rule.

---

4   *Solomon v Cromwell Group plc* [2011] EWCA Civ 1584.
5   *Dyson Ltd v Hoover Ltd* [2002] EWHC 2229 (Pat).
6   [2005] EWHC 1317 (Ch).
7   [2010] EWHC 2699 (QB).

12.2.1.1.3   *Offer on an issue in the claim*

The distinction between an offer relating to part of the claim and an offer relating to an issue in a claim is significant. That is because where an offer relates to part of a claim the court has a discretion on costs under CPR 36.10(2). If, however, an offer is made on an issue in the claim the terms of CPR 36.10(1) will apply, on acceptance within the relevant period, giving the court no discretion as to costs.

Crucially, an offer on liability is an offer on an issue in the claim rather than part of the claim: *Onay v Brown*.[8]

Accordingly, even when the defendant expressed the offer as being specifically on the issue of contributory negligence, the claimant gained the benefit of the costs provisions provided for under CPR 36.10(1) when that offer was accepted within the relevant period: see *Onay*.

The approach in *Onay* was followed in *Sonmez v Kebabery Wholesale Ltd*.[9] In that case the defendant made an offer on liability of 75 per cent, whilst the claimant maintained no deduction for contributory negligence was appropriate. The court entered judgment on liability for 80 per cent in the claimant's favour. The defendant contended this was a 'win' in the face of an outright denial of any contributory negligence by the claimant.

However, in *Onay* the court had concluded that even if there were no deemed costs order applicable on acceptance of the relevant offer, the claimant would still have 'won' and hence been entitled to costs in accordance with the general rule found in Part 44 that the unsuccessful party will pay the costs of the successful party. Similarly, in *Sonmez* the claimant was held entitled to recover costs from the defendant. As Goldring LJ observed:

> 'Contributory negligence will inevitably be intertwined with the defendant's liability for the accident.'

The same approach was taken yet again in *Sutherland v Turnbull*[10] where the relevant offer was to pay a percentage of the damages that would have been assessed on full liability, but only for some of the injuries suffered by the claimant (to reflect issues on causation that arose in relation to other injuries).

On acceptance of that offer, within the relevant period, an issue arose as to whether the offer related to an 'issue' in the claim, giving rise to the deemed costs order under CPR 36.10(1), or to 'part only of the claim', giving the court a discretion as to the appropriate costs order in accordance with CPR 36.10(2).

The court held, rejecting an argument by the defendant, that *Onay* was distinguishable because the offer here reflected issues on causation – the offer was on the 'issue' of liability not just a part of the claim. Moreover, there had been no abandonment of the remaining parts of the claim, which would have been necessary for effective acceptance under CPR 36.10(2).

---

8   [2009] EWCA Civ 775.
9   [2009] EWCA Civ 1386.
10   [2010] EWHC 2699 (QB).

Accordingly, the claimant was entitled to costs under CPR 36.10(1), which excluded arguments that might have been advanced as to the incidence of costs if the terms of CPR 36.10(2) had been applicable and the court was considering how to exercise the discretion on costs conferred by that sub-section.

In *Sutherland* the court also made an important ruling on one aspect of the definition of 'costs of the proceedings' which Parts 36.10(1) and (2) provide that the claimant will be entitled to.

12.2.1.1.4 *'Costs of the proceedings'?*

There may, at first sight, appear to be a conflict between the ability to make a pre-issue Part 36 offer, which by definition can be accepted before court proceedings have been commenced, and the entitlement, on acceptance of a Part 36 offer within the relevant period, to the 'costs of the proceedings' conferred by CPR 36.10.

Following the introduction of the CPR, with associated protocols, the term 'proceedings' had been given a wide definition, so as to include pre-issue steps: *Crosbie v Munro*.[11] This approach has subsequently been endorsed in the specific context of the term 'costs of the proceedings' found in CPR 36.10.[12]

In *Solomon* Moore-Bick LJ held:

> 'It is quite true that the word "proceedings" normally refers to proceedings already pending and Part 36 as a whole is primarily directed to that situation. In that context the extension of the Rules to enable Part 36 offers to be made before proceedings have been started might be considered to be somewhat anomalous, but the terms of Part 36 as a whole make it quite clear, in my view, that steps taken in contemplation of proceedings are to be regarded as "proceedings" for the purpose of rule 36.10(1). That is the natural meaning of the language used and if it were not so the rules would be silent on the consequences of accepting a Part 36 offer made before proceedings had been issued. I think it unlikely that the Rule Committee simply overlooked that. It is far more likely that it intended the word "proceedings" in rule 36.10(1) to be construed in the way I have indicated. I am fortified in that conclusion by the fact that a similarly broad approach to the construction of the word "proceedings" was taken, albeit in another context, in *Crosbie v Munro* [2003] EWCA Civ 350, [2003] 2 All ER 856, paragraphs 26–33, citing *Callery v Gray (No 1)* [2001] EWCA 1117, [2001] 1 WLR 2112. The effect of accepting a Part 36 offer made before a claim has been issued, therefore, is that the claimant is entitled to recover costs he has incurred in contemplation of the proceedings up to the date of acceptance insofar as they would have formed part of his recoverable costs if proceedings had already been issued.'

Consequently, if a Part 36 offer is made and accepted before court proceedings have been issued the claimant will, generally, be entitled to assessment of those costs, on the standard basis, because, in this context, the term 'proceedings' is broad enough to cover work done in contemplation of court proceedings. This confirms the approach taken in *Re Gibson's Settlement Trusts*[13] (see **1.13.3**).

Where, however, the provisions of section II or IV (from April 2013 section III) of Part 45 apply, then CPR 44.12 A(4A) confirms the court must assess costs in accordance

---

[11] [2003] EWCA Civ 350.
[12] *Thompson v Bruce* (QBD 28 June 2011); *Solomon v Cromwell Group plc* [2011] EWCA Civ 1584.
[13] [1981] 1 All ER 233.

with those provisions. In *Solomon* the Court of Appeal confirmed those fixed costs will apply despite the terms of CPR 36.10 referring to assessment. Moore-Bick LJ explained how this apparent discrepancy could be resolved when he observed:

'In a case such as the present, however, there are by definition no proceedings in which an order can be made, unless and until the receiving party issues a claim under Part 7 or one of the parties issues Part 8 proceedings under rule 44.12A. In my view rule 44.12 must be read and understood in that context. An order for costs cannot exist in a vacuum divorced from any substantive proceedings and accordingly an order for costs cannot be deemed to have been made under rule 44.12(1)(b) if a Part 36 offer is made and accepted before any proceedings have been commenced.'

Whilst the parties could expressly agree that fixed costs would not be applicable, the claimant would then also need to avoid making use of the procedure found in CPR 44.12A when seeking to recover costs. Moore-Bick LJ explained that was because:

'In my view the Rules must be read in accordance with the established principle that where an instrument contains both general and specific provisions, some of which are in conflict, the general are intended to give way to the specific. Rule 36.10 contains rules of general application, whereas Section II of Part 45 contains rules specifically directed to a narrow class of cases. Reading the Rules as a whole, I have no doubt that the intention is that Section II of Part 45 should govern the cases to which it applies to the exclusion of other rules that make different provision for the general run of cases. It is true that the procedure in rule 44.12A is not exclusive and that a claimant may start proceedings under Part 7 or Part 8 to recover costs under the terms of a settlement agreement; paragraph 17.11 of the Costs Practice Direction makes that clear. However, it is very doubtful whether he could recover more than the fixed costs for which Section II of Part 45 provides. It is unnecessary to decide that question in the present case, however, because both claimants issued proceedings under rule 44.12A. Accordingly, subject to any agreement between the parties to the contrary, neither can recover more or less by way of costs than is provided for under the fixed costs regime.'

If the claimant has issued court proceedings, at least by the date the Part 36 offer has been accepted, CPR 44.12A is inapplicable. That is because proceedings have been started so the fixed costs provided for under Part 45, even if these would have applied pre-issue, will have been superseded (as the scope of CPR 45.7 is confined to costs only proceedings under CPR 44.12A or proceedings for approval of a settlement under CPR 21.10(2)): *Shah v Elliot*[14] and *Letts v Royal Sun Alliance Plc.*[15]

If it is suggested court proceedings have been commenced prematurely (in effect without the claimant complying with timescales provided for in the relevant protocol) the court, even when there is a deemed costs order following acceptance of a Part 36 offer within the relevant period, can consider, when assessing costs under CPR 44.5, the issue of prematurity by deciding what costs have been reasonably incurred and hence are recoverable: *Letts v Royal Sun Alliance Plc*[16] (see **1.11.4** and **12.2.7.5**).

Where the claimant is entitled to the 'costs of the proceedings' under CPR 36.10 that will be the costs of the whole claim even if the relevant offer is on an issue only: *Sutherland v Turnbull.*[17]

---

[14]   [2011] EW Misc 8.
[15]   [2012] EWHC 875 (QB).
[16]   [2012] EWHC 875 (QB).
[17]   [2010] EWHC 2699 (QB).

That approach was endorsed by Tomlinson LJ in *Medway Primary Care Trust v Marcus*[18] where he concluded the term 'costs of the proceedings', found in both Parts 36.10(1) and (2) should be approached on the following basis:

> 'It is in my view implicit in this rule that in such a situation the starting point is that the costs recoverable will include those referable to the entire claim hitherto pursued but, by acceptance of an offer relating to part only of the claim, subsequently in part abandoned.'

That, as Tomlinson LJ noted when giving judgment, can present difficulties for a defendant who does not make, for whatever reason, an adequate Part 36 offer at a sufficiently early stage, because if made once significant costs have been incurred then provided that offer is accepted within the relevant period such costs will, subject to assessment, be recoverable.

A party, particularly a defendant, who wishes to make an offer to settle must be very mindful of the application, and potential scope, of the costs provisions found in CPR 36.10, particularly where the offer is accepted within the relevant period. When it is not intended that those consequences should follow, perhaps because there are issues about costs being restricted to those fixed under the small claims track or the offeror wishes to argue for an order other than the defendant paying the costs of the proceedings, the offeror may wish to make a non-Part 36 offer: *Hall v Stone*.[19] A non-Part 36 offer does not, however, always have the same potential costs consequences as an offer made under Part 36 (see **12.2.4.3**).

12.2.1.1.5   Counterclaim

Provided the Part 36 offer states that it takes into account the counterclaim, the claimant's costs will, in accordance with CPR 36.10(6), include any costs incurred dealing with the defendant's counterclaim.

12.2.1.1.6   Permission

Whilst the terms of CPR 36.9(2) confirm that, usually, a Part 36 offer may be accepted at any time, this rule is subject to CPR 36.9(3) which identifies a number of circumstances in which the court's permission is required to accept a Part 36 offer (see **11.4.11.3.1**).

Where permission to accept a Part 36 offer is required there will be no automatic entitlement to costs under Parts 36.10(1) or (2), and hence no deemed costs order under CPR 44.12(1) (from April 2013, CPR 44.9) when court proceedings have been issued, because CPR 36.9(4) stipulates, unless the parties have agreed costs, the court will have to make an order dealing with costs. Moreover, as the rule provides the court 'may' order the costs consequences in CPR 36.10 to apply, that indicates there is a discretion whether or not, in any particular case, to do so.

---

[18]   [2011] EWCA Civ 750.
[19]   [2007] EWCA Civ 1354.

12.2.1.2 Deemed order in favour of the defendant

CPR 38.6 provides that, unless the court orders otherwise, a claimant who discontinues is liable for the costs which a defendant, against whom the claimant has discontinued, incurred on or before the date notice of discontinuance was served.

Whilst the court may order otherwise a claimant, thinking of discontinuing, needs to bear in mind that once the claim has been discontinued CPR 44.12(1) (from April 2013 CPR 44.9(1)(c)) will generate a deemed costs order, on the standard basis, in favour of the defendant.

Consequently, a claimant who does not wish for those consequences to apply, on discontinuance, will either need to seek the defendant's agreement for the claim to be discontinued on different terms, for example that there be no order for costs, or apply to the court, given the discretion on costs provided for under CPR 38.6, seeking an order other than payment of the defendant's costs by the claimant.

If application is made, the claimant will have the burden of persuading the court to depart from the general rule that costs against the claimant will follow when a claim is discontinued.[20]

A claimant, who discontinues, also needs to be mindful that the terms of CPR 44.12(1), in the context of discontinuance under Part 38, may not deprive the court of jurisdiction to order that costs payable under CPR 38.6 should be assessed on the indemnity basis, see *Atlantic Bar & Grill v Posthouse Hotels Ltd*.[21]

The defendant will also have the benefit of a deemed costs order under CPR 44.12(1) (from April 2013 CPR 44.9(1)(a)) where the claimant's claim is struck out, under CPR 3.7, for non-payment of court fees.

12.2.1.3 Other deemed costs orders

CPR 44.13 (from April 2013, CPR 44.10) provides for a general rule that where the court makes an order which does not mention costs then, subject to the terms of this rule, no party is entitled to costs in relation to that order.

Where, however, the court makes an order granting permission to appeal or any other order sought by a party on an application without notice that order, if it does not mention costs, will be deemed to include an order for the applicant's costs in the case. The rule also makes specific provision for any party affected by this order, though deemed, to apply at any time to vary the order.

Given the terms of the general rule it is important, whenever the court makes an order when there is no such deeming provision, that this does deal appropriately with costs.

---

[20] *Walker v Walker* [2005] EWCA Civ 247; *Messih v McMillan Williams* [2010] EWCA Civ 844.
[21] (Unreported) 2 November, 1999 (ChD).

12.2.1.4   Interest

CPR 44.12(2) (from April 2013, CPR 44.9(4)) provides that interest, under the Judgments Act 1838, on costs deemed to have been ordered under paragraph (1) of the rule, shall begin to run from the date on which the event which gave rise to the entitlement to costs occurred.

12.2.2   The court's discretion on costs

When there is no deemed costs order, or at least entitlement to assessment of costs without specific agreement to this effect, a party who wishes to recover costs will need to rely on the court exercising discretion to make an appropriate order in favour of that party.

That order may be a ruling on costs as part of a judgment dealing with the substantive issues. More frequently, terms on costs will be agreed by the parties, following settlement of the substantive issues, in anticipation of the way in which the court would exercise discretion when making an order dealing with costs, following the terms agreed, if called upon to do so.

Occasionally, having otherwise agreed terms, the parties may invite the court to make a ruling just on the issue of costs. Whilst, from time to time, it will be appropriate to determine the issue of costs in these circumstances the court will, generally, be reluctant to do so for the reasons explained in *BCT Software Solutions Ltd v C Brewer & Sons Ltd.*[22]

12.2.2.1   The discretion

The court's discretion as to costs is dealt with by CPR 44.3 (renumbered from April 2013 as CPR 44.2 but with the number of the sub-rules still following the same sequence).

CPR 44.3(1) confirms the court has discretion as to whether costs are to be payable by one party to another and, if so, a discretion on the amount of those costs as well as when such costs are to be paid.

The exercise of that general discretion is shaped by the further terms of CPR 44.3.

12.2.2.2   The general rule

CPR 44.3(2)(a) provides that if the court decides to make an order about costs, the general rule is that the unsuccessful party will be ordered to pay the costs of the successful party (though CPR 44.3(2)(b) confirms the court may make a different order).

---

[22]   [2003] EWCA Civ 9399.

12.2.2.2.1   *Starting point*

This general rule must, therefore, be the starting point for the court when deciding what order to make about costs. In many cases this starting point will also be the finishing point for reasons explained by Jackson LJ in *Fox v Foundation Piling Ltd*[23] when he said:

> 'There has been a growing and unwelcome tendency by first instance courts and, dare I say it, this court as well to depart from the starting point set out in rule 44.3(2) (a) too far and too often. Such an approach may strive for perfect justice in the individual case, but at huge additional cost to the parties and at huge costs to other litigants because of the uncertainty which such an approach generates. This unwelcome trend now manifests itself in (a) numerous first instance hearings in which the only issue is costs and (b) a swarm of appeals to the Court of Appeal about costs, of which this case is an example.'

The case-law on this issue, to which Jackson LJ was referring in *Fox*, was reviewed by Coulson J in *Brit Inns Ltd v BDW Trading Ltd*[24] where, after considering relevant authorities, a number of general principles, and the cases these can be drawn from, were identified:

- In a commercial case the successful party will usually be the party that recovers money from the other.[25]

- The only certain way for a defendant to shift potential cost liability is to make a Part 36 offer which it betters at trial.[26]

- An exaggerated claim may deprive the claimant of some or all of costs otherwise payable.[27]

- However, it is usually only where the exaggeration is deliberate that the claimant has been ordered to pay the defendant's costs.[28]

- In general terms, for costs to be shifted as a result of conduct, there needs to be a more or less total failure on the issues that went to trial[29] or a failure to accept a Part 44 offer that would have put the claimant in a better position than going on.[30]

It is important, when exercising discretion on costs under Part 44, that the court does start by identifying the successful party and hence with the general rule. Failure to do so may well be an error of law.

12.2.2.2.2   *Claims about money*

In *Barnes v Time Talk (UK) Ltd*[31] Longmore LJ observed that when deciding who was the successful party 'the most important thing is to identify the party who is to pay

---

23   [2011] EWCA Civ 790.
24   [2012] EWHC 2489 (TCC).
25   *Multiplex Constructions (UK) Ltd v Cleveland Bridge UK Ltd* [2008] EWHC 2280 (TCC); *Gibbon v Manchester City Council* [2010] EWCA Civ 726.
26   *Gibbon v Manchester City Council* [2010] EWCA Civ 726; *Fox v Foundation Piling Ltd* [2011] EWCA Civ 790.
27   *Islam v Ali* [2003] EWCA Civ 612; *Fulham Leisure Holdings Ltd v Nicholson Graham and Jones* [2006] EWHC 2428 (Ch).
28   *Painting v University of Oxford* [2005] EWCA Civ 161; *Ford v GKR Construction Ltd* [2001] 1 WLR 1397.
29   *Hullock v East Riding of Yorkshire County Council* [2009] EWCA Civ 1039.
30   *Fulham Leisure Holdings Ltd v Nicholson Graham and Jones* [2006] EWHC 2428 (Ch).
31   [2003] EWCA Civ 402.

money to the other'. That approach was endorsed by Waller LJ in *Straker v Tudor Rose*[32] and confirmed again by Ward LJ in *Widlake v BAA Ltd*[33] where he held:

> 'Although it was a case set in a commercial context, Waller LJ was surely right in *Straker* to endorse Longmore LJ's views that the most important thing is to identify the party who is to pay money to the other even in a case of personal injury. The claimant had to come to court to establish her claim, a genuine claim, because she had suffered an injury through the admitted negligence of the defendant. The judgment in her favour is a vindication of her stance.'

Personal injury cases are indeed, like commercial cases, generally about money, at least in terms of the remedy the court can provide, so this approach to determining who is the successful party seems entirely apposite.

12.2.2.2.3   Claims about more than money

Occasionally, however, a case may be about more than money which can make discerning the successful party more difficult. Even so the court may prefer, particularly if considering the impact of a Part 36 offer, to consider costs in the context of whether Part 36 costs consequences would be 'unjust' rather than artificially determining who has been the successful party: *Smith v Trafford Housing Trust.*[34]

Where a claim is clearly about more than just money, the test for the judge, in determining who has been the successful party was identified by Sir Thomas Bingham MR in *Roache v News Group Newspapers Ltd*[35] when he held:

> 'The judge must look closely at the facts of the particular case before him and ask: who, as a matter of substance and reality, has won? Has the plaintiff won anything of value which he could not have won without fighting the action through to a finish? Has the defendant substantially denied the plaintiff the prize which the plaintiff fought the action to win?'

12.2.2.2.4   Multiple defendants

The general rule applies equally to claims against multiple defendants. Where, however, there are unsuccessful defendants and successful defendants the court may order that the costs of successful defendants be costs the claimant can recover, as part of the costs of the claim, from unsuccessful defendants. When that occurs the court also has discretion to provide that such costs be paid:

- direct by the unsuccessful defendant to the successful defendant: *Sanderson v Blyth Theatre Company*;[36] or

- by the claimant to the successful defendant but with the right to recover those costs from the unsuccessful defendant: *Bullock v London General Omnibus Co.*[37]

Either of these orders will only be appropriate if the claimant is considered by the court to have behaved reasonably in suing more than one defendant, so that it would not be unjust for a defendant to be ordered to pay the costs of another defendant.

---

[32]   [2007] EWCA Civ 368.
[33]   [2009] EWCA Civ 1256.
[34]   [2012] EWHC 3320 (Ch).
[35]   Court of Appeal, 19 November 1992.
[36]   [1903] 2 KB 533.
[37]   [1907] 1 KB 264.

In *Moon v Garrett*[38] the Court of Appeal held that whilst, for such an order to be just, it will usually be necessary for the claimant to have sued the relevant defendants in the alternative, that is not always essential. Waller LJ explained that:

> 'It seems to me that ... there are no hard and fast rules as to when it is appropriate to make a *Bullock* or *Sanderson* order. The court takes into account the fact that, if a claimant has behaved reasonably in suing two defendants, it will be harsh if he ends up paying the costs of the defendant against whom he has not succeeded. Equally, if it was not reasonable to join one defendant because the cause of action was practically unsustainable, it would be unjust to make a co-defendant pay those defendant's costs. Those costs should be paid by a claimant. It will always be a factor whether one defendant has sought to blame another.'

In *Moon* the Court of Appeal also confirmed that the pre-CPR jurisdiction to make such an order had survived, given the terms of CPR 44.3.

Where Part 20 claims are taken, an unsuccessful Part 20 claimant will normally be ordered to pay all the Part 20 costs of the successful Part 20 defendant unless that would be unjust, for example where the claimant joined the successful Part 20 defendant and failed in that claim as well as the claim against the original defendant: *Green v Sunset & Vine Production Ltd.*[39]

Where the claimant is successful against some defendants but not others, it is preferable for the agreement, or order, to spell out the precise costs consequences. In *Nassif v Augusta Offshore SPA*[40] the claimant issued proceedings against three defendants. Eventually, judgment was entered with provision for the first defendant to pay the claimant's costs of the claim. On the basis of that order the claimant was not entitled to recover costs against the second defendant and the third defendant, although the claimant's position was made more problematic because the claims against those defendants had previously been discontinued, hence the words 'the claim' were held to be applicable only to the remaining live claim.

12.2.2.2.5 Counterclaims

Difficulties can also arise, applying the general rule, where there is a claim and a counterclaim.

What may be termed common costs will not be apportioned between the claim and counterclaim but may be divided.[41]

If the parties wish costs to be approached in a different way, sometimes appropriate because the insurers of each party will pay the costs of the claim and counterclaim respectively, any agreement should record that the principle of not apportioning costs will be inapplicable.

Issues can also arise where there is an apportionment on liability in a case where there is a claim and a, at least potential, counterclaim: *Parkes v Martin.*[42] Where, however, the

---

[38] [2006] EWCA Civ 1121.
[39] [2009] EWHC 1610 (QB).
[40] [2009] EWHC 90143 (Costs).
[41] *Medway Oil and Storage Co Ltd v Continental Contractors Ltd* [1929] AC 88; *Hay v Szterbin* [2010] EWHC 1967 (Ch).
[42] [2009] EWCA Civ 883.

only issue is contributory negligence, a claimant who succeeds on the issue of primary liability is likely to be regarded as the successful party[43] (see **12.2.1.1.3**).

12.2.2.2.6   Appeals

The general rule will also have application to an appeal hearing.

Moreover, CPR 44.13(2) (from April 2013, CPR 44.10(4)) confirms that the appellate court may, unless it dismissed the appeal, make orders about the costs of the proceedings giving rise to the appeal as well as the costs of the appeal. Consequently, the general rule may, in effect, be applied with hindsight once the outcome of the appeal, if successful, is known.

12.2.2.3   Departing from the general rule

The starting point for the exercise of the court's discretion on costs, that if there is to be a costs order the unsuccessful party will pay the costs of the successful party, may not always be the finishing point. That is because CPR 44.3(4) requires the court, when exercising discretion as to costs, to have regard to all the circumstances and goes on to identify some circumstances which, if applicable, will always be relevant to this discretion.

Before, however, considering circumstances relevant to the exercise of the general discretion referred to in CPR 44.3, and in particular the circumstances which indicate the court should depart from the general rule, it is appropriate to consider how a relevant Part 36 offer may modify, and potentially restrict, the general discretion on costs found in Part 44.

The costs consequences of Part 36 will override the application of the general discretion found in Part 44 when a party accepts a Part 36 offer after expiry of the relevant period or, when judgment is entered, the court has to compare the terms of a judgment with an extant Part 36 offer. Hence the observation by Coulson J in *Brit Inns Ltd* that a Part 36 offer is the only way of securing certainty on the costs consequences of an offer, a point previously recognised by Moore-Bick LJ in *Gibbon v Manchester City Council*[44] when he held:

> 'In seeking to settle the proceedings, therefore, parties are not bound to make use of the mechanism provided by Part 36, but if they wish to take advantage of the particular consequences for costs and other matters that flow from making a Part 36 offer, in relation to which the court's discretion is much more confined, they must follow its requirements.'

Hence the costs consequences of any relevant Part 36 offer should be the starting point for the court, once the successful party has been identified, in determining whether there should be any departure from the general rule, before going on to consider other circumstances including those specifically identified by CPR 44.3(4).

---

[43]   *Onay v Brown* [2009] EWCA Civ 775; *Sonmez v Kebabery Wholesale Ltd* [2009] EWCA Civ 1386.
[44]   [2010] EWCA Civ 726.

12.2.3 Costs consequences of Part 36 offers

Parts 36.10 and 36.14 deal with the cost consequences of the rule.

Whilst CPR 36.10 deals with the costs consequences on acceptance of an offer made under the rule, CPR 36.14 deals with the costs consequences of such an offer following judgment.

Where an offer to settle the whole claim, or issue in the claim, is accepted within the relevant period, specific costs consequences are deemed to apply by CPR 36.10(1) (see **12.2.1.1**).

In other circumstances, under both CPR 36.10 and CPR 36.14, the court will be exercising a discretion as to costs, but a much more restricted discretion than that conferred by CPR 44.3 given the prescriptive nature of both CPR 36.10 and CPR 36.14.

12.2.3.1 Preliminaries to costs consequences under Part 36

CPR 36.1(2) confirms that if an offer is not made in accordance with the terms of CPR 36.2 it will not have the consequences specified in CPR 36.10 and CPR 36.14. Accordingly, it is vital the rules on form and content are complied with if an offer is to carry costs consequences under Part 36 (see **11.5.4.1**).

More fundamentally there must, before this is clothed with potential costs consequences under the rule by reference to Part 36, be an 'offer'.

Consequently, a proposal which, in effect, seeks total capitulation on the part of the offeree may not be an offer at all: *AB v CD*[45] (see **11.5.5.1**).

Similarly, a proposal must have the necessary degree of finality, if accepted, to constitute an offer, so an interim payment would not suffice for these purposes: *Ali v Stagecoach*[46] (see **11.2.1**).

Furthermore, a Part 36 offer carries costs consequences of CPR 36.10 and CPR 36.14 only in relation to the costs of the proceedings in which that offer is made and, specifically, not to any appeal from a final decision in those proceedings.

This rule means it is essential, in the event of an appeal against a final order, that the parties consider whether any further Part 36 offer is appropriate in order to secure the potential consequences provided for under CPR 36.14(1), in relation to the appeal, whilst remaining mindful of the costs consequences in the event of such an offer being accepted within the relevant period.

A party may make a Part 36 offer in appeal proceedings which are subject to the CPR even if the decision being appealed was made in a forum, such as a tribunal, where Part 36 would not applicable: *Blue Sphere Global Ltd v Revenue & Customs Commissioners*.[47]

---

[45]   [2011] EWHC 602 (Ch).
[46]   [2011] EWCA Civ 1494.
[47]   [2010] EWCA Civ 517.

Blue Sphere Global Ltd also confirms an offer made in appeal proceedings, by a claimant who is the respondent in that appeal, can be very effective for the purposes of CPR 36.14.

If there is an offer, but not an effective Part 36 offer, acceptance will be governed by the general law of contract, rather than the terms of Part 36, and any costs consequences solely by the terms of CPR 44.3 (see **12.2.4.3**). If an offer is effective under Part 36 then the terms of that rule will prevail over the common law, so far as acceptance is concerned, and, crucially, provide for very specific costs consequences in relevant circumstances identified in the rule.

Finally, CPR 36.13 does prevent the court being referred to a Part 36 offer in certain circumstances, notably when the trial of preliminary issues has taken place but the claim as a whole is not resolved (see **11.2.4**).

12.2.3.2   Costs consequences on acceptance of a Part 36 offer within the relevant period

Where a Part 36 offer is accepted within the relevant period there will be costs consequences in favour of the claimant (see **12.2.1**).

Where the court's permission is required to accept a Part 36 offer, even though this may be sought within the relevant period, CPR 36.9(4) requires the court, unless this issue is agreed by the parties, to make an order dealing with costs. That rule also provides that the court may order the costs consequences set out in CPR 36.10 will apply, hence if application for permission to accept the offer is made within the relevant period the court might order the costs consequences provided for under CPR 36.10(1) may apply (or perhaps CPR 36.10(2) if the offer accepted related to part only of the claim and the claimant abandons the balance of the claim).

12.2.3.3   Costs consequences on acceptance of a Part 36 offer after the relevant period

CPR 36.10(4) deals with costs consequences on the acceptance of a Part 36 offer after expiry of the relevant period (as well as acceptance of any Part 36 offer made less than 21 days before the start of trial). This rule provides that if the parties do not agree the liability for costs then the court will make an order as to costs.

Once again the terms of CPR 36.9(4) will be applicable if permission to accept the offer is required by CPR 36.9(3). If costs are not agreed the court may order the consequences set out in CPR 36.10 will apply. In other words, where permission to accept an offer is required, the starting point for the court is likely to be the consequences applicable under CPR 36.10, depending upon whether or not the offer has been accepted within the relevant period. Where an offer is accepted within the relevant period CPR 36.10(1) will apply (see **12.2.1**) but otherwise the terms of CPR 36.10(5) will be relevant.

CPR 36.10(5) effectively creates a presumption that where a Part 36 offer is accepted after expiry of the relevant period the claimant will be entitled to the costs of the proceedings up to the date on which that relevant period expired and the offeree will be liable for the offeror's costs thereafter.

This rule, at face value, suggests late acceptance will confer the costs benefits provided for under CPR 36.14(2) on a defendant, against a late accepting claimant, but not necessarily those set out in CPR 36.14(3) in favour of a claimant, against a late accepting defendant.

12.2.3.3.1 Claimant accepting late

The presumption created by the terms of CPR 36.10(5), although that rule does not expressly use this word, may result, by analogy with CPR 36.14, in the court applying this presumption unless that would be 'unjust': *Lumb v Hampsey*;[48] *SG v HK Hewitt*[49] (both applying *Matthews v Metal Improvements Co Inc*[50] though that case was concerned with the pre-2007 version of Part 36 where the equivalent rule expressly used the word 'unjust').

The defendant's conduct may have a bearing on whether the costs consequences set out in CPR 36.10(5) would be unjust when a claimant accepts a Part 36 offer late.

Consequently, where the claimant was a litigant in person and the defendant had not spelt out the costs consequences likely to follow in the event of late acceptance, the presumption the claimant would have to meet the defendant's costs after the end of the relevant period was displaced: *Kunaka v Barclays Bank plc.*[51]

In *Thompson v Bruce*[52] the court ruled that CPR 36.10 does apply prior to the issue of court proceedings so the presumption in CPR 36.10(5) was the appropriate starting point on late acceptance of a pre-issue offer. The judge emphasised, however, that this rule gives the court a discretion to displace when is in effect a presumption. On the facts of the case that presumption was displaced given that, in particular, the defendant had been granted extensions of time by the claimant to provide a response to the letter of claim, under the relevant Pre-action Protocol, and had never suggested the response, when it arrived, would be accompanied by a Part 36 offer. An argument by the defendant that the offer could have been assessed, when made, because the claim should have been valued before sending the letter of claim, was rejected by the court as the relevant protocol does not envisage the claim will have been fully quantified before the letter of claim, requiring at that stage only an outline of the financial loss incurred and an indication of the heads of damage to be claimed. Consequently, the defendant was ordered to meet the claimant's costs down to and including the hearing which sought approval by late acceptance of the offer. Whilst recognising the claimant might have sought an extension of time to accept the offer, the judge concluded that this was no more than an oversight and may well have arisen because of the cordial way the parties had been dealing with each other.

In *PGF II SA v OMFS Co*[53] the defendant's failure not to respond to a suggestion of mediation was relevant, following the claimant's late acceptance of a Part 36 offer by the defendant, because the defendant had been unreasonable in refusing to mediate when

---

48 [2011] EWHC 2808 (QB).
49 [2012] EWCA Civ 1053.
50 [2007] EWCA Civ 215.
51 [2010] EWCA Civ 1035.
52 (Unreported) 28 June, 2011 (QBD).
53 [2012] EWHC 83 (TCC).

there was a prospect that mediation would have been successful. Consequently, no order for costs between the parties was appropriate from the expiry date of the relevant period.

Whilst it will not be unjust for the presumption in CPR 36.10(5) to apply simply because the claimant is a child or protected party, and hence will need court approval of any settlement, the claimant's status is a factor the court must take into account when deciding whether applying the terms of CPR 36.10(5) would be unjust.

In *Matthews v Metal Improvements Co Inc*,[54] under the pre-2007 version of Part 36, and in *Lumb v Hampsey*,[55] under the current version of Part 36, the fact the claimant, in each case, was a protected party did not, of itself, mean it was unjust to apply the presumption now found in CPR 36.10(5).

However, the significance of the claimant being a child or protected party, as a factor to be taken into account when deciding whether the costs consequences of CPR 36.10(5) would be unjust, was confirmed by the Court of Appeal in *SG v Hewitt*.[56]

In *SG* the claimant suffered a serious head injury caused by the negligence of the defendant. In 2009 the defendant made a Part 36 offer at a stage when the claimant's advice was that it is impossible to put a definitive value on the claim as the prognosis, for the injury caused by the defendant, was unsettled. By 2011 further expert evidence gave a more definite prognosis and the defendant's offer, which had never been withdrawn, was accepted.

When the claimant applied to the court for approval of the settlement an issue arose about the incidence of costs between 2009 and 2011. The judge at first instance held it would not be unjust for the usual order under CPR 36.10(5) to be made but the Court of Appeal took a different view.

Whilst recognising decisions on costs would always be fact-sensitive the judge at first instance was held to have erred in failing to give appropriate weight to all relevant factors, including the following:

- The mere fact approval was required was not definitive in the claimant's favour, but the judge erred in failing to put this factor properly into the balance.
- The offer was made before the claimant commenced proceedings at a time when the prognosis was uncertain.
- Uncertainties about the evolution of the injury did not fit easily under the rubric 'an ordinary contingency of litigation'.
- The offer was not rejected.
- The defendant knew further reports were being obtained, not merely to improve or expand the claim but to ascertain the prognosis.
- The defendant not only had the advantage of choosing when to make the offer but also the option to withdraw it at a later stage (but chose not do to so).

---

54   [2007] EWCA Civ 215.
55   [2011] EWHC 2808 (QB).
56   [2012] EWCA Civ 1053.

Taking account of these factors the appeal was allowed and the defendant was ordered to pay the claimant's costs throughout.

It is notable that the facts of *SG* differed from those in *Matthews*. Crucially, in the former case, the uncertainty of the prognosis was inherent in the injury caused by the defendant whilst in the latter the uncertainty about the future, when the offer had been made, was for reasons unconnected with the injury suffered as a result of the defendant's negligence.

Even where the presumption in CPR 36.10(5) is applicable where the case involves a child or protected party, the claimant ought still to recover the costs of seeking approval, given that this would have been required in any event.

Whilst the claimant can recover, as incidental, costs incurred in contemplation of proceedings, the defendant is not necessarily able to do so. That is because the defendant, even though proceedings were subsequently issued, has been held to have been unable to recover costs of dealing with matters raised pre-issue but not pursued in the proceedings: *McGlinn v Walsham Contractors Ltd*.[57] Moreover, if no court proceedings are commenced the court does not usually have jurisdiction to make an order that a potential party pay the costs of another potential party: *Bethell Construction Ltd v Deloitte and Touche*.[58]

These potential difficulties for the defendant are, therefore, a very relevant consideration in the event of the claimant accepting a Part 36 offer late but before court proceedings have been commenced.

The distinction between the position of a claimant, who may force the issue of costs by commencing court proceedings, and the defendant, who may at least not so readily be able to do so, might be significant if there is late acceptance by the claimant of a defendant's Part 36 offer at a stage when court proceedings have yet to be commenced. A defendant may not have instructed lawyers, and hence incurred costs, at that stage but even if costs have been generated these may simply not be recoverable in the absence of court proceedings.

Thus a claimant faced with a very early Part 36 offer, which cannot properly be assessed, may, rather than relying on the court later refusing to make an adverse costs order in the event of late acceptance, prefer to defer issuing proceedings until an assessment of the offer can be made given that, unless withdrawn or changed, a Part 36 offer will remain open for acceptance at any time.

If, of course, the claimant has commenced Part 7 proceedings, the defendant will have a strong argument for recovering costs, even those incurred prior to issue of those proceedings. It is less clear whether Part 8 proceedings would generate the same entitlement. The point did not arise in *Thompson* and, in any event, would not have been determinative given the decision in that case.

---

57   [2005] EWHC 1419 (TCC).
58   [2011] EWCA Civ 1321.

12.2.3.3.2   Defendant accepting late

If a defendant accepts a claimant's Part 36 offer after the end of the relevant period, that defendant will be the 'offeree' and the claimant 'offeror', so the presumption under CPR 35.10(5) is that the defendant will pay the claimant's costs up to acceptance.

Once again, as effectively a presumption, such an outcome may be displaced by the court if that would be unjust.

In these circumstances, however, can the claimant obtain the benefits conferred by CPR 36.14(3), normally the reward where judgment is entered on terms which are at least as advantageous to the claimant as the claimant's own offer?

A negative answer to this question was given in *Fitzpatrick Contractors Ltd v Tyco Fire & Integrated Solutions (UK) Ltd (No 3)*,[59] a case where the claimant's offer was accepted by the defendant a year after it was made.

This ruling was, perhaps, influenced by the basis on which submissions were made for the claimant, which focused upon what the costs position would have been under CPR 36.14 following 'trial'. Whilst the pre-2007 version of Part 36 did indeed use, in this context, the word 'trial', the current rule refers to 'judgment'. Thus there needs to be a 'judgment', but not necessarily a 'trial', to raise the presumption that the costs consequences, set out in CPR 36.14 will apply, unless that would be 'unjust'.

A different answer to the same question was given in *Bunch v The Scouts Association and Guides Association*[60] where the defendant accepted, again well outside the relevant period, a Part 36 offer on liability made by the claimant. Crucially, the court entered judgment for the claimant in the terms then agreed. The court then held that it was not 'unjust' for the claimant to receive the benefits provided for under CPR 36.14, rejecting an argument by the defendant that upon acceptance the claim was stayed, to the extent of the agreement reached, thereby precluding the entry of judgment.

Similarly, in *Andrews v Aylott*[61] the defendant accepted the claimant's offer on liability outside the relevant period but, again significantly, judgment was then entered in those terms. Rejecting the defendant's argument the claim was thereby stayed the court gave, in principle, the claimant the benefits provided for under CPR 36.14(3), although subsequently it was ruled that interest on damages did not extend to the capitalised value of future periodical payments.

Tactically, therefore, a claimant whose Part 36 offer is accepted late by the defendant might be advised to seek judgment and then argue the consequences of CPR 36.14, for indemnity costs and enhanced interest, are not unjust.

In *Jolly v Harsco Infrastructure Services Ltd*,[62] however, the court concluded the terms of CPR 36.11 precluded there being a judgment, with the costs consequences that would then follow under CPR 36.14, but accepted issues such as the basis of assessment should, in these circumstances, be held over to detailed assessment.

---

[59]   [2009] EWHC 274 (TCC).
[60]   QBD Master Rose, 3 December 2009.
[61]   [2010] EWHC 597 (QB).
[62]   [2012] EWHC 3086 (QB).

The approach followed in earlier cases was, however, adopted once again in *Ontulmus v Collett*.[63]

Even without a judgment ensuring parity between a late accepting claimant and a late accepting defendant this would suggest that the consequences provided for, respectively, under CPR 36.14, when judgment is entered, ought to apply on late acceptance, unless this would be unjust.

The issue of parity between the parties is a relevant consideration given that the current version of Part 36 was drafted with that factor very much in mind. In the consultation paper, preceding the introduction of the new rule in 2007, the Department for Constitutional Affairs observed:

> 'Policy Objectives
> 6.   The policy objectives behind these proposals are, while preserving the effectiveness of the system in encouraging early settlement of cases:
>   •   to make it easier and more attractive to use Part 36 by removing unnecessary burdens/processes, in particular by:
>   –   allowing some categories of defendant to make written offers to settle without requiring a payment into court to support the offer, because it can be assumed that their offers are genuine and would be honoured if accepted;
>   –   allowing parties to accept offers after the initial time limit has expired without requiring the court's permission and, to balance that, allowing unaccepted offers and payments to be withdrawn after the time for acceptance has expired;
>   •   to provide equal or equivalent treatment of claimants' and defendants' offers;'

On this analysis a defendant who accepts the claimant's Part 36 offer late ought to do more than just show that this was a reasonable way of dealing with the matter.

Moreover, as the focus under CPR 36.14 is always on the terms of the judgment, with the claimant needing to establish this is 'more advantageous' than the defendant's offer or 'at least as advantageous' as the claimant's own offer, parity would suggest the claimant ought to be at liberty to seek judgment even if that involves the court lifting any stay imposed by CPR 36.11.

12.2.3.4   *Costs consequences of a Part 36 offer on judgment (whole claim)*

CPR 36.14 deals with the costs consequences of a Part 36 offer 'upon judgment being entered' where either:

•   a claimant fails to obtain a judgment 'more advantageous' than a defendant's Part 36 offer; or

•   judgment against the defendant is 'at least as advantageous' to the claimant as the proposals contained in a claimant's Part 36 offer.

---

[63]   [2014] EWHC 4117 (QB).

The specific costs consequences are set out in CPR 36.14(2), where the claimant fails to obtain a judgment more advantageous than the defendant's Part 36 offer, and in CPR 36.14(3), where judgment against the defendant is at least as advantageous to the claimant as the claimant's own offer.

Those consequences will be applicable unless the court considers that would be 'unjust'. However, such consequences will not apply to a Part 36 offer that has been withdrawn or changed (unless the offeree beats the offer as changed) or to an offer made less than 21 days before trial (unless the court have abridged the relevant period for that offer).

The applicability of costs consequences set out in CPR 36.14 depends upon a number of issues.

12.2.3.4.1   Part 36 offer

There must, as a preliminary, be an offer against which any subsequent judgment can be compared: see *Ali v Stagecoach*.[64] Moreover, as CPR 36.1(2) makes clear, an offer not made in accordance with the rules on form and content found in CPR 36.2 will not have the consequences specified in CPR 36.14.

12.2.3.4.2   Judgment

If there is an effective Part 36 offer, that must be compared with the terms of any judgment entered before deciding whether the consequences provided for under CPR 36.14 may be applicable.

The 2007 version of Part 36 provides for costs consequences of Part 36 offers to apply on 'judgment' rather than, as it was pre-2007, following 'trial'. Consequently, for example, a successful application for summary judgment would now bring the cost consequences found in CPR 36.14 into play. The court may enter judgment in other circumstances, without a trial, as illustrated in both *Bunch v The Scouts Association and Guides Association*[65] and *Andrews v Aylott*[66] although doubt has since been expressed on whether judgment can be entered when a stay is imposed by the acceptance of a Part 36 offer: *Jolly v Harsco Infranstructre Services Ltd*[67] (see **12.2.3.3.2**).

There must also be an 'offer' against which any subsequent judgment can be compared. That, given the terms of CPR 36.1(2), means an offer made in accordance with relevant provisions of the rule, including CPR 36.2 and, where applicable, CPR 36.4, 36.5, 36.6 and 36.15.

Consequently, an offer, even if referring to Part 36, which does not comply with the rule should not trigger the cost consequences of CPR 36.14. Anything which does not even amount to an offer cannot, by definition, suffice for these purposes (see **12.2.3.1**).

---

[64]   [2011] EWCA Civ 1494.
[65]   QBD Master Rose 3 December 2009.
[66]   [2010] EWHC 597 (QB).
[67]   [2012] EWHC 3086 (QB).

12.2.3.4.3 CPR 36.14 consequences for the defendant

CPR 36.14(1)(a) and CPR 36.14(2) provide that (unless the court considers this would be unjust) where a claimant fails to obtain a judgment more advantageous than a defendant's Part 36 offer the defendant is entitled to:

- costs from the date on which the relevant period expired; and
- interest on those costs.

There is no provision under CPR 36.14(2), unlike CPR 36.14(3), for costs to be assessed on the indemnity basis. That may be appropriate, under Part 44, but does not follow automatically and will require some unusual feature which justifies such an order (see **12.2.6.2**).

The reason why the claimant can recover costs on the indemnity basis under CPR 36.14 but the defendant cannot was explained by Simon Brown LJ in *Kiam v MGN Ltd*[68] when he said:

> 'If the claimant thought that, even if he were to make and then beat an offer, he was going to get no more than his costs on the standard basis, why would he make it? It would afford him no advantage at all. He would do better simply to claim at large and recover his costs whatever measure of success he gained. His position is, in short, quite different from that of the defendant who plainly has every incentive to make a settlement offer, generally by way of payment into court, irrespective of the basis on which any costs order will be made. Take any ordinary damages claim. A defendant wishing to protect himself will pay money into court. The incentive to do so is self-evident. The incentive does not need to be created or stimulated by raising the defendant's expectation as to the level of costs he will recover. And, consistently with this, where payments in are not beaten, defendants routinely recover their costs on the standard basis; I know of no rule or practice in such cases for making indemnity costs orders.'

This approach was adopted in *F & C Alternative Investments (Holdings) Ltd v Barthelemy*[69] where Davis LJ held:

> 'Part 36.14 represents a departure from otherwise established costs practice. It imposes a deliberately swingeing costs sanction, by Part 36.14(3), on a claimant who fails at trial to beat a defendant's Part 36 offer. That is, for policy reasons, designed to encourage a sensible approach of claimants to offers and to promote settlement ...'

12.2.3.4.4 CPR 36.14 consequences for the claimant

CPR 36.14(1)(b) and CPR 36.14(3) provide that if judgment against the defendant is at least as advantageous to the claimant as the proposals contained in a claimant's Part 36 offer (unless the court considers this would be unjust) the claimant is entitled to:

- interest on the whole or part of any sum of money (excluding interest) awarded at a rate not exceeding 10 per cent above base rate for some or all of the period starting with the date on which the relevant period expired;
- costs on the indemnity basis from the date on which the relevant period expired;
- interest on those costs at a rate not exceeding 10 per cent above base rate; and (for offers made on or after 1 April 2013)

---

[68] [2002] EWCA Civ 66.
[69] [2012] EWCA Civ 843.

- an additional amount, namely 10 per cent of the amount awarded up to £500,000 and 5 per cent on any amount awarded above £500,000 up to £1,000,000, on the sum awarded to the claimant by the court, where the claim is or includes a money claim, or on the sum awarded to the claimant by the court in respect of costs, where the claim is only a non-monetary claim, subject to a maximum of £75,000.

The context in which a claimant may be awarded indemnity costs under CPR 36.14 was explored by Lord Woolf in *Petrotrade Inc v Texaco Ltd*[70] where he held:

> 'However, it would be wrong to regard the rule as producing penal consequences. An order for indemnity costs does not enable a claimant to receive more costs than he has incurred. Its practical effect is to avoid his costs being assessed at a lesser figure. When assessing costs on the standard basis the court the court will only allow costs 'which are proportionate to the matters in issue' and 'resolve any doubt which it may have as to whether costs were reasonably incurred or reasonable proportionate in amount in favour of the paying party'. On the other hand, where the costs are assessed on an indemnity basis, the issue of proportionality does not have to be considered. The court only considers whether the costs were unreasonably incurred or for an unreasonable amount. The court will then resolve any doubt in favour of the receiving party. Even on an indemnity basis, however, the receiving party is restricted to recovering only the amount of costs which have been incurred (see Part 44.4 and Part 44.5).
>
> The ability of the court to award costs on an indemnity basis and interest at an enhanced rate should not be regarded as penal because orders for costs, even when made on an indemnity basis, never actually compensate a claimant for having to come to court to bring proceedings. The very process of being involved in court proceedings inevitably has an impact on a claimant, whether he is a private individual or a multi-national corporation. A claimant would be better off had he not become involved in court proceedings. Part of the culture of the CPR is to encourage parties to avoid proceedings unless it is unreasonable for them to do otherwise. In the case of an individual proceedings necessarily involve inconvenience and frequently involve anxiety and distress. These are not taken into account when assessing costs on the normal basis. In the case of a corporation, corporation senior officials and other staff inevitably will be diverted from their normal duties as a consequence of the proceedings. The disruption this causes to a corporation is not recoverable under an order for costs.
>
> The power to order indemnity costs or higher rate interest is a means of achieving a fairer result for a claimant. If a defendant involves a claimant in proceedings after an offer has been made, and in the event, the result is no more favourable to the defendant than that which would have been achieved if the claimant's offer had been accepted without the need for those proceedings, the message of Part 36.21 is that, prima facie, it is just to makes an indemnity order for costs and for interest at an enhanced rate to be awarded. However, the indemnity order need not be for the entire proceedings nor, as I have already indicated, need the award of interest be for a particular period or at a particular rate. It must not however exceed the figure of 10 per cent referred to in Part 36.'

The same point was made by Chadwick LJ in *McPhilemy v Times Newspapers Ltd*[71] where he held:

> 'An order, under paragraph (3) of CPR 36.21, for the payment of costs on an indemnity basis does not give rise to a risk of double compensation. The purpose for which the power to order the payment of costs on an indemnity basis is conferred, as it seems to me, is to enable the court, in a case to which CPR 36.21 applies, to address the element of perceived

---

[70] [2000] EWCA Civ 512.
[71] [2001] EWCA Civ 933.

unfairness which arises from the fact that an award of costs on the standard basis will, almost invariably, lead to the successful claimant recovering less than the costs which he has to pay to his solicitor.'

The court has a discretion on the enhanced interest rate and, when this will apply, case-law reflecting ranges of awards up to and including the maximum 10 per cent.

No interest, under the terms of CPR 36.14(3), was awarded on that part of the judgment relating to future periodical payments in *Andrews v Aylott*.[72]

12.2.3.4.5 Costs consequences of withdrawn or changed Part 36 offers

CPR 36.14(6) provides, significantly, that the costs benefits potentially available under CPR 36.14 do not apply to an offer that has been withdrawn or changed so that its terms are less advantageous to the offeree, provided in the latter case the offeree has beaten the less advantageous offer.

This rule means that:

- if an offer is withdrawn, the costs consequences otherwise provided for under CPR 36.14 do not apply; and

- if an offer is changed so that the terms are less advantageous to the offeree, and the offeree fails to beat the less advantageous offer as changed, the original offer will be effective for costs purposes (presumably, therefore, back to the date when the 'relevant period' of that original offer expired); but

- if an offer is changed so the terms are less advantageous to the offeree, but the offeree beats the less advantageous offer as changed, the offer will not have the costs consequences otherwise provided for under CPR 36.14 (even if the offeree fails to beat the offer as originally made).

There may, unusually, be circumstances in which an offer has not been withdrawn or changed, cannot be accepted, yet may remain effective for the purposes of CPR 36.14.

In *Pankhurst v White*[73] there was a preliminary trial on the issue of liability at which the claimant obtained judgment at least as advantageous as his offer on that issue. The version of Part 36 then in force had no provision equivalent to that now dealing with the consequences of withdrawing an offer. The claimant's offer was held to still have 'costs potency' up to the time the defendant made a Part 36 offer to settle the whole claim, which offer the claimant ultimately failed to beat at the trial of quantum.

Under the current version of Part 36, the offer on liability could not have been accepted, at least without permission of the court, once trial of that issue started, and could not have been accepted once judgment on that issue was given. However, without withdrawal or change that offer should have remained effective for costs purposes (though given the terms of the defendant's subsequent offer to settle the whole of the claim it might well have been 'unjust' for those consequences to have applied thereafter).

Tactically, rather than simply withdrawing an offer, it may be preferable to change that offer so that it is less advantageous to the offeree given that if the offeree ultimately fails

---

72 [2010] EWHC 597 (QB).
73 [2010] EWCA Civ 1445.

to beat the offer as changed the original offer will remain effective for costs purposes but, once changed, is incapable of acceptance in its original form.

Where an offeror makes, as will more usually happen, offers which are increasingly more advantageous to the offeree, the making of those further offers does not amount to a withdrawal of the earlier offers which therefore retain the potential for costs consequences. An argument to the contrary was rejected by Cox J in *Mahmood v Elmi*[74] who held:

> 'Were it otherwise, a defendant who makes a Part 36 offer before proceedings are issued would be protected in costs only if he made no subsequent offers. There would be no incentive for him to make a further offer, as the trial date approached, because he would thereby be deprived of all the costs protection he had acquired until then. This would hardly encourage or promote the sensible and realistic settlement of cases, in accordance with the aim of the CPR, once litigation has commenced.'

12.2.3.4.6 'Unjust'?

The costs consequences on judgment provided for under CPR 36.14 are only presumptions but the court must order those consequences unless it would be unjust to do so.

When considering whether the usual costs consequences would be unjust, CPR 36.14(4) requires the court to take into account all the circumstances of the case. That rule also identifies some specific circumstances which, as with all similar rules in the CPR setting out a structured decision-making process, the court must take into account where applicable.

The specific circumstances identified in CPR 36.14(4) are:

* the terms of any Part 36 offer;
* the stage in the proceedings when any Part 36 offer was made;
* the information available to the parties at the time when the Part 36 offer was made; and
* the conduct of the parties with regard to the giving or refusing to give information for the purposes of enabling the offer to be made or evaluated.

There is, however, no limit to the type of circumstances which may, in any particular case, make it unjust the costs consequences set out in CPR 36.14 should follow: *Lilleyman v Lilleyman*.[75]

A number of cases have illustrated how the court should approach the question of what would be unjust for the purposes of CPR 36.14 and which, by analogy, may well be relevant in deciding whether the presumption as to costs found in CPR 36.10(5) should prevail where there is late acceptance (see **12.2.2.3**).

---

74   [2010] EWHC 1933 (QB).
75   [2012] EWHC 1056 (Ch).

Because of the incentive indemnity costs offer to the claimant it will not be unjust for these to be awarded in the absence of any unreasonable conduct by the defendant: *Kiam v MGN Ltd*;[76] *F & C Alternative Investments (Holdings) Ltd v Barthelemy*.[77]

In *Kiam v MGN Ltd*[78] Simon Brown LJ set the context for claimant Part 36 offers, and indirectly what might be 'unjust' about relevant costs consequences applying, when he said:

> 'If the claimant thought that, even if he were to make and then beat an offer, he was going to get no more than his costs on the standard basis, why would he make it? It would afford him no advantage at all. He would be better simply to claim at large and recover his costs whatever measure of success he gained. His position is, in short, quite different from that of a defendant who plainly has every incentive to make a settlement offer, generally by way of payment into court, irrespective of the basis on which any costs order will be made.'

This approach was adopted in F & C Alternative Investments (Holdings) Limited v Barthelemy[79] where Davis LJ held:

> 'Part 36.14 represents a departure from otherwise established costs practice. It imposes a deliberately swingeing costs sanction, by Part 36.14(3), on a claimant who fails at trial to beat a defendant's Part 36 offer. That is, for policy reasons, designed to encourage a sensible approach of claimants to offers and to promote settlement ...'.

In *Huck v Robson*[80] the defendant declined an offer made by the claimant of 95 per cent on liability. Even though the case was 'all or nothing', so the court would never have awarded 95 per cent on liability, the Court of Appeal held that it was not 'unjust' for costs consequences under Part 36 to follow. Whilst the trial judge had found it would be 'unjust' for the offer to carry cost consequences, because the discount on liability was 'derisory'. Schiemann LJ, in the Court of Appeal, emphasised that:

> 'The crucial question to be addressed by the judge ... was ... will it be unjust to award the claimant his costs on an indemnity basis? It is important to bear in mind that this is the way the question is phrased. The question is not: will it be unjust not to award the claimant his costs on an indemnity basis?'

Noting a claimant who betters his Part 36 offer has a prima facie entitlement to indemnity costs, Schiemann LJ concluded:

> '... I do not categorise the defendant's reaction in the present case as unreasonable. Nor would he have been behaving unreasonably if he had accepted the claimant's Part 36 offer. I however see nothing unjust in awarding a claimant his indemnity costs in circumstances where the defendant chooses not to accept an offer to settle for less than that to which the claimant is entitled.'

Schiemann LJ did recognise, however, that there might be circumstances where the claimant recovered in full after making a Part 36 offer with a purely nominal discount and would not be awarded costs on the indemnity basis as when he said:

---

[76]   [2002] EWCA Civ 66.
[77]   [2012] EWCA Civ 843.
[78]   [2002] EWCA Civ 66.
[79]   [2012] EWCA Civ 843.
[80]   [2002] EWCA Civ 398.

'... a claimant's Part 36 offer must represent at the very least a genuine and realistic attempt by the claimant to resolve the dispute by agreement. Such an offer is to be contrasted with one which creates no real opportunity for settlement but is merely a tactical step designed to secure the benefit of the incentives. That is not to say that the offer must be one which it would be unreasonable for the defendant to refuse; that would be too strict a test ...'

Schiemann LJ also observed:

'I do not consider that Part 36 was intended to produce a situation in which a claimant was automatically entitled to costs on the indemnity basis provided only that he made an offer pursuant to Part 36.10 in an amount marginally less than the claim.'

The question of what might amount to a purely nominal discount was explored by Tuckey LJ who observed:

'... if it was self-evident that the offer made was merely a tactical step designed to secure the benefit of the incentives provided by the Rule (e.g. an offer to settle for 99.9% of the full value of the claim) I would agree with Jonathan Parker LJ that the judge would have a discretion to refuse indemnity costs. But that cannot be said of the offer made in this case, which I think did provide the defendant with a real opportunity for settlement even though it did not represent any possible apportionment of liability.'

In the same vein Norris J observed in *Wharton v Bancroft*[81] that:

'All Part 36 offers are tactical in the sense that they are designed to take advantage of the incentives provided by Part 36. A low offer in a case where the offeror considers that the offeree's position has no merit cannot be written off as self evidently "merely a tactical step".'

The Court of Appeal applied the approach in *Huck* to a defendant's offer, which the claimant failed to beat, in *Matthews v Metal Improvements Co Inc*.[82] In that case the claimant's prognosis changed for the better, following which the claimant promptly took steps to accept an earlier Part 36 offer made by the defendant. The judge, at first instance, ordered the defendant to pay the claimant's costs of the claim, including costs after the Part 36 offer. The Court of Appeal concluded the judge had made an error of law because it was only if she could properly conclude that it was unjust to order the claimant to pay the costs in question that she could depart from the usual order. That approach did not change simply because the claimant was a patient. Stanley Burnton J observed:

'Moreover, the Deputy District Judge's approach is based on a misunderstanding of the function of a Part 36 payment or offer. The defendant may make a conservative payment in the hope that it will tempt the claimant to accept a conservative estimate of the value of his claim. He may make a generous Part 36 payment because he is reluctant to incur the risks and costs of going to trial, and hopes thereby to avoid them. The defendant may quite properly make a low payment in the hope that events or evidence will favour him: for example, that his expert will advise favourably in due course; that a prognosis of the claimant's injuries which are the subject of his claim will prove over-pessimistic; that cross-examination of the claimant or his witnesses may be successful; or that the trial judge will quantify general or special damages modestly. Conversely, there is nothing unreasonable in a competent claimant rejecting a Part 36 payment in the hope that at trial the judge will take a generous view of his damages. The risks that the parties run are costs risks, in the case of the defendant that he will have to pay all of the claimant's costs, notwithstanding his

---

payment, and in the case of the claimant that he will have to pay the defendant's costs from the last date when he could have accepted the payment. In other words, the function of a Part 36 payment is to place the claimant on that costs risk if, as a result of the contingencies of litigation, he fails to beat the payment.'

The claimant's unsettled prognosis was a contingency inherent in the litigation meaning there was nothing 'unjust' about the costs consequences under Part 36 applying.

Although the claimant's capacity is not a factor specifically identified in CPR 36.14 it is one of the 'circumstances' of the case and must, therefore, be a factor taken into account when deciding what will be unjust. Consequently, where the claimant accepted, late, a Part 36 offer for an injury which, crucially, had been caused by the defendant's breach of duty (unlike the contingency in *Matthews* which was unrelated to the defendant's negligence) it was unjust for the costs consequences in CPR 36.14 to apply: *SG v Hewitt.*[83]

Given the terms of CPR 36.14(4), and in particular the significance of information which enables the offer to be evaluated, the absence of clarification, where requested, even without an order from the court that this be provided, may be relevant in determining whether the costs consequences under CPR 36.14 would be unjust: *Colour Quest Ltd v Total Downstream UK plc.*[84] For these purposes information has been held to mean factual information rather than the way an issue on the law is to be argued: *PGF II SA v OMFS Company.*[85]

Even without a request for clarification where a party has withheld material relevant to the offer, thereby making a proper appraisal of that party's case more difficult, that may have the effect of making the costs consequences under CPR 36.14 unjust: *Factortame Ltd v Secretary of State for Transport, Local Government and the Regions.*[86]

If there is a pre-action protocol which provides for exchange of information, such as disclosure, it may be unjust for the consequences of CPR 36.14 to apply when the exchange of information envisaged by the protocol had not taken place: *Webb Resolutions Ltd v Waller Needham & Green.*[87]

In *Ford v GKR Construction Ltd*[88] the defendant, after getting a late adjournment of the trial, obtained and adduced surveillance evidence. That evidence led the court to award the claimant, at the adjourned trial, less than a Part 36 payment made by the defendant. The surveillance evidence would not have been available when the case was originally going to be tried and hence not available when the claimant had to assess the defendant's Part 36 offer. That surveillance evidence could, and should, have been obtained and disclosed sooner so that the claimant could have assessed the merits of the offer at the time it was made. Lord Woolf MR held that:

'If a party has not enabled another party properly to assess whether or not to make an offer or whether or not to accept an offer which is made because of non-disclosure to the other

---

83 [2012] EWCA Civ 1053.
84 [2009] EWHC 823 (Comm).
85 [2012] EWHC 83 (TCC).
86 [2002] EWCA Civ 22.
87 [2012] EWHC 3529 (Ch).
88 Court of Appeal, 22 October 1999.

parties of material facts or if a party comes to a decision which is different from that which would have been reached if there was proper disclosure, that is a material matter for the Court to take into account in considering what Order should be made.'

That approach reflects the need to conduct litigation, for the purposes of the overriding objective, in a way that allows other parties to know where they stand at the earliest possible stage and make informed decisions about the prospects and conduct of the case at the lowest practicable cost. Nevertheless, if the claimant has not complied with the timetable for case management directions the defendant may secure the normal costs consequences under Part 36 if there is a corresponding delay in disclosing surveillance evidence: *Uttley v Uttley*.[89]

In *Walsh v Singh*[90] the aggregate value of the claims for which the claimant obtained judgment was £61,500. The defendant had made a Part 36 offer of £85,000. However, the trial judge held that the cost consequences in CPR 36.14 would be unjust because the defendant had sought to rely on material obtained by the use of spyware on a laptop used by the claimant revealing, amongst other things, privileged material and because much of the cross-examination had been calculated to belittle and discredit the claimant. The trial judge concluded a well-judged Part 36 offer did not give full licence to conduct a trial thereafter in whatever way without fear of costs reprisals. In all the circumstances of the case justice was held to be done by making no order as to costs. The Court of Appeal did not interfere with the exercise of discretion on costs by the judge.

In *Epsom College v Pierse Contracting Southern Ltd*[91] the claimant had possession of, but misplaced, an important piece of real evidence. That evidence was eventually located, and produced, but meanwhile the claimant had made a Part 36 offer. At trial the claimant obtained judgment against the defendant in terms which were at least as advantageous to the claimant as the offer made. The court concluded it would be unjust for the cost consequences of CPR 36.14 to apply from the end of the relevant period in the offer, rather those consequences applied after the missing evidence was produced to the defendant on the basis that, once this evidence had become available, the defendant could have re-assessed the merits, accepted the claimant's Part 36 offer and argued the question of costs on the basis of the issues surrounding late production of the evidence.

In *Hutchinson v Neale*[92] the conduct of a party made the costs consequences provided for under CPR 36.14 unjust. That was because the defendant, whilst making an offer which was at least as advantageous to the claimant as the judgment obtained, was found by the court to have acted dishonestly and, compounding that, to have made unfounded allegations of dishonesty against the claimant.

In *Smith v Trafford Housing Trust*[93] the court concluded it would be unjust for the claimant, who had a money judgment entered for less than a Part 36 offer made by the defendant, to suffer the costs consequences of CPR 36.14 when the case was not primarily, for either party, about money.

Generally, however, the courts are likely to take the view that, in the absence of some particularly relevant circumstances, it will not be unjust for the consequences provided

---

[89]   [2001] All ER (D) 240.
[90]   [2011] EWCA Civ 80.
[91]   [2011] EWCA Civ 1449.
[92]   [2012] EWCA Civ 345.
[93]   [2012] EWHC 3320 (Ch).

for under CPR 36.14, where otherwise applicable, to prevail. That is because, under Part 36 as opposed to Part 44, indemnity costs are not to be seen as penal, or carrying any stigma, given that even on the indemnity basis a receiving party may only recover costs which have actually been incurred: *Petrotrade Inc v Texaco Ltd*;[94] *Home Office v Lowndes*.[95]

It is, therefore, wrong to characterise the benefits conferred on the claimant under CPR 36.14 as a windfall because the rules confer, in appropriate circumstances, that entitlement, and unless relevant costs sanctions are imposed there would be no incentive on a defendant to take offers made by the claimant seriously: *Dugmore v Swansea NHS Trust*.[96]

Consequently, as Ward LJ tenchantly observed in *Nixon v Chanceoption Developments Ltd*:[97]

'Part 36 will not work unless we ensure that it has teeth which leave their mark on the purse of the losing party.'

In *Blue Sphere Global Ltd v Revenue & Customs Commissioners*[98] the Court of Appeal held it was not unjust for a claimant to have the benefits of CPR 36.14 even though the claim concerned alleged VAT fraud and the defendant contended the appeal had been fought in the public interest.

Similarly, in *Hemming v Westminster City Council*,[99] whilst the defendant licensing authority contended the costs consequences provided for under CPR 36.14 would be unjust because the case involved a point of principle which could affect other licensing authorities, such as the defendant, in other cases that argument was not accepted as the particular claim could have been compromised without prejudice to the stance that might be adopted in other cases.

On the general basis that Part 36 must have effective sanctions if it is to play a proper part in helping achieve the settlement of claims, the costs consequences provided for under CPR 36.14 were not held to be unjust in *Crema v Cenkos Securities Plc*[100] and *Seeff v Ho*.[101]

Even where the relevant Part 36 offer was made at a very late stage the additional amount was held not to be 'unjust' in *Davison v Leitch*.[102] The additional amount was also awarded in *Watchorn v Jupiter Industries Ltd*.[103] However, in *Elsevier Ltd v Munro*[104] a different approach was taken where the offeree had received the offeror's witness statements at a late stage and the judge concluded it was unduly harsh to criticise the offeree for not accepting the offer promptly in these circumstances.

---

[94] Court of Appeal, 23 May 2000.
[95] [2002] EWCA Civ 36.
[96] [2003] 1 All ER 333.
[97] [2002] EWCA Civ 558.
[98] [2010] EWCA Civ 517.
[99] [2012] EWHC 1582 (Admin).
[100] [2011] EWCA Civ 10.
[101] [2011] EWCA Civ 401.
[102] [2013] EWHC 3092 (QB).
[103] [2014] EWHC 3003 (Ch).
[104] [2014] EWHC 2728 (QB).

Consequently, imposing an additional amount would involve an unjust element of penalty and that was not, therefore, awarded.

In *Downing v Peterborough & Stamford Hospitals NHS Foundation Trust*[105] Sir David Eady cautioned against any departure from the presumption the benefits conferred by CPR 36.14 on a claimant would not be unjust when he observed:

> 'It is elementary that a judge who is asked to depart from the norm, on the ground that it would be "unjust" not to do so, should not be tempted to make an exception merely because he or she thinks the regime itself harsh or unjust. There must be something about the particular circumstances of the case which takes it out of the norm.'

12.2.3.4.7 'Advantageous'?

CPR 36.14 uses the word 'advantageous' in both sub-paragraph (2) and (3), for the purposes of comparing any judgment with a Part 36 offer made by either the claimant or the defendant.

For the purposes of CPR 36.14(2) the term 'more advantageous' means taking a broad view about whether the judgment, when compared with the relevant offer, was 'worth the fight': *Carver v BAA Plc*.[106]

However, the approach taken in *Carver* has been considered as only appropriate where one party has engaged in ADR and the other has not: *Multiplex Constructions (UK) Ltd v Cleveland Bridge UK Ltd*.[107]

Similarly, the approach in *Carver* was not followed in *Morgan v UPS*,[108] even though the defendant's offer was only beaten 'by a whisker', because the claimant had engaged in reasonable negotiations.

Morgan was approved, and the same approach adopted, in *Fox v Foundation Piling Ltd*.[109]

In *Gibbon v Manchester City Council*[110] the Court of Appeal, whilst not endorsing the analysis in *Multiplex Constructions (UK) Ltd*, held that, save for exceptional cases, the test of what was 'more advantageous' would be measured in purely fiscal terms.

Carnwath LJ summarised the position:

> 'Accordingly, the judgment in *Carver* should not be interpreted as opening the way to a wide ranging investigation of emotional and other factors in every case, even where the financial advantage is significant. I agree with Moore-Bick LJ that in most cases success in financial terms will be the governing consideration.'

---

[105]   [2014] EWHC 4216 (QB).
[106]   [2008] EWCA Civ 412.
[107]   [2008] EWHC 2280 (TCC).
[108]   [2008] EWCA Civ 1476.
[109]   [2011] EWCA Civ 790.
[110]   [2010] EWCA Civ 726.

This approach was followed in *McGinty v Pipe*[111] where the court gave the claimant judgment, following trial, in the sum of £365,260.10 when the defendant had made a Part 36 offer, two years earlier, of £350,000. Whilst the defendant contended an increase in damages, of 4.3 per cent, was not 'worth the fight', the judge concluded the comparison between offer and judgment had to be made from the litigant's perspective and with a money award the amount involved was likely to outweigh other factors in determining whether the judgment was 'more advantageous' than the offer.

The meaning of the phrase 'at least as advantageous' in CPR 36.14(3) was considered by the Court of Appeal in *Blue Sphere Global Ltd v Revenue & Customs Commissioners*.[112] Reflecting the difference in wording between CPR 36.14(2) and CPR 36.14(3) Moses LJ held:

> 'I reject straight away the suggestion that BSG only beat the offer by a small margin and that that affords a basis for reaching the conclusion that it would be unjust to give effect to 36.14. It is of note that Rule 36.14(1) draws a contrast between the failure of a *claimant* to obtain a judgment *more advantageous* than a defendant's Part 36 offer (36.14(1)(a)) and a judgment obtained against a defendant which "is at least as advantageous" to the claimant as proposals contained in a claimant's Part 36 offer (36.14(1)(b)). It should not be forgotten that where a claimant's Part 36 offer is refused the claimant is compelled to continue in order to recover at least the sum for which the claimant is prepared to settle. In those circumstances it is to be expected that the Rule would acknowledge the predicament of a claimant whose only choice is either to abandon the appeal or to press on.'

Hence the approach in *Carver*, in this context deciding whether the sum by which the claimant beats the claimant's own offer was 'worth the fight' will not be applicable for the reasons explained by the Court of Appeal in *Acre 1127 Ltd (in liquidation) v De Montfort Fine Art Ltd*[113] where the claimant's judgment, on appeal, was reduced to £442,442.04. The claimant had made a Part 36 offer, prior to the first instance decision, of £500,000 which was stated to be 'inclusive of interest until the relevant period has expired'. When comparing the offer and judgment the proper comparison was held to be between the figures in the offer of £500,000 and the judgment sum of £442,442.04, together with such discretionary interest as it was appropriate to award on the latter in respect of the period between accrual of the cause of action and the expiry of the relevant period. On this basis the value of the judgment, as comparator sum, was £510,113.44. That was, the Court of Appeal held, 'at least as advantageous' as the claimant's own offer. The court went on to hold that the situations addressed by Parts 36.14(1)(a) and (b) were not analogous, as sub-rule (b) requires the court to examine the advantage to the claimant. It would, the Court of Appeal held, have been difficult on that basis to justify a conclusion that the outcome, even after the appeal, was not at least as advantageous to the claimant as the proposal to settle for £500,000.

If the court does take account of factors other than success in financial terms, this approach will apply equally to a claimant, when deciding whether judgment is at least as advantageous as the claimant's own offer, as it does to a defendant: *Diageo North America Inc v Intercontinental Brands (ICB) Ltd*.[114]

---

[111] [2012] EWHC 506 (QB).
[112] [2010] EWCA Civ 1448.
[113] [2011] EWCA Civ 130.
[114] [2010] EWHC 172 (Pat).

The approach taken in recent case-law to the interpretation of CPR 36.14 has been endorsed by the Civil Procedure (Amendment No 2) Rules 2011 which provide that after CPR 36.14(1) there shall be inserted:

> '(1A) For the purposes of (1), in relation to any money claim or money element of a claim, "more advantageous" means better in money terms by any amount, however small, and "at least as advantageous" shall be construed accordingly.'

Paragraph 1(4) of these rules confirms that the new rule applies to offers to settle made in accordance with CPR 36.2 on or after 1 October 2011. However, given case-law such as *Gibbon*, a court seems likely to adopt the same approach to pre-October 2011 offers.

When comparing offer and judgment in a non-money claim, or on the non-money element of a claim, CPR 36.14(1A) will not apply but guidance on the correct approach can be obtained from earlier case-law, in particular *Huck v Robson*.[115] That would suggest, certainly when dealing with offers on an issue such as liability, the view in *Gibbon* that an offeree ought to be entitled to evaluate an offer on the basis of a 'rational assessment' by a straightforward comparison between the offer and the judgment.

If a party seeks more than monetary damages, that may be a factor in determining what is 'advantageous' but if the case really is 'all about money' then the comparison will be made on that basis alone: *Force India Formula One Team Ltd v Malaysia Racing Team SDN BHD*.[116] In this context, therefore, what the claimant has gained by pressing ahead will be just as relevant to answering the question of what is more 'advantageous' as it is to the, usually, anterior question of who has won (see **12.2.2.2**).

The court must compare like with like when contrasting offer and judgment. Accordingly, when comparing the defendant's offer with the judgment entered, any interest adding to the value of the judgment from the date of the offer must be disregarded: *Blackham v Entrepose UK*.[117] Similarly, when comparing a claimant's Part 36 offer with any judgment entered, interest must be calculated on the judgment sum up to the date the relevant period in the offer expired so as to make an accurate comparison: *Acre 1127 Ltd (in liquidation) v De Montfort Fine Art Ltd*.[118]

Given the obligation under CPR 36.15 on a defendant who makes a Part 36 offer to deal with CRU, that element of the claim may have an important bearing on whether or not any subsequently judgment is 'more advantageous' to the claimant than the offer.

Where the defendant elects to make a Part 36 offer which includes deductible benefits, CPR 36.15(8) confirms that, when deciding what is 'more advantageous', the comparison must be made between the net amount of the offer and the net amount of the judgment, in each case after CRU deduction. That is why it is important that any Part 36 offer by the defendant complies with the requirements of CPR 36.15(3) and, where deductible benefits are included in the offer, gives the information stipulated in CPR 36.15(6).

---

[115] [2002] EWCA Civ 398.
[116] [2012] EWHC 1621 (Ch).
[117] [2004] EWCA Civ 1109.
[118] [2011] EWCA Civ 130.

Where there is a change in the CRU certificate, reducing the amount of deductible benefits, between offer and judgment or if the court, when giving judgment, restricts the amount of deductible benefits, the claimant may recover less, gross, than the relevant offer but nevertheless obtain a judgment which is 'more advantageous' than the offer because the net sum payable has increased: *Fox v Foundation Piling Ltd*.[119]

Where an offer is made without regard to any liability for recoverable benefits, the notional gross amount of both offer and judgment, including any benefits, will be irrelevant, the comparison being made between the offer and net sum payable to the claimant.

If the defendant makes an offer including any deductible benefits and, following acceptance, either party appeals the deduction, any refund should go to the claimant as the claimant has effectively accepted the gross sum: *Hilton International v Martin-Smith*.[120]

If the offer is made 'without regard to any liability for recoverable amounts' under CPR 36.15(3)(a), the claimant will have effectively accepted a net figure, so in the event of an appeal any refund should be due to the defendant as that was never part of the offer.

It is the significance of CRU on the issue of what is 'advantageous', as well as the implications of any subsequent CRU appeal, that makes it important the defendant's Part 36 offer does comply with the requirements of CPR 36.15 rather than, for example, being silent about CRU, stating the offer is 'net of CRU' or even 'gross of CRU' (see 11.5.4.4).

12.2.3.5 Costs consequences of a Part 36 offer on judgment (preliminary issue)

A Part 36 offer made on any issue tried as a preliminary is likely to be relevant to the costs of that issue, depending upon who made the offer and how the judgment compares with that offer.

However, given the terms of CPR 36.13, communication to the court of any relevant offer may be prohibited until such time as the claim as a whole has been determined (see 11.2.4).

Where there has been a Part 36 offer on an issue, that may have a bearing on the costs of that issue, even when the claim as a whole is tried.

Where the only Part 36 offers are to settle the whole claim, there is conflicting case-law about the costs consequences of such offers where the court details with a preliminary issue.

In *HSS Hire Services Group PLC v (1) BMB Builders Merchants Ltd (2) Grafton Group (UK) PLC*[121] the Court of Appeal held that where preliminary points have been decided

---

[119] [2011] EWCA Civ 790.
[120] QBD, 5 October 2000.
[121] [2005] EWCA Civ 626.

by a court at first instance but there is a Part 36 offer of settlement, and quantum is still unknown, the best person ultimately to rule on costs will be the trial judge.

In *Kew v Bettamix*,[122] however, there was a preliminary trial on the issue of limitation and, although succeeding in part, on that issue, the claimant was ordered to pay the defendant's costs for the issue on which the claimant did not succeed, despite the claimant having made a Part 36 offer to settle the whole claim which, of course, the claimant might ultimately have matched or bettered.

The approach in HSS Hire Services Group PLC has subsequently been followed by the Court of Appeal in RTS Flexible Systems Limited v Morkerei Alois Müller GmbH & Co KG.[123]

At face value it does seem curious if a claimant who has made a Part 36 offer of outright settlement and is unsuccessful on a preliminary issue should be ordered to pay the costs of that issue there and then whilst a defendant, in essentially the same situation, can defer determination of the costs issue until such time as the outcome of the case as a whole is known.

In these circumstances a party who has made a Part 36 offer of settlement can, at the very least, argue the costs of a preliminary issue, which goes against that party, might not be determined until all aspects of the case are concluded. If, however, the relevant issue is a discrete one, which can readily to be seen to have added to the overall costs of the case, the court may feel able to make a costs ruling there and then, notwithstanding the offer of outright settlement.

A distinction can be drawn between costs following the trial of preliminary issues and costs orders made for interim hearings, whether the case management hearings or the hearing of an application.

In *Jean Scene Ltd v Tesco Stores Ltd*[124] the judge reflected this distinction by observing:

> 'It is undesirable for a judge to make even a partial costs order if it is in relation to part of the costs of the action generally, as opposed to a freestanding application ...'

Where there is a freestanding application the court may be more ready to conclude costs should follow the event in that application, certainly where it might be said one party has generated the need for that application and hence incurred costs that could otherwise have been avoided. In that context the approach advocated in *Kew* can be readily appreciated. The Court of Appeal might, in that case, be seen as having applied the test appropriate to freestanding interim hearings but in the slightly different context of the trial of a preliminary issue.

It might be argued, even so, that where a party has made an offer to settle which ultimately proves to have been well-judged then any further costs, including costs of interim applications, are generated by the other party having not accepted the offer, unless the conduct of the offeror does merit a sanction in costs. With case management hearings, of course, costs will usually be in the case and, if anything, the prospect of

---

[122]   [2006] EWCA Civ 1535.
[123]   [2009] EWCA Civ 26.
[124]   [2012] EWHC 1275 (Ch).

Part 36 offers later having an impact on the incidence of such costs only endorses the appropriateness of such an order in the vast majority of case management hearings even where it might be said one party or the other is, to a greater or lesser extent, successful or unsuccessful on particular issues.

12.2.3.6   *2007 transitional provisions*

Part 36 offers made prior to the introduction of the current version of the rule on 6 April 2007 may still be relevant so far as the costs consequences are concerned.

Rule 7 of the Civil Procedure (Amendment No 3) Rules 2006 dealt with transitional arrangements for existing Part 36 offers on the introduction of the new Part 36.

- A valid Part 36 offer or Part 36 payment made 21 days before 6 April 2007 which would have had costs consequences under the old Part 36 will have the consequences of the new CPR 36.10, 36.11 and 36.14. However, if court permission would have been required to accept the offer under the old rule permission of the court will still be required.

- For offers made in the 21 day period before 6 April 2007, the old rule will apply initially but the new rule applies following the expiry of 21 days from the date of that offer or payment unless the trial started within that period.

- Where an offer complying with CPR 36.10, as it was, had been made before 6 April 2007, the court will take that offer into account under the new Part 36 and the permission of the court will still be required to accept such an offer after proceedings have been commenced (which effectively removed the obligation to follow up a pre-issue offer with a payment into court within 14 days of service of proceedings).

12.2.3.7   *2013 transitional provisions*

Paragraph 22(7) of the Civil Procedure (Amendment) Rules 2013 provides that the amendment to Part 36.14(3), which implements the Offers to Settle in Civil Proceedings Order 2013, does not apply to a claimant's Part 36 offer which was made before 1 April 2013.

That amendment provides for the claimant to recover an 'additional amount' if judgment is at least as advantageous to the claimant as the claimant's own Part 36 offer (see **12.2.3.4**).

Consequently, a claimant may wish to make a further Part 36 offer, in the terms of any earlier Part 36 offer the claimant stands by, after 1 April 2013 as, under Part 36, there is no prohibition on multiple offers: see *L G Blower Specialist Bricklayer Ltd v Reeves*.[125]

12.2.4   Circumstances relevant to the court's general discretion on costs

The court's discretion as to costs is dealt with by CPR 44.3 (renumbered from April 2013 as CPR 44.2 but with the number of the sub-rules still following the same sequence).

---

[125]   [2010] EWCA Civ 726.

Subject to the application, in appropriate circumstances, of costs consequences found in Part 36 the court will, although starting with the general rule that the unsuccessful party will pay the costs of the successful party, need to take into account all relevant circumstances, including those specifically identified as relevant by the terms of CPR 44.3(4), when deciding what, if any, order to make about costs.

Having taken into account all relevant circumstances the court may, in accordance with CPR 44.3(2)(b), decide to depart from the general rule that the unsuccessful party should pay the costs of the successful party.

The circumstances identified by the terms of CPR 44.3(4) include admissible offers to settle which do not carry costs consequences under Part 36 as well as issues of conduct, further defined by CPR 44.3(5), and the extent to which the successful party has succeeded even if not wholly successful.

CPR 44.3 does, therefore, provide a structured decision-making process making it appropriate to look at the circumstances identified by the rule itself in turn.

12.2.4.1   The conduct of all the parties (CPR 44.3(4)(a))

What amounts to relevant conduct, for these purposes, is dealt with by CPR 44.3(5).

CPR 44.3(5) identifies relevant conduct of the parties as including:
* conduct before, as well as during, proceedings, in particular whether any relevant pre-action protocol was followed: (44.3 (5)(a));
* whether it was reasonable for a party to raise, pursue or contest any particular allegation or issue: (44.3(5)(b));
* the manner in which a party has pursued or defended his case or any particular allegation or issue: (44.3(5)(c));
* whether a claimant who has succeeded in his claim, in whole or in part, exaggerated his claim: (44.3(5)(d)).

12.2.4.1.1   Conduct causative of costs

Case-law suggests that, in this context, the term 'conduct' means conduct which has caused costs to be incurred which might otherwise not have been incurred. That is illustrated by comparing a number of decisions.

In *Home Office v Lownds*[126] the court specifically identified how a lack of co-operation might render necessary costs which would otherwise be unnecessary and that these should therefore be paid for.

Similarly, in *Charles v NTL Group Ltd*[127] costs were reduced because there clearly had been significant exaggeration which had led directly to additional costs being incurred.

---

[126] [2002] EWCA Civ 36.
[127] [2002] EWCA Civ 2004.

However, in *Hall v Rover Financial Services (GB) Ltd*[128] conduct, namely dishonesty, which may have led to the proceedings in the first place but was otherwise extraneous to the litigation, was held not to be relevant for these purposes.

12.2.4.1.2 ADR

The approach of the successful party to ADR may also influence the court's approach on costs. Although not specifically referred to in relation to conduct under CPR 44.3(5) the court is likely to take account of the duty on the parties, under CPR 1.3, to further the overriding objective and so look at conduct in relation to ADR.

In *Halsey v Milton Keynes General Hospital Trust*[129] the Court of Appeal determined the fundamental principle was that a successful party should not be deprived of costs as a result of refusing ADR unless that party had acted unreasonably in so doing. The court also identified relevant factors in assessing whether a party has acted unreasonably. In particular:

- the nature of the dispute;
- the merits of the case;
- whether other settlement methods have been attempted;
- if the costs of mediation would be disproportionately high;
- delay; and
- whether the mediation had a reasonable prospect of success:
  - a party might be reasonable in refusing mediation if the other party has adopted a position of intransigence; and
  - a party's own obduracy could not be a proper reason for concluding the refusal to mediate was reasonable even though this would mean it had no prospect of success.

Hence, even where the application was not actually made, if a party would have succeeded in an application for summary judgment that may justify refusing ADR on the merits, but refusing to agree ADR because that party thought he would win should be given little or no weight by the court when considering whether such refusal was reasonable. Consequently, a party who neither applies for summary judgment nor engages in ADR may be at some risk.

On this basis more than merely token engagement with ADR would seem necessary. Hence, a party who agreed to a mediation but then took an unreasonable position in the mediation was held to be in the same position as a party who unreasonably refused to mediate at all: *Earl of Malmesbury v Strutt & Parker*.[130]

Where there is encouragement by the court to enter ADR then, the stronger the encouragement, the easier it will be for the unsuccessful party to discharge the burden of showing the other party's refusal was unreasonable.

---

[128]   [2002] EWCA Civ 1514.
[129]   [2004] EWCA Civ 576.
[130]   [2008] EWHC 424 (QB).

In *Halsey* the court considered more general use could be made of the power to give a direction for ADR in personal injury cases, and if such a direction is given it may be difficult for the party declining ADR to show that this was reasonable.

In *Dunnett v Railtrack plc*[131] although the respondent was wholly successful in resisting the appeal there had been a complete failure to engage in the Court of Appeal ADR scheme. That was despite the court, when giving permission to appeal, suggesting such means be used by the parties. It was appropriate, therefore, for this to carry costs consequences.

The Court of Appeal again emphasised the importance of engaging, where appropriate, in ADR when giving judgment in *Burchell v Bullard*.[132]

In *Painting v University of Oxford*[133] Longmore LJ observed:

> 'Negotiation is supposed to be a two-way street, and a claimant who makes no attempt to negotiate can expect, and should expect, the courts to take that into account when making the appropriate order as to costs.'

Although, in that context, dealing with a claimant who failed to engage in negotiations, and hence ADR, the same could be said of a defendant who fails to reciprocate efforts at negotiation made by a claimant.

In *PGF II SA v OMFS Company*[134] both the claimant and the defendant made Part 36 offers, the claimant also suggesting a mediation to which the defendant never made any response. Following late acceptance of the defendant's Part 36 offer by the claimant, the court concluded that whilst the defendant's refusal to mediate was not relevant conduct for the purposes of CPR 36.14(4), making the usual costs consequences under that rule unjust, it was relevant to the more general discretion on costs under Part 44. Applying *Halsey* there had been a reasonable prospect that mediation would have been successful, hence it was unreasonable for the defendant to have refused to mediate.

The sanction for failing to make appropriate efforts towards settlement may, therefore, sound in costs (see **11.10**).

12.2.4.1.3   Particular allegations or issues

This factor inevitably overlaps with the terms of CPR 44.3(4)(b). Generally, certainly in a personal injury claim, a claimant should not be penalised because some allegations or issues are not established (see **12.2.4.2**).

12.2.4.1.4   Manner of pursuing or defending a case

Occasionally the manner in which a claim is pursued or defended may amount to conduct which has an impact on costs, for example *Walsh v Singh*.[135]

---

[131] [2002] EWCA Civ 303.
[132] [2005] EWCA Civ 358.
[133] [2005] EWCA Civ 161.
[134] [2012] EWHC 83 (TCC).
[135] [2011] EWCA Civ 80.

12.2.4.1.5 *Exaggeration*

This factor focusses on the claimant and, consequently, it is not unusual for an unsuccessful defendant to argue it is relevant a claimant has succeeded but recovered less, sometimes far less, than the claim made.

Personal injury claims invariably start as unquantified claims for damages. Damages for pain, suffering and loss of amenity, as well as other non-pecuniary claims, will not be quantified by a specific sum. A lower value claim, comprising just past losses, may set out full details of expenses and losses in a schedule at the outset but where there are future losses and expenses claimed these, too, are likely to be unquantified.

Because it is often difficult to accurately quantify the claim, particularly for future losses and expenses, until all relevant evidence is available, the claimant does need to be wary of attempting to do so, given the risk that the defendant will later argue there has been exaggeration when costs are being dealt with. With, perhaps, an eye on arguments about exaggeration, or in the hope a cautious claimant will guard against that risk by undervaluing the claim, it is not unusual for the defendant to press for a detailed schedule before that is viable and hence the need for the claimant to be wary of acceding to any such demand (see **2.8.3**).

A decision which appears to support the argument that a claimant who has exaggerated might be deprived of costs, but on closer analysis is an exceptional case, is *Painting v University of Oxford*.[136]

In *Painting* the claimant beat, at trial, a Part 36 offer made by the defendant. The Court of Appeal concluded the issue at trial had been that of exaggeration on which the defendant had won and thus, under the general rule, should recover costs, after the date of the Part 36 offer.

That decision was based on unusual circumstances because the trial was concerned overwhelmingly with the issue of exaggeration on which the defendant won. Furthermore, the claimant never manifested a willingness to negotiate or put forward a counter offer to the defendant's Part 36 offer.

A more typical case is *Jackson v Ministry of Defence*[137] where the defendant made a Part 36 offer of £150,000 and the claimant recovered £155,000 at trial. On the basis the trial judge found the claimant was involved in a significant degree of exaggeration, when giving evidence, the defendant was order to pay 75% per cent of the claimant's costs. The defendant appealed, arguing the case was essentially the same as *Painting*. That appeal was dismissed as the defendant was held perfectly able to protect itself against the risk of an exaggerated claim by making an early, and adequate, Part 36 offer. In any event *Painting* was regarded as an exceptional case.

Similarly, in *Hall v Stone*[138] the judge awarded the claimants 60 per cent of their costs on the basis that, although not dishonest, there was some exaggeration and the injuries were less serious than alleged. The Court of Appeal held the claimant should recover costs in full as the successful party. This was not a case like *Painting* in which the

---

136 [2005] EWCA Civ 161.
137 [2006] EWCA Civ 46.
138 [2007] EWCA Civ 1354.

defendant could claim to have won on such an important issue he could properly regard himself as the victor even though the claimant had beaten a Part 36 offer. Smith LJ held:

> 'The mere fact that the defendant has succeeded in keeping the damages down below the sum claimed by the claimant will not necessarily make him the victor or even a partial victor. Of course, where, as in *Painting*, the main issue in the case was whether the claimant had grossly exaggerated the claim and that issue had important costs consequences, it will be open to the judge to hold that the defendant was the victor. But if the claimant's exaggeration was no more than to put his case rather high, it does not seem to me that a defendant who has not made an effective and admissible offer can be regarded as the victor.'

In *Hall* Smith LJ went on to conclude that it was not appropriate to 'cut down the costs of the successful party merely because he has not done quite as well as he had hoped', unless the judge was able to conclude the losing party actually won on one or more issues in the case for the purposes of CPR 44.3(4)(b).

In *Straker v Tudor Rose*[139] the court agreed with the approach in *Barnes v Time Talk UK Ltd*[140] where Longmore LJ said 'the most important thing is to identify the party who is to pay money to the other'.

All these cases were carefully reviewed by the Court of Appeal in *Widlake v BAA Ltd*.[141]

In *Widlake* the claimant was found, by the trial judge, to have deliberately concealed a history of low back pain from the medical experts to try and increase the damages she might recover. On this basis, despite an award of damages totalling £5,522.38 which comfortably beat the defendant's Part 36 offer of £4,500, the judge ordered the claimant to pay the defendant's costs.

The Court of Appeal concluded that it was necessary to exercise the discretion on costs afresh as the trial judge had misdirected himself by failing to correctly determine the starting point of who was the successful party. On the facts that was plainly the claimant who came to court to establish her claim and judgment in her favour was a vindication of that stance.

In determining whether the general rule, that the unsuccessful party should pay the costs of the successful party, should not apply CPR 44.3(4)(a) required the court to have regard to conduct but in the context of 'a particular allegation or issue'. This helped to reconcile the apparently conflicting authorities, by regarding exaggeration as an 'allegation' relevant to the 'issue' of quantum. That was because it was then not necessary to determine who was the 'winner' but only to establish whether it was unreasonable for the claimant to pursue a particular allegation. If it was, then that was conduct the court had to take into account.

The way in which regard should be had to that conduct was principally to enquire into its causative effect, in other words to cause the incurring or wasting of costs.

The court held that similar consequences apply under CPR 44.3(5)(d) which asks whether a claimant has exaggerated.

---

[139] [2007] EWCA Civ 368.
[140] [2003] EWCA Civ 402.
[141] [2009] EWCA Civ 1256.

In any event, the court was entitled in an appropriate case to say misconduct was so egregious that a penalty should be imposed on the offending party by depriving that party of costs. However, despite recognising the findings of dishonesty by the trial judge Ward LJ observed:

> 'I sound a word of caution: lies are told in litigation every day up and down the country and quite rightly do not lead to a penalty being imposed in respect of them. There is a considerable difference between a concocted claim and an exaggerated claim and judges must be astute to measure how reprehensible the conduct is.'

The Court of Appeal noted, importantly, the shield available to defendants when dealing with false or exaggerated claims was Part 36. Whilst coming close to such an offer might sometimes have an impact on costs, the fact the defendant did not make a sufficiently high offer counted against it. Ward LJ summarised the position:

> 'The basic rule is that the claimant gets his (or her) costs if the defendant fails to make a good enough Part 36 offer ...'

A factor which counted against the claimant, however, was the failure to negotiate, as whilst not obliged to do so the refusal could impact on costs that otherwise might be recovered.

Having taken all these factors into account it was then necessary for the court to see where the balance would lie.

The starting point was the claimant should recover costs because she was the successful party and beat the defendant's offer. Making an exaggerated claim, with the result the case became heavily contested, was a relevant factor, but an order for costs against the claimant was less justified where the defendant failed to make an adequate Part 36 offer. The claimant's dishonesty also had to be penalised. Additionally, the claimant's failure to negotiate was a relevant factor.

When all these factors were balanced, the right order was that there should be no order for costs.

The approach in *Widlake* was followed by the Court of Appeal in *Gregson v Hussein & CIS Insurance*[142] and at first instance in *Morton v Portal Ltd*.[143]

The same approach was taken in *Fox v Foundation Piling Ltd*[144] where Jackson LJ held:

> 'Indeed the fact that the claimant has deliberately exaggerated his claim may in certain instances not be a good reason for depriving him of part of his costs: see *Morgan v UPS*. A defendant who has obtained video surveillance evidence is perfectly well able to protect his position on costs by making a modest offer under Part 36.'

In *Fox* Jackson LJ went on to observe that the facts in *Widlake* were so extreme that the claimant, as even a successful party, was nevertheless ordered to bear all of her own costs.

---

[142] [2010] EWCA Civ 165.
[143] [2010] EWHC 1804 (QB).
[144] [2011] EWCA Civ 790.

Jackson LJ went on to hold:

> 'I readily accept that the claimant's ultimate recovery fell far short of the original pleaded claim. This was in part because the video surveillance evidence showed the claimant to be less disabled than he alleged. Also it was in part because the accident of 11 April 2003 had accelerated pre-existing degenerative change, rather than caused an injury which the claimant would otherwise have escaped. The claimant realistically faced up to these matters when he accepted the defendant's final offer of £31,702.59 net.'

Hence Jackson LJ concluded:

> 'In my view, there is no justification for departing from the usual starting point as set out in rule 44.3 (2) (a), namely that the unsuccessful party should pay the successful party's costs. The judge exercised his discretion on the wrong basis, namely the assumption that the defendant was the successful party. It therefore falls to this court to re-exercise that discretion.'

When re-exercising that discretion the conclusion, in the words of Jackson LJ, was that 'I can see no reason to depart from the starting point that the claimant, as the successful party, should recover all his costs assessed on the standard basis'.

12.2.4.2   Whether a party has succeeded on part of his case, even if he has not been wholly successful (CPR 44.3(4)(b))

The court may, in appropriate circumstances, make an issue-based costs order, with costs following the event on such issues.

In practice, the court may prefer to award the successful party a specified percentage of the overall costs, to reflect costs associated with the unsuccessful issues, if it is decided to make an order reflecting those issues.

In *AEI Rediffusion Music Ltd v Phonographic Performance Ltd*[145] Lord Woolf MR observed:

> 'The most significant change of emphasis of the new rules is to require courts to be more ready to make separate orders which reflect the outcome of different issues. In doing this the new rules are reflecting a change of practice which has already started. It is now clear that too robust an application of the "follow the event principle" encourages litigants to increase the costs of litigation, since it discourages litigants from being selective as to the points that they take. If you recover all your costs as long as you win, you are encouraged to leave no stone unturned in your effort to so.'

The court will not, however, necessarily make an order based on the costs of issues even when the successful party has not been wholly successful. In *Burgess v British Steel plc*[146] Swinton Thomas LJ held that:

> 'It is, in my judgment, unusual to deprive a defendant who has paid a sum of money into court well in excess of the claim of any part of his costs because he was unsuccessful on a particular evidential issue, although it may be open to the court to deprive that party of the

---

[145]   [1999] 2 All ER 299.
[146]   (2000) 144 SJLB 58.

costs relating to the issue itself. In the same way it would be unusual to deprive a claimant of his costs in a personal injury claim if he had beaten the payment into court but had not been successful on certain evidential issues.'

Similarly, in *Goodwin v Bennetts UK Ltd*[147] Jackson LJ held:

'The ultimate result of this litigation is that the claimant has succeeded on some of her heads of claim and has failed on others. The defendant could have protected itself by making an offer which would have exceeded the modest sum finally awarded by this court. The defendant did not make any offer of settlement – the claimant had to go to trial, indeed had to come to this court in order to recover any damages whatsoever. It is unsurprising and not unusual that the claimant did not succeed on all of her alleged breaches of duty or allegations of negligence. Looking at all the circumstances of this case, I do not consider that any discount should be made from the normal order for costs.'

Jackson LJ made the same point in *Fox v Foundation Piling Ltd*[148] when he said:

'In a personal injury action the fact that the claimant has won on some issues and lost on other issues along the way is not normally a reason for depriving the claimant of part of his costs: see *Goodwin v Bennett UK Ltd* [2008] EWCA Civ 1658. For example, the claimant may succeed on some of the pleaded particulars of negligence, but not on others.'

12.2.4.3 Any admissible offer to settle which is not an offer to which costs consequences under Part 36 apply (CPR 44.3(4)(c))

CPR 44.3(4)(c) provides that in deciding what order to make about costs the court must have regard to all the circumstances including 'any admissible offer to settle ... which is not an offer to which cost consequences under Part 36 apply'.

An offer for the purposes of CPR 44.3(4)(c) must be an 'admissible offer'. Accordingly, there must not only be an offer but it must have expressly been made 'without prejudice except as to costs' rather than on a wholly 'without prejudice basis' (see **11.2.2** and **11.2.3**).

Additionally, even if originally made as a Part 36 offer, the offer must not be one to which the costs consequences found in Part 36, namely CPR 36.10 and CPR 36.14, have applied.

Accordingly, if any of the costs consequences provided for under Part 36 already apply, that offer should not have any further bearing on costs. Otherwise, however, the fact there has been a Part 36 offer may be a relevant consideration when the court exercises the general discretion as to costs conferred by Part 44.

An offer which was never intended to have the costs consequences of Part 36, an offer which was intended to have those consequences but failed to comply with the requirements as to form and content found in Part 36, and also an offer that was effective under Part 36 but was then withdrawn, may all be relevant for the purposes of this sub-rule.

---

[147] [2008] EWCA Civ 1658.
[148] [2011] EWCA Civ 790.

In *Fox v Foundation Piling Ltd*[149] Jackson LJ observed:

> 'In relation to the circumstances of the case, there has been much debate about whether the defendant's Part 36 offer can be taken into account at all. In my view, it plainly can be considered. A Part 36 offer which is subsequently withdrawn ceases to attract the consequences set out in rule 36.14. Such an offer then constitutes an "admissible offer to settle" within rule 44.3(4)(c).'

12.2.4.3.1   Use by the offeror

In *Biffa Waste Services Ltd v Maschinenfabrik Ernst Hese GMBH*[150] the court had regard to Part 36 offers, not carrying Part 36 consequences, to the advantage of the offeror, when considering what order to make as to costs under Part 44. The claimant incurred costs of over £1 million in a claim seeking damages just under £2 million. Judgment was entered for just over £140,000. The claimant had made various Part 36 offers, latterly to accept £125,000. The defendant had only responded to these proposals belatedly and the judge held the fact that the claimant had made offers coupled with the absence of any timely response to those offers by the defendant were relevant considerations, as even with exaggeration by one party it must be remembered the other party can make a Part 36 offer. Accordingly, the defendant was ordered to pay the claimant's costs to be assessed, despite the claimant incurring very substantial costs in the recovery of only a small part of the sum claimed, without any preliminary order restricting the claimant to part only of those costs.

Similarly, in *J Murphy & Sons Ltd v Johnston Precast Ltd*[151] an issue-based costs order against a defendant who was the successful party overall was not considered appropriate partly because the defendant had made offers to the claimant and the claimant would have been in a much better position, compared with the judgment given, had either of those offers been accepted.

Where a defendant successfully defends the claim but had made a Part 36 offer to settle, even if withdrawn, that may be a relevant factor in determining whether to award indemnity costs: *Community Gateway Association Ltd v Beha Williams Norman Ltd*.[152]

The fact a party has made an offer to settle which proves to be optimistic should not be held against that party when the question of costs is considered under Part 44.

12.2.4.3.2   Use against the offeror

In *Quorum A/S v Schramm*[153] the court concluded that a claimant who recovered more than the claimant's own Part 36 offer should not be deprived of costs by comparing judgment with that offer.

In *Rolf v De Guerin*[154] the claimant, in a building dispute, ultimately obtained judgment for £2,500 against the defendant. The claimant had previously made a Part 36 offer of £14,000 which also invited the defendant to attend a formal mediation or round table

---

[149]   [2011] EWCA Civ 790.
[150]   [2008] EWHC 2657 (TCC).
[151]   [2008] EWHC 3104.
[152]   [2011] EWHC 2994 (TCC).
[153]   [2002] 2 All ER (Comm).
[154]   [2011] EWCA Civ 78.

meeting. The judge, at first instance, ordered the claimant to pay the defendant's costs from the end of the relevant period for that offer. Allowing an appeal the Court of Appeal noted the consequences of the Part 36 offers were regulated by Part 36 itself and observed the terms of CPR 44.3(4)(c) would make no sense if the offer to settle were to be held against the offeror. In any event, a willingness to accept less than the formal claim, when the size of that formal claim had already been taken into account for the purposes of determining costs, could hardly be a reason for penalising the offeror.

12.2.4.3.3   Withdrawn offers

CPR 36.14(6)(a) expressly provides that the costs consequences set out in CPR 36.14 will not apply where a Part 36 offer has been withdrawn.

Hence in *Epsom College v Pierse Contracting Southern Ltd*[155] whilst the first instance judgment was upheld, that was on alternative grounds, as it was an error simply to apply the consequences of CPR 36.14 to an offer that had been withdrawn. As the Court of Appeal recognised the exercise of discretion under Part 44 is a quite different exercise to determining whether the costs consequences of Part 36 apply, even though it may sometimes lead to the costs consequences set out in CPR 36.14 being applied.

Similarly, the Court of Appeal was clear in *Fox v Foundation Piling Ltd*[156] that the defendant's withdrawn Part 36 offer ceased to attract the consequences set out in CPR 36.14 and could only be considered under CPR 44.3(4)(c).

A decision which may give a misleading impression of the law, away from the particular context of the case, is *Owners and/or Bareboat Charterers and/or Sub Bareboat Charterers of the Ship Samco Europe v Owners of the Ship MSC Prestige*[157] where the court had to determine the incidence of costs following a decision apportioning responsibility for a collision at sea.

It is important to note that, as an admiralty case, Part 61 of the CPR, as well as Part 36, was applicable and that offers to settle made by the parties expressly referred to Part 61 as well as Part 36.

The judge observed Part 61 applies to admiralty claims, with offers to settle collision claims being dealt with by CPR 61.4. That rule provides that where an offer to settle is made, in accordance with the rule, and the maker of the offer obtains at trial an apportionment equal to or more favourable than the offer then, unless the court considers it unjust, the maker of the offer will be entitled to all costs from 21 days after the offer and earlier costs in the percentage to which he would have been entitled had the offer been accepted. There is no equivalent provision to CPR 36.14(6), that a withdrawn offer will not carry these costs consequences.

Consequently, under Part 61, the issue for the court was whether it would be unjust to award costs in accordance with that rule when the outcome was a judgment at least as advantageous to the claimant as the claimant's own offer, albeit an offer that had subsequently been withdrawn. In that context the judge found that it would be just for the claimant's offer to carry the costs consequences provided for under Part 61. The

---

[155] [2011] EWCA Civ 1449.
[156] [2011] EWCA Civ 790.
[157] [2011] EWHC 1656 (Admlty).

decision is not, therefore, an authority for withdrawn offers carrying the specific costs consequences provided for under Part 36. Rather, such offers will only fall to be considered under the general discretion conferred by Part 44.

Furthermore, the review of earlier case-law, dealing with offers that have been withdrawn, should now be viewed with some caution given the subsequent Court of Appeal ruling in *French v Groupama Insurance Co Ltd*[158] which considered, when looking at what might be termed quasi-Part 36 offers, the potential costs consequences of such an offer which had been withdrawn.

It is important to be clear about whether a Part 36 offer is being withdrawn, as illustrated by *Lilleyman v Lilleyman*.[159]

In *Lilleyman* the claimant sought reasonable financial provision from her late husband's estate. In July 2011 the defendant made two, simultaneous, offers, one of which was made under Part 36 and the other just on a 'without prejudice' basis. In January 2012 the defendant made a further 'without prejudice' offer which, referring back to the offer made in July 2011, indicated that this offer was now withdrawn.

Following judgment the issue was whether the Part 36 offer made in July 2011 had been withdrawn in January 2012. Whilst the court held the letter was clearly intended to withdraw only the 'without prejudice' offer, reflecting the need for a Part 36 offer to be expressly withdrawn, it is, perhaps, always safest to be clear, where there is more than one offer, precisely which offer is being withdrawn.

A Part 36 offer which has been withdrawn, or for any other reason does not have the cost consequences provided for in that rule, may still be relevant to the exercise of the court's general discretion on costs under Part 44 as Jackson LJ explained in *Fox v Foundation Piling Ltd*:[160]

> 'In relation to the circumstances of the case, there has been much debate about whether the defendant's Part 36 offer can be taken into account at all. In my view, it plainly can be considered. A Part 36 offer which is subsequently withdrawn ceases to attract the consequences set out in rule 36.14. Such an offer then constitutes an "admissible offer to settle" within rule 44.3(4)(c).'

The significance of a withdrawn Part 36 offer under Part 44 may well depend upon whether, within the time the offer was open, it was reasonable for the offeree to make a decision on that offer, for example because the information necessary to make that decision was unavailable: *Rehill –v- Rider Holdings Ltd*.[161]

12.2.4.3.4   Changed offers

CPR 36.14(6)(b) confirms that the costs consequences found in CPR 36.14 will not apply to a Part 36 offer that has been changed so that its terms are less advantageous to the offeree, provided the offeree has beaten the less advantageous offer.

---

[158] [2011] EWCA Civ 1119.
[159] [2012] EWHC 1056 (Ch).
[160] [2011] EWCA Civ 790.
[161] [2014] EWCA Civ 42.

12.2.4.3.5 *Quasi-Part 36 offers*

Prior to the April 2007 amendments to Part 36, the court had discretion to treat a purported Part 36 offer, not complying fully with the rules as to form and content, as effective. This topic was explored by the Court of Appeal in *Trustees of Stokes Pension Fund v Western Power Distribution Power Distribution (South West) plc.*[162]

The current version of Part 36 contains no equivalent provision but, of course, there are still offers extant which were made before April 2007.

So it was that in *French v Groupama Insurance Co Ltd*[163] the Court of Appeal dealt with issues summarised by Rix LJ as:

> '... how a pre-litigation offer to settle should be treated in the light of CPR provisions to be found in Part 36, as amended over the period concerned, and in the light of *Trustees of Stokes Pension Fund v Western Power Distribution Power Distribution (South West) plc* [2005] EWCA Civ 854.'

In *French* the claimant alleged breach of contract by the defendant, her insurers, in connection with a claim for reinstatement of her home following subsidence.

The defendant made, on more than one occasion, an offer of £115,000.

Whilst the claimant obtained judgment for £132,247.41, that included an award for damage suffered after the offer leading the judge to conclude she would have been at least £20,000 better off had she accepted the defendant's offer when made and used that to reinstate her property there and then.

Consequently, when dealing with costs, the judge, applying *Stokes*, concluded the defendant had made a quasi Part 36 offer, hence after 21 days from the date of that offer the claimant should recover no costs and have to pay the defendant's costs.

The Court of Appeal noted the defendant's offer failed to meet the requirements of the original Part 36, then in force, in a number of ways:

• being made before proceedings;
• not being supported by a payment into court following issue; and
• being time limited (and therefore effectively withdrawn).

Hence, there was no requirement the court would even take the offers into account let alone apply the cost consequences of Part 36.

The *Stokes* case was decided in the context of the original Part 36, particularly how Part 36 offers not accompanied by a Part 36 payment ought to be treated under the court's general discretion, then found in Part 36 itself and also Part 44. The court concluded, provided certain conditions were met, a Part 36 offer should usually be treated as having the same effect as a Part 36 payment. In this case, however, the conditions identified in *Stokes* were not met.

---

[162] [2005] EWCA Civ 854.
[163] [2011] EWCA Civ 1119.

Moreover, in *Stokes* the court also considered whether withdrawal of the offer made any difference to the potential costs consequences. The critical consideration, on this point, was whether the offer should have been accepted within the time it remained open. The question, as the Court of Appeal noted in *French*, was not whether a withdrawn offer should be *taken into account* but whether *Part 36 consequences* should follow, a question that became all the more important when the offer was only a quasi-Part 36 offer.

Furthermore, coupled with the changes to Part 36, making clear a withdrawn Part 36 offer would not carry with it the costs consequences of the rule, CPR 44.3 was amended so this no longer provided for the court's general discretion on costs to take account of an offer 'whether or not made in accordance with Part 36' but only an 'admissible offer to settle ... and which is not an offer to which the costs consequences under Part 36 apply.'

The Court of Appeal, in *French*, concluded these amendments reflected a new determination to specify carefully what did or did not count as a Part 36 offer with Part 36 consequences, other admissible offers being relevant to the exercise of discretion under Part 44 but not carrying the costs consequences of Part 36.

On this basis the Court of Appeal concluded it was now harder to formulate an approach to the Part 44 discretion that some offers which were not Part 36 offers should nevertheless be treated as such for the purposes of applying Part 36 consequences. Accordingly, although not necessary for the decision in the case, as the relevant offer was not a quasi-Part 36 offer, *Stokes* should be regarded now as dealing primarily with the specific problem where a Part 36 payment was a formal requirement in circumstances that added nothing to the value of the offer.

Consequently it was necessary for the discretion on costs to be exercised afresh by the Court of Appeal under Part 44, untrammelled by *Stokes*. After weighing up all the circumstances of the case the court concluded the fair result was that there should be no order as to costs other than that the claimant should have her costs down to 21 days after the making of the defendant's latter offer.

Hence the decision in *Stokes* should, perhaps, now be treated with some caution. Perhaps all that can be said with any certainty is that in *French* the Court of Appeal affirmed the observations in *Stokes* that where an offer was open for a limited period or time and it was not reasonable for the claimant to have accepted the offer within that timescale, the offer would be unlikely to carry costs consequences.

A better approach to determining the costs consequences of an offer no longer open, under Part 44, may be to confine any consequences to the period in which the offer could have been accepted. That is in line with earlier Court of Appeal authority, not cited in *Stokes*, namely *Capital Bank Plc v Stickland*.[164] Such an approach is also consistent with the general approach that only offers on the table are likely to facilitate settlement and that, indeed, offers which are no longer open, but might carry costs consequences, are likely to hinder, rather than help, settlement.[165]

---

[164] [2004] EWCA Civ 1677.
[165] *Sampla v Rushmoor Borough Council* [2008] EWHC 2616 (TCC); *C v D* [2011] EWCA Civ 646.

In *Rowles-Davies v Call 24-7 Ltd*,[166] where the court had to consider the potential costs consequences under Part 44 of the purported acceptance of a Part 36 offer after the trial had started (which was treated as a counter offer), the judge concluded the defendant would have done well to have allowed the claimant to accept that offer. Accordingly, whilst the defendant argued it was difficult to think through all the implications of such a situation arising in the middle of a trial, some provision should be made to reflect the fact the defendant was responsible for losing the opportunity of avoiding two days' costs of trial on both sides.

The defendant also argued the judgment was not 'more advantageous' than the defendant's offer, because the amount of irrecoverable costs would almost inevitably have exceeded the amount by which the judgment would have exceeded the amount offered. The judge held that whilst *Carver v BAA plc*[167] was binding, not much weight should be attached to that decision, even on the basis the unrecoverable costs would exceed the amount by which the judgment exceeded the Part 36 offer.

12.2.4.3.6 Time limited offers

It is now well established that a time limited offer cannot be a Part 36 offer.[168]

Accordingly, like a withdrawn offer, a time limited offer can only be relevant to the exercise of the court's general discretion as to costs under Part 44.

A court should, perhaps, adopt the same approach to the efficacy of such an offer as it would to a withdrawn offer, in other words focussing only the period of time the offer was open and, at the very least, determining whether the offer should have been accepted within that timescale.

12.2.4.3.7 Near Miss Offers

The terms of CPR 36.14(1A) mean that, at least to Part 36 offers made on or after 1 October 2011, what might be termed a 'near miss' offer will not carry the costs consequences of that rule.

Whilst such an offer might still be taken into account, when the court considers costs, under CPR 44.3(4)(c) it seems unlikely the courts will allow the uncertainty that would generate. In *Hammersmatch Properties (Welwyn) Ltd v Saint-Gobain Ceramics & Plastics Ltd*[169]the approach taken by Chadwick LJ in *Johnsey Estates (1990) Ltd v Secretary of State for the Environment, Transport and the Regions*[170]where he said:

> 'It seems to me that a court should resist invitations to speculate whether offers to settle litigation which were not in fact made might or might not have been accepted if they had been made. There are, I think, at least two reasons why a court should not allow itself to be led down that road. First, the rules of court provide the means by which a party who thinks that his opponent is not open to reason can protect himself from costs. He can make a

---

[166] [2010] EWHC 1695 (Ch).
[167] [2009] 1 WLR 113.
[168] *C v D* [2011] EWCA Civ 646; *Thewlis v Groupama Insurance Co Ltd* [2010] EWHC 3 (TCC); *PHI Group Ltd v Robert West Consulting Ltd* [2012] EWCA Civ 588; *Shaw v Merthyr Tydfil County Borough* [2014] EWCA Civ 1678.
[169] [2013] EWHC 2227 (TCC).
[170] [2001] EWCA Civ 535.

payment in; he can make a Calderbank offer; now, under the Civil Procedure Rules 1998, he can make a payment or an offer under CPR Part 36. The advantage of the courses open under the rules is that they remove speculation. The court can see what offer was made, when it was made, and whether it was accepted. Secondly, speculation is likely to be a most unsatisfactory tool by which to determine questions of costs at the end of a trial.'

Ramsey J, on this basis, held that:

'Whilst CPR 44.2(4)(c) will clearly have application where there is an open offer made for more than is recovered or an offer purportedly under Part 36 for a sum in excess of the sum recovered but where, for some reason it does not have the Part 36 costs consequences, I do not consider that it should alter the costs consequences in a case such as this.'

Ramsey J added:

'I am doubtful that, on analysis, a "near miss" offer can generally add anything to what otherwise would be conduct in the form of unreasonable refusal to negotiate. To do so would raise the difficulties in Johnsey and seek to base an exercise in discretion on offers which neither party made at the time but which, with the benefit of hindsight, one party should have made and the other party should have accepted.'

The Court of Appeal, however, appeared to take a broader view about the potential effect of offers under Part 44 in *Coward v Phaestos Ltd*.[171]

12.2.4.3.8   Exercise of discretion

The costs consequences of an offer taken into account under Part 44 will be much less certain than where an offer carried costs consequences under Part 36. That is because, under Part 44, the offer is just one of the factors which the court must take into account, whilst under Part 36 the specific consequences provided for under the rule will, unless any of the exceptions apply, prevail.

The relationship between Part 44 and Part 36, and the different scenarios within which those rules might need to be applied, was reviewed in *Fox v Foundation Piling Ltd*.[172] Jackson LJ, with whom the other members of the court concurred, summarised those different scenarios.

'First, where one party makes a Part 36 offer and then achieves a more advantageous result than that proposed in his offer, the provisions of rule 36.14 modify the court's general discretion in respect of costs.

Secondly, parties are quite entitled to make "Calderbank" (that is an offer expressed to be without prejudice except as to costs) offers outside the framework of Part 36. Where a party makes such an offer and then achieves a more advantageous result, the court's discretion is wider than under Part 36. Nevertheless, it may well be appropriate to order the party which has optimistically rejected the "Calderbank" offer to pay all costs since the date when that offer expired: *Trustees of Stokes Pension Fund v Western Power Distribution (South West) Ltd* [2005] EWCA Civ 854.

A not uncommon scenario is that both parties turn out to have been over-optimistic in their Part 36 offers. The claimant recovers more than the defendant has previously offered to pay,

---

[171]   [2014] EWCA Civ 1256.
[172]   [2011] EWCA Civ 790.

but less than the claimant has previously offered to accept. In such a case the claimant should normally be regarded as "the successful party" within rule 44.3(2). The claimant has been forced to bring proceedings in order to recover the sum awarded. He has done so and his claim has been vindicated to that extent.

However, an adjustment may be required to reflect the costs referable to a discrete issue which the successful party has lost. An adjustment may also be required to compensate the unsuccessful party for costs which it was caused to incur by reason of unreasonable conduct on the part of the successful party.

For these purposes in a personal injury action the fact that the claimant has won on some issues and lost on other issues along the way is not normally a reason for depriving the claimant of part of his costs: *Goodwin v Bennett UK Ltd* [2008] EWCA Civ 1658.

Similarly, even deliberate exaggeration of the claim may not be good reason to deprive the claimant of costs as a defendant may always make a Part 36 offer.'

Given the terms of the Court of Appeal judgment in *French*, the second point made by Jackson LJ may need to be refined in the light of that further ruling. Otherwise, this summary should, perhaps, be taken to accurately reflect the law in this area, particularly on the crucial point that recovery of damages above and beyond the amount, if any, offered by the defendant, whether or not as a Part 36 offer, will be sufficient vindication to render the claimant the successful party.

In *Widlake v BAA Ltd*[173] the Court of Appeal confirmed the need, when the court considered the effect of an admissible offer not carrying costs consequences under Part 36 on the general discretion found in Part 44, for a balancing exercise which took into account all relevant circumstances. Consequently, whilst the primary question was to determine who had been the unsuccessful party, for the purposes of the general rule in Part 44, it was then necessary to assess all other factors when deciding if it was appropriate to depart from that general rule. Ward LJ framed the following question for the court when addressing this secondary question:

'Having tried to represent these considerations in a balance sheet, where does the balance lie?'

A similar approach was adopted by the Court of Appeal in *Saigol v Thorney Ltd*[174] and again in *Coward v Phaestos Ltd*.[175]

12.2.5 Costs orders

After considering all relevant circumstances, the court's general discretion as to costs, can be exercised by making an order, under CPR 44.3(6) (from April 2013, CPR 44.2(6)), that a party pays:

- a proportion of another party's cost;
- a stated amount in respect of another party's costs;
- costs from or until a certain date only;
- costs incurred before proceedings have begun;

---

[173]   [2009] EWCA Civ 1256.
[174]   [2014] EWCA Civ 556.
[175]   [2014] EWCA Civ 1256.

- costs relating to particular steps taken in the proceedings;
- costs relating only to a distinct part of the proceedings; and
- interest on costs from or until a certain date.

Any such order should be made at the time of judgment rather than assessment, as assessment is a different procedure from deciding whether a party is to be awarded all or only part of the costs: *R v Westminster City Council ex parte Chorion plc*.[176]

Consequently, the judge assessing costs cannot alter the order for costs made by the judge giving judgment but, nevertheless, is still entitled to take account of relevant factors, found in CPR 44.5, when deciding the amount of costs: *O'Beirne v Hudson*.[177]

A judge assessing costs must, however, be careful not to subject a party, where the costs order already made reflects one of the orders permitted by CPR 44.3(6) to what might be termed 'double jeopardy': *Northstar Systems Ltd v Fielding*.[178]

Jackson J (as he then was) reviewed the case-law dealing with the range of costs orders available to the court in *Multiplex Constructions (UK) Ltd v Cleveland Bridge UK Ltd and Cleveland Bridge Dorman Long Engineering Ltd*[179] from which he derived a number of principles including those relevant to the excise of discretion under CPR 44.3(6):

- In considering how to exercise its discretion the court should take as its starting point the general rule that the successful party is entitled to an order for costs.
- The judge must then consider what departures are required from that starting point, having regard to all the circumstances of the case.
- Where the circumstances of the case require an issue-based costs order, that is what the judge should make. However, the judge should hesitate before doing so, because of the practical difficulties which this causes and because of the steer given by CPR 44.3(7).
- In many cases the judge can and should reflect the relative success of the parties on different issues by making a proportionate costs order.
- In assessing a proportionate costs order the judge should consider what costs are referable to each issue and what costs are common to several issues. It will often be reasonable for the overall winner to recover not only the costs specific to the issues which he has won but also the common costs.

Indeed, CPR 44.3(7) expressly requires the court, if considering making an order relating to a distinct part of the proceedings, to make instead, if practicable, an order for payment of a proportion of another party's costs or an order for costs from or until a certain date only.

12.2.6 Basis for the assessment of costs

Where the court is to assess the amount of costs payable under a costs order, whether by summary assessment or detailed assessment, those costs, in accordance with CPR 44.4(1) (from April 2013, CPR 44.3(1)), will be assessed either on the standard basis or on the indemnity basis.

A costs order may provide for part of the costs to be assessed on the standard basis and part on the indemnity basis.

If the court makes an order about costs without indicating the basis on which those costs are to be assessed, or an order for costs to be assessed on a basis other than the standard basis or the indemnity basis, CPR 44.4(4) (from April 2013, CPR 44.3(4)) confirms those costs will be assessed on the standard basis.

The basis for the assessment of costs, under Part 44, is effectively part of the court's general discretion on costs. It is, therefore, a broader discretion than when the terms of CPR 36.14(3) apply.

12.2.6.1 Indemnity costs under Part 36

CPR 36.14(1)(b) applies where judgment against the defendant is at least as advantageous to the claimant as the proposals contained in a claimant's Part 36 offer.

When that rule applies then, unless this would be unjust, the clamant will, in accordance with CPR 36.14(3)(b), be entitled to costs on the indemnity basis from the date on which the relevant period in the offer expired.

Consequently, the only issue for the court, when CPR 36.14(1)(b) applies, is to determine whether the consequence of indemnity costs would be unjust (see **12.2.3.4.6**).

Accordingly, in this context, indemnity costs should not be seen as carrying any stigma requiring unreasonable conduct to generate such an order: *Petrotrade Inc v Texaco Ltd*.[180]

12.2.6.2 Indemnity costs under Part 44

A different approach to indemnity costs, from that under Part 36, is applicable where the court is exercising the general discretion, as to the basis of assessment, found in Part 44.

After identifying the correct approach to these issue under Part 44 it is worth considering how that has been applied in a number of different situations.

---

[180] Court of Appeal, 23 May 2000.

12.2.6.2.1   *General approach*

In *Reid Minty v Taylor*[181] Kay LJ made a general observation about the proper approach to the discretion on the basis for the assessment of costs under Part 44 when he said:

> 'The approach of the CPR is a relatively simple one: namely, if one party has made a real effort to find a reasonable solution to the proceedings and the other party has resisted that sensible approach, then the latter puts himself at risk that the Order for costs may be on an indemnity basis. What would be a reasonable solution will depend on all the circumstances of the case, and might, in a case which is clearly of no merit, include pointing out, in such detail as is appropriate, the fundamental weaknesses of the case being presented by the other side and inviting consideration of abandonment.'

That does not mean a claimant who fails to accept an offer from the defendant, even a Part 36 offer, and subsequently does worse than the offer should normally bear indemnity costs. In *Reid Minty* May LJ held that:

> 'It cannot be right that every defendant in every case can put themselves in the way of claiming costs on an indemnity basis simply by inviting the claimant at an early stage to give up, discontinue, and pay the defendant's costs on a standard basis.'

However, May LJ went on to observe that:

> 'It might be different if a defendant offers to move some way towards a claimant's position and the result is more favourable to the defendant than that.'

In *Kiam v MGN Ltd*[182] Simon Brown LJ put the comments made in *Reid Minty* into perspective when he observed:

> 'I for my part, understand the Court there to have been deciding no more than that conduct, albeit falling short of misconduct deserving of moral condemnation, *can* be so unreasonable as to justify an order for indemnity costs. With that I respectfully agree. To my mind, however, such conduct would need to be unreasonable to a high degree; unreasonable in this context certainly does not mean merely wrong or misguided in hindsight. An indemnity costs order made under Rule 44 (unlike one made under Rule 36) does, I think, carry at least some stigma. It is of its nature penal rather than exhortatory.'

Consequently, Simon Brown LJ continued:

> 'It follows from all this that in my judgment it will be a rare case indeed where the refusal of a settlement offer will attract under Rule 44 not merely an adverse order for costs, but an order on an indemnity rather than standard basis.'

Simon Brown LJ concluded:

> 'It is very important that *Reid Minty* should not be understood and applied for all the world as if under the CPR it is now generally appropriate to condemn in indemnity costs those who decline reasonable settlement offers.'

---

[181]   [2001] EWCA Civ 1723.
[182]   [2002] EWCA Civ 66.

Case-law suggests this general approach requires something 'out of the norm' to generate an order for indemnity costs.

It is, therefore, exceptional for the court to order that, under Part 44, there should be indemnity costs because such an order is regarded as penal and carrying a degree of stigma. In *Epsom College v Pierse Contracting Southern Ltd*[183] Rix LJ summarised the law on this point when he observed that before indemnity costs were imposed under Part 44 it was necessary that:

> '... the case in question falls outside the norm, and that conduct must be unreasonable to a high degree (*Reid Minty (a firm) v Taylor* [2001] EWCA Civ 1723, [2002] 1 WLR 2800, *Excelsior Commercial & Industrial Holdings Ltd v Salisbury Hammer Aspden & Johnson* [2002] CP Rep 67) can be met where there has been an unreasonable failure to accept offers of settlement, or a party has unreasonably resisted a sensible approach to finding a solution to the proceedings; even if such a case deserving of indemnity costs has been described as "a rare case indeed" (*Kiam v MGN Ltd* (No 2) [2002] 2 All ER 242, *per* Simon Brown LJ at [13]).'

Similarly, in *Barr v Biffa Waste Services Ltd*[184] Coulson J, having reviewed the authorities, concluded that:

> 'The relevant principles in relation to indemnity costs to be gleaned from the authorities can perhaps be summarised as follows:
>
> (i) Unreasonable conduct "to a high degree" is necessary for an order for indemnity costs: see *Kiam v MGN Ltd* [No 2] [2002] 2 All ER 242. In *Excelsior Commercial & Industrial Holdings Ltd v Salisbury Hammer Aspden & Johnson (A Firm)* [2002] EWCA Civ 879, the Court of Appeal said that an order for indemnity costs was appropriate only where "there was some conduct or some circumstance which took the case out of the norm".
>
> (ii) The pursuit of claims which could be fairly described as "speculative, weak, opportunistic or thin" gives rise to a high risk that, if the claim fails, indemnity costs will be ordered: see Tomlinson J (as he then was) in *Three Rivers District Council & Ors v The Governor & Company of the Bank of England* [2006] EWHC (Comm) 816 at paragraph 25 and Gloster J in *JP Morgan Chase Bank & Ors v Springwell Navigation Corp* [2008] EWHC 2848 (Comm) at paragraph 7.
>
> (iii) A claimant's refusal of a defendant's Part 36 offer which the claimant subsequently fails to beat may, subject to the Court's discretion, be determinative of his liability to pay indemnity costs: see *Reid Minty (A Firm) v Taylor* [2002] 2 All ER 150. But it should not be thought that it is generally appropriate to condemn in indemnity costs those who decline reasonable settlement offers: see *Kiam* and *Excelsior*.'

It is, therefore, important that a claimant who wishes to secure, amongst other benefits, indemnity costs, in the event any judgment is at least as advantageous to the claimant as the claimant's own offer, makes a Part 36 offer. That is because, unless there is something exceptional about the defendant's conduct which merits such a sanction under Part 44, an order for indemnity costs is unlikely to be made even when the claimant obtains judgment at least as advantageous as the claimant's own, non-Part 36, offer. As Davis LJ explained in *F & C Alternative Investments (Holdings) Ltd v Barthelemy*:[185]

---

[183] [2011] EWCA Civ 1449.
[184] [2011] EWHC 1107 (TCC).
[185] [2012] EWCA Civ 843.

'... there is no reason or justification, in my view, for indirectly extending Part 36 beyond its expressed ambit. Indeed to do so would tend to undermine the requirements of Part 36 and the repeated insistence of the courts that intended Part 36 offers should be very carefully drafted so as to comply with the requirements of Part 36.'

12.2.6.2.2   Failing to beat an offer

Where the defendant fails to beat a claimant's Part 36 offer then, unless that would be unjust, the court should make an order for indemnity costs in accordance with CPR 36.14(3). If the relevant offer is not a Part 36 offer the claimant, to obtain an order for indemnity costs, will have to show there is something that takes the case 'out of the norm'.

Where the claimant fails to beat a defendant's offer there is no such distinction between a Part 36 offer and a non-Part 36 offer. In either situation the defendant will have to show indemnity costs are justified on the basis of the discretion under Part 44: *Reid Minty v Taylor*;[186] *Kiam v MGN Ltd*.[187]

Where, however, a claimant's case was always very weak and ultimately failed the fact the defendant had made a Part 36 offer, even though that offer was later withdrawn, this was a relevant factor in the court deciding part of the costs payable by the claimant should be assessed on the indemnity basis: *Community Gateway Association Ltd v Beha Williams Northern Ltd*.[188]

12.2.6.2.3   Breach of court orders

In *Baron v Lovell*[189] it was held that where a party is in breach of a direction given by the court it may be appropriate to order indemnity costs against that party. Brooke LJ said, in relation to the discretion of the judge on costs, that:

'If he considers that that party has acted unreasonably in this way in connection with the litigation in breach of the direction of the court, there may come a time when he decides that it is appropriate to make an Order for indemnity costs against that party, or to exercise his power to award interest on damages at a much higher rate than what is usual, if those powers are available to him.'

12.2.6.2.4   Issues

Where a party pursues issues inappropriately, that may be sufficient to take the case out of the norm and lead to an order for indemnity costs.

In *Craig v Railtrack plc*[190] a finding in favour of the claimant on liability was inevitable, the only issue being which of the defendants would be liable. The court held, consequently, that in these circumstances the claimant was entitled to have costs assessed on the indemnity basis as the defendant should have ensured the issue of liability was disposed of at an early stage with the claimant and then sorted out that issue between themselves.

---

[186] [2001] EWCA Civ 1723.
[187] [2002] EWCA Civ 66.
[188] [2011] EWHC 2994 (TCC).
[189] Court of Appeal, 27 July 1999.
[190] [2002] EWHC 168 (QB).

In *Greaves v Watchorn*[191] the defendant maintained an argument that the claimant was not wearing a seat belt when that point seemed to have no real merit. The defendant subsequently admitted liability just before trial and the judge ordered indemnity costs under Part 44. This was on the basis that the claimant had tried to persuade the defendant not to pursue a point with no merit and it was appropriate for the defendant to incur costs consequences when the defendant continued to take that point.

Similarly, costs may be appropriate when a party conducts himself on a wholly false basis when the true state of affairs was within his knowledge, or at least capable of ascertainment if properly investigated, and the proceedings were thereby significantly prolonged and costs increased. Hence in *Cooper v P & O Stena Line Ltd*[192] the defendant made allegations of fraud by malingering when an investigation of its own records would have suggested this was inappropriate.

12.2.6.2.5 Allegations

Allegations of fraud, which are not substantiated, may well result in an order for indemnity costs because it is important a party against whom such allegations are made can deal properly with them.

In *Zurich Insurance Co Plc v Hayward*[193] Smith LJ explained that where allegations of fraud were made against a claimant and not substantiated:

'If he has not been dishonest, he will win and will recover all his costs. Zurich is solvent and I would have thought that, if the fraud allegation were held to be wholly without foundation, there would be a good argument for indemnity costs.'

Indeed, allegations falling short of fraud, such as 'sharp practice' may, at least partly, result in an order that costs be assessed on the indemnity basis. In *Halliwells LLP v Austin*[194] an argument, based on sharp practice, of unconscionability was developed in a skeleton argument. On this point Warren J observed:

'Sharp practice may be not as derogatory a term as fraud but it is not something of which one expects honest people to be guilty.'

Consequently, when it came to costs, the judgment held:

'I do not consider that this is a case for indemnity costs on the whole but I do think, and I will come to this in more detail in a moment, that the very serious un-particularised allegations against Mr Burns do warrant some measure of disapproval by the Court and given the very late stage at which dishonesty, not fraud, but dishonesty in the sense of sharp practice or the requirement to give full disclosure were raised, as I said, at a very late stage, it would be appropriate to order that the costs of the hearing itself, that is the cost of attendance of solicitors and Mr Potts' entire brief fee, should be paid on an indemnity basis.'

If the defendant wishes to allege fraud that should be the subject of an express allegation in the defence rather than an insinuation: *Hussain v Amin*[195] (see **3.6.7.5**). The

---

[191] [2003] CLY 341.
[192] [1999] 1 Lloyd's Rep 734.
[193] [2011] EWCA Civ 641.
[194] [2012] EWHC 3140 (Ch).
[195] [2012] EWCA Civ 1456.

defendant may seek to insinuate in order to guard against the risk of indemnity costs in the event the allegation is not substantiated.

12.2.6.2.6   Conduct

The way the claim is conducted, particularly when allegations which cannot be substantiated are made, may justify an order for indemnity costs.

Consequently, where the paying party ran the case that sought to ridicule the successful party it was held that there was a difference between fighting a case firmly and properly and fighting a case on the basis of a wholesale attack on the integrity of the opponent without justification: *Somatra Ltd v Sinclair Roche & Temperley*.[196]

In *Clarke v Maltby*[197] the claimant sought indemnity costs on the basis of the conduct of the defence, and allegations made by the defendant. Owen J made a number of observations about the conduct of the claim by the defendant relevant to the basis of assessment.

> "... the ... counter-schedule called into question the genuineness of the symptoms described by the claimant. The clear implication was that she was deliberately exaggerating her symptoms. Furthermore that was the basis upon which the prolonged cross-examination of the claimant, and that of other witnesses was conducted. Whilst I accept that it was appropriate for the defendant to test the degree to which the claimant was under a permanent disability as a consequence of the injuries sustained in the accident, the degree to which such disability adversely affected her capacity to function as a solicitor at partner level carrying out banking related work, and in particular to explore why she had reduced her working hours to three days a week, the manner in which the case was conducted went far beyond that. The allegation of deliberate exaggeration, an allegation that the claim was fraudulent, was not pleaded as it ought to have been if it was to be pursued.
>
> Critically there was simply no support for the allegation of deliberate exaggeration in any of the medical evidence upon which the defendant relied, including evidence from a consultant psychiatrist and a neuro psychologist. On the contrary, each expert in turn specifically disavowed any suggestion of deliberate exaggeration on her part.
>
> I also take account of the fact that the allegation of deliberate exaggeration to substantiate a fraudulent claim was being made in relation to a solicitor.
>
> Furthermore the counter-schedule implied serious professional impropriety on the part of the solicitors representing the claimant. The inference was that her solicitors had influenced her to reduce her working hours in order to inflate the value of her claim. In their written opening, served on the defence in advance of the hearing, counsel for the claimant understandably expressed concern at the inference to be drawn from the terms of the counter-schedule.'

On this basis the judge concluded, so far as costs were concerned, that:

> 'In the exercise of my discretion I have taken account of all the circumstances, and have come firmly to the conclusion that the conduct of the defence as summarised above plainly takes the case out of the norm. There will therefore be an order that the defence pays the claimant's costs of the claim on an indemnity basis.'

---

[196] [2002] All ER (D) 231.
[197] [2010] EWHC 1856 (QB).

12.2.6.3 The significance of indemnity costs

Whether the court assesses costs on the standard basis or the indemnity basis, costs which have been unreasonably incurred or are unreasonable in amount will not be allowed.

Additionally, where costs are assessed on the standard basis, the court will only allow costs which are proportionate to the matters in issue and will resolve any doubt about whether costs were reasonably incurred or reasonable and proportionate in amount in favour of the paying party.

Where costs are assessed on the indemnity basis, there is no requirement that those costs be proportionate to the matters in issue and the court will resolve any doubt about whether costs were reasonably incurred or reasonable in amount in favour of the receiving party.

In practice the distinction between assessment on the standard basis and assessment on the indemnity basis can sometimes be significant, for example in a case of modest value that has been run to trial where the issue of proportionality, if costs are assessed on the standard basis, may be a particular problem for the receiving party.

Even in higher value claims, where the issue of proportionality may be much less of an issue, the resolution of doubt in favour of the receiving party, rather than the paying party, may be a significant factor.

In *Colour Quest Ltd v Total Downstream UK Plc*[198] David Steel J recorded that:

> 'It was for instance the experience of the claimants' solicitors that in respect of a claim for costs it was typical that a recovery of between 70 and 75% of the sum claimed would be made on a standard basis. It was suggested that the disparity between the costs awarded on a standard basis and those awarded on an indemnity basis might be as much as 20%.'

In *F & C Alternative Investments (Holdings) Ltd v Barthelemy*[199] Davis LJ observed that the costs sanction imposed by CPR 36.14(3), which includes indemnity costs, was 'deliberately swingeing'.

It is also important to note that costs budgets are a significant factor in determining the amount of costs, but only when the court is assessing those costs on the standard, rather than the indemnity, basis.

12.2.7 Assessment of costs

Assessment of costs by the court will be influenced by a number of factors.

Costs, or at least some elements of the costs allowable, may be fixed and hence largely exclude the court's discretion.

---

[198] [2009] EWHC 823 (Comm).
[199] [2012] EWCA Civ 843.

In other circumstances the amount of costs allowed will reflect hourly rates applied and the time allowed, taking account of whether the assessment is being made on the standard basis or the indemnity basis (because crucially, that will determine whether the test of proportionality applies).

The court, when assessing costs, must also have regard to a number of specific factors identified in CPR 44.5(3) (from April 2013, CPR 44.4(5)) as well as costs estimates given and, from April 2013, costs budgets where these have been set.

12.2.7.1   Fixed costs

There are a number of circumstances in which costs of the claim, or part of the claim, are fixed by the CPR.

Where costs are fixed that will effectively dictate what the court may allow.

12.2.7.1.1   The small claims track

Part 27 deals with the procedure for claims that have been allocated to the small claims track and limits the amount of costs which can be recovered in respect of such a claim.

Whether the costs regime of Part 27 applies to a claim will be determined by the track to which the claim is allocated rather than the amount of damages ultimately awarded, though if the claim could have been allocated to the small claims track that may be a factor in determining what costs have been reasonably incurred.[200]

12.2.7.1.2   RTA Protocol and EL/PL Protocol

Where a claim enters, and is resolved in, the RTA Protocol or the EL/PL Protocol costs are fixed in accordance with CPR 45.18 (see **1.12.4**).

12.2.7.1.3   Ex-RTA Prorocol and EL/PL Protocol case

Part 45 also sets out fixed costs for ex-RTA protocol and ex-EL/PL Protocol cases.

Fixed costs where a claim no longer continues under the RTA Protocol are set out in table 6B.

A. If parties reach a settlement prior to the claimant issuing proceedings under Part 7.			
Agreed damages	At least £1,000, but not more than £5,000	More than £5,000, but not more than £10,000	More than £10,000, but not more than £25,000

---

[200] *O'Beirne v Hudson* [2010] EWCA Civ 52; *Dockerill v Tullett* [2012] EWCA Civ 184.

Fixed costs	The greater of- (a) £550; or (b) the total of: (i) £100; and (ii) 20% of the damages	The total of- (a) £1,100, and (b) 15% of damages over £5,000.	The total of- (a) £1,9310; and (b) 10% of damages over £10,000.

B. If proceedings are issued under Part 7, but the case settles before trial

Stage at which case is settled	On or after the date of issue, but prior to the date of allocation under Part 26	On or after the date of allocation under Part 26, but prior to the date of listing	On or after the date of listing but prior to the date of trial
Fixed costs	The total of- (a) £1,160; and (b) 20% of the damages	The total of- (a) £1,880; and (b) 20% of the damages	The total of- (a) £2,655; and (b) 20% of the damages

C. If the claim is disposed of at trial

Fixed costs	The total of- (a) £2,655; and (b) 20% of the damages agreed or awarded; and (c) the relevant trial advocacy fee

D. Trial advocacy fees

Damages agreed or awarded	Not more than £3,000	More than £3,000, but not more than £10,000	More than £10,000 but not more than £15,000	More than £15,000
Trial advocacy fee	£500	£710	£1,070	£1,705

Fixed costs where a claim no long continues under the EL/PL Protocol, if an employers' liability claim, are set out in table 6C.

Table 6C

A. If Parties reach a settlement prior to the claimant issuing proceedings under Part 7

Agreed Damages	At least £1,000, but not more than £5,000	More than £5,000, but not more than £10,000	More than £10,000, but not more than £25,000
Fixed costs	The total of- (a) £950; and (b) 17.5% of the damages	The total of- (a) £1,855; and (b) 12.5% of damages over £5,000	The total of- (a) £2.500; and (b) 10% of damages over £10,000

B. If proceedings are issued under Part 7, but the case settles before trial

Stage at which case is settled	On or after the date of issue, but prior to the date of allocation under Part 26	On or after the date of allocation under Part 26, but prior to the date of listing	On or after the date of listing but prior to the date of trial
Fixed costs	The total of- (a) £2,630; and (b) 20% of the damages	The total of- (a) £3,350; and (b) 25% of the damages	The total of- (a) £4,280; and (b) 30% of the damages

C. If the claim is disposed of at trial

Fixed costs	The total of- (a) £4,280; and (b) 30% of the damages agreed or awarded; and (c) the relevant trial advocacy fee

D. Trial advocacy fees

Damages agreed or awarded	Not more than £3,000	More than £3,000, but not more than £10,000	More than £10,000 but not more than £15,000	More than £15,000
Trial advocacy fee	£500	£710	£1,070	£1,705

Fixed costs where a claim no longer continues under the EL/PL Protocol, if a public liability claim, are set out in table 6D.

Table 6D

A. If Parties reach a settlement prior to the claimant issuing proceedings under Part 7			
Agreed Damages	At least £1,000, but not more than £5,000	More than £5,000, but not more than £10,000	More than £10,000, but not more than £25,000
Fixed costs	The total of- (a) £950; and (b) 17.5% of the damages	The total of- (a) £1,855; and (b) 10.5% of damages over £5,000	The total of- (a) £2.370; and (b) 10% of damages over £10,000

B. If proceedings are issued under Part 7, but the case settles before trial			
Stage at which case is settled	On or after the date of issue, but prior to the date of allocation under Part 26	On or after the date of allocation under Part 26, but prior to the date of listing	On or after the date of listing but prior to the date of trial
Fixed costs	The total of- (a) £2,450; and (b) 17.5% of the damages	The total of- (a) £3,065; and (b) 22.5% of the damages	The total of- (a) £3,790; and (b) 27.5% of the damages

C. If the claim is disposed of at trial
Fixed costs   The total of- (a) £3,790; and (b) 27.5% of the damages agreed or awarded; and (c) the relevant trial advocacy fee

D. Trial advocacy fees				
Damages agreed or awarded	Not more than £3,000	More than £3,000, but not more than £10,000	More than £10,000 but not more than £15,000	More than £15,000
Trial advocacy fee	£500	£710	£1,070	£1,705

As these costs are fixed by Part 45, the indemnity principle should not apply (see **1.12.2.5**)

12.2.7.1.4   Fast track trial costs

Part 46 (from April 2013 section VI, Part 45) prescribes fixed costs for advocacy in fast track trials (see **4.2.3.2.2**).

Where a case has been allocated to the multi-track, a costs judge, assessing costs is not entitled just to rule that costs should be assessed on the fast track basis, including fixed costs for advocacy, although it is permissible, when assessing costs to take into account, if that be the case, that the claim should have been allocated to the fast track.[201]

12.2.7.2   Hourly rates

The Guide to the Summary Assessment of Costs gives guideline rates for hourly rates of solicitors in a large number of courts across the country. Those hourly rates, though they may be applied in other circumstances, are intended primarily for summary assessment of costs.

In appropriate cases hourly rates exceeding those guidelines may well be justified.

Issues can arise about the appropriate hourly rate when a non-local firm of solicitors deals with a claim. Where that happens the court is likely to adopt the approach in *Wraith v Sheffield Forgemasters Ltd.*[202]

12.2.7.3   Time spent

Once the hourly rate has been determined, that can be applied to such time as the court considers it is appropriate to allow, having regard to the requirement, in CPR 44.4, that costs which have been unreasonably incurred or are unreasonable in amount will not be allowed.

When considering whether any step, and hence time spent, is reasonable, the correct viewpoint is that of a sensible solicitor considering what, in the light of his then knowledge, was reasonable in the interest of the client.[203]

Hence costs for any work done which is incidental to the proceedings, in which the costs are being assessed, may be allowed. For example:

*   work done prior to the issue of court proceedings;[204] and
*   the costs of attending an inquest in a fatal claim.[205]

For these purposes the importance of file notes, not just recording the time but explaining how that time was spent, cannot be over emphasised.

---

[201] *Drew v Whitbread Plc* [2010] EWCA Civ 53.
[202] [1998] 1 WLR 132.
[203] *Francis v Francis and Dickerson* [1955] 3 All ER 836.
[204] *Re Gibson's Settlement Trusts* [1981] 1 All ER 233.
[205] *Roach v The Home Office* [2009] EWHC 312 (QB).

12.2.7.4 *Proportionality*

Even if costs have been reasonably incurred and are reasonable in amount those costs in accordance with CPR 44.4(2)(a), when assessed on the standard basis, will only be allowed if proportionate to the matters in issue.

Guidance on approaching proportionality, in the assessment of costs, was given by the Court of Appeal in *Lownds v Home Office*.[206]

In *Lownds* the court recommended a two-stage approach to the issue or proportionality. First, a global approach will indicate whether the total sum claimed for costs is, or appears to be, disproportionate. If the total sum claimed for costs is not disproportionate all that will be required, for the costs to be allowed, is that each item should have reasonably been incurred and the item itself be reasonable in amount.

If, however, the total sum claimed for costs appears, at first sight, to be disproportionate, it is necessary for the second stage of the test to be applied which will require the court to be satisfied that the work in relation to each item was necessary and, if it was, that the cost of the item was reasonable.

On this analysis proportionality involves limiting the costs of necessary items to what would have been reasonable if the litigation had been conducted in a proportionate manner.

Lownds reflected the definition of proportionality in the Costs Practice Direction, as defined in turn by the overriding objective, and recognised a number of factors:

- The relationship between the total of the costs incurred and the financial value of the claim may not be a reliable guide as to what is proportionate. In any event, proportionality has to be approached on the basis of the sum the claimant believed it was reasonable he might recover at the time the claim was made.

- In any proceedings there will be costs which will inevitably be incurred and which are necessary for the successful conduct of the case.

- Solicitors are not required to conduct litigation at rates which are uneconomic and so in a modest claim the proportion of costs is likely to be higher than in a large claim and may even equal or possibly exceed the amount in dispute. Otherwise, access to justice would be impeded.

The approach in *Lownds* was adopted and approved in *Motto v Trafigura Ltd*.[207]

Changes to the CPR in April 2013 introduce a new test on proportionality. CPR 44.3(2)(a) confirms the court will only allow costs which are proportionate to the matters in issue but goes on to provide expressly that costs which are disproportionate in amount may be disallowed or reduced even if they were reasonably or necessarily incurred. Furthermore, again from April 2013, CPR 44.3(5) provides the costs are proportionate if they bear a reasonable relationship to:

- the sums in issue in the proceedings;

- the value of any non-monetary relief in issuing the proceedings;

---

[206] [2002] EWCA Civ 365.
[207] [2011] EWCA Civ 1150.

- the complexity of the litigation;
- any additional work generated by the conduct of the paying party; and
- any wider factors involved in the proceedings, such as reputation or public importance.

No further guidance is given to the courts on how to approach this test and that is, therefore, likely to be determined by further case-law. It may be the courts will adopt the approach set out by Lord Justice Jackson in his Final Report when he wrote:

> 'I propose that in an assessment of costs on the standard basis, proportionality should prevail over reasonableness and the proportionality test should be applied on a global basis. The court should first make an assessment of reasonable costs, having regard to the individual items in the bill, the time reasonably spent on those items and the other factors listed I CPR rule 44.5(3). The court should then stand back and consider whether the total figure is proportionate. If the total figure is not proportionate, the court should make an appropriate reduction. There is already a precedent for this approach in relation to the assessment of legal aid costs in criminal proceedings: see *R v Supreme Court Taxing Office ex p John Singh and Co* [1997] 1 Costs LR 49.'

The Civil Procedure (Amendment No 2) Rules 2013 confirm that the new CPR 44.3(7) will not apply to any work carried out on claims where court proceedings have been issued prior to 1 April 2013 nor to work carried out prior to 1 April 2013 in cases where court proceedings are issued after that date. Rather, the work not covered by the new rule, the terms of CPR 44.4(2)(a), as it was in force prior to 1 April 2013, will remain applicable.

12.2.7.5   *Relevant factors in deciding the amount of costs*

When the court is deciding the amount of costs to be allowed under the terms of an order for costs the court, as well as working within the framework set out in CPR 44.4 for assessment, must have regard to factors identified specifically in CPR 44.4(3) which are:

- the conduct of the parties, including conduct before as well as during proceeding (see above);
- efforts made before and during proceedings to try and resolve the dispute;
- the amount or value of any money or property involved;
- the importance of the matter to all the parties;
- the particular complexity of the matter or the difficulty or novelty of the questions raised;
- the skill, effort, specialised knowledge and responsibility involved;
- the time spent on the case;
- the place where and the circumstances in which work or any part of it was done; and
- (from April 2013) the receiving party's last approved or agreed budget.

Although these factors do, to some extent, duplicate the matters the court should take into account when deciding whether to make a costs order under CPR 44.3(6) (from April 2013, CPR 44.2(6)) the court, provided this does not involve what might be termed 'double jeopardy', can take account of matters which might have, but did not, influence the costs order made when determining the amount of costs payable.[208]

The court cannot, however, when deciding the amount of costs effectively override an order, such as an order allocating the case to a particular track, but may, when deciding the extent to which costs have been incurred reasonably, allow for this factor.[209]

12.2.7.6 Costs estimates/budgets

The former Section 6 of the Costs Practice Direction dealt with estimates of costs which may also have a bearing on the amount of costs allowed on assessment. This remains relevant for cases not subject to costs budgeting.

An estimate of costs, for the purposes of the Costs Practice Direction, means an estimate of base costs including disbursements, but excluding additional liability and VAT. In *Leigh v Michelin Tyre Plc*[210] the court stressed that costs estimates are required to include estimates of the overall costs to be incurred on the assumption that the case will not settle (and not merely estimates of future costs up to some date on which it is thought the case is likely to, or might, settle).

In *Leigh* the Court of Appeal gave guidance on how costs estimates should be used when assessing costs. Where there is no substantial difference between the amount of the costs estimates and the costs claimed on assessment, the Costs Practice Direction would not need to be applied. If, however, there was a substantial difference, on the basis that the estimate should provide a yardstick by which the reasonableness of the costs finally claimed may be measured, costs may be restricted unless the receiving party could give a satisfactory explanation and, even then, difficulties might be faced if the paying party had relied on the estimate or that had influenced case management directions given by the court.

Subsequently, paragraph 6.5A of the Costs Practice Direction has expressly provided that if there is a difference of 20 per cent or more between the base costs claimed by a receiving party on detailed assessment and the costs shown in an estimate of costs filed by that party, the receiving party must provide a statement of the reasons for the difference. If the court then concluded that the receiving party had not provided a satisfactory explanation for the difference, and the paying party reasonably relied on the estimate, the court may regard the difference as evidence that the costs claimed are unreasonable or disproportionate.

Consequently, care and precision are necessary in the preparation of costs estimates.

Whilst paragraph 6.1(1) of the Costs Practice Direction recognises costs estimates given by different parties may be compared, when assessing reasonableness and proportionality, the Court of Appeal observed in *Leigh* that 'it is common ground that ordinarily a claimant's legal representative shoulders a greater burden than his counterpart', effectively acknowledging the claimant's costs are likely to be higher than the defendant's.

---

[208] *Northstar Systems Ltd v Fielding* [2006] EWCA Civ 1660; *O'Beirne v Hudson* [2010] EWCA Civ 52; *Letts v Royal Sun Alliance Plc* [2012] EWHC 875 (QB).
[209] *O'Beirne v Hudson* [2010] EWCA Civ 52; *Drew v Whitbread Plc* [2010] EWCA Civ 53.
[210] [2003] EWCA Civ 1766.

From April 2013 the court, when deciding the amount of costs, will have regard to any costs budget. Costs management, which deals with budgets, is introduced by a new section II in Part 3. The court may depart from a budget, when assessing costs, but will need good reason to do so. What might amount to 'good reason', in the context of the pilot Defamation Proceedings Costs Management Scheme was considered in *Henry v News Group Newspapers Ltd*.[211] Whilst emphasising the importance of the approved or agreed budget, in the future, as providing a prima facie limit on the amount of recoverable costs, the Court of Appeal recognised that, when deciding whether there was good reason to depart from a budget, it was still necessary to look at all the circumstances of the case.

Costs budgeting should not be about simply costs capping because it is inextricably linked with case, and from April 2013 costs, management by the court.

12.2.7.7   The indemnity principle

Assessment of costs is subject to the indemnity principle.

This principle is that the order for party and party costs may not be more than an indemnity, that is the amount which the receiving party has to pay his or her own solicitor.[212]

A valid conditional fee agreement is a specific exception to the indemnity principle, but unless valid such an agreement will inevitably infringe the indemnity principle, meaning that costs incurred cannot be recovered. Hence it is this principle which has underpinned technical challenges launched against conditional fee agreements.

Consequently, it is essential any conditional fee agreement complies with the statutory provision, allowing such agreements, found in section 58 of the Courts and Legal Services Act 1990 (as amended by the Legal Aid Sentencing and Punishment of Offenders Act 2012 and reflected by the Conditional Fee Agreements Order 2013.[213]

12.2.8   Base costs and additional liabilities

If the claim has been funded on the basis of a conditional fee agreement, which provides for a success fee, made between 1 April 2000 and 31 March 2013, additional liabilities may be recovered as part of the costs of the claim.

12.2.8.1   Definitions

The CPR and the Costs Practice Direction contain some important definitions:
* 'Base costs' is defined by para 2.2 of the Costs Practice Direction as costs other than the amount of any additional liability.
* 'Additional liability' is defined by CPR 43.2(1)(o) as, amongst other matters, the percentage increase on base costs.

---

[211] [2013] EWCA Civ 19.
[212] *Gundry v Sainsbury* (1910) 1 KB 654.
[213] SI 2013/689.

- 'Percentage increase' is defined by CPR 43.2(1)(l) as the percentage by which the amount of the fee can be increased in accordance with a conditional fee agreement which provides for a success fee.
- 'Insurance premium' is defined by CPR 43.2(1)(m) as a sum of money paid or payable for insurance against the risk of incurring a costs liability.

12.2.8.2   Information about the funding arrangement

Appropriate, and timely, information about all relevant funding arrangements must be given if the party receiving costs is to recover additional liabilities (see **5.2.4.1**).

In default, however, the court may give, if that is appropriate, relief from sanctions (see **9.1.5**).

12.2.8.3   Percentage increase

The percentage increase allowed on base costs is fixed for certain types of claim, but otherwise will need to be assessed by the court, taking account of the particular circumstances of each individual case.

12.2.8.3.1   Costs Practice Direction

Section 11 of the Costs Practice Direction deals with the approach the court should adopt in considering whether a percentage increase is reasonable:

- Section 11.7 provides that '... when the Court is considering the factors to be taken into account in assessing an additional liability, it will have regard to the facts and circumstances as they reasonably appear to the Solicitor or Counsel when the funding arrangement was entered into ...'.
- Section 11.8 identifies relevant factors in deciding whether a percentage increase is reasonable as including:
  - The risk that the circumstances in which the costs will be payable might or might not occur.
  - The legal representatives' liability for any disbursements.
  - What other methods of financing the costs are available to the receiving party.

  A percentage increase will not, however, be reduced simply on the ground that, when added to base costs which are reasonable (and where relevant proportionate) the total appears disproportionate.

12.2.8.3.2   Case-law

In *Callery v Gray*[214] the Court of Appeal held that in a moderate and straightforward road traffic accident case, which settled pre-issue, a success fee of 20 per cent was reasonable.

In *Callery* the Court of Appeal accepted solicitors could operate in a similar fashion to insurers (the success fee equating to an insurer's premium): underwriters setting

---

[214]   [2001] EWCA Civ 1246.

premiums by using their knowledge of the market to calculate a 'burning cost', namely the predicted frequency of loss multiplied by the predicted quantum of loss.

Some assistance, in assessing the risk, or 'burning costs', by reference to particular types of case, can be drawn from the Compensation Recovery Unit. So, for example, CRU statistics reveal that, for 2002/3, the percentage of successful claims were are follows:

- Motor: 87 per cent.
- Employers' liability: 77 per cent.
- Public liability: 60 per cent.
- Clinical negligence: 46 per cent.

The approach in *Callery* recognised that it would not be correct to view a straightforward case as being appropriate for a 0 per cent percentage increase, a middle-risk case as having an appropriate percentage increase of 50 per cent and a high-risk case at 100 per cent. That is because the actuarial formula for calculating risk can be expressed as follows:

Prospect of failure x 100
Prospect of success

Hence, in *Designer Guild Ltd v Russell Williams (Textiles) Ltd*[215] Master Hurst observed 'it is generally accepted that if the chances of success are no better than 50% the success fee should be 100%'.

In *Sarwar v Alam*[216] a percentage increase of 100 per cent was allowed (in relation to the costs issues which went to the Court of Appeal) and the views of Master Hurst in *Designer Guild* were expressly approved.

A number of cases have since considered the appropriate percentage increase that should be allowed across a wide range of personal injury claims, many involving issues rather more complex than *Callery*.

Cheshire County Council v Lea[217] was a tripping case with a success fee in the conditional fee agreement at 100 per cent. The defendant appealed a decision allowing a success fee of 50 per cent:

- At the date the conditional fee agreement was entered into there was held to be no more than a 50 per cent chance of success, giving an uplift of 100 per cent applying the 'no hindsight' principle.
- If that was correct it was irrelevant the case was straightforward, as a case with a 50 per cent change of success remains so regardless of complexity.
- Whilst the uplift of 50 per cent given by the district judge was thought to be on the high side it was within the generous ambit within which reasonable disagreement was possible.

---

[215] [2000] 1 WLR 2416.
[216] LTL 23/3/2003.
[217] LTL 8/7/2003.

Smiths Dock Ltd v Edwards[218] was a mesothelioma case with a success fee fixed in the conditional fee agreement at 87 per cent:

- This was held to be a very different case to *Callery*.

- As at the date of the conditional fee agreement it was possible to be very optimistic some liability would be established, but that was not certain and the risk not negligible.

- 87 per cent was, in the circumstances, reasonable.

Atack v Lee[219] was an accident involving a collision between motor vehicles on a roundabout:

- Liability was denied, proceedings were issued and the case allocated to the multi-track. Liability was tried as a preliminary issue and determined in favour of the claimant, following which the claim was resolved promptly.

- The denial of liability was held to be a regular feature of such cases, which did not prevent many reaching settlement after issue.

- Furthermore, the conditional fee agreement did not put the claimant's solicitors at risk of not being paid if a Part 36 payment was not beaten.

- The risk assessment conducted by the claimant's solicitors was held not to reveal his reasonable thought processes, so the costs judge had to consider the matter afresh from the standpoint of a reasonably careful solicitor assessing the risk. On this basis the judge allowed 50 per cent for the success fee.

- Although the Court of Appeal considered some costs judges might have allowed a success fee of up to 67 per cent, the uplift of 50 per cent fixed by the costs judge was held to be within the range reasonably available to him.

In *Ellerton v Harris*[220] the claimant was knocked down, in a supermarket car park, as the defendant was reversing his motorcar:

- Liability was promptly admitted, though proceedings were subsequently issued.

- Whilst the defendant had left the scene immediately after the accident the court considered that he had been easily traceable.

- Though the conditional fee agreement was modified, to protect the claimant in the event of a Part 36 payment, that was held to be just one of the rare risks which justified a success fee as high as 20 per cent in such a simple claim.

In *Callery* the Court of Appeal also highlighted the opportunity of agreeing a staged success fee and the prospect this would carry of justifying a higher success fee if the case progressed to a later stage. Lord Woolf observed:

> 'A two-stage success fee would have the advantage that the uplift would more nearly reflect the risks of the individual case, so that where a claimant's solicitor had to pursue legal proceedings, this would be in the knowledge that, although a significant risk of failure existed, the reward of success would be that much the greater. Where, on the other hand, the claim settled as a consequence of an offer by the defendant, he or his insurer would have the satisfaction of knowing that he had ensured that the success fee would be reduced to a modest proportion of the costs.

---

[218] [2004] EWHC 1116 (QB).
[219] [2004] EWCA Civ 1712.
[220] [2004] EWCA Civ 1712.

> We have considered the risk that a two-stage success fee would encourage claimant's solicitors to take claims past the protocol stage in order to benefit from the higher uplift. Such conduct would, however, be prevented by a defendant who was prepared to settle by making a formal settlement offer, putting the claimant at risk as to costs.'

Moreover, the Court of Appeal in *Callery* confirmed it was entirely appropriate for a conditional fee agreement to be entered, and an ATE insurance policy arranged, at the outset (uncertainty about risks being reflected, as appropriate, in a staged success fee) Lord Woolf observing:

> 'In these circumstances, we consider that, from the viewpoint of both the claimant and his solicitor, it will normally be reasonable for a CFA to be concluded and ATE cover taken out on the occasion that the claimant first instructs his solicitors.'

In both *Atack* and *Ellerton* the Court of Appeal held it was not permissible to adopt fixed rates for success fees when assessing the reasonableness of a success fee. The court also endorsed the two stage success fee approach recommended in *Callery* which would allow a success fee of up to 100 per cent if the claim did not settle within the protocol period. To some extent these comments may be contrasted with the observations that, for the purposes of risk, it was a 'regular feature' for liability to be disputed throughout the protocol period and even after issue of proceedings.

KU v Liverpool City Council[221] confirmed that the court did not have power under the Costs Practice Direction to direct that a fixed success fee in a conditional fee agreement was recoverable at different rates for different periods of the proceedings, including a detailed assessment of costs. That is not the same, of course, as the claimant providing, in the conditional fee agreement, for a staged success fee.

Despite the encouragement to use staged success fees there are occasions when a single success fee of 100 per cent will be appropriate bearing in mind the need for the underlying risk assessment to be viewed not with hindsight but on the basis of the information available at the time it was made. Hence, for example, a single success fee of 100 per cent was allowed in a potentially complex clinical negligence claim: *Oliver v Whipps Cross University Hospital NHS Trust*.[222]

Generally, however, the courts have been reluctant, even in complex claims such as clinical negligence, to allow a very high single staged success fee but have been more ready to accept a high success fee when that is staged and the event triggering the relevant stage occurs. Consequently, a single success fee of 100 per cent was reduced, on assessment, to 67 per cent in *Barham v Barking, Havering and Redbridge NHS Trust*.[223]

Conversely, if the success fee is staged the court is less likely to reduce the success fee for subsequent stages when such stages are reached and more likely to accept the percentage increase provided for as occurred, for example, in *Peacock v MGN Ltd*.[224]

---

[221] [2005] EWCA Civ 475.
[222] [2009] EWHC 1104 (QB).
[223] (Unreported) Central London County Court, 15 June 2007.
[224] [2010] EWHC 90174 (Costs).

Even where, however, the success fee is staged, the court will not necessarily allow the success fee sought for the latter stages if the reality was that there was no real risk of losing the case: *Fortune v Roe*.[225]

That is because whilst hindsight should not be applied there are cases in which the prospect of a 'win' is very good from the outset, for example where the only issue is contributory negligence. This will be very relevant to what is an appropriate success fee even where the conditional fee agreement is modified so that the solicitors bear Part 36 risks: *C v W*.[226]

12.2.8.3.3   CPR fixed success fees

If the claim arises out of a road traffic accident on or after 5 October 2003 and has been funded by a conditional fee agreement providing for a success fee, then that success fee is fixed by s III of Part 45 of the CPR:

- For solicitors at 12.5 per cent except where a trial takes place when the success fee will be 100 per cent.
- For counsel at 12.5 per cent except:
  - where the case concludes at trial when the success fee will be 100 per cent; or
  - a multi-track case concluding within 21 days before trial when the success fee will be 75 per cent; or
  - a fast track case concluding within 14 days before trial when the success fee will be 50 per cent.

If the claim arises out of a employers' liability accident on or after 1 October 2004 and has been funded by a conditional fee agreement providing for a success fee, then that success fee is also fixed by s III of Part 45:

- For solicitors at 25 per cent except where a trial takes place when the success fee will be 100 per cent; or
- For counsel at 25 per cent except:
  - where the case concludes at trial when the success fee will be 100 per cent; or
  - a multi-track case concluding within 21 days before trial when the success fee will be 75 per cent; or
  - a fast track case concluding within 14 days before trial when the success fee will be 50 per cent.

CPR 45.18 provides that a party may apply for a different percentage increase if the parties have agreed damages of an amount greater than £500,000 or the court awards damages of an amount greater than that sum. For these purposes any finding, or likely finding, of contributory negligence will be disregarded and the provision will also apply if damages include periodical payments of equivalent value.

A case will be concluded at trial if the hearing commences, even though the claim then settles, but not if a settlement is concluded before the hearing has begun: *Amin v Mullings*.[227]

---

[225] [2011] EWHC 2953 (QB).
[226] [2008] EWCA Civ 1459.
[227] [2011] EWHC 278 (QB).

Similarly, where the court conducted a summary assessment after settlement of the claim, so that a hearing of the substantive issues never even commenced, that was not a trial resulting in a 100 per cent success fee: *Thenga v Quinn*.[228]

Consequently, even if the hearing only consists of an application to adjourn, that will amount to a final contested hearing for the purposes of the fixed success fee: *Loizou v Gordon*.[229]

The fixed success fee applicable when there has been a trial will apply even if the claimant fails to beat a Part 36 offer made by the defendant: *Lamont v Burton*.[230]

Fixed success fees do not apply where the damages exceed £500,000. In these circumstances the court will need to assess the success fee without applying hindsight or the fixed amount which would otherwise have applied. Value, of itself, does not necessarily generate risk: *C v W*.[231] However, if the case had potential complexities, which might have meant the claim being unsuccessful, those factors must be viewed as known to those conducting the risk assessment at the time it was made: *Halford v Bakkavour Foods Ltd*.[232]

12.2.8.4 Insurance premium

When deciding whether an insurance premium is reasonable, and hence recoverable, the court must, to a large extent, respect actuarial assessments made when fixing the premium: *Kris Motor Spares Ltd v Fox Williams LLP*.[233]

12.2.8.5 Proportionality

The Costs Practice Direction confirms that, for the purposes of deciding whether costs are proportionate, additional liabilities will be left out of account.

VAT should also be excluded, for the purposes of considering proportionality, as it is a tax the impact of which has no bearing on the steps taken in the litigation or the cost of those steps: *Giambrone v JMC Holidays Ltd*.[234]

12.2.8.6 Disclosure

If the claimant seeks to recover additional liabilities, relevant details will need to be disclosed at the stage costs are assessed, whether this be summary assessment or detailed assessment.

The information required is identified by section 32 of the Costs Practice Direction.

---

[228] [2009] EWCA Civ 151.
[229] SCCO, 22 August 2012.
[230] [2007] EWCA Civ 429.
[231] [2008] EWCA Civ 1459.
[232] (Unreported) Doncaster County Court, 2 September 2011.
[233] [2010] EWHC 1008 (QB).
[234] [2002] EWHC 2932 (QB).

If there may be a summary assessment, the receiving party may wish to prepare a separate bundle, relating to additional liabilities, as it will generally be inappropriate to disclose that information until the substantive issues have been resolved.

The documentation which will need to be disclosed at the appropriate stage to assist the court in assessing additional liabilities is likely to include:

- the conditional fee agreement or a summary of the key information required for the purposes of section 32 of the Costs Practice Direction;

- risk assessment; and

- policy schedule or other information confirming the amount of the ATE premium.

12.2.8.7 Transitional provisions

From April 2013, CPR 48.1 confirms the terms of Parts 43 to 48, and related provisions of the Costs Practice Direction, will continue to apply in relation to a conditional fee agreement made before 1 April 2013, in the terms those provisions were in force immediately before that date.

Such an agreement is included in the definition of a 'pre-commencement funding arrangement' found in the new CPR 48.2 which also defines a 'pre-commencement funding arrangement' as including funding arrangements made in relation to insolvency-related proceedings, publication and privacy proceedings or mesothelioma claims. Consequently, for such claims, the ability to recover additional liabilities will remain even for conditional fee agreements made on or after 1 April 2013.

Otherwise, the success fee will not be recoverable as part of the costs of the claim where the conditional fee agreement is entered into from 1 April 2013.

Similarly, the insurance premium will remain recoverable where there is a 'pre-commencement funding arrangement', as defined by the new CPR 48.2 introduced in April 2013, and also, to a limited extent, under the Recovery of Costs Insurance Premiums in Clinical Negligence Proceedings Regulations 2013, but otherwise no longer form part of the recoverable costs.

12.2.9 Interest on costs

Pre-CPR section 17 of the Judgments Act 1838 provided for every judgment to carry interest from the time of entering up the judgment until that judgment was satisfied while section 18 provided that all court orders whereby any sum of money or any cost should be payable by any person, would have the effect of judgments.

In *Hunt v AM Douglas (Roofing) Ltd*[235] the House of Lords confirmed the effect of these two sections was that interest on costs ran from the date the order for costs was made not the date on which the costs were subsequently assessed or agreed.

---

[235] [1990] 1 AC 398.

However, in *Thomas v Bunn*[236] the House of Lords confirmed that where there was a split trial, interest on costs ran from the date of judgment or agreement on quantum but otherwise endorsed *Hunt*.

Concurrent with the introduction of the CPR, s 17 of the Judgments Act 1838 was amended to provide for interest at 8 per cent and for rules of the court to provide that all or part of interest might be disallowed. Within the CPR, rule 40.8 gave the court power to order that interest should run from a date different to that when judgment was given.

The approach to interest on costs under the CPR was reviewed by the Court of Appeal in *Simcoe v Jacuzzi UK Group Plc*.[237]

The first issue for the court was, under the CPR, whether interest on costs ran from the date of the order for costs as agreed or assessed (the 'incipitur' date) or from the date the sum was agreed between the parties or assessed by the court (the 'allocatur' date).

The Court of Appeal held that the normal rule was for interest to run on costs from the 'incipitur' date.

On the next issue for determination the Court of Appeal confirmed that general rule applied when the case was funded by a conditional fee agreement, as the purpose of the uplift was to provide compensation for the risk of recovering nothing in costs if the claim did not succeed rather than compensation for any delay in receiving money under the costs order.

Consequently, interest on costs, whatever the funding arrangement, will be payable, under the Judgments Act, calculated from the 'incipitur' date to the date such costs are paid.

12.2.10   Methods of assessing costs

CPR 44.7 (from April 2013, CPR 44.6) provides that the court, when it orders a party to pay costs to another party, may order assessment to take place by way of summary assessment or detailed assessment.

12.2.10.1   Summary assessment

Section 13 of the Costs Practice Direction confirms that the court should always consider whether to make a summary assessment of costs and should make a summary assessment:

- at the conclusion of the trial of a case which has been dealt with the on the fast track; or
- at the conclusion of any other hearing which has lasted not more than one day.

Summary assessment will be dealt with by the judge who has dealt with the hearing immediately prior to that assessment.

---

[236] [1991] 1 AC 362.
[237] [2012] EWCA Civ 137.

If there has been no hearing it may not be appropriate to conduct a summary assessment: *Mahmood v Penrose*;[238] *Thenga v Quinn*.[239]

Where costs may be assessed summarily, any party who wishes to seek an order that the costs be paid by another party should prepare a statement of costs in form N260 so that such an assessment can, if appropriate, be made. Where it would be useful to put the basic information on the statement of costs in context, it may be helpful to provide some additional narrative dealing, in particular, with the factors relevant to the amount of costs found in CPR 44.4(3) (see **12.2.7.5**).

Even summary assessment must involve an assessment not just the application of what might be termed a 'tariff'. In *1-800 Flowers Inc v Phonenames Ltd*[240] the judge, conducting the summary assessment, assessed the figure by reference to the sort of figures the judge had seen in other cases of the same kind rather than the detail of the work done in the particular case. Allowing an appeal the Court of Appeal concluded the judge had 'erred in principle when he in effect applied his own tariff to the case, without carrying out any detailed examination or analysis of the costs actually incurred by the opponent as set out in its statement of costs'.

Jonathan Parker LJ held that:

'In my judgment the jurisdiction to assess costs summarily is not to be used as a vehicle for the introduction of a scale of judicial tariffs for different categories of case. However general the approach which the court chooses to adopt when assessing costs summarily, and however broad the brush which the court chooses to use, the assessment must in my judgment be directed to and focused upon the detailed breakdown of costs contained in the receiving party's statement of costs.'

Moreover, the court, when making a summary assessment, should adopt the same approach to determining the amount of costs, including approaching proportionality on the basis of *Lownds*, as it would when conducting a detailed assessment: *Morgan v Spirit Group Ltd*.[241]

In *Drake v Fripp*[242] Lord Neuberger observed that:

'On a detailed assessment, the costs judge should first look at the overall base figure and consider whether it seems proportionate. If it does, then the costs judge will allow a reasonable sum for each item on the receiving party's bill which it was reasonable to incur. If the base figure does not seem reasonable, then the costs judge will allow a reasonable sum for each item on the bill only if satisfied that the item was necessarily incurred. That this is the correct approach is clear from *Home Office v Lownds (Practice Note)* [2002] EWCA Civ 365, [2002] 1 WLR 2450 para 31 as approved and applied in *Motto v Trafigura Ltd* [2011] EWCA Civ 1150, paras 43-50.

I can see no good reason why a similar approach should not be adopted when the court is carrying out a summary assessment. Indeed, it would be rather bizarre if different principles applied in relation to the two methods of assessment.'

---

238 [2002] EWCA Civ 457.
239 [2009] EWCA Civ 151.
240 [2001] EWCA Civ 721.
241 [2011] EWCA Civ 68.
242 [2011] EWCA Civ 1282.

12.2.10.2   Detailed assessment

Where there is to be a detailed assessment, CPR 47.1 provides that the general rule is that the assessment will not take place until the conclusion of the proceedings, although the court may order otherwise, though once an order for detailed assessment has been made the court can order a payment on account of costs yet to be assessed (see **12.2.11.1**).

Detailed assessment will involve a separate hearing, which is likely to be dealt with by a different judge, from the hearing of the substantive issues when the order for costs, now being assessed, was made.

A detailed assessment will be appropriate when a hearing falls outside the scope of Section 9 of the Costs Practice Direction or there is good reason for there not to be a summary assessment. That might, for example, be:

- where there are substantial grounds for disputing the sum claimed which cannot be dealt with summarily; or
- there is insufficient time to carry out the summary assessment; or
- where the receiving party is an assisted person; or
- where the receiving party is a child or protected party.

Detailed assessment will require the preparation of a detailed bill of costs on the part of the receiving party to which the paying party is likely to respond by points of dispute which, in turn, may require replies.

If the parties remain unable to agree the amount of costs, assessment will take place, the court determining the amount of costs allowable by reference, in particular, to the factors in CPR 44.4(3) (see **12.2.7.5**).

Because there is some overlap between the factors relevant to the amount of costs, in CPR 44.4(3), and the circumstances which are relevant to the exercise of discretion as to whether the costs order should be made in the first place, found in CPR 44.3 (from April 2013, CPR 44.2), the court may take into account, when assessing costs, issues such as conduct even if these were not reflected in the costs order made, equally the court must be careful not to penalise the receiving party twice if relevant matters were reflected in the original costs order (see **12.2.5**).

A judge assessing costs may take into account factors identified in CPR 44.5, such as conduct, even though there has been a trial and no issues such as conduct have affected the exercise of the court's discretion when deciding what order to make as to costs in accordance with CPR 44.3: *Northstar Systems Ltd v Fielding*.[243]

Where detailed assessment proceedings are commenced after 1 April 2013, the court will undertake a provisional assessment (in accordance with CPR 47.15 introduced into the CPR from that date).

---

[243]   [2006] EWCA Civ 1660.

12.2.10.3   Costs only proceedings

If the claim settles before proceedings have been issued, but costs cannot be agreed, it may be necessary to take costs only proceedings to resolve the issue.

CPR 44.12A (from April 2013, CPR 46.14) sets out a procedure which may be followed when the parties to a dispute have reached an agreement on all issues, including which party is to pay the costs, made or confirmed in writing but where they have failed to agree the amount of those costs and no proceedings have been started.

The procedure is set out in section 17 of the Costs Practice Direction.

12.2.11   Payments on account of costs and interim costs certificates

The CPR facilitate obtaining at least part payment of costs prior to any detailed assessment by the rules providing for payments on account of costs and for interim costs certificates.

Effective use of these provisions can improve cash flow as well as helping to narrow the issues on costs and reduce the likelihood of a detailed assessment being necessary.

12.2.11.1   Payments on account of costs

CPR 44.3(8) (from April 2013, CPR 44.2(8)) provides that the court, when a party has been ordered to pay costs, may order an amount to be paid on account before the costs are assessed.

This is a useful provision and should always be utilised when the court, following trial, directs costs be dealt with by detailed assessment. This rule can also be used to ensure that, if terms of settlement are reached, those terms include provision for a payment on account of costs.

The court should generally exercise the power to make such an order. In *Mars UK Ltd v Teknowledge Ltd (No 2)*,[244] the payment on account was set at two-thirds of the costs which, on a rough estimate, the receiving party would be awarded.

Where there is a hearing at which one party is ordered to pay the costs of another, to be the subject of a detailed assessment, a payment on account of those costs should always be sought there and then. It is preferable for the order to be made by the judge who has dealt with the hearing, rather than another judge on subsequent application, as the latter judge may not have sufficient knowledge of the case to make an assessment of the appropriate level of any payment on account: *Dyson Appliances Ltd v Hoover Ltd.*[245]

Where there is a deemed costs order on acceptance of a Part 36 offer within the relevant period, that will suffice to generate the entitlement to a payment on account of costs: *Barnsley v Noble*[246] (see **12.2.1.1**).

---

[244] [1999] 2 Costs LR 44.
[245] [2003] EWHC 624 (Ch).
[246] (Unreported) 7 March 2012 (ChD).

Where terms of settlement are reached, which include provision for payment of costs which will be the subject of a detailed assessment, efforts should be made to include, within the agreement, provision for a payment on account of those costs.

If there is an order for detailed assessment of costs, when there has not been a hearing, if a payment on account of those cannot be agreed an application, for an appropriate order, would seem necessary.

The court may need some details of the costs of the receiving party in order to fix the appropriate level of any payment on account. Similarly, if the parties are to agree a payment on account of costs there will need to be some information made available, by the receiving party, about the costs incurred. For these purposes costs estimates exchanged during the proceedings may suffice.

From April 2013 CPR 44.2(8) provides that where the court orders a party to pay costs subject to detailed assessment it will order that party to pay a reasonable sum on account of costs, unless there is good reason not to do so. Consequently, payments on account of costs, in such circumstances, should become the norm.

12.2.11.2   *Interim costs certificates*

CPR 47.15 (from April 2013, CPR 47.16) provides that the court may, at any time after the receiving party has filed a request for a detailed assessment hearing, issue an interim costs certificate for such sum as it considers appropriate. This power, therefore, can only be exercised when a request for a detailed assessment hearing has been made.

The court then has a complete discretion as to the amount considered appropriate for an interim costs certificate.

Encouragement to issue a interim costs certificate has been given on the basis this is likely to narrow the issues and so reduce the likelihood of a fully contested detailed assessment hearing: *Dyson Appliances Ltd v Hoover Ltd.*[247]

12.2.11.3   From April 2013, CPR 47.20 deals with the costs of detailed assessment proceedings. CPR 47.20(4) expressly provides that the terms of Part 36 will apply to the costs of detailed assessment proceedings, so parties are likely to make Part 36 offers and should secure the benefits provided for in CPR 36.14, though in relation to costs assessed, in the event of an outcome which is 'more advantageous' or 'at least as advantageous' as the relevant offer.

12.2.12   Time for complying with an order for costs

CPR 44.8 (from April 2013, CPR 44.7) provides that a party must comply with an order for the payment of costs within 14 days of:

- the date of the judgment or order if it states the amount of those costs;
- but if the amount of those costs, or part of them, is decided later by way of detailed assessment then the date of the certificate which states the amount; or
- in either case such later date as the court may specify.

---

[247] [2003] EWHC 624 (Ch).

12.3 RECOVERY OF DAMAGES AND COSTS

When damages are payable, on the successful conclusion of a personal injury claim, payment should be made by the date specified in the court order or agreed between the parties.

Similarly, costs are payable by the agreed date or the date set out in the relevant court order, though if no date for payment of costs is given the terms of CPR 44.8 (from April 2013, CPR 44.7) generally require payment to be made within 14 days of the costs being assessed.

If either damages or costs are not paid by the due date, steps will need to be taken to enforce the agreement reached or any order made.

12.3.1 Availability of enforcement

To take enforcement proceedings there must be a judgment.

That is why it is generally advantageous for the claimant to have the benefit of a judgment, even when terms are agreed, rather than a 'Tomlin' order.

Where the parties have agreed to a stay of the claim, by using a 'Tomlin' order, it will be necessary, if the terms are not complied with, to apply back for the stay to be lifted and appropriate further steps then taken.

Where the claim has been concluded on acceptance of a Part 36 offer there may be no judgment.

Given the terms of CPR 36.11(6), payment of the sum due on acceptance must be made within 14 days of acceptance. Furthermore, under CPR 36.11(7) if that sum is not paid the claimant may enter judgment for the unpaid sum. If the Part 36 offer accepted is not for a single sum of money then, under CPR 36.11(8) a party who alleges the other party has not honoured the terms of the offer may apply to enforce the terms without the need for a new claim.

Where CPR 36.11(7) applies it would appear no application is required and, consequently, it should suffice for a letter to be sent to the court inviting entry of judgment which should, for the sake of completeness, also recite the appropriate terms as to costs consequent on the acceptance. If court proceedings have already been issued, and Practice Direction 36A complied with, the court will already have documentation confirming the terms agreed, but if not, copies of the documents confirming offer and acceptance will need to be filed with the request for judgment.

If settlement is reached before court proceedings have been commenced, without acceptance of a Part 36 offer, the claimant may issue proceedings for breach of contract though may prefer, particularly if the value of the claim does not exceed £5,000 in order to avoid arguments about allocation of the claim, to issue the personal injury claim, that would have been issued had terms not been reached. That claim will need to plead the agreement reached and seek a declaration that a binding compromise in those terms has been concluded.

Once, by whatever means, a judgment, for a specified sum of money and/or costs has been entered, that may be enforced.

12.3.2   Means of enforcement

There are a variety of means by which a judgment can be enforced including:

- warrant of execution;
- third party debt order;
- charging order and order for sale;
- attachment of earnings;
- appointment of receiver;
- sequestration;
- bankruptcy; and
- company liquidation.

An assessment about the most appropriate method of enforcement will be necessary, taking account of a variety of factors, but principally which method is likely to secure payment soonest.

12.3.3   Parties to enforcement

If damages for personal injury are not paid the practical problem, when it comes to enforcement, is that the nominal defendant may not be able to meet that judgment and that, where there is an insurer, it is the insurer against whom the claimant will wish to enforce the judgment.

In this situation the claimant may wish to rely on the terms of the Third Parties (Rights Against Insurers) Act 1930.

The 1930 Act was due to be replaced but, regrettably, implementation has been delayed leaving the claimant, where reliance on the 1930 Act is necessary, with the somewhat complex preliminaries of taking appropriate steps against the nominal defendant before moving on to enforce against the insurer.

If there is an issue about indemnity it may be appropriate to join the insurer into the proceedings at the outset and, of course, where the claim arises out of a road traffic accident the European Communities (Rights Against Insurers) Regulations 2002 allow the claim to be pursued directly against the insurer in any event which, in turn, will allow a judgment to be entered against that insurer and enforced without any of the difficulties generated by the terms of the 1930 Act.

12.3.4   Retainer and instructions

If action to enforce a judgment is necessary, a check should be made to ensure the current retainer with the claimant covers such steps, and if not an appropriate retainer agreed.

The claimant should also be advised about the action considered necessary and instructions sought to take appropriate steps.

12.3.5 Costs of enforcement

Fixed costs are applicable to some enforcement steps which will simply be added to, and recovered as part of, the judgment.

With other methods of enforcement further costs, which will have to be assessed, will be incurred.

12.3.6

Costs of implementation

Costs of implementing an order, so as to carry the terms of that order into effect, are likely to be treated as part of any order one party pay the costs of the action to another party: *Wallace v Brian Gale & Associates*.[248]

12.3.7 Interest

When payment of damages and/or costs is delayed, because of the need to take enforcement steps, interest, under the Judgments Act, should be added to allow for delay from the date payment was due until the date payment is made.

Even where payment is late, but made before enforcement steps are taken, it will usually be appropriate to pursue the claim for interest unless the sums involved is minimal and the client is happy to forego that interest.

Interest, on this basis, will be payable from the date the judgment fell due until the date of payment.

12.4 UNSUCCESSFUL CLAIMS

If the claimant's claim has been unsuccessful further steps, to conclude the claim, may be required, in particular dealing with the costs of the defendant.

12.4.1 Legal aid

If the claimant has pursued the claim with the benefit of a legal aid certificate, the court may still make an adverse costs order, if the claim is unsuccessful, against the claimant, but that order will usually have the proviso that it not be enforced without leave of the court.

---

[248] [1997] 2 Costs LR 15.

Leave to enforce the order may be obtained, or obtained to a limited extent, if the claimant has made a legal aid contribution or should the claimant later come into sufficient funds.

If the claimant has been partially unsuccessful, but nevertheless recovered damages, and hence faces an adverse costs order, the court may direct a set-off of the defendant's costs against the damages awarded: *Lockley v National Blood Transfusion Service*.[249]

12.4.2   Non-legal aid funding made prior to April 2013

If the claimant has made arrangements to fund the case prior to April 2013, other than by legal aid, it is likely, if the claim is wholly or partially unsuccessful, the court will make an adverse costs order against the claimant which can be enforced.

If the claimant has ATE or BTE insurance it is likely those insurers will provide an indemnity against adverse costs, at least up to the limit of any indemnity provided under the policy, and hence such insurers must be notified of any adverse costs order. If the costs have not been assessed there and then the insurers may wish to deal with that assessment. Consequently, it is essential any insurers are advised, as soon as possible, of any adverse order which may result in a claim on the policy.

If there is no, or no adequate, insurance cover the claimant will be at risk of the defendant enforcing any order for costs once assessed.

12.4.3   QOCS (qualified one-way costs shifting)

From April 2013 s II of Part 44 of the CPR deals with QOCS.

QOCS will apply to proceedings which include a claim for damages:

*   for personal injuries;
*   under the Fatal Accidents Act 1976; or
*   which arise out of death or personal injury and survive for the benefit of an estate by virtue of s 1(1) of the Law Reform (Miscellaneous Provisions) Act 1934.

However, pre-action applications are not included.

Moreover, QOCS will not apply to proceedings where the claimant has entered into a pre-commencement funding arrangement, as defined by CPR 48.2, which will be a conditional fee agreement pre-dating 1 April 2013 or a conditional fee agreement entered into after that date where recoverability of additional liabilities survives.

The effect of QOCS is that any orders for costs made against a claimant may be enforced without the permission of the court but only to the extent that the aggregate amount in money terms of such orders does not exceed the aggregate amount in money terms of any orders for damages and interest made in favour of the claimant.

---

[249]   [1992] 1 WLR 492.

In general terms that means an unsuccessful claimant, where QOCS applies but subject to the specific exceptions identified in s II of the new Part 44, will not have to pay the defendant's costs while a partially successful claimant will have liability for costs but only to the extent of damages and interest recovered.

There are a variety of situations in which a claimant who recovers damages may nevertheless face adverse costs orders. For example, there may be adverse orders made at interim hearings, the claimant may fail to obtain judgment which is more advantageous than the terms of a Part 36 offer made by the defendant, or the court may make an adverse order under the general discretion as to costs found in Part 44.

There are three exceptions to the general rule preventing a claimant who does not recover any damages being responsible for costs:

- Orders for costs may be enforced to the full extent against the claimant, without permission of the court, where proceedings have been struck out on the grounds that:
    - the claimant has disclosed no reasonable grounds for bringing proceedings;
    - the proceedings are an abuse of the court's process; or
    - the conduct of:
        (i) the claimant; or
        (ii) a person acting on the claimant's behalf and with the claimant's knowledge of such conduct,
        is likely to obstruct the just disposal of the proceedings.
- Orders for costs may be enforced to the full extent against the claimant, with the permission of the court, where the claim is found on the balance of probabilities to be fundamentally dishonest.
- Orders for costs may be enforced to the full extent against the claimant, with permission of the court and to the extent that the court considers it just, where the proceedings include a claim made for the financial benefit of a person other than the claimant or a dependant within the meaning of the Fatal Accidents Act 1976 (other than a claim in respect of the gratuitous provision of care, earnings paid by an employer or medical expenses) or a claim is made for the benefit of the claimant other than a claim to which s II of the new Part 44 applies.

12.4.4 Technical challenges

Over the last decade, on the basis of the indemnity principle, defendants have made numerous technical challenges to costs claimed by claimants.

The indemnity principle does, of course, apply equally to defendants who seek to recover costs.

Many defendant lawyers now act on the basis of a conditional fee agreement, even though this may be of the 'no win – reduced fee' variety with no success fee the defendant will seek to recover from the claimant and hence not necessarily requiring service of Notice of Funding.

Consequently, if there is a potential liability for the costs of the defendant it may be worth enquiring:

- whether the defendant has been acting on the basis of a conditional fee agreement; and if so
- relevant details of the agreement to ensure compliance with the statutory scheme and hence no breach of the indemnity principle.

12.4.5   Non-party costs orders

If the claim is unsuccessful, particularly if the defendant cannot recover costs from the claimant, it is possible the claimant's solicitors will face an application for a non-party costs order.

For solicitors to become liable for costs as a funder it will be necessary for the litigation to have been controlled in some way and for the lawyers to have done more than simply act as might be expected under a conditional fee agreement: *Tinseltime Ltd v Roberts*.[250]

12.5   PRIVATE CLIENT WORK

The claimant may have requirements for private client work, following successful conclusion of a personal injury claim, particularly if the damages are substantial.

There are a number of potential requirements to consider.

12.5.1   Wills

If the client is to receive damages, particularly substantial damages, it is appropriate to offer advice on the need for a will, or an updated will.

12.5.2   Personal injury trust

If the client is receiving income-based state benefits, appropriate advice should be given on the possibility of setting up a personal injury trust, or referral made to specialist solicitors for this purposes.

12.5.3   Family law

Damages recovered in a personal injury claim may be subject to a financial order made in family proceedings: *Wagstaff v Wagstaff*;[251] *Mansfield v Mansfield*.[252]

Consequently, appropriate advice should be given, where the size of the award justifies this, on steps such as:

- a pre-nuptial agreement;
- a post-nuptial agreement;
- use of a personal injury trust;
- use of periodical payments orders;

---

[250] [2012] EWHC 2628 (TCC).
[251] [1992] 1 FLR.
[252] [2011] EWCA Civ 1056.

- how the total damages are broken down into constituent parts (as the court may be more likely to treat general damages as funds available for division).

12.6 ADMINISTRATION

There are some important administrative steps to take following conclusion of a personal injury claim.

12.6.1 Report

The client should receive a final report, explaining the terms on which the case has been concluded and outlining any further action that may be appropriate in the future.

12.6.2 File closing

Once all aspects of the claim have been concluded, appropriate steps should be taken to close the file.

12.6.3 File retention

Particular care is required to ensure the retention of any file which involves a child or protected party as well as cases where there has been an award of provisional damages or a periodical payments order.

12.6.4 Payments

The client should be accounted to, as soon as practicable, with damages recovered and payments made to third parties, where these are outstanding, either from payments on account of costs or costs once agreed and recovered.

12.6.5 Recovery of costs

CPR 47.7 provides that the time limit for commencing detailed assessment proceedings is three months from the relevant judgment or order, date of service of notice of discontinuance or acceptance of a Part 36 offer or payment.

If this time limit is not complied with the paying party may seek an order requiring commencement of detailed assessment proceedings within a specified period, in accordance with CPR 47.8. Such an order will normally be more appropriate and proportionate than an order disallowing costs altogether under CPR 44.14: *Botham v Khan*.[253]

Consequently, whilst efforts will usually be made to try to agree costs, it is important to start any detailed assessment proceedings in time.

---

[253] [2004] EWHC 2602 (QB).

The defendant may, initially, be supplied with a summary of costs though it may be more expedient to have a full bill of costs prepared at the outset as the defendant will often insist upon the detailed information of a bill before entering negotiations likely to result in agreement of costs.

If a bill is prepared that may still be sent to the defendant on the basis that time for serving points of dispute will be extended if it seems likely negotiations will result in agreement, though if not points of dispute may as well be called for.

As with the claim itself the parties should be ready and willing to pursue negotiations and reach agreement on costs without the need for a detailed assessment hearing if possible.

If, once assessed, costs are not paid, appropriate steps, to recover those costs, can be taken (see 12.3.2).

12.7 CONCLUSION

The claim may have been unsuccessful but, nevertheless, ensured the claimant has received proper access to justice.

If the claim has been successful, the practitioner responsible for running that claim will have navigated the path from initial instructions to recovery of damages and costs. That inevitably reflects hard work and the application of knowledge and skill.

Achieving a successful outcome in a personal injury claim is never easy, particularly when such claims are invariably responded to by experienced and well-resourced insurers of the nominal defendant.

Well done!

INDEX

References are to paragraph numbers.